Blue & Gold and Black

TEXAS A&M UNIVERSITY

115

MILITARY HISTORY SERIES

Blue & Gold and Black

and Black

Racial Integration
of the U.S. Naval Academy

Robert J. Schneller Jr.

TEXAS A&M UNIVERSITY PRESS

College Station

Library of Congress Cataloging-in-Publication Data

Schneller, Robert John, 1957–
Blue & gold and black : racial integration of the U.S. Naval Academy /
Robert J. Schneller
p. cm. — (Texas A&M University military history series ; no. 115)
Includes bibliographical references and index.
ISBN-13: 978-1-60344-000-4 (cloth : alk. paper)
ISBN-10: 1-60344-000-3 (cloth : alk. paper)
1. United States Naval Academy—History. 2. African American soldiers.
3. Sociology, Military—United States. 4. United States—Race relations.
I. Title. II. Title: Blue and gold and black.
UB418.A47S46 2008
359.0071'173—dc22
2007022333

To midshipmen

Contents

List of Illustrations

Galleries of images follow pages 84, 238, and 374.

Part 1

Part 2

Part 3

Preface and Acknowledgments

In the summer of 1965, Pres. Lyndon Johnson ordered United States Naval Academy superintendent R. Adm. Draper Kauffman to double that institution's black enrollment before fall classes began. Until then, Academy officials had ignored racial issues, African Americans constituted only a token presence among the brigade of midshipmen, and equal opportunity eluded them. The president's order was "very successful in shaking the very dickens out of us," recalled Admiral Kauffman.[1] From then on, racial issues appeared near the top of the leadership's agenda as the Academy developed policies to increase minority representation, celebrate diversity, and curb discrimination. These policies helped complete the Academy's transformation from a racist institution to one that ranked equal opportunity among its fundamental tenets.

Blue & Gold and Black is a history of the integration of African Americans into the Naval Academy. It examines how the Academy's policies and culture changed in response to demands for equal opportunity and how these changes affected the lives of black midshipmen.

Throughout its history, race relations at the Naval Academy reflected race relations in America. After the first African American graduated from the Academy in 1949, the Navy made little headway in race relations for the next decade and a half. Although official written policy called for equal opportunity, the Navy's leaders did not enforce it. At best, the leadership neglected racial issues; at worst, the leadership tolerated discrimination. Although the service accepted qualified blacks, it took no consistent positive action to diversify its uniformed personnel or civilian workforce. As a result, the proportion of blacks serving in the Navy or working for the Navy remained below the percentage of blacks in American society.

The Naval Academy followed a similar course. No African Americans joined the faculty or staff, nor did the Academy develop a minority recruiting program, and an average of only three African Americans became midshipmen and two graduated each year between 1949 and 1968. Because Academy officials ignored race, the amount of racially motivated mistreatment suffered by African American plebes varied with the racial attitudes of the individuals in their companies, and black midshipmen did not have the same opportunities as their white classmates.

While the Navy and Naval Academy's racial policies languished, race relations in American society underwent a revolution. The civil rights movement swelled from a handful of voices challenging the "separate but equal" doctrine in federal court to a massive chorus demanding nothing less than full voting rights for African Americans and an end to Jim Crow segregation. Bus boycotts, sit-ins, freedom rides, street marches, and other forms of nonviolent protest in Montgomery, Selma, Birmingham, Greensboro, and a thousand other cities and towns precipitated passage of the Civil Rights Act of 1964 and the Voting Rights Act of 1965. This legislation accorded black Americans the fundamental rights of citizenship that most whites had long taken for granted.

Since the Navy was an arm of the federal government and the Naval Academy a national institution, they too felt pressure to reform. On 26 July 1963, Secretary of Defense Robert S. McNamara released a directive that inaugurated an aggressive new racial policy for the Department of Defense, one that sought to increase participation and opportunities for black officers and enlisted men and women throughout the armed forces. The Navy reexamined and rewrote its own racial policy along the lines of the directive. In January 1965, the secretary of the navy issued an equal opportunity manual that articulated the new policy.

But it was Lyndon Johnson who really started the process of racial reform at the Naval Academy. Upon taking office, President Johnson made "equal rights for all Americans whatever their race or color" his top priority, and "affirmative action" became embedded in the lexicon of rights-consciousness during his administration. In the midst of securing passage of the voting rights legislation during the summer of 1965, Johnson took personal notice of the dearth of African American midshipmen at the Academy. That August, NAACP leader Roy Wilkins "beefed" to him that the Academy had only nine black midshipmen in its 4,100-man student body, citing the figure as a conspicuous example of discrimination in the armed forces. Immediately after the meeting, Johnson telephoned the secretary of the navy, and their conversation resulted in the genesis of the Academy's minority recruiting program.

While the Navy developed and implemented its new equal opportunity policy over the next decade, the Academy developed its minority-recruiting program and incorporated racial awareness training into the curriculum. These steps did not eliminate racially motivated mistreatment of black midshipmen, but they did reduce discrimination and level the playing field, culminating in 1976 in the appointment of the first African American as the top-ranking midshipman. More than any other factor, however, it was the presence of black midshipmen throughout the brigade and their attainment of social equality that reduced discrimination at the Academy. In succeeding years the Academy's racial policy evolved to the point that no white upperclassman in his right mind would openly harass a black plebe because of race. At the same time, the proportion of black midshipmen at the Academy nearly reached the proportion of black people in America.

With the introduction of women to the Academy in 1976, gender eclipsed race as the chief social issue facing midshipmen and Academy officials. The Tailhook scandal of 1991 spurred Academy officials to develop and enforce more stringent antidiscrimination policies.

By the end of the twentieth century these developments had greatly reduced but did not eliminate racial discrimination at the Academy, for the system used to indoctrinate plebes and inculcate leadership qualities provided bigots and sexists with opportunities to act out their prejudices without revealing their true motives. Discrimination will likely remain a problem at the Academy as long as the hierarchical system gives some midshipmen power over others and parents teach prejudice to their children.

Most institutional history is written from the top down, and most social history is written from the bottom up. Based on the documentary record as well as the memories of scores of midshipmen and naval officers, *Blue & Gold and Black* includes both perspectives. By examining both the institution and individuals, the book provides a clearer picture of the course of racial integration at the Naval Academy than would have been possible with a top-down or bottom-up approach alone.

This book takes a biographical approach to social history. Through memory sources, defined here as written correspondence, responses to questionnaires, memoirs, and oral histories, African American midshipmen recount their experiences in their own words. Their humanity and individuality are not adrift in oceans of statistics. Memory sources provide insights into the Academy's culture that cannot be gained from official records.

Obtaining memory resources involved asking Academy alumni lots of questions. I sent cover letters describing the project along with lists of questions to hundreds of black alumni and a few white alumni. Many of these queries resulted in written correspondence and oral history interviews with black Academy graduates and nongraduates. Black alumni provided the bulk of memory resources.

Many people decided *not* to respond to my queries. Most of them did not tell me why, so I can only surmise the reasons. Perhaps they didn't have a strong feeling about the subject. Maybe they were concerned that responding might hurt their naval career. Perhaps their busy schedules did not permit time to respond, particularly among young officers and those retired from the Navy but deeply involved in "second careers." There could have been suspicion that I, an official Navy historian, would tell the tale without the warts. In many instances the contact information I had was out of date, particularly for younger officers at sea or rotating between tours of duty. A few of those who promised to participate simply never got around to it.

Several people who chose not to participate did, in fact, tell me why. One alumnus gave an interview but later retracted it. "It's too early in my life to have such details publicly written," he said. "My experiences at USNA represent a small portion of my . . . life adventures and challenges." Another alumnus expressed concern about my approach. "I am not sure I understand what you hope to accomplish with your book," he said. "I tend to be hostile toward 'group' projects of any kind and am generally disgusted with works that tend to ignore the diversity of African American culture. Most of my friends at the Academy (regardless of their race) were absolutely unique individuals. In my opinion, developing a group biography that ignores this individuality would be a profound injustice to all of my classmates." Comments like the last led me to eschew cliometrics (history based on statistics) and to tell the tale in a way that highlights black midshipmen's individuality.

Some white people who decided not to participate also said why. "The question of racial tensions [at the Academy] has rarely been mentioned as a problem," declared a former commandant of midshipmen. An ex-superintendent said that my "approach could be divisive or counterproductive to our desire to bring people together as one team." These replies reflect the denial of racism and the unwillingness to confront it that enabled discrimination to exist at the Academy.

This book consists of three parts. Each part covers a different period and includes five chapters: a chapter on the Academy's racial policies during that period, a chapter on the backgrounds of African Americans who became midshipmen during that period, two chapters on their plebe years, and a chapter on their experiences as upperclassmen and the impact the Academy made on the rest of their lives. The policy chapters examine the forces outside and inside the Academy that shaped its racial policies. The background chapters examine the racial attitudes African American midshipmen encountered while growing up and the mechanisms they learned for coping with racism, as these attitudes and mechanisms shaped their adaptations to the Academy's culture. The plebe-year chapters examine the period during which black midshipmen were most vulnerable to racism at both the individual and institutional levels. The last chapter of each part (chapters 5, 10, and 15) explores black midshipmen's opportunities as upperclassmen and beyond and ends with a conclusion that summarizes the argument in that part.

Any tale of black people's integration into one of America's most venerable institutions is bound to spark debate. I trust, however, that the history of the evolution of the Academy's racial policies, along with how these policies affected the experiences of black midshipmen—from Wesley Brown, class of 1949, through Jacqueline Jackson, class of 1999—will provide valuable insights on how the Naval Academy's culture shed its segregationist underpinnings and became an unparalleled opportunity for African Americans.

I am fortunate to work for the United States Naval Historical Center, the U.S. Navy's official history office. Many people at the Center made this book possible. I thank Rear Admiral Paul E. Tobin Jr., U.S. Navy (Ret.), director of naval history, and Dr. William S. Dudley, former director of naval history, for their leadership and encouragement from the book's inception through its publication. I also thank William Vance, Jay Thomas, Todd Creekman, James Carlton, Andy Hall, Duane Heughan, and Pete Wheeler, successive deputy directors during that period. I am particularly grateful to Gary Weir and Ed Marolda, my immediate supervisors, for their guidance and support.

Every one of my friends and colleagues at the Naval Historical Center helped in one way or another. Several of them deserve special mention. I am indebted to Gina Akers, Bernard Cavalcante, John Hodges, Ariana Jacob, Ken Johnson, Kathy Lloyd, Tim Pettit, Mike Walker, and Wade Wyckoff of the Operational Archives as well as Barbara Auman, David Brown, Linda Edwards, Davis Elliott, Glenn Helm, Jean Hort, Shirley Martyn, Heidi Myers, Young Park, and Tonya Simpson of the Navy Department Library for invaluable research support. I thank Jeff Barlow, Bob Cressman, Mike McDaniel, Randy Papadopoulos, Rick Russell, and John Sherwood of the Contemporary History Branch for research leads and constructive criticism. I am grateful to senior editor Sandy Doyle for editorial input. I thank Sabreena Edwards, Jack Green, Jill Harrison, Ruby Hughlett, Ella Nargele, Randy Potter, Donna Smilardo, and Maxine Ware for providing various kinds of administrative support.

I thank Gina Akers, Alan Gropman, Diane Batts Morrow, Alex Roland, Brian Shellum, and John Sherwood for reviewing the entire manuscript and offering valuable suggestions for its improvement. Although these people helped make this book better, responsibility for its flaws remains with me.

I thank the staffs of the Library of Congress, Howard University's Moorland-Spingarn Research Center, the Naval Historical Foundation, the National Archives, the U.S. Naval Academy's Nimitz Library, and the U.S. Naval Institute. I am particularly indebted to Gary LaValley and Beverly Lyall of Nimitz Library's Special Collections and Archives Division for preserving and making available the Naval Academy's records. I thank Mary Lenn Dixon at Texas A&M University Press for shepherding this book into print.

Most of all I wish to express my gratitude to the Naval Academy alumni who shared their recollections with me. Their names appear in the bibliography. Without their help, I would never have been able to write the book.

Blue & Gold and Black

PART 1
Official Neglect

TOKEN REPRESENTATION,
1945-1965

"We Make No Special Effort"

I N 1961, future admiral Joseph Paul Reason decided to become a midshipman at the U.S. Naval Academy. Many of his friends and neighbors thought it was the dumbest thing he could do. "You know how the Navy treats black people," they would tell him.[1]

Although African Americans had served at sea throughout American history, the Navy's official racial policy had long been one of discrimination. No black officers had been commissioned before World War II. African Americans who enlisted early in the war could expect to serve only in the messman's or steward's branches as cooks or officers' servants. Ashore at home, American society forced black sailors to live by local segregation laws and customs. Ashore abroad, Jim Crow followed black sailors as white shipmates did their best to enforce American racial customs in foreign ports. Black sailors bristled at being relegated to "chambermaids of the braid," and protests against discrimination from the black community flooded the Navy Department throughout the war.[2]

Under pressure from the black press, the NAACP, and civil rights activists, President Franklin Roosevelt ordered Secretary of the Navy Frank Knox to expand the role of African Americans in the fleet. The Navy began accepting blacks for "general service" in June 1942 but maintained segregation in training and by occupation.[3]

A modified version of this policy adopted in 1943 offered no real improvement. It restricted most black sailors to shore duty, assigned them to menial jobs with little prestige and few chances of promotion, excluded them from the WAVES (Women Accepted for Volunteer Emergency Service) and the Nurse Corps, and denied them commissions in the officer corps.[4]

The situation changed dramatically when James Forrestal became secretary of the navy after Knox died of heart failure on 28 April 1944. Under Forrestal's leadership the Navy revolutionized its written policy. "In the administration of naval personnel," he declared in a directive issued in December 1945, "no differentiation shall be made because of race or color." Two months later, the Bureau of Naval Personnel (commonly called "BuPers") issued Circular Letter 48–46, which lifted "all restrictions governing types of assignments for which Negro naval personnel are eligible." BuPers' enormous responsibilities included administration of all naval officers and enlisted men and women.[5]

Despite the change on paper, a gap between policy and practice remained. The Navy developed no program for recruiting black sailors for the enlisted general service. Indeed, some recruiting officials erroneously informed black sailors that their enlistment would be *limited* to the steward's branch. As a result, the proportion of black sailors in the enlisted force declined from a wartime high of 5.5 percent to just 3.7 percent five years later. In mid-1948, 62 percent of the blacks serving in the Navy remained in the steward's branch, and all the stewards were black.

The situation for African Americans in the Navy's officer corps was worse. With great reluctance and only after much prodding, in February 1944 Secretary Knox authorized the commissioning of the first thirteen black naval officers, later dubbed the "Golden Thirteen." African American presence in the officer corps remained negligible for the rest of World War II. On 31 August 1945, the Navy had only sixty-four black officers, including two WAVES and four nurses. These sixty-four men and women accounted for less than 0.02 percent of the Navy's total of 325,074 warrant and commissioned officers, and none of the black officers were regulars.[6] After the war, black reserve officers who had entered the Navy with academic credentials or technical expertise resented the underutilization of their talents in all-black labor units and the like and wanted out. Black reservists who wanted to remain in the Navy experienced bitter frustration. During the war they had not been allowed to serve in billets that fitted them for promotion, and not one received a regular commission in the first eighteen months after V-J Day. As a result, by the end of 1946 only three black officers remained on active duty.[7]

The Naval Academy had produced zero black officers during the war. Since Reconstruction, African American politicians, editors, clergymen, and other leaders had been trying to integrate the Naval Academy as a step toward gaining full civil rights for black people in America. Their efforts resulted in some three dozen blacks appointed to the Academy through World War II. Only six gained admission, three during the 1870s, two during the 1930s, and one in

1945. Doubtless the inferior education provided to black people during the Jim Crow era prevented more African Americans from entering. The first five black midshipmen never made it past the first year. Racist white midshipmen hazed them unmercifully, physically assaulted them, or ignored them; each one left Annapolis under dubious circumstances; and the Academy's administration to varying degrees condoned the ill treatment.[8]

After the war the Navy launched a modest effort to recruit black officers. In December 1946, BuPers sent Lieutenant Commander Edward S. Hope, a black reservist assigned to officer procurement, "on a long trip to visit a number of Negro colleges to 'show the uniform,'" as he put it, "and speak on the 'unthinkable' possibility of a career as a commissioned officer in the regular navy." After addressing black educators at the annual convention of the Association of Colleges and Secondary Schools in Tuskegee, Alabama, Hope visited thirty-one black high schools and colleges in Texas, Louisiana, Alabama, Georgia, Tennessee, North Carolina, and Virginia, states with large black populations. At each stop he outlined the Naval Reserve Officers Training Corps (NROTC) program and discussed its racial policy. Hundreds of black students expressed an interest in applying for an NROTC scholarship.[9]

Since the Naval Academy could not produce enough ensigns each year to meet the Navy's need for officers without radical alteration, the Navy Department had devised a plan to expand NROTC to make up the difference. Strategy at that time envisioned the largest peacetime navy in American history, with a personnel strength of approximately 50,000 officers and 500,000 enlisted people—more than five times the numbers in service in 1936. The new plan left the Academy unchanged, but a "Regular" NROTC program offered competitive scholarships to fifty-two civilian colleges across the country.[10] Selection boards dominated by local civilians screened the applicants for the schools in each state. Not one black person served on any of these state boards. State law prohibited the admission of blacks in fourteen of the fifty-two NROTC schools, and policy and tradition barred blacks in many others.[11]

Although BuPers regarded Hope's "long trip" as a genuine effort to increase the number of black officers, it proved to be an exercise in tilting at windmills, for none of the all-white selection board members in the states Hope visited would even consider sending a black candidate to a white school. As a result, of the 5,600 students who enrolled in the new NROTC program in 1947, only fourteen were black.[12]

Negative perceptions of the Navy in the black community exacerbated the problem of recruiting black officers. Despite the promise of equal opportunity, most African Americans believed that all a black person could reasonably expect to do in the Navy was cook food and wait on officers. This gap between policy and practice, a hangover from World War II, gave the Navy a headache for decades. Many African Americans felt disgust, disillusionment, and resentment toward the Navy. Black veterans in particular distrusted any announcement of a new program "applicable to all citizens." Bitter experience had taught them that, unless the announcement specifically said so, the program was not open to blacks. Hope found that most black people were uninformed about the Navy's new racial policy, or worse, indifferent to it. The wartime flood of African American complaints received in the Navy Department had slowed to a trickle after the war, confirming this growing apathy.[13]

The reality for African Americans in the other services was equally dismal. The Army expanded opportunities for blacks but retained segregation in mess halls, barracks, and all-black units. The Army Air Forces accepted black pilots and integrated pilot training in 1946, but it permitted segregation in recreation, messing, and social activities on bases where Jim Crow prevailed in the surrounding civilian communities. The Marine Corps clung to a rigid pattern of segregation and minimal opportunity for African Americans. In sum, in the absence of outside pressure, the armed services continued to resist integration.[14]

Politics spurred President Harry Truman into applying that pressure. As in the two previous presidential elections, segregation was a major campaign issue in 1948. Truman determined that to win the election he would need the black vote, so he decided to take executive action against discrimination within the armed services. On 26 July 1948 he issued Executive Order 9981, which declared, "There shall be equality of treatment and opportunity for all persons in the armed services without regard to race, color, religion, or national origin." The directive led to the establishment in January 1949 of the President's Committee on Equality of Treatment and Opportunity in the Armed Forces to investigate compliance. When asked at a press conference whether he envisioned the eventual end of segregation in the armed services, Truman said yes.[15]

Truman's civil rights actions netted him 69 percent of the black vote in twenty-seven major cities, according to an NAACP poll. The results of the 1948 election demonstrated that black political strength in the states with the largest electoral votes had gained sufficient strength to determine the outcome of a closely contested national election. As NAACP voting analyst Henry Moon observed, African Americans had become a "balance of power" force in national politics.[16]

The President's Committee on Equality of Treatment and Opportunity in the Armed Forces became known by the name of its chairman, soft-spoken Georgia lawyer Charles Fahy. The Fahy Committee included, among others, John H. Sengstacke, editor and publisher of the *Chicago Defender,* a leading black newspaper with a national readership. The committee members began their work with a formal meeting at the White House on 12 January 1949. Over the next nineteen months, they heard testimony from sixty-seven witnesses, perused reams of official documents, toured ships, schools, and installations, and rigorously analyzed the services' racial policies.[17]

At first the Navy perceived no need to alter its racial policy in light of Truman's executive order. Indeed, the Fahy Committee was impressed by the fact that in just five years after Pearl Harbor "the Navy had moved from a policy of complete exclusion of Negroes from general service to a policy of complete integration in general service."[18]

Even so, the committee concluded that the Navy was not in compliance with the spirit of Truman's order. The central problem was minority recruiting. During hearings on 26 April 1949, Sengstacke asked Captain J. H. Schultz, assistant chief of naval personnel for naval reserve, whether the Navy had a program to recruit blacks into the Naval Reserve. "We make no special effort to get any race, creed, or color," replied Schultz. Later Fahy asked what the Navy was doing to increase the number of black Naval Reserve officers. "We aren't doing anything special to procure Negro officers or Negro enlisted men," said Schultz. In short, the Navy had no minority recruiting program. Dennis Nelson, a training and public relations specialist in BuPers, pointed out that black people still believed the only branch of service open to them was the steward's branch. "Since the Navy makes no effort to carry the information to them other than the usual media," he observed, "they probably just don't get the word that the opportunities exist." Sengstacke agreed. "You've got to make some special effort to get them in," he said. "You can't do it by keeping silent on it." Similarly, the Navy did not publicize opportunities for African Americans at the Naval Academy.[19]

The Fahy Committee expressed concern to President Truman over the small number of black sailors in the enlisted force and disappointment in the results of efforts to increase the number of black officers. To facilitate the latter, the committee suggested that the Navy publicize the fact that all of its officer programs were open to blacks on an equal basis. The secretary of the navy formally accepted these recommendations on 7 June.[20]

During the next several months, the Navy returned five black reserve officers to active duty for recruiting service and hosted a delegation of black journalists on the cruise of the battleship *Missouri* in the summer of 1949. Later that year, in conjunction with the National Urban League, BuPers sent a team of three black officers on a speaking tour of forty-nine black schools, civic groups, and other organizations in seventeen southern cities to recruit NROTC candidates.[21]

These extra efforts to procure African American reserve officers were also disappointing. Although some 2,700 blacks in the seventeen southern cities filled out applications to take the preliminary scholastic examination, only 250 actually took the test. Of these 250, only one passed and also qualified physically. Although black people received an inferior education under segregation because black schools received inferior resources, it is difficult to believe that so many African Americans could have failed a fairly administered and graded test. The recruiting team made another tour of black high schools and colleges across the Southeast in 1950, with roughly the same dismal results. Because of the high cost and low return of these tours, BuPers discontinued them. The Fahy Committee blamed the results on the poor education blacks received in some parts of the country and the stiff competition for scholarships. "Until Negroes receive more appointments to Annapolis, and until they can compete with greater success for [NROTC] scholarships," lamented the committee, "it is unlikely that the number of Negro officers will be much increased."[22]

What the Fahy Committee did not point out was that many NROTC schools would not accept any African American, no matter how qualified, and that the Navy still lacked a consistent program for recruiting black officers. The tours of the South by black recruiters were ad hoc measures, not part of a long-term plan. And with no change in the NROTC state selection committee setup, the second two tours were just as much of a windmill joust as Commander Hope's tour had been.

In the absence of sound minority recruiting efforts, the Navy backslid in terms of proportional representation. In 1956, African Americans accounted for 9.5 percent of Navy enlistees. For the next six years, however, the proportion of incoming blacks fell to an average of 3.1 percent. Although the proportion of African American officers doubled from 0.1 percent in 1954 to 0.2 percent in 1962, their numbers remained negligible, the lowest of all the services.[23]

In light of these figures, BuPers reexamined the Navy's recruiting policy to determine whether it discriminated against minorities. In a 24 January 1959 report to the secretary of the navy, the bureau declared the policy nondiscriminatory and argued against developing a minority recruiting program. To recruit African Americans, the report said, the Navy would have to establish quotas, "which might result in more accusations of discrimination." The report recommended "that the Navy continue to recruit, train and assign personnel without consideration as to race." In short, the bureau chose to do nothing to increase the number of black sailors in the Navy.[24]

Despite the Navy's bad reputation in black communities, civil rights advocates paid little attention to the service during the 1950s. Their eyes were on a much bigger prize. During Earl Warren's tenure as chief justice (1953–69), the Supreme Court reversed a century-old trend by calling for federal intervention to protect the civil rights of African Americans. The Warren Court attacked segregation in housing and interstate transportation and enabled many black people to return to the polls. These decisions fueled the growth of black political power, even in the South. In 1940, only 2 percent of blacks of voting age in twelve southern states were qualified to vote. In 1947, 12 percent, or more than 600,000 black people, were qualified. By 1952, the number had reached 1.2 million.[25]

In the 1930s, NAACP attorney Thurgood Marshall had launched a long-range, carefully orchestrated litigation campaign to challenge the "separate but equal" doctrine established by *Plessy v. Ferguson*. At that time, for every two dollars spent on black education in the South, seven dollars was spent on whites. In 1951, Marshall began to coordinate a series of lawsuits charging that segregation in education was discriminatory. The NAACP campaign reached its zenith when the Supreme Court heard the case of *Oliver Brown et al. v. Board of Education of Topeka, Kansas*. The Court's decision, handed down on 17 May 1954, overturned *Plessy* and found school segregation unconstitutional. "Separate educational facilities are inherently unequal," the Court declared, and it ordered the desegregation of school systems "with all deliberate speed." Soon hundreds of districts in Arizona, Delaware, Kansas, Kentucky, Maryland, Missouri, New Mexico, Oklahoma, Utah, West Virginia, Wyoming, and the District of Columbia quietly integrated their schools. The *Brown* decision became the sine qua non of the civil rights movement and dealt a severe blow to Jim Crow, for it provided a legal basis for overturning segregation in both public and private life.[26]

Southern politicians mounted a campaign of massive resistance to school desegregation. On 12 March 1956, 101 southern congressmen signed a "Declaration of Constitutional Principles" asking their states to refuse to obey the desegregation order and promising to try to reverse *Brown*. To evade implementation of the order, states cut off aid to desegregated schools, denied licenses to teachers who taught at those schools, and barred NAACP members from public employment. The rebel battle flag reappeared over capitols in states of the old Confederacy and, in some cases, in official state flags, to symbolize opposition to desegregation. White citizens' councils and other white supremacy groups sprang up in numerous southern towns. Many white leaders condoned the harassment and abuse of black children to precipitate their departure from white schools. African Americans were killed for daring to assert their rights or for violating Jim Crow etiquette. One of the most notorious incidents involved Emmett Till, a black fourteen-year-old who was murdered because he whistled at a white woman in a grocery store in Mississippi.[27]

In 1957, Arkansas governor Orval Faubus organized white mobs and National Guard troops to prevent nine black children from entering Little Rock's Central High School. This disgraceful event forced President Dwight Eisenhower to dispatch the 101st Airborne Division to the city to enable the children to enter the school. Armed troops escorted the "Little Rock nine" to their classes for the next two months, and federalized Arkansas National Guardsmen patrolled Central High for the rest of the year.[28]

During the 1960s the civil rights movement became a powerful political force as large numbers of blacks as well as whites demanded an end to segregation and full voting rights for African Americans. Bus boycotts, sit-ins, freedom rides, street marches, and other forms of nonviolent protest took place in Montgomery, Selma, Birmingham, Greensboro, and a thousand other cities and towns across the South. Some of these demonstrations targeted a particular ordinance or business; others sought to eliminate Jim Crow entirely. In cities like Nashville, Galveston, and Houston the white establishment desegregated lunch counters, restaurants, and other places of public accommodation. By the summer of 1960 more than thirty southern cities, mostly in border states, established organizations to conciliate the local black community.

But the forces of Jim Crow did not cave in easily. In Birmingham, Alabama, and Orangeburg, South Carolina, the white establishment refused to desegregate anything and white citizens resorted to violence. Hecklers jabbed lighted cigarettes into the backs of girls seated at lunch counters, blew cigar smoke in the faces of protestors, hurled food and insults at them, spit at them, kicked them, and beat them. On the streets, police loosed dogs on protesters, fired tear gas at them, turned water hoses on them, and arrested them by the thousands. In Frankfort, Kentucky, unknown assailants fire-bombed the gymnasium of a black college. In Atlanta, Georgia, an unknown assailant threw acid in the face of a sit-in leader. In Houston, Texas, three masked men seized a black man, flogged him with a chain, carved "KKK" on his chest with a knife, and hung him by his knees from an oak tree.

Resistance to integration of institutions of higher learning received national attention. On 20 September 1962, James Meredith, a twenty-eight-year-old Air Force veteran, tried to register at the University of Mississippi. Mississippi governor Ross Barnett stood between Meredith and the admissions office. Attorney General Robert F. Kennedy dispatched five hundred federal marshals to Ole Miss to protect Meredith as he entered college. On the thirtieth, an angry crowd pelted the marshals with bottles, bricks, and buckshot. The marshals fought back with clubs and tear gas. The next day President John F. Kennedy ordered the first of five thousand soldiers onto the campus. They quelled the riot and federal guards protected Meredith until he graduated from Ole Miss in 1963. On 11 June, two black students planned to register at the University of Alabama. Alabama governor George Wallace vowed to bar the way. "I say, segregation now! Segregation tomorrow! Segregation forever!" Wallace had shouted at his inauguration. When the two students tried to register, Wallace stood in front of the admissions office until federal marshals ordered him to move.[29]

That same evening, President Kennedy addressed the nation on national television. The disgraceful behavior of George Wallace and others had led him to reevaluate his position on civil rights. Upon entering office in 1961, Kennedy viewed the civil rights movement as a "conundrum to be managed," as historian Harvard Sitkoff put it, "not a cause to be championed." Kennedy had faith in integration and believed Jim Crow to be wrong, yet he preferred to act slowly and at what he deemed the proper time. He considered demands for freedom now to be just as irresponsible as calls for segregation forever. Eager to curry favor with southern Democrats so that he could win again in 1964, fight the Cold War abroad, and foster a healthy economy at home, Kennedy shied away from civil rights legislation. But now he said that the time had come to confront "a moral issue" that was "as old as the Scriptures" and "as clear as the American Constitution." He warned the Wallaces of the land that their day was over. He declared his intention to ask Congress to eliminate racial discrimination from American life and law. The speech marked a turning point in the civil rights movement. To one historian it signaled the beginning of the "Second Reconstruction," a coherent effort by all three branches of government to secure African Americans their full civil rights. That June, Kennedy asked Congress to enact the most comprehensive civil rights act ever. In the following weeks, he made personal appeals to a broad range of educators, lawyers, business executives, and politicians to support the bill. Although it hurt his standing in the South, the President remained committed to this new course.[30]

Civil rights advocates organized a massive rally in the capital to demand federal support for black rights and to build momentum behind the proposed civil rights legislation. On 28 August 1963, more than a quarter of a million black and white people gathered near the Lincoln Memorial in Washington, D.C., to rally for "jobs and freedom." It was the largest political assembly in American history. Martin Luther King Jr., the most prominent black leader of the civil rights movement, gave the closing speech. It was powerful yet formal recitation of the trials of black people struggling for freedom against the shackles of racist oppression. As he was getting ready to sit down, black gospel singer Mahalia Jackson called out from behind him, "Tell them about your dream, Martin! Tell them about the dream!" King turned toward the crowd and spoke as if the Holy Spirit had taken hold of him. "I have a dream," he declared, that one day this nation will rise up and live out the true meaning of its creed: "We hold these truths to be self-evident—that all men are created equal." I have a dream that one day on the red hills of Georgia the sons of former slaves and the sons of former slaveowners will be able to sit down together at the table of brotherhood. I have a dream that one day even the state of Mississippi, a desert state sweltering with the heat of injustice and oppression, will be transformed into an oasis of freedom and justice. I have a dream that my four little children will one day live in a nation where they will not be judged by the color of their skin but by the content of their character. . . . When we let freedom ring, when we let it ring from every village and every hamlet, from every state and every city, we will be able to speed up that day when all of God's children, black men and white men, Jews and Gentiles, Protestants and Catholics, will be able to join hands and sing in the words of the old Negro spiritual, "Free at last! Free at last! Thank God almighty, we are free at last!"

At that moment, King's ideal of interracial brotherhood seemed within reach. It was one of the most moving orations in American history.[31]

Sadly, inspired rhetoric was not enough to overcome the prejudice so deeply ingrained into so many generations of white Americans. Hours after President Kennedy's televised address, Medgar Evers, field secretary for the NAACP in Mississippi, was killed by a shotgun blast in the back outside his home in Jackson. Less than three weeks after Dr. King articulated his dream, four black girls were killed in the Sixteenth Street Baptist Church in Birmingham by an exploding bomb.

These events transformed civil rights into the country's central political and social issue by 1964. Lyndon B. Johnson, who took office after the assassination of John F. Kennedy on 22 November 1963, called for "nothing less than the full assimilation of more than 20 million Negroes into American life." Although the big Texan had once obstructed civil rights legislation, Johnson entered the White House as one of the nation's foremost champions of racial equality.[32]

Johnson brought all of his legendary political skill to bear in lobbying for passage of the civil rights legislation. After much presidential politicking, the longest filibuster in Senate history, and several compromises on the legislation, Congress passed the Civil Rights Act of 1964 on 2 July. Although the act sought only legal equality, not social equality, it was the most far-reaching and comprehensive law in support of racial equality that Congress had yet passed. It gave the U.S. attorney general additional power to protect citizens against discrimination and segregation in voting, education, and the use of

public facilities. It forbade discrimination in most places of public accommodation. It established the federal Equal Employment Opportunity Commission, required the elimination of discrimination in federally funded programs,
and authorized termination of federal funds upon failure to comply. Finally,
it authorized the U.S. Office of Education to assist communities in school
desegregation.[33]

While Congress was passing the civil rights bill, the Student Nonviolent Coordinating Committee (SNCC), a national civil rights organization,
launched the Mississippi Freedom Summer Project to attack disfranchisement
in the Magnolia State. Some nine hundred college students, most of them
white, volunteered to travel to Mississippi to work for the project. The workers sought to persuade rural black Mississippians to register to vote and set up
"freedom schools" to teach them how to read and write. White racists, led by
the Ku Klux Klan, mounted a ferocious counterattack. The Mississippi state
legislature and most municipalities enacted dozens of ordinances to interfere
with the project and harass the volunteers. Project workers were beaten, jailed,
and shot at, and the buildings they were using as schools were bombed. By
the end of August, four workers had been murdered and four others seriously
wounded, eighty had been assaulted, hundreds had been arrested, and more
than sixty black churches had been bombed or burned. Despite the danger,
many black people registered to vote in Mississippi.[34]

In 1965, Martin Luther King carried the struggle for enfranchisement into
Alabama. On "Bloody Sunday," 7 March 1965, King set out with six hundred
people on a march from Selma to Montgomery to focus public attention on
voting rights. On the Edmund Pettis Bridge at Selma's outskirts, Dallas
County sheriff Jim Clark and Alabama state troopers wearing Confederate
insignia attacked the marchers with billy clubs, tear gas, electric cattle prods,
bullwhips, and rubber tubing wrapped in barbed wire, putting seventy people
in the hospital. Television cameras captured police brutality against children
and old women. Later that day Clark's deputies rioted in Selma's black section
and, in one instance, threw a young black man through a stained glass window
at a black Baptist church. On the twenty-first, another group of marchers,
numbering in the thousands and including whites, northerners, and the greatest gathering of civil rights leaders since the March on Washington, set out
from Selma. When they reached Montgomery four days later, they noticed
the Confederate stars and bars flying under the Alabama state flag above the
capitol dome. That night, four Klansmen murdered a white Detroit housewife
who had participated in the march.[35]

Outraged by the events in Selma, President Johnson went before Congress
on 15 March and made an impassioned plea for a strong new voting rights law.
"Their cause must be our cause, too," he declared. "Because it is not just Ne-

groes, but really all of us who must overcome the crippling legacy of bigotry and injustice." For the next several weeks, Johnson and his aides applied unrelenting pressure on Capitol Hill for passage of the bill. Less than four months after its formal introduction, Congress passed the Voting Rights Act of 1965 on 6 August. The Voting Rights Act enjoyed broader, more sustained public support than any previous civil rights measure. It changed politics overnight, broke the back of disfranchisement in the South, and helped to increase the registration of eligible black voters in six southern states from 30 percent to 46 percent within a year. One of the many whites put out of office by the surge in black voters was Sheriff Jim Clark.[36]

Pressure from the civil rights movement led the Kennedy and Johnson administrations to direct the services, including the Navy, to reexamine their racial policies. Although Kennedy trod lightly around the issue of segregation in the South during his first few months in office, he attacked discrimination in the federal government openly from the start. In March 1961, he established the Committee on Equal Employment Opportunity, chaired by Vice President Johnson, and the Civil Rights Subcabinet Group, chaired by presidential assistant Frederick G. Dutton, to coordinate the administration's civil rights actions. The latter group regularly scrutinized the racial programs of the various departments, demanded reports and investigations of racial matters, and ensured that federal agencies adhered to administration policy.

Kennedy's secretary of defense, Robert McNamara, long a member of the NAACP, was equally committed to equal opportunity. On 24 March 1961, he signed a memo directing the service secretaries and heads of other defense agencies to review existing programs to ensure that they complied with the president's basic equal opportunity policy. The memo also told defense officials to ensure that "Negro institutions are fully informed of employment opportunities within the Department of Defense and are included in visits to schools and colleges in connection with recruitment activities."[37]

In keeping with McNamara's emphasis on the issue, Secretary of the Navy John B. Connally on 12 May sent a "personal letter" to all officers in command to remind them of the Navy's racial policy and to urge them to encourage minority group members to take advantage of officer training programs, including the Naval Academy. The secretary added that officers should assure minority group members that they would not encounter prejudice. In the following months the secretary and the Navy Office of Industrial Relations issued a flurry of instructions and notices promulgating and clarifying the Navy's racial policy.[38]

In August 1961, the Leadership Conference for Executive Action on Civil Rights, a group of representatives from some fifty civil rights groups chaired by Roy Wilkins of the NAACP, submitted to the president a list of proposals aimed at ending federally supported segregation. The group touched on the dearth of black officers in the armed forces and the racial composition of the Navy's steward's branch. Other civil rights advocates as well as Kennedy administration officials also raised questions about the Navy's racial policy.[39]

To address these questions, presidential assistant Harris L. Wofford arranged a meeting at the White House on 22 September between Vice Admiral William R. Smedberg III, chief of naval personnel, and representatives from the NAACP, the National Urban League, and other civil rights organizations. James Evans, counselor for the assistant secretary of defense, also attended. The discussion made it clear that black sailors were making inroads into a broad range of occupational specialties, including radio, radar, and electronics, and that many of the problems with the steward's branch had been resolved. Nevertheless, Navy recruiting efforts had failed to convince black high school students that the Navy would provide them with the same opportunities as whites, and the black community still looked askance at the steward's branch. It also became clear that blacks who wanted to become naval officers faced hurdles that whites did not face. No NROTC units had been established at black colleges, and the problem of discrimination in NROTC state selection boards persisted.

A significant part of the discussion focused on the Naval Academy. James Evans realized that information about the Academy's entrance requirements failed to reach many black students until it was too late for them to prepare adequately to meet them. This failure had dire consequences for the number of black officers in the Navy. Although each recent graduating class had produced more than five hundred ensigns, only eighteen black midshipmen had graduated to date from the Academy. "Obviously," Evans noted, "approaches toward equity of participation here call for increased Negro cadet input if the output of naval officers of color is to approach the population proportion or even the officer proportion found in the other Services." As Evans put it in a memo to Carlisle P. Runge, assistant secretary of defense for manpower, "the Navy welcomes Negro cadets at Annapolis, and Negro youths in general to Navy opportunities, but the Negro citizen is not so convinced."[40]

After reviewing minority officer procurement and training in all the services, Runge on 7 November 1961 sent a memo to the under secretaries of the Navy, Army, and Air Force on the subject. Frederick Dutton had declared that "the problem of adequate minority representation in officer training is another example in which affirmative action is needed to ensure that qualified Negro applicants are recruited or given the opportunity for special training in order to meet required standards. . . . As a matter of urgency, therefore," Runge continued, "each military department will institute specific active measures to increase the participation of Negroes in existing officer procurement and training programs." He directed the services to make "special efforts" to inform black students at the secondary school and college levels about the opportunities for officer training in the services; to encourage black college students to participate in officer training courses; and to "institute active public information programs . . . to reach potential Negro candidates as a specific objective."[41]

The cry to increase black representation at the service academies soon came from another quarter as well, amid a chorus of voices protesting the discrimination uniformed African Americans encountered in civilian communities next to naval installations and military bases. In 1960, blacks who joined the service entered an integrated institution. To be sure, unequal treatment persisted in assignments, promotions, and the application of military justice, but blacks in uniform enjoyed a much higher level of job equity than black civilians outside the Department of Defense. But as integration became the norm on base, racial inequity off base became increasingly more irksome to black servicemen and women. Because schools on military bases could not usually accommodate all of the children whose parents were assigned there, many uniformed African Americans had to send their children to segregated schools off base. Moreover, on-base government housing had room for only about half of married servicemen. African Americans who had to live off base found it difficult if not impossible to find decent housing and encountered Jim Crow in civilian restaurants, theaters, and other places of public accommodation. Base commanders generally ignored these problems.[42]

Representative Charles Diggs Jr. (D-Mich.) had been protesting the miserable living conditions black servicemen endured off base since before Kennedy's election. Diggs had entered Congress as the first black representative from his state and campaigned tirelessly for civil rights throughout his career. Born in Detroit, Michigan, on 2 December 1922, Diggs was educated in Detroit's public school system, graduated from law school in 1951, took a seat in the Michigan state senate that same year, and won election to Congress in 1954. Diggs considered himself a representative of all Americans, not just those from Michigan's 13th District. For the next fifteen years he championed the cause, whether stumping for racial equality or heralding the importance of emerging African nations. His efforts earned him the nickname "the Mississippi Congressman at Large" and got him barred from South Africa. In 1969, he helped establish and became chairman of the Congressional Black Caucus. He remained in office until 1980.

Throughout his time in the House, Diggs promoted integration of the armed forces. Himself a veteran, he had been drafted in the Army Air Force in 1943, commissioned a second lieutenant in 1944, and honorably discharged in 1945. During the war he became the youngest administrative officer at Tuskegee Army Air Field. As a congressman he challenged successive administrations to redress the legitimate grievances of minorities in the armed forces.[43]

Ever since Diggs had taken office, black servicemen had been deluging him with complaints of discrimination. Diggs, in turn, had been pressing the Defense Department to investigate them. In April 1959, he introduced a bill to prohibit discrimination against uniformed personnel, only to be rebuffed by the House Judiciary Committee. In 1960, he toured military bases and naval installations across the Pacific to investigate the status of integration in the services. He found discrimination wherever he went. The "major complaints," as he later put it in a letter to President Kennedy, included "double standards for promotions as between white and Negro servicemen, failure to promote Negro servicemen, lack of communication between command and personnel, discrimination and segregation in on- and off-base recreational facilities and off-base housing, participation of Armed Service Command and Officer personnel in local community discriminatory practices, inequality of treatment of dependent accompaniment, use of symbols of racial intolerance on bases, intimidation of complainants concerning racial discrimination, and severe comparative penalties for offenses committed by Negro Service personnel." Diggs concluded that the services had not fully implemented Truman's Executive Order 9981. Beginning in 1961, he sent McNamara a series of letters protesting inequality in the department and demanding action. That August, Diggs urged McNamara to create a citizens' committee like the Fahy Committee to investigate and report on discrimination in the armed services. On 12 February 1962, he urged McNamara to investigate the conditions of servicemen at home and abroad.[44]

Largely as a result of Diggs's cry for reform, President Kennedy invoked Executive Order 9981 to convene another group to examine the progress the services had made toward racial integration since the Fahy Committee had finished its work. In June 1962, Kennedy announced the formation of the biracial Advisory Committee on Equal Opportunity in the Armed Forces. Its purpose was to determine what should be done to improve equality of treatment and opportunity inside the services as well as to eliminate discrimination against minority military personnel in civilian communities. Chaired by Washington, D.C., attorney Gerhard A. Gesell, its membership included six prominent lawyers and civil rights advocates, among them John Sengstacke. McNamara directed the services to cooperate fully with the Gesell Committee, as it came to be called.[45]

Gesell and his colleagues examined the recruitment, assignment, and promotion of African Americans in each service; discrimination on naval and military bases; and the off-base discrimination that uniformed blacks encountered in civilian communities. They heard testimony from base commanders, Defense Department officials, service representatives, and others; visited military bases and naval installations; and interviewed and surveyed officers and enlisted men and women of all ranks.

Secretary of the Navy Fred H. Korth attended a luncheon with the Gesell Committee on 24 January 1963. Korth realized that the committee was comparing the participation of blacks in the various services. He also realized that as the figures now stood, "the Department of the Navy is in the least favorable light," as he put it to Under Secretary of the Navy Paul B. Fay Jr. That same day, Korth directed Fay to "take personal cognizance" of minority affairs in the Navy and to prepare a Secretary of the Navy Instruction setting forth the Gesell Committee's objectives and realistic methods for meeting them.[46]

Fay asked the committee members to share their initial impressions of the Navy's racial policies. "Disappointing," replied Gerhard Gesell. "The Navy seems to be falling behind the other services." Gesell recommended the Navy start by doing something about recruiting. "Less than one-tenth of one percent of Navy officers are Negroes," he said. "This is a shocking condition which should be remedied." Gesell suggested expanding the recruiting teams in black communities, developing special training programs and methods for recruiting African Americans, and setting up recruiting stations on the campuses of black colleges.[47]

On 7 February, Under Secretary Fay outlined the major problems with the Navy's racial policy in a memo to Secretary Korth. The most salient problem, Fay said, was the dearth of black officers. He attributed the dearth to "the lack of well-qualified applicants of all ethnic groups." In turn, the lack of qualified applicants, he argued, stemmed from the fact that the Navy's officer corps had to compete with industry for the same pool of college graduates. Unfortunately, the Navy could not match private industry in pay, nor was separation from loved ones appealing. Furthermore, the Navy suffered from a poor image in the black community. And although the Navy's racial policy was one of equal opportunity, the Navy had done little to trumpet the opportunities it had to offer in the black community. "In fact," noted Fay, "in certain cases efforts have been made to limit publicity concerning Negro personnel under the theory that publicizing the achievements of an individual might operate to the detriment of the individual concerned." To address these problems, Fay recommended that Korth reaffirm the Navy's equal opportunity policy to officers in command, launch a publicity campaign in the black community, and resurrect the "all-Negro recruiting team" to recruit blacks into the NROTC.[48]

Over the next several months, the Navy renewed its efforts to reach the black community. The chief of naval personnel sent personal letters to 102 college presidents and fifty high school principals reminding them about the opportunities available to African Americans in the NROTC program and Officer Candidate School. An interracial team of Navy and Marine representatives piggybacked onto Department of Labor conferences in Atlanta, Nashville, and Houston to present information on Navy career opportunities to black educators in the South, where most of the nation's black people lived. BuPers sent letters to active-duty black officers imploring them to help improve the Navy's image in the black community, revised recruiting literature and training films to increase depictions of blacks in the Navy, instructed recruiters and district commanders to emphasize equal opportunity in all programs, and assigned a black lieutenant commander to officer recruiting duty in the bureau. BuPers also published articles on the Navy's equal opportunity policy in *All Hands* and the *Flag Officer's Newsletter.* That July, the under secretary began making semiannual reports on the status of "Equal Opportunity in the Navy" to the secretary.[49]

Meanwhile, the Gesell Committee was reaching its own conclusions about how to fix the Navy's racial policy. After a year of gathering and analyzing mountains of data, the committee issued an initial report in June 1963. Since 1950, "the Armed Forces have made an intelligent and far-reaching advance toward complete integration" and "substantial progress toward equality of treatment and opportunity," the committee declared, but it was "not enough."

The report dealt with off-base discrimination, but it also addressed recruitment of African Americans. Although blacks accounted for 11 percent of the American population in 1962, the percentage of black enlisted men and women stood at 12.2 in the Army, 9.1 in the Air Force, 7.7 in the Marine Corps, and 5.1 in the Navy. The percentage of black officers stood at 3.2 in the Army, 1.2 in the Air Force, 0.2 in the Marines, and 0.2 in the Navy. To improve the participation of African Americans, the Gesell Committee recommended that the services develop minority recruiting programs. Such programs should include recruiting at black colleges, creating recruiting literature that appealed to blacks, and making wider use of black officers in recruiting assignments. The committee also made recommendations to ensure the fair assignment and promotion of black servicemen and women.

The initial report noted that African Americans were attending all of the service academies: ten at the Naval Academy, fourteen at the Military Academy, and fifteen at the Air Force Academy. "To increase the pitifully small number of Negro officers," the Gesell Committee declared, "energetic efforts must be made to raise the number of Negroes in the Academies."[50]

Soon after the Gesell Committee released the initial report, Secretary McNamara directed the service secretaries to comment on it. For the most part,

Navy secretary Korth found the committee's recommendations to be "sound and progressive" but had "serious cause for disagreement" on a few points. In response to the Gesell Committee's recommendation that "energetic efforts . . . be made to raise the number of Negroes in the academies and in all officer programs," Korth argued that the Navy could not control who received appointments to the Academy. "All persons who apply and qualify are considered," he declared, "without regard to race, religion, color, or national origin." Korth's gist was that appropriate action to improve equal opportunity in the Navy was already under way.[51]

McNamara, however, perceived the need for radical change. On 26 July 1963, he released Directive 5120.36, inaugurating an aggressive new racial policy for the Defense Department. The policy sought to increase the number of black officers, enhance the opportunities for qualified minority officers to hold command positions, and enlist and retain larger numbers of black recruits. The policy was aimed to eliminate discrimination not only inside the armed forces but in the civilian communities surrounding installations as well.[52]

Directive 5120.36 required the services to submit an outline plan for implementing the new policy. The Navy's plan, put forward that August, included provisions for preparing equal opportunity manuals for base commanders, recruiters, and housing officers; insertion of statements about the Navy's equal opportunity policy into existing recruiting and housing manuals; appraisals of command equal opportunity programs by the inspector general and the Navy Department; and semiannual reports of progress by the chief of naval personnel to the secretary of the navy and by the latter to the secretary of defense. Norman S. Paul, assistant secretary of defense for manpower, approved the Navy proposal along with those of the other services.[53]

Implementing the new policy took longer than Paul had anticipated, because service officials dragged their feet and the Defense Department proved reluctant to enforce the new policy in the aftermath of Kennedy's assassination and while Congress was debating the bill that became the Civil Rights Act of 1964.

Nevertheless, the Navy invested a significant amount of time and energy developing plans and guidelines to carry out Directive 5120.36. The secretary of the navy created an ad hoc committee in BuPers to run what was now being referred to as the Navy's equal opportunity "program." The bureau broadened the Navy's outreach into the black community by sending representatives to meetings of civil rights organizations and to black high schools and colleges. In January 1965, the secretary of the navy issued the Navy's first equal opportunity manual, SECNAV Instruction 5350.6, "Equal Opportunity and Treatment of Military Personnel." The manual articulated the Navy's basic racial policy and guided commanders in discharging their civil rights responsibilities both on and off base.[54]

Ironically, although Secretary of the Navy Forrestal had pioneered a policy of racial integration in the 1940s, by 1965 the Navy had backslid to being a reluctant follower of the Defense Department's lead. The Navy had entered the 1950s with a racial policy it considered "sound and practical." For the next decade and a half it claimed to offer equal opportunity to African Americans, denied the existence of discrimination inside the service, and perceived no need to change its racial policy. The naval establishment believed that, once an African American entered the Navy, he or she should have equal opportunities in occupation, training, and promotion. But the establishment was concerned neither with what happened to black officers and sailors off base nor with the number of blacks who entered the service or black promotion rates. While the Department of Defense was attacking off-base discrimination before passage of the Civil Rights Act of 1964 and emphasizing increased participation of African Americans in the services, especially the number of black officers, the Navy was resisting the development of minority recruiting programs and commissioning the smallest percentage of black officers of the services. In short, the Navy's racial policy affirmed the concept of equal opportunity but attached no importance to the proportional representation of minorities.

Throughout this period, the Naval Academy's racial policy followed the course charted by the Navy Department and BuPers. It was Congress, however, that dominated the process for selecting midshipmen. Regulations varied from year to year, but by and large senators and representatives controlled roughly 60 percent of the nominations until 3 March 1964, when Congress passed a law increasing its control to about 75 percent. Throughout this period, senators and representatives could appoint whomever they chose, without reference to objective criteria. Many members of Congress did in fact rely upon competitive exams to select nominees, but for the rest political patronage remained embedded in the process.

The president and secretary of the navy controlled the bulk of the noncongressional appointments. Presidential nominations went to the sons of regular military personnel and deceased veterans. Secretarial nominations went to regular and reserve enlisted men of the Navy and Marine Corps, honor graduates of select educational institutions, NROTC students, and a handful of other categories. The secretary of the navy could also nominate candidates whom members of Congress had designated as "alternates" and, under certain circumstances, a small number of "competitors" from noncongressional sources.[55]

Fifty-one African Americans were admitted to the Naval Academy between

1945 and 1964. These men accounted for 0.2 percent of the total of 22,392 midshipmen who entered in the classes of 1949 through 1968. Members of Congress appointed thirty-one of the fifty-one black midshipmen, or 61 percent. The secretary of the navy appointed the remaining twenty midshipmen, or 39 percent. Of these twenty, eleven were Navy enlisted men, four were Naval Reserve enlisted men, three were Marine Corps enlisted men, and two were "qualified alternates and competitors." These percentages compare favorably with the sources of appointment for midshipmen as a whole. For example, 56 percent of incoming plebes in the class of 1963 entered the Academy in 1959 with congressional appointments, and 33 percent were regular and reserve sailors and marines as well as qualified alternates and competitors appointed by the secretary of the navy.[56]

For midshipmen with congressional appointments, however, the sources of black appointments differed markedly from the larger picture during this period. Overall, midshipmen received nominations from every state in the union and the District of Columbia, with the most populous states sending the most congressional appointees. The black midshipmen in the classes of 1949–68 received appointments from only twelve states, none of which had been part of the Confederacy. Although U.S. senators and representatives from the eleven former Confederate states accounted for 20 percent of congressional appointments to the class of 1963, for example, no twentieth-century black midshipman entered the Academy with a nomination from any of those states until 1967, after passage of the voting rights act. With rebel flags flapping over former Confederate capitals in defiance of federal desegregation orders and southern politicians flinging racial epithets about in public, it is not difficult to understand why no blacks entered the Academy with a nomination from that section of the country. Thus, the system of appointments, with its heavy reliance on Congress, kept the black population at the Academy down as long as Jim Crow reigned in the South.[57]

Of the thirty-one black midshipmen in the classes of 1949–68 with congressional appointments, nine received their nominations from New York; seven from Illinois; three from California; two each from Michigan, Missouri, and Pennsylvania; and one each from Connecticut, Kansas, Maryland, Massachusetts, Ohio, and Rhode Island. Six of William Dawson's (D-Ill.) African American appointees entered the Academy between 1945 and 1964, more than any representative during this period. Adam Clayton Powell Jr. (D-N.Y.) and Edna F. Kelly (D-N.Y.) tied for second, each with three African American appointees admitted. Charles Diggs and Jeffrey Cohelan (D-Calif.) each had two, and Robert J. Dole (R-Kans.), Edward A. Garmatz (D-Md.), Theodore F. Green (D-R.I.), Torbert H. MacDonald (D-Mass.), Albert P. Morano (R-Conn.), Morgan M. Moulder (D-Mo.), Robert N. C. Nix (D-Pa.), Barratt

O'Hara (D-Ill.), Edmund P. Radwan (R-N.Y.), James Roosevelt (D-Calif.), Robert T. Ross (R-N.Y.), Herman T. Schneebeli (R-Pa.), John B. Sullivan (D-Mo.), Robert Taft Jr. (R-Ohio), and Herbert Zelenko (D-N.Y.) each had one. Sixteen of the nineteen representatives and Senator Green were white. All were born and raised in northern states except Garmatz, who hailed from Baltimore; Moulder and Sullivan, both from Missouri; and Ross, who was reared in North Carolina but moved north at age twenty-six.[58]

Four of the twenty members of Congress whose black appointees entered the Academy during this period were themselves black: William Dawson, Robert Nix, Adam Powell, and Charles Diggs. Together they accounted for twelve of the thirty-one (38.7 percent) black midshipmen appointed from congressional sources to the classes of 1949–68.

Black congressmen had been leading the efforts to integrate the Naval Academy since the Civil War and had nominated most of the blacks appointed to the Academy through World War II. White politicians considered it political suicide to send African Americans to the service academies for most of this period. After Reconstruction, no African American entered Congress until the people of Chicago's "Bronzeville" district elected Oscar DePriest in 1928. From then until the end of World War II, the Bronzeville district representative remained the only African American in Congress, with Arthur Mitchell succeeding DePriest in 1934 and William Dawson succeeding Mitchell in 1942. Although DePriest, Mitchell, and Dawson appointed blacks to the Naval Academy throughout their terms in office, none of their appointees were admitted until after World War II.

Adam Powell, who became the second African American in Congress (at one time) after winning a seat in 1944, the next year appointed the first black midshipman to graduate from the Naval Academy. Powell had earned a national reputation as an outspoken, flamboyant, and energetic activist and spokesman for the black community. Ending segregation in the armed forces sat near the top of his agenda. Particularly disturbed by the fact that very few African Americans had gradated from West Point and none from Annapolis, Powell immediately sought qualified black candidates for the service academies. Powell's first appointee to the Naval Academy, Wesley Brown, '49, succeeded in becoming its first black graduate.[59]

In part because he used service academy appointments as political capital, Powell sent fewer blacks to the Naval Academy than might be expected during his long career in the House. Although critics charged that William Dawson was more loyal to the Chicago political machine and the national Democratic Party than to the cause of civil rights, he consistently appointed blacks to the Naval Academy throughout his own long career in the House. Nix, who took office in 1959, had more success in having appointees admitted to the Academy after 1965 than before. Similarly, Augustus F. Hawkins, the only other African American in Congress during this period (elected in 1962), saw none of his black appointees admitted to the Academy until after 1965.[60]

Charles Diggs had been trying to get black youth into the Naval Academy ever since taking his seat in the House in 1955. After five years of fruitless efforts, he brought up the subject in a conversation with the dean of men at Howard University. "I have nominated ten young Negro men to be midshipmen at the Naval Academy," Diggs said, but not one had been admitted. Several of his appointees had successfully entered the Military and Air Force academies, "but I have no midshipman at Annapolis and never have had one. I need to find whether this is bias at work, or whether my candidates have been weak."

The dean pored over the list of students enrolled at Howard, looking for potential candidates, and came up with Joseph Paul Reason. Diggs's wife, Anna, had also heard of Reason; her brother was one of Reason's childhood friends. Diggs contacted Reason and asked him to participate in an experiment to see whether there was indeed discrimination at the Academy. Would Reason accept an alternate appointment and go through the application process?

The offer hit Paul Reason like a bolt from the blue and rekindled his ambition to become a naval officer, which had been snuffed out when his application for the NROTC program had been rejected. Even though he had nearly finished his third year of college, he decided to accept. He easily met all of the entrance requirements. At the end of the physical examination, a senior medical officer, a Navy captain, debriefed him. "You've more than exceeded our standards," said the captain. "But you're in your junior year of college. You don't want to leave the university now and come here and start as a plebe, do you? You really need to learn more about this place. I mean, you're a year away from graduation. You'll do just fine. You don't need to come here." Despite the captain's efforts to dissuade him from entering the Academy, Reason decided to do so anyway, joining the class of 1965.[61]

Diggs also sent another black Washingtonian to the Naval Academy that year, Stanley Jerome Carter. Carter's decision to enter the Naval Academy did not stem from a long-standing ambition to become a naval officer. He wanted to go to college, but his family would be hard pressed to afford it. The idea of entering a service academy occurred to him late in his junior year at Roosevelt High School in Washington after he read an article in the paper that said that Adam Clayton Powell had five vacancies available for appointment to Annapolis and three vacancies for West Point. "I have waited patiently all year and have received no applications," the article reported Powell as saying. "This has happened repeatedly, year after year." A day or so later, Carter overheard his history teacher discussing Powell's article with Carter's best friend. The teacher urged the lad to apply to a service academy. This overture made Carter a little jealous. He considered himself every bit as qualified as his friend, and the prospect of a free education had an enormous appeal. He decided to seek an appointment to a service academy himself, preferably West Point. So one day he put on his best suit, skipped school, and went downtown to the House Office Building carrying a list of all the black congressmen. He tried Powell's office first. Ironically, despite Powell's article, Carter was rebuffed. Since Carter was not from New York, one of Powell's staffers explained, the congressman could do nothing for him. This situation, too, was ironic, given the fact that the first two of Powell's black appointees admitted to the Naval Academy had come from Washington.

Carter went to Diggs's office next. There he received a much better reception. Diggs's administrative assistant talked to him for an hour or two and, although Carter had dropped in without an appointment, Diggs also spent ten or fifteen minutes with him. Carter told the congressman about his ambition and qualifications. Diggs promised to do what he could. As it turned out, Diggs had no openings at West Point that year and had already filled the principal slot to the Naval Academy, so he offered Carter an appointment to Annapolis as first alternate. Although Carter knew almost nothing about the Naval Academy, he accepted. When Diggs's principal appointee failed to meet the entrance requirements, Carter joined the class of 1965. In an interesting coincidence, two more black Washingtonians entered the class of 1965 with Carter and Reason, each with an appointment from William Dawson, making four blacks in an incoming class of 1,234 plebes, or 0.3 percent.[62]

Edna Kelly's appointment of three blacks to the Academy resulted from both political motives and an honest, color-blind effort to represent her constituency. During nearly twenty years in Congress (8 November 1949–3 January 1969), Kelly, like many other New York Democrats, strongly supported federal social and economic programs. She proposed legislation to extend rent control and provide working mothers with tax relief and introduced many bills to provide equal pay for equal work for women. Nothing in her record marked her as an outspoken proponent of civil rights, but her district included a large proportion of black voters.[63]

In 1954, New York state assemblyman Bertram L. Baker and other black politicians in Brooklyn petitioned Kelly to appoint blacks to the service academies. Baker suggested several possible candidates, including Malvin Davidson Bruce, who lived across the street from him. Bruce had grown up proud of his West Indian heritage and, with his family's emphasis on getting a good education, was destined for college. He dreamed of studying engineering and becoming a naval officer, so in 1953 he entered Rensselaer Polytechnic Institute in the contract NROTC program. After Baker proposed Bruce's name to Kelly, Bruce went down to the congresswoman's office for an interview. Kelly told Bruce that she usually selected her nominees by their performance on competitive exams. Bruce took the exam and made the second-highest score. Kelly told him that the black candidate who got the highest score, George Matthew Fennel Jr., wanted to go to the Naval Academy too. She offered Bruce a choice: he could have the principal appointment to West Point that year, or he could have the principal appointment to Annapolis the following year, if he was willing to wait. Bruce decided to wait. Thus Edna Kelly appointed George Fennel to the class of 1958 and Mal Bruce to the class of 1959.[64]

Like Bruce, Patrick Michael Prout, Kelly's third black appointee admitted to the Naval Academy, also grew up in Brooklyn proud of his West Indian heritage, college bound, and with dreams of becoming a naval officer. To help her son realize his dream, Prout's mother joined the local Democratic Club, got to know Edna Kelly, and told the representative about her son's desire. Kelly had Prout take the Civil Service Competitive Exam and he did well enough to earn her principal appointment. Prout entered the Academy in the class of 1964.[65]

Jeffrey Cohelan's nominations stemmed from a conscious effort to increase black enrollment at the Academy. Cohelan represented Berkeley, California, and sat on the House Armed Services Committee. In May 1959, he requested information from BuPers on nonwhite appointments to the Naval Academy. Specifically, he wanted to know the number of nonwhites appointed or admitted, the source of the appointments, the performance of those admitted, and the circumstances behind the success or failure of each one. The chief of naval personnel forwarded the request to the superintendent, who was the Academy's top-ranking officer and one of the chief's top subordinates. Both BuPers and the Academy searched their records. The superintendent's staff compiled information on Japanese, Filipinos, and African Americans admitted to the Academy but did not have information on all nonwhite appointments. In his reply to the congressman, the superintendent reported that, as of 19 June 1959, thirty-two blacks had been admitted to the Academy. Of these, fourteen had graduated and five remained in attendance. Of the thirteen who were separated, ten left for Academic reasons, one was discharged for unsatisfactory conduct, one resigned voluntarily, and one died. The superintendent pointed out that the attrition rate for black appointees stood at 40.6 percent, compared to an Academy-wide average attrition rate of 29.6 percent over the previous five years. Of the fourteen who finished, five graduated in the top half and nine in the bottom half of their class. All but one of the graduates received a commission.[66]

The relative paucity of appointments from congressional sources is not the only reason so few blacks entered the classes of 1949–68. According to a 1955 report by the American Civil Liberties Union, one Negro congressman, probably Powell, complained that he could not find black applicants for his appointments. This complaint foreshadowed Under Secretary Fay's 1963 observation about the scarcity of qualified applicants and underscores the fact that finding good people has always been and will always be a difficult task for recruiters.[67]

The Navy's World War II hangover remained one of the principal reasons so few African Americans sought to enter the classes of 1949–68. As late as the mid-1960s, many black people believed that all an African American could be in the Navy was a messman or steward. Don't even think about becoming a naval officer, they figured, for the Navy's officer corps was lily white. Most African Americans had heard of West Point or had seen a black Army officer, but few knew that the Naval Academy existed or had seen a black naval officer. Abraham R. Stowe, who enlisted in the Navy in 1959, never saw a black warrant officer until he became one himself in 1967 and saw his own reflection in the mirror. Stowe grew up near the Willow Grove Naval Station near Philadelphia, Pennsylvania, but many black people who did not live near a naval installation gave little thought to the Navy or knew nothing about it. Chancellor A. "Pete" Tzomes, an African American graduate of the class of 1967 from Williamsport, Pennsylvania, made a similar observation: "In my community, when you thought military," he recalled, "you really thought Army and Air Force. I never got exposed to anyone who had been in the Navy until I got to the Academy." The few articles about the Academy that appeared in the black press during this period shed little additional light on the subject.[68]

In a perfect example of what Under Secretary Fay said in 1963 about the Navy's tendency "to limit publicity concerning Negro personnel under the theory that publicizing the achievements of an individual might operate to the detriment of the individual concerned," Naval Academy policy exacerbated the lack of information about the school reaching the black community. In November 1950, various reporters requested photographs of Lawrence C. Chambers, '52, Reeves R. Taylor, '53, and the two African Americans admitted into the class of 1954, John D. Raiford and Bobby C. Wilks. The Academy's executive department allowed the midshipmen to decide for themselves whether to consent to the request, but not before an academic board official advised them that the Academy discouraged any form of publicity "for individual midshipmen." Not surprisingly, the black midshipmen declined to release photos of themselves to the press.[69]

Eight months later, another reporter requested material for a feature on blacks at the Academy. "It has long been the Naval Academy's policy not to

publicize any midshipman because of his race, creed, color, or nationality,"
declared the official reply. "When special requests, such as yours, are received,
the midshipmen concerned are asked whether or not they desire any such
publicity, and if they do not, their wishes are respected and their privacy protected by the Academy." The reporter received no material from the Academy.
A similar request by another reporter that fall met the same fate.[70]

Reporters from the black press clamored for a story on Reeves Taylor on
the occasion of his graduation in June 1953. After the ceremony in Dahlgren
Hall, Taylor ducked out a side door to evade them. A reporter and a photog-
rapher from the *Afro-American* almost caught up to him as he was heading
back to Bancroft Hall. "Uh, oh," thought Taylor. "Cameras." The newly
minted ensign cut across a nearby volleyball court to avoid having to talk to
them. "At first it was thought that colored graduates at the Academy had been
advised not to submit to interviews," said an article in the *Afro-American,*
"but naval authorities made it clear . . . that such actions were 'personal' with
the men."[71]

The Academy also received requests for data on the participation of blacks
at the Academy, such as the number currently enrolled, the number of graduates, and the number admitted. At first the Academy released the information.
But in 1958, the superintendent directed that replies to future such requests
state, "Our records are not kept in such a manner as to enable us to readily
furnish you the desired information." Thus, rather than publicize the presence
of black midshipmen, the Academy suppressed public release of information
about them. No doubt this policy contributed to the dearth of black applicants to the Academy during the 1950s.[72]

Some African Americans did know what the Academy was all about and
considered attending but were discouraged from seeking appointments. Pete
Tzomes was one of the few blacks in his junior high school class. When he
sought information from the school's guidance counselor, the counselor said
that it was unreasonable "to expect that a Negro could go to the Naval Academy." Bill Norman, who had grown up under segregation in Norfolk and
who, during his senior year in high school, was president of his class and
president of the student government, went to a Navy recruiter's office and
asked how to apply to the Academy. "He simply wouldn't give me any information," recalled Norman. "And he said he didn't want me to waste my time
going through the tests." Ron Stowe had enlisted in the Navy with the idea
of eventually becoming an officer, but he had such a hard time getting the
enlisted training he wanted that the thought of going to the Academy never
even crossed his mind. And even as Paul Reason stood on the Academy's
threshold, a Navy doctor tried to convince him not to step across. No doubt

many other qualified young blacks with an interest in the Naval Academy were similarly discouraged.[73]

During the 1950s, neither BuPers nor the Naval Academy itself made an effort to increase minority enrollment. Until 1961, Naval Academy policy toward recruiting African Americans mirrored the BuPers policy toward recruiting black sailors—that is, the Academy did nothing specific to recruit blacks. But the Kennedy administration's assault on discrimination in the federal government, the Gesell Committee's campaign for greater representation of blacks in the officer corps, McNamara's Directive 5120.36, and the various observations inside and outside the Navy secretariat that black people had a bad impression of the Navy or knew nothing about the Naval Academy, prompting various calls for "public information programs," led BuPers to begin actively recruiting African Americans for the Academy. In 1962 and 1963, the chief of naval personnel sent letters to the heads of some one hundred historically black colleges and two thousand predominantly black high schools requesting opportunities to inform students about the Academy and other Navy programs and soliciting suggestions on how to increase black enrollment in them. No doubt this letter campaign was precipitated by Assistant Secretary Runge's 7 November 1961 directive to "institute specific active measures to increase the participation of Negroes in existing officer procurement and training programs." The campaign resulted in hundreds of visits by Navy recruiters to black high schools and colleges. In May 1963, the Navy recruiters that attended the Secretary of Labor Conference in Houston included the Naval Academy in their pitch to black educators. These ad hoc efforts were, however, fire-fighting measures; they were not conceived as part of a permanent program to recruit blacks for the Academy.

In early 1964, Alfred B. Fitt, deputy assistant secretary of defense for civil rights, an office under the assistant secretary of defense for manpower established to run the Defense Department's equal opportunity program, helped BuPers recruit African Americans for the Naval Academy. Fitt persuaded several members of Congress to use some of their appointments to increase minority enrollment at the service academies. He also persuaded the academies to accept as many qualified black candidates as he could supply. He found candidates by writing to the superintendents and principals of schools in selected cities across America and assuring them that the academies were indeed open to all who qualified. Fitt was surprised to discover how little school superintendents, principals, and guidance counselors in black schools knew about career opportunities for officers in the armed forces. Even though Fitt launched his "micro-personnel operation," as he later called it, halfway into the academic year, long after the usual admittance process had begun, it resulted in nominations for ten African Americans for all three academies, two of whom entered the Naval Academy class of 1968. Fitt's imaginative effort proved that special efforts to increase minority enrollment at the academies could work. But it was a one-time-only deal, for Fitt's successor chose not to repeat the operation. When the class of 1965 graduated, the Navy still lacked a minority recruiting organization or an ongoing minority recruiting program for the Naval Academy.[74]

Growing Up under Segregation

FIFTY-ONE AFRICAN Americans became midshipmen between 1945 and 1964. Segregation and the struggle for racial equality formed the backdrop of their childhoods. The racial attitudes they encountered and the mechanisms they learned for coping with racism while growing up influenced how they adapted to the Naval Academy's culture. These attitudes and mechanisms proved as diverse as their backgrounds.[1]

In 1950, more than 15 million black people lived in the United States, making up 10 percent of the population. Of these 15 million, 10.2 million lived in the South, 2.2 million in the Midwest, 2 million in the Northeast, and 0.6 million in the West. By 1960, the black population had climbed to over 18 million (10.5 percent of the total population), with more than 11 million African Americans living in the South, 3 million in the Midwest, 3 million in the Northeast, and 1 million in the West.[2]

Even as the civil rights movement was gaining the force necessary to sweep it away, segregation remained legal in the South through the mid-1960s. Signs reading "white only" or "colored" hung over theaters, waiting rooms, bathrooms, and water fountains. Laws mandated segregation in parks, ice cream parlors, public transportation, and homes for the aged, indigent, blind, and deaf. Public facilities reserved for African Americans, such as schools and hospitals, received less funding than those for whites and were markedly inferior. African Americans also had shabbier housing and recreational facilities. "Separate but equal" was not simply a non sequitur but a lie. Jim Crow etiquette accompanied the legal strictures. It included taboos against blacks and whites dancing, swimming, eating, or drinking together. The biggest taboo was interracial sex or marriage, particularly for black males. Black people who defied the doctrine of white supremacy risked being tortured to death by white lynch mobs.

Above the Mason-Dixon Line, restrictive covenants, zoning ordinances, and neighborhood associations excluded black people from many white neighborhoods. African Americans were expected to use different beaches and not to patronize certain dance halls, hotels, and restaurants. Although black people had the right to vote and enjoyed better living conditions and economic opportunities, more protection under the law, and greater freedom as human beings up north than they did down south, by no means did they have the same rights and opportunities as white people.

All African Americans suffered the consequences of prejudice. In 1960, fewer than half as many black people finished high school, proportionally speaking, as white people. Whereas 8 percent of white people finished four or more years of college, only 3 percent of black people did so. Poorer education meant fewer job prospects. Between 1949 and 1964, the unemployment rate for African Americans doubled that of whites. More than 80 percent of black people who did have jobs worked at the bottom of the economic ladder, compared to 40 percent for whites. In 1969, black people with eight years of schooling earned a median income of $4,472, while whites with the same schooling made $7,018. In 1970, one in three blacks existed below the poverty line, while only one in ten whites did.[3]

The black midshipmen from the classes of 1949–68 who grew up in the South experienced racism at its worst. John Raiford, '54, was raised on a farm in Hazelhurst, Mississippi. Prejudice "was built into every aspect of the local culture," he recalled. He was taught to "keep away from whites as much as possible because they don't like you or respect you." Harold Bauduit, '56, spent his early childhood in New Orleans. His father was bitter about segregation and regarded many white people as demons. His mother had a more positive view of whites but remained bent on getting the family out of the South. Charlie Bolden, '68, grew up in Columbia, South Carolina, where name calling was common and black people were expected to "stay in their place." When Frank Simmons, '68, was asked what kind of racial attitudes he encountered in youth, he replied, "Birmingham, Alabama, 1943–1961: no further explanation required."

Those from border areas also encountered legal or de jure segregation. Wes Brown, '49; Larry Chambers, '52; Stan Carter, '65; Floyd Grayson, '65; and Paul Reason, '65, all grew up in Washington, D.C. During their childhoods the nation's capital was a segregated city. Black civil servants worked separately from whites. Black Washingtonians were barred from public playgrounds, tennis courts, and swimming pools. African Americans could watch spectator sports in Uline Arena, Washington's largest indoor sports facility, but were not permitted to ice skate there. Most restaurants and theaters refused to serve black people. Downtown nightclubs employed blacks but did not cater to them. Even barber shops and eateries on Capitol Hill were segregated.

Wesley Brown and his parents Rosetta and William lived with Rosetta's mother, Katie Shepherd, in her house near Logan Circle. Wesley felt a tremendous sense of community while growing up. Neighbors were friends. "We never locked our door," he recalled. William drove a truck for a fruit and vegetable wholesaler, delivering produce to restaurants and hotels. He was one of the few men on the block who held a job throughout the Depression. Rosetta pressed clothes at a laundry.

With both parents working, Wesley was raised by his grandmother. Katie Shepherd was the family's matriarch. With a mixture of love and iron, she instilled in Wesley a strong work ethic and sense of morality, saw to it that he went to church, and insisted that he did well in school. She also drilled into him her belief that each succeeding generation should strive to do better than the last, frequently reminding the family that her own mother had been born in slavery and that her late husband's parents had been slaves.

Wesley became aware of segregation in kindergarten. He would ask his parents to take him to a movie. "You can't go there," they would reply. Jim Crow laws prohibited black kids from playing in white playgrounds, so Wesley and his friends played in the streets and alleys, even when the white playground nearby was empty. Sometimes they played on the lawn in Logan Circle until the park police drove them off. When Wesley grew old enough to take the trolley by himself, he would go exploring. On one occasion he disembarked in a white neighborhood. A policeman approached him. "Get back on the trolley," he said. "Go back to where you belong." Segregation remained so pervasive that Brown had little contact with white people. Any interaction he did have stemmed from school, church, or community activities and, later, government jobs, but it was formal and circumscribed by events. Black Washingtonians simply did not socialize naturally or informally with whites. "We more or less lived in our own world," he recalled.[4]

Larry Chambers's background resembled Brown's in many ways. Chambers was born in Bedford, Virginia. His father, a World War I naval veteran, died when Larry was four years old. His mother, Charlotte, never remarried. Larry and his two brothers and two sisters remained in Bedford with their grandparents while Charlotte moved to D.C. to find work. She soon landed a job as a clerk in the War Department. For the next several years, the children saw their mother about once every other month, for it was the Depression and Charlotte couldn't afford to visit them more frequently. When Larry was in the fourth grade, he and his siblings and grandparents moved to Washington.

Chambers grew up in close-knit communities in both Bedford and Washington. "Everybody looked out for everybody," he recalled. "If I got in trouble anywhere, my family knew about it before I got home." It was a support system that "gave you the feeling that somebody cared."

After the family reunited, Larry's grandmother remained the matriarch, running the house, taking care of the kids, and administering discipline with a switch. Larry often put the other kids up to doing things, often got caught, and often got punished for things he didn't do. His grandmother figured that it balanced out the things he got away with.

Larry's grandfather never disciplined the children. The son of slaves, he read to them; he talked to them about the family's history, the plight of black people in America, and the unfolding events of World War II; and he let them argue with him. None of the other adults tolerated arguments from the children. Despite the Depression and segregation, he remained optimistic. He "had the habit of making us all feel like we were ten feet tall," Chambers recalled.

Segregation was legal throughout Chambers's youth. "Mostly you stayed in your section of town," he recalled. "You ran with your friends." Chambers and his family lived in a house at 7th and T Streets Northwest in a tough neighborhood. Some of the older folks were addicted to heroin; some of Chambers's peers had alcohol problems. Chambers and his friends were horrified by what drugs and drink did to people, so they steered clear. Instead they played sports and went to Howard Theater to see the world's first rock and roll bands when they could afford tickets. Chambers never had social contact with white people. In fact, he rarely had contact with white people at all except when he visited the Smithsonian, the Library of Congress, and the like. The segregated bathrooms and water fountains in such places didn't bother him. "That was part of growing up," he recalled. "It's just the way it was." Still, he despised prejudice. His grandfather's optimism and advice helped him cope with it. "You're better than those people," his grandfather would say. "You can stand on your own two feet." The cohesiveness of the community also helped him cope. The Depression lingered longer in black communities than it did in white communities, so people in his neighborhood continued to help each other out.

Although born in 1940, Bill Jones, '64, might just as well have grown up during the Depression. Bill was raised in the Gilmor Housing Projects in Baltimore. His parents divorced when he was ten or eleven, after which his mother raised Bill and his two brothers and sister by herself. Although she had a nursing degree, she could not find a position in the Baltimore hospitals, so she worked as a domestic when she could. Bill and his siblings worked after school to help support the family. Although Bill's mother refused to go on welfare, she and her children learned to use the powdered eggs, powdered milk, peanut butter, and yellow-dyed margarine given to families on welfare because they were inexpensive. Although black people in Baltimore could sit in any seat they pleased on the bus, they could neither eat in certain restaurants nor try on clothes in department stores.

Bill went to high school at Baltimore Polytechnic Institute shortly after it was integrated. He was one of only a dozen black students in the school. Sometimes he encountered hostility and racial prejudice. "You solved those problems with physical violence," he recalled. "You beat somebody up or they beat you up or you just ignored it. I chose to ignore it most of the time. I usually had enough white friends who would keep it from happening." These interracial friendships had limited scope, however. "We were friends at school and that's where the friendship ended," recalled Jones. "When you left school, you went back to your own environment."

Stanley Carter, Floyd Grayson, and Paul Reason grew up in the generation that experienced the beginning of integration. Stan Carter spent his early childhood in Ivy City, a section of northeast Washington near West Virginia and Montello Avenues. Blacks lived on one side of the street and whites on the other. "You didn't go across the street unless you were passing through," Carter recalled. He learned that people who looked like him were unwelcome in certain stores and couldn't eat at lunch counters with whites. His parents taught him that it was not good enough for a black person to be as good as a white person. "If you are going to succeed," they would say, "you have to be better." When Carter was about eight, the family moved to Parkland Apartments in Anacostia, where he attended Garfield Elementary School. Outside of school, Carter learned to cope with gangs and gang warfare in Anacostia by befriending the leaders but not joining any of the gangs. When Carter was in junior high school, his parents moved the family uptown to Fort Totten Drive in Northeast D.C. to get away from the gangs. Since their new house was only a block from North Capitol Street, Carter went to school in Northwest D.C., attending McFarland Junior High and Roosevelt High. Both schools were integrated. When Carter first attended Roosevelt High, some 80 percent of the student body was white. By the time he graduated, the percentage of white students had fallen off precipitously because of "white flight," as white people moved out of the city to the suburbs or enrolled their children in private schools so that they wouldn't have to go to integrated schools. "It was almost a stampede," he recalled. Throughout his high school days, black students and white pretty much socialized separately.

Paul Reason grew up near Howard University, where his father was professor of romance languages. His mother was a high school biology teacher. Paul lived for most of his youth in a house on Girard Street, Northeast. When the family moved there in 1944—Paul was three—the neighborhood was also in the midst of white flight. Other Howard professors and black professionals remained, however. Although Reason attended segregated schools during his early childhood, his parents sensed that America was moving toward integration, so they took pains to expose Paul and his sister to white society. The family spent a week or two every summer at a camp on Lake Winnepesauke in New Hampshire. Paul and his sister were usually the only black children there. At home, his parents had friends of many different ethnicities. Paul grew up in a multiracial environment, and he was just as comfortable among white people as he was among black people. Nevertheless, he didn't have many white childhood friends. Most of the white kids he knew while growing up he met at summer camp or the Washington Junior Academy of Sciences. "They were not social friends," he recalled. "They weren't people I'd go out and play baseball with. They weren't people I'd go to movies with. You couldn't go to movies together. It just wasn't allowed."

Reason refused to let such things bother him. "If you're of a race different from most of the people around you," he recalled, "it's noticed by everybody. After a while you get to the point that you must move forward and accomplish your goals and eat your meals and sleep your nights, no matter what race you are. You don't worry about it anymore. You focus on the other things. And when you hit a stone wall, whether because of your race or something else, you detour, or you climb over it. You don't break through it. You can hurt yourself breaking through. If you got around to the other side by a way that didn't injure you, you're intact. You can move forward and do good things. I was precluded from doing many things that a young person of my age would have done, just because I was black. I was not allowed to let that upset me. My parents taught me that 'It will change one day, and when it changes, you have to be able to read. You have to be able to write. You have to have skills that allow you to succeed once you have that path opened to you. But if you go out and become an arch-militant and you engage in violence, you probably won't be alive to see that day.'"

Floyd Grayson's parents also sensed that segregation wouldn't last forever. His father, who landscaped houses in suburban subdivisions, believed that integration was inevitable because the country simply couldn't afford "separate but equal" facilities. Pleasant experiences working for white people, including U.S. senators and representatives, reinforced his conviction that black people and white people could get along. Floyd grew up in Kenilworth, a pleasant black neighborhood in Northeast D.C. near the Maryland line. Kenilworth was an integrated neighborhood when the Graysons and other black families first moved there, but white flight soon rendered it homogeneously black. The junior high and high schools Floyd attended remained virtually all black even after D.C. schools were officially integrated. Occasionally somebody would call Floyd a "dirty nigger," but otherwise he didn't think much about race until a white Boy Scout leader tried to prevent him from becoming an eagle scout by flunking him on the test for the lifesaving badge. Floyd later passed the same test at the YMCA, got the badge, and became an eagle scout.

Grayson had his first sustained contact with white people in college. Before entering the Academy, he spent two years at Capital University, a small Lutheran school in Columbus, Ohio, where Floyd was one of a half dozen blacks in a student body of about two thousand. Many of the whites he came into contact with harbored stereotyped images of black people. "White people just didn't know much about us," he recalled. "In some cases, they were very afraid." On one occasion, Grayson was washing his hands at the bathroom sink when a white student emerged from a stall and wiped his hands on Grayson's shirt. Grayson turned around and decked the guy, then went to the dean to explain what had happened. Grayson was not punished, and the white student was ashamed of what he had done. Grayson had many good experiences with white students at Capital University as well, and he remained open-minded about white people.

Some black northerners had relatively few problems with racism in their youth. Reeves R. Taylor, '53, grew up in a blue-collar family in Providence, Rhode Island. His father struggled throughout the Depression. For several years Reeves had to live with his grandmother because his own parents could not afford to care for their only child. Things got better at the beginning of World War II, when Reeves's father found a job as a stevedore. Although Providence had no Jim Crow laws, the more expensive hotels and restaurants nevertheless refused to serve African Americans. Still, the city had an integrated school system, and Reeves had many white friends while growing up. He attended Hope High School, where he was elected class president and, in the spring of 1947, graduated in the top of his class. That fall he entered Brown University.

Lou Adams, '58, grew up in a West Indian neighborhood in Manhattan. The neighborhood was mostly black, Adams attended mostly black schools, and he encountered little prejudice. Mal Bruce, '59, also grew up in a West Indian neighborhood, in Brooklyn. Mal went to a mostly white high school, had white friends, and had no problems with prejudice. Mal's father and uncle instilled in him pride in his heritage and the belief that he was equal to anyone. His father was proud when the British national cricket team became integrated. Mal, too, regarded the black cricket players as heroes, but they did not loom as large in his pantheon as baseball player Jackie Robinson.

James Frezzell, '68, grew up black but experienced a similar degree of acceptance from white people in his hometown. Frezzell was born and raised in Monessen, Pennsylvania, a steel town near Pittsburgh. James's father worked as a laborer in a steel mill. His mother took care of the house and the kids. When James was six, the family moved into an integrated neighborhood so that James and his brother and three sisters could go to better schools. James encountered little discrimination in Monessen. Most of the neighbors also worked in steel mills. His father often said that it was so dark and dirty from the soot that everyone in the mill was black.

Passion for football also dampened prejudice. Football was king in the steel towns of western Pennsylvania, which produced such gridiron legends as Tony Dorsett, Mike Ditka, Dan Marino, Cookie Gilchrist, and Joe Namath. In Monessen, high school football games often drew fifteen to twenty thousand spectators. "The whole town would close down to see a football game," Frezzell recalled. "Winning a game was front page news." He was a star fullback and cornerback for the Monessen High Greyhounds. The drive to win and rigors of two-a-day practices fostered camaraderie and companionship among black and white teammates, not prejudice and racism.

Other black northerners did encounter some degree of racism during their youth. Lucius Gregg, '55, was raised mostly in an all-black ghetto on the south side of Chicago. He attended all-black schools and had little interaction with whites except for white high school teachers and customers at a downtown florist for whom he delivered flowers throughout the Windy City after school. Although his mother was qualified to teach in Chicago public schools, she was denied a certificate because of her race. She cleaned houses in the suburbs and later worked making sundaes and milk shakes at a fashionable ice cream store downtown. Robert Lucas, '68, grew up in Springfield, Ohio. He attended a high school that was 50 percent black and 50 percent white and was the first black student to be elected class president. He lived in an integrated neighborhood and had lots of white friends. Nevertheless, white people sometimes called him names and people who looked like him still could not get certain jobs or eat in certain restaurants in Springfield. Pete Tzomes, '67, grew up in a black neighborhood in Williamsport, Pennsylvania, where one of the streets was literally named "Nigger Hollow." His parents taught him to act differently around white people than he did around black people and not to enter certain business establishments. Yet Tzomes joined many of the same clubs in the community that whites did, including the Key Club, the Future Teachers of America, and the National Conference of Christians and Jews. Like Lucas and Taylor, Tzomes attended an integrated school.

Newcomers to the North were surprised by the prejudice they encountered there. When John Raiford was twelve, his family moved to Illinois. In terms of prejudice, they found that Illinois wasn't much different from Mississippi. Harold Bauduit's family moved from New Orleans to New York City when Harold was fourteen. In New Orleans, Bauduit had had very little contact with white people. In New York, he attended an integrated school and had white friends. But the racial attitudes he encountered up north resembled those he had grown up with down south. "I felt that the people in New York didn't really want blacks," he recalled, "but they couldn't stop blacks. That's the difference between New York and New Orleans. In New Orleans, they just put up a sign that said 'white only.' In New York they couldn't do that, but you felt it from the people." Pat Prout, '64, was born and raised in Trinidad in the West Indies. His family moved to Brooklyn when he was twelve. "In Trinidad, the population was about 40 percent of African descent, 40 percent of East Indian descent, 10 percent Chinese, and 10 percent others," recalled Prout, "so race was not that much of an issue at all, because people mingled and interacted very easily in that society." In some ways, his new home resembled the old one. He went to school with white people and had friends of all colors. But in other ways, New York differed markedly. Brooklyn neighborhoods were segregated by race and, for the first time in his life, white kids called Prout derogatory names because of the color of his skin.

Black midshipmen from the classes of 1949–68 entered the Naval Academy for a variety of reasons. Many developed the ambition to become midshipmen in high school or earlier, with the express purpose of going to the Naval Academy and being commissioned in the Navy. Some sought to enter the Academy for the educational opportunity without giving much thought to a naval career. Others sort of stumbled unintentionally into the Academy from the enlisted service. Still others were recruited to play varsity football. A few became midshipmen to facilitate integration of the Academy, at least in part.

Wesley Brown entered the Naval Academy with the ambition to become its first black graduate. After finishing Dunbar High School in 1944, Brown attended Howard University in the Army's Specialized Training Reserve Program, intent on serving his country and becoming an engineer. He intended to seek an appointment to West Point during his freshman year at Howard. But when Adam Powell offered him an appointment to the Naval Academy, Brown pondered the offer. Did he really want to go to Annapolis? The Military Academy seemed a safer bet, since several African Americans had already graduated from there. But the possibility of breaking the color barrier at the Naval Academy intrigued him. It awakened a yearning to emulate the African American military heroes he had grown up with in Washington—his godfather, Hewlett Smith, who had joined the army during the Spanish-American War; three Dunbar High alumni who had graduated from West Point; and

Colonel Henry O. Atwood, head of the Cadet Corps (the equivalent of to-day's Junior ROTC program) at Washington D.C.'s black high schools. At-wood had been working with black members of Congress since the 1930s to find black candidates for West Point and to be the first to graduate from Annapolis. He had always tried to steer the best and brightest toward a service academy, and Brown had been cadet colonel, the top cadet among the 1,500 participants from Washington's four black high schools, during his senior year. Brown decided to accept Powell's offer. Fully aware of the pioneering role he would play and the difficulties he would face, he made a conscious decision to try to break the color barrier at the Naval Academy, to serve his country and serve his race.[5]

Larry Chambers's and Paul Reason's motivation included making sure that the Naval Academy's color barrier stayed broken. A push from Colo-nel Atwood propelled Chambers into the Academy. Like Brown, Chambers became Cadet Corps colonel during his senior year in high school. Atwood remained keen on sending black students to the Naval Academy. With Wes Brown a first classman at the time and about to "break the ice," Atwood thought it was crucial to get an African American into the plebe class to keep it from refreezing, as Chambers phrased it. He convinced Chambers to follow in Wesley Brown's footsteps.

Colonel Atwood arranged an interview with Representative William Daw-son for Chambers and several other seniors. Dawson decided to nominate Chambers as first alternate to the Naval Academy. When Dawson's principal nominee failed to meet the entrance requirements, Chambers took his place. In April 1948, he passed the Academy's entrance examination.

Atwood might also have influenced the decisions of Washingtonians Ed Sechrest and Richard Drew to enter the Academy. Atwood was head of the Cadet Corps while Sechrest was going to Dunbar and Drew was going to Armstrong High School.

Initially, Paul Reason set his sights on becoming a naval officer because it seemed the most economical way to get the education he wanted. Rea-son excelled in science and math, earned enough merit badges to become an eagle scout, lettered in tennis, and became a platoon commander in the Cadet Corps.[6] Known as a "fix-it kid," he once learned how to install a new roof on his family's garage just by watching roofers in the neighborhood. Although he spent most of his youth under segregation, his experiences in an integrated Boy Scout troop and his outgoing nature facilitated the integration of McKin-ley Technical High School in 1955. Academically, athletically, and socially, he was ideally qualified to become a naval officer.

Reason became interested in the NROTC program during his senior year (1957/58) of high school. His physics teacher, a naval officer during World

War II, often used naval examples in class. Occasionally the teacher remarked that the NROTC program could finance a college education. Interested in optics, Reason identified the University of Rochester as having one of the best optics programs in the country, in part because of its proximity to Eastman Kodak. The University of Rochester also had an NROTC program. Reason figured he could get the education he wanted there and have the Navy pay for it. He applied for the program and took the full battery of tests.

Not long afterward, he received a rejection letter. The following Saturday, a Navy commander knocked on the Reasons' door. Reason invited him inside. The commander sat down in the living room. "I was not sent here by the Navy," he explained rather haltingly. "I'm sort of here on my own. I know that you received a letter this week, telling you that you were not selected for naval ROTC. I'm here because you should understand that it is not the Navy that makes the choice as to who gets the program. It is a board made up of educators from the universities that have naval ROTC within your region. Your region proceeds from Washington to Atlanta and this board was not willing to select a black." Of the three hundred who competed, Reason ranked number two. The officer had come because he was ashamed of the racism inherent in the selection process and felt he owed Reason an explanation. The revelation did not devastate Reason, however; having grown up under segregation, it came as no surprise.

After being rejected by the NROTC program, Reason spent his freshman year at Swarthmore College, his sophomore year at Lincoln University in Pennsylvania, and his junior year at Howard University. He had just about finished his junior year when Charles Diggs approached him to apply to the Academy. "I wanted to be truly supportive of Congressman Diggs and his efforts to determine whether or not discrimination was in place," he recalled.

Talks with people who had gone to Annapolis and West Point cemented Reason's ambition to go to the Naval Academy. A white midshipman from the class of 1961 whose brother knew Reason's sister spent an evening at the house talking with Paul about the Academy. "He was very positive in describing his experience," Reason recalled, "and he, probably more than anyone else, really encouraged me to come. 'The Naval Academy needs you there,' he said, 'because there are not many people like you there.'" A soon-to-be alumnus, John Shelton,'61, encouraged Reason as well. Shelton happened to be a black Washingtonian, too. "I spent an afternoon with John," Reason recalled. "John had been the brigade boxing champion. He was a very popular figure at the Naval Academy. My experience with him was positive. He was a very gregarious, engaging fellow. So I thought if many people there were like him, and if he had excelled and was happy, then certainly I could get along."

Reason's soon-to-be father-in-law, James Fowler, thought that going to the Naval Academy would be a good thing. Fowler had graduated from the Military Academy in 1941 after Franklin Roosevelt had put a stop to the abuse heaped upon him by racist upperclassmen during his plebe year. At the time, Reason was engaged to Fowler's daughter, Diane. "I learned very little about his trials and tribulations at the Military Academy," Reason recalled. "He felt it was a positive move for me to go to the Naval Academy, even if it was the *Naval* Academy. He extolled the virtues of the technical education I would gain. He talked about the camaraderie. He talked as you would expect any academy graduate to speak to a potential enrollee about the virtues of an academy."

Reeves Taylor, Mal Bruce, Pat Prout, Floyd Grayson, Pete Tzomes, and Charlie Bolden cited the traditional ambition of becoming a midshipman and a naval officer as their primary motivation for entering the Naval Academy. They all wanted a college education, but they wanted to get it at the Academy instead of at a civilian institution of higher learning.

Although Reeves Taylor was already a student at Brown, what he really wanted to do was to become a midshipman. A voracious reader as a boy, he had devoured Edward Ellsberg's *Ocean Gold, Thirty Fathoms Deep,* and *Treasure Below,* as well as books on naval aviation. Even before entering high school, Taylor had developed the ambition to go to the Naval Academy and to become a naval aviator. In an era when naval aviation was still closed to African Americans, it was an uncommon dream. "You're not going to be able to do that," other black people would tell him. "Don't waste your time trying." His parents, however, never tried to discourage him.

Taylor was the first twentieth-century African American to enter the Naval Academy without the influence of Henry O. Atwood. At age fifteen, Taylor began researching how to get into the Academy. He learned that Senator Theodore F. Green and other Rhode Island congressmen sponsored competitive examinations every year to select their appointees. Taylor took the exam twice. The first time, during his senior year in high school, he did not do well enough to win an appointment. The second time, during his freshman year in college, he received the highest score, so Senator Green nominated him as principal. Taylor also received appointments to the Kings Point Maritime Academy and the NROTC program that year, but with a principal appointment to the Naval Academy there was no question that he would go anywhere else. After passing the entrance exams, Taylor entered the Academy in the class of 1952.

Mal Bruce knew that he was going to go to college. His father and uncle had drilled that into him. But ever since he was a little kid, Bruce had leaned toward a naval career. During World War II, his uncle had worked at the Brooklyn Navy Yard, where they turned out a new destroyer every ninety days or so. His oldest brother was a Navy enlisted man. On several occasions he saw newsreels of newly minted ensigns tossing their caps skyward on graduation day. These images sparked a desire to join the Navy that merged with the family's demand that he get a college education to form his ambition to enter the Academy.

Pat Prout, Floyd Grayson, Pete Tzomes, and Charlie Bolden identified the television show *Men of Annapolis* as a significant source of inspiration. The prime-time series first aired in 1957 and continued into 1958. It depicted life at the Academy as it had been since the time of Teddy Roosevelt, with background footage filmed in the Yard, as the Academy campus was called.[7] Charlie Bolden was in the ninth grade when he first watched *Men of Annapolis* on TV. "I was very, very impressed by the life of a midshipman and decided that's what I wanted to do," he recalled. No doubt the series inspired many white kids to become midshipmen as well.

Bolden began applying to the Academy in ninth grade. Each year he received replies telling him that he was too young, but he kept on sending in applications anyway, "just so they wouldn't forget me," as he later put it. During his senior year, he tried to get an appointment from his senator, Strom Thurmond, and representative, Albert W. Watson, but was he told, in essence, "no way." Bolden explored other avenues, ultimately securing an appointment to the Naval Academy from William Dawson.

Pete Tzomes wanted to be a professional baseball player until the eighth grade, when a midshipman came to his school to talk about the Academy. The midshipman's presentation included the film *Ring of Valor.* Tzomes was enthralled. He talked to his guidance counselor about the Academy. When the counselor told him that it was unreasonable "to expect that a Negro could go to the Naval Academy," Tzomes decided then and there that he would do just that.

Pat Prout's father was a sailor in the merchant marine and had traveled extensively in Latin America, Europe, and Asia. Whenever he returned home from a voyage, he regaled the family with tales of the exotic lands he had seen. The stories enthralled young Pat. He dreamed of traveling and having adventures like his father. He knew he was going to go to college, so why not go to a school that would enable him to pursue his dream? The Naval Academy seemed just such a school. Prout's interest in the Academy blossomed into a passion after he heard a presentation by a Navy recruiter at career day during his junior year of high school. He watched *Men of Annapolis* religiously. The following summer, he mentioned his dream of going to the Academy to the owner of the dry cleaner's where he was working. The owner happened to know Mal Bruce, so he gave Bruce's address at the Academy to Prout. Bruce invited Prout to visit Annapolis. The trip cemented Prout's ambition.

During his senior year of high school, he applied to only one college—the Naval Academy. Since he was only sixteen at the time—below the minimum age—he was not accepted. He enrolled in Hunter College in New York and vowed to keep applying to the Academy until he succeeded. Finally, after his second year at Hunter, he did.

John Raiford, Harold Bauduit, Stan Carter, and Gil Lucas viewed the Naval Academy primarily as an educational opportunity. Raiford developed the ambition to enter the Academy after enlisting in the Navy at the end of his sophomore year in high school. He sought an appointment to get an education and to enhance his chances of getting a good job. "I got a fleet appointment via the Naval Academy Preparatory School," he recalled. "One night I was a watch officer's messenger, and I asked the officer about the big, fat gold ring on his finger. He told me about this school that trained naval officers, where everyone got one of these rings. It sounded like he was making it up; it was so removed from anything that I had experienced. But I later saw an announcement that anyone could apply to go to that very school. I applied, went to NAPS, and made a score high enough on the entrance exam to get a secretary of the navy appointment." Enlisted candidates for the Naval Academy who demonstrated exceptional potential in leadership, athletics, or academics but whose skills needed improvement for admission received an appointment to the Naval Academy Preparatory School (NAPS) in Newport, Rhode Island, for one year. In the 1970s, the Navy opened NAPS to civilians as well. With a student body of some three hundred midshipman candidates, NAPS mirrored the Naval Academy in developing military, moral, physical, and academic skills.

Harold Bauduit reached college age during the Korean War. He wanted to join the Navy to avoid being drafted into the Army. "I wanted a clean bed to sleep in," he recalled. "I didn't want to sleep in a muddy foxhole." He saw the Naval Academy as a splendid opportunity to get a free education. "I never thought much beyond the education," he recalled. "I didn't think of what happened after the Academy."

If pragmatism shaped Harold Bauduit's decision to enter the Academy, patriotism shaped Stan Carter's decision. "At that time, you had the draft," he recalled, "so everybody was going to go into the military and I wanted to go to college. We weren't the most affluent family in town. What better way to accomplish all these goals than going to something like the Academy?" Carter would have preferred West Point, but he didn't want to wait a year for the principal appointment from Representative Diggs. He wound up at Annapolis because he could get in right after high school. Gil Lucas wanted a good, technical education without financially burdening his family, but he couldn't get a big enough scholarship from a civilian school. He had heard good things about West Point from his uncle, Robert W. Green, a Military Academy graduate of the class of 1950. Lucas didn't think he wanted to be in the Army, however, so he considered the Naval Academy. He decided to apply and told his high school guidance counselor so. "You don't need to apply," said the counselor, "because you'll never get in." Like Tzomes, being told he couldn't do something hardened Lucas's resolve to do it. He took a competitive civil service exam, scored well, and received an appointment from Robert Taft Jr. (R-Ohio).

Lu Gregg, Lou Adams, and Bill Jones got into the Naval Academy by accident. Lu Gregg excelled not only in academic work during high school but also in the JROTC unit, becoming its commander. The experience inspired him to join the Marine Corps Reserve with a view toward entering the University of Illinois ROTC program. About a month after he graduated from high school, however, the Korean War started and his reserve unit was activated. Instead of going to college, he went to boot camp. After making it through boot camp and cold-weather training at Camp Pendleton, he became an MP at the Marine base in Barstow, California. While he was there, the assistant to the base chaplain suggested that Gregg seek admittance to the Naval Academy. He took the suggestion as a joke, one that his mother would appreciate, so he mentioned it to her in a letter. His mother took the suggestion seriously, however, and repeated it to the principal of Lu's high school. The principal, in turn, took the matter to Representative William Dawson. Two months later, Lu received orders to NAPS and entered a class that had already been in session for six months. He and the other 1,200 midshipman candidates were slated to take the Academy's entrance exam in thirty days. Despite his late arrival, Lu passed the exam and entered the Academy.[8]

Lou Adams joined the Navy right after he graduated from high school in 1952. "My brother was in the Army over in Korea," Adams recalled. "I joined the Navy so I could go and help him out." While in boot camp, Adams took a typing test, pecking out fifteen words per minute. That was better than any other boot had done that day, so the Navy sent him to teleman's school and afterward assigned him to work the teletype in the Navy recruiting office at 90 Church Street in New York City. One of the officers billeted there, a white lieutenant (j.g.) from Mississippi, saw potential in Adams. The lieutenant suggested that Adams take the exam for NAPS. "I had no desire to go to the Naval Academy," Adams recalled. But the lieutenant persisted. Adams qualified for NAPS, did well there, and entered the Academy with a fleet appointment. It didn't dawn on him that going to the Academy was a big deal until his mother gushed with excitement when he told her the news.

About a year after graduating from high school, Bill Jones decided on a whim to enter the armed forces. He went down to the Baltimore Custom

House, where recruiters from each of the services were posted. He scrutinized their uniforms. The sailor's uniform looked "girly." The soldier's and
airman's uniforms looked nondescript. The marine, wearing tailored dress
blues, looked sharp and trim. Jones enlisted in the Marine Corps. As long
as he could remember, he wanted to fly. Soon he began taking every test
he could to become a commissioned aviator, including the exam for NAPS.
He passed them all. His first choice was to enter the Marine Aviation Cadet
(MARCAD) program, but it was not to be. "You can turn the officer program
down for the Naval Academy," his commanding officer told him, "but you
can't turn the Naval Academy down for another officer program." Thus, Bill
Jones entered the Academy via NAPS.

James Frezzell faced a difficult but pleasant decision in the winter of
1962/63 as graduation day approached. Being a football star for Monessen
Senior High had opened a world of opportunity for him. Some fifty universi-
ties, including West Virginia, Pittsburgh, Penn State, Nebraska, and Arizona,
had offered him athletic scholarships. At that same time, Tony Urbanik and
Steve Belichick were trying to break the color barrier in Navy's varsity football team. No African American had ever played varsity football for Navy.
Urbanik was recruiting for West Virginia and Pittsburgh as well as the Naval
Academy at that time, so he was aware of Frezzell's prospects. Urbanik and
Belichick approached him about playing for Navy. "They just picked me out
of nowhere," Frezzell recalled. He had seen *Men of Annapolis* on TV. He liked
the look of the Navy football uniforms. Navy football was enjoying one of its
golden eras, with Heisman Trophy–winning quarterback Roger Staubach,
'65, at the helm. And like Wesley Brown, the challenge of being a "first" appealed to Frezzell. He accepted Navy's offer. After a year at NAPS and with
an appointment from Representative Robert N. C. Nix (D-Pa.), he entered
the Academy in the summer of 1964. James Frezzell became one of the first
African Americans recruited by the Academy to play football.

The families, friends, and neighbors of most of the black midshipmen responded positively to their decision to enter the Academy. "My family and
the immediate community thought the world of what I was doing," recalled
Harold Bauduit. "They were all behind me 100 percent. They felt it was
a great opportunity." Floyd Grayson received a similar reception at school.
"My teachers were very proud that I had the guts to try," he recalled. When
news of Bill Jones's assignment to the Academy reached home, his family and
friends treated him as "God's gift to the world," as he put it. "A little boy
from the projects in this white Good Humor uniform. Some of them were
throwing their daughters at me. It was great." When Lu Gregg transferred
trains in Chicago on the way to NAPS from California, a large party met him
at the station, including his family, high school principal, and photographers.

His high school ROTC unit greeted him with crossed swords! The next day his story appeared on the front page of Chicago newspapers.

But there were trepidations as well. John Raiford never told his family about his becoming a midshipman. They had never heard of the Academy, and John felt they wouldn't grasp the significance of the appointment. Besides, John figured he might not make it to graduation, anyway. Gil Lucas's family and friends were proud of him for going to the Academy, but many other people in Springfield, Ohio, black and white, had no idea what the Naval Academy was all about. Some thought the Naval Academy was located in Indianapolis, not Annapolis. Pat Prout's father also harbored misconceptions about the Academy. He had grown up in Trinidad and spent much of his adult life at sea in the merchant marine. He worried that Pat would wind up in the enlisted service if he went to Annapolis. Reeves Taylor's parents had always supported his aspiration to become a naval aviator, but many of his friends and neighbors were not at all encouraging. "You're not going to be able to do that," they would say. "Don't waste your time trying." Floyd Grayson's mother believed that, because of the Navy's reputation for discrimination, her son would stand a better chance of getting into West Point. Still, she never discouraged him from trying for the Naval Academy. Paul Reason's mother was less than enthusiastic about her son's decision to enter the Academy. Nobody on either side of the family had ever served in the armed forces, and Paul had only one more year to go before graduating from Howard University with an engineering degree. Reason's friends and neighbors had mixed reactions. Some thought it was a wonderful opportunity. Even if he "utterly detested Academy life," they said, "the end result would justify four years of drudgery" because he would get a wonderful education and, after graduation, valuable experience in the fleet, both of which would serve him well in a post-naval career in engineering.[9] "Others thought it was the dumbest thing I could ever possibly do," Reason recalled. "You know how the Navy treats black people," they would tell him. Pete Tzomes's mother was disappointed that her son wanted to enter the Academy. She wanted him to be a doctor or lawyer, not a naval officer.

Whatever reception their decisions had received, the black midshipmen themselves had few if any trepidations about the journey upon which they were about to embark. They certainly didn't worry about discrimination. "I thought that I would be treated like anyone else," recalled Mal Bruce. Floyd Grayson felt the same way. "I went there with high hopes that I would be able to do as well as anybody," he recalled.

Larry Chambers harbored no real concerns about being a black man in a virtually all-white environment, especially after a meeting with Wesley Brown arranged by Congressman Dawson. To be sure, Chambers had heard horror stories about previous black midshipmen who had gone through hell and then bilged, but Brown, resplendent in his summer whites, stood as living proof that an African American could make it as a midshipman. Brown encouraged Chambers to give the Academy his best shot. Chambers resolved to do just that.

Sweep It under the Rug

THE COLLISION with reality during "plebe summer" sorely tested black midshipmen's preconceptions of the Academy. Having been outstanding in their previous lives, newly minted midshipmen were reduced to near nothingness after being sworn in. They enjoyed precious few privileges, had no prestige whatsoever, and were subjected to systematic indignities.

A newly minted midshipman of this era occupied the lowest position in the Academy hierarchy, a status reflected in his nickname, "plebe," derived from the word *plebian*. The superintendent, the Academy's highest-ranking officer, handled the Academy's overall administration, commanded the officers assigned there, and supervised the civilian employees. The commandant of midshipmen, the second-ranking officer, was responsible for the care and feeding of midshipmen. Midshipmen from the sophomore, junior, and senior classes, known collectively as the upper classes, outranked plebes and enjoyed privileges denied them. Sophomores, juniors, and seniors were known formally as third classmen, second classmen, and first classmen and informally as youngsters, segundos, and firsties.

Midshipmen were organized into twenty-four to thirty-six companies, six battalions, and two regiments, constituting the "Brigade of Midshipmen." Navy and Marine Corps officers served under the commandant as battalion and company officers in the executive department. Battalion and company officers were responsible not only for administration and discipline but also for counseling and guidance of the midshipmen.

Firsties assumed many responsibilities in training plebes. The superintendent appointed midshipman officers from the first class to give them experience in the exercise of military authority and to provide military and adminstrative leadership for the brigade. Three sets of midshipman officers, called "stripers" for the stripes worn on their sleeves, served as brigade, regimental, battalion, and company officers during the academic year. The superintendent selected the "fall" and "winter sets" from the first class on the basis of their previous records and the "spring set" from the best of the midshipman officers in the first two sets. Midshipmen also served as watch officers in Bancroft Hall. All upperclassmen shared responsibility for enforcing discipline.[1]

Regulations governed almost every aspect of a midshipman's life. Infractions fell into two categories. Class A, or "honor," offenses involved serious breaches of discipline. They included, among other things, lying, cheating, stealing, intoxication, marrying, hazing, and offenses indicative of "moral turpitude." Midshipmen guilty of Class A offenses were generally dismissed, or "separated," from the Academy. Class B, or "conduct," offenses involved comparatively minor infractions such as unauthorized use of chewing gum; untidiness in dress or person; improper haircut, shave, or shoeshine; arriving late to formation; and room in disorder. "Violations of the innumerable rules and regulations," explained a prospective midshipman's primer, "are numerous, inevitable and expected."

To report a midshipman for an infraction, in Academy slang, was to "fry" him. Any officer or upperclassman could fry a plebe for a Class B infraction by submitting a "delinquency" or "conduct" report, as it was formally called, to the battalion office. One of the commissioned Navy officers posted there investigated the charge and then either cancelled the report or approved it and forwarded it to the commandant. The commandant also either cancelled or approved the report. If the latter, he assigned the appropriate number of demerits and forwarded the report to the superintendent, for his information. Demerits served both as a record of misconduct and as a basis for determining punishment.

A midshipman could challenge a delinquency report, but this was a perilous course of action, since it was a Class A offense to file a false report. Such situations generally boiled down to one person's word against another's, and plebes usually lost.

Punishments for Class B offenses included restriction; reprimand; deprivation of leave, recreation, or privileges; suspension; or reduction in midshipman rank. The usual punishment was extra duty, which generally consisted of rowing a heavy boat or marching back and forth in a prescribed area. Plebes who accumulated more than 300 demerits were subject to dismissal.[2]

In addition to the regulations that all midshipmen had to follow, plebes were also required to observe a series of "rates" as part of their indoctrination. Rates included information plebes had to know, things they had to do, and privileges accorded to upperclassmen but denied to them. For example, plebes "rated" giving up their seats to upperclassmen, double-timing it to all formations, keeping to the center of corridors, and memorizing the menu for the next meal.

Plebes also rated learning every bit of information and trivia in *Reef Points*, the "plebe bible," for upperclassmen regularly quizzed them on it. The book described the various buildings and monuments in the Yard, extracurricular activities available to midshipmen, and Academy sports. It included information about ships, aircraft, organization of the fleet, and Navy traditions; lyrics to songs such as "Anchors Aweigh"; and the names of all the Academy's athletic coaches. Its glossary introduced plebes to officially approved jargon such as "anchor man," the midshipman with the lowest standing in his class; "bull," the nickname for English and history; and "crab," a girl from "Crabtown" (Annapolis). There were also poems given as answers to stock questions, such as "How long have you been in the Navy?" Plebes were expected to sing the songs, name the names, recite the poetry, or answer the questions on demand. An upperclassman could stop a plebe at any time to ask him questions or give him a spot inspection.[3]

"Plebe summer" immersed plebes in Naval Academy culture during the summer before their first freshman semester. A "fast-paced boot-camp style orientation," as a midshipman's parent's primer put it, plebe summer made "never ending" "physical and mental demands upon the plebes' time."[4]

Black midshipmen's experiences at the Academy were as diverse as their backgrounds. Most African Americans had little difficulty making the transition from their previous lives into plebes during plebe summer, particularly those who had been enlisted men before becoming midshipmen. Wes Brown's year in the Army before entering Annapolis helped him adjust easily to the rigorous schedule. "During those first few weeks we had more to do than there were hours in the day," Brown recalled. "We ran to formation, learned customs and regulations, memorized 'can's and can'ts' until our eyes popped." The plebes took refresher courses in basic math, English, and history; learned how to tie knots, row cutters, and sail; and studied naval tradition. Having been cadet colonel at Dunbar and taken engineering at Howard, Brown had no trouble with either the military or academic aspects of plebe summer. "Things were much easier than I had expected," he recalled.[5]

John Raiford, Harold Bauduit, Lou Adams, Frank Simmons, and James Frezzell had joined the Navy, survived boot camp, and spent a year at NAPS before coming to Annapolis. Raiford found plebe summer easier than boot camp. To Bauduit and Adams, plebe summer resembled boot camp. Frezzell had not spent much time around the water before, but he was used to doing chores and working even when he had two football practices a day, so the full schedule was no shock to him. Lu Gregg and Bill Jones had been enlisted men in the Marine Corps before becoming midshipmen. To Jones, plebe summer was nothing compared to Parris Island. "I've got more time in the pay line," he would say to the second classmen in charge of the plebes, "than you've got in the chow line."

Many black plebes who had no prior military experience before entering the Academy had no problems making the adjustment either. How to fold shirts a certain way, to make the bed just so, and to do the countless other things that plebes had to do to get by came easily to Reeves Taylor and Mal Bruce. Pat Prout had wanted to be a midshipman so badly that he focused his whole being on doing whatever it took to succeed. "Nothing was going to get in the way of my graduating from the Naval Academy," he recalled. Paul Reason adjusted easily to plebe summer because he knew what he was missing on the outside. He had been to frat parties and had done the things that civilians do in college, so he never felt deprived by the Academy's reveille-to-taps schedule. And he had entered with a good inkling of what to expect, from discussions with friends attending the various service academies and from reading books on the Naval Academy at the Library of Congress.[6] Reason's classmate Floyd Grayson also adjusted to plebe summer rather easily. "It was hard work," Grayson recalled, "and it could be difficult at times, but it was fun. I coasted right through it."

Other black plebes found the adjustment more trying. Pete Tzomes entered the Academy with no inkling of what to expect. Plebe summer "wasn't fun," he recalled, "but I knew I wanted to be there, so I gutted it out." To Stan Carter, plebe summer was "a culture shock." "I had never been in a white environment," he recalled. "Having to deal with white folks was a learning experience." To Charlie Bolden, the most striking thing was "the pace and intensity." "I had never been through anything like that before," he recalled. "Like a lot of my classmates, I decided that I wanted to go home." Bolden stuck it out, in part, because of his parents' encouragement. But the main reason he stayed was to defy two racist upperclassmen who told him that they were going to run him out. Bolden's classmate Gil Lucas had a similar experience. Lucas characterized the transition from civilian life to Academy life as "a living hell." Like Bolden, much of Lucas's misery resulted from racist upperclassmen bent on driving him out.

Larry Chambers wanted to quit on the first day. He strongly disliked the way plebes were treated. "I thought, at the time, that the hazing was childish, trivial, petty, and mean," he recalled later. "I didn't see the value of it. Until combat." A week later he tried to quit again. Colonel Atwood talked him out of it.[7] "It was a difficult transition," recalled Chambers. He had been an outstanding student in high school. At the Academy everyone was outstanding.

Life for any plebe became harder when the upper classes returned from their summer activities and the academic year began. For all the difficulties fourth classmen experienced in making the transition from civilian life during plebe summer, they did not have to contend with a full academic program. "Throughout the academic year the daily events in the life of a midshipman are governed by a rigid schedule," noted a pamphlet describing the Academy. Reveille sounded at 6:20. Forty seconds after the first note, room inspection began. Midshipmen had twenty-five minutes to shave, shower, and dress before reporting at 6:45 to breakfast formation, where they underwent personal inspection. Afterward they marched to breakfast, ate, and marched back to clean their rooms. Classes started at 7:45. From Monday through Friday, the academic day was divided into six hour-long periods, with two morning periods reserved for study. Lunch formation and another inspection took place at 12:20. Fifth period began at 1:10, followed by either a long afternoon drill or the sixth period and a short drill. The drills ended at 4:10 or 4:30, and from then until the dinner formation (and inspection) at 6:40 midshipmen engaged in athletics or extra duty. The evening study period lasted from 8:00 until 9:50, with taps blown at 10:05. Plebes caught not studying during study period or out of bed after taps went on report. Saturday mornings were split between recitation and drill, and afternoons were free for those who had no extra duty. On Sundays reveille sounded at 7:15, followed by mandatory church attendance. Sunday afternoons were free.[8] "Only the utilization of every precious minute of the sixteen waking hours will enable midshipmen to take part in the extracurricular activities without detriment to their academic work," cautioned one alumnus.[9]

In addition to a full academic schedule, plebes had to deal with the full complement of upperclassmen. During the summer, relatively few upperclassmen had been around to give them a hard time. Now many eyes watched their every move. All upperclassmen shared responsibility for plebe indoctrination. Many took special pains to ensure that plebes knew their rates.

Mealtimes were particularly difficult, for the mess hall was the principal forum in which they were tested on *Reef Points* and other so-called plebe knowledge. A fourth classman had to answer questions while sitting rigidly on the edge of his chair, "keeping his eyes in the boat" (gazing steadily ahead unless responding to an upperclassman), and "eating a square meal" (raising the fork perpendicularly from the plate until level with the mouth, then conveying the food horizontally to its destination). A plebe who screwed up might have to "shove out," which meant having to remain in a seated position without actually touching the chair.[10]

To enforce plebe rates and minor infractions of the regulations without resort to conduct reports, the Academy condoned a method known as "coming around." If a plebe made a faux pas in the mess hall, answered a question improperly in a corridor, or chuckled while in ranks, an upperclassman could invite him to come around to his room that night for what *Reef Points* called "a fitting reprimand." Many of the punishments were rather mild, such as making a fourth classman learn a Frank Sinatra tune or having a southern plebe sing "Marching through Georgia." Typically the plebe had to do the number of push-ups corresponding to his class year.[11]

The system permitted an upperclassman a great deal of latitude. Sometimes he might have a plebe come around for personal reasons. It might be that he disapproved of the plebe's attitude, hometown, or education, or that he simply disliked him. A plebe often had no way of knowing the real reason behind an invitation to come around. All told, it was almost impossible never to break a rule, and an upperclassman "out to get" a plebe could easily find a pretext for making his life difficult.

Soon after joining the brigade at the end of plebe summer, most of the black midshipmen who entered the Academy between 1948 and 1964 discovered that they were the only African Americans from their class in their respective companies. With the number of blacks entering the classes of 1949–68 averaging three per year, such a distribution seemed inevitable. Although there is no evidence that Academy officials deliberately avoided assigning more than one black plebe per company, it happened to work out that way throughout this period. A few black plebes joined companies with African American upperclassmen but, again, the distribution might have occurred by chance and not by design. As a plebe, Mal Bruce served in the 4th Company with Ed Sechrest, then a first classman, and Ken Slaughter, '57, then a second classman. Similarly, Pat Prout, Stan Carter, and Pete Tzomes were all in the same company during Prout's first-class year. Paul Reason's experience, however, was more typical. "I never had another black midshipman in my company during all four years," he recalled. "Because the numbers were so small, the chances of having two blacks in the same company were remote."

Wes Brown also had an exceptional experience. He roomed alone all four years. Academy officials must have harbored apprehensions about blacks and whites rooming together, so they never assigned him a roommate. Instead of fretting, however, Brown reveled in the privacy after having had four roommates at Howard.[12]

Reeves Taylor spent plebe summer of 1948 in a room by himself. When the plebes joined the brigade that fall, he again found himself assigned to a room alone. Taylor immediately requested to speak with the officer-in-charge of the fourth class, Commander Norvell Gardiner Ward. Respectfully but emotionally, Taylor voiced objections to not having a roommate. "Is this the way you're going to treat me in the Navy?" he said. "How am I going to be a naval officer if you're going to isolate me?" He asked why he wasn't assigned a roommate. Commander Ward said that the executive department wanted to avoid a "situation" where someone might take exception to rooming with a black person. Taylor said that he would rather resign from the Academy than go through plebe year without a roommate, adding that he would tell Senator Green why he left. Ward relented. When Taylor returned to his room, he found a roommate there already. Oddly enough, Taylor's classmate Larry Chambers was assigned roommates from the start. Black midshipmen who followed were also assigned roommates from the start.[13]

As Larry Chambers observed, the racial attitudes black midshipmen encountered at the Naval Academy were those of America. "We were all part of where we grew up," he recalled. "Kids came from all over. They brought their attitudes with them."

During this period the Academy's culture reflected the racial attitudes of the American South. Many black plebes soon noticed the fact that racism was built into that culture. Racial slurs figured into the standard questions upperclassmen fired at plebes. "What's playing at the Star?" (a movie theater in a black neighborhood) went one such question. The approved answer, recalled a 1961 alumnus, was, "I didn't know you were dragging this weekend, sir." The answer implied that the upperclassman was dating a black female and derided him for doing so. The Navy song "Bible Stories" included the word "darkies" in the chorus. Another Navy song declared that the solution to the "vexing Chinese question" was to send "a hundred negro reg'ments" to China to "start a Coon Republic." Generations of white midshipmen referred to the janitors in Bancroft Hall, all of whom were black, as "mokes," an old racist slang term for "monkey." The 1936 edition of *Reef Points* defined *moke* as a "colored corridor boy or mess attendant." Although the word had disappeared from *Reef Points* by Wes Brown's plebe year, midshipmen continued referring to black janitors as mokes for decades to come. Such institutionalized racism both reflected and reinforced negative attitudes and stereotypes that midshipmen and naval officers had grown up with.[14]

Some black midshipmen encountered negative attitudes from one or more of their classmates. One group of plebes habitually referred to Wes Brown as "that damned nigger" when talking among themselves out of Brown's earshot. Others expressed their feelings by refusing to sit beside him at meals or in chapel, by occasionally whispering nasty comments anonymously in ranks, or by simply ignoring him. Larry Chambers occasionally heard a classmate who didn't know he was within earshot say the word "nigger." Nevertheless, he got along well with most of his classmates. Similarly, Stan Carter overlooked insulting remarks about black people made by southern whites from rural areas because the remarks seemed to stem more from ignorance than prejudice. "It was a learning experience for them, too," Carter recalled. "Some of them had not been around black folks before." Carter bore no ill will toward such people. He would simply explain to them that even words spoken without the intent to harm could inflict damage.

No one deliberately made racist remarks to Reeves Taylor either. "They may not have talked to me," he recalled, "but they never said anything to me that was insulting." Most of his classmates kept their distance from him. Such deliberate avoidance was no less discriminatory than name calling.[15] But enough of Taylor's classmates went out of their way to be friendly to make plebe year tolerable.

Pat Prout saw his first "white only" signs in Washington in 1958 while on his way to Annapolis to visit Mal Bruce. The very idea of segregated bathrooms and water fountains struck him as so absurd that he laughed out loud. But the signs drove home as nothing before the depth of racial strife in America. In Annapolis, he listened with concern to Bruce's black classmates talking about how white midshipmen sometimes tried to set up black midshipmen for demerits by throwing things in their lockers or soiling their uniforms. Such stories did nothing to diminish Prout's ardor for the Academy. Still, when he walked through the gates on induction day, the lilting beauty of southern accents did not enthrall him but made him anxious, for he had come to believe that white southerners just did not like black people. In the coming weeks he steered clear of white southerners.

A white classmate from Florida soon reinforced Prout's perception. On one occasion during plebe summer, the entire fourth class gathered in Mac-Donough Hall for an evening of boxing, including a match between one of Prout's black classmates and one of his white classmates. The excitement mounted as the boxers danced around the ring throwing punches at each other. At one point the white midshipman, who had been losing, started to gain the upper hand. Swept up by the moment, the white Floridian, sitting two rows behind Prout, leapt to his feet. "Get that nigger!" he shouted. "Get that nigger!" The words struck Prout like a hammer blow. He turned around and glared at his classmate. When the Floridian noticed Prout frowning at him, he caught himself and sat down. Prout had been called names and had lived under de facto segregation in New York, but he had never encountered prejudice so deeply ingrained and uninhibitedly expressed. The chagrined classmate later tried to befriend Prout, but the black New Yorker had no interest in becoming anything more than an acquaintance. For Prout, the event precipitated an epiphany nearly as intense as when he first saw the "white only" sign, and it sensitized him to prejudice. Negative racial attitudes among his classmates proved the exception rather than the rule, and Prout sometimes misconstrued innocent remarks, but there were just as many times when he could discern the true meaning of a seemingly innocuous remark or action.

Many of Gil Lucas's white classmates were friendly toward him in the Yard but behaved like strangers in town, especially when they were going to places that did not welcome African Americans. Lucas found that those who rowed crew and ran track with him were more likely to act as friends outside the walls as well as inside.

Floyd Grayson had similar experiences with white midshipmen. Although he got along well with most of his classmates, "there were some who clearly had problems with you," he recalled, "in not wanting to talk to you or not wanting to be around you." His plebe-year roommate was from Kansas. The fellow clearly felt uneasy around Grayson at first, but as the weeks passed he adjusted well to rooming with a black person. "We became reasonably close," recalled Grayson.

Like Lucas, Grayson experienced coldness in town from some of his white shipmates who had treated him warmly in Bancroft Hall. "You'd see classmates or upperclassmen in your company that you knew well," recalled Grayson, "and they would turn their head and not even say anything to you. You could walk right by and they wouldn't even acknowledge that you were there." These experiences particularly angered Grayson when he was in town with his parents and a white classmate out with his own parents would behave as if he was "ashamed to know you because you're black and have a black family." "My mother and father were sharp people," he recalled. "I had nothing to be ashamed of. Both my parents were very proud and very wise and very good people, so I didn't cotton to my classmates' behavior very well." But not every white midshipman behaved this way. Football star Roger Staubach, for example, treated Grayson with the same friendliness outside the Yard as he did inside. People who were comfortable with themselves tended to act "the same way no matter where they were," Grayson observed, "because they were secure."

Negative attitudes among white classmates proved the exception, not the rule. In most instances, black plebes encountered no overt racial hostility from their white classmates. "We were great buddies," Lou Adams said of his classmates. "Maybe it was because we were in the same boat." Mal Bruce also got along with his classmates splendidly. "There's nothing like suffering through it together," he recalled. John Raiford found his classmates' racial attitudes "very good for those times." "I always assumed that whatever problems arose between me and other midshipmen were due to reasons other than race. This was not because I was so righteous, but because I wanted to spare myself the deleterious effects of the anger and frustration that would otherwise prevail. I don't recall ever having to deal with a personal problem of race." Pete Tzomes observed that white classmates sometimes behaved awkwardly around him, but he attributed it to inexperience or immaturity, not racism. Tzomes enjoyed being around white people who had never been around black people before, such as farm boys from the Midwest. He also enjoyed changing southerners' attitudes about African Americans by performing his duties as well as or better than they did. He never encountered hostility from classmates. Paul Reason's gregariousness overwhelmed whatever misgivings any of his white classmates might have had about his race. "Even to this day," he recalled years later, "I'm not in the same room with someone when I don't strike up a conversation with them. And when we part, even if it's after only five or ten minutes, I'll either know his name or know why he's there or know who he is." Social interaction with people, whatever their color or ethnicity, simply came naturally to him. "Paul was always 'Mr. Smooth,'" recalled Bill Jones. "He knew the right thing to say to people."

Some black midshipmen rarely encountered overt racial hostility from upperclassmen. "I don't think they thought about race," recalled Harold Bauduit. "The subject never came up." "My upperclassmen were great," recalled Lou Adams. "They really looked after me. The second classmen who ran the plebes would make remarks, but the remarks were made to toughen me up, not to insult me."

Other black midshipmen often encountered overt racial hostility from upperclassmen. Pat Prout overheard several upperclassmen remarking that they did not want blacks at the Naval Academy. On separate occasions three different white upperclassmen told Paul Reason flat out in the privacy of their rooms during come-arounds that, since there was no place in the Navy for a black officer, there was no place at the Academy for a black midshipman, so he should leave. Several white upperclassmen had no compunction about telling race jokes when Floyd Grayson was within earshot. Pete Tzomes was frequently called "nigger" when he was outside his company area. For Charlie Bolden, Mal Bruce, and Gil Lucas, the prejudice of some upperclassmen manifested itself primarily through racially motivated mistreatment.

By and large, however, most white midshipmen seemed to have neutral or positive racial attitudes. For the most part, relations between black and white midshipmen were cordial and friendly. Only a minority of white midshipmen displayed open prejudice. Still, even a few bigots could make life difficult for black plebes.

Most faculty members and commissioned officers assigned to the Academy maintained their professional comportment at all times. No doubt many harbored prejudice, but "people in the military do on the surface what it is proper to be observed doing," observed Pete Tzomes. No doubt others harbored no prejudice at all. But whether they approved or disapproved of African Americans at the Academy, most of the officers and faculty accorded black midshipmen all the propriety and respect due the uniform.

A few, however, openly exhibited prejudice. Tom Hudner, who was a first classman when Wes Brown was a plebe, recalled hearing a southern-born civilian professor from the department of English, history and government say, in class, that the "nigger" would "never get through." Brown, however, perceived no prejudice from instructors.

During a training session, John Raiford's wrestling instructor paired the plebes in his group by size, except for Raiford and black classmate Bobby Wilks, '54.[16] "Bobby was much smaller than I," Raiford recalled, "and he complained. The instructor ordered Bobby to wrestle me, without responding to Bobby's complaint. When Bobby hesitated, the instructor wrote him up for disobeying an order, which was considered a serious offense for a plebe."

Mal Bruce and his marine engineering instructor had not been getting along. The instructor, who had taught at Georgia Tech, had recently come on board the Academy faculty. One day, in class, he called Bruce a "nigger." Bruce reported the incident to his company officer. The dean ordered the instructor to issue a formal apology to Bruce in class. The instructor complied. Despite the ill feelings the instructor must have harbored, Bruce made an A in the course. Math was Pat Prout's strong suit, so he was assigned to a special section. When he walked into class the first day, the instructor asked him whether he had entered the room by mistake. The instructor did not bother to check the roster before asking the question. Prout believed the instructor had simply assumed that no black midshipman could qualify for the advanced course. "I'm going to show this bastard that I can do it," Prout thought. He, too, made an A. Gil Lucas's linear algebra professor revealed his attitude on the first day. "You will never get an A in my class," he told Lucas. The midshipman concluded that the professor was prejudiced. "I'd never met the man before in my life," Lucas recalled. "What other reason would there be? He didn't say that to anybody else." Lucas did not make an A. During plebe summer the commissioned officer in charge of Floyd Grayson's company took Grayson aside for a private talk. Grayson excelled in drill. In high school he had been a battalion commander in the Cadet Corps, and at Capital University he had won the Convair Cadet of the Year award, given to the outstanding Air Force ROTC cadet in each school. Grayson's experience and performance in commanding a platoon of fellow plebes impressed the officer. "You ought to be able to command this company and probably the battalion," the officer told Grayson. "But we can't let you do it because we have too many southern guys here, too many people that are uncomfortable with blacks." Grayson didn't think the officer was prejudiced. "He was really just trying to prepare me for disappointment," Grayson recalled, "and the fact that I wasn't going to get a command position." Whatever the officer's intentions might have been, the reality of the situation disturbed Grayson deeply. No matter how well he performed, he couldn't aspire to a position of leadership because he was black.

Black midshipmen also encountered prejudice outside from white people in Annapolis. On one occasion a white midshipman's parents spotted Lou Adams and exclaimed, "Oh, they got one of those again." On several occasions Adams heard civilians mutter racist epithets under their breath as he walked by.

Most of the problems stemmed from the fact that, before the mid-1960s, Annapolis was segregated. African Americans accounted for about a third of the city's population. Jim Crow laws and customs confined them to separate sections of town. Black Annapolitans attended separate schools, attended separate churches, ate in separate restaurants, patronized separate movie theaters and taverns, and were buried in separate cemeteries. Most black Annapolitans depended on the Naval Academy for their livelihood. Their jobs entailed maintenance of buildings and grounds and cooking and cleaning in Bancroft Hall. "The segregated environment *around* the Naval Academy was a bad, bad scene," Lu Gregg recalled. He avoided trouble by avoiding the white-owned businesses in town.[17]

Reeves Taylor recalled that one night during the examination period, just before he was sworn in, he and several classmates went out to the movies. They bought their tickets and sat down together. A few minutes later, the manager of the theater and several ushers appeared by Taylor's row, shining a flashlight in his face. They asked him to leave. Unused to such practice and horrified and embarrassed by the incident, Taylor did so. He received better treatment in town once he donned the midshipman's uniform. The first time his mother visited him at the Academy, she, her friend, and Taylor went to a restaurant. Taylor happened to be in uniform and they had no trouble getting served. The next day Taylor's mother and her friend returned to the same restaurant without Taylor. The proprietor asked them to leave. Taylor himself never had a problem getting served while in uniform.

Mal Bruce had similar experiences. He arrived in Annapolis early on the day in the summer of 1955 that he was to report to the Academy. He wanted a cup of coffee, so he went into a restaurant outside Gate 3 and sat down. He was wearing civilian clothes. No one said anything to him. He noticed that people who were arriving after him were getting coffee almost immediately. Still, no one said anything to him. Finally the man behind the counter walked over. "If you want take-out you can go around back," he said, "but we don't serve you in here." Bruce was mortified. Nothing like this had ever happened to him in New York. Later, after plebe summer, a group of classmates invited him to go out to town. "I don't know if I ought to," said Bruce. "I'm not welcome." He had not been to town since the coffee incident, but his class-mates insisted, so he joined them. They went to the movies and then stopped at a restaurant for a soda. "Oh my God," Bruce thought as he walked through the door. "This is that place I was in." But now he was in uniform, with other midshipmen, and had no trouble getting served. For the rest of his time in Annapolis, he never had a problem while in uniform.

During parents' weekend at the end of plebe summer 1965, Paul Reason, his sister, and a friend got a bite to eat at restaurant inside the seven-mile radius from the Academy in which midshipmen were required to wear their uniforms. "We sat there for a good little while and ate and talked," Reason wrote in a letter to his parents. "All the waitresses looked at us pretty hard but there was no question about being served."[18] Later that fall, Reason told his parents that Annapolis was "having a wave of sit-ins." "Some of my old friends from Howard are here in jail," he wrote. "They have been on a hunger strike for the last two days."[19] At least one restaurant refused to serve Gil Lucas, even while he was in uniform. Stan Carter and Pete Tzomes simply avoided known "redneck" places or other establishments that did not serve blacks.

John Raiford mostly avoided white people in town, too, with one excep-tion. "I attended the local white Methodist church as part of an Academy church party," he recalled, "and I developed a pleasant relationship with the minister and his family."

Most of the plebe indoctrination and associated physical hazing black midship-men went through resembled what white midshipmen experienced. Reeves Taylor never thought he was receiving undue attention from upperclassmen because he was black. John Raiford recalled experiencing nothing out of the ordinary, "even though some first classmen could say 'mister' with such a sneer that it sounded like an epithet!" "In general," he added, "the regi-mented but fair living conditions at the Academy were sort of an oasis from pervasive racist practices just beyond the Academy gates." Pat Prout endured the usual barrage of come-arounds, push-ups, and *Reef Points* questions from the first classmen in his company. "When they felt satisfied that I was squared away," he recalled, "I was left alone. The second half of plebe year was a walk in the park for me because they then focused on the people who were not squared away."

Larry Chambers was hazed more than many of his classmates, but he at-tributed it to his attitude, not his race. He knew that several of his classmates were getting it worse and he never believed he was being discriminated against. He did suspect, however, that some of the seemingly normal plebe treatment he was receiving might have been racially motivated. To avoid unnecessary exposure to prejudiced upperclassmen or to upperclassmen who didn't know him, he remained in his company area as much as he could.

Paul Reason, too, experienced the usual plebe treatment. Sometimes after he answered an upperclassman's question, the upperclassman would ask, "Do you bet your ass on that?" Reason soon learned not to guess. "Some people were more adept at swinging an atlas [as a paddle] than others were," he recalled. Reason also "swam to Baltimore" two or three times. The closets in some of the rooms in Bancroft Hall were partitioned off from the main space by a wall that did not quite reach the ceiling. "Swimming to Baltimore," a traditional plebe punishment, involved balancing on the stomach on the 6-inch ledge between the closet and the room and simulating a crawl stroke. "I had a plebe year," concluded Reason.

So did Pete Tzomes. "I don't think my share of push-ups and things like that were any more significant than anybody else's," he recalled. Toward the end of plebe year a first classman fried Tzomes unjustly, but not for racial reasons. Tzomes had a clean conduct record and the firsty couldn't stomach the idea of a plebe finishing the year with no demerits. Bill Jones didn't get fried for racial reasons either. "I never got demerits because I was black," he recalled. "It was usually because I did something wrong and I got caught."

Mal Bruce suffered the usual indignities, including the "water torture" and "carrier quals." The former involved shoving out while holding a strong box at arm's length. The upperclassman would then ask questions on *Reef Points* or other required plebe knowledge, and for every wrong answer he would pour a cup of water into the box. "If you spill that," he would say, "you're going to have to lick the water up off my floor." "Carrier quals" involved placing a mattress near one end of the hallway and having the plebes run toward it from the other. "The upperclassman would give you a cut," recalled Bruce, "and you had to dive for the mattress. Sometimes you made the mattress. Sometimes you fell just short of it." Once when Bruce was on his way to formation, a firsty from another battalion accused him of failing to square a corner and had him come around every night for nearly two weeks. There were always six or seven other plebes in the room. The firsty had them do push-ups or play handball in the shower in their inspection shoes, which meant that they had to get up at 4:00 A.M. to build the polish back up to avoid demerits. Although Bruce never complained, his own first classman figured out what was going on and put a stop to it. Bruce didn't think the first classman from the other battalion was a racist. "He was just an asshole," Bruce said. The experience enabled Bruce to observe that the intensity of the hazing varied from one company to the next. He didn't think his own company was that bad.

Lu Gregg got the impression everyone was treading lightly around him. "I had this sense that upperclassmen from the South were careful not to be too hard on me so their classmates from the North wouldn't think they were singling me out," he recalled. "And the ones from the North were careful with me, thinking I was getting a hard time from the others. I still got demerits, however."

Gil Lucas, on the other hand, landed in a particularly rough company, the "Terrible 10th," notorious for terrorizing plebes. Lucas took cold comfort in the fact that the upperclassmen in the 10th practiced equal opportunity hazing. "A lot of white midshipmen got horrible treatment, too," he recalled. "All kinds of crazy stuff went on when nobody was around. A lot of people who were physically hurt were white. People had knees blown out and big marks put on them. All kinds of bad things happened." Years later, when the novel *A Sense of Honor* was published, Lucas bought a copy. Written by Lucas's white classmate James Webb, the novel portrays a campaign by a gung-ho first classman to shape up a plebe having a difficult time adjusting to Academy life. "I couldn't get through the first chapter," Lucas admitted. "I threw the book away. It brought up too many bad memories." For Lucas, even the ordinary hazing was repugnant. "Back then," Charlie Bolden aptly concluded, "it was not unusual to have some upperclassmen harassing plebes and others turning their backs."

Many black midshipmen also underwent hazing with a decidedly racist edge. During the first month of Wes Brown's first semester, demerits rained down on him by the bucketful. He got fried for things that were nearly impossible to disprove, such as talking in ranks or marching out of step on the way to class. He also received demerits for offenses that would normally be overlooked, such as a speck of dust in his room. A classmate considered Brown a "marked man." One first classman believed that a group of a dozen or so southern-born seniors were deliberately giving Brown undeserved conduct reports in the hopes that he would exceed the demerit limit and be separated. Another first classmen knew an individual classmate who wanted Brown out and was filing false conduct reports. The executive department took action to prevent further mistreatment of Brown. The commandant passed the word to the battalion officers that no more unfair conduct reports on him would be tolerated. The battalion officers, in turn, advised the midshipman officers of this policy, and the midshipman officers passed the word down the chain. Brown finished his first semester with 103 demerits. Next semester he received only five, for a total of 108 for his plebe year.[20]

Brown's experience was not unique. Although most white upperclassmen treated black plebes equally, a significant minority used the arbitrary power accorded them by the plebe indoctrination system to act on their prejudices. Probably half of the black midshipmen from the classes of 1949–68 suffered some degree of racially motivated mistreatment at the hands of such upper-classmen. Moreover, it has been alleged that two black midshipmen who did not graduate and did not respond to my queries also suffered racially motivated hazing.

Many black midshipmen who said they experienced no racially motivated mistreatment went through plebe year in the 1950s. It might be that racism became more overt when the civil rights movement gained momentum in the 1960s. It is also possible that, with Jim Crow still firmly entrenched in American society during the 1950s, black plebes overlooked a lot of things that would have rankled later generations.

Pat Prout, who did everything by the book, was so squared away that if anyone had singled him out for hazing racism would obviously have been the motive. "He was perfect," Bill Jones recalled of his classmate. "His mind was like a vice. He knew what to do and how to do it." Stan Carter agreed. "He was an athlete," he said of Prout, and "super smart. He had the type of personality that endeared him to a lot of folks. He had a very high standing in the company."

Bill Jones was squared away too, but just to make sure, he projected a bad-ass attitude designed to stop hazing before it got started. "How could they get me for not being able to march?" he said. "I came out of the Marine Corps. How could they get me for not having shined shoes? My military dress was superior to theirs. My military bearing was better than theirs. I walked ramrod straight. I was the guidon bearer at boot camp. Militarily, there's nothing they could teach me that I didn't already do better than they could, so they'd ask dumb questions at the table, like 'Who were the Triple Crown winners?' I could care less. 'Why are you asking me that?' That's what I was thinking. I never said that out loud to most of them, but they learned not to question me because I would intimidate them in some way, or, in some cases, threaten them with bodily harm. I don't know how it got around, but they started thinking I knew voodoo and that I was a voodoo priest, and I would threaten them with needles in the doll, and these fools believed it."

Floyd Grayson projected a bad-ass attitude too. Stan Carter described Grayson as "the militant of the group." Grayson stood 6'2" and weighed 200 pounds. "When he scowled at you," said Carter, "you stayed clear of his path. He felt that white folks were not to be trusted. You always had to watch your back." Although many blacks felt that way to some degree, noted Carter, it was not evident in their demeanor. "In his, it was," Carter said. "Everybody knew how Floyd felt." Bill Jones agreed. "Nobody messed with Floyd," he recalled. "I thought I intimidated others. Floyd intimidated me. He didn't tolerate no crap. The whole world was a white-black issue with him. Floyd was

H. Rap Brown and all of the black power movers wrapped up into one." "It's not that I didn't like white people," said Grayson, "I just wasn't having any of their foolishness. But if I found someone who had character and could stand up, man, he was my buddy."

Many black midshipmen identified skin color as the motive behind some of the hazing they suffered. The most common manifestation of racially motivated hazing was excessive come-arounds. Stan Carter, James Frezzell, Floyd Grayson, and Paul Reason believe that they received more than the average number of come-arounds because of their race. Carter got many of his from a southern-born second classman who made it clear that he just didn't like him. Grayson had no doubt whatsoever that racism lurked behind his own excessive come-arounds.

Paul Reason was more circumspect about the motives behind his come-arounds. "No one would ever obviously single me out," he said. There were always five or six white plebes in an upperclassman's room with him. Afterward, the other plebes often wondered aloud whether Reason was the target and they were victims of circumstance. "I don't know why I've got to come around to this guy," they would say, "except he knows I'm your roommate," or "he saw us at the same time." "Nah," Reason would reply, "I was there because he was out to get *you*." Reason did not attribute the come-arounds to racism. "It wasn't a black-white thing," he said. Another plebe in his company, Marvin Rosenberg, was also getting more than his fair share of come-arounds. Reason remembered Rosenberg as "one of the brightest, most unassuming and trusting members of the company." "Marv was very obviously, by name and by manner and appearance, Jewish," Reason said. "It wasn't anti-Semitism, just like for me it wasn't anti-black. It's just that we were different." Perceiving that someone is different because of physical characteristics—not "one of us"—as well as targeting someone because of his physical characteristics are, however, indeed manifestations of prejudice.

Racially motivated mistreatment appeared in other forms as well, like name calling, threats, hazing of roommates, and physical violence. Floyd Grayson periodically heard racial epithets or jokes about Harry Belafonte or Sammy Davis Jr. muttered by white midshipmen hidden in a crowd where they could not be identified. A white upperclassman once called Gil Lucas a "stinking half-breed." Several weeks into the first semester, Mal Bruce realized that he was getting fried unjustly. On one occasion his roommates' shoes passed inspection while he was written up. "My shoes shined better than any of theirs," he recalled. In a manner eerily reminiscent of Wesley Brown, Bruce tallied up some 50 demerits during the first five weeks. Most of the chits came from the same half-dozen upperclassmen from his company, most of whom happened to speak with southern drawls. Similarly, Gil Lucas concluded that several up-

perclassmen were bent on driving him out. Whenever one particular individual saw Lucas standing in a formation, he would reach in and punch the name
tag on his chest hard enough to draw blood. Behind closed doors during
some come-arounds, white upperclassmen would beat Lucas with a broom or
punch him repeatedly. Lucas's white roommate was getting it worse. "They
didn't like him either," Lucas recalled, "and they would make him wear two
pairs of sweat gear and work out until he sweated enough to stick a penny to
the wall." In fact, Lucas saw so many of his white classmates receive equally
horrible treatment that he couldn't say for sure whether it was racism or sadism that was driving his own hazing. A second classman from South Carolina
openly threatened Charlie Bolden. "I'm going to make it my business to make
sure that you don't survive plebe year," he told him. At the time, Bolden
was getting high marks in academics, conduct, and military performance.
"There was no doubt in my mind that it was racially motivated," he recalled.
A white second classman from Birmingham, Alabama, joined forces with the
South Carolinian in trying to drive Bolden out. Although they administered
large doses of traditional plebe punishments—shoving out, "uniform races"
(changing from one uniform to the next in rapid succession, with only a minute or so allowed for each change), and "rigging the rifle" (holding a rifle at
arm's length to exhaustion)—they never brought Bolden to a point that he
seriously considered quitting.

The black midshipmen from the classes of 1949–68 had a support network to
lean on when things got bad. Many of their white classmates provided help,
loyalty, and camaraderie. "I had good support from my classmates," recalled
John Raiford, "particularly those with whom I served at NAPS." Lu Gregg
and white classmate Don Martin struck up a friendship while rowing together
on the plebe crew team. Martin asked Gregg to be his roommate. Gregg
agreed. They got along so well, they roomed together for the rest of their
time at the Academy. "He helped me with humanities and social studies and I
helped him with math and science," Gregg recalled. "He didn't tell me until
our senior year that his parents in Montgomery, Alabama, strongly objected
to me as his roommate."

Leighton Smith, '62, another white midshipman from Alabama, also
took some grief from his family for supporting black midshipmen. "My father was one of the most biased individuals that I ever met," Smith recalled.
One Christmas the family discussion turned toward rumors about the im-
peding integration of the local high school. "None of my children are going
to school with a nigger!" Smith's father exclaimed. "Well if that's the case,
Daddy," Smith replied, "I've got to quit the Naval Academy, because we've
got a couple of good guys up there. You would call them 'niggers.' I just call

them classmates." "He stopped absolutely cold," Smith recalled. "He could not believe what he had just heard. I never heard him make a remark like that again." Smith remained in the Navy until 1996, retiring as a full admiral.[21]

Two of Wes Brown's classmates, Harvey Conover and Robert Jess Salomon, offered to room with him. Brown declined. Given what he had learned about the experiences of black midshipmen and cadets in the past, he figured that sooner or later someone would give him a hard time because of his race. When that happened, he did not want a roommate to have to share the burden, nor did he want the guilt of someone being harassed because of him. Some of Brown's classmates treated him like anyone else and had no apprehensions about talking to him, running with him, or playing tennis with him. A few considered themselves his friends.

Stan Carter was facing a crucial physics exam. No matter how hard he studied, he just could not grasp the material. Finally he asked for help. Two of his white classmates spent several days tutoring him. Carter passed the exam with flying colors. Gil Lucas also studied with white classmates, but he was the one doing the tutoring. Studying and suffering together forged strong bonds between Lucas and his fellow plebes, regardless of race. "My classmates are among the finest people I know," he declared.

Mal Bruce was having trouble in swimming. His lean, wiry frame carried almost no body fat, giving him negative buoyancy. Whenever he tried to tow his roommate the required two lengths of the pool in the lifesaving drill, both of them ended up under water. Bruce just couldn't get a passing grade. John B. Funderbunk Jr., a white classmate from South Carolina, offered to be his partner. Funderbunk was a short, stocky guy who floated like a cork and had enough buoyancy for them both. Bruce towed him the required two lengths of the pool with ease. "Mr. Bruce," the swimming instructor said. "I guess you've been practicing." Bruce passed the test. Such instances of teamwork and loyalty are what Bruce remembers most about his days at the Academy. "To this day, we're still a very close-knit class," he said. "I guess we'll be that way until we die."

Many black midshipmen from far away had no family to visit on weekends unless a classmate invited them home. One of James Frezzell's white roommates, Stephen B. Grey Jr.,'68, invited Frezzell to his house. "His parents took me right into their home," Frezzell recalled, "and we've remained good friends over the years." Similarly, Bill Jones was befriended by the family of one of his white roommates, even though the family came from Georgia.

Every now and then midshipmen tired of Academy fare and went into town for a bite to eat. On one such occasion, Floyd Grayson and some ten white classmates sat down at a lunch counter. The person behind the counter refused to serve Grayson. "If he can't eat here," said one of Grayson's classmates, "we're not eating here." The midshipmen walked out en masse and got something to eat somewhere else.

Midshipmen from different parts of the country often forged bonds by finding common ground with one another. Paul Reason developed close friendships with several white classmates in his company who had also been to college before becoming midshipmen. "We had things to talk about and experiences to share," he recalled.

In one extraordinary case, a white plebe used his body to shield a black classmate from racially motivated mistreatment. During plebe year 1964/65, Chris L. Katsetos, a white plebe from Rhode Island, James K. Orzech, a white plebe from a suburb of Cleveland, and Emerson F. Carr, a black plebe from Minneapolis, were assigned to the same squad. Orzech had grown up in a place where white people did not want black people moving into their neighborhoods, and he had interacted only infrequently with black people before, so he was a bit standoffish with Carr. But he was still surprised when a few of his white classmates openly expressed their resentment of a black midshipman by making racist remarks. Even more surprising to Orzech was the attitude of Chris Katsetos. While virtually every other plebe tried his best to remain invisible, Katsetos would deliberately provoke upperclassmen. "Who is this nut case Katsetos?" Orzech often wondered. After plebe summer, Katsetos, Orzech, and Carr joined the 14th Company. Soon, the three of them found themselves coming around together to a room occupied by upperclassmen from the Deep South. "They were definitely gunning for Carr," recalled Orzech. "I don't ever remember them issuing a racial slur or anything like that, but you knew damn good and well they were running Carr extra hard because he was a black." It seemed to Orzech that, whenever Katsetos felt that the southerners were going too far, he would deliberately provoke them into punishing him instead of Carr. Orzech remained braced up and tried to blend into the background while all of this was going on. "I was kind of like the innocent bystander," he recalled. "But I got to do all these extra things." The come-arounds lasted for several weeks. Ultimately, they failed to prevent Carr from graduating, but he was turned back into the class of 1969. Katsetos graduated with honors, the first midshipman to graduate with a bachelor's and a master's degree, but died as a passenger in the crash of a military aircraft in 1973. Orzech served thirty years in the Navy and Naval Reserve, retiring as a captain.

Many black plebes also received support from white upperclassmen. Several first classmen went out of their way to support Wes Brown and prevent others from treating him unfairly. In particular, two seniors, Howard Allen Weiss and Joseph Patrick Flanagan, offered to be Wes Brown's "first classman." Custom dictated that every plebe was adopted by a first classman, who served as the newcomer's guide, mentor, and protector. "The relationship between them is unique," noted a primer on the Academy. It approximated "that of a somewhat aloof older brother with his kid brother, without the fraternal tie and possibly without any special affection between them. The purpose of this odd relationship is to give the plebe a friend at court; an older counselor who is experienced in the ways of the Naval Academy and who may guard his younger charge in a semi-official capacity from running afoul of the rocks that beset his course." A plebe usually visited his first classman a few minutes before each meal formation to have his appearance checked and to get advice. "I wanted to help him," recalled Howie Weiss, "and see to it that things went all right. I don't think I was waving a flag for anything or anybody. I just knew there was going to be trouble." Weiss indeed proved very helpful and supportive to Brown. Joe Flanagan, who became a second first classman to Brown at the commandant's request, also proved helpful and supportive.[22]

"I had a very warm friendship with my first classman, Richard O. Mongrain, '51, of Minnesota," recalled John Raiford. Lou Adams found that he could rely on the upperclassmen in his company. "They really looked after me," he said. Several white first classmen tried to intervene on behalf of Pete Tzomes when they learned that Tzomes was unfairly fried by the firsty who couldn't stand plebes having clean conduct records, but they were too late, and the demerits stood. Reeves Taylor became close to two second classmen who lived across the hall.

Although Taylor never felt that he was experiencing undue attention because of his race, his white first classman, Ernest B. Brown, '49, felt differently. An Irish Catholic born in 1926 and raised in Houston, Texas, Brown grew up amid stricter Jim Crow laws than had his father, born forty years earlier. He found Taylor to be "a nice young man" and decided to become his first classman because nobody else had picked him and he felt sorry for him. "The half-Irish ethnicity could have come into play here," Brown recalled. On one occasion, Brown discouraged a classmate from treating Taylor unfairly by frying the classmate's plebe. The classmate subsequently left Taylor alone.[23]

At the behest of Wesley Brown, Milton Gussow became Chambers's first classman. "Mickey" Gussow had met Brown during plebe summer and the two had remained friends ever since, despite being in different companies. A Jew from Newark, New Jersey, Gussow had seen his parents treat people the same, regardless of race, creed, or color, so that was how he treated people. Gussow never encountered anti-Semitism at the Academy, nor had he known what Brown had gone through during plebe year. Nobody ever gave Gussow a hard time because of his relationship with Wesley Brown or even made a passing comment about it. From Gussow's perspective, the subjects of race, religion, or ethnicity simply never came up at the Academy. To be sure, he had heard the usual run of ethnic jokes, but he never took them seriously. So when Gussow decided to become Chambers's first classman, the thought that the black plebe might encounter racial problems never crossed his mind. Howie Weiss had become Wesley Brown's first classman specifically to help Brown cope with discrimination, but for Gussow the race factor never entered the equation. Indeed, for the rest of the academic year Gussow neither saw nor heard of anyone discriminating against Chambers. None of Gussow's classmates made disparaging remarks to him about being a black plebe's first classman. From Gussow's point of view, Chambers's being black was irrelevant to his being a midshipman.[24]

When Mal Bruce joined the 4th Company, Ed Sechrest and white classmate Harlan D. Swanson Jr., '56, the regimental subcommander, discussed who should be Bruce's first classman. They decided that it would be better for the black plebe to have a white first classman, so H. D. Swanson volunteered. Bruce had assumed that Sechrest was going to be his first classman, so he was surprised and a little dismayed to learn that Swanson intended to fill that role, because Swanson was from Chattanooga, Tennessee. Bruce need not have worried, for Swanson did right by him. It was Swanson who put a stop to Bruce's extended come-arounds to the first classman in the other battalion, and when H. D. arrived at the conclusion that his plebe was getting fried unjustly he put a stop to that too. Bruce believed that Swanson was motivated by an innate sense of fairness.

Pat Prout believed that most white upperclassmen treated him fairly. In fact, he developed long-term friendships with several of them. Initially Prout harbored doubts about his first classman, Kenneth W. Waldorf, '61, who came from a Navy family out of San Diego. Prout took Waldorf's aloofness to mean that he did not want a black plebe. Prout figured he was in for trouble, but he need not have worried. Waldorf "sheltered me a great deal during the first six months," Prout recalled. Waldorf had Prout come around often. The first classman would ask questions, but "it wasn't intense." And with Prout coming around to Waldorf's room, he was unavailable for potential come-arounds to upperclassmen who might have given him a hard time.

Similarly, the white second classman who was persecuting Stan Carter was eventually stopped by the second classman's roommate. Evidently the segundo was not getting along with his roommate. One day, while standing in formation, the segundo said something that pushed his roommate over the edge. The roommate turned to Carter, who was standing next to him. "Stan," he said, "if you can arrange to throw that SOB in the shower, I'll spoon you." "Spooning" was an Academy custom in which an upperclassman would shake hands with a plebe, thereby closing the formal distance between them and becoming friends. "You better believe he went in the shower," recalled Carter. After drying off, the livid segundo eagerly awaited the next come-around. When the time arrived, Carter entered the room braced up and loudly announced his arrival in the usual fashion. The segundo was about to light into him when his roommate came in. "Stan, what are you doing?" he said. "You're my buddy. You don't have to do that in this room." The segundos glared at each other. "I thought the two of them were going to go to war right there," recalled Carter. "But hey, that was the way it was. If one roommate spooned you, there was nothing the other one could do. Boy, did I walk away with that one clean." Carter also had a good relationship with his first classman, who happened to be from Texas. "He was a good counselor," Carter recalled. "He'd try to settle me down at times when he thought that I was despondent or when he thought that things weren't going well for me. He would bring me in and sort of cheer me up, give me a pep talk, try to get me going back in the right direction."

Gil Lucas had a supportive white first classman as well, Stephen B. Allman, '65, from Ohio. "More than once I overheard him screaming at people that they shouldn't treat me so badly," Lucas recalled. Other white upperclassmen also tried to stop the hazing of Lucas and his classmates, but to no avail. Only a major change in policy would succeed in reducing the severity of the plebe indoctrination system.

Paul Reason and his white first classman, Gordon Stewart Lingley, '62, had mutual friends in Washington, and both had graduated from high school in 1958. "Stew" gave Reason a come-around from time to time, but just to have a chat. "He pretty much treated me as a peer all along," Reason recalled. "I was never braced up. When I went in, it was automatic 'carry on.'"

Floyd Grayson developed a good rapport with a white second classman from Philadelphia, Edward L. Walsh, '63. Ned Walsh helped Grayson understand why he could not get a higher leadership position during plebe summer. "I was very fond of him," recalled Grayson. Grayson had a less satisfactory relationship with his white first classman, who hailed from Albany, New York. "He was a decent first classman," Grayson recalled, "but he couldn't really help me cope with racism." "You have to ignore it," the first classman would advise Grayson. It was this sweep-it-under-the-rug attitude much more than the open expressions of racism that finally shattered Floyd Grayson's preconception of the Academy as a place where performance could transcend prejudice.

"Tolerated without Further Attention"

WHATEVER RELATIONSHIPS African American plebes forged among white classmates and upperclassmen, their best friends often turned out to be other black midshipmen. Wherever they hailed from and whatever their backgrounds, being black gave them a common bond. Whether they had grown up under de jure segregation below the Mason-Dixon Line or de facto segregation above it, all black midshipmen had dealt with racism on some level for most of their lives. No matter how much a white midshipman might try to empathize with a black midshipman, he could no more truly understand what it was like to be black than a non-parent could truly understand what it was like to be a parent.

The common experience of being black often erased the traditional boundaries between plebes from different companies. Midshipmen tended to spend most of their time with classmates from the same company. Company mates lived along the same corridors in Bancroft Hall, drilled together, and generally formed their closest friendships at the Academy with other company mates. Black midshipmen, however, tended to adhere to the same patterns of socialization they had followed before entering the Academy—not spending much time with their white friends outside of school or school-related activities. Classmates Harold Bauduit and Ed Sechrest got to know each other quite well despite being in different companies. Likewise, the four African Americans in the class of 1959 became good friends, even though they were in different battalions. It was the same for the five black midshipmen in the class of 1964 (one of whom did not graduate). The black midshipmen in the class of 1965—all from Washington, D.C.—became especially close.

The common experience of being black also tended to break down the traditional barriers between plebes and upperclassmen. As a result, the relationships between black plebes and black upperclassmen were often much closer and more informal than those between whites from different classes, at least during off-duty hours. Despite the fact that Wesley Brown, Larry Chambers, and Reeves Taylor were in different companies, they went out of their way to become acquainted with one another. Brown went over to Taylor's room a couple of times and Taylor visited Brown's room once or twice. The sheer size of Bancroft Hall prevented more frequent contact. "It had seven miles of corridors," recalled Taylor. "It seemed like three miles to go to Wesley Brown's room." Brown saw more of Chambers, both at the Academy and in Washington. Brown reassured Chambers and Taylor that what they were going through was, in the vast majority of instances, normal plebe stuff. Chambers and Taylor derived some comfort from the fact that they were being treated the same as their classmates—like maggots.[1]

Although Ed Sechrest did not select Mal Bruce as his plebe, he spooned Bruce and occasionally took him along when he visited friends in town. Most black plebes met black upperclassmen when they joined the brigade at the end of plebe summer. Bill Jones and his classmates in the class of 1964 became particularly close to the black midshipmen in the next class. "We made friends with them the day they walked in the door," he recalled. Paul Reason met Jones and the other black upperclassmen in the usual plebe manner. "The first thing they do is they blast open your door and you come to attention and brace up," Reason said. "They came around and sought me out and introduced themselves." "We sized them up real quick," said Jones. During their plebe year, the black midshipmen from the class of 1965 often took black upperclassmen home to Washington on Saturday afternoon for dinner with their parents or to parties with their friends. "We were family," Stan Carter observed about those relationships. The upperclassman Paul Reason knew the best was Holger Gustav Ericsson Jr., '63. Eric, as he was called, was one of the first African American midshipmen to introduce himself to Reason. "We had a lot of things in common," Reason recalled. "We were close to the same age. He was a good guy." The two developed a close friendship, and Eric became the first upperclassman to spoon Reason. Because Eric was from Brooklyn, he also became good friends with Pat Prout, so Reason spent a lot of social time during his plebe year with Prout as well. When Reason, Carter, and Floyd Grayson became upperclassmen themselves, they grew as close to the black plebes of the classes of 1967 and '68 as the black midshipmen of the classes of 1963 and '64 had been to them. During their first-class year, Paul Reason and Stan Carter regularly socialized with black plebes James Frezzell, Charlie Bolden, and William Stanton "Buddy" Clark Jr. "We all knew each other's parents, brothers, sisters, cousins, godparents," recalled Floyd Grayson. "Everybody."

On weekends, midshipmen did not have to sit with their company at the mess table; they could sit wherever they wanted. The black midshipmen tended to sit together, regardless of class or company affiliation. "We segregated ourselves," observed Carter. "If it had not been for that, it would really have been a lot more difficult for me."

Only rarely did black plebes have black first classmen. When Pat Prout selected Pete Tzomes to be his plebe, he didn't even know Tzomes was African American. Tzomes had light-colored skin and straight hair. "Do you have a problem having a firsty who is black?" Prout asked. Tzomes struggled to stifle a smile. Prout frowned. "Mister, what are you smirking at?" he asked. "Wipe that smirk off your face." Tzomes did so. Prout reiterated the question. The smile reappeared on Tzomes's face. Prout grew angrier. Tzomes burst out laughing. "I'm black," he said. "What?" said Prout. The two soon developed a close friendship.

Black upperclassmen sometimes assumed a role that might be described as "special assistant first classman for minority affairs" for black plebes who felt uncomfortable discussing racial issues with white upperclassmen. Mal Bruce took pains to get to know each incoming black plebe. "If there is anything you don't feel you could discuss with your first classman," he would say to them, "you can come down and see me." Only once did a black plebe approach Bruce with what the plebe thought was a case of racially motivated mistreatment, but when the two sat down and sorted it out, they concluded that the plebe had misconstrued an act of normal plebe hazing. Pat Prout never discussed racial matters with his first classman or any other white midshipman; he felt comfortable talking only to other black midshipmen about racial matters. As a youngster, he figured that incoming black plebes would feel the same way, so when Stan Carter joined his company, Prout took him under his wing, as Carter put it, even though third classmen usually left plebe mentoring to the first and second classes. After surviving their own plebe year, Carter and Paul Reason helped incoming African Americans survive their plebe year. "We were very protective of each other," recalled Stan Carter. "Gil Lucas was smart as a whip," Reason recalled, "but he was really intimidated by Bancroft Hall, initially. I could work with him and get him to calm down. He was always trying to be perfect. 'Hey, you can't be perfect,' I said. 'You've got to accept a little less than that.'" As an upperclassman, Floyd Grayson spooned black plebes and offered them help as a matter of course. He felt that black midshipmen had to stick together and believe in each other and help each other.

Most black upperclassmen did not spoon black plebes automatically. Whatever his race, an upperclassman usually did not spoon a plebe until they became friends, or unless they had been friends before coming to the Academy, or without some geographic or family connection. Spooning did not happen often before the Army-Navy game in any case. As Paul Reason observed, "You'll grow into a spoon before you get one." Still, the strictures of segregation and their small numbers thrust black midshipmen together socially, regardless of class, and made spoons between black upperclassmen and black plebes more common than they were among white upperclassmen and white plebes.

Black midshipmen often spent what little free time they had among black people in Annapolis. Whether they were following the familiar segregationist patterns they had grown up with or simply felt unwelcome in white business establishments, uniform or no uniform, black midshipmen gravitated toward the black section of Annapolis when they had town liberty on Saturday afternoons.

Wes Brown spent most Saturday afternoons visiting black people in town. He had met several Annapolitans in Washington before coming to the Academy. He had become acquainted with Aris T. Allen, for example, at Howard, when both were going through the Army Specialized Training Reserve Program. Allen introduced him to other folks in Annapolis's black community, where Brown's name was well known. Several people stopped him in the street and invited him to drop by any time. Soon everyone, white or black, got to know him, but Brown became a hero in the black community.[2]

The black citizens of Annapolis opened their arms to each new African American midshipman with as much ardor and pride and joy as they had for Brown. "There were relatively few places where one could go socially in Annapolis if you were black, other than into Ward Four [the black section of town]," recalled Paul Reason. "And in Ward Four, there was nothing really to do except go to the homes of friends."

Wes Brown introduced Larry Chambers and Reeves Taylor to Dr. Hi Johnson and other black Annapolitans, who welcomed the black plebes into their homes as they had Brown. Like Brown, Chambers and Taylor enjoyed visiting black families in town when they didn't have extra duty and welcomed the opportunity to sit down, relax, and take a break from the stress of being a plebe. As an upperclassman, Chambers introduced incoming black plebes to Dr. Johnson and other black families in town so that they too would have a place to go on Saturday afternoon. Reeves Taylor also became good friends with Tommy Baden, a black man who worked in the Academy's tailor shop, with whom he shared an interest in photography. The Badens befriended Lu Gregg as well.

"There were a number of black people that went out of their way to make life pleasant for me," recalled John Raiford. "They were generally very supportive and happy to see me when I walked around in town. I remember seeing pre-teenage children standing on the sidewalks exclaiming 'There he goes!' and cheering as I marched by. An important factor in my social life was the fact that I had a fiancée, Roberta Randall, during three and a half of the four years that I was at the Academy. Her home was my home whenever I had liberty. Her family and friends always treated me as an honored guest."

Lu Gregg also has fond memories of black people in town. "They reached out to me and I to them," he said. "From the kids I would speak to as I passed the playgrounds at the all-black Bates High School, to the adults on Calvert Street, including some who were Navy stewards in the mess hall. Some families became special—the Badens out on West Street, the Crowleys in Eastport. All became a source of motivation and a home-away-from-home."

Before Mal Bruce entered the Academy, he had become acquainted with Ray Richardson, whose father was a black physician in town. When Ray heard that Mal was going to become a midshipman, he extended him an open invitation. One Saturday after plebe summer ended, Bruce went out to visit the Richardsons. He was amazed by the reception he received from black people in town. "God bless you, son," they would say. "We're proud of you. Work hard." Some would point him out to their children. "See, he's a midshipman," they would say. Others would stop what they were doing to shake his hand. When Bruce arrived, Dr. Richardson told him how black Annapolitans kept track of how many black midshipmen were in each class and who they were and so forth. "It gave me an eerie feeling," recalled Bruce, "like it was some underground telegraph." The intensity of their sentiment warmed his heart. Dr. Richardson also invited the other black midshipmen over, and it was there that Bruce and his three black classmates often got together. Bruce also took pains to introduce incoming black plebes to black families in town.

The preferred meeting place for black midshipmen soon became the home of Lillie Mae Chase. Different versions exist of the origins of Mrs. Chase's special relationship with black midshipmen. In one version, she was sitting on her porch talking with her mother in 1955 when three black midshipmen strolled by and struck up a conversation. Mrs. Chase invited them in and her home soon became known as a place where black midshipmen could gather and have sandwiches and cookies.[3]

In another version, toward the end of the summer of 1955 the commandant summoned the four black plebes in the class of 1959 to his office. He asked whether their mothers and fathers wanted to come to parents' weekend just before the end of plebe summer. Since none of the local hotels were open to African Americans, the commandant had arranged for their parents to stay with black families in Annapolis and Arundel on the Bay. One of the people who volunteered their home was Lil Chase, who worked as a custodian at the

Naval Academy Museum. Lil and her mother, Louise Stewart, lived in a house just outside Gate 3 on College Avenue. Mal Bruce's aunt and uncle were planning to attend, so Bruce arranged for them to stay at Lil's. When their plans fell through, Mrs. Chase invited Bruce to drop by. Bruce did so, thus inaugurating a tradition that was to last for years.

Whatever the origin of their relationship, Lillie Mae Chase became "a mother away from home" for black midshipmen. Later in life she joked that she had more than three dozen sons, "all from a different dad," whom she affectionately dubbed her "couch lizards." "She took us as we came here as plebes," recalled Charlie Bolden, "and helped us get through the Naval Academy." "I was fresh out of high school, somewhat confident, almost cocky, but the environment at the Naval Academy had proved to be a little more than I had bargained for," Bolden added. "Refuge at Lil's on the weekend always served to recharge my batteries and give me inspiration and hope that I could survive no matter what anyone did or said back on the Yard."

One of the first things black upperclassmen did for black plebes was introduce them to Mrs. Chase. Small in stature but big of heart, Lillie Mae brimmed with nervous energy and personal warmth. She was a lifelong resident of Annapolis, a faithful member of the Mount Moriah A.M.E. Church, and extremely devoted to family and friends. Over the years she worked at the Blue Lantern Inn, the Annapolis Yacht Club, the Naval Academy Chapel, and the David Taylor Naval Research and Development Center, as well as at the Naval Academy Museum, retiring in 1976 with more than twenty years of federal civil service.[4]

Mrs. Chase's home became a sanctuary for black midshipmen, a place where they could loosen their ties, put up their feet, and relax in a wholesome environment. Stan Carter and his black classmates went there almost every weekend. "You could sit on the sofa and talk about the kind of things you'd be talking about if you were home with your own parents," he recalled.

Black midshipmen regularly met at Mrs. Chase's house to make their weekend plans. After the noon meal on Saturday, they would rendezvous there, find out what was happening, and go off and do their thing. By going to Lil's first, those who had no plans often found something to do. Before returning to the Academy, they often went to Lil's to decompress after their weekend activities. Her home was also a place where they could meet their dates or families or friends. "Lil Chase really helped make our life a lot easier," recalled Floyd Grayson.

When white midshipmen's dates came into town for social events, they usually stayed with white families or at one of the hotels in town. The Academy attached so much importance to its hops and balls that it employed a full-time social director whose job, in part, entailed arranging accommodations for "drags" (dates) and explaining social protocol to them. One of the preferred hotels was Carvel Hall, a 125-room hotel in the center of Annapolis that grew up around a house built in 1763 by William Paca, one of Maryland's signers of the Declaration of Independence. The only African Americans allowed to set foot in Annapolis hotels during the Jim Crow era, however, were people like Marcellus Gabriel Hall, who worked as a doorman, bell captain, desk clerk, and almost everything else in Carvel Hall for fifty years beginning in 1913. As an old man, Hall wore a navy-blue coat festooned with the gold stripes of a fleet admiral and one gold star for each decade he worked at the hotel. White midshipmen always paid their respects to "old Marcellus," as they called him, when they picked up their drags, and old Marcellus never turned in a midshipman he caught sneaking up the fire escape. Black women, however, were denied accommodations at Carvel Hall throughout the half century that Marcellus worked there, and many of the social director's services were therefore unavailable to black midshipmen.[5]

Lillie Mae Chase made her house available to black midshipmen's dates and she knew the protocol for all of the Academy's social events. She would tell the women when they needed to wear a straw hat or gloves, and if they didn't have them she would lend them hers.

Mrs. Chase's house provided a forum for black midshipmen from different companies to share their experiences and for black upperclassmen to hand down oral traditions to incoming black plebes. It was there that Mal Bruce heard about Wes Brown's experience. "It was passed on to Chambers, to Bauduit, to Sechrest, to me," Bruce recalled, "and you realized, 'Hey, if he could do it under those conditions, what we're doing is a piece of cake.'" Mostly the stories comforted and reassured the plebes, who realized that the upperclassmen had survived the same treatment they were going through. The upperclassmen constituted living proof that an African American could succeed at the Academy.

Mrs. Chase also told stories herself. If a midshipman was having a problem, Lillie Mae would tell a story about how another midshipman solved a similar problem, whether it entailed studies, sports, or girlfriends. Sometimes she would serve food. "That's where I learned to eat crabs," recalled Pete Tzomes. But, most important, she provided a home away from home for black midshipmen.

Despite the close ties black plebes forged across company and class lines to other African American midshipmen, if they were having racial problems, as often as not they kept it to themselves. Pat Prout was in the same company with Stan Carter when Prout was a youngster and Carter was a plebe. Prout suspected that Carter was having difficulties with some of the white upperclassmen in the company, but Carter never said anything about it. As an upperclassman, particularly as a firsty, Floyd Grayson kept a weather eye open for racially motivated hazing of black plebes. "I would've been right on it," he recalled, "but I don't remember anybody complaining. I think we were too silent then. People talked about it, but didn't think about doing anything about it because we were in such a minority that you just knew the main way to get through it was just to endure it." Whether from pride, temperament, or blind adherence to the midshipman's credo—"never bilge a shipmate"— many black plebes never told anyone else about the racial problems they were having.

Sometimes the price of such silence was steep indeed, for in some cases hazing precipitated the departure of black midshipmen. Stan Carter recalled that his classmate Darryl Andre Hill, '65, left the Academy because he did not like how the rules prevented him from seeing his girlfriend in Washington. Floyd Grayson was in the same battalion as Hill, but in a different company. Hill's room was up on the fourth deck, where, as Grayson put it, the upperclassmen "were the sourest, most cantankerous people. Something about the halls being closed in up there on that fourth deck affected those guys' attitudes and dispositions. They were mean." According to Grayson, Hill reached his breaking point one day in the spring of 1962. "He and I were walking braced up," recalled Grayson. "We had been outside talking and we were on the first deck walking down the hall, and all of a sudden, he hollered out, 'Grayson is a nigger!' It was that night he went over the wall. He just left and never returned." Grayson does not believe Hill's hazing was racially motivated. "I think everything had gotten to him," he said. "I think Darryl left because of the atmosphere on the fourth deck." Hill accepted an offer to play halfback and receiver for the University of Maryland, where he became a star player and the first black football player in the Atlantic Coast Conference.[6]

Clyde Hobart Robinson Jr., '64, also left the Academy because of hazing. Among the five black midshipmen who started out in the class of 1964, Robinson was the youngest, having entered the Academy right out of high school. Instead of trying to develop Robinson's potential, the upperclassmen in Robinson's company "rode him pretty hard," as Prout put it. "His grades suffered as he tried to make the transition." Officially, Robinson left because he was deficient in his studies during the second term.[7] Prout believed that upperclassmen went out of their way to cook up justifications for frying Robinson. Bill Jones agreed. Robinson "piled up demerits like crazy," he said. "They drove him out." Neither Pat Prout nor Bill Jones specifically attributed Clyde Robinson's departure to racially motivated hazing.

The story was different for James Frezzell, however. Frezzell did not compile a stellar academic record at NAPS. He finished the course standing 174th in a class of 187. Still, he scored well above the minimum on the entrance examination. According to his officer-in-charge at NAPS, Frezzell was somewhat quiet and withdrawn. But the officer also considered Frezzell a "courteous, sincere student well motivated toward a naval career." Frezzell's "performance of military duties was generally acceptable," the officer added, "and his military appearance very good." The officer noticed that, though Frezzell had difficulty with technical subjects, he was "conscientious in the preparation of assignments, active in class participation, and genuinely concerned about his academic achievement."

But Frezzell was not coming to the Academy to be a scholar. He was coming to play football. His officer-in-charge at NAPS said that on the gridiron Frezzell "demonstrated an outstanding ability, an unflinching spirit and an indomitable will to win." Tony Urbanik and Steve Belichick had high hopes that Frezzell would help improve the Academy's image in the black community. "Although the services were integrated, TV broadcasts of the Army-Navy game showed only white ballplayers," recalled Frezzell. "It didn't look good." Urbanik and Belichick were also concerned that black midshipmen playing Navy football would upset some of the white players. "Don't talk about civil rights," they advised him. "Just go and be a midshipman and play ball." Frezzell didn't think that his race would be a problem at Navy, anyway. After all, his prowess on the gridiron had negated any prejudice that might otherwise have come his way in Monessen, so he figured it would be the same at the Academy. The desire to win games, he believed, would overcome resentment toward a black man being on the team. Frezzell believed he was good enough to help Navy win.

But it was not to be. Frezzell entered the Academy on 30 June 1964 in fine football trim, weighing in at 190 pounds. A group of second classmen began working him over right away. Every time one of the segundos spotted Frezzell in the hallway, he would make the black plebe do push-ups or jumping jacks. "I was exercising a lot more than I was supposed to," recalled Frezzell—so much, in fact, that within about two months his weight dropped to 165 pounds. The hazing took a toll on his health as well as his waistline. On 25 August 1964, he entered sick quarters for four days with a case of strep throat. Two days after being discharged, he went right back into sick quarters for three more days, then spent a twelve-day stretch in the hospital with mononucleosis.

The hazing continued after Frezzell got out of the hospital and classes began. Second classmen, almost exclusively from outside his company, would have him come around on the slightest pretext, especially when TV news programs reported stories about civil rights demonstrations. "*Frezzell*," some of them would say. "What kind of name is that? Where did you get that from?"—as if Frezzell wasn't a proper name for a black person. Others put down Darryl Hill, who had also been recruited to play football. They said that Hill was "chicken" and "gutless" and "scared" and lacked talent. There were white plebes on many of these come-arounds as well, but the segundos often let them stand at ease while keeping Frezzell braced up. Frezzell also had to remain braced up at the dining tables on numerous occasions when white plebes were allowed to "carry on." Quiet by nature and advised by Urbanik and Belichick not to mention discrimination, Frezzell never discussed his harassment with anyone. "Grin and bear it" was his attitude. And he was as stubborn as he was quiet. "They couldn't break me," he recalled. "Not being able to break me made them madder."

Frezzell's roommate, Kevin F. Delaney, '68, a white plebe from Wolcott, Connecticut, knew that Frezzell was getting a lot more come-arounds than many of their classmates. He also knew that Frezzell's grades were suffering as a result. Delaney concluded that a concerted effort was under way by a handful of upperclassmen to get Frezzell. "The system at that time allowed that minority of bigots to prevail," Delaney recalled, "and to really ruin the future of a gentleman who I consider a fine human being and a person who would've made an exceptionally good naval officer."

Delaney had grown up in an all-white New England town and had never been south of Yankee Stadium before coming to Annapolis, but he had also never before encountered virulent racism. None of his classmates seemed bothered by the color of Frezzell's skin, and he could not understand why the upperclassmen would be. "Jimmy was a good friend," he recalled. "I had a lot of respect for him. He was giving 110 percent to get through whatever he had to get through and to live that dream of becoming a commissioned naval officer. He could taste it. He could feel it. He just didn't quit. He was a player all the way to the day he left, fighting to live that dream."

Delaney himself received extra attention from these same upperclassmen simply because he was Frezzell's roommate. Whenever the upperclassmen would burst into their room, Delaney and Stephen R. Hart, '68, another white roommate, were just as likely as Frezzell to receive unfair conduct reports or be made to do push-ups. Delaney was also getting more than his share of come-arounds from these upperclassmen. Nobody ever said anything overtly to indicate that the harassment resulted from racial prejudice. But "it was very clear that our room became much more of a target than other rooms in the company," recalled Delaney.

Several white upperclassmen tried to help Frezzell by having him come around to rest or study, so those out to get him couldn't have him doing push-ups all night. But these sympathetic midshipmen never took direct action against his persecutors. "There were upperclassmen who kind of empathized with my plight and they would try to help as much as they could," Frezzell recalled. "But at the time, the prevailing ethic was not to interfere."

There were no black upperclassmen in Frezzell's company, and Frezzell never told the black upperclassmen he saw at Lillie Mae Chase's house what was going on. Paul Reason, however, knew that Frezzell was having a tough time. "Jim was a harried plebe," Reason recalled. "He probably got more focus than the others." But Reason was far enough removed from Frezzell's company that he could not say for certain whether the extra attention Frezzell was receiving stemmed from racism or from other causes.

Whatever the cause, the harassment soon interfered with Frezzell's academic performance. "I just wasn't allowed to study," he recalled. "I guess they figured that would be the way to get me out. I had to study by flashlight at night for exams because I was constantly being interrupted." Frezzell failed two courses the first semester.

At that point his coaches stepped in. Frezzell had played well on the freshman team as running back on offense and cornerback on defense, until an injury he sustained while tackling future legendary Miami Dolphin running back Larry Czonka sidelined him for the rest of the season. The coaches wanted Frezzell to return next season, so they arranged for him to have a chance to retake the final examinations, if he was willing to cut short his Christmas break and return to the Academy to study. Frezzell took the offer. With no one around to haze him, he absorbed enough to pass the reexaminations.

The coaches' intervention brought only a temporary halt to Frezzell's harassment. Soon after the second semester started, the come-arounds began all over again. Frezzell still refused to bilge his persecutors, even though he probably would have had support from the coaches had he done so. Frezzell believed that the coaches knew what was going on and felt that it was their responsibility to stop his harassment. He began to wonder whether he was part of an experiment to see if white midshipmen could accept a black football player without interference from above. He concluded that keeping the team lily-white was more important to the upperclassmen on the team than winning.

Frezzell started the second semester on academic probation. The harassment continued to degrade his classroom performance. He finished the semester with one F, four Ds, and a B. The academic board convened to discuss his case along with those of other midshipmen found academically deficient. Moments before Frezzell went in for his hearing, a commissioned junior officer from the executive department suggested that Frezzell file a discrimination complaint with a black congressman. His jaw agape, Frezzell stared at the officer. "If you knew this was going on all year, why didn't you do something about it?" Frezzell thought. He politely declined the officer's suggestion. He had had a bellyful of the Academy and did not wish to remain. The academic board granted him an "honorable separation due to academic deficiency under conditions not prejudicial to his eligibility for reappointment." On Frezzell's Evaluation Summary Report, completed upon a midshipman's graduation or separation, Frezzell's company officer rated him low in academic potential; satisfactory in academic effort, bearing and appearance, ability to get along with peers and superiors, respect for regulations, and breadth of interests; and high in dependability, initiative, self-reliance, and enthusiasm. The Academy was keeping the door open for Frezzell, but he had no desire to return. "I'd had enough," he said.

After the hearing Frezzell went over to Lillie Mae Chase's house. He told her that he had been discharged. He was sad that his Navy career had to end this way. Lil told him that it was God's will. "He has another purpose for you," she said. "Just keep the faith and that purpose will become evident."

Frezzell finished his college education at California State University in western Pennsylvania, where he graduated with a B.S. in mathematics and a minor in physics. He then began a long career as a manager in government and private industry. When the class of 1999 graduated, Frezzell was executive director of a corporation in upstate New York that rehabilitated houses in minority areas and enabled first-time home buyers to obtain mortgages. Today Frezzell is an active member of the Albany chapter of the Naval Academy Alumni Association, helping to recruit minority midshipmen. When asked how he could reconcile his treatment at the Academy with his willingness to help, he replied, "It's the Christian way of doing things."

Frezzell's refusal to file discrimination charges against his persecutors, whether motivated by Urbanik and Belichick's admonition not to mention civil rights, the midshipman's credo "never bilge a shipmate," or his own pride and temperament, enabled his persecutors to get away with racially motivated harassment. If racism contributed to the separation of other black midshipmen during this period, none of them formally protested to the authorities either. The silence of these black midshipmen contributed to the executive department's belief that there were no racial problems at the Academy.

Throughout the period from Larry Chambers's matriculation in the summer of 1948 through Paul Reason's graduation in the summer of 1965, the Academy executive department neither articulated nor disseminated any racial policy at all. The attitude among higher-ranking executive department officers throughout the 1950s and early '60s seemed to be "why fix it if it ain't broke?" They considered the Academy's racial problems to have been solved with the graduation of Wes Brown.

This point of view reflected the prevailing attitude that had surfaced among Navy leaders in the wake of World War II. By the end of the war, the written racial policy promulgated by James Forrestal had lulled many naval officials into a false sense that equal opportunity had become a fact of life in the Navy, and they remained complacent about equal opportunity for fifteen years. Except for some minor alterations to the steward's branch, it was only when the Gesell Committee began to scrutinize the services' racial policies that the Navy sputteringly resumed the process of racial reform.

Until the tide of reform generated by Defense Secretary McNamara's response to the Gesell Committee began lapping at the shores of the Naval Academy in the summer of 1965, neglect of racial issues and toleration of discrimination remained the rule in Annapolis. Until then, promulgating any sort of policy or statement about the consequences of racial discrimination simply did not occur to Academy officials. Neither did developing training programs for executive department officers and midshipmen to enhance their awareness of racial issues. Academy officials expected the existing culture to absorb black midshipmen just as it did white midshipmen. At the same time, Academy officials created no extracurricular activities or organizations designed to appeal to African Americans. Instead of making provisions for racial or ethnic diversity among midshipmen, Academy officials expected all midshipmen, whatever their background, to assimilate into the existing culture. "I doubt the Academy faculty had any concept of 'diversity,' let alone making any attempt to promote it," recalled John Raiford. "I think that we blacks were just tolerated without further attention."

V. Adm. Charles S. Minter served at the Academy for much of this period, first as executive officer of the physical education department from June 1953 to August 1955, then as commandant of midshipmen beginning in June 1961. When R. Adm. Charles C. Kirpatrick, the superintendent, had a heart attack in January 1964, Minter became superintendent, a position he held until June 1965. Born on 23 January 1915 and raised in Pocahontas, Virginia, Minter graduated from the Naval Academy in 1937. In each of his Academy billets, Minter paid little attention to racial issues. "The black problem just didn't arise," he said. "We had such a very small number of black midshipmen—two, three, four in each of the classes during the time when I was there. I recall no racial incidents relating to those young people. I don't recall any mast or any heavy conduct reports. It was just something that wasn't really thought about very much." Minter never thought it necessary to take any steps to ensure the fair treatment of black midshipmen, nor did he ever receive instructions or communications from the Navy Department in regard to racial policy. "Race just wasn't that much of an issue," he said.

Wesley Brown and his mother, Rosetta Brown, with Naval Academy diploma, 3 June 1949. Copyright *Washington Post;* reprinted with permission of the District of Columbia Public Library.

Lawrence C. Chambers, Class of 1952.
Midshipman Personnel Jacket, Nimitz Library,
United States Naval Academy.

Malvin D. Bruce, Class of 1959. *Lucky Bag*,
1959, Nimitz Library, United States Naval
Academy.

Lillie Mae Chase, c. 2000. Courtesy of William C. Jones.

Floyd Grayson, Class of 1965. *Lucky Bag,* 1965, Nimitz Library, United States Naval Academy.

Joseph Paul Reason, Class of 1965. *Lucky Bag,* 1965, Nimitz Library, United States Naval Academy.

James Frezzell, Class of 1968. Courtesy of James Frezzell.

Outside the Mainstream

THE ONLY occasions on which race did receive official attention in those days were the mandatory Sunday afternoon dancing classes, universally known as "tea fights." Beginning in the mid-1950s, the Academy held tea dances six Sundays per year in Memorial Hall and later Dahlgren Hall for plebes and some four hundred to a thousand young women from cities along the eastern seaboard.[1] Plebes were required to attend four of the six dances. The midshipmen would line up on one side of a partition while the women lined up on the other for the first dance. When a plebe got to the front of the line at the head of the partition, he paired up with whoever happened to be in the corresponding place on the other side. After the first dance, the participants could choose any partner they pleased. The purpose was to teach plebes ballroom dancing and evidently good manners. "It's good training for the middies to take a date through a receiving line," an upperclassman on the hop committee once told a reporter, "and to carry on a conversation with a girl they didn't know before."[2]

The presence of African Americans complicated the picture. If they followed the normal procedure, the result would be black men dancing with white women. The code of social behavior during the Jim Crow era strictly forbade interracial dancing, for it conjured up the image of the racist's worst nightmare, a black man having sex with a white woman. Accordingly, black midshipmen were not permitted to dance with white women in the segregated town of Annapolis.

As a result, tea fights were usually very awkward for African American midshipmen. Nobody told Gil Lucas how to handle the situation. "The tea dances were a living hell for me," he recalled. "Since there were usually no black women to dance with, I just had to kind of walk around and look stupid." An acquaintance of his happened to attend one of the dances, a white coed from Hood College. "We started talking in the middle of the dance floor," Lucas said. "There were probably hundreds of people out there. All of a sudden we noticed that everybody had stopped dancing. They made this big circle around us and were staring. She got really embarrassed and disappeared in the crowd. I never saw her again." Eventually Lucas solved the tea dance problem by simply not attending.

Bill Jones and Paul Reason found happier solutions. Mrs. Mary A. Marshall, the brigade hostess and social director, permitted them to invite their girlfriends to the dances, to the chagrin of white classmates who would have liked to invite their own girlfriends. Thereafter black plebes were excused from going through the line. They met their dates at the door instead.[3] Still, this creative solution sent a signal that the Academy regarded black midshipmen as outside the mainstream.

Of the fifty-one African Americans admitted into the classes of 1945–68, thirty-three, or 66 percent, graduated. The failure rate of 34 percent for blacks does not differ significantly from the failure rate of 35 percent for all midshipmen from the classes of 1955–75.[4] Thus, although blacks had a harder time getting admitted to the Academy than whites did, black midshipmen during this period stood an equal chance of graduating.

Of the seventeen black midshipmen admitted into the classes of 1945–68 who did not graduate, ten were discharged for academic deficiency, four for misconduct, two resigned voluntarily, and one died. The last was Richard Albert Drew, '56, whose uncle Charles Drew had developed the process for separating plasma from blood. Drew finished his plebe year standing 174th in a class of 852 and served his youngster cruise on board the destroyer escort *DeLong* (DE-684), where he earned a 4.0 (the highest grade) in conduct. Midshipmen spent part of each summer on board a ship at sea. These "practice" cruises introduced them to shipboard life and to the various branches of the service while providing practical experience in gunnery, navigation, seamanship, engineering, and communications.

It had not been easy for Drew to do so well. During his second semester, he began having severe headaches. Harold Bauduit urged him to go to sick bay, but Drew was afraid the doctors would give him a medical discharge if he did. Finally the pain got so bad that Drew sought help. He spent most of May 1953 in the naval hospital in Annapolis. The next month he began to wear glasses and the headaches stopped, enabling him to go on cruise. At sea he began having difficulty with his vision, despite the new glasses. His eyes just didn't seem to work together. More ominous, he began to experience a burning sensation down his right side. After returning from sea in August, he was admitted to the neurological unit of the U.S. Naval Hospital in Bethesda, Maryland. Suspecting a brain tumor, the doctors performed several operations but could find no definitive evidence of one. Drew's condition continued to deteriorate. Finally, on 24 May 1954, he died. The funeral service took place four days later at the First Baptist Church in Washington and he was buried in Arlington National Cemetery. Lu Gregg, Ed Sechrest, and six white class-mates served as pallbearers.

Of the four discharged for misconduct, two were dropped after the first semester, one after the second, and one, Holger Ericsson, in his first-class year. "Eric" was smart, talented, and squared away. Toward the end of his plebe year in the spring of 1960, he numbered among the midshipmen selected to accompany President Eisenhower to a summit conference in Paris.[5] Later Eric developed the computer course that Stan Carter and his classmates took as plebes. Although he intended to go into the Marine Corps after gradua-tion, according to Stan Carter, Eric's company officer, a white Marine major, didn't want Eric to join the Corps, so the major fried him on a trumped-up Class A offense during June Week. Given the opportunity to resign, Eric chose to do so. The details remain murky, for neither Carter nor Paul Rea-son remembers exactly what happened, and I was unable to contact Ericsson myself. Whatever the true cause, Eric resigned on 20 June 1963, fifteen days after his classmates graduated, giving him the dubious distinction of being the farthest along upon being separated among the black midshipmen who failed to graduate.

Two of the black graduates in this group were "turnbacks" to the next class, graduating in five years instead of four. Emerson Carr turned back to the class of 1969 as a result of his plebe-year academic performance. Reeves Taylor fell ill with pneumonia at the end of his first-semester youngster year and spent most of December 1949 in the Annapolis naval hospital. His grades suffered as a result and he was discharged on 9 February 1950. Reappointed by Representative Aime J. Forand (D-R.I.), he was readmitted to the Acad-emy in the class of 1953.

Of the seventeen black midshipmen who did not graduate, only three survived plebe year: Ericsson, Drew, and one other. Of the ten discharged for academic reasons, six were dropped after the first semester, two were dropped after the second, one was dropped at the end of his second-class year, and one, Lou Adams, was honorably discharged after his youngster cruise. Adams had earned passing grades in marine engineering second semester, except for boilers. He returned to the Academy after youngster cruise prepared for a re-examination in boilers. What he didn't understand was that the reexamination was on the entire course, not just part of it. He passed the boilers part of the reexam but failed the rest, thereby precipitating his discharge. This unhappy ending constituted Adams's only negative experience at the Academy. On the whole, if a black midshipman survived plebe year in this period, he had an 89 percent chance of making it to graduation.[6]

With no prior college experience before becoming a midshipman, Larry Chambers found class work tough, but he had no major difficulties. "The hardest subject I had was German," he recalled, "but the hard sciences were easy for me." Chambers graduated 119th in a class of 783. Although John Raiford had entered the Navy with a decided educational disadvantage, he had no undue difficulties with class work and graduated 729th in a class of 854. Mal Bruce's prior college work enabled him to sail through his plebe-year courses. Academics became harder for him midway through youngster year when he first began to encounter material he had not already studied, but he still continued to excel in math and science. He finished 610th in a class of 800. Bill Jones never liked school, so he didn't take his studies seriously at the Academy. None of his courses was particularly difficult, and he did just enough work to get by. During exam week, he preferred playing pinochle to studying. On graduation day he stood 816th out of a class of 932. Similarly, Stan Carter never cared about excelling academically, only surviving.

For the most part, academics came easily to Floyd Grayson and Paul Reason. Of the 802 members of the class of 1965, Reason stood 302nd, Grayson 449th, and Carter 774th. Pete Tzomes did well in math, physics, and Russian but not so well in English. He graduated 254th in a class of 893. After struggling with chemistry and calculus plebe year, Charlie Bolden became a star student until his second-class year, when he failed a course in electrical engineering and lost interest in studying. Gil Lucas remained focused on academics and consistently outperformed most of his classmates. He stood 122nd out of 841 members, while Bolden finished 361st.

Other black midshipmen from the classes of 1949–68 also excelled in the classroom. Lu Gregg found the transition from a ghetto high school to the Academy challenging academically. He ended plebe year in the bottom quartile of his class. Thereafter he improved dramatically. During second-class year he received the highest grade in his class on the electrical engineering final. He graduated in the top 10 percent of his class, with distinction, standing 74th in a class of 742. George Fennell, '58, graduated with distinction, standing 116th in a class of 900. Pat Prout finished a respectable 268th in a class of 932.

Some did not fare so well in the classroom. Harold Bauduit stood only a few numbers above the anchor man, finishing 662nd in a class of 682. Kent Withers Slaughter, '57, graduated 810th in a class of 848. Robert Chester

Newton, '63, finished 870th in a class of 887. Nevertheless, the academic hurdle was not as high for black midshipmen as it would later become.[7]

On the whole, however, the black midshipmen who entered the Academy between 1945 and 1965 (including Emerson Carr) did a little worse in class standing than most of their peers, graduating, on average, in the 36th percentile. Academic performance alone did not account for class standing or "order of merit." Conduct grades and "aptitude for the service" ratings were also factored in. Midshipmen received an aptitude rating each term and during summer practice cruises. According to the regulations, the aptitude rating was supposed to reflect a midshipman's "officerlike qualities; that is, those qualities which reflect his ability as a leader, his sense of duty, his military attitude and bearing, and his desirability in time of war." A midshipman's aptitude rating for each term was derived from "grease chits" received from his instructors, executive department officers, and every first classman in his company. There was no specified set of objective criteria for determining grease marks. Indeed, the whole process was rather arbitrary. Some midshipmen considered it little more than a popularity contest.[8]

In some cases, white midshipmen and officers evaluated black midshipmen fairly. "Invariably I stood in the upper third of the class in military aptitude," recalled Mal Bruce. "The upper class sort of ranked me high among my classmates in aptitude." Pat Prout also had good "grease"—the midshipmen's nickname for aptitude for the service. "Through my youngster year I was number two in grease in the brigade," he recalled.[9]

Grease, however, gave bigots a golden opportunity to express their prejudices. White midshipmen and officers who had nothing against black midshipmen personally but who believed that African Americans should not be naval officers could, with impunity, give black midshipmen much lower grease marks than they deserved. So could out-and-out bigots. Many black midshipmen believe they would have done better in order of merit had the white midshipmen evaluated their aptitude for the service fairly. "I would have been a hell of a lot higher in my class standing had it not been for grease," recalled Larry Chambers. "Cost me a lot of numbers." Floyd Grayson had the same impression. "I felt that oftentimes I didn't get the grade I deserved," he recalled. "I just felt . . . ignored." Racism accounted for a significant part of black midshipmen's lower average class standing.[10]

In some respects, the experiences of African American upperclassmen differed little from those of their white classmates. After class, all midshipmen participated in sports. Reeves Taylor helped his company rack up points against the other companies by winning cross country races. Mal Bruce ran track and played handball and squash. He later regretted not developing an interest in a "carry-over" sport like golf. Stan Carter tried soccer and 150-pound football but didn't think he was good enough to pursue them to the varsity level. Floyd Grayson played one year of junior varsity lacrosse and rowed crew for three years. Paul Reason played volleyball and field ball. Pete Tzomes tried out for 150-pound football but injured his knee on the second day of practice and had to have surgery. After that he stuck with company sports. During second-class year, he helped establish weightlifting as an intramural sport at the Academy. Gil Lucas participated in four varsity sports: cross country, indoor track, outdoor track, and heavyweight crew. He found crew to be a great bonding experience because, as he put it, "there's no sport where you work any harder."

For many midshipmen, extracurricular activities consumed whatever free time remained after academics, sports, and military responsibilities. Reeves Taylor played tenor sax in the "NA-10," the midshipman band that performed at hops. Stan Carter and Paul Reason served in the public relations committee, whose members sat in the press box at every Navy sporting event, serving as spotters and announcers. During big football games broadcast on national television, committee members told sportscasters who was making the plays and passed them notes with anecdotes for color. Paul Reason also participated in the antiphonal choir, one of two choirs that sang in every Naval Academy chapel service on Sunday mornings. Gil Lucas later sang in the antiphonal choir.

In the summers, midshipmen gained firsthand experience with the fleet on cruises. Mal Bruce underwent the usual greenhorn treatment on his youngster cruise, including standing "mail buoy watch" in the middle of the ocean and being sent to the boatswain's locker for "six fathoms of shoreline." Pat Prout got seasick off Cape Hatteras after eating greasy pork chops during his own youngster cruise and decided then and there that he did not want to go surface navy. Paul Reason was proud to be one of sixty-five midshipmen from the class of 1965 who spent the first half of their youngster cruise on board the carrier *Enterprise* (CVAN-65).

Back in Annapolis, black upperclassmen varied in the degree to which they participated in indoctrinating plebes. "I was probably as big a pain in the butt as any of my other classmates," recalled Larry Chambers, "but I tried to ask technical questions." John Raiford took the opposite tack. "I did almost no 'running plebes,'" he recalled. "It just wasn't my thing." Mal Bruce said that although he and the other firsties in his company wanted "to give them a plebe year," as he put it, they tried to be reasonable. As long as plebes knew the basics, they left them alone. In their view, the purpose of plebe indoctrination was to inculcate leadership qualities and the ability to follow orders and regulations, not to vent sadistic impulses. Bill Jones simply refused to participate in indoctrinating plebes. Stan Carter worked mostly with black plebes, helping them learn the ropes instead of asking them a lot of questions. Paul Reason had plebes come around to his room regularly, but he had them there to study or listen to his radio, not to answer questions. Gil Lucas had hated the treatment he received as a plebe, so as an upperclassman he strove mightily to be fair and to stop classmates from going too far.

Most black firsties had white plebes. Floyd Grayson's plebe came from Columbus, Ohio. Grayson picked him because he grew up near Capital University, where Grayson went to college before entering the Academy. "I did my best to try to help him to make the transition and cope," he recalled. Paul Reason never could get his plebe to loosen up. The plebe called Reason "sir" all year long, even though Reason spooned him on the day he chose him.

Several black midshipmen got married in the Naval Academy Chapel soon after graduation. Ed Sechrest became the first to do so, ending the ceremony with the traditional walk out the chapel door under an arch of swords held by classmates. Hours later, classmate Harold Bauduit and his bride exchanged wedding vows in the chapel. In 1964, Bill Jones and black classmate Benjamin F. Thomas each had his wedding there.[11]

Most black upperclassmen continued to get along well with most of their white classmates. Larry Chambers had no racial difficulties as an upperclassman. Bill Jones considered his white roommates to be friends. Despite his initial trepidations about southerners, Pat Prout developed a close friendship with Joseph W. Prueher, '64, a white classmate from Tennessee. Stan Carter became good friends with white classmate John R. Musitano, '65. They often visited each other's homes on liberty. Paul Reason developed a close relationship with white classmate Daniel V. Flanagan Jr., '65, from California. During their second- and first-class years, Reason's bride to be, Diane Fowler, was attending Wayne State College in Detroit. Flanagan also had a girlfriend living in the Motor City. The fiancée of another classmate, Richard J. Sharpe, was attending Wayne State as well. Once a semester when they had a long weekend—from 4:00 Friday afternoon until evening meal formation on Sunday—the trio would drive to Detroit and back. They did it by pre-positioning a car in town, driving straight through, and sleeping only in the car on the way out and the way back. They always got back in time. Lu Gregg was one of the few in his class to meet the requirements to skipper one of the Academy's 44-foot yawls. On several occasions he and five or six classmates and their dates spent a weekend together on a yawl, sailing into the bay. Race never entered the picture on these outings.

Nevertheless, much of the socializing outside of Academy-sponsored activities remained segregated. Despite his friendship with John Musitano, Stan Carter spent most of his time away from the Yard with other black people. "They basically did their thing," he recalled. "We did ours." For John Raiford, the awkwardness of socializing with white people at the Academy came home most poignantly through his fiancée. "When I brought Roberta to dances within the Yard," he recalled, "none of my classmates ever asked her for a dance. And I never asked anyone else to dance with me. I remember that Roberta was given dance cards with blank spaces to be filled in by the different dance partners who might dance with her. My name was the only one ever entered in any of those cards over the entire period."

Despite the generally congenial racial climate for black upperclassmen at the Academy, the occasional incident would remind them that they were different. Wes Brown tried to join the choir, but the director very apologetically informed him that the Academy just wasn't ready for a black tenor. On one occasion Paul Reason and Stan Carter were pressed into service with the Glee Club, when it put on a joint concert with Misericordia College, a women's school in Wilkes Barre, Pennsylvania. Misericordia's glee club included two black women. The director of the Academy's Glee Club did not want them to feel left out during the social festivities that followed the concert, so he arranged for Reason and Carter to make the trip. At the time, Reason was the only African American that sang in any choir at the Academy. Carter, who didn't sing well, lip-synched his way through the concert.

Some black midshipmen experienced racial problems while on cruise. "During second-class summer there was a joint two-week Military Academy–Naval Academy amphibious landing exercise (CAMID) at Little Creek, Virginia," recalled John Raiford. "Afterwards, the local Chamber of Commerce sponsored a dance dubbed the 'CAMID Ball.' The black YMCA contacted me to be the 'Guest of Honor' for a dance that was being held at the exact same time as the Camid Ball. I don't know how the YMCA got my name, race, and address. I hesitated until I was told that the Chamber of Commerce had promised to donate a large sum of sorely needed money to the black Y if I attended. I did." The only negative racial experience Lou Adams had during his Academy stint occurred during his youngster cruise on the cruiser *Des Moines* (CA-134) while the ship was in port in England. Adams was walking with a white Englishwoman on deck past the turret when some white sailors uttered rude and racist remarks to them. Stan Carter felt that the commissioned officers at sea scrutinized his performance more closely than that of his white classmates. Carter believed he had to outperform his peers to get an equal evaluation. On the other hand, Carter had no difficulties with the enlisted men, particularly the black sailors. During one cruise, everybody else's laundry came back "rough dried." "Mine came back pressed," he recalled. His first-class cruise was the best. "I was lucky," he said. "I was on a ship with two black officers and I had no problems because they looked after me." Pete Tzomes spent the second half of his youngster cruise in Norfolk for amphibious training. The social highlight of the summer was the midshipman's ball. Just before the ball started, a Navy commander had a few words with Tzomes and black classmate Calvin W. Huey, '67, the first African American football player to start on the varsity squad. "I hope you understand the Navy's integrated," the commander drawled, "but the young women of Norfolk aren't." Two black girls were invited to the dance so that Tzomes and Huey could attend. Tzomes spent part of his first-class summer on a submarine out of Key West. The town held a dance for the midshipmen, but Tzomes was specifically not invited. The skipper of his submarine protested, but to no avail. Tzomes sat the dance out while the rest of his classmates attended. Dances were about the only time as a midshipman he felt singled out because of his race.

Although Reeves Taylor got along well with his classmates, he received lower grease marks than he thought he deserved. When the time came during first-class year for duty assignment selection, he chose destroyers. Shortly thereafter, the commandant of midshipmen summoned Taylor to his office. The Navy was not putting "colored officers" on small vessels, he said. Taylor's choice was limited to two or three larger vessels. He wound up on the cruiser *Columbus* (CA-74), the same ship Larry Chambers had sailed on a year earlier.

One evening in the fall of 1954 during second-class year, Harold Bauduit received an order to report to the commandant of midshipmen. The commandant met him in the reception area and awkwardly inquired whether he had ever experienced any problems at the Academy because of his race. Bauduit soon learned that two reporters from the *New York Times* were waiting inside the commandant's office to interview him. The commandant was trying to find out in advance what Bauduit might say to them. Although miffed by the commandant's inability to just come out and ask what was on his mind, Bauduit told the reporters, honestly, that he had never experienced any racial troubles at all as a midshipman. He later noted that this episode marked the only time the subject of race arose in his experience at the Academy.

Several weeks later, the commandant summoned Lu Gregg to his office. He reminded Gregg that Navy was playing the University of Mississippi in the Sugar Bowl at New Orleans as a result of its outstanding 1954 season. He told Gregg that stadium officials had changed their policy and would allow him to sit with his classmates instead of in the segregated section. African American fans of Ole Miss, however, could not even enter the stadium, because the University of Mississippi limited ticket sales to white people. The black press argued that, in light of the Supreme Court's recent *Brown v. Board of Education* decision, Navy should refuse to play. The Academy, however, never considered backing out of the game. By deciding to play, fumed James L. Hicks, editor of the *Afro-American*, a black newspaper with a national circulation, "the Navy's top brass insulted, desecrated, and defiled the watery graves of every colored sailor who has died in the defense of his country." "Through this one act," Hicks continued, the Navy "has all but nullified all its work in integration during the past few years. So far as I'm concerned at the moment, when the Navy speaks to me of integration—I will hear a prostitute speaking of love." Whatever impact Hick's statement had on Gregg and his black shipmates, it could not have helped the Navy's image in the black community.[12]

Pat Prout believed that the purpose of plebe indoctrination was to develop plebes professionally. As a second classman, he served on plebe detail, focusing on basics like military bearing, marching, and table manners. At the end of the summer, a plebe from Alabama joined Prout's company. One day Prout had him come around to his room to see how he was doing on his *Reef Points*. After answering a few questions, the plebe told Prout that he was a member of the Ku Klux Klan and began spouting some of the Klan's racist doctrine. Prout's jaw dropped. He wondered how the plebe could be so brazen, so stupid. From then on, Prout grilled the plebe at every opportunity. The plebe bilged before the end of the year.

One evening some two months before their graduation, Charlie Bolden and Frank Simmons drove to a restaurant in town noted for serving beer to midshipmen illicitly. Bolden and Simmons stepped up to the bar next to several white classmates and ordered beers.

"I'm sorry," said the bartender, "I can't serve you."

"We got a problem," Bolden protested, "because we want to be served just like everybody else."

The bartender frowned. "Well, if you go out back," he said, "I'll get you a beer."

"I'm not going in the back," said Bolden.

"If you don't leave," the bartender said, "I'll have to call the police."

"How about letting me have the phone," Bolden shot back, "because what you are doing is illegal." Indeed, although the Civil Rights Act of 1964 had outlawed refusing to serve African Americans, the bartender knew that Bolden's classmates were violating the regulations by drinking inside the seven-mile radius of the chapel, so he probably figured he could get away with it. The confrontation escalated, with raised voices and an attempt to throw Bolden out. Disgust finally overwhelmed Bolden, and he and Simmons left peacefully. Not one of their white classmates, who sat there watching the whole ugly scene unfold, rose to join them. These white midshipmen's attitude, reflected by the Academy's leadership, seemed to be that it was better to ignore discrimination than to confront it. Although black midshipmen encountered far less racial hostility among white midshipmen as upperclassmen than they had as plebes, the feeling of existing outside the mainstream never fully left them.

The absence of black midshipmen in top brigade leadership positions cemented this sentiment. So-called "stripers," firsties with the rank of midshipman lieutenant junior grade or higher, held leadership positions in the brigade or in their regiment, battalion, company, platoon, or squad. Stripers were selected through a complex process involving interviews, grease, and Academy records. Roughly 20 percent of the firsties in the classes of 1949–65 were stripers during each set, and some 46 percent held the midshipman rank of second petty officer or lower. The third or spring set, covering roughly the last five or six weeks before graduation, was the honor set, featuring mild weather and the high visibility of June Week[13] with its myriad parades, concerts, Blue Angels flights, and other colorful events, culminating in the graduation ceremony.

Twenty-seven black midshipmen graduated in the classes of 1949–65. Of these twenty-seven, only two—or 8 percent—were stripers in the third set, and 50 percent were midshipman second petty officers or lower. Pat Prout achieved the highest rank in the group: midshipman lieutenant (j.g.) assigned to a battalion staff. During the first set he had stood even higher, as a four-striper (midshipman lieutenant commander) regimental subcommander. He considered striving to become company commander of the color company in the third set, but he was discouraged from trying. "They'll never make you company commander," his classmates said, "because they wouldn't want to have a black color girl for June Week." Statistically and socially, the chances of a black midshipman becoming a striper in the high-visibility third set during this period were slim to none.[14]

Floyd Grayson left the Naval Academy much more pessimistic about race relations than he had been when he entered. "There were many whites who did not believe in racism and did not want to treat you unfairly," he recalled, "but they would not take a stand against their friends. They wanted to be well liked and wanted to be one of the boys, so even though they may not openly have done anything to hurt you, they didn't prevent anyone else from hurting you. That's what I noticed more than anything. People did not take a stand against someone who was being unfair. That, to me, was really the problem of racism."

A 2005 report echoed Grayson's view with regard to sexual harassment at the service academies, but it might just as well have been addressing racism: "Midshipmen who observe harassing behavior and fail to intervene and correct it, in effect, condone that behavior. This tolerance, even if only by a few, of the attitudes demonstrated by offenders, undermines the standards essential to successful leadership development. Accordingly, midshipmen . . . must assume more responsibility for holding others accountable by intervening, confronting, and correcting each other for failure to live up to the required standards."[15]

The Sunday before June Week, Floyd Grayson went for a walk with Paul Reason. They talked about their dreams and aspirations. Grayson was dubious about his prospects in the Navy. "Paul," he said, "they don't want us here and they sure enough aren't going to want us in the Navy. There's no way we'll see a black admiral in our lifetime."

Whatever their experience, most African Americans from the classes of 1949–68 have no regrets about having attended. Even some of those who did not graduate look back on their Naval Academy days with fondness. After leaving the Academy, Lou Adams earned a bachelor's degree from Morgan State College and was working on a Ph.D. in experimental psychology at Penn State when he received a job offer from IBM. He has remained in the corporate world ever since and now works as an engineer for Lockheed Martin Management and Data Systems. Adams recalls his Academy experience as a "great period" and gets together with classmates from time to time. His only regret is that he did not graduate. James Frezzell enjoys seeing other former midshipmen at Academy alumni events and remains grateful to Tony Urbanik and Steve Belichick for giving him the opportunity to play football for Navy. He still admires his friends and supporters at the Academy for being unafraid to do the right thing. "These are people of character," he declared.

Many of those who did graduate look back with mixed feelings. Larry Chambers served for thirty years in naval aviation, rising to the rank of rear admiral and becoming the first black Academy graduate to attain flag rank. Nearly twenty years passed after graduation before he set foot in Annapolis again. Finally, as his youngest daughter was thinking about becoming a midshipman, his wife convinced him to go back for a football game. "While I had some good memories," he recalled, "I also had some tough memories."

After the tour on the *Columbus*, Reeves Taylor embarked on a naval aviation career during which he logged 3,500 hours in jet aircraft and made 408 carrier traps (landings). He retired as a captain and spent most of his second career working for Shell Oil Company. "I learned a lot," he said of the Academy. "Both educationally and socially, it definitely prepared me for what I was getting into. There were easier ways to have done it, but that's the way I did it."

John Raiford graduated from the Academy but was not commissioned in the Navy. "I had entered into a purported marriage at age fifteen," he recalled. "My purported wife was pregnant by another man at the time, and I did not know it. When I found out a few weeks later, I sent her home to her family and sent the marriage license back to the issuing county clerk in Holly Springs, Mississippi. I considered myself single from that point on." However, regulations stated that no one who is married or who has ever been married could be a midshipman. Academy officials learned about Raiford's marriage during the usual investigation of all midshipmen on the eve of graduation.

"The Navy charged that I lied about my marital status and informed me that I would be given a dishonorable discharge," Raiford said. "I was allowed to contact an attorney, who arranged for me to go to East St. Louis and get an annulment *ab initio* (from the beginning). The annulment decreed that the marriage never existed. Several black lawyers in two different cities gave of their time and talent to achieve this, because I had no resources at the time. The Navy still declined to offer me a commission. But I was allowed to graduate with my class and given a discharge 'under honorable conditions.' It could have been worse; it could have been better. I went to Cornell Law School the following fall and got my law degree from there in 1958. I worked as an engineer for the Underwood Corp. in Hartford, Connecticut, from 1958 to 1960; as a staff engineer with RCA in West Los Angeles, California, from 1960 to 1962; and as a member of the technical staff and contract negotiator at Hughes Research Laboratories in Malibu, California, from 1962 to 1989. I joined the state bar of California in 1966 and was licensed to practice law there until I retired on 1 January 1999. I practiced before the U.S. Patent Office in 1979 and before the U.S. Supreme Court in 1980."

Despite the unhappy ending, Raiford remained upbeat about his Academy experience. "I had some of the most enjoyable times of my life there," he said. "It was a boost to my self-esteem that I ate in the same dining hall with kings, queens, presidents, admirals, and generals. There was also a degree of respect that was accorded me that I had not previously enjoyed. I also felt that it was nice to have the opportunity to be the first black enlisted person to come up from the fleet through NAPS and graduate."

Wes Brown spent his naval career in the Civil Engineer Corps, building houses in Hawaii, a nuclear power plant in Antarctica, and a desalinization plant at Guantanamo Bay, Cuba. The largest-scale projects he worked on were in the Philippines: construction of the air station at Cubi Point which, at the time, was the largest earthmoving undertaking in the world after the Panama and Suez canals, and construction of the aircraft carrier wharf at Subic Bay, where he served as project officer and operations officer. His career included special assignments to Liberia, Chad, the Central African Republic, and Costa Rica, for which he received a commendation for achievement from Secretary of the Navy Paul H. Nitze in 1964. He retired a lieutenant commander on 30 June 1969 after twenty years of service. He believed that an unfair fitness report from a racist commanding officer had kept him from making commander. Otherwise, he never had racial problems with any other Seabees.

Brown continued working as an engineer, first for the State University of New York at Stony Brook, Long Island, until 1976, then in the facilities planning department at Howard University, until his second retirement in 1988. Since then he has lectured at college campuses, played tennis, traveled with his wife, Crystal, and spent time with his four children and seven grandchildren. Public service remained an important part of his life throughout his career and retirement. He was a member of the Association for the Study of African American Life and History; the NAACP; the American Civil Liberties Union; the John Wesley A.M.E. Zion Church; and the National Naval Officers Association. He served as a Naval Academy alumni trustee, a member and chairman of the D.C. delegate's congressional nominations review board for U.S. service academies, and a member of the secretary of the navy's advisory subcommittee on naval history. To recognize his pioneering role and to thank him for his continuing involvement with the Navy, in the spring of 2002, V. Adm. John R. Ryan, the superintendent, named a new field house after him.[16]

Lu Gregg wanted to go into naval aviation after graduation. At the physical, however, Navy doctors detected a slight myopia in his left eye. They suggested he go surface navy and apply to flight school later. Gregg then took an Air Force physical. Air Force doctors detected the same myopia, concluded that he had been favoring his right eye while studying, and suggested he cover his right eye while studying. If the doctors saw improvement in two months time, he would be accepted directly into pilot training upon graduation from the Academy. His eyes did improve, so he entered the Air Force.

Gregg graduated from pilot training near the top of his class, then became the youngest pilot with his own crew flying for the Military Airlift Command, including VIP flights from Andrews Air Force Base to Paris and back. The Air Force sent him to Massachusetts Institute of Technology, where he received a master's degree in aeronautics and astronautics in 1961. During the next four years he served as a project scientist in the Office of Aerospace Research and the Air Force Office of Scientific Research and continued to fly as mission commander in the VIP squadron at Andrews. In 1965, he left active duty to become associate dean of sciences at Northwestern University. The next year he was listed in *Who's Who in America* and named "One of the Outstanding Young Men of Chicago." In 1972, he held the first in a series of executive positions in leading business corporations, initially as vice president of First National Bank of Chicago and finally as vice president for corporate communications of Hughes Aircraft and Hughes Electronics. After retiring from Hughes in 1999, Gregg began working part time as vice chairman and executive vice president of NeTune Communications, a global broadband digital satellite networking company serving motion picture and TV filmmakers.

In his spare time, Gregg served on numerous committees, including the Academy's academic advisory board, the chief of naval personnel's Civilian

Advisory Board, the Committee on NASA-University Relations, Harvard University's Visiting Committee on Physics, and the National Academy of Sciences' Commission on Human Research. He has also served as chairman of the White House Fellows Selection Committee, Midwest; chairman of the National Academy of Sciences' Committee on Minorities in Science; and vice chairman of the board of directors for the Corporation for Public Broadcasting. "My Academy experience helped me to both identify and exploit opportunities," he recalled. "Despite the segregated environment that surrounded the Academy, many of my professional achievements in life began to accelerate at the Academy and continued thereafter." "All incidents *within* the Academy bring good memories," he added.

After leaving the Academy, Harold Bauduit served thirteen years in the Air Force, one of the hundreds of midshipmen who chose the lighter blue uniform until 1979, when the Navy shut down interservice transfers.[17] After leaving the Air Force in 1969, Bauduit earned a law degree from the University of Colorado and hung his shingle in a town near Denver. Bauduit remained positive about his days as a midshipman. "It is something I would never go through again," he said, "but I would never trade the experience for anything." Harold Bauduit died in 2000.

Mal Bruce served for twenty-nine years in the surface navy, retiring as a captain in 1988. He then spent ten years as president and chairman of the board of a small cabinet manufacturing company in California before retiring from the second career to pursue his interest in photography. He looks back on the Academy as a "wonderful experience," for it was there that he forged some of the strongest friendships of his life.

Pat Prout became a Marine infantry officer, saw combat during two tours in Vietnam, and left the Corps after four years. He then earned an M.B.A. from Harvard Business School, worked for IBM, Philip Morris, and Chase Manhattan Bank, and in 1996 took a job with Heidrich and Struggles as a recruiter of top-level executives in the financial services industry. "It's like any experience," he said about Annapolis. "You have some good and some bad. Overall, I enjoyed my four years at the Naval Academy and if I had to do it all over again, I would."

Bill Jones returned to the Marine Corps after graduation, served a tour as a platoon leader, went to flight school, and flew nearly 160 missions in the back seat of an F-4 Phantom jet fighter over Vietnam. His most difficult undertaking occurred seven months into the tour, when he had to accompany his brother's body home. In his last tour, he served as a Marine recruiter on college campuses. Radicals from the Students for a Democratic Society or the Black Panthers would occasionally ask him how a black man could kill Asian babies on behalf of a racist country. "I just push a button and the babies die," he would say. "Napalm." Such tough and flippant talk scared away the radicals, but it also masked—or perhaps revealed—the fact that he was sick of military service. He left the Corps in July 1970 because he did not want to fight in a war "that our political fathers did not have the will to win," as he recalled. But more important, the "campus rabble rousers" with their college deferments reinforced his perception that poor and black soldiers were doing a disproportionate share of the dying in Vietnam. After leaving the service, he worked for Proctor and Gamble until the mid-1980s, when he opened his own real estate business. Throughout his civilian career, he never allowed pursuit of the almighty dollar to interfere with the deep, abiding love he has for his wife and two children.

Looking back on his midshipman days, Jones has love-hate feelings about the Academy. While he hated "school" and felt stifled by the routine and straitjacketed by regulations, he loved the cruises and the challenges posed by getting over the wall and back without being caught. "When I wasn't bored," he recalled, "it was fun. They took me places I would have never gone. I loved summers because you got to go on cruises. How else would I have ever gone to Europe? The Mediterranean? To hang out in Cannes, France? Or Malta? To play on the crap tables in Monte Carlo or to ride around the Vatican on a motor scooter? That's because I was on a Med cruise. Or the Caribbean cruise. How else would I have ever gotten to see what voodoo was really like?"

Stan Carter served his naval career in the surface navy, including a tour as a company officer at the Academy and a tour as advisor to the chief of naval personnel on minority and women's affairs before retiring in 1988. Thereafter he spent a year as assistant dean at the School of Business at Florida A&M University, then started a highly successful Ford dealership in North Carolina. He merely endured the Academy, but he enjoyed his naval career. Now, in his spare time, he serves as president of the Rotary, president of the chamber of commerce, a board member for Habitat for Humanity, and a Blue and Gold recruiter, helping others get into the Naval Academy.

Pete Tzomes started out in the Marines dreaming of becoming an aviator, but when that didn't work out he embarked on a career in nuclear submarines, becoming the first African American officer to do so. Apart from the occasional sailor muttering that he "wasn't taking orders from no nigger officer," he found the submarine community free of prejudice, an attitude he attributed to the camaraderie that developed from close-quarter living on board submarines. In May 1983, he became the first African American submarine skipper. Five years later, he became special assistant for equal opportunity (OP-01J) to the deputy chief of naval operations for manpower, personnel and training (OP-01)/chief of naval personnel. He retired as a captain in 1993 and has since pursued a second career, mostly with Commonwealth Edison. Tzomes summed up his Academy experience as "rewarding." "The rules were such that if you followed them," he said, "you were going to succeed."

Gil Lucas became the second African American officer to enter the submarine force, returning to the Academy in 1973 for a two-year tour as 35th Company officer. He left the Navy after eleven years of active duty and took a series of jobs involving remediation and cleanup of nuclear weapons and radioactive waste sites. What Lucas remembers most about his Academy experience are shipmates. "The Naval Academy attracts a lot of super people," he said. "They're the best people I've known."

Charlie Bolden became a Marine aviator and logged more than six thousand hours of flying time in more than thirty models of fixed and rotary wing aircraft as a test pilot and combat pilot, including more than one hundred missions over North and South Vietnam, Laos, and Cambodia in the A-6A Intruder. Selected as an astronaut candidate by NASA in 1980, Bolden qualified as a space shuttle pilot and logged more than 680 hours in space during four missions, including the successful deployment of the Hubble space telescope in 1990. He returned to earth in Annapolis, serving as deputy commandant from June 1994 to June 1995. In July 1998 he was promoted to the rank of major general and two years later became commanding general of the 3rd Marine Aircraft Wing. [18] In a 2000 interview, Bolden looked back on the Academy as "the premier form of officer education for the naval service." "The leadership principles you're exposed to and the opportunities to practice them at the Naval Academy equipped me quite well to go into the Marine Corps and to do the things that I've done in the thirty-some odd years that I've been a marine," he said.

Three days after graduation, Paul Reason married Diane Fowler in the Naval Academy chapel. He became a surface nuclear officer and rose steadily through the ranks. As a junior officer he served on board the *Enterprise* for two deployments to the Southeast Asia and Indian Ocean areas during the Vietnam War. As commander, he served as naval aide to President Jimmy Carter. As captain, he skippered the nuclear-powered guided-missile cruiser *Bainbridge* (CGN-25). As vice admiral, he served as the deputy chief of naval operations for plans, policy, and operations (N3/5). In 1996, he assumed command of the Atlantic Fleet (CINCLANTFLT) and became the first African American naval officer to wear four stars and, to date, the only African American naval officer to achieve that rank. "You learn things about yourself and about the Navy that you'd never be exposed to anyplace else," he said of the Academy. "I've never been a great one to jump off a high dive into a swimming pool. But there, you climb up a vertical ladder way up into the rafters of the natatorium, and you jump off. That's to simulate having to jump over the side of a ship. You can't walk backwards, because there's a stream of one hundred people behind you. When you get to the edge, they tell you what to do. You duck-walk off and your eyes get big. You say, 'Holy shit!' But you survive, and so from that point on, you know that, 'Hey, it's no big deal.' And then you have to stay in the water for three hours. Don't care what you do while you're in the water, but you can't stand on the bottom, and you can't hold on the side. It's important to know that you have done that successfully when you spend most of your adult life in the middle of an ocean with water all around you. Where else do you learn that sort of stuff?"

Floyd Grayson entered the surface navy after graduating from the Academy and embarked on the destroyer escort *Hammerberg* (DE-1015) for his first tour of duty at sea. At the counseling session after his first fitness report, the skipper told him that he was taking to the job well, handling the men well, doing everything well. "But I still can't help but think of you as colored," the skipper said. Grayson received a less than top-notch fitness report. With this and several other instances of prejudice, Grayson saw the writing on the wall. "I realized that my future was not under my control," he said. He left the Navy after serving the minimum five-year commitment, attended Harvard Business School, earned an M.B.A., and took a job with a home building company in Baltimore. In the fall of 1975 he took control of his future and started his own company, Grayson Homes, which over the years became one of the top ten homebuilders in Baltimore.

Thoughts of Paul Reason's success in the Navy sometimes bring tears to Floyd Grayson's eyes. "I never would have believed that Paul would become commander-in-chief of the Atlantic Fleet," he said. "It speaks well of America that through the years we can change. I'm a believer in America and its opportunities, despite what I went through."

After revolutionizing its written racial policy in the mid-1940s, the Navy made relatively little headway in its racial practices before the mid-'60s. Although the written policy called for integration and equal opportunity, the Navy neither provided equal opportunities for black sailors nor strove for proportional representation of African Americans in the enlisted service or officer corps. As a result, the percentage of blacks in the Navy remained below the percentage of blacks in American society, and uniformed African Americans as well as civilians who sought a commission still encountered racial barriers. Likewise, the Naval Academy did not strive for proportional representation of black midshipmen. As a result, only fifty-one African Americans entered the Academy and thirty-three graduated in the classes of 1949–68, with black graduates in each class never numbering more than four, and none in the classes of 1950, 1951, 1960, and 1966.[19] Between the graduation of Wesley Brown in 1949 and Charlie Bolden in 1968, an average of three African Americans became midshipman and two graduated each year. In short, black midshipmen had little more than a token presence at the Naval Academy during this period.

So few blacks entered the Naval Academy before 1965 for two main reasons: racism and toleration of racism. The Navy's racist policy in the early days of World War II struck a discordant note that reverberated for decades in the black community. Mention of the Navy conjured up images of black sailors shining the shoes of lily-white officers, serving their food, or washing their dishes. As the World War II experience receded into the past, these negative images began to fade. Still, when black people who did not live near a naval installation thought of a military career, they usually thought of the Army or Air Force, not the Navy.

For many black youth who pondered the journey to Annapolis, racism stopped them before they ever got started. They simply did not have the same chance to enter the Academy as whites did. In many parts of the country, high school guidance counselors talked black students out of applying to the Academy. Until the civil rights movement dethroned Jim Crow, no southern congressman was likely to jeopardize his political career by appointing an African American. Blacks who did receive appointments often got them because of civil rights agendas like those of Charles Diggs, Edna Kelly, and Jeffrey Cohelan. Rarely did blacks get appointed in the "normal" way in those days, as the result of a senator's or representative's honest effort to represent his or her constituency.

The Navy's equal opportunity policy demanded that, if a black received an appointment, he would get an equal shot at entering. It might not be a fair shot, given the inferior education he had received under segregation or the potential for bias in grading, but he did get to take the same entrance examinations as white appointees, and if he passed he would be admitted. For many of the untold number of African Americans who were appointed but failed the exams, an inferior education or bias in grading kept them out. And who knows how many who passed all the tests were turned away at the last minute by a discouraging debriefing from an Academy official?

Toleration of discrimination resulted from both lingering racism and the belief that the Navy's racial problem had been solved. Ignoring discrimination enabled it to survive. For example, the Navy ignored the fact that bigoted selection boards denied black students in a large portion of the country the opportunity to enter the NROTC program, and even if a black did get selected for a school in a Jim Crow region, stated policy or unwritten tradition would keep him out. The Navy stopped special efforts to inform black southerners about the opportunities in the officer corps in 1950 because these efforts failed to bring about an increase in minority enrollment in either the Academy or the NROTC program. But instead of trying something else, not to mention filtering out the discrimination inherent in the process, the Navy did nothing for a decade.

The lack of an organization or permanent program dedicated to minority recruiting in BuPers also served to keep the number of black midshipmen low. Throughout the 1950s, the Navy continued to "recruit, train and assign personnel without consideration as to race," as the bureau put it, even if it meant that the proportion of blacks in the fleet would decline.[20] The bureau's decision not to develop a minority recruiting program stemmed from the belief that it would have to set quotas to do so. Since the existence of quotas would lead to charges of discrimination, bureau officials reasoned, it was better to do nothing.

The Naval Academy's recruiting policy reflected the bureau's policy. During the 1950s, the Academy did nothing to recruit minorities, nor did it do anything about the discrimination inherent in the admission process, such as the dearth of appointments from Jim Crow states.

The situation began to change after the Kennedy administration arrived in Washington. As more and more young black people got involved in civil rights activities, the movement reached critical mass, forcing the government to act. Events in Greensboro, Birmingham, and cities throughout the South underpinned McNamara's efforts to reform the Defense Department's racial policy. As a result, neglect began to give way to affirmative action throughout the Defense establishment. The services could no longer get by with token selection. They now had to strive for proportional representation of minorities.

During the 1960s, civil rights advocates expressed the desire to increase minority enrollment at the Academy as one solution to the problem of underrepresentation of blacks in the officer corps. Increasing minority participation in the armed forces went hand in hand with the larger goal of ending off-base discrimination in the eyes of the Gesell Committee.

During the first half of the '60s, the Navy dealt with the new racial policy by ad hoc measures, literally setting up an "Ad Hoc" group in BuPers which, presumably, would institute the new policy, then go away. The bureau established no permanent organization or program for dealing with equal opportunity and affirmative action. With regard to minority recruiting for the Naval Academy, the bureau's ad hoc letter writing efforts and conference visits in 1962 and 1963 might have evolved into a permanent program, but since the bureau did not repeat these efforts in 1964 they proved a false start. Alfred Fitt's novel operation to recruit blacks for the academies foreshadowed the program later developed at the Academy, but since his successor did not continue the operation, Fitt's feat was also a false start.

In sum, racism and ignoring discrimination limited the number of blacks attending the Academy during these years. Racism tarnished the Navy's image in the black community, discouraged young men interested in the Academy from trying to enter, and denied blacks equal opportunity to get in. Ignoring discrimination prevented the establishment of a permanent minority affairs organization or program charged with recruiting blacks for the Academy.

By and large, African American midshipmen got along well with white midshipmen and had few problems with the administration during this period. Nevertheless, the majority of black midshipmen from the classes of 1949–68 did encounter racism during plebe year from a minority of prejudiced class-mates and upperclassmen. To whatever degree an individual African American encountered racism, the experience made success that much more difficult for him to obtain than it was for his white classmates. The officers of the ad-ministration perceived no racial problems and did nothing to enhance racial awareness. Their policy toward black midshipmen was, at best, one of benign neglect.

Although the black midshipmen who entered the Academy in this period made a positive impact on the attitudes and behavior of numerous individu-als, they were too few in number to change the nature of race relations at the institutional level. Nor did any impetus for change trickle down to the Naval Academy from above. As a result, the Academy lacked a racial policy through-out the period. Not only was there no minority recruiting program, but no one in the administration deemed it necessary to issue any sort of statement, directive, guideline, or regulation prohibiting racial discrimination against black midshipmen.[21]

The only racial issue upon which the administration consistently weighed in was enforcement of the customary Jim Crow separation of black men and white women at tea fights. Otherwise, except for the handful of times a re-porter wanted to talk to a black midshipman or an activity needed a black face for an event involving black civilians, like Paul Reason's guest appearance with the Glee Club, the administration ignored race.

Whether by ignoring racism or remaining unaware of its presence, the administration enabled it to exist, thereby denying black midshipmen equal opportunity. In the absence of input from commissioned officers, the mid-shipmen themselves became the arbiters of race relations. Most midshipmen either harbored no prejudice or did not discriminate, but some did openly display racial hostility toward black plebes. In many instances, this racial hos-tility manifested itself in unfair treatment or hazing of black plebes. In at least one and probably several more instances, such treatment precipitated the de-parture of a black plebe. Although most black midshipmen never experienced anything so extreme, they did encounter varying degrees of hostility or racially motivated mistreatment. The amount of discrimination a black midshipman experienced depended on his proximity in Bancroft Hall to prejudiced upperclassmen. If, after plebe summer, he happened to land in a company free of bigots, he had few problems because of race. If he happened to land in a nest of bigots, rough weather lay ahead. Regardless of where black midshipmen resided in Bancroft Hall, however, the crux of the racial problem remained the white majority who did not personally discriminate but who failed to speak up when others did so. Accordingly, a black midshipman entering the Academy in 1964 stood the same chance of encountering discrimination from upperclassmen as a black midshipman who had entered the Academy in 1954.

Most black midshipmen, whether by the attitudes they encountered or the treatment they received, even if only from a minority of white midshipmen and even if only to a small degree, were made to feel different, not one of the boys, outside the mainstream. Official inattention to race, except to enforce Jim Crow customs at tea fights and to condone segregation in Annapolis, especially when it came time to secure accommodations in town for black families, reinforced this sentiment, as did the dearth of black stripers.

In sum, during this period the Naval Academy was like a club that admitted minority members and gave them access to most of its facilities but still barred them from several of the most important rooms open to majority members. Although much of the Academy's culture accommodated black midshipmen, significant elements of it did not.

To facilitate adapting to Academy life and acquiring the things that the larger culture denied them, black midshipmen created their own subculture within the mainstream Academy culture. This subculture provided them with an alternative mutual support structure and means for socialization. The subculture consisted of three main elements: a greater readiness to cross company and class lines to seek each other out and to form friendships, a tendency to spend town liberty in the black community, and a unique lore.

Some degree of apartheid existed in most parts of Jim Crow America, if not at school then in places people frequented after school. By and large, midshipmen of different colors had not socialized with one another after school before donning the uniform, so until they got used to it they were a little awkward at it. Most black midshipmen had grown up living among black people and not socializing with white people outside of school and school-related activities, so at the Academy they fell into a familiar groove by developing their closest relationships with other black people. Thus, when a black plebe was having a problem, he was more likely to turn to another black person for help. This support made him more ready to form relationships across company and class lines than his white classmates. For their part, black upperclassmen were more willing to associate with black plebes than white upperclassmen were with white plebes because there were so few black midshipmen around.

Segregation in Annapolis reinforced this pattern. With many white busi-

nesses begrudgingly accepting their patronage, black midshipmen gravitated
toward the black community while on town liberty. During Academy events
involving dates or families of black midshipmen, segregation impelled them
toward the black community. The dates and families of white midshipmen
could stay where they pleased, but those of black midshipmen were barred
from Carvel Hall and other traditionally favorite places. To enable black midshipmen to participate in tea fights, their dates to go to hops, and their mothers and fathers to come to parent's weekend, the administration as well as
the black midshipmen themselves created an alternative network of accommodations in the black community, including the homes of Lillie Mae Chase
and black families in the Fourth Ward and outside of town. Although these
accommodations enabled black midshipmen not to be conspicuously dateless
or parentless at important events, the necessity of separate accommodations
prevented black midshipmen and their families from socializing freely with
white midshipmen and their families outside the Yard.

The lore of the black midshipmen's subculture consisted of the stories and
rumors about black alumni or upperclassmen handed down to black plebes.
Those stories and rumors that dealt with discrimination in town, racial hostility from classmates, or racially motivated hazing from upperclassmen were
unique to the black experience. The lore functioned as a survival mechanism,
providing black plebes with the cold comfort that others had survived what
they were undergoing.

The black subculture was not a counterculture. It was neither at odds with
nor designed to subvert the mainstream culture. It was, instead, a tool to help
black midshipmen adapt to the mainstream Academy culture and an antidote
to the racism they faced.

PART II
Racial Policy Revolution: African Americans Assimilate, 1965–1976

"Shaking the Very Dickens Out of Us"

ON 3 July 1965, President Lyndon Johnson began a memo to Secretary of the Navy Paul Nitze with the observation that there were only nine African Americans in the Naval Academy's 4,100-man student body. The president then asked how "we might encourage Negroes to apply for and obtain admittance to the Academy." This memo sparked development of the Naval Academy's minority recruiting program and a revolution in its racial policies.[1]

President Johnson's desire to increase minority enrollment at the Naval Academy stemmed directly from his larger domestic agenda. Civil rights topped that agenda for most of his presidency. Johnson took office with a vision of providing greater opportunities to the disadvantaged. Five days after Kennedy's assassination, Johnson laid out the issues he deemed most important in an address before Congress: "education for all of our children," "jobs for all who seek them," "care for our elderly," and, above all, "equal rights for all Americans whatever their race or color." In his State of the Union message in January 1964, he declared "unconditional war on poverty in America." In a speech to the graduating class of the University of Michigan the following May, he articulated a dream of building a "Great Society," where "men are more concerned with the quality of their goals than the quantity of their goods."

Johnson took his landslide victory in 1964 as a mandate to launch the Great Society. He prodded a Democratic Congress into enacting the most significant domestic legislation since FDR's first term, including federal aid to education, Medicare for the aged, Medicaid for the poor, reform of immigration law, creation of the National Endowments for the Arts and Humanities, and the Voting Rights Act of 1965.[2]

"Affirmative action" became embedded in the lexicon of rights-consciousness during Johnson's presidency. John F. Kennedy had introduced the term in Executive Order 10925 of 6 March 1961, which forbade discrimination in all companies doing business with the federal government and required them to take affirmative action to prevent discrimination. The order seemed to call for employers to recruit, hire, train, and promote minorities, but it did not specify results. On 24 September 1965, Johnson issued Executive Order 11246, reiterating the principle that all phases of employment should be handled on a meritocratic and color-blind basis. The order authorized withholding federal funds from discriminatory contractors and using affirmative action to open up skilled jobs to African Americans. In May 1968, the Labor Department set "goals and timetables" that increased pressure on corporations to recruit, hire, and promote minorities to reflect their proportion in the general population. Although the directive stopped short of setting quotas for any racial or ethnic group, it cleared the way for making "benign" racial preference to achieve proportional minority representation a legitimate public policy.[3]

Johnson's 3 July 1965 memo to Secretary of the Navy Nitze provided the spark that set the Academy in motion toward proportional representation. "There is some hesitancy on the part of qualified young Negroes to seek out an appointment or apply for admission," said Johnson. He asked Nitze to suggest ways to encourage more blacks to try. The issue arose again during Johnson's meeting with NAACP head Roy Wilkins on 3 August in preparation for an upcoming White House conference on implementing new civil rights legislation. Wilkins told the president that a conspicuous example of discrimination in the armed forces had recently come to his attention—the low number of black midshipmen at the Naval Academy. The Military Academy had twenty-nine blacks in a student body of 2,700, or 1.1 percent. The Air Force Academy had seventeen blacks in a student body of 2,900, or 0.6 percent. The Naval Academy's nine blacks in a student body of 4,100 accounted for just 0.2 percent. Immediately after the meeting, Johnson telephoned Nitze and told him to find out why so few blacks were attending the Naval Academy and to double the number enrolled there right away. The president said that he wanted "the same degree of racial equality to operate at Annapolis as it does in the rest of the government."[4]

Secretary Nitze immediately summoned the Academy's superintendent to Washington. Rear Admiral Kauffman arrived that evening. Draper L. Kauffman had entered the U.S. Naval Reserve a month before Pearl Harbor. During World War II, he organized the first Navy Demolition Teams, the ancestor of the Underwater Demolition Teams and SEALs, and saw combat in the Pacific, for which he received numerous decorations including the Navy Cross with Gold Star. After the war, he rose through the ranks of the surface navy, becoming Academy superintendent in June 1965.[5]

Although Kauffman had internalized a degree of racial prejudice while growing up the son of a vice admiral, he did his best to overcome it. In the summer of 1964, Mary Marshall, the Academy's social director, asked Kauffman's wife, Peggy, if she and the admiral would open their home on weekends to midshipmen who had no family or friends in the Annapolis area. The Kauffmans agreed. From then until the admiral became superintendent, their basement recreation room became a weekend dorm for some two to six midshipmen about once a month. With Draper spending most of his time setting up and running the Office of Program Appraisal, Peggy became the primary host. That November, Mrs. Kauffman told her first midshipman protégé that he could invite five other midshipmen to stay over the first weekend of Christmas leave. She also planned to have a dance in the recreation room that Saturday night. The protégé later telephoned to ask whether the Kauffmans minded if one of the six was black. "Of course not," said the admiral, who had answered the phone.

"My answer was hypocritical," he later recalled. "We considered ourselves quite liberal on civil rights, but that night we found we were far more liberal in theory than in practice. We had never had a black houseguest before and to think of having such a young man in the house with our two daughters about his age was thought provoking, to say the least. Our parents, all four of them, would have had a stroke. What should we do for a date for him at the dance? How would the children react? Of course, the last two problems were not problems. Our kids were miles ahead of us and Kelsey had a black classmate at the Cathedral School whom she liked very much and would invite. . . . The weekend went beautifully. Thanks to our own kids, we did not overreact and, anyway, Gil Lucas, the black midshipman concerned, was a very fine young man, very well mannered, though understandably a bit shy. He returned twice more that year." Gil Lucas never sensed any of Draper and Peggy's trepidations. "I just can't say enough about how wonderfully his family treated me," he recalled. "They were fantastic."

When Kauffman arrived in Washington on the evening of 3 August 1965, Secretary Nitze told him of the president's order to double the Academy's black enrollment. The order posed a difficult problem. The class of 1969 had already started plebe summer, yet Johnson expected the Academy to find and enroll nine more qualified African Americans by the time classes began in September. Kauffman telephoned the commandant and dean of admissions, and then he and Nitze discussed the problem. Kauffman doubted that the Academy could find and enroll even two qualified blacks, let alone nine, in the time allotted. More important, he believed that conspicuously inserting a group of blacks near the end of plebe summer "would make their lives miserable and might well cause an unfortunate racial reaction on the part of white midshipmen," as he recalled. Nitze agreed. He promised to persuade the president that it would not be in the Academy's best interest to augment the plebe class at this late date. In return, Kauffman promised to match or exceed the number of blacks enrolled at the other academies in future years without lowering admission standards. The next day, the secretary asked the president to relent on his order to double the number of black midshipmen immediately. Johnson did so but said that he wanted the Academy to enroll thirty new black plebes a year. "President Johnson knew that if he came up with such a sweeping order," Kauffman later reflected, "even if we were not able to follow it, we would darned well be working hard to improve the situation. He was very successful in shaking the very dickens out of us."[6]

Secretary Nitze sent President Johnson a written reply on the fifth. He reviewed the Navy's efforts in recent years to establish "increasing contact" with predominantly black high schools and colleges as part of its general minority recruiting effort. He suggested that few blacks had applied to the Academy recently because those who could have qualified had so many opportunities in the private sector. Naval service, with its long deployments and family separations, seemed relatively unattractive. Nitze promised to consult with Roy Wilkins, other black leaders, congressmen, and members of organizations like the Navy League for advice and support in minority recruiting. "I can assure you," Nitze concluded, "that the Navy desires and will take all appropriate measures to achieve a significant multiplication of Negro midshipmen at the Academy."[7]

In the weeks following his return to the Academy, Admiral Kauffman and his subordinates gave a lot of thought to the problem of increasing black enrollment. First they tackled the question of why the other service academies were attracting more African Americans than the Naval Academy was. They came up with numerous answers, "some nonsensical," as Kauffman put it, "some fairly sensible." One officer suggested that blacks did not know how to swim, were afraid of the water, and therefore did not like being at sea. "This idea was backed up by the fact that almost every black midshipman in the past ten years had been on the swimming sub squad for most of his time at the Academy," Kauffman recalled. The Academy required all midshipmen to be proficient swimmers. Those who could not pass the annual swimming test were assigned to a "sub squad," which practiced in the pool several hours a week until they met the swimming standards for their class. Another theory had it that blacks did not like the idea of living in crowded shipboard spaces surrounded by white officers.

Later, after discussing the matter with black midshipmen and black civilians, Kauffman learned the true answer. The Navy's World War II hangover was keeping blacks away in droves. "There was no doubt that the parents of the young men who we were trying to recruit were far more bitter against the Navy than against the other services," he recalled. "The Navy was looked on as the epitome of color snobbery. They believed that our old rule that blacks could only be servants correctly reflected the Navy's attitude toward the black community." When the six black midshipmen from the classes of 1967 and 1968 returned to the Academy that September, Admiral Kauffman formed them into an advisory group and met with them frequently. The group "couldn't have been more cooperative," Kauffman recalled. "All of them obviously knew all about Gil Lucas's visits to our house and they accepted me as being more honest and understanding than I suppose I really was. They were also very frank." During the first meeting, when Kauffman used the term "colored," the group quickly pointed out that the preferred term was "black." When the admiral learned that a friend of Charlie Bolden's family operated a black radio network in the Southeast, he asked him how you could have a black network. Bolden replied that, within a minute of turning on the radio, he could tell a black station from a white one by the language being used or the music being played. "I was woefully ignorant in this whole area," Kauffman later admitted. "These young men had to do a lot of educating of their white superintendent, frequently to my chagrin, and even more frequently to their amusement." Until Johnson had shaken the dickens out of him, Kauffman, like most of his predecessors, had never given any thought to racial issues at the Academy.[8]

Admiral Kauffman also got the black upperclassmen involved in minority recruiting. Working with the midshipman radio club, the group put together thirteen half-hour radio segments on the life of African Americans at the Academy, which were broadcast over black radio stations in Georgia and the Carolinas. At Kauffman's request, all six—including four youngsters—participated in Operation Information, a privilege heretofore reserved for firsties and segundos. Operation Information, part of the Academy's overall recruiting effort, involved midshipmen getting four more days of leave at Christmas and spring break so that they could speak to students and civic groups and make radio and television appearances in their hometowns. Charlie Bolden wrote an article about the lives of black midshipmen for *Tuesday Magazine,* a black publication with a circulation of 1.4 million.[9]

On 5 November 1965, for the first time ever, the Naval Academy Board of Visitors addressed the topic of black midshipmen in its biannual report. Consisting of distinguished academicians and members of Congress, the board evaluated the Academy's administration, curriculum, and facilities. The report noted the dearth of black representation at the Academy. "This situation can be remedied only through a positive program of recruitment," it declared. Board members attributed the low numbers to word about the Academy not reaching the black community. They suggested using NAPS as an avenue to qualify more blacks for admission and encouraging commanding officers to persuade promising black enlisted men to apply to NAPS. They also suggested that Navy recruiters do a better job of recruiting young blacks right out of high school. Thereafter updates on minority recruiting and other issues became a regular feature of the board's report. That particular board happened to include the first African American member, Dr. James M. Nabrit Jr., president of Howard University, a Johnson appointee.[10]

The Department of Defense helped service academies tackle the problem of increasing their minority enrollments. In keeping with the Johnson administration's emphasis on affirmative action and his own aim of increasing the number of black officers in the services, Secretary McNamara prepared a "Memorandum for Educators" in October 1965. The memorandum briefly described the opportunities available to qualified individuals at the service academies, emphasized the Defense Department's policy that "military careers are free from discrimination and that opportunities for admission, assignment and advancement are completely equal," and urged school officials to submit the names of promising students to the Department of Defense. The department repeated this effort annually for the duration of McNamara's tenure.[11]

The Defense Department's minority recruiting drive for the service academies received attention in the black press. A June 1966 *Ebony* magazine article that discussed McNamara's Memorandum for Educators noted that the service academies had now joined big corporations, government agencies, and major colleges in "the national quest for the bright, highly trainable, 'instant Negro.'" The article went on to tout the academies' "current push for more Negro students" and included information on entrance requirements and military career opportunities. Under the heading "Academies Repudiate History of Anti-Negro Bias," the article declared that "the new open-door policy on Negro enrollment in the service academies is a dramatic break with the past."[12]

In 1967, BuPers launched a recruiting program designed to double the number of black officers in the Navy and Marine Corps within two years and hired an advertising firm to promote minority recruitment. That summer, the secretary of the navy sent out letters to all black officers asking them to help with minority recruitment. That fall, BuPers sent thirty-two black officers to predominantly black schools to try to sell young African Americans on the idea that the Navy was genuinely interested in having more black officers. The next year, BuPers assigned minority affairs officers to area recruiting staffs.

One of the officers involved in the recruiting effort was Reeves Taylor. BuPers assigned him to minority recruiting duty in 1966. The Navy just could not seem to attract African Americans, and it was Taylor's job to "figure out what was wrong," as he put it, "and try to correct it." He visited more than a hundred historically black universities across the country and talked to faculty, students, administrators, and people in town. He found that most African Americans still perceived the Navy as a racist service that limited black sailors to cooking or serving food. "It was incredible," he recalled. "Everyone from college presidents to street cleaners all had the same opinion." One college president even accused Taylor of being a fake because he believed that the Navy had no black commanders, Taylor's rank at the time. To combat this negative image, Taylor set up recruiting stations in black neighborhoods and accelerated the incorporation of black people and cultural themes into recruiting advertisements. His job also entailed recruiting black college students and establishing reserve officer training programs at historically black colleges. At his recommendation the Navy set up new NROTC units at three historically black schools: Prairie View A&M College in Texas in the spring of 1968, Southern University and A&M College in New Orleans in the fall of 1971, and Savannah State College in Georgia that same fall.[13]

Recruiting films, posters, and advertisements in newspapers, magazines, and television began to feature black sailors and officers. Early efforts depicted African Americans in racially integrated activities. A 1965 Naval Academy feature published as a Sunday supplement to the *New York Times* included a photograph of a black midshipman studying. A 1968 promotional insert in the *Chicago Daily News* featured on its cover a black midshipman leading a formation. Later efforts, such as some of the posters created in the late 1960s and early '70s, incorporated a "Black is Beautiful" theme. One depicted a young black sailor with an Afro and a bush comb, with the caption, "Can you dig it?" Another depicted two African American men wearing dashikis, one of whom sported an Afro. "You can be Black," the caption declared, "and Navy too."[14]

As a result of these efforts, the proportion of African Americans in the Navy's officer corps climbed from 0.3 percent in 1965 to 0.7 percent in 1970. Meanwhile, black officers slowly began moving up to the higher ranks. By September 1970, three black naval officers had reached the grade of captain. In 1971, Samuel L. Gravely Jr. became the first black naval officer to reach flag rank.[15]

In the fall of 1965, the Navy launched a recruiting campaign designed specifically to increase black enrollment at the Academy. The secretary of the navy's office, BuPers, and the Academy itself each played a part, pursuing minority recruiting along three avenues: informing the black community of opportunities available at the Academy, encouraging qualified young men to apply, and assisting them in obtaining nominations. The Navy followed these same avenues throughout Admiral Kauffman's superintendency. Each October, the Academy sent out recruiting letters to one thousand African American national merit scholars in their senior year of high school. Black midshipmen remained active in Operation Information. BuPers screened and processed the applications of all prospective midshipmen and in 1966 instituted a special minority recruiting program within its Naval Academy Midshipman Branch (Pers B66). Regular Navy recruiters worked with high school officials to identify and establish personal contact with potential minority candidates. Interested individuals received medical and scholastic examinations as a preliminary screening to determine their eligibility. BuPers used the School and College Aptitude Test (SCAT) as an indicator of performance on the College Boards, which the Academy had recently adopted as its entrance exam. If a candidate's SCAT results indicated the probability that he could score the minimum acceptable result on the College Boards, the recruiter urged him to apply and BuPers forwarded his name to the special civilian assistant to the secretary of the navy for congressional liaison work. The special civilian assistant lobbied members of Congress to appoint the most promising candidates. The goal was to admit thirty new black plebes per year, as the president had ordered.[16]

After two years the three-pronged recruiting effort more than doubled black enrollment at the Academy. In the fall of 1965, BuPers screened some seven hundred minority candidates and forwarded thirty-three names to the secretary of the navy's office, which obtained congressional appointments for twenty-three. Ten of the twenty-three passed the College Boards, and seven entered. Five more African Americans received noncongressional appointments that season, and a total of twelve African Americans entered the Academy in the summer of 1966. That fall, BuPers screened 957 candidates and forwarded eighteen names to the special civilian assistant, who obtained nominations for thirteen. Eight of these candidates passed the College Boards and four of them entered. Eight more received noncongressional appointments, for a total of twelve African Americans entering in the summer of 1967. By the end of that year, black enrollment stood at twenty-six: four in the class of 1968, two in 1969, nine in 1970, and eleven in 1971. These twenty-six black midshipmen accounted for 0.6 percent of the student body. Although Lyndon Johnson never followed up on his order to double the black enrollment at the Naval Academy, Under Secretary Charles F. Baird thought it prudent to inform him that his order had been carried out, despite the fact that the Academy had fallen well short of the goal of enrolling thirty black plebes per class.[17]

The special civilian assistant to the secretary of the navy, John Rhinelander, admitted to Baird that the new recruiting effort had achieved slim results. One reason was that civilian colleges as well as the other service academies were competing for the same pool of highly qualified African Americans. Three applicants referred by BuPers to Rhinelander in the fall of 1966 received full, four-year scholarships to Duke, Stanford, and Syracuse. Another reason was low test scores. Each year the SCAT and College Board results and the Civil Service Designation Exam used by members of Congress to screen potential nominees tagged fewer than a dozen qualified candidates from hundreds of interested individuals. Rhinelander knew that Dr. James B. Conant, a prominent educator, was calling for abolition of the College Boards, arguing that the tests were biased against minorities and created de facto segregation in higher education. But no one had come up with a viable alternative to the College Boards. Many individuals who had scored poorly on them were well qualified in all other areas. To help such individuals qualify for the Academy, the Navy invited them to enlist in the Naval Reserve and attend NAPS for a year and then try again. The minimum College Board scores were 500 verbal and 550 math and, as a rule of thumb, a year at NAPS raised an individual's scores by 50–75 points. To increase minority enrollment at the Academy, Rhinelander recommended increasing minority input into NAPS and exploring the possibility of having the Naval Academy Foundation send promising candidates to private prep schools.[18]

Admiral Kauffman echoed these views. "We and BuPers are making Herculean efforts in the area of minority group recruiting," he told the Naval Academy Alumni Association near the end of his tour in the spring of 1968, but "the results have not been anything commensurate with the effort because every good school in the country is after exactly the same young man we want." Kauffman agreed that the best hope for increasing minority enrollment in the future lay in NAPS and the foundation.[19]

Under Rear Admiral James F. Calvert, who relieved Admiral Kauffman as superintendent in July 1968, the Academy's minority recruiting program evolved into its modern form. Raised in Ohio, Admiral Calvert graduated from the Academy in the class of 1943. While serving in submarines during World War II, he became one of the Navy's most decorated officers. After the war, he became the third skipper to command a U.S. nuclear submarine. In 1959 his ship, the *Skate* (SSN-578), broke through the ice and surfaced at the North Pole, the first vessel ever to do so. In 1965, Calvert became the youngest rear admiral in the Navy and took command of part of the Sixth Fleet in the Mediterranean.[20]

As a submariner Calvert had encountered very few black sailors and never a black officer. Nevertheless, he realized that the country was changing and had no problem with black officers when he became the Academy's forty-sixth superintendent. When the secretary of the navy and the chief of naval operations (commonly known as the CNO) added a fourth year to his tour, it became the longest of any superintendent in some eighty years.[21]

Admiral Calvert faced recruiting problems from the start. When he arrived in Annapolis in June 1968, Admiral Kauffman told him that the Academy had come within thirteen people of not being able to fill the class of 1972 with qualified midshipmen. The total enrollment had dropped 6 percent since 1967. Kauffman believed that widespread student protest against the war in Vietnam was fostering a general antimilitary attitude among college-age youth.[22]

Before then, the Academy never really had to "recruit" anyone except athletes and, recently, minorities, for qualified majority applicants had always outnumbered available berths. Since 1962 the Academy's primary recruitment effort had been the Naval Academy Information Program, commonly called the Blue and Gold Program, administered by the Academy's candidate guidance office, established that same year. The Blue and Gold Program consisted of a network of Academy alumni, Naval and Marine Corps Reserve officers, and civilians who provided information and assisted prospective midshipmen in the admissions process. Blue and Gold officers interviewed candidates, visited high schools, represented the Academy at local college nights, and generally served as a "field force" for the Academy. Besides Operation Information, little more extensive organization or effort had been necessary.

In 1969 the Academy instituted a more formalized recruiting organization. On 14 March, Admiral Calvert formed a recruiting committee, with himself as chairman, to direct and plan the Academy's recruiting effort and to coordinate and the various agencies involved in it, including the candidate guidance office, BuPers, the Naval Academy Foundation, and the Naval Academy Alumni Association. Recruiting committee members included the superintendent, commandant, academic dean, dean of admissions, and head of the Naval Academy branch of BuPers. That summer (25 July 1969), Admiral Calvert changed the "candidate guidance office" to the "recruitment and candidate guidance office," assigned a Navy line captain as its director, and charged it with spearheading the midshipman recruiting effort. The recruitment and candidate guidance office continued to direct the Blue and Gold Program, including the program's five regional directors; administered Operation Information and similar programs; and ran the Educator Visit Program, which provided information on the Academy to selected secondary school educators. It also published the *Blue and Gold Newsletter* and trained people to become Blue and Gold officers.[23]

The new organization helped Admiral Calvert address the Academy's minority recruiting problems. A report submitted by a member of the admissions committee in August 1968 pointed out several deficiencies in the current approach. The few black midshipmen participating in Operation Information could reach only a limited audience. The letters sent to black national merit scholars targeted the very individuals most sought by recruiters everywhere and thus were unlikely to yield large numbers of candidates. Despite the doubling of black enrollment since 1965, African Americans still made up less than 1 percent of the student body. The report concluded that the Academy needed to rethink its approach. It suggested broadening the dissemination of information to include Upward Bound and other programs for inner city minority youth and having recruiters work more closely at the personal level with interested individuals. The Academy began contacting Upward Bound, College Bound, Aspira, and other such programs in the spring of 1969.[24]

Black enrollment climbed slowly but steadily during the next few years. In 1968, sixteen African Americans entered the Academy with the class of 1972. The next year, eighteen blacks entered. In 1970, twenty-one entered the class of 1974. Six African Americans graduated that year (1970), the largest number to graduate in a single class to date.[25]

Meanwhile, BuPers laid a new minority pipeline to the Academy through NAPS. In 1968, the bureau developed the Broadened Opportunity for Officer Selection and Training (BOOST) program to prepare educationally deprived minorities for the Naval Academy, NROTC, and Navy Enlisted Scientific Education Program by means of a special college preparatory course at NAPS. BOOST was a two-year program for enlisted men selected by BuPers who scored poorly on standardized tests but demonstrated promise in other areas. Civilians who signed up for an eight-year enlistment in the Naval Reserve (four active and four inactive) and completed basic training were also eligible for BOOST. The first-year curriculum focused on remedial work in language skills, math, science, and reading at the high school college-prep level. During the second year, BOOST students entered the regular NAPS program. All successful BOOST graduates were guaranteed an NROTC scholarship but had to compete for a Naval Academy appointment like other enlisted men. In 1969, BuPers surveyed all enlisted men to find minorities who met the basic eligibility requirements for admission to NAPS. The bureau identified one thousand potential candidates for BOOST and sent letters to 809 of them, encouraging them to apply. Of the 220 who did apply, 130 met both the physical and scholastic requirements. In June 1969, a pilot group of twenty-one black midshipman candidates entered NAPS under the BOOST program, and twenty-three more did so a year later. In 1973, management of BOOST shifted from the CNO's office to the office of Commander Naval Education and Training. With the BOOST program, the Navy had added a fourth prong to its minority recruiting effort for the Academy. In addition to informing black youths about the Academy, encouraging them to apply, and assisting them in getting nominations, the Navy now sought to educate them as well, to assist them in meeting the scholastic admission requirements.[26]

The efforts of the late 1960s were not increasing the proportion of black officers in the Navy fast enough to suit Admiral Elmo R. Zumwalt Jr. During his tour as CNO (July 1970–July 1974), Zumwalt did more than any of his predecessors to improve race relations in the Navy. After graduating with the class of 1943, Zumwalt rose through the ranks of the surface navy. On 30 September 1968, he became Commander Naval Forces, Vietnam, commanding the naval forces engaged in operations along South Vietnam's coastal and inland waters.

Admiral Zumwalt became CNO amid the trepidations of the Navy's senior leadership. At that time the service was facing serious problems, among them the block obsolescence of warships, diversion of funds from new construction to fight the war in Vietnam, and waning strength in the face of a growing Soviet naval threat, as well as low morale, drug use, and racial tension in the enlisted force. Defense Secretary Melvin R. Laird and Navy Secretary John H. Chaffee had jumped Zumwalt into the berth over the heads of thirty-three of his seniors because they believed that the Navy needed rapid reform and that Zumwalt was the man for the job. Intelligent, aggressive, charismatic, and the youngest man to become CNO, Zumwalt already had a reputation for being unorthodox, and he took office committed to changing Navy policy in a variety of areas.[27]

With aging ships requiring more and more maintenance, the antiwar movement in full swing, malaise gripping America's armed forces, and the withdrawal from Vietnam and the end of the draft both imminent, Zumwalt identified retention as the Navy's biggest personnel challenge. "It seemed to me," he recalled, "that there were four kinds of things the Navy could do to make the service more attractive and more satisfying." First, bring the regulations and practices dealing with dress, grooming, and so forth into line with the customs and tastes of the 1970s. Second, revise operational schedules to reduce sailors' long separation from their families during deployments. Third, give enlisted men and women more responsibility and greater opportunities for advancement. Fourth, "and most important," Zumwalt declared, "throw overboard once and for all the Navy's silent but real and persistent discrimination against minorities."[28]

Zumwalt sought to bolster retention through "people programs," which he launched by means of highly unorthodox and controversial "Z-grams." The directives liberalized dress and haircuts and did away with "mickey mouse" rules to make life easier for enlisted men and women. Many of the

Navy's senior leaders voiced strong objections to Zumwalt's people programs, arguing that overturning traditions would erode discipline.[29]

Zumwalt was not totally naïve about the Navy's racial problems when he took office. He had grown up in Tulare, California, among Hispanics and African Americans, several of whom he considered good friends. His parents had taught him that skin color or racial origin "provided no clue to a person's character or worth," as he put it. Like many naval officers, Zumwalt had little contact with either black sailors or racial problems early in his career. An incident that highlighted the Navy's institutional racism for him as none had before occurred during the briefing he received upon taking over the job of detailer for lieutenants in BuPers in 1957. "The officer I was relieving told me that the routine for assignment of minority officers was to send them to dead-end billets so that their promotion beyond middle rank would be unlikely," he recalled. "I did not follow that prescription, but I cannot say that beyond not following it I could think of a way that a junior commander could alter a policy that, evil though it was, was clearly winked at or even encouraged by the captains and admirals he worked for." When he became CNO, he deemed the proportion of blacks in the officer corps (0.7 percent) "shameful" and believed that the Navy was marching "in the rear rank of the military services" in breaking down racial barriers. Minority issues had been on his agenda from the beginning, but not at the top, for he believed that, compared with the civilian community, the Navy had relatively few racial problems.

Admiral Zumwalt soon realized that he had "underestimated by far the seriousness of the Navy's racial problem." During his early months as CNO, he along with Secretary Chaffee and other officials attended Friday morning briefings on the progress of problem-solving and study groups representing various type commands, geographic areas, or specialized skills. On 6 November 1970, Zumwalt had his Friday morning meeting with a group of black naval officers and their wives to discuss discrimination. Two weeks later, he met with a similar group of black enlisted men and their wives. These meetings sparked an epiphany for the CNO. "I was astonished," Zumwalt said shortly after the meetings.

> I thought I was philosophically prepared to understand the problems of minority groups. . . . I came to realize for the first time that the Navy did even worse things to its minority people than give them demeaning jobs and stunt their careers. Day after day it inflicted upon them, sometimes without even knowing it was doing so, personal slights, affronts, and indignities of a peculiarly humiliating kind. . . . Perhaps the most revealing incident at the officers' meeting came in the course of a discussion of housing for black Navy families. One of the members of the

group had just delivered an eloquent description of the difficulties he had had finding decent living quarters for his family as he had moved around the country, and of the lack of help he had received from the administrative people at the bases to which he had been assigned. An admiral demurred. . . . He said, "Now when I was commanding in Charleston I had this boy working for me who was having a little trouble getting located and I found him a right nice place to live." One of the wives asked, "How old was this boy?" The admiral answered, "Oh, thirty or thirty-five, I reckon." "I see," the wife said, and the discussion resumed at the point at which it had been interrupted. I saw, too, and I know John Chafee saw. As much as anything that exchange showed me how urgent it was to get started and the long hard way we all had to go.[30]

On 17 December 1970, Zumwalt issued Z-66, "Equal Opportunity in the Navy," which he later said "was probably the most important and certainly the most heartfelt of the 121 Z-grams." Z-66 confessed that the Navy had been insensitive to the problems of minority groups and promised to launch an in-depth investigation of discrimination in the Navy and how to end it. Unlike previous directives that paid lip service to minority issues, Z-66 called for specific action quickly. Among other things, every base, station, ship, and aircraft squadron commander was to appoint a minority officer or senior petty officer as his special assistant for minority affairs; Navy exchanges, ship's stores, and major commissaries were to stock cosmetics, grooming aids, foods, and produce used by minority families; and books and magazines of interest to African Americans were to be made available in reading areas, all by 15 January 1971. Z-66 announced that Zumwalt's own special assistant for minority affairs, Lieutenant Commander William Norman, would be visiting major naval activities to meet with commanding officers and minority families to discuss the problems they were facing. "Ours must be a Navy family that recognizes no artificial barriers of race, color or religion," Z-66 concluded. "There is no black Navy, no white Navy—just one Navy—the United States Navy." In the next two years the Navy formulated and began to implement some two hundred programs aimed at eradicating racism and improving life for all naval officers and enlisted people.[31]

Admiral Zumwalt had not been long in the job before he noticed that black enrollment at the Naval Academy still constituted little more than 1 percent of the brigade. "Despite efforts begun three years ago to recruit more blacks," declared an Associated Press article he read in August 1970, "the Navy officer corps remains a virtual lily-white organization with Negroes accounting for less than one per cent of the Navy's 80,000 officers." One black officer quoted in the article derided the Navy's current recruitment effort as "accelerated tokenism." The article pointed out that only fifty-two African Americans had entered the Academy to date. The article led Zumwalt to take personal interest in the Academy's black enrollment. From this point forward, minority recruiting for the Academy became an OPNAV (Office of the Chief of Naval Operations) issue.

On 23 November 1970, Admiral Ralph W. Cousins, vice chief of naval operations, addressed minority recruiting in a message to Vice Admiral Dick H. Guinn, chief of naval personnel. Admiral Zumwalt believed that a black enrollment of 3–4 percent "should be an easily achievable initial goal." "Such a goal would mean doubling or tripling the number of Black Midshipmen per class," Cousins noted, "and accepting a higher than average attrition rate for the first couple of years." Cousins directed Guinn to submit to a plan of action and milestones for achieving that goal and to investigate minority recruiting methods and results at the other service academies and civilian universities.[32]

R. Adm. Sheldon Kinney, former commandant of midshipmen (1964–67) and now the acting chief of naval personnel, replied on 15 December. Kinney noted that the black enrollment stood at 2.0 percent in the Military Academy, 1.7 percent at the Air Force Academy, and 1.2 percent at the Naval Academy. West Point did all of its minority recruiting from its admissions office by mail and telephone. Air Force had a network of twenty black recruiters in district offices around the country, sent black high school guidance counselors recruiting brochures and included them in "educational airlifts," had black cadets make presentations in their hometowns like the Academy's Operation Information, and sent letters to black national merit scholars.

Civilian schools did somewhat better than the service academies in terms of proportional representation, but not in comparison with the 11 percent black population of the United States. The black enrollment stood at less than 2 percent at MIT, 3.2 percent at Harvard, 3.3 percent at Michigan, 3.8 percent at the University of Maryland, 4.3 percent at Stanford, and 5.2 percent at Yale. Several of these schools used some of the same minority recruiting methods as the service academies, including having black students make presentations in their hometowns, sending literature to guidance counselors, and contacting minority merit scholars. But they also did things that the academies didn't do, such as advertising in *Ebony* magazine; "redefining" College Board scores for disadvantaged groups, a euphemism for lowering entrance standards; and hosting work study programs on campus for high school students. People working in the admissions offices of these schools believed that their most productive tactic was the student and staff member speaking engagements analogous to the Academy's Operation Information program.

To increase black enrollment at Annapolis, Kinney preferred to intensify the recruiting effort and expand the selection base of qualified black candidates rather than reduce academic qualifications or lower academic entrance standards for black candidates. To achieve Zumwalt's goal of 3–4 percent black enrollment, Kinney recommended a goal of bringing in thirty-five black midshipmen in June 1971, with an increase of at least ten per year through June 1974. Factoring in attrition, this goal would yield a black enrollment of 3.75 percent by the latter date.

Kinney reviewed Academy minority recruiting methods already under way, including assignment of specific minority recruiting duties to the assistant head of the Naval Academy branch in BuPers, participation of increasing numbers of black midshipmen in Operation Information, sending letters to national merit scholars, and the BOOST program.

Kinney then described some of the Navy's recently adopted recruiting methods. Minority recruiting officers had been assigned to each of the eight offices of the directors of navy recruiting and were slated to be assigned to each of the Navy main recruiting stations by 1 March 1972. These officers were working with the BuPers Naval Academy branch. BuPers had begun distributing annually a notice on opportunities for minorities at the Academy. Taking a cue from the Air Force, the recruitment and candidate guidance office had begun "airlifting" black educators from around the country to Annapolis for briefings and sales pitches. The firm of Young and Rubicàm had been hired to prepare an advertising campaign to target the black community for officer recruiting.

In addition to these efforts, Kinney recommended that the Academy expand recruitment of black candidates through the Blue and Gold organization, relax the requirements for extracurricular activities and athletics for academically qualified blacks, advertise in the black media, and use the Naval JROTC program in black schools to identify and select prospective candidates.[33]

Admiral Zumwalt directed Lieutenant Commander Norman, his special assistant for minority affairs, to review Kinney's proposals. Trained as a naval flight officer, Norman had been a history instructor at the Academy during his previous tour, the first uniformed African American to serve on the faculty. Norman agreed that the best way to increase the number of black midshipmen was to intensify recruiting efforts and expand the selection base of qualified black candidates. However, he deemed Admiral Kinney's enrollment goals inadequate. "Certainly 50–57 black midshipmen entering in June 1971 and 75–100 black midshipmen per class in the next three years is a feasible and realistic goal," he asserted. To achieve that goal, he recommended assigning fifty black Blue and Gold officers to every naval district; obtaining two hundred black guidance counselors, principals, and teachers as Blue and Gold affiliates; amplifying efforts to inform black high school students about the Academy through high school visits and advertisements in black media; notifying black candidates of acceptance as early as possible to preempt other academic institutions; including black educators and community leaders in *all* Naval Academy "airlifts"; and increasing efforts to recruit black athletic stars, particularly basketball and football players.

The chief of naval personnel approved Norman's proposals to enhance the minority recruiting effort. Admiral Zumwalt concurred and set a goal of enrolling fifty to fifty-seven black midshipmen in June 1971 and seventy-five to one hundred per class thereafter, so that the proportion of black midshipmen at the Academy would reflect America's black population. By 1976, the Academy had adopted most of the procedures Norman had recommended for intensifying the minority recruiting effort and broadening the selection base of qualified black candidates.[34]

Meanwhile, in the fall of 1970, Admiral Guinn telephoned Admiral Calvert. Without discussing Admiral Kinney's or Commander Norman's proposals, the chief of naval personnel ordered the superintendent to increase minority enrollment at the Academy to achieve Admiral Zumwalt's goal of proportional representation. For the rest of his tour as superintendent, Admiral Calvert investigated and implemented organizational and procedural changes to increase African American enrollment. Subsequent reports noted Admiral Calvert's "personal interest in and emphasis upon increasing the number of black midshipmen."[35]

Fortunately for Admiral Calvert, a new officer had just arrived in Annapolis to spearhead the minority recruiting effort. Lieutenant Kenneth Johnson had been assigned to the recruitment and candidate guidance office as the Academy's first minority affairs officer in August 1970. Johnson grew up in Hallandale, Florida, where his father was a hotel cook. After graduating from Iowa State University in 1963, he joined the Navy and entered Officer Candidate School. He then went to sea on board three different ships before coming ashore in Annapolis.

Johnson's job was to help the director of recruitment and candidate guidance identify and assist qualified members of minority groups interested in attending the Academy. "When I first came here," he told a reporter near the end of his tour, "there had been really no active recruitment of blacks. I figured there'd be about 150 black kids—and I would have considered that small." In fact, the 4,300-man brigade included only fifty-two African American midshipmen when he came on board.

Johnson perceived three obstacles standing in the way of increased black enrollment: the Navy's five-year service obligation for an Academy education, the Academy's lily-white image, and the negative publicity surrounding racial incidents in the armed services. He found it difficult not to be discouraged. As he told a reporter for the Baltimore *Evening Sun*, "So many things are against us." Interest among minority high school students in becoming mid-shipmen, even in Baltimore, the Academy's backyard, was "negligible." Most students at Baltimore's all-black Edmonson High School preferred to enter historically black colleges where, as Edmonson's head guidance counselor put it, "they are assured a good reception." As Johnson told a reporter for the Annapolis *Evening Capital,* "Young black prospects are just not getting the word." "Ours is an 'image' problem," he added, "and it's a bad one. You tell them all the benefits the Navy can offer them, and you feel you've got them in your corner. Then they go home and their parents tell them, 'No way, the Navy's Jim Crow.'" Johnson later elaborated on the image problem. "I don't feel . . . that minority kids turn down the Navy because of an antimilitaristic attitude held by some white youngsters," he said. "To them it's more of an antiwhite attitude, or antisystem. And when you say system to most minority youngsters, that means white."

Johnson concluded that the solution was dissemination of information. He devised a two-pronged strategy to increase the Academy's outreach into the black community. The first prong involved marketing. Johnson spent the fall and winter of 1970–71 traveling to black communities around the country and talking to high school students, principals, guidance counselors, and minority organizations about the opportunities for African Americans and other groups at the Naval Academy. In one month alone, he visited high schools in Dallas, Texas; Pensacola, Florida; Trenton, Willingboro, and Camden, New Jersey; Colorado Springs, Colorado; and Detroit, Michigan. He found that students in black high schools, even in nearby Baltimore, knew little about the Academy or had little interest in it. Slowly but surely, he established personal contact with increasing numbers of potential black candidates.

The second prong of Johnson's outreach strategy involved integrating the Blue and Gold organization. When Lieutenant Johnson first arrived in Annapolis, the organization included only one black officer. Johnson invited black teachers and youth program counselors to participate in the Blue and Gold Program as affiliates. Johnson also asked 442 minority Naval Reserve officers to participate in the Academy's recruiting effort. By April 1971, sixty-eight of them, including forty-three black officers, had agreed to become Blue and Gold officers.[36]

Lieutenant Johnson's efforts produced dramatic results. In the summer of 1971, forty-six African Americans entered with the class of 1975, marking an important turning point. Blacks had accounted for an average of 1 percent of each incoming class entering the Academy between the summer of 1965 and the summer of 1970. In the summer of 1971, 3.5 percent of the incoming plebes were black. Never again would the proportion drop below that number. In the summer of 1972, a record seventy-eight African Americans, largely due to Johnson's extensive traveling and the efforts of the new black Blue and Gold officers and affiliates. Between 1971 and 1975, an average of seventy-nine blacks entered the Academy each summer and accounted for 5.6 percent of incoming plebes. Similarly, between 1976 and 1998, Annapolis admitted an average of seventy-four African Americans per year, accounting for 5.5 percent of each incoming class.[37]

To keep up the momentum, Lieutenant Johnson added a section on minority recruiting in each issue of the *Blue and Gold Newsletter*. The sections included statistics as well as advice. Johnson suggested that Blue and Gold officers establish ties with black ministers and other community leaders as well as the black press and organizations such as the NAACP and Urban League. "Some of the organizations may not be receptive to your appeal," he noted in the September 1971 issue, but "you should not let that prevent you from approaching them again." That same issue encouraged Blue and Gold officers to also establish ties with the Navy's minority recruiting officers at main recruiting stations. In a later issue he urged Blue and Gold officers to follow up their initial meetings with interested youths with "something beyond a cursory phone call."[38]

Johnson also sought to mobilize African American naval officers. In 1971, he and several other naval officers involved in minority recruiting discussed forming an organization to help them do their work. They realized that the Navy had fewer than one hundred minority officers and that less than half of them were African American. In 1972, the group founded an organization they dubbed the National Naval Officers Association during a meeting at the Hilton Inn in Annapolis. The members dedicated themselves to supporting the sea services in recruitment, retention, and career development of minority officers. The association soon gained support from the superintendent of the Naval Academy, the BuPers chief, and the secretary of the navy. The organization held its national conference annually during July. At the time of its thirtieth anniversary in 2002, the National Naval Officers Association had forty-two chapters.[39]

Meanwhile, Defense Department policies and growing racial unrest in the Navy cemented affirmative action and equal opportunity near the top of the CNO's agenda. During Zumwalt's tour, President Richard M. Nixon redefined affirmative action as a means for protecting groups. This came as a shock, for Nixon was no friend to African Americans. His "southern strategy" for winning reelection in 1972 was designed to appeal to southern whites, the western Sun Belt, blue-collar ethnic voters in the North, and the suburban middle class. Although he did not attempt to reverse the major legislative gains of the civil rights movement, he sought to hold the line against further legislation, and he turned a deaf ear to civil rights leaders.

Nevertheless, for political reasons, beginning in 1970 Nixon promulgated regulations requiring employers to set aside what in effect were quotas for various groups. These regulations governed all federal hiring and contracting and thereby affected more than one-third of American labor. Thereafter employers could fend off charges of discrimination only by demonstrating a statistical parity between the racial composition of their workforces and that of local populations. Critics charged that, instead of color-blind treatment based on merit, affirmative action now gave preferential treatment to members of certain minority groups and fostered reverse discrimination. From then on, whenever a black person got a particular job or promotion or scholarship, many white people attributed it to race, not to merit. Nevertheless, Nixon's alterations to affirmative action represented a significant gain for black people. The threat of litigation induced increasing numbers of businesses to open opportunities to black people. Affirmative action now included the notion of proportional representation of minorities to reflect the general population.[40]

In 1970, the Nixon administration extended Executive Order 11246 and its implementing regulations to the armed forces, thereby imposing its affirmative action policy on the Navy. In June 1971, the Department of Defense directed the services to launch race relations education programs to enhance the racial awareness of servicemen and women and to improve equal opportunity in the services. The Defense Department established the Race Relations Education Board to administrate the programs and set up the Defense Race Relations Institute to train instructors and develop curricula.[41]

On 9 July 1971, Secretary Chaffee issued Instruction 5350.10A, "Equal Opportunity within the Department of the Navy," to bring the Navy's racial policy in line with the latest Defense Department directives. Among other things, it ordered all ships and stations to take action to eliminate on- and off-base discrimination, including, if necessary, sanctions against discriminatory landlords, and to develop "aggressive affirmative action programs" including "numerical goals and timetables" for civilian employees. That same day, BuPers directed all commanding officers to include in officers' fitness reports an evaluation of their performance in equal opportunity areas.[42]

Implementation of the various programs initiated by Zumwalt and the Defense and Navy departments proceeded unevenly. Some commanding officers paid little attention to equal opportunity, according it a low priority. Others had a poor understanding of the Navy's various racial policies, often using the terms "equal opportunity" and "affirmative action" interchangeably. Many higher-ranking officers and senior enlisted people involved in recruiting took affirmative action to mean a monthly quota for minorities.

Inattention and misunderstanding on the part of commanding officers enabled racial problems to persist. People charged with equal opportunity and race relations duties often spent more of their time on collateral duties or responding to crises than conducting the programs designed to prevent them. Meanwhile, black sailors received a disproportionate share of punitive discharges, nonjudicial punishment, and extra instruction. The number of black officers remained so small that white sailors often greeted them with a look of incredulity.[43]

Zumwalt's reforms came too little too late to prevent racial tension in the fleet from boiling over into violence. After 1965, the racial tension and violence afflicting American cities infiltrated the armed forces. In Vietnam, brawls between black front line soldiers and white rear echelon troops rose in frequency. When news of Martin Luther King's assassination reached Cam Ranh Bay in April 1968, a group of white sailors donned KKK-like hoods, burned a cross, and hoisted a rebel flag on the flagstaff in front of headquarters. That summer, a savage race riot broke out at the U.S. Army stockade at Long Binh, South Vietnam, resulting in the death of one white soldier and injuries to several others. During the first eight months of 1969, some 160 violent incidents between black and white marines occurred at Camp Lejeune. In May 1971, a four-day race riot at Travis Air Force Base in California involving a brawl among some two hundred airmen at its height resulted in the death of one person and injuries to thirty others.

In 1972, President Nixon scaled down the draft and at the same time stepped up the air war against North Vietnam. After the communist Easter offensive in March 1972, Nixon doubled the number of carriers on Yankee Station off North Vietnam from three to six, which meant that the Navy had to find men for the additional carriers as well as their escorts. The average duration of an overseas deployment for ships in the Seventh Fleet grew from six to nine months. The increased manpower needs combined with decreased availability of draftees compelled BuPers to recruit a higher proportion of more poorly educated sailors. Although this policy increased the number of black enlistees, many of them lacked the education needed to advance in the Navy. More unfortunate, the Navy failed to develop a remedial education program to bring such recruits up to speed. Of 12,000 blacks recruited in 1972, only a third had high enough scores to qualify for technical training. The combination of extended line tours and the sudden introduction into the fleet of large numbers of poorly educated sailors put an extra strain on greenhorns and veterans alike at "a time when strain was already excessive," as Zumwalt put it.

On 12 October 1972, tension exploded on the carrier *Kitty Hawk* (CVA-63) while the ship was steaming from Subic Bay to the Tonkin Gulf. A black apprentice seaman who was being questioned for allegedly refusing to obey an order and assaulting a petty officer during a brawl ashore at the last port suddenly stormed out of the interrogation. For the next seven hours, groups of black sailors armed with chains, wrenches, bars, and broomsticks roamed through parts of the ship, beating white sailors. The riot involved some 4 percent of the 5,000-man crew and resulted in the injury of forty-seven sailors, all but six of whom were white. Eventually twenty-six black sailors were charged. Four days later on 16 October, ten black sailors from the fleet oiler *Hassayampa* (AO-145), angered by the theft of money from one of their wallets, proceeded through the ship beating seven white sailors and inflicting minor injuries. Ultimately, six of these black sailors were charged. Some two weeks later, a two-day sit-down strike took place on the carrier *Constellation* (CVA-64) during training exercises off San Diego. The carrier had recently received on board an unusually large number of poorly educated enlistees. On 2 November, false rumors that 250 mostly black first-term crewmen were going to be discharged to make room for mostly white aviators and technically trained sailors needed for combat operations off Vietnam precipitated a meeting of black sailors, about ninety of whom staged a sit-in and refused to perform their duties. When the crewmen remained unwilling to disperse after meeting with members of the ship's minority affairs program, the skipper surrounded the space with seasoned officers and petty officers to contain the protesters. Ultimately, the Navy discharged forty-seven of these men (thirty-six honorably) and transferred seventy-four to new assignments. Scores of other more minor incidents erupted on ships and bases throughout the Navy.

Zumwalt blamed the incidents on naval leaders who failed to implement his programs. On 10 November 1972, he addressed a gathering of all the ranking admirals in Washington. "The Navy has made unacceptable progress in the equal opportunity area," he declared. "The reason for this failure was not the programs but the fact that they were not being used." He attributed the incidents on the *Kitty Hawk, Hassayampa,* and *Constellation* to unrelieved racial pressures that arose not from lower standards or permissiveness, but from the failure of Navy commands to implement racial programs with a "whole heart." Zumwalt declared racial integration to be a top priority.[44]

After Zumwalt's speech, implementation of the Navy's racial policy accelerated. On 14 November 1972, the Navy launched Phase I of the new Race Relations Education Program developed by BuPers early the previous year in anticipation of the June 1971 Defense Department directive. The program was part of the Navy's broader Human Resource Management Program, another new program that also included drug and alcohol education and other training and management tools. The goals of Phase I were to make naval officers and enlisted men and women aware of the debilitating effects of institutional and personal racism and to stimulate action by commands and individuals to eliminate racism. The program made naval officers and enlisted people aware of the Navy's racial problems during two- and three-day seminars conducted by facilitators trained at the Defense Race Relations Institute and at the newly established Navy Race Relations School in Millington, Tennessee. Eventually, everyone in the fleet was supposed to attend an Understanding Personal Worth and Racial Dignity (UPWARD), Executive, or Flag seminar. Aggressive and confrontational, these seminars mirrored the "encounter groups" in vogue in American society during the 1970s. Facilitators urged participants to vent their true feelings about people of different races, to reveal their inner prejudices, and to express openly their anger and frustration at whatever injustices they perceived in the Navy equal opportunity program. The authors of Phase I hoped that, once skippers became aware of the racial problems in their commands, they would develop and implement command affirmative action plans to resolve them.[45]

By mid-1974, about 70 percent of all naval officers and enlisted men and women had completed an UPWARD, Executive, or Flag seminar. These seminars succeeded in increasing individual awareness of racial issues throughout the fleet. An evaluation of Phase I conducted in 1973 demonstrated that the seminars gave naval officers and enlisted people a better appreciation of black people's dignity and made them aware that racial discrimination still existed in the Navy. New recruits continued to receive Phase I type training after the program ended in 1974 for those already in the fleet.

Phase I failed, however, to foster organizational changes to eliminate discrimination. The 1973 evaluation revealed that the program had less effect on white senior enlisted men and senior officers than on junior officers and sailors, and that only a few commands generated affirmative action plans. In other words, although the seminars increased participants' awareness of racism, they precipitated little change in the existing policies and practices of naval commands. In most cases, the best a skipper could do was to create a "climate of equal opportunity," for it was usually beyond his or her authority to recruit, detail, or promote minorities into areas in which they were underrepresented.

By the time Zumwalt retired in 1974, most of his racial reforms had been incorporated into a new equal opportunity manual (OPNAV Instruction 5354.1) issued that same year. This new directive reiterated the policy of equal opportunity and required Navy commands to develop affirmative action plans. Among its stated objectives was "to achieve increased representation of minority personnel in the various categories and grades of the service which is proportional to the demography of the source populations."

To facilitate achievement of these objectives, the Navy launched Phase II of its Race Relations Education Program. Phase II required all commands to develop, implement, and monitor affirmative action plans but emphasized consultation over confrontation. Facilitators were retrained to help commanding officers meet the new requirements. To ensure that equal opportunity and affirmative action remained ongoing processes, Phase II required all commands to form training teams, sponsor workshops, establish human relations councils, and maintain minority statistics. These requirements were designed to facilitate upward and lateral movement of minorities, recognize the cultural and ethnic diversity of naval personnel, and fight discrimination on a continuous basis. Phase II held all commanding officers and commanders accountable for addressing policies, procedures, and practices which, wittingly or unwittingly, contributed to discrimination or unequal opportunity. By 1977, the Navy considered Phase II fully implemented and self-sustaining, with affirmative action plans, human resource councils, and command training teams in place and functioning at most commands.[46]

By the time the all-volunteer force replaced the draft in 1973, the Navy had once again raised educational standards for recruits and quietly culled the ranks of substandard men in the fleet by discharging them under honorable conditions. Between 1971 and 1974, the proportion of black sailors in the enlisted service climbed from 5.4 percent to 8.1 percent. By April 1974, African Americans accounted for 11 percent of first-term volunteers for the service, marking the first time this figure paralleled the black proportion of the U.S. population.[47]

In November 1975, Admiral James L. Holloway III, Zumwalt's successor as CNO, formed a task force to review the Navy's progress in equal opportunity and race relations and to develop an updated service-wide plan for affirmative action. The result, entitled the Navy Affirmative Action Plan (NAAP) and issued by Holloway in June 1976, institutionalized equal opportunity and affirmative action in the Navy. The NAAP mandated and provided guidance for the development and implementation of affirmative action plans throughout the Navy hierarchy. It also required an annual review and assessment of the progress made in affirmative action at all command levels. With the adoption of the NAAP, the CNO committed the Navy to the elimination of racial bias and the proportional distribution of minorities across pay grade and rank categories and occupational groups. The NAAP also committed the Navy to increasing the total number of minorities in the service, particularly in the officer corps.[48]

As if to symbolize the Navy's commitment to equal opportunity and affirmative action, Vice Admiral James D. Watkins, the chief of naval personnel, hosted a breakfast with key NAACP leaders during the NAACP annual convention in Memphis on 2 July 1976, two days before the nation celebrated its bicentennial. Admiral Watkins admitted that the Navy had not pushed its racial program as vigorously as it might have and promised that it would "launch additional efforts to expand opportunities for minorities and . . . ensure that equal opportunity is available at every level of naval operations." Dr. William Montague Cobb, who sat on the NAACP's board of directors, noted a "new spirit in the Navy." He likened the Navy to the apostle Paul, who persecuted Christians until a vision transformed him into the greatest missionary of all time. Cobb promised to lend the Navy the NAACP's full cooperation. After the meeting Admiral Watkins sent a bus to Washington and took two dozen black boys and girls from Dr. Cobb's neighborhood to Annapolis for a tour of the Naval Academy.[49]

The Navy's institutionalization of equal opportunity and affirmative action cemented concern about the number of black midshipmen entering the Academy each year onto the CNO's agenda. V. Adm. William Paden Mack relieved Admiral Calvert as superintendent in June 1972. From the start of his tour, Admiral Mack strove to attain Admiral Zumwalt's goal of increasing the percentage of blacks at the Academy until it reflected the proportion of blacks in America.[50]

Soon after Admiral Mack became superintendent, the job of recruiting midshipmen was shifted from BuPers to the Academy itself. The name of the recruitment and candidate guidance office was changed back to "candidate guidance office." Effective 1 October 1972, the Naval Academy admissions branch of BuPers was transferred to Leahy Hall at the Academy and placed under the authority of the director of candidate guidance. The candidate guidance office now had full responsibility for identifying, recruiting, and counseling candidates for admission to the Academy. Finally, a congressional liaison officer billet was established in the candidate guidance office and its incumbent charged with full-time duty as liaison with congressional staff members responsible for nominations to the service academies. Two years later, the superintendent authorized another minority affairs officer billet, now designated "minority affairs counselor," to aid as a field recruiter.[51]

Meanwhile, Academy-affiliated organizations began recruiting black members. In 1971, Lu Gregg joined the academic advisory board. Formed in 1966, the board consisted of distinguished educators, business leaders, and naval officers convened primarily to help develop a new majors program. In the fall of 1972, the board of trustees of the Naval Academy Alumni Association, a private, nonprofit charitable organization that raised funds for Academy programs, began seeking African American members, especially "outstanding black personalities of national reputation and athletic background." By November, Rafer Johnson, the 1960 Olympic decathlon gold medalist and widely regarded as the world's best athlete of that time, had joined the organization. The board continued soliciting membership among black Academy alumni.

The minority recruiting procedures established under admirals Kauffman and Calvert remained in use under Admiral Mack and his successor, R. Adm. Kinnaird R. McKee. The Academy continued to mail application information to black youth from lists generated by the Educational Testing Service, the National Merit Scholarship program, and the National Scholarship Service and Fund for Negro Students, but the most productive minority recruiting method remained face-to-face contact during school visits by the Academy's minority affairs staff, midshipmen participating in Operation Information, and Blue and Gold officers and affiliates.

In 1973, 120 African Americans entered with the class of 1977. This figure marked a peak that has not been surpassed at this writing. The next year, ninety-four blacks entered with the class of 1978. Admiral Mack attributed the "dip" to increased competition from civilian institutions. Capt. W. A. Walsh, the CNO's assistant for special projects, however, attributed it to the increase of the minimum SAT score in math from 550 to 580. "If last year's standards had been applied," Walsh argued, "a minimum of 40–50 additional black applicants could have been accepted this year." The Academy accepted all black applicants who qualified under the 1974 standards while rejecting some five hundred fully qualified majority applicants. In 1975, the Academy again raised the minimum SAT score in math, from 580 to 600, because so many qualified candidates applied that the administration thought it could be more selective. That summer, however, the number of blacks who entered in the class of 1979 fell to fifty-five. Even more telling, the number of blacks applying to the Academy had plummeted from 619 for the class of 1977 to 331 for the class of 1979.[52]

The plunge alarmed naval leaders. One of the CNO's special assistants implied that the superintendent's concern for minority recruiting seemed to languish until end-of-the-year pressure caused the Academy to "scramble" for African Americans each spring. The special assistant suggested that "external pressure" from up the chain of command would focus the superintendent's efforts on minority recruiting more consistently throughout the year. Neither the chief of naval education and training nor the chief of naval personnel had enough clout, however, because both were junior to the superintendent. "The only effective pressure that has been brought to bear on USNA," the special assistant told his boss, "has come directly from the CNO."[53]

Admiral Holloway expressed concern to the chief of naval personnel that the minority recruitment program at the Academy had "lost considerable momentum." "We are not able to maintain at least our status quo with each incoming class," he lamented. He suggested cooperative effort between the Academy and the Navy Recruiting Command in minority recruiting.[54]

Admiral Mack had already initiated such an effort. In February, he informed V. Adm. David H. Bagley, the chief of naval personnel, of the "obstacles" the Academy was facing "in attracting quality Black students." Together they devised a joint national advertising campaign for both the Academy and the NROTC, featuring ads in *Ebony, Black Enterprises*, and other black publications as well as direct mailings to high school seniors and juniors.

The Academy itself had done little advertising to this point because it had rarely suffered from want of majority applicants. To be sure, BuPers and the Navy Recruiting Command had been advertising in the black community since 1967, and the Academy had occasionally placed promotional features in newspapers, but the Academy itself had never mounted a sustained advertising effort in black media, despite Admiral Kinney and Commander Norman's recommendations to do so as early as 1970. The drop in the number of blacks entering in 1975 from its peak two years earlier finally spurred the Academy into action.

The Academy and the Navy Recruiting Command launched a nine-month pilot program in August 1975. Most of the ads appeared in fall 1975 and spring 1976 issues, "addressing high school students at the time they are contemplating their college choice," as Bagley put it to Mack. The ads targeted prospective candidates, their parents, and their educators and focused on themes of education, leadership, pride, professionalism, and tradition. Funding for the campaign came from the Navy Recruiting Command, which canceled lower-priority programs to pay for it. That same year, the Academy increased the minority affairs counselors' travel budget and featured a black midshipman on the cover of the Naval Academy catalog.[55]

In 1976, the Academy authorized a third minority affairs counselor billet for the candidate guidance staff. The Academy and Navy Recruiting Command continued the NROTC/Academy advertising campaign that year and produced a pamphlet designed specifically for the minority candidate.[56]

These efforts failed to reproduce the dramatic results of 1973. The number of African Americans admitted to the Academy each year had reached somewhat of a plateau, with an average of sixty-five entering in each class for the next ten years. No doubt the continuing competition from colleges and other service academies, the end of the draft in 1973, and the relative saturation point being reached by the Academy's minority recruiting effort contributed to the leveling off of the number of blacks entering.[57]

Nevertheless, the Academy had revolutionized its racial policy. The superintendent had been relatively unconcerned about black representation in the brigade until President Johnson shook the very dickens out of him and spurred him into launching a minority recruiting program in the fall of 1965. The program evolved into its modern form during the early 1970s, largely as the result of Admiral Zumwalt's reform of racial policy. Henceforth the number of African Americans entering each class was a fixed item on the agenda of the CNO as well as the superintendent.

7

Growing Up in Turbulent Times

THE MINORITY recruiting program brought 476 African Americans into the classes of 1969–79. Race riots in American cities, cries for black power, protest against the war in Vietnam, and busing to achieve racial integration formed the backdrop of their youth and shaped their adaptation to the Academy's culture as well as their impact upon it.

By the mid-1960s, about half of the U.S. population of African Americans lived in the North and West, largely in urban areas. Although the white majorities in these areas had assimilated ethnic groups like Irish and Italians, they had not assimilated African Americans. Black people remained concentrated in the inner cities as white flight or private pledges not to sell or lease to black people hindered integration. Many African Americans paid premium prices for slum housing in ghettos that suffered higher incidences of poverty, illiteracy, juvenile delinquency, and murder than surrounding areas.

While rural black southerners were dismantling Jim Crow, urban black northerners were more concerned about economic issues. Color lines continued to channel urban blacks into low-paying "Negro jobs" with little prospect for advancement. Most still worked as domestics or unskilled laborers. The median income of black people stood at just over half that of white people, and the unemployment rate for blacks doubled that of whites. Nearly half of all black families lived below the poverty line. Integration as a means to full citizenship meant little to northern blacks, who already could vote and enjoyed many of the civil rights for which southern blacks were still struggling. "The black cat in Harlem wasn't worried about no damn bus," snapped a disgruntled Urban Leaguer in New York. "He'd been riding the bus for fifty years. What he didn't have was the fare."

Black bitterness spewed forth between 1965 and 1968 in a succession of "long hot summers" as some three hundred race riots and disturbances erupted in cities and towns across America. Most of the riots exploded spontaneously, sparked by police action. Rioters looted and destroyed both black- and white-owned tenements and businesses, particularly those reputed to exploit African Americans, but avoided damaging black churches, libraries, and schools. The violence resulted in the deaths of 250 black people, the wounding of more than eight thousand, and the arrest of some fifty thousand. By one estimate, a total of a half million black people participated in the riots, a number equal to the number of Americans serving in Vietnam in 1968. In some places, nearly half the adult population of the ghetto took part. In almost all others, the participants constituted a cross section of the black community, with neither teenagers nor criminals predominating. The National Advisory Commission on Civil Disorders, appointed by President Johnson in 1967, attributed the riots to bitterness arising from poverty, unemployment, slum housing, and segregated education caused by white racism.

As nonviolence gave way to violence, expressions of rage drowned out strategies for social change among some black leaders. Before 1965, most civil rights advocates shared the common goals of gaining access to schools, polling booths, and public accommodations. By and large, integration remained the end and nonviolence the means. After the Watts riot in the summer of 1965, civil rights leaders agreed that the movement needed to go beyond the traditional agenda toward improving the living conditions of poor rural and ghetto blacks. However, no one could agree on how to solve the complex problems of slum housing, dead-end jobs, and second-rate education. Black activists whose self-sacrifice had helped bring about the end of de jure segregation and disfranchisement in the South grew increasingly frustrated with the fact that nonviolence had done little to mitigate the effects of de facto segregation up north. The riots added an exclamation point. Continuing school and residential segregation and economic disparity convinced younger militant blacks that Martin Luther King's vision of an integrated society was an impossible dream. They began to transform the struggle for desegregation into a battle for self-determination. Many young African Americans began to identify more with radical black separatist Malcolm X than with Martin Luther King.

By 1966, many members of two of the leading civil rights organizations, the Congress of Racial Equality (CORE) and the Student Nonviolent Coordinating Committee (SNCC), believed they had turned the other cheek too often with too little to show for it. Too many vicious beatings by sadistic

Klansmen and jailings by racist sheriffs convinced them that the time had come to fight back. Floyd McKissick, elected national director of CORE in January, spoke of nonviolence as "a dying philosophy." Stokely Carmichael, who became head of SNCC in May, talked about blacks becoming "the executioners of our executioners."

The disintegration of unity among civil rights leaders became apparent in the summer of 1966, when James Meredith, the same man who had integrated the University of Mississippi four years earlier, set out on a march from Memphis to Jackson hoping to inspire black Mississippians to exercise their right to vote. Barely ten miles into his journey, a Klansman shot him in the back, wounding him seriously. Leaders of major civil rights organizations, including King, Carmichael, McKissick, Roy Wilkins of the NAACP, and Urban Leaguer Whitney Young, rushed to Memphis. Wilkins and Young wanted to finish what Meredith had started as an interracial march to support new civil rights legislation. McKissick and Carmichael wanted to make it an all-black trek to "put Johnson on the spot." King's attempt to serve as a moderating influence failed. The new black nationalist militancy of CORE and SNCC diverged so sharply from the traditional nonviolent, interracialism of the NAACP and National Urban League that Wilkins and Young abandoned the march. Despite King's presence, CORE and SNCC dominated what came to be called the Meredith March Against Fear from its opening rally on 9 June 1966. When King preached nonviolence, young black militants shouted, "White blood will flow!" When King spoke of Christian love, the militants shouted, "Seize power!" When King's followers tried to sing "We Shall Overcome," the militants drowned them out with the SNCC version, "We Shall Overrun." The climax of the march came in Greenwood, Mississippi, when Carmichael leaped onto a flatbed truck, raised his arm in a clenched-fist salute, and led the crowd in chanting "Black Power!" Thereafter, "Black Power" replaced "Freedom Now" as the slogan of choice among young black militants.

Black Power came to have many meanings. It was always more of a slogan than a program. Stokely Carmichael kept redefining it to suit various audiences. Martin Luther King condemned it as a "nihilistic philosophy born out of the conviction that the Negro can't win." Roy Wilkins repudiated it as "the father of hatred and the mother of violence." Most other black spokespersons applied the Black Power label to their own agendas. As historian Harvard Sitkoff put it, "Revolutionaries used it to preach guerrilla warfare, liberals to demand reform, and conservatives to emphasize self-help. Both separatists and integrationists employed it, as did proponents of love and of confrontation, of violence and nonviolence." At bottom, black power proponents believed that white people could not be trusted to help black people. Racism ran too deep for integration to ever succeed, they reasoned, so black people should take control of their own political, economic, and social institutions. If white people resisted with violence, then black people had to fight back.

The slogan "Black is Beautiful" soon emerged as a corollary to black power. African Americans discarded hair straighteners and skin bleaches in favor of clothes, music, food, dialect, and elements of style that celebrated their culture and heritage. They established black studies programs in universities across America, rejected the term "Negro" as a vestige of slavery and insisted upon being termed "black" or "Afro-American," and wore their color, as Langston Hughes put it, "like a banner of the proud."

As the 1960s waned, many of the leading black power advocates became so radical that they lost their following. In July 1967, CORE eliminated the term "multi-racial" from the membership clauses of its constitution, thereby alienating liberal whites and moderate blacks alike. Stokely Carmichael expelled whites from SNCC's executive committee, talked of "offing the pigs" and "killing the honkies," and abandoned all pretense of working within the civil rights movement. His rhetoric and that of his successor, H. Rap Brown, who equally imprudently urged black people to shoot white people, caused SNCC's membership and financial support to melt away. By 1967, SNCC had lost white support, alienated black politicians and civil rights leaders, gone bankrupt, and shrunk to some forty hardcore militants.

In February 1968, SNCC merged with the Black Panther Party for Self Defense. Huey Newton and Bobby Seale had formed the Black Panthers in October 1966 in Oakland, California, to monitor police behavior and combat police brutality in the ghetto. Black Panther chapters sprang up in several big cities as party leaders advocated full employment, self-determination, and exemption from military service for black people as well as freedom for all imprisoned African Americans. Although the Black Panthers set up free health clinics and breakfast programs for children, their Marxist leanings, paramilitary activities, open display of firearms, shootouts with police, racist rhetoric, and leadership's criminal behavior prevented them from ever attracting more than a few thousand members. After 1969, the group virtually ceased to exist, in part because of pressure from the FBI and the Nixon administration.[1]

Richard M. Nixon won the 1968 presidential election in part because he promised to end the war in Vietnam. Protest against America's involvement in Vietnam began in earnest in the spring of 1965, as "teach-ins" against the war took place on many college campuses and the organization Students for a Democratic Society (SDS) staged the first national antiwar demonstration in Washington, attended by fifty thousand people. The expansion of the antiwar movement kept pace with the escalation of the war, featuring a broad array of participants and tactics, including legal and illegal demonstrations, grassroots organizing, congressional lobbying, electoral challenges, civil disobedience, draft resistance, and political violence. Some peace activists and black power advocates including Stokely Carmichael traveled to Hanoi to offer political support to the North Vietnamese, earning the everlasting enmity of many American servicemen and women. Like many African Americans, boxer Muhammad Ali considered the conflict a "white man's war." Although drafted, he refused to be inducted into the U.S. Army. "No Vietcong ever called me 'nigger,'" he explained. In April 1967, more than three hundred thousand people demonstrated against the war in New York. Six months later, fifty thousand demonstrators surrounded the Pentagon, leading to some seven hundred arrests. Smaller antiwar demonstrations sprang up across the country, often ending in violent clashes between college students and working Americans.

In March 1968, President Johnson decided to stop escalating the war. His attempt to finance the war and the Great Society simultaneously, without significantly raising taxes, hobbled both efforts and sparked the double-digit inflation, soaring unemployment, and mounting federal debt that would hound the economy into the 1980s. On 31 March 1968, Johnson announced on television that the United States would restrict the bombing of North Vietnam and seek a negotiated settlement with Hanoi. He also announced that he would not seek reelection.

Nixon negotiated with the North Vietnamese and followed a policy of "Vietnamization"—withdrawing American troops and turning over more and more of the fighting to the South Vietnamese. At the same time he stepped up the bombing of the north, widened the air war into Laos, and sent ground forces into Cambodia. By the end of the war the tonnage of bombs dropped on Vietnam far exceeded the combined total dropped on Germany and Japan during World War II. Meanwhile, a growing awareness that the American people no longer supported the war caused morale among American fighting men to plummet and incidents of insubordination, drug use, and racial tension to soar.

Antiwar protest peaked as U.S. forces withdrew from Vietnam. In October 1969, more than two million people took part in Vietnam moratorium protests across the country. The next month, half a million demonstrated in Washington. The movement was attracting a broader base of participants, including students, draft resisters, veterans, and members of the "silent majority" who did not believe that the war was immoral but did believe that it was unwinnable. The Nixon administration tried to blunt the movement by mobilizing support, smearing protest leaders, and, in 1973, ending the draft. Protest on college campuses reached a crescendo in 1970 following the invasion of Cambodia and the shooting of antiwar demonstrators at Kent State University in Ohio and Jackson State College in Mississippi as a national student strike shut down more than five hundred colleges. Protest activities waned as U.S. troops returned home, where they were too often shunned or denigrated instead of welcomed. Years would pass before America admitted that they had been good soldiers in a bad war.

Meanwhile, both sides wearied of the fighting. In October 1972, the United States and North Vietnam agreed on a cease-fire, the return of American prisoners of war, at least a temporary continuation of the existence of the South Vietnamese government, and permission for North Vietnamese Army regulars to remain in the south. The signing of the Paris Peace Agreements on 27 January 1973 reaffirmed the October terms. Three months later, all that remained of U.S. military presence in Vietnam were a few embassy guards and attachés. With U.S. forces gone, the North Vietnamese continued to fight a steadily weakening South Vietnamese army. In the spring of 1975, a North Vietnamese thrust into the central highlands precipitated the final rout of South Vietnamese forces. On 30 April, as communist troops entered the South Vietnamese capital of Saigon, the last remaining Americans abandoned the U.S. embassy in a dramatic rooftop evacuation by helicopter.[2]

Nixon's withdrawal from Vietnam quelled antiwar protest, but his stance on racial issues inflamed civil rights advocates. He had entered the White House on the conservative backlash to the turbulence in America, campaigning against open housing and busing for racial balance, promising "law and order," and denouncing Great Society programs, liberal Supreme Court decisions, and protestors. "For the first time since Woodrow Wilson," lamented the president of the NAACP, "we have a national administration that can be rightly characterized as anti-Negro."

Nixon deliberately decelerated the pace of school desegregation. In 1969, in *Alexander v. Holmes County,* the Supreme Court ordered all school districts to end segregation "at once." Two years later, in *Swann v. Charlotte-Mecklenburg Board of Education,* the Court upheld the use of busing to achieve integration speedily. Nixon opposed busing for personal reasons and because most whites did so too. The idea of liberal judges forcing white kids to attend school with black kids repelled white parents who cherished the neighborhood school concept or who harbored prejudice. More black parents opposed busing than supported it, preferring not to send their children in twos and threes into hostile white classrooms. In March 1972, shortly before launching his reelection campaign, Nixon appeared on television and appealed to Congress to impose a moratorium on busing. Two years later, in *Milliken v. Bradley,* the Supreme Court stymied court-ordered busing between white suburbs and black urban areas.

Scandal wrecked Nixon's second administration. News of what reporters dubbed "Watergate" began breaking even before the last U.S. combat units pulled out of Vietnam. One revelation followed another: secretly taped conversations in the Oval Office, missing portions of tapes, wiretapping, break-ins at the Democratic National Committee offices at the Watergate complex in Washington, D.C., and a crude, illegal, and ultimately botched cover-up. The scandal set off a constitutional crisis that precipitated Nixon's resignation on 8 August 1974. Gerald Ford, Nixon's vice president, took office the next day. By and large, Ford maintained the racial status quo.[3]

No thanks to Nixon, African Americans were better off when he left the White House than when Lyndon Johnson entered it because of civil rights legislation passed before 1969. Black people's economic power had increased substantially. The median income gap between black and white people decreased significantly during the Johnson and Nixon years. Broader job opportunities for African Americans enabled increasing numbers of black people to enter the middle class. The proportion of black families living below the poverty line decreased from about half in 1960 to just under a third in 1974. Black people's political power had also increased substantially. The number of African Americans holding political office climbed, for example, from six member of Congress and ninety-seven state legislators in 1966 to sixteen members of Congress and more than two hundred state legislators in 1973. By the latter date, Cleveland, Los Angeles, and several scores of small southern towns had elected black mayors. Desegregation of schools had progressed in spite of Nixon. The proportion of black children attending integrated schools in the South rocketed from 32 percent in the 1968/69 school year to 86 percent in the 1974/75 school year. All told, black people had taken substantial strides toward equality by America's bicentennial in 1976, but they still had a long road ahead.[4]

The 476 African Americans who entered the Naval Academy in the classes of 1969–79 reflected the broadening of the Academy's black recruiting base, the growing political power of African Americans, and the diversity of the communities from which they came. These 476 accounted for 3.1 percent of the total of 15,145 midshipmen admitted into these classes.

The minority recruiting procedures developed during the early 1970s yielded a crop of black midshipmen who arrived at the Academy from different sources and along different routes than white midshipmen. Approximately 27 percent of these 476 black midshipmen entered with regular congressional appointments, 45 percent came in as qualified alternates and competitors, and 28 percent received other noncongressional appointments. Before 1965, the relative proportion of black midshipmen appointed from congressional and noncongressional sources reflected that of midshipmen as a whole. African Americans from the classes of 1969–79, however, differed from the overall picture. From the class of 1973, for example, 45 percent of all midshipmen

entered with regular congressional appointments, 35 percent came in as qualified alternates and competitors, and 20 percent received other noncongressional appointments.[5]

It was Congress's reform of the service academy admissions process in
1964 that enabled more African Americans to enter Annapolis as qualified alternates and competitors. Historically, members of Congress submitted to the
Academy a list of both principal nominees and qualified alternates who could
replace a principal who declined the nomination or proved unable to attend.
The rules adopted in 1964 permitted the secretary of the navy to appoint 150
qualified congressional alternates each year and to fill any last-minute vacancies with qualified alternates.[6]

Many African American noncongressional appointees entered Annapolis
via the NAPS route. By the spring of 1973, NAPS had become what the Academy superintendent described as "the nucleus of the Naval Academy program
to increase the total numbers of minority midshipmen." By the 1972/73
academic year, the number of African American candidates enrolled at NAPS
had risen to forty-six. Commander Ken Johnson visited NAPS frequently to
counsel and guide black students there.[7]

Of the 476 black midshipmen entering the Academy in the classes of
1969–79, 127 came in with congressional appointments. Black congressional
appointees in these classes received nominations from twenty-nine states and
the District of Columbia. Before 1965, no African American midshipman had
entered with an appointment from a member of Congress from a state in the
old Confederacy. By 1976, at least one African American had entered from
every state in the old Confederacy except Mississippi. California supplied the
most black congressional appointees between 1965 and 1975 (fourteen), followed by New York (eleven), Pennsylvania (ten), Illinois (ten), Texas (nine),
Ohio (eight), District of Columbia (eight), Michigan (six), Indiana (six), and
Georgia (six), with five or fewer from the rest. Black members of the House
made twenty-seven of the 127 black nominations, or 21 percent, with Robert Nix of Philadelphia and Ralph Metcalfe of Chicago each appointing five;
William Dawson of Chicago, John Conyers Jr. of Detroit, and Charles Ran-
gel of New York each appointing three; and William L. Clay of St. Louis,
Louis Stokes of Cleveland, Andrew Young of Atlanta, and Shirley Chisolm
of Brooklyn each appointing two. Thus, the demographics of the Academy's
black population more nearly reflected the demographics of America's black
population during this period than during the previous period.[8]

By and large, black midshipmen who entered the classes of 1969–79 grew
up aware that their race set them apart from mainstream America. Although
integration and affirmative action were under way during their youth, prejudice and discrimination were slow to recede. Nevertheless, most of them could

sense that change was in the air and, for many, the racial situation improved during their junior high and high school years.[9]

Joseph Bertram Freeman, '70, spent most of his youth in a mixed neighborhood in Philadelphia. His father, a postal worker, and mother, a toy factory employee, moved there when he was about six. They were the first black family on the block. From Bert's perspective, their arrival caused no problems among the neighbors and he made many friends in the new neighborhood. By the time he finished high school, however, the majority of white families had moved out. In the interim he attended majority white parochial schools and got along well with his white classmates. Nevertheless, most of his closest friends were black.

Bruce A. Henry, '70, grew up in a black section of Plainfield, New Jersey. His father worked as a pharmacist and a buyer for a large supermarket chain. His mother was an associate professor at a junior college. They taught him that people should be judged on merit and not skin color, but in the real world black people experienced prejudice. Sometimes black people had to be twice as good as white people to get the same opportunities. When he and his mother visited Plainfield High School after he finished junior high, the guidance counselor, without looking at his record, simply assumed he was going into the vocational program. His mother quickly set the counselor straight. Henry had white friends at school but socialized largely with other blacks outside of school and school-related activities.

Everett L. Greene, '70, grew up in the predominantly black neighborhood of Mount Auburn in Cincinnati. His father worked in a General Motors factory and his mother kept house. The neighborhood had been all white until his family moved in, becoming the first black family on the block. "After several community meetings," Greene recalled, "the white families sold their homes and moved to other neighborhoods." During the riots of the 1960s, Greene overheard white people say that, if black demonstrators tried to enter white neighborhoods, they "would be opposed with force." Greene encountered prejudice himself. On one occasion, a white couple refused to sit next to him in a movie theater. On another occasion, he jogged through a neighborhood unknown to him, which, as he soon learned, turned out to be the "wrong" neighborhood. Some of the residents called him "nigger" as he ran by. On yet another occasion, a pair of white policeman pulled him over after he had dropped his father off at work. They said he looked too young to drive, but it seemed to him rather a case of racial profiling.

Anthony J. Watson, '70, grew up in Cabrini Green, a notoriously tough Chicago community. His childhood memories included being robbed at knifepoint in an elevator and paying "protection dues" to avoid being beaten up while he was a safety patrol in elementary school. His father worked at a printing plant and his mother worked as an administrative assistant at Edward Jenner Elementary School. They taught Tony and his two brothers and three sisters to be tolerant and to respect everyone, regardless of race. "We moved into Cabrini-Green when I was a year old," he recalled. "We were one of the very first black families to move in. We grew up with Italians, Irish, African Americans, and Jewish folks. By the time I reached high school the neighborhood was all African American. The elementary school I went to was of mixed races. By the time I was in seventh or eighth grade, it was virtually all black. When I entered Lane Tech High School, an all-boys school, I was one of only twenty-five African American students among four to five thousand boys. That's when I really started learning that there was a big difference. The first day I walked in the school, somebody spit in my hair. I was starting high school ten miles away from where I lived and it was a quite different environment for me. I didn't know how to react. I was scared to death. Lane Tech High was a very athletically competitive school. I ended up playing on the football team, which I think helped me establish a presence there at the school. Nobody ever bothered me after that." In fact, most of his friends at Lane Tech were white.

Leo V. Williams, '70, spent his early years under segregation in Norfolk, Virginia, living in a black neighborhood and attending black schools. Although the neighborhood generally insulated its residents from prejudice, Leo couldn't help but notice the "white only" and "colored only" signs above restrooms and water fountains in the local Sears department store. His father had a master's degree in education and worked as a school administrator; his mother took care of the house and raised the children. His parents taught him and his brother and sister to take pride in their heritage. Some of his parents' friends as well as some of his older friends were active in the civil rights movement during the '60s. Leo, too, became involved just after the passage of the Civil Rights Act of 1964. "A fairly large group of us decided that we were going to be at least among the first," he recalled. "We all put on coats and ties to go to the movie theater. We were very, very conscious of our image and we didn't want to present any negative impression." Jeering crowds of whites dressed in jeans greeted them upon their arrival at the theater downtown. Other whites stood by in silent support of the black youths. Nervous policemen stood by as well. Fortunately, no violence ensued. Leo later participated in a march on the local school board to demand a swimming pool and chemistry lab for the black school equal to those in the white school.

Richard G. Samuels, '73, lived on U.S. Air Force bases until his parents separated when he was about seven. His mother then took Ric and his six siblings to Cleveland and settled in a black neighborhood and supported the family by working as a waitress and nurse's aide. Ric attended integrated schools, made friends among the white kids, and had no particular difficulties with bigots. On the other hand, he always had to deal with a certain amount of name calling and other types of prejudice from a minority of the white people he encountered. Such experiences faded when he transferred into South High School, where he played football. In spite of whatever prejudice he encountered, his mother taught him that "everybody was okay until proven otherwise."

Robert Watts, '73, grew up in New York City. His parents taught him that he had to work twice as hard and be twice as good as whites to succeed. Once during a family vacation in North Carolina he unwittingly drank from a "white only" fountain, and several grown white men chased him down the street. His alcoholic father walked out on Bobby and his seven brothers and sisters when he was thirteen. His mother settled the family in a black enclave in Farmingdale, Long Island, where she struggled to make ends meet on welfare and working as an unskilled laborer. Bobby noticed that white people treated black people with indifference and perceived them to have stronger bodies but weaker minds. He coped by becoming a football and track star at the predominantly white schools he attended. Prejudice seemed to spring up everywhere when some white girls began flirting with him. Both black girls and white boys were hostile toward these white girls. The same white boys were also hostile toward him.

Donald Montgomery, '74, spent his early years in Cartersville, Georgia, and his teen years in Baltimore. His father worked in the post office and his mother in a factory and as a nurse's aide. Don remained unaware of Jim Crow segregation in Cartersville during the '50s. He thought his family sat in the balcony at the movies because the view was better. Traveling was a different matter. His father hated to stop to use "colored only" bathrooms, so he just kept going. Nevertheless, his parents taught him to love everyone, regardless of their color. In Baltimore he was among the first black students who integrated Robert Poole Junior High School. "Man, they did not want us there," he recalled. "That was probably the most traumatic thing I've ever experienced." He remembers frequently being suspended for fighting, "because every time somebody called me a name, I was fighting." A classic people person, Don overcame the prejudice by getting involved in school plays and sports. "Eventually I won over the school," he said. He went to high school at Baltimore Polytechnic, the same school that Bill Jones, '64, had attended. Montgomery encountered prejudice at Poly as well, but it was class snobbery instead of racism. As in junior high, the antidote was academic and athletic excellence. Throughout his teen years in Baltimore he lived in integrated neighborhoods and had both white and black friends.

Boyd "Eddie" Graves, '75, was born and raised in an integrated neighborhood in Youngstown, Ohio. He never considered a person's skin color when making friends. "My best friend was a Hungarian Catholic next door," he recalled. "My other best friend was an immigrant German around the corner. My white friends were my closest friends. There was never any teaching on race. There was no emphasis on 'the white man this or that' back then. I didn't buy into the race stuff. I thought it was detestable." Eddie's father supported the family by working in the steel mill by day and at a hospital by night, and his mother taught German in high school.

Will Merrell, '75, was raised in Lockport, Illinois. His father was a maintenance man at a supply depot for Veterans Administration hospitals. His mother was a cook in a nursing home. His parents taught him never to judge a person by race or color. They said that, although many white people harbored prejudice, "there were some good white people in the world." Some of his white friends' parents would not allow him into their homes; others welcomed him for dinner or to sleep over. Dating a white girl, however, remained taboo.

Charles Cole, '76, came from a mostly black suburb of Cleveland, where his father worked in an aluminum plant and his mother worked as a clerk in the city court system. Although he did not encounter much racism in his neighborhood, he was, as he put it, "aware of who I was and what I was." One day when he was about five, his four-year-old brother came home and told his mother that he was white. When his mother explained to him that he was black, he started to cry. "He didn't want to be black," Cole recalled. "People had told him that that wasn't very good." Cole had vivid memories of white resistance to black people moving into ritzy Cleveland suburbs. He also remembered the riots in Cleveland that such resistance helped create. "I lived about half a mile into East Cleveland, so I was within walking distance of the Cleveland border," he said. "During the riots, the East Cleveland police were stationed on the border to make sure that people from Cleveland didn't come into East Cleveland and try to burn something."

Cary Hithon, '77, was raised in a mostly black section of Severna Park, Maryland. His father, a sheet metal worker, died when Cary was about ten. His mother, who worked as a domestic, taught him to treat all people equally. From the sixth grade on, he attended integrated schools. He encountered no real racial hostility in school except for nasty comments from a handful of individuals, including the assistant football coach in high school, who once told him to get his "black ass" out onto the field. Although radical black power type attitudes were in vogue during his high school days, he believed that the James Brown song "I'm Black and I'm Proud" was too provocative. He had white friends on the high school football team and felt accepted by most white people at school, but he noticed that white and black kids tended to segregate themselves at school dances.

Cary Hithon's Naval Academy classmate Jeffrey K. Sapp, '77, lived in a white neighborhood and attended mostly white schools in Colorado Springs, Colorado, from seventh grade on. Arthur and Barbara Sapp raised Jeff to be "color-blind." A gifted athlete who rarely watched TV and didn't read the newspaper regularly, Jeff grew up only dimly aware of the civil rights movement and black power. Most of his friends were white and race rarely became an issue. One of the few times race did become an issue was when Jeff began dating a white girl in junior high. It never occurred to him that there would be a problem until the girl's father made it clear that he did not like his daughter going out with a black guy. Art Sapp weighed in, too. Although he had rarely spoken to Jeff about race before, he told his son that in Georgia, where Art had grown up, a black male risked being shot for dating a white female. "If you're black in America," Art said, "some people will help you, but others will go out of their way to hurt you." Jeff's relationship with the girl ended when she told him that her father was making it too difficult to go on seeing him.

Byron Marchant, '78, grew up in Chicago, where his father worked as a draftsman for the city engineering bureau and his mother worked as a journalist. His parents taught him that he should treat everyone equally, that everyone should treat him equally, and that he should not let the behavior of individuals taint his view of their race. He steered clear of gang activities and drug use during his teen years by playing sports—hockey, football, basketball, baseball, everything. He found that athletic prowess tended to erase color lines, although he did encounter prejudice upon being bused from a black neighborhood to predominantly white junior high and high schools. He did make white friends at school, but his best friends were other black kids he knew from the neighborhood and from riding the bus to and from school.

Black midshipmen raised on military bases tended to encounter less prejudice and discrimination than blacks raised in the civilian world. Military bases were more integrated than American society during the 1960s and early '70s.

John Porter, '71, the son of a fighter pilot, a Tuskegee Airman, was raised on U.S. Air Force bases mostly in Texas and Delaware. His parents taught him that he always had to do better than white people to be considered as good. "Open racial prejudice was socially acceptable in the '50s and '60s," he recalled, "so my experiences were typical of the times." John was among the first African Americans to attend Dover High School in Dover, Delaware. "I experienced some blatant racism from some," he said, "but I also made some lifelong Caucasian friends."

James T. Jackson, '75, grew up on various U.S. Air Force bases. His father was a dentist and his mother a junior high school teacher. "We were always in integrated neighborhoods," he recalled. "It was a very good, very supportive environment." He remained aware of his racial identity but encountered no instances of prejudice beyond "typical childish teasing." Still, his parents taught him that blacks had to be a little bit better than whites to make the football team, the band, the school play.

Kerwin Miller, '75, spent his youth either on U.S. Army bases or in the D.C. area. His father was an officer in the Army Medical Service Corps and his mother a housewife. On Army bases, he was often the only African American at base housing and at school. In D.C., he resided in black neighborhoods and attended mixed schools. "I lived mostly in majority settings all my life," he recalled. "I always felt that I could compete with anybody because I grew up with everybody." Miller discovered that he was usually more comfortable around white people than they were around him. He was used to socializing with whites, but many of the white people he met had not socialized with black people before. Sometimes white kids called him names, but he usually had no trouble with white people once they got to know him. He could make friends easily with black people or white people. He did, however, experience impersonal, institutional discrimination from time to time. He remembered not being able to use "white only" facilities while traveling in the South and having to urinate beside the road. He recalled that his father often had difficulty finding off-base housing. And once he was not allowed to have the lead role in a school play because the teacher believed that it wasn't a "black" part.

Mason C. "Chuck" Reddix, '76, was also an Air Force kid. His father was a surgeon and his mother kept the books. Both of his parents came from Louisiana. They decided not to raise their children with Jim Crow, so they lived mostly in the Southwest, usually becoming the first black family on the block in each town. His parents' strong emphasis on education and extensive travel with their children minimized the prejudice they were exposed to. "Race just wasn't a factor," recalled Reddix. "I never really grew up wanting to be white. I wasn't really concerned about being black, either." Nevertheless, white friends who saw news stories about race riots on TV expected him to be an authority on black people's thinking.

Despite the fact that military bases were more integrated than the larger society, prejudice sometimes stalked black people on bases. Bruce Franklin, '76, part Native American and part African American, was raised on Parks, Edwards, Travis, Weisbaden, Ramstein, and McClellan Air Force bases. His father was a sergeant major, his mother a junior high English teacher. Bruce and his brothers and sisters were called names and physically attacked nearly everywhere their father was stationed, always by kids with less education or lower economic status.

Like African Americans admitted to the Naval Academy before 1965,

many of those admitted between 1965 and 1975 entertained traditional notions of becoming an officer in the Navy or Marine Corps. In some cases their
ambition to become midshipmen arose independently of Navy recruiting efforts. Ev Greene's high school guidance counselor suggested he apply to the
service academies. Influenced by his uncle's tales of serving at sea during the
Korean War, Greene picked Annapolis. By the time he completed his application, he was envisioning a twenty- to thirty-year career in the Navy. The
TV program *Men of Annapolis* sparked Bobby Watts's ambition to enter the
Academy. When he was a little older, his aunt married a Navy enlisted man.
Bobby was so impressed with his demeanor and confidence that it cemented
his ambition. Lamar Chapman, '75, had long held aspirations of becoming
an officer in the Marine Corps. To prepare himself, he served for four years in
the JROTC, where he became the highest-ranking cadet in his school. Charlie
Boyd, '76, developed an awareness of the Naval Academy when he was very
young because the Army-Navy game was played in his hometown, Philadelphia. Later he dreamed of flying jets off aircraft carriers. James Jackson's conservative nature and military family inspired him to apply to service academies.
His parents pushed him toward the Naval Academy because it was only an
hour away from their home in Silver Spring, Maryland. When James visited
the Academy and saw the drum and bugle corps, it "was the frosting on the
cake," as he put it. Marv King, '78, grew up in an Air Force family, became
the second-ranking officer in his high school JROTC program, and wanted a
military career. He picked the Naval Academy over the Military and Air Force
academies because he believed it presented the greatest challenge.

Kerwin Miller had long planned to attend West Point and had nominations to the Military Academy from five different sources. He figured he was
a shoo-in, until he took the physical late in the fall of his senior year of high
school. Because he had hay fever, the doctors disqualified him. After Christmas he received a call from Commander Ken Johnson, who asked if he wanted
to apply to the Naval Academy. Miller said that West Point had disqualified
him for having hay fever. "You don't have to worry about hay fever at sea,"
Johnson said. Miller agreed and received an appointment to Annapolis from
Representative William Clay (D-Mo.) of St. Louis.

Likewise, Byron Marchant originally had his heart set on West Point.
Marchant's father was a lieutenant colonel in the Army National Guard.
Marchant watched him go off for training each summer, developed an interest in exploration and adventure, and had no desire for a nine-to-five job, so
he decided to go to the Military Academy. He applied, received an appointment, and figured he was in. Then one day he saw a black naval officer pull up
in front of his house in a Corvette convertible to pick up an airline stewardess
who lived on the block for a date. Dazzled by the man's white uniform and

mesmerized by his gold aviator's wings, Marchant went over and struck up a conversation. The officer was Alfred B. Coleman, one of twelve black graduates in the class of 1972, nicknamed the "Dirty Dozen" after a movie. Coleman encouraged Marchant to apply to the Naval Academy and to follow up by contacting the local Blue and Gold officer. Marchant did so and eventually picked Navy over Army because it seemed more glamorous and life at sea held a better promise of adventure than life in an isolated Army post.

Chuck Reddix also chose the Naval Academy as a fallback position. He originally wanted to become an Air Force pilot, but he "didn't have the eyeballs," as he put it. "If you were an Air Force officer and you didn't fly," he recalled, "you were nothing." He did some research and found that he could get into the Naval Academy with less than perfect vision. He also found the Academy's half-civilian faculty attractive. Even though he was accepted by Harvard, Stanford, and Michigan State, he chose the Naval Academy.

Many of the black midshipmen of the classes of 1969–79 entered the Academy for economic reasons, attracted by the prospect of a "free" education or guaranteed employment upon graduation. "I wanted to have a job when I got out of college," recalled Chuck Cole. "When I got out of high school in 1972, there was talk of a recession or a depression coming. I knew people who were coming out of college and working in the post office or in gas stations. I didn't want to do that. I wasn't sure exactly what I wanted to do with my life. There were also financial issues. My parents didn't have a lot of money."

For some, the desire for a military career dovetailed with economic considerations. Bruce Franklin was accepted at the Naval Academy, West Point, the Merchant Marine Academy, and several civilian colleges. He chose a military school over a civilian one so his parents could afford to send his brothers and sisters to college and because his father was in the military, and Navy over Army because, as he put it, "I'd rather ride than walk."

In contrast to African Americans admitted before 1965, most of those admitted between 1965 and 1975 had little or no thought of a naval career when they sought to enter the Academy. Kenneth Dunn, '74, decided to go to Annapolis "to obtain the best education possible and to play 'big-time' college football," as he put it. Dunn's classmate Don Montgomery was recruited by the Academy to play football. Montgomery had offers from several other schools as well. He picked Navy because he didn't like what he saw when he visited some of the other colleges—drug use and so forth—and because the high school lacrosse manager, who aspired to go to the Academy himself, said that Montgomery would never make it.

Ric Samuels's high school guidance counselor introduced him to the advantages of attending the Naval Academy. "I had no ambition to become an officer," Ric recalled, "no desire to go to the Naval Academy." The guidance counselor suggested he fill out an application. He didn't bother. She contacted Ric's congressman anyway. Later, Lee Corso, the defensive back coach for Navy, came to the school and talked to Ric, a high school football star, for nearly an hour. "He had me convinced that there were only two schools worth going to—Navy or West Point," Samuels recalled. "Navy was the good guys. We wore the white hats." Corso talked about all the opportunities in the Navy available to Academy graduates. Samuels was particularly intrigued by the possibility of being able to fly jets off aircraft carriers. The fact that his scholarship did not depend on his playing football, in case of injury or some other eventuality, convinced him to go to Annapolis.

It was a push from his father that propelled Jeff Sapp into the Naval Academy. Art Sapp had served as an enlisted man in the Army for nearly twenty-two years before retiring in 1962 and becoming a real estate broker. Art had dreamed of becoming an officer, but the Army's racial policies had prevented him from getting the education he needed for a commission. As the chance of fulfilling that dream faded, he developed an ambition to send one of his sons to a service academy to become an officer and live the life he had wanted for himself. Jeff's mother Barbara supported her husband's ambition. An article in *Ebony* magazine featuring African American midshipmen inspired Art to target the Naval Academy for Jeff. He arranged for Jeff to meet retired rear admiral Norman Coleman, a business acquaintance and Blue and Gold officer. He also arranged a meeting for Jeff with Lieutenant Commander Ken Johnson, who flew out to Colorado to make the Naval Academy pitch in person. Art and Barbara even enlisted the help of Jeff's high school sweetheart, who told Jeff that she wouldn't mind becoming an officer's wife.

Like James Frezzell, Jeff Sapp found himself in the enviable position of having a wealth of opportunities. In high school he had lettered every year he was eligible in football, wrestling, gymnastics, and track, had become team captain or co-captain in each sport, and had been voted all-state in football. During his senior year, Sapp received letters of intent from sixty-two colleges offering athletic scholarships. He looked forward to becoming the first in his family to finish college but had never considered the Naval Academy before his father launched the campaign. In fact, the only image of the Navy his mind held before then had come from a recruiting poster nailed up near the high school.

Nevertheless, Art Sapp convinced Jeff that the Naval Academy would give him the education and character he needed to prosper. "It's not what you are, but who you are," Art would say. "You've got to become part of something bigger than yourself. You've got to learn to make it on your own, to stand out in the crowd." The young athlete did not yet understand the full meaning of these words, but he got the gist. Jeff Sapp decided to go to the Naval Academy to please his parents.

For many other African Americans, it was the Navy or Naval Academy's recruiting effort that first planted the idea of becoming a midshipman into their heads. In fact, many black midshipmen in the class of 1970 entered as a direct result of the recruiting effort launched by Admiral Kauffman's pledge to President Johnson to double the black enrollment. Bert Freeman had never considered a service academy until a pair of Navy chiefs visited his school, St. Joseph's Preparatory School, in the fall of 1965 during his senior year. "The last thing in the world I was thinking about was being in the Navy for the rest of my life," Freeman recalled. "I really wanted to go to college, and this was an opportunity to get there."

Tony Watson had a similar experience. "It wasn't my ambition at all to go into the Navy or the military," he recalled. "In fact, as a senior in high school I made myself two promises. One was that I'd never go to another all-boys school. The other was that I'd never join the military. Naval Academy football team people came to recruit me at Lane Tech in the fall of 1965. There were two of us on the team whose grades were good enough. They flew us both out to the Naval Academy for a weekend. I thought it was pretty sharp. I thought maybe this would be nice to do, but I never thought I'd get a chance to do it. I was motivated by the chance to go to school and to have it paid for. But also in the back of my mind was the ambition to become an astronaut. I had just never anticipated doing it in the Navy. I knew of Annapolis and its stature, but I really never thought that a guy growing up in a public housing community would be a fit."

Leo Williams had pretty much made up his mind to go to Yale until October of his senior year, when a pair of Navy chiefs—perhaps the same pair who had recruited Bert Freeman—came to Booker T. Washington High School. Williams already had the Navy in his blood, not only because he had grown up in Norfolk. His grandfather had served during World War I as a boatswain and his father had served during World War II as one of the Navy's first black corpsmen. Williams knew something about the Academy from watching *Men of Annapolis* and from talking to William Powell, '59, who at one time was dating one of his father's teaching associates. But it was the pitch by the chiefs and the fact that Navy was free—whereas Yale had offered only a 50 percent ride—that convinced Williams to apply. His classmate Edwin Shirley also applied as a result of the Academy recruiting effort. Both Williams and Shirley received nominations from Congressman Charles Diggs of Detroit.

In high school Bruce Henry had "no conception of what the Naval Academy was like," he recalled. "In the fall of my senior year, a Blue and Gold team came to my high school looking for prospective minority candidates. I was one of four individuals from my school called down to the guidance office to meet the Blue and Gold team and discuss the Naval Academy. Until then I had planned to go to Rutgers University to pursue pre-med."

Cary Hithon was dozing in his senior black studies class in the fall of 1972 when the teacher startled him with a question. "Cary," she asked, "what are you going to do with your life?"

"Well," he answered, "I'm going to college."

"Have you ever thought about the Naval Academy?" she asked.

"My grades aren't good enough for that," he demurred.

"I don't know about that," she said. "I think I'm going to have my husband come in." The teacher happened to be Bernadette Johnson, Ken Johnson's wife. Commander Johnson did come to the school, met with Hithon, and convinced him to apply. It was the Academy's prestige and the opportunity for a free education that attracted him. He applied to no other schools.

Advertisements to "join the Navy and see the world" sparked Chuck Cole's interest. But he didn't know what the Naval Academy was about until his junior year of high school. "I used to watch the Army-Navy football game. I knew that West Point was a military school for Army officers, but I didn't know where the Navy guys came from. I didn't even know there was a Naval Academy until one day a midshipman came to the school on Operation Information." Cole applied to the Naval Academy, but his congressman, Charles Vanik (D-Ohio), wanted to send him to West Point. Cole did not want to go to West Point, however, because he did not want to go to Vietnam. "That's where I figured I'd be headed at the time," he recalled. When one of Vanik's aides telephoned to offer him the appointment to the Military Academy, Cole expressed resentment at not being given the Naval Academy nomination, since he was the best candidate from the congressman's district. His mother's eyes widened as she listened to her son tell off the congressional aide. "Are you crazy?" she seemed to be thinking. "What do you mean you don't want an appointment to West Point?" Cole, however, remained adamant. He telephoned the Naval Academy admissions office, seeking help. Commander Johnson arranged for Cole to come to Annapolis with an appointment from Shirley Chisolm (D-N.Y.).

Operation Information also sparked interest in Navy for Edward J. Gilmore, '76. Gilmore originally wanted to go to the Air Force Academy, but during his junior year of high school an Air Force recruiter told him his grades were not good enough. Not long after that, a midshipman came to his school to make a pitch for the Naval Academy. "I had no idea what the Naval Academy was," he recalled. "As a matter of fact, when the person who introduced him said 'Annapolis,' I thought he said 'Indianapolis.'" As the midshipman's presentation continued, it dawned on Gilmore that he was talking about An-

napolis, Maryland, just four hours away. After the presentation, the midshipman handed out brochures. Gilmore was hooked. He decided to apply to the
Naval Academy.

The decision to attend the Academy drew mixed reactions from some of
the family members, friends, and neighbors of the black midshipmen in the
classes of 1969–79. Ev Greene's family, close friends, and immediate neighbors
were excited about his decision, but some of his peers "did not appreciate" it
because "they were dodging military service to avoid going to Vietnam," as
Greene recalled. Moreover, many of the black people in his community still
perceived the Navy negatively because of the World War II hangover.

Greene's classmate Anthony L. Jackson, '70, encountered similar feelings.
Jackson's father, who had served as an Army officer during World War II and
had since become a pacifist, tried to talk him out of going. Everyone else was
"excited and pleased" about his decision to become a midshipman, Jackson
said, despite the perception in his community of the Navy as "a high-handed,
racist, supercilious outfit."

The Navy was largely unknown in Tony Watson's community in the mid-
1960s, but there was a great deal of antimilitary sentiment there. Those who
did know something about the Navy perceived the Academy as lily-white.
"You're not gonna make it there," they told Watson, "because it's for rich
white kids." Nevertheless, his parents were thrilled with his decision to go to
the Academy.

People in Ric Samuels's community considered the Navy the most prejudiced service. "You very seldom saw any black naval officers," he recalled.
"The thought was, 'Hey, when you go into the Navy, you're probably going
to be a steward.'" Samuels's white friends considered his appointment to the
Academy a great opportunity. His black friends didn't know what the Academy was. His older brother, an Army officer, was proud. His younger brother
opposed the war in Vietnam and thought Ric's decision was a mistake and
that a black person who went into the military was a sellout. A new guidance
counselor, who started at his school his senior year, told him he ought to go to
Princeton instead. "Her point was that black men did not have to go into the
military any more," Samuels said. "There were other avenues available. Why
restrict yourself by going to the Naval Academy?"

Kerwin Miller's father was pleased about his appointment but worried
that the Navy had fewer opportunities for African Americans than the Army.
Miller's uncle had been one of the Navy's first black dentists. "Don't go," he
told Kerwin. "If you need money, I'll help you go to a regular college. My
experiences as a black officer were not good."

Chuck Cole's teachers were enthusiastic about his becoming a midshipman, but a few family members had reservations about his going to a military

school because of Vietnam. Plus his grandfather told him he could do better for himself than go into the military. Similarly, everyone applauded James Jackson's decision except his sister, who harbored antiwar sentiment and tried to dissuade him from going. Everyone supported Charlie Boyd's decision to become a midshipman except the science teachers who believed he would be better off at Johns Hopkins, MIT, or one of the Ivy League schools to which he had been accepted. Byron Marchant's guidance counselor at his predominantly white high school, as well as some of his peers, hinted that he might not be able to make it. His parents and other peers, however, expressed enthusiasm.

Bert Freeman's parents were proud and his friends and neighbors supportive. The older folks in Bruce Henry's community were excited, because the prospect of an African American pursuing a commission was new to them. Although people in Bobby Watts's community considered the Navy the most prejudiced service, they were proud because he was the first student from his high school, black or white, to be accepted at the Academy. And although nobody in the community knew what the Academy was about, when he explained it, they looked upon his acceptance as a victory for the neighborhood. Lamar Chapman's family, friends, neighbors, and high school teachers were all proud of him for rejecting offers from several civilian schools in favor of the Academy. Eddie Graves's community overwhelmed him with support. Ed Gilmore received lots of respect and no discouragement for his decision to become a midshipman. Most of the poor people in Cary Hithon's community considered the Naval Academy an unattainable dream. When they found out about his acceptance, they were thrilled to the point of putting him on a pedestal. Marv King's family and closest friends were proud of him, but few people in the community knew anything about the Academy. Most were supportive when they found out that a congressional appointment was involved. Similarly, although the Navy was unknown in John Porter's community, people supported his decision to go the Naval Academy.

CHAPTER

Forms of Discrimination

WINDS OF change blew through Annapolis for African Americans who became midshipmen between 1965 and 1975. During this period the Naval Academy's culture shifted from ignoring diversity to embracing it.

Nevertheless, for black midshipmen from the classes of 1969–79, plebe year retained its age-old ability to shock the daylights out of them with its instant discipline and reveille-to-taps schedule. To put a new twist on an old phrase spoken by a black soldier during the Civil War, the top rail was on the bottom now, as young men who had been big fish in their hometown ponds were minnows again.

Some black midshipmen had difficulty making the transition. Plebe summer was Tony Watson's first time away from Chicago. "My fear kicked in while I was checking in," he recalled. "I was filling out this card that required you to indicate all the things you were involved in. The guys next to me were putting down that they were president of their class, captain of the football team, members of the National Honor Society, and all this other stuff. All I could put down was I was on the football team. I wasn't president. I wasn't in the National Honor Society. I wasn't in any of that stuff. At that moment, I thought that maybe the people back in Chicago who said that the Academy was for rich white kids were right; maybe I'm not competitive with these folks. These guys are all heavy hitters and I'm just a regular guy from a public housing community in Chicago. At that moment I decided that I was going to have to work harder than everybody else to try to keep up. And that's what I did for that whole plebe year."

Many of those who did not know what to expect had a hard time. "I went to the Academy pretty blind," recalled Bruce Henry. "I had nothing in my background and no one to help prepare me mentally or physically, but particularly mentally, for what I was getting ready to go through. I heard it might be like boot camp, but what did I know of boot camp? It was tough for everybody, white or black." Bobby Watts found the transition from civilian to plebe "very traumatic." "I didn't have a clue," he recalled. "I showed up ignorant. I had my own ideas of what it was going to be like. The day I stepped on the Academy grounds, I went into shock. It was a totally different world. Everybody was yelling at you. Nobody was your friend. The plebes eventually banded together as a class to protect one another, but it took some time to learn how to do that."

Jeff Sapp arrived in Annapolis with a sense of dread. For him plebe summer was like "stacking bowling balls." The physical aspects and the yelling didn't bother him, but the Academy's round-the-clock regimentation did. In Colorado Springs he could do what he wanted when he wanted, but in Annapolis he had to sleep, eat, shave, and do everything else on a rigorous schedule in which he had no say.

Other black midshipmen found plebe year a mixed bag. "It wasn't that hard for me because I was very disciplined and structured anyway," recalled Chuck Cole. "So all the things about folding your clothes and lining them up a certain way, that was easy for me." "The physical stuff was a little bit hard," he added, "because I wasn't real physical. By the time plebe summer was over, I'd gotten into shape and everything was okay." Cary Hithon was used to football coaches yelling at him and calling him names, so when second classmen did the same, it didn't bother him. "It just rolled off my back," he said. The hardest part was "thinking about all the fun my friends were having at home while I was here suffering." At one point he got so homesick that he telephoned his mother and told her he was coming home, but she told him to gut it out. Chuck Reddix had moved around a lot while growing up because of his dad's Air Force career. It made him "adaptable." Reddix found that his lifelong fascination with things military and extensive reading about ships, planes, and other military hardware helped. "We'd be marching along," he recalled, "and a helicopter would fly by. 'Mr. Reddix,' they'd ask, 'what kind of helicopter is that?' I'd say, 'An H-3 Sea King, sir.' They were amazed and basically left me alone, because generally, if they asked me something, I would probably come up with the right answer." Reddix was less sanguine about plebe summer's physical education program, however. "I hated that," he recalled. "I'd wake up and curse, because I knew I was going to go out on that field and sweat for an hour and a half."

Black midshipmen from the classes of 1969–79 with military backgrounds had little or no difficulty with the transition from civilian to plebe. Kerwin

Miller had grown up a military dependent and had few problems adjusting. "I had been around military people," he recalled. "I had been around discipline. My father was a disciplinarian because of his background." Don Montgomery's father instilled discipline in his children as well. "Everyone older than you were was 'sir,'" Montgomery recalled. "We were taught to do something right the first time so you didn't have to do it over again. I used to shine my dad's boots. He would give me a quarter when he could see his face in them." James Jackson went to boot camp during the summer of 1970 before he entered NAPS. "They were geared up for young people who were going off to Vietnam," he recalled. "It was serious and straightforward, very disciplined." After boot camp, plebe summer was "fruit." "The marching, the yelling, the military discipline of the Naval Academy was not a big social shock to me," he said.

For others, family life and school activities had prepared them for the plebe summer grind. Bert Freeman had been in the high school band and already knew how to march. "Plus the fact that my mother taught me to make the bed so well," he recalled. "I could make up the bed better than the people who were showing me how." Ev Greene had grown up respecting people in positions of authority and doing what he was told, so he had no problems adjusting to the Academy's discipline. Ric Samuels found plebe summer not much more difficult than two-a-day football practices. And he enjoyed being issued all the gear. "I was pretty poor growing up. I didn't have anything," he recalled. "People throwing all these clothes at me, though they were uniforms, was great."

A few black midshipmen even liked plebe summer. "I pretty much enjoyed most of plebe summer," recalled Leo Williams. "I was not easily intimidated. I was for the most part very confident. I fairly quickly got to be in a leadership position." Likewise, Lamar Chapman seemed to thrive on plebe summer's rigors. "There was basically no transition for me to make," he recalled. "I was mentally, physically, and emotionally prepared to elevate my military life from JROTC to the next level." Tony Jackson had learned to march and handle an M-1 rifle in a JROTC program. He came to Annapolis brimming with idealism. He loved learning how to shoot a pistol and sail a knockabout. "There was a lot about the summer that appealed to me," he recalled. Byron Marchant delighted in plebe summer's physical and mental challenges. "I actually thought it was pretty exciting and kind of fun," he recalled.

Like their predecessors, many black plebes in the classes of 1969–79 encountered little racial hostility from classmates. "Most midshipmen were not prejudiced," recalled Ev Greene. Neither Ken Dunn, Bert Freeman, Don Montgomery, Charlie Boyd, Chuck Reddix, nor Jeff Sapp discerned prejudice among white classmates. "Most of my classmates were too busy with being midshipmen to worry about race," Boyd recalled.

Many black midshipmen developed close friendships with white classmates. "I got along well with just about everybody in the company," Tony Watson recalled. Jeff Sapp believed that his company shipmates didn't see "color." Byron Marchant became good friends with his white roommate, Kevin Lynch, '78, a white Irish Catholic from New England. "I learned more from him about black music than anybody else I'd known," recalled Marchant. "He grew up in a family that was absolutely tolerant of racial difference." Many of the midshipmen he spent a lot of time with happened to be white Irish Catholics. He hung out with black friends, too. During the little free time available plebe year, Marv King hung out mostly with his roommates. "One was a laid-back southerner from Alabama," he recalled, "the other a short Jewish guy from Wisconsin."

About as many black plebes encountered at least some prejudice from their classmates as those who encountered little or none. "There was a small but significant segment of the brigade that did not welcome minorities," recalled Ev Greene. Bruce Henry got along with some of the classmates in his company very well. But several of them wanted nothing to do with him and called him "the Groid" behind his back. One day while Bobby Watts was chopping through the halls, a classmate called him a nigger. Watts wanted to punch the guy but restrained himself. Months later the classmate apologized to Watts, confessing that he was trying to provoke a fight in hopes of getting Watts kicked out. Ric Samuels was galled by white classmates from Boston who voiced opposition to integration when that city started busing minorities to white schools.

Several black midshipmen were nicknamed "Pimp" because of their taste in music or civilian clothing.[1] Some of Chuck Cole's white classmates nicknamed him "Coon," "Ten-percent," and "Charcoal," the last a combination of his name and skin color. Cole attributed this more to the tenor of the times than to racism. "Blacks took more grief back then than they take today," he recalled. "People just said things. Now, there's more sensitivity." John Porter found his classmates' racial attitudes to be "typical for the time." "I had previously assumed racist attitudes were due to ignorance or lack of education," he recalled. "I was very disappointed to see that the 'nation's finest' were trained to have similar beliefs. I quickly learned that these more intelligent people harbored much contempt for people they perceived as lesser beings."

Some white midshipmen expressed prejudice subtly. "There were those who covertly would let you know that they didn't want blacks there," recalled one African American alumnus. "Remarks behind your back. Undertones. Non-inclusion in different gatherings or outings or social events. They might come in the room and invite the two white roommates to an event and not you." Bruce Franklin dubbed such behavior "East Coast institutional racism." "Many midshipmen didn't want minorities there," he recalled. "After class, black midshipmen were abandoned by the white midshipmen, socially. All of some people went in this direction and all of other people went in that direction. Nothing was said." Franklin had never encountered such behavior while growing up on the West Coast. "It was new to me and I hated it," he said. Byron Marchant also encountered a degree of social segregation at the Academy. "There was still a fundamental element of races separating on a social level," he recalled. "For the most part, the black midshipmen would go to parties where there were predominantly black people and the white midshipmen would go to parties where there were predominantly white people, and ne'er the twain really met." Prejudice among classmates also manifested itself in peer evaluations. Ev Greene, Will Merrell, and others received lower "grease" scores than they thought they deserved.

Lamar Chapman encountered lots of racial hostility from classmates. "My classmates had zero to very low tolerance for racial differences," he recalled. "The twelve blacks in my class and the fifteen other African American midshipmen developed an every man for himself, survive at all cost mentality. Tolerate the name-calling and insults from your white classmates. Don't complain or make waves. I was called a 'nigger' several times a day." One incident in particular stands out in his memory: "On the evening ending parents' visitation, our midshipman company commander initiated a shaving cream fight in our company area to keep the plebes' minds off their parents and girlfriends leaving. I was getting the best of one of my classmates by unloading almost an entire can of foam in his face. The upperclassmen found it to be funny. My white classmate ran to his room and returned less than five minutes later with a white sheet over his head. He held two pencils tied together into a cross with metal paper clips. With the aid of lighter fluid the cross was burning! This racially charged insult was directed at me. I grabbed my assailant and threw him to the floor. Before I could ignite his sheet with his own burning cross, my other classmates pulled me off of him. My company officer only asked if I was okay and if I wanted to bring my classmate up on charges. The grin-and-bear-it strategy I observed from my fellow African American classmates was the only answer I could think of at the time. This is just one of hundreds of stories I could share." The credo "never bilge a shipmate" doubtless prevented other black midshipmen from reporting similar incidents.

To Leo Williams, "it was fairly obvious" that many white classmates in his company were "uncomfortable" around black people. "My first roommate was a young man from Atlanta who had never spent any time around African Americans," he recalled. "For him to look up and find me as a roommate was something that he found pretty distasteful." Neither one spoke to the other for about two or three weeks. "We got beyond it," Williams added. "The Academy had decided either you get over it or you get out of it. Ultimately it got to the point where we had to depend on one another to do certain things. The whole plebe experience is about team building as well as character building."

Similarly, Ric Samuels discovered that many of his white classmates had not had much exposure to black people before coming to the Academy. Most of the racial problems he had with such people arose out of ignorance, not malice. Some of Ken Dunn's white classmates had more trouble adjusting to him than he did to them. "My roommate had to make a bigger transition than I did," Dunn recalled. "He came from a bedroom community in New Jersey and had no contact with black Americans at all before we met." Likewise a white classmate told Jeff Sapp that he was the first black person to whom he had ever spoken. Kerwin Miller met several white people in his company who had not been around black people before and were uncomfortable around him. Miller, on the other hand, had grown up among white people and was not uncomfortable around them. "I won them over because I flowed," he recalled. "But had they been with somebody else who might not have flowed as well, they would have had a problem."

Some of Miller's black classmates who had not spent time around white people before felt uncomfortable among white midshipmen at the Academy, especially if the white midshipmen had not spent time around black people before. "We'd do some things a little differently," Miller recalled. "We'd wear stuff when we went to sleep that they weren't used to. 'What is that you are wearing on your head?' they would say. A lot of my black classmates said, 'These people just don't understand.'" The feeling created racial tension. It made some black midshipmen oversensitive and prone to perceive racial slights where none were intended. Miller, however, had no such tension in his relationships with the white midshipmen in his own company. "When other blacks would come visit me," he recalled, "they would say, 'Your guys act a lot differently than the guys in my company.' I said, 'Well, I think it's because of me. I act a lot differently than you do. You kind of have an attitude with these folks. I'm a little bit more patient with them. I don't question everything they say as if it's a personal thing.'"

Compromise played key a key role in working out differences. The display of Confederate flags annoyed Ric Samuels, especially if the midshipmen displaying them were not from the South. "When you're from Indiana and you have a rebel flag, that I didn't understand," he recalled. "What message are you trying to get across? Are you a member of the KKK?" Samuels found that bigotry followed the rebel flag in some cases, but not in all. He had many a heated discussion over the flag. Some classmates refused to take it down. Others did so without ado when they learned that Samuels found it offensive. Kerwin Miller liked Motown. His white roommate preferred country and western. They worked out their differences by listening to different kinds of music at different times of the day.

Most African American plebes encountered racial hostility from only a minority of classmates. By and large, fourth classmen grew close to one another, regardless of race. "There is an extremely close bond between us from the plebe experience," recalled Charlie Boyd, "even if we're not in touch with each other often." Chuck Cole found that prejudice subsided as the crucible of plebe indoctrination forged a camaraderie among the plebes. "My classmates in my company and I were all pretty close," he recalled. "You had to pitch in and do things together. I helped out white guys and white guys helped me out all through my time there." "I probably had stronger bonds to the guys in my company than I did to some of the other black midshipmen," he added. Similarly, Eddie Graves made stronger friendships among his white classmates in his company than with anybody else at the Academy. Despite the social segregation he experienced, Bruce Franklin found many of his white classmates to be "very helpful." "To those people," he said, "I will be eternally grateful." Cary Hithon received help from white classmates whenever he needed it. Hithon would sometimes complain to white friends about the lack of black girls at tea fights, but generally blacks and whites did not sit down together to discuss racial issues. Lloyd Prince, '78, and his white classmates hit it off well right from the start. "The support of classmates in our company was excellent!" he recalled. "I made friendships in the first few days that are as strong today as they were then."

Many African American plebes discerned little or no prejudice among first, second, or third classmen. Ev Greene considered the vast majority of upperclassmen "fair and honorable individuals." Bert Freeman never heard an upperclassman call him a name or utter a racist comment. It was the same for Byron Marchant. "Some of the upperclassmen were jerks," he recalled, "but I never perceived racial prejudice from any of them." Will Merrell discerned an attitude of "reserved acceptance" among white midshipmen.

Nevertheless, *most* black plebes, in fact, did encounter negative racial attitudes from *some* upperclassmen. Bruce Henry was a youngster when Martin Luther King Jr. was assassinated. "I remember that day as one of great sadness," he said. "I was walking down the hall to my room in disbelief, in shock, like the nation was, and I passed an upperclassman's room. I overheard him say, 'I'm glad that nigger is dead.'" Henry had to restrain himself from doing something that would have made a bad day even worse.

Tony Watson had a virtually identical experience. "The biggest drama I had at the Naval Academy from a racial standpoint occurred in 1968 on the day that Martin Luther King was assassinated," he recalled. "Up to that point the Naval Academy had always taught us all that we were all part of a big melting pot; that we were all the same. In spite of things, I really believed that. When I heard the news of King's assassination, I went back to my room, feeling like my second father had been taken from me. And I heard a midshipman walking past my door say to another midshipman, 'I'm glad that nigger's finally dead.' It just took my breath away. I'll never forget that sinking feeling. I realized that we're not all the same and that it's not a big melting pot. I realized that I needed to be more aware of the people around me than I had been. Even though people might be saying one thing in front of me, they might well be saying stuff behind my back. 1968 was a very traumatic time in the country's history. Martin Luther King got killed, Bobby Kennedy got killed, the Vietnam War was at its peak, Chicago was being burned down, and here I was kind of isolated at a place where I thought we were all fighting for the common good of the country. It just took the wind out of me in a big way and affected me for the rest of my life. We're really not part of a big melting pot at all. We're more like a salad. Even though you may put some dressing on it and stir it all up together, you still have distinct elements. You can tell the lettuce from the cherry tomatoes from the onions. It's not a melting pot. It's a very diverse community in which each group has its own distinct attributes."

Ev Greene discovered that a small but significant segment of upperclassmen did not welcome minorities. On one occasion, he heard an upperclassman refer to a black belt as a "nigger belt." On another occasion, he saw an upperclassman scrawl racist epithets on a poster of Dr. King. All too often he heard derogatory comments about the black janitors who worked in Bancroft Hall. A handful of upperclassmen told Bobby Watts flat out that they did not want blacks at the Academy. Cozy Bailey, '75, had a run-in with an intoxicated upperclassman. "If a smart-mouthed nigger like you came into my neighborhood," the upperclassman said, "I'd sic my dog on him."[2] Jeff Sapp had a similar encounter. "If I could rename you," a racist upperclassman once told him, "I would call you 'nigger.'" Lamar Chapman perceived that upperclassmen "were constantly reminding African American midshipmen that they were not really part of the brigade."

Many black plebes encountered the attitude that African Americans did not deserve to be midshipmen or were not qualified to be midshipmen. Black people became midshipmen, went such reasoning, only because of quotas resulting from political pressure for integration. Bruce Henry, Bobby Watts, Will Merrell, and Bruce Franklin each ran across first and second classmen who shared this belief. "Others felt that the large numbers of blacks who were starting to enter were being accepted at lower standards," Merrell recalled. "Some believed that blacks had their appointments handed to them." The upperclassmen who told Bobby Watts that they didn't want blacks at the Academy believed minorities "hadn't done anything to help make this country what it is. They felt that I had not earned my right to be there. The only reason we had this opportunity was because the North beat the South."

Some black midshipmen encountered well-meaning whites who insulted them while trying to be helpful. "One upperclassman told me that he was going to protect me and I was going to be his 'nigger,'" said Bobby Watts. "My mother had sent me a care package. He came into my room and saw it and started looking through it and taking stuff out of it as upperclassmen would do. He wasn't one of those yelling, screaming first classmen. He was a guy from the South. He truly meant that he was going to take care of me. He thought that I *should* be there and that I was a good guy. The word 'nigger' was everyday language to him. It was his southern upbringing. He was just ignorant about how to relate to black people." Cozy Bailey received an unintended insult in his first fitness report, written by an upperclassman. "Although Mr. Bailey is black," it said, "he does well."[3]

In Charlie Boyd's case, a well-intended policy backfired somewhat. "During plebe summer, the upperclassmen of our company thought it would be a good experience for everyone to have roomed with someone black for a while," he recalled. "There were only two of us in the company. They made us move over and over again instead of having others move in with us. They may not have meant it to be a negative experience, but since the rooms always had to be in class-A condition, it was a major pain." Cary Hithon remembered being chewed out by a firsty at the end of plebe summer. After he finished yelling, the firsty softened his tone. "He was sort of apologetic for being so hard on me," Hithon recalled. "Then he said, 'I want to see your kind make it.' That's the part I will never forget. 'If I ever run into him again,' I thought, 'I'm going to punch his lights out.'"

Sometimes upperclassmen called black plebes to account for racial issues over which they had no control. On one occasion, a firsty had Bobby Watts come around and asked what he thought about the Black Panthers. "I told him there were two routes you could take," Watts recalled. "Either the radical approach, where you could go out and fight against the government, or the nonviolent approach, such as that adopted by the SCLC. 'Both of them have merit,' I told him. 'One takes a lot longer than the other, even though the more violent one may be short-lived, you get people to focus on you right away.' That's all I told him. I didn't tell him which one I favored, which was neither. Nevertheless, he labeled me as a radical and said that I shouldn't be there and called me a Black Panther and all this other kind of stuff. I thought, 'Where did he get all this from?'"

When riots erupted after the King assassination in Washington, D.C., the Academy suspended liberty there. The decision angered one racist first classman. "Porter had better stay out of my way," the firsty warned one of John Porter's roommates. Porter did so but resented the idea of someone taking his frustrations out on him because he was black.

Similarly, Kerwin Miller's color brought him unwanted attention because of an incident that happened during a lecture delivered by women's rights activist Gloria Steinem. Something Steinem said prompted Midshipman 1/C Charles H. Rucks, '72, to stand up. "He started talking about racism at the Naval Academy," recalled Miller. "I can't remember all his words, but the place was silent. You could have heard a pin drop. He put it out there. He basically challenged the Academy to do more because of what he had seen." After the lecture, some of the upperclassmen in Miller's company had him come around. Miller entered each room braced up and stood at attention. "Miller," the upperclassmen would ask, "are we racists?"

"What the hell!" Miller thought. "What am I going to tell you? I'm a plebe. Ask me this next year and I'll tell you what's going on, but not right now." Miller had always tried as much as his personality would allow to blend inconspicuously into the background, the traditional plebe survival tactic. Rucks's assertions, however, made that impossible. "Some of the white upperclassmen were genuinely concerned," Miller said. "'Are you getting treated any differently?' they would ask." Miller would have preferred not to have the extra attention, however. He did not want anyone to think he was getting special treatment.

Cary Hithon found that many upperclassmen behaved awkwardly around him. "They treated you differently," he recalled. "They wouldn't yell at you the same way, or they would get on you for something a little more picayune, but nothing that would bring any attention upon themselves." Hithon believed that such upperclassmen were treating him this way out of ignorance, not prejudice. They simply had never dealt with black people before coming to the Academy.

Fortunately, most white midshipmen did not behave this way. Instances of overt racism stunned Jeff Sapp precisely because they were so rare. Ron Grover, '75, put it best: "A degree of prejudice existed similar to what existed in society." Most black plebes found negative racial attitudes confined to a minority of upperclassmen.

Black midshipmen still encountered discrimination in town, although racial hostility there was on the wane. "Every now and then you'd be out on liberty in town walking around," recalled Chuck Reddix, "and somebody would whiz by in a car and yell 'nigger' at you. And I remember one time, I was walking in town with a young lady who happened to be white. Somebody speeding by in a car called her 'nigger lover' and tried to splash us with a mud puddle." Charlie Boyd had similar experiences. "There were a few isolated incidents of racism from whites in the community," he said. "I remember people driving by and shouting insults or throwing beer bottles at us when we were in town."

Like their predecessors, black midshipmen from the classes of 1969–79 occasionally encountered negative racial attitudes among faculty and staff. "There were a few instructors who were obvious bigots," recalled Leo Williams. Chuck Reddix encountered similar instructors. "Some of the faculty members, especially the old guys, seemed to have a low opinion of blacks," he said. "One of my professors first-class year referred to blacks as Negroes. And then he made a comment like, 'They rut like deer.' Other than that comment, which I really thought was really kind of strange, I don't remember any prejudice being directed against anybody, except plebes as a whole." During a boxing match an assistant boxing coach shocked Lamar Chapman. "Go in there and hurt that white boy or the judges will steal it from you because you're a nigger," the coach said. He later apologized for using the word "nigger," but the damage had been done.

The manner and extent to which racist upperclassmen could make black plebes' lives miserable, or even worse, changed between 1965 and 1976. Academic reform during that period brought about fundamental reforms in the plebe indoctrination system that affected the lives of all midshipmen, black or white.

From time immemorial, it seemed, midshipmen had marched to class and had taken the same prescribed "lockstep" curriculum, whether they entered the Academy with two years of college or right out of high school. The only choice they could make themselves was the foreign language elective. In the mid-1950s, the civilian members of the faculty and the Board of Visitors began calling for academic modernization.

In 1959, the Academy began reforming the curriculum in earnest. That September, the superintendent approved the introduction of a validation program and elective courses. During the 1959/60 academic year, the Academy offered thirty-five electives in seven different departments. In September 1960, the Academy put into effect a new core curriculum that emphasized principles and analytic methods instead of techniques. The change rendered marching to class impractical, so that tradition also went by the wayside, much to the dismay of many older alumni. These reforms marked a fundamental divergence from past practice.

In the spring of 1963, the Academy inaugurated the Trident Scholars program of independent study, which excused outstanding firsties from classes to conduct approved research projects. That same year, letter grades replaced numerical grades to enable Academy alumni to compete on a more equal basis with civilians in applying to engineering graduate schools. Coupled with the switch to letter grades was a reduction in the traditional emphasis on daily grades and daily recitation, a move that cultivated a more stimulating classroom atmosphere.

The Naval Academy upgraded its faculty as well. Civilians with Ph.D.s were hired, and the proportion of commissioned instructors with master's degrees was increased. In August 1963, the Academy hired a civilian educator of national prominence, Dr. A. Bernard Drought, dean of engineering at Marquette University, as academic dean.

In September 1964, the Academy inaugurated a minors program. Under this program, core courses constituted 85 percent of the curriculum. About half of the core courses were in science and engineering, a quarter in the humanities and social sciences, and a quarter in professional naval subjects. The remaining 15 percent of the curriculum consisted of electives to constitute the minor. By validating courses or taking them on an overload basis above the required 137 credits, a midshipman could earn a major.

Rear Admiral Kauffman, who became superintendent in June 1965, dubbed these reforms the "Academic Revolution." "During the last five years we have made enormous progress academically and intellectually," he wrote Admiral David L. McDonald, the CNO, in April 1966. A report by a team of civilian academics that evaluated the new curriculum the month before concluded, "The strongest and firmest impression we have is one of rapid academic growth and a well-conceived effort to align the Academy's academic programs with those of the better colleges and technical institutes."[4]

The academic revolution did not end when Draper Kauffman stepped down as superintendent. His successor, James Calvert, instituted some of the most sweeping curriculum reforms in the Academy's history, starting with a complete overhaul of the curriculum in 1969. Admiral Calvert cut back the core courses, almost doubled the hours allocated to professional subjects, and, that September, introduced a majors program. In fact, Calvert was kept on for a fourth year largely to ensure the success of the majors program. Initially the Academy offered twenty-four majors ranging from hard sciences to liberal arts. By 1975, policy set the ratio of majors in engineering/science/math to humanities at 80:20. Meanwhile, the number of courses grew from 366 in 1968 to 550 in 1975.[5]

During the late 1960s, the academic revolution sparked a revolution in the plebe indoctrination system that severely reduced the "mickey mouse" stuff plebes had to endure and drastically reduced physical hazing. Ideally plebe indoctrination converted civilians into midshipmen, instilled in them a pride in belonging, and imbued them with the ideals of duty, honor, and loyalty. It also tested the mettle of plebes, weeded out those not suited to a naval career, and taught the survivors to be part of the Navy team. But, as in any hierarchical system, abuses occurred because the system accorded arbitrary power to individuals ill equipped to handle it. Throughout the Academy's history, the experience of plebe indoctrination could be lighthearted and fun or brutal and demeaning, depending on the maturity and proclivities of the individual upperclassmen doing the indoctrinating.

In the mid-1960s, the new emphasis on scholarship resulting from the academic revolution began to conflict with the old plebe indoctrination system. The first inkling that something was amiss arose from observations on how plebes spent their most precious commodity—time. Plebes "were supposed to be short on time, to teach them to set priorities," as Admiral Calvert put it. "The Academy asked them to do more than they could possibly do. They had to set priorities and get the most important things done."[6]

Concerns arose about the amount of time plebes were spending on indoctrination activities, particularly come-arounds and "professional questions" at the expense of their studies. The system in effect before 1965 permitted large numbers of upperclassmen to make demands on a plebe's time. Any first or second classman in a plebe's battalion could have the plebe come around. Come-arounds took place behind closed doors, were authorized during any of four periods each day, and were not necessarily limited to "correctional" purposes. Sometimes upperclassmen had plebes exercise to the point of physical exhaustion. Come-arounds after the evening meal often extended well into plebes' study hours. Plebes were sometimes "booked" for come-arounds for weeks ahead. Answering professional questions could consume even more time. First and second classmen asked plebes professional questions at meals, during come-arounds, or in the passageways of Bancroft Hall. If a plebe didn't know the answer, he would have to look it up. The questions were supposed to be limited to required plebe knowledge—including *Reef Points;* the front page of the day's newspaper and everything in the sports section concerning Navy; the menus for the next two meals; the officers of the watch; the number of days until the Army game, Christmas leave, the Ring Dance, and graduation; the movies in town; sports events in the Yard; and the like—but all too often answers to questions like "What was the name of the lead elephant in Hannibal's column when the Carthaginians crossed the Alps to invade Italy" or "How long have you been in the Navy" (the "correct" answer is a lengthy poem from *Reef Points*) required extensive research or memorization of lengthy passages. Many plebes were getting up in the middle of the night to prepare their answers, thus losing sleep. At meals, plebes were sometimes questioned so heavily that they had little time to eat. Too many plebes were spending so much time going to come-arounds and answering professional questions that their grades were suffering.[7]

The first step toward reform came in August 1964 when the commandant promulgated a new instruction on plebe indoctrination. The instruction emphasized that successful leadership stemmed from personal example and moral responsibility. It forbade "time-consuming, frivolous or childish requirements," especially those that denied a plebe time to study, time to sleep, and a chance to eat a "full and complete meal." The instruction appeared to signal an intolerance of hazing. "Upperclassmen will not touch a fourth classman under any circumstances except to administer first aid," it declared. The instruction limited physical punishment to approved exercises listed in a manual issued by the physical education department. The instruction also set guidelines for professional questions. It authorized only first and second classmen to ask professional questions. It limited the questions to *Reef Points,* American naval history, the honor concept, naval organization, and other types of information relevant to midshipmen and naval officers that could be readily found in a list of prescribed sources. Plebes doing unsatisfactory academic work could be asked only questions related to their studies. Considering what Gil Lucas, Jim Frezzell, and many of their classmates went through during plebe year (1964/65), however, this instruction made little real impact on the experience of plebe indoctrination.[8]

A much more significant change came in April 1965 when the Academy introduced the squad leader system. Its purpose was to improve the leadership and organization of upperclassmen and prevent them from abusing plebes. The new system did away with the old one-to-one, plebe-to-first classman, mentor-protector arrangement familiar to every black midshipman from Wesley Brown to Paul Reason. Under the old system, any firsty or segundo could "run" any of the plebes in their battalion, although in practice they usually focused only on the plebes in their company. The plebe's first classman tried to shield him from overzealous participants, but tradition prevented him from interfering too much. Under the new instruction, beginning with the class of 1969, each plebe had to answer only to his squad leader—a first classman— and the other firsties and segundos in his squad. Other upperclassmen could participate in plebe indoctrination only with the squad leader's permission. The squad leader was responsible for the physical and academic health and well-being of the plebes in his squad, usually four. The squad leader saw to it that his plebes got enough sleep, food, and time to study. "The squad leader will keep himself informed of the progress and performance of his midshipmen fourth class in all matters, including academics, professional training, aptitude, conduct and physical fitness," read a revised instruction on plebe indoctrination issued by the commandant in August 1965, and the squad leader was to ensure "that time-consuming or useless requirements are not imposed on his plebes."

The new instruction also changed the procedures for come-arounds, which had existed at the Academy since the dawn of the twentieth century. It permitted any firsty or segundo to "correct" plebes on the spot, but it limited them to giving come-arounds only to plebes in their squad. No longer could any upperclassman target any plebe. Only midshipman officers could still give come-arounds to plebes outside their squad. Just as significant, the new instruction reduced the number of authorized come-around periods from four to three, eliminating the period after the evening meal. Furthermore, come-arounds were no longer to be done behind closed doors; the door now had to be left open.[9]

Even these changes did not go far enough, as Admiral Kauffman soon discovered. While attempting to gauge the impact of recent curriculum reforms, he inadvertently brought intense adverse publicity to the plebe system. As the dust from the academic revolution began to settle, Kauffman thought it "a perfect time to take stock, to find out all of the problems which may have arisen in the wake of a change that was both drastic and rapid." He asked the Middle States Association of Colleges and Secondary Schools to send an evaluation committee to the Academy during the 1965/66 school year. He wanted a distinguished group of educators "to make the most detailed, searching and critical analysis possible of every aspect of the Academy." The evaluation committee met on 20–24 March 1966. The chairman planned to submit the committee's findings to Kauffman around 1 May.[10]

The press caught wind of the evaluation committee's findings in early April. One of the committee members or a disgruntled faculty member involved in the evaluation process might have leaked the story to reporters. Whatever the source, the leak plunged Admiral Kauffman into a storm of controversy over the plebe indoctrination system. A series of articles appearing in the *Washington Post* early that month alleged that military requirements were stifling midshipmen's academic performance. Amid allegations of "grade-fixing," midshipmen "coasting" at the "gentlemen's C" level, sleeping in class, and low faculty morale, the articles reported that the evaluation committee intended to recommend that the Academy deemphasize sports and military requirements in favor of academics. Admiral Kauffman thought these articles were sensational and showed only the bad side of the school. He considered them "lethal."[11]

The storm worsened on 7 April when Senator Jennings Randolph (D-W.Va.) addressed his colleagues on the revelations in the *Post.* "There is excessive subordination of academics to so-called plebe indoctrination—which really is plebe harassment," he declared. "Plebes are acquiring foundation experience in the traditions of the brigade, but in too many cases it is to the detriment of academic foundations." Senator Randolph said that two of his three nominees who entered the Academy in 1964 and 1965 "experienced inordinate difficulties or disillusionment." One of them claimed to have spent three-fifths of his unscheduled study time going to come-arounds, answering questions, or running personal errands for upperclassmen in his company, expressly forbidden by both the 1964 and 1965 plebe indoctrination instructions. "Most upperclassmen are fine fellows and are genuinely desirous of helping plebes to acclimate themselves," said the former plebe in a letter to Randolph that the senator read to his colleagues, "but there always seem to be a few who possess cruel tendencies."[12]

The cases of three plebes run out of the Academy by upperclassmen fueled the indoctrination system controversy for months. An especially ruthless and atypical firsty targeted a plebe who was the son of a congressional staff assistant. The staffer told his boss that his son had gotten a "dirty deal." The congressman pressured Under Secretary of the Navy Robert Baldwin to review the case in detail. In the process of doing so Baldwin examined several similar cases. Anxious about the bad publicity the plebe indoctrination system had just received, Baldwin feared that if "one more such incident" broke in the press it would "leave a bad scar on the Academy's reputation" and threaten "plebe indoctrination in its entirety . . . with complete abolishment." Baldwin suggested that the Academy reform the system, particularly with regard to come-arounds and professional questions, before another scandal forced a "fundamental change in our policy."[13]

Admiral Kauffman believed that enforcing the rules already in place would suffice. He placed particular emphasis on making upperclassmen aware that they would face dire consequences if they broke two of the new taboos: touching a plebe except to render first aid, and infringing on the study period. He was wary of carrying the reforms too far. "I feel very strongly that a *positive but controlled* Plebe Year is essential," he noted in a letter to Vice Admiral B. J. Semmes, chief of naval personnel. "It is the primary difference between the Naval Academy and Princeton." Kauffman pointed out that plebes came from "widely varying backgrounds" and were not "very well screened." Most entered the Academy with a congressional appointment, and all they needed to do to get in was pass the physical exam and admissions test. "We do not get 1,300 *law abiding, mature* young *gentlemen* in here each summer," he said. Some of them would "never make an acceptable Naval Officer no matter what we do." For the rest, unpopular rules and their enforcement were necessary to mold them into naval officers.

In a nod to the under secretary, however, Kauffman did alter the rules a little. Another new instruction issued in August 1966 forbade upperclassmen from threatening a plebe with dismissal or pressuring a plebe to resign. It also discouraged upperclassmen from having plebes come around to their room more than once for a given correction. Later that month, the administration tried to substitute the term "special instruction" for "come-around," but the euphemism never caught on.[14]

The ousting of the second plebe fanned the flames of controversy. This plebe happened to be the younger son of Captain Wayne Hoof, '41, head of the Academy's department of English, history, and government. The separation of his son so upset Hoof that he skirted the chain of command and appealed directly to the chief of naval personnel and secretary of the navy. Hoof declared that the plebe indoctrination system did not serve the best interests of either the plebe or the Academy. Basically he reiterated the argument that the system prevented plebes from getting enough sleep, food at meals, and time to study. He strongly recommended that the Academy limit the indoctrination period to plebe summer and accord plebes the same status as third classmen during the academic year.[15]

Associate Professor Robert Seager II joined the fray in the fall of 1966, criticizing not only the plebe system but the entire "military-academic relationship." Seager had taught history at the Academy for five years. Educated at the Citadel, Merchant Marine Academy, Rutgers, Columbia, and Ohio State, Seager had turned down better offers because he wanted to take part in the academic revolution. After joining the faculty, he helped establish a successful Fulbright Scholar program and advocated greater civilian governance of the Academy.

Seager was a card-carrying member of the American Association of University Professors (AAUP), the leading organization dedicated to protecting academic freedom. Its mission involved advancing academic freedom and shared governance, defining fundamental professional values and standards for higher education, and ensuring higher education's contribution to the common good. The organization encouraged members to speak out.[16]

On 19 October 1966, Seager wrote a letter to Admiral Kauffman, declaring that the recent reforms in the plebe system were nothing more than "nice-sounding phrases committed hopefully to paper by the commandant's office and committed quickly to the wastebasket by everyone else" in Bancroft Hall. He described the atmosphere of Bancroft Hall as "corrosive and destructive of everything the learning process at the college level involves." He asserted that the commissioned company officers were "ill-educated," had no desire to control the upperclassmen who ran the plebe system, and viewed education as a hindrance to the real task of squaring away midshipmen. He described at length several incidents of hazing he had witnessed personally. Recently, while he was eating lunch in Bancroft Hall, a second classman began to heap "crude, dirty-minded and profane" language on a plebe at their table. Seager asked his midshipman host to intervene, but the firsty declined to do so. "That plebe is no damn good," he told the professor. "We're trying to get him out of here before Christmas." Seager claimed that such scenes were all too typical. He praised the recent directives designed to reform the plebe system but castigated the executive department for not enforcing them. "Psychological hazing has replaced physical hazing and the Company Officers are not sophisticated enough to see that the former is just as destructive of human dignity as the latter and in most instances more dangerous physically to the well-being of the individual." Echoing Hoof, Seager concluded by recommending that indoctrination be done away with after plebe summer.[17]

The case of the third plebe drew particularly close attention because he was African American. Born and raised in Washington, D.C., Tony Jackson graduated from Woodrow Wilson High School and entered the Academy in June 1966. In high school Jackson had been an above-average student, a Cadet Corps captain, and a member of the drill team. Although four civilian colleges had accepted him, financial considerations and the influence of role models led him to choose the Naval Academy. His parents were divorced when he was about three, and although he had received partial scholarships to all four civilian schools, his mother would be hard pressed to pay the difference. She persuaded him to go to the Academy and helped him obtain an appointment from William Dawson through her father, a friend of the congressman. Two positive role models—black officers Benjamin Cloud, a naval aviator and friend of his mother who was later involved in quelling the racial disturbance on the carrier *Kitty Hawk*, and Paul Reason, an acquaintance from the Civil Air Patrol—influenced his decision to attend the Academy.

Upperclassmen treated Jackson fairly during plebe summer and he enjoyed having another black midshipman in his company. When the summer ended, however, he was transferred to the 25th Company because the Academy wanted to spread African American midshipmen throughout the brigade. That's when his troubles began.

Jackson had no friends in the new company. He had personality clashes with several classmates and, worse, upperclassmen, some of whom harbored prejudice. Jackson frequently heard racist remarks or jokes in the halls and at the mess table. On one occasion an upperclassman stood him up against a wall in Bancroft Hall and called him a "nigger." Jackson spent a lot of time standing at attention outside his room in foul weather gear, racing up and down the hallway, and doing push-ups. He found himself going to come-arounds more often than his classmates on the flimsiest pretexts, almost always to the same handful of rooms. He also found himself being fried for the most trivial of offenses.

Jackson discussed his problems with classmate Bruce Henry. Although they were in different companies and involved in different sports, they had enough common ground to commiserate about their lot. There was little else they could do.

The pressure on Jackson mounted quickly. Hard on the heels of a conduct warning from his company officer on 26 September came one from his battalion officer on 6 October. Thereafter the chaplain, a clinical psychologist working for the Academy's mental hygiene unit, the commandant, and Professor Seager each talked to Jackson as well. Nevertheless, by the end of the month, Jackson's demerit total reached 180 and the sleep deprivation resulting from the come-arounds was hurting his grades. He fell into a deep depression.

The clinical psychologist, a Navy lieutenant commander, saw Jackson three times. He found the black plebe to be "an intelligent, rigid, serious, and covertly hostile Midshipman who evidenced a somewhat condescending attitude." "He has a long history of conflict in interpersonal relationships which has persisted at the Academy. . . . He has had difficulty accepting authority and has felt that he did not 'belong' here."

At about that time one of the top midshipman officers in the brigade offered Jackson his help. "He said that men of my caliber needed to be in the service," Jackson recalled. "He wanted to know if I thought I was being treated unfairly." Unfortunately, the offer came too late. "I really didn't take advantage of his willingness to intervene," Jackson added. "I didn't see anything that he could really help with."

Depressed and unwilling to fight back, Jackson reached the breaking point. "One morning the bells went off and I just couldn't get up," he recalled. "I must have lain in the rack for ten or fifteen minutes before I finally got up and got dressed. I took my time. I thought, 'I can't do this anymore.'" Jackson submitted his letter of resignation on 1 November. "I have been unable to adjust to Naval Academy life," he wrote in the letter, adding that the Academy was not providing the kind of education he wanted.

Jackson's company officer strongly recommended that his resignation be accepted. "Midshipman Jackson's problems stem from the fact that he seems to be fighting the system, passively ignoring orders, USNA Regulations and advice by his Squad Leader," noted the company officer. "He has lost his motivation toward becoming a Naval Officer. . . . It is obvious that Midshipman Jackson resents authority and feels that he doesn't belong in a military environment. Although academically sound, his conduct to date has been very unsatisfactory." In another report the company officer declared that Jackson seemed "to want to be treated as a 'special case' to go about doing as he pleases."

Jackson's battalion officer concurred. Jackson "failed to learn to live with the system," noted the battalion officer. "In view of his inability to adapt himself to life at the Naval Academy and his loss of motivation to become a Naval Officer, I recommend that Mr. Jackson's resignation be accepted." "Mr. Jackson stated that there were no plebe indoctrination violations and that no discrimination is involved in his case," he added, "although people seemed to watch him extra carefully because he was a Negro."

When the commandant of midshipman, Captain Sheldon H. Kinney, found out that Jackson intended to resign, he summoned the black plebe to his office. "He asked me bluntly whether I was resigning because of race or racism," Jackson recalled. "I told him no. I think that was accurate. There was racism there. I wanted to tell him that there was something of a plantation attitude there among a lot of the midshipmen. But the truth of the matter was that for me, racism wasn't the primary ingredient in success or failure at the Academy." Jackson added that he would have resigned even if he had encountered no racism at all. "The key issues for me were loneliness and depression," he added. "My success or failure at the Academy had far more to do with my immaturity and my particular temperament and my disposition toward depression than did the racial episodes, although they certainly didn't help." Kinney noted that Jackson considered scholarship as "primary" and everything else "secondary" during "college" years. This was precisely the attitude that caused many older officers to resent the academic revolution.

The decision to leave filled Jackson with a mixture of relief, frustration, and guilt. "I knew the Academy wasn't where I needed to be," he recalled, "but I wasn't sure whether it was my fault or a problem with the system. I carried that around for a long time." Since his mother would not sign the papers necessary to release him, he had to remain at the Academy until his eighteenth birthday nine days later. He then went on leave pending separation. On 6 January 1967, the secretary of the navy approved his resignation.

Professor Seager wrote Admiral Kauffman five months later, forwarding a recommendation he had written for Jackson to Princeton. Seager noted "that a high ranking midshipman officer in the 25th Company" had "participated in the cabal that forced Mr. Jackson out of the Naval Academy." This midshipman "considered Mr. Jackson not only a liar but a thief as well," Seager said. "For this and for other reasons he frankly confessed that he too had taken it upon himself to 'run Jackson out of here.'" "My informant is a decent young man and a fine student," Seager added. "He is going to be an excellent naval officer. He had simply become, quite inadvertently it would seem, a minor functionary in a system of psychological hazing so corrosive, so insensitive, and so thoroughly ingrained in Bancroft Hall that he himself was probably not aware of the injustice of the judgments he pronounced on Mr. Jackson."

Seager had tried to discuss Jackson's case with his company officer, but "talking to him was like communing with the open sea."

In his recommendation for Jackson, Seager noted to Princeton's admissions director that the former midshipman was "a bright, sensitive, highly motivated young man" who "got caught up in a system of physical and psychological hazing that boggles the imagination of any rational person this side of Captain Bligh." "He was not prepared for this disgraceful treatment, understandably resisted it, and in so doing earned the renewed and special attention of those eager upperclassmen who take it upon themselves to 'square away' the Plebes." "He had an extremely rough few months. The wonder is that he managed to do passing work while he was here; he had no opportunity whatever to approach what appears to be his academic potential. . . . He was harassed, insulted and put upon from the moment he walked in here."[18]

In the end, it might well have been racism that precipitated Jackson's downfall. From the beginning, most of his hazing had a decidedly racist edge. Instead of rolling with the punches and striving to fit in, Jackson reacted to the hazing with passive resistance and arrogance. The fact that he accorded the classroom a higher status than Bancroft Hall, a reversal of priorities most upperclassmen found objectionable, worsened the situation. Racism knocked Jackson into a downward spiral of depression and hostility that exacerbated his hazing and culminated in his departure from the Academy. Jackson's case involved neither subtle nor unintentional forms of discrimination but blatant, in-your-face racism.

The executive department made an honest effort to determine whether racism factored into Jackson's resignation. A midshipman officer, a battalion officer, and the commandant himself each asked Jackson that question point blank. When Jackson replied in the negative each time, the executive department stopped pursuing that line of inquiry. Had Jackson been willing or able to fight back against his persecutors, the administration might have confronted racism at the Academy. But with Jackson unwilling to do so, the opportunity was lost. Although discrimination did in fact occur, nobody, not even Seager, followed through on the racial aspect of the case. For Seager the primary question was academic.

Other professors from the department of English, history and government also expressed concern about the incompatibility of the academic revolution and plebe indoctrination system, although their comments did not approach the stridency of Hoof's and Seager's. Admiral Kauffman considered this criticism "a very strong attack on the whole system." He later said that the attack was "very sincerely supported by a member of the Secretariat in Washington." No doubt that person was Under Secretary Baldwin.

Seager remained on the faculty until the end of the academic year. The

Academy did not renew his contract. As for Hoof, Kauffman considered transferring him because he had gone outside the chain of command and caused no end of grief. But Hoof was terminally ill with Parkinson's disease. Kauffman regarded him as mentally unstable and viewed his actions as those of a distraught father with an incurable disease, so he permitted Hoof to serve out his tour and career at the Academy. Nevertheless, Hoof resigned at the end of the academic year, too.

The attacks by Hoof and Seager prompted Admiral Kauffman to undertake a thorough review of the plebe system during the winter of 1966/67. Kauffman formed a committee to study the impact of indoctrination on plebes' eating, sleeping, and studying habits. The committee concluded that the recent restrictions on the physical punishments upperclassmen could dole out to plebes had indeed led to an increase in the time plebes were having to spend looking up the answers to professional questions. As Kauffman told the Board of Visitors in April 1967, the upper classes were "over-compensating in the more cerebral areas." In the old days the typical punishment consisted of a few dozen push-ups that took only a few minutes to do. Now the typical punishment involved finding the answer to a question that could take a half an hour or more. In fact, the investigation found that plebes were spending an average of 90 minutes per day researching the answers to professional questions which, all too often, "were far from being professional," and that come-arounds ate up even more time. Kauffman admitted that the critics in the department of English, history and government had "one completely valid argument—that Plebes did not have enough time to study."

The plebe indoctrination committee made more than two dozen recommendations that became the basis for another round of reforms of the plebe system early in 1967. The new reforms involved the first class in formulating the rules for plebe indoctrination and charged them with the responsibility for enforcing them, preventing abuses, and punishing offenders, including their own classmates. They also limited the amount of time plebes spent on mastering plebe knowledge to 30 minutes per day and limited the source of professional questions to their current assignment in *Naval Indoctrination,* the textbook for their course on naval orientation.

Reform of the plebe indoctrination system continued under Admiral Calvert. During Tony Watson's second-class year (1968–69), Calvert appointed him head of a midshipman plebe indoctrination committee. "It was a difficult assignment," Watson recalled, "because he basically charged the committee to assess every single thing in the plebe world, including whether people should tuck their chins in, brace up, all those things, even whether there should be a plebe indoctrination system at all. We put a team of people together and looked at this for months and made recommendations that resulted in some substantial changes. Many classmates weren't fond of some of these recommendations because it appeared that they would soften the plebe system that they grew up under, but every class says that the class after them had it easier."

The new rules marked a dramatic departure from past practice. They limited the on-the-spot punishment for plebe deficiency to ten and only ten push-ups. Gone were the days when an upperclassman could have a plebe do the number of push-ups corresponding to his class year. The new rules forbade upperclassmen from making plebes do physical activity in their rooms and limited the physical activity upperclassmen could demand of plebes outside to uniform and relay races. Swimming to Baltimore, the water torture, and the like were now taboo. The new rules drastically reduced and firmly delineated the type and amount of plebe rates and professional knowledge plebes were responsible for reciting on demand. They freed plebes from having to learn the names of athletic team managers, the stars of current movies, the weights of Navy football players, and a host of other trivia. To be sure, plebes had to learn and recite an abundance of information, but that abundance was now more clearly and narrowly circumscribed. Upperclassmen could no longer fry a plebe for indoctrination deficiencies. Instead, they had to file a Plebe Performance Report (Form #3) with the plebe's squad leader, who could then assign the errant plebe a maximum of three morning runs or exercise. These changes reduced the amount of demeaning experiences plebes had to endure and cut off many of the traditional avenues upperclassmen had used to "get" plebes. They also largely relegated physical hazing to the dustbin of history. The title of an article in the *Washington Post* neatly summed up the impact of the revolution in plebe indoctrination: "Annapolis Looks Brighter without the Haze."[19]

The reforms did not prevent plebe indoctrination from serving its traditional purposes. Ric Samuels recalled being run after parents' weekend at the end of plebe summer. "One of the toughest things is when your parents come and visit you for that weekend and then they go," he said. "Our platoon leader just ran the stew out of us that night. I remember all of us laughing because we were just getting hammered, but it was so funny that you didn't think about mom and the family leaving. You just thought, 'Man, we're really getting our fannies handed to us.' It built unity in the group and got your mind off of being homesick."

Plebe indoctrination still had its dark side, as well. "Things went on even though they were illegal," recalled Samuels. "They could physically stress you, but they were very careful about things that could injure people. That was the dividing line. You could do anything as long as you didn't permanently hurt somebody." By the time of Chuck Cole's plebe year (1972–73), things like shoving out, swimming to Baltimore, and the water torture had gone with the wind. "I came in during the time when they were starting to enforce the plebe indoctrination manual," Cole recalled. Nevertheless, it was woe to the plebe who dared complain about whatever treatment the upperclassmen were meting out. "'Oh, you want to go by the book?' they would say. 'Well, let's go get the book and see how closely we can follow it.' Then they'd throw the whole book at you," Cole said. "It was all legal, but there was so much of it, you were better off not saying anything." The intensity of indoctrination still varied from one company to the next.

Upperclassmen proved ingenious in inventing new indignities. A perennial favorite was inviting a plebe to "hang around and listen to music." The more artful firsty or segundo conveyed the impression that he was finally beginning to view the plebe a human being. Soon after the plebe arrived at the upperclassman's room, however, he was quickly disabused of any such notion. "You came in and you hung by your arms from the shower curtain rod while they played music," Kerwin Miller recalled. Another favorite was "calling home," where upperclassmen made plebes take a shower in their uniform while pretending to dial a telephone. Still another indignity involved having plebes brace themselves spread-eagled into the alcove above the bunk bed, then holding bayonets under their stomachs and timing how long they could stay up there. "There were uniform races," Miller said. "Come arounds in socks, jocks, locks, and boondocks. That's all you'd have on. That was clearly degrading."

But for sheer humiliation, nothing beat the "atomic sit-up." "It was a set up, really," Miller recalled. "The upperclass would get a plebe and say, 'Hey, you can't do this atomic sit up.' And they'd always get another plebe in on it. 'Didn't you do an atomic sit up?' They'd show you another upperclass. He'd get down. They'd have people hold his shoulders. And he's blindfolded. They act like he's trying to do the sit up. They're holding him back. 'You can't do it. It's an atomic sit up.' They explain the forces involved and why this doesn't work. When you get down there, the set-up is, after they put your blindfold on, they get this other guy who drops his drawers and puts shaving cream on his behind. And sure enough, they'd always get the biggest, fattest guy with the biggest ass to put shaving cream on. He's leaning over you. You're trying to push up against somebody. Then they let you go. You come all the way up. You end up with your head right in the crack of the guy's behind. They'd take your picture." Marv King described such indignities as "college prank stuff."

Bruce Franklin sensed anger among upperclassmen who resented not being allowed to treat plebes as badly as they had been treated. "It was as if they had gotten trashed when they came through and they just felt it necessary to trash somebody," he recalled. "But they couldn't do it, so they resorted to the psychological." Franklin endured a stretch of all-call come-arounds, where he was "booked" for every authorized come-around period before each meal. Upperclassmen gave him an assignment at each one. Some he could do easily using *Reef Points*. Others required more extensive research. Come-arounds and questioning at meal times were interfering with ability to sleep, to eat, and to study. Franklin did not, however, specifically attribute the treatment to racism.

Leo Williams could identify nothing in his treatment as being racially motivated. Neither could Bert Freeman, Tony Watson, Ric Samuels, Charlie Boyd, Ken Dunn, Cary Hithon, Jeff Sapp, or Marv King. "I was treated pretty much as one of the plebes," King recalled. "I got no more or less harassment than the rest." Upperclassmen had Chuck Cole doing push-ups and coming around to their rooms, but no more so than his white classmates. Ric Samuels had the same view. "I never felt like I would get run out because I was black," he recalled. "I knew I wasn't going to get any slack, but I never felt threatened."

Kerwin Miller did receive extra attention, but not necessarily because he was black. "I used something which has worked for me in most cases when under stress," he recalled, "and that's comic relief. We would be in tense situations. Getting yelled at, screaming, people falling out, a couple of guys crying, and all that, and I would crack a joke and break the tension. It would bring stuff on me, but then it would lighten up everybody else." "I got demerits like anybody," he added. "I'd get demerits for being a smart ass. I knew the upper class would eventually think it was funny. But I cleaned my room. I made sure my stuff was squared away. I knew my rates."

Black midshipmen who experienced no discrimination themselves believed that it existed at the Academy. Although Bert Freeman never thought he was mistreated because of his race, black classmates told him they thought they were. Similarly, Ed Gilmore had no racial problems himself, but he knew another black midshipman who did. Some of Kerwin Miller's black classmates told him that they too were having racial problems. One African American alumnus had two black classmates who believed they were hazed so severely because of their race that it led to their departure. One of them was made to spend so much time looking up the answers to professional questions that he bilged academically.

About as many plebes did have firsthand experience with racially motivated mistreatment as those who did not. Sometimes an upperclassman would order a plebe to "moon" another upperclassman. On one occasion an upperclassman told Bruce Henry to "run down to so-and-so's room and show him the dark side of the moon." Chuck Reddix never encountered anything so blatant. "I wouldn't say that there was anybody who was definitely gunning for you," he recalled. "Of course every now and then you'd find somebody who probably didn't like blacks and therefore would try to make your life a little bit more miserable. You would not be able to figure out the guy's motivations. You have a choice. You can decide that he's down on your case because you're a plebe, or he's down on your case because you're black. Which choice you make is a matter of personal make-up. By and large, for me, personally, not too many of the upper class seemed to be gunning for me because I was black. I had one second class later on in plebe year who I think probably gave me a harder time because I was black. He was from Texas, also. But make no mistake, the man was fair. I thought he was unreasonable, but the man never went out and out to kill me. He might have leaned on me a little harder, but I can't say that he ever mistreated me. Still, I hate the Dallas Cowboys to this day because of him."

Black midshipmen also had to endure more subtle, perhaps even unintentional, forms of discrimination. "My white classmates never noticed that I would stand at attention longer than them because the upperclass never gave me carry on," recalled Kerwin Miller. "They just never saw that as something that happened because I was black. My roommates were spooned by people who didn't spoon me. When upper class came into the room, I would be standing at attention the whole time while they were there. They were calling my roommates by their first names. Then they'd look over, and say 'Oh yeah, you can carry on.' I'd been standing at attention for an hour. I thought, 'Why couldn't you have said that when you first came in?' I don't know whether it could be said to be racially motivated or what, but there were a lot of people who had spooned my roommates and hadn't spooned me."

An even more grueling instance of hazing left Miller wondering whether the motivation was racial. "I had the experience of sleeping up on the roof," he recalled. "They made a white guy sleep up there too. 'The only reason that I'm up here is because they don't like you,' the guy said. 'They didn't want it to look like they were targeting you, so they made me sleep up here.' Well, he was a good guy. He was squared away. They'd come get us at ten o'clock and we'd go up there. One of us would have to stay awake to make sure the other one didn't fall. I don't know if anybody else in my company experienced that. But once again, could you say it was racial when, in fact, it was a black midshipman and a white one up there? No. Explicitly, I can't point to anything racially motivated. If you've ever been in a situation that you have a gut feeling that you're being treaty differently, but you have no evidence of it, you still have the gut feeling."

In its severest form, racially motivated mistreatment could drive a black plebe out of the Academy. Although Lamar Chapman bilged academically during his first semester, he believed that the real reason for his departure was racism. "I was too angry to stay at Annapolis," he recalled. "The daily racism and prejudice was much more than I was prepared to handle at the time. Boxing was an outlet for me. However, I wasn't boxing for the sport of boxing. I wanted to hurt someone in the ring just because I was hurting outside of the ring. I made several applications to resign from the Academy. The company officer and battalion officer always seemed to misplace my resignation form. The academic board even offered me the chance to attend NAPS while I continued to box for Navy. It was an offer I gladly refused."

"We're Not Going to Stand for It"

LIKE THEIR predecessors, black midshipmen from the classes of 1969–79 had several sources of support to lean on when things got rough. By and large, they encountered little prejudice from their sports teammates. In fact, a team generally became a primary source of support for everyone on it, particularly at the varsity level. Athletes helped other athletes, regardless of race. "I don't give a hoot what you played," recalled varsity football player Cary Hithon. "If you were an athlete, other athletes looked out for you." James Jackson recalled that "coaches and the officer representatives for teams made sure that there was no undue or illegal harassment, period." Jeff Sapp, who became an outstanding nose guard on the varsity football team as a walk-on, received invaluable support and encouragement from football coaches Jack Cloud, Rick Lantz, and George Welch as well as athletic director Bo Coppedge, all of whom were white.

Since midshipmen could not play varsity football their first year, Don Montgomery played on the plebe team during his first fall in Annapolis. "We were tight," he recalled. "I never had a problem with my classmates. They were good people. We went nine and one." After plebe year, however, Montgomery discovered that some of the upperclass players remained infected by the kind of attitude that had dogged Darryl Hill and Jim Frezzell. Black football players were still persona non grata as far as these people were concerned. Such an attitude was new to Don Montgomery. "In my experience, the object was to win," he recalled. "It didn't matter what color the guy next to you was." One day while watching highlight films, a white youngster on the team called him a "nigger" and tried to pick a fight with him. "I'd like to whip his butt today," he recalled. "The only reason that I didn't beat the living daylights out of him was that I wanted to graduate." Montgomery, a 6′5″, 240-pound offensive lineman, vented his frustrations on the practice field. "I took it out on everybody," he said. "I used to just pancake those suckers. At practice, I'd be munching them and knocking the living daylights out of them. I was just hateful, man. I think they resented that. I was supposed to be a teammate. We were supposed to work hard, but you're not supposed to enjoy it as much as I was."

Nevertheless, the team pulled for Montgomery during his hour of darkness. "My mom died my sophomore year," he recalled. "It was just before the Duke game. I was coming off the practice field. As I was walking back Coach Forzano was standing out there. His face was real red and he had a big old lump in his throat. 'Coach,' I said, 'What's wrong?' 'Your mom's in a coma,' he said. I hated everybody except for my mom. I didn't care about anybody else, only my mom. She died later in the week. We had a funeral in Baltimore for our friends there and then we had a funeral in Cartersville. As the funeral in Baltimore was just getting started, the doors opened and the whole football team came in; all the coaches and the whole team. I had no idea they were coming. As hateful as I was, I didn't know anybody even cared. When they showed up, it was an eye-opener for me. That changed everything. Because the person who was getting all my love was my mom. And after they did that for me, I became a teammate and I wanted to graduate. For my mom. And every day after that it got better and better."

The situation for African Americans on the football team got better, too. Cary Hithon played offensive lineman all four years, making the varsity squad the last two and starting as a firsty. He encountered no racism from teammates. In 1976, Jeff Sapp became the first African American to become co-captain of the varsity football team, an honor accorded him by the vote of his teammates, most of whom were white.

Like the black midshipmen from previous classes, Leo Williams and his classmates found a refuge from the Academy's rigors and a home away from home at Lillie Mae Chase's house. "Hank Shaw and I had been out in town one Sunday afternoon," recalled Williams. "We came back to change clothes at Lil's before we had to be back in the gate. This Marine captain came into the house and asked us who we were and how we had the gall to be out of uniform in town. Lil just stood there with her face as straight as could be, without cracking a smile, and let him go through this whole routine. Hank and I were standing at attention almost to the point that our trousers were around our knees, because this Marine captain was dressing us down. When he had finished, he and Lil looked at each other and just burst out laughing. 'Hey, you guys, this is Pat Prout,' she said. 'He went through exactly what you're going through, so don't take any guff off of him.' We just wiped our brows. Lillie Mae was one of those people who was always there when we needed her."

During Leo Williams's midshipman years, Lillie Mae Chase handed the baton to Peggy Kimbo as the mother away from home for black midshipmen. By the late 1960s, Lillie Mae had grown too old and the black midshipmen too numerous for her to open her home to them all. Nevertheless, she continued serving as unofficial sponsor for many black midshipmen until the early 1990s. She died of heart failure at her home on 6 March 2001. Many of her former "couch lizards" attended her funeral. The pall bearers and flower bearers included Robert Newton, '63, Buddy Clark, '68, Tony Watson, Floyd Grayson, Frank Simmons, Bruce Henry, Stanley Carter, and Leo Williams. The program for her funeral service listed all the places at which she had been employed. "Her most important job," it concluded, was "sponsor for the black midshipmen." An obituary in the local newspaper hailed her as "unsung but vital support in the Academy's effort to retain minority students." On 21 February 2004, the city of Annapolis honored her by designating a portion of College Avenue near her former home "Lillie Mae Chase Way."[1]

Peggy Kimbo's involvement began on Thanksgiving Day 1966. "That was back in the days when you couldn't go home for Thanksgiving," recalled Tony Watson. "We had to be at the Naval Academy." Lillie Mae Chase wanted to invite the black midshipmen for dinner, but there were too many for her to have them all over, so she asked Peggy Kimbo to take some of them. Peggy agreed. "That was the night we created family with Peggy Kimbo," said Tony Watson.

After that, Peggy Kimbo did for black midshipmen what Lillie Mae Chase had done. "The classes before mine were raised, for the most part, by Lilly Mae Chase," recalled Leo Williams. "Beginning with my class, and through about the class of '72, '73, some of '74, we largely migrated to Peggy Kimbo, but we still maintained our ties with Lillie Mae." Bert Freeman recalled that "Peggy Kimbo's home was always open to us. If you wanted to go some place to sit down, talk, relax, and just chill out or act like it was home, we would go to Peggy's house. We went there all the time." Tony Watson has similarly fond memories of Peggy. "We could be there day or night, raid her refrigerator, and she never asked us for anything," he recalled. "She's as much a part of the fabric of who we are as any member of our class."

The Naval Academy has always figured prominently in Peggy Kimbo's life. She was born in 1930 and raised on College Avenue in Annapolis. Her mother worked as a domestic; her father worked at the Academy laundry for more than forty years. "We were part of the Academy," she recalled of her childhood. "We played ball up against the wall. We always made friends with the midshipmen back in those days. They gave us tennis rackets. They'd bring us out tennis balls. They were really great."

Peggy Kimbo worked at the Galway Bay Irish Restaurant on Maryland Avenue, formerly the Little Campus restaurant. She started there in 1957, working behind the soda fountain. When the last show let out in nearby Circle Theater on Saturday, midshipmen poured into the restaurant. Peggy worked hard serving them milkshakes and banana splits. Midshipmen also crowded into the place for breakfast after the Sunday morning service in the chapel. Peggy later worked as a waitress and eventually became the maître d'. She has been photographed with members of Congress, Maryland governors, even President Bill Clinton.[2]

"Peggy Kimbo is 'Miss Annapolis,'" said Tony Watson. "She's only about 4'8", but she's ebullient, packed full of enthusiasm; just one of the greatest people on earth. She loves the Naval Academy and she loves the Navy." Leo Williams described her as "a folk hero in the Annapolis community." "Everybody knows her," he said. "Annapolis is a very small town. Many of the blacks in Annapolis are related somehow. Once we got to know Peggy, and people knew that Peggy was kind of our godmother, so to speak, they really protected us within that community. We felt very safe and secure there and it gave us the social outlet that we were looking for at the same time. She had kids who were younger than we were. It was kind of an extended family."

Bert Freeman found this welcoming attitude throughout the black community of Annapolis. "The entire African American community was just so welcoming to the black midshipmen," he recalled. "It was just amazing, on a day-to-day, minute-to-minute basis, everywhere we went, we were just absolutely supported in a lot of different ways. It was nice to see regular people." The McManus and Diggs families soon opened their homes the way Lil Chase and Peggy Kimbo had. Black Annapolitans considered Cary Hithon a local person, took him under their wing, and followed his career after he graduated. "The minority community in town was very supportive," recalled Charlie Boyd. "We could tell they were pulling for us to succeed."

Bert Freeman found this especially true among the Academy's black civilian workers. "They loved us," he said. "They were absolutely supportive of us. They always had wonderful and encouraging words to say. They were always glad to stop to take a minute to talk to us. They always made me feel good, and you could feel the bond among the civilian blacks who worked there as well as the bond that we had with each other." The black workers did whatever they could to help. "You need something, let me know," they would say to black midshipmen. "Somehow I'll get it to you."

Black midshipmen also received support from local churches. Lillie Mae Chase introduced many of her couch lizards to the Mount Moriah A.M.E. Church in Annapolis. The First Baptist Church and the Mount Zion A.M.E. Church, of which many of the Academy's black workers were members, also "made life better for black midshipmen," as James Jackson explained. "The pastors of these churches occasionally preached at the Academy and infused black culture to all involved."[3] Many black families from St. Paul's Lutheran Church, the church Ev Greene attended, invited him to their homes after Sunday services.

Black plebes found their black classmates to be another important source of support. "The biggest thing in plebe summer was to meet other blacks who were in my class," recalled Kerwin Miller. "We had people to relate to who had similar backgrounds. That helped us out a lot. It boosted our hope that we were going to make it through." Just seeing another black midshipman helped. "I remember once when I was marching during plebe summer," recalled Bobby Watts, "and I hadn't seen another black face the whole time I was there, maybe two or three weeks, and I saw another black midshipman in another company marching in another direction and I just stopped and pointed at him. And of course, the other midshipmen behind me marched into me." Bert Freeman supported black classmates who thought they were having difficulties because of their race by talking with them about it. Similarly, Bruce Franklin commiserated with black classmates who were having as difficult a time as he was.

Like the black midshipmen who entered the Academy before 1965, the African Americans in the classes of 1969–79 tended to cross company and class boundaries more readily than white midshipmen to develop and maintain friendships. As long as fewer than three dozen African Americans entered with each class, the Academy deliberately spread out incoming black plebes, usually one per company, in the belief that it would enhance integration. "Our opportunity to meet was on weekends," recalled Bruce Henry. "During the week, we sat with our companies at our assigned dining tables in the mess hall. But on the weekends, we could sit where we wanted to. The class of '68 would say to the class of '70 when we were plebes, 'Come join us at this table.' And we would all sit together. It was a table of black midshipmen and this is when we communicated. It was the most effective way for all of us to catch up with who was doing what, who was encountering what problems, who had some tips, suggestions, or what was going on socially." Black plebes often brought their white roommates along. As they became upperclassmen themselves, the black midshipmen in the class of 1970 invited the African Americans in the next three classes to join them at weekend meals.

The fact that African Americans liked to sit together bothered some white officers. "As a first classman, I remember sitting at the head of a dining table one weekend noon meal," Bruce Henry recalled. "That particular day, I was at the head of one of two tables, both of which were mixed, but very heavily skewed black. It was easy to pick us out in a sea of white midshipmen. I was sitting next to the main aisle. I heard the officer of the day (OOD) coming down the aisle because he was wearing his sword and it was clanking. He stopped behind my chair and everybody at my table and in the area became silent. I knew that something was getting ready to happen.

'Who is the senior man here?' said the OOD.

'I am, commander,' I said as I stood up. 'Can I help you, sir?'

'What's the story on this table?' he said.

I knew exactly what was on his mind, but I said, 'I don't understand, sir.'

'This table here and the table next to it,' he said, 'they're all black.'

I looked at the table where I was sitting and at the next table. I then looked around the entire mess hall doing a 360 while I was in front of him. Then I looked right back at him. 'Commander,' I said, 'the only color I see here is Navy blue.'

He looked at the two tables and then he looked around the mess hall. 'And so it is,' he said. 'Carry on.'"

"A number of white midshipmen felt concerned about that," recalled Bobby Watts. "'Why do you guys want to sit together?' they would ask. 'What are you guys plotting?' I told my classmates who asked me that, 'What do you think twelve black midshipmen are going to do against four thousand? It doesn't make any sense. If you look around, you see tables and tables full of white midshipmen. You don't think anything about it. But you see one table with black midshipmen and you get all excited. Even if we didn't sit together, you would still see table after table of white midshipmen. I don't understand your concern.'" As Watts told one of his white company mates, "You sit with guys who aren't in the company who you know and like and want to be with, so why can't I do the same?" "He didn't have an answer for that," Watts recalled. "They had this perception that when blacks got together, there would be problems. Maybe it stemmed from some of the things that were happening in the fleet on the various ships." On one occasion, a white upperclassman threatened to charge the blacks sitting at two tables together with mutiny. "He backed down when a black upperclassman challenged him," Watts said. Even a group of black midshipmen standing together in town aroused suspicion, he added.

On one Saturday afternoon when Tony Watson was a second classman, the commandant happened to see all the black midshipmen sitting together. "At the time we had maybe twenty-four black midshipmen at the Academy," Watson recalled. "We took up two tables. Each table had twelve seats." Watson happened to be brigade commander of his class, so the commandant summoned Watson to his office the following Monday. "Midshipman Watson," he said, "what is this thing going on with all these black midshipmen at these tables on Saturday?" Watson was standing at attention before his desk, with his "eyes in the boat" (looking straight ahead). The question stunned him. "Well sir," he said, "There are only two tables with twelve black midshipmen. There are probably five hundred tables with twelve white midshipmen. I've never heard anybody complain about the tables with the twelve white midshipmen." The commandant pondered Watson's reply during a long, uncomfortable silence. "You've got a point," he said at last. "You're dismissed." "Frankly, that event really angered me," Watson said. "I've never forgotten it. I can remember it as clear as day. The commandant called me in and hauled me on the carpet for something like that."

Many black midshipmen in the classes of 1969–79 got to know their black classmates through the swimming sub squad. "Quite a few of us came from city-type environments and hadn't had the opportunity to swim," recalled Bobby Watts. "I thought I knew how to swim. When I got there, I found out I didn't, so I was on the sub squad. And you looked around, and I guess 95 percent of the midshipmen on the sub squad were black. That's how I realized there was more of us than just the one guy I saw marching." Ev Greene met most of his black classmates on the sub squad. "There were a lot of us in that pool," recalled Cary Hithon. African American midshipmen were so prevalent on the swimming sub squad that it was nicknamed "the black tide."[4]

Most black plebes found black upperclassmen to be their best source of support. Just as the blacks in the class of 1965 had mentored those in the class of 1968, the latter mentored those in the class of 1970. Charlie Bolden, Buddy Clark, Frank Simmons, and Gil Lucas took Bruce Henry and his black classmates under their wing, as Henry recalled. "If we were having problems academically, they would certainly assist us, either to get tutoring or extra instruction of some sort. Or if an upperclassman was giving us undue pressure, then they would speak with that upperclassman to understand why. I never had to ask them for extra instruction or ask them to get an upperclassman off my back, but there're a couple of others who did take advantage of that. But, if you weren't doing what you were supposed to do to be a good midshipman, they'd tell you that too."

"The blacks in the class of '68 made it a point to make themselves known to us," recalled Bert Freeman, "particularly Charlie Bolden. He was very visible to us. We met his family and did many different kinds of things with them, and he made it a point to sit down and talk to us about different things. It was very helpful." The black midshipmen in the class of 1970 continued the tradition. "Time passed and the class of '68 graduated and moved on," Bruce Henry recalled. "And we, the class of '70, moved up."

In fact, Leo Williams and his classmates created a slightly more formal arrangement for helping black plebes. "We were very focused on making sure that the African Americans who were in the classes behind us knew that they had a support organization," Williams recalled. "We actually formed a loose organization, a loose African American network, if you will. We called them all in, much to the disapproval of the Naval Academy establishment. I mean, at that time there were no African American support groups. It was something that was seen as, for the most part, I think, either insubordinate or perhaps even subversive. Hank Shaw, who started with us in the class of '70 and was turned back and graduated in the class of '71, was the initiator of the first meeting. Tony Watson and I collaborated with Hank in doing that, but it was Hank's idea. 'Hey look,' he said, 'we need to get these guys together and let them know that there's really a support organization there.' 'Okay,' we said, 'let's go do it.' And the three of us actually put the first meeting together. That was in '68. We were second class at that time. It was not a formal organization. It was ad hoc and it was just to let everyone know that we were there when they needed us."

Ric Samuels recalled that black upperclassmen looked out for him and his fellow black plebes. "Walt Crump, '72, would come down to my room, pretending to harass us," Samuels recalled. "But he was checking on us to make sure everything was okay. Most of the guys would take any opportunity they got to take the stripes off and talk man to man without regard to rank or class standing. They'd look out for you."

The black midshipmen from the classes of 1971, '72, and '73, in turn, continued the tradition for the classes that followed. When he was an upperclassman, Ric Samuels found that many black plebes who came from predominantly black neighborhoods wondered how they would fit in. "Hey," Samuels would tell them, "contrary to what you're going to hear from a lot of your classmates and a lot of the upper class, you're not in here because somebody's giving you a handout. You've earned the right to be here. You were selected from a large group of highly qualified people. You can perform as well as any of these guys." "When you shot straight with them," Samuels recalled, "they realized you weren't going to give them preferential treatment, but you were going to watch their back. They knew that if they were getting harassed unnecessarily, that they could come to somebody like me or one of my classmates. It was a tight-knit group. When I came there, there were forty-four of us total before the class of '75 came in. We all knew each other. During June Week, we all partied together. The plebes could party with the upperclass because it was such a small, tight community."

Bobby Watts provided similar help. "I talked to all the black plebes," he recalled. "I sat down and I would counsel all of them. I would find out what was going on. I would say most of the black midshipmen knew me. I'd give them my two cents as to what they needed to do. I would give them guidance on a regular basis and I would smack them upside the head, verbally, if need be."

Commander Ken Johnson strengthened the support network early in 1972, while in the process of forming the National Naval Officers Association. "We're about to start this organization," Johnson said at a meeting of the black midshipmen. "We're going to provide not only more black input into the Academy, but we're going to provide a support network for you who are already here." Chuck Reddix recalled several meetings with Johnson. "Periodically we'd meet with him and he'd talk with us to monitor how we were doing," Reddix said. As a plebe, Kerwin Miller found it heartening to have black upperclassmen show genuine concern for his well-being and progress at these meetings. "Just to have them hit you on the back and say, 'Hey, how are things going?' That was very uplifting to a lot of us," he said.

The tradition continued through the class of 1979. "The upperclass black midshipmen took it upon themselves to look out for us," noted Charlie Boyd, recalling his plebe year. "In fact, if it wasn't for their help, many of us might not have made it out. They gave us hope, set an example, and made sure we had a chance to relieve some of the stress from time to time."

Black midshipmen who socialized together and supported each other referred to themselves by several informal nicknames, such as the "El Dorado Social Club."[5] The most prominent nickname was the "Seventh Battalion" or "Seventh Batt." Seventh Batt met informally to plan parties and social events, usually associated with the Army-Navy game and June Week. James Jackson recalled how the group called its meetings. "It was probably not going to be politically correct to say, 'We want all the black midshipmen to go to a meeting in Room 101,'" he said. In the early 1970s, the Academy tested minority midshipmen for sickle cell anemia as part of the physical examination. "So to outsmart the administration, when we wanted to call a meeting of all the black midshipmen, we just had an announcement made over the loudspeakers before dinner requesting all people who got tested for sickle cell to please report to Room 101."

Jeff Sapp considered the group his primary source of support. "I wouldn't have made it without Seventh Batt," he recalled. Sapp became acquainted with the group through other black football players.

But it wasn't skin color that drew African Americans together. As Cary Hithon recalled, Seventh Batt "was born out of a real need to bond. People group themselves with those that they feel more comfortable with or have something in common with. It's a cultural thing. Even though we may have been from different parts of the country, we all had like stories or like experiences. We individually may have been a lot different, but our cultures were probably very similar. When you wanted to say something to someone who would understand what you were going through, you couldn't turn to your white roommate, because he wouldn't understand."

Jeff Sapp believed that the bonds black midshipmen forged with each other created a heartfelt sense of duty to mentor younger shipmates. The essence of that sense of duty stayed with him for the rest of his life. "You've got to bring other people along," he said during a 2006 interview. "As they get stronger, you get stronger."

James Jackson thought that the presence of black upperclassmen prevented negative racial attitudes from manifesting themselves. "No black upperclassman would let one of his classmates use a racial slur against a black plebe," he recalled. "That just wasn't going to happen." As black plebes became upperclassmen, they too prevented classmates from using racial slurs. "When I was a sophomore, junior, and senior," Jackson said, "I would let all the typical plebe things go on—challenging the plebes to learn their rates and yelling and screaming—but I would not for a second allow one of my roommates or classmates to use a racial slur. If black upperclassmen found out that something was going on, we as a group would go to the upperclassman who was doing it and say, 'Hold it, that's off limits, we're not going to stand for it.' Incidents would happen maybe two or three times a year. We would hear of an overzealous upperclassmen using racial slurs and would go have a talk with him. When I was a first classman and a company commander and a striper, I got a chance to stand watch throughout the Academy. If a junior or sophomore was using racial slurs toward a plebe, I could nail them for demerits and conduct unbecoming a midshipman. And because my white classmates and I had been through hell together, it would be absolutely abnormal for one them, in my presence, to use a racial slur. We had too much loyalty. That's what kept down slurs. The white upperclassmen didn't allow it either."

Black upperclassmen managed to stop the racially motivated mistreatment of black plebes in several instances. Will Merrell was given all-call comearounds and made to brace up permanently by a firsty who objected to his reading *Muhammad Speaks,* a black newspaper published in Chicago. After about three weeks of such treatment, Charlie Rucks, then a firsty serving on the regimental staff, intervened and put a stop to it. "The blacks at the Academy formed one of the strongest support networks I have ever seen," Merrell recalled.

Help from a black upperclassman enabled Eddie Graves to survive an effort to run him out of the Academy. One particular segundo had Graves on all-call come-arounds. He made Graves stand braced up outside his door before every meal, even on weekends. "I was his lawn jockey," Graves recalled bitterly. "He was dead set on running my black ass out of there." The segundo grilled Graves incessantly while allowing white plebes into his room to play the stereo. He also grilled Graves at tables. The constant questioning deprived Graves of food at meals and time to study in the evenings. Graves didn't know

whether the segundo's motivation was racial or personal. He did know, however, that he was the only plebe the segundo was running this way and the
only African American in his class in the company.

The hazing almost pushed Graves over the edge. "One day in the mess
hall," he recalled, "one of the upperclass was trying to get me to answer
questions without eating. Every time I picked up the fork, he would ask me a
question. So I had to put the fork down. I couldn't even get the three chews
and a swallow. Finally, after about the sixth question, I pulled back from the
table and said, 'Let's go,' meaning, 'What else is there?' We marched out of
the mess hall and went upstairs. It seemed like they already had this set up.
He took me into a room. There were six of them. They were all around me,
each shouting orders, instructions, barking this and that, pulling me from one
side to the other, just like a jack in the box." Graves considered turning in his
resignation but decided to gut it out.

Bobby Watts, himself a segundo, figured out what was going on after
encountering Graves at his usual post outside his persecutor's door one weekend. "It's 6:15 on Saturday night," Watts asked. "What are you doing braced
up, Graves?"

"Sir!" Graves answered. "The second classman has me braced up, sir!"

"He's got you coming around and bracing up and he's not even here?"

"Yes sir!"

Watts and several classmates, black and white, confronted Graves's persecutor. "Why are you riding this guy as hard as you are?" Watts asked. "He's
proven himself." The harassment petered out after that.

On two separate occasions, black plebes who thought upperclassmen were
running them unfairly complained to Ric Samuels. Samuels asked them their
rates. They couldn't answer correctly. "If you don't know your rates," Samuels said, "then you deserve to get your butt run."

In some cases, black upperclassmen were harder on black plebes than their
white classmates. Kerwin Miller recalled a harrowing encounter with Charlie
Rucks during plebe summer. "There were twelve black midshipmen who were
first class when we were plebes," Miller said. "These guys were rough. They
had been through a lot. You could tell. Well, you were never supposed to go
out without your name tag on. When you didn't wear your name tag, you had
to go find seventy-five name tags—your class year—from your classmates, or
you could find upper class name tags. I think one first-class name tag equaled
ten plebes. They knew how difficult it was to try to get a first class to give you
a name tag. So if you didn't wear yours, you had to go outside your company and find seventy-five and come back and show your upper class you had
seventy-five. I saw Rucks, plebe summer, second set, first black upper class
I saw. He was the only one, probably, in the whole summer program. I just

thought it was good to see a brother in uniform. I stopped him and I said, 'Sir. Midshipman Miller, Fourth Class. May I have your name tag?' This guy got right up in my face and started screaming all kinds of obscenities. I thought, 'My God!' I must have stood there braced up for about an hour with this guy just yelling at me. 'Who the hell do you think you are?!' he screamed. 'You better get the fuck out of my face!!' That was the only time I remember actually being afraid the whole summer. He did eventually give me the name tag. I had to pay for it, though. We became real good friends after that."

A black second classman, Larry W. Calhoun, '73, subjected Chuck Cole to his worst come-arounds. "If I survived him," Cole recalled, "I could survive anybody else." Bobby Watts gave Isaiah Owens, '76, a hard time to help prepare him for what he believed were hard times to come. "Ike Owens was a real jock, a heavily recruited football player," Watts recalled. "During plebe summer he was invited over to the commandant's house, or the superintendent's house, one of them, and of course, all the upperclassmen are like, 'We're going to get this guy.' The coaches were trying to protect him. And he was a cocky kind of guy. He didn't think he needed to know any of his rates. He and I had a long discussion. I took personal care of him for the summer. He had a very difficult summer. But that helped him to survive. 'The coaches aren't going to be there for you all the time,' I told him. 'There's going to be an off-season and you're going to be on your own. These guys are out to get you and I'm not going to protect you. I'm going to make it so you will survive here.' I had a concern. 'Is this going to look like I'm treating him harder because he's black and I'm black?' I thought about that, but I thought, 'If I don't do this to him, he's not going to survive. If I don't do this to him, he won't make it through.' And he survived."

Even as black upperclassmen continued to look out for black plebes and black midshipmen continued to cross company and class lines to forge friendships, by the mid-1970s African American midshipmen began to blend into the brigade more and segregate themselves less. "Black unity kind of waned," recalled Ric Samuels. "When the class of '75 came in, there wasn't the tight-knit group we had during my first couple of years. It was kind of strange when this huge group came in. There were blacks you didn't know. During my plebe year, everybody knew each other. We stay in touch today, not only with the guys in our class, but in previous classes. When the large groups started coming in, you lost a lot of that unity." Bobby Watts formed the same impression: "As we got larger numbers of black plebes, it was interesting to watch the dynamics. The plebes interacted more with their white counterparts, went out with them and so forth, much more so than we did when we were plebes. The Academy was going out and aggressively recruiting more minorities. They were broadening their scope outside of the inner cities. They were getting kids who came from predominantly suburban schools, which had a very small black population. More and more suburban blacks entered, and they came there with less baggage, I guess, than our generation came with. Society was changing, even in that short span. These kids had grown up just a little bit differently. Their relationship with their white counterparts in high school was different. They didn't necessarily live in little black enclaves like I did, and so they were a little bit more comfortable."

When he was a firsty, Floyd Grayson, '65, knew all of the black midshipmen in his class and in the three classes below as well as their families. At that time, however, there were fewer than a dozen black midshipmen in all four classes. When Cary Hithon was a firsty, there were some two hundred black midshipmen in all four classes, and he never knew them all. Chuck Cole never knew all the African Americans in his own class, not to mention in the whole the brigade.

Although Bert Freeman got along well with white classmates inside the Yard, he socialized largely with other black midshipmen outside. He also found that other black midshipmen were his biggest source of support. "Most of the help we got was from people who looked like us," he recalled.

During the mid-1970s, black midshipmen didn't necessarily socialize only with other black midshipmen. Chuck Cole had no problems socializing outside of the Yard with white classmates. "I probably had stronger bonds to the guys in my company than I did to some of the other black midshipmen," he recalled, "just because I was with them more often in the company area." In fact some black midshipmen did not socialize much with other black midshipmen at all. A group of black midshipmen would "meet down by the Coke machine in one of the exits of King Hall," Don Montgomery recalled. "They'd go there and talk trash and stuff. I was never a part of that." Chuck Reddix observed that social groupings of midshipmen tended *not* to form along racial lines. "Plebes seemed to associate more with the people who were in their squad, or their roommates, or their company mates than anybody else," he recalled. "That's probably because of forced cohabitation, for lack of a better word. Over time, you end up associating with guys in your particular classes in your major, guys you met and like and want to spend time with. Ethnically speaking, there were several groups going. There were some guys who would just hang around with anybody and everybody. Some of the black guys would tend to hang around together, because they either knew each other from before, or knew each other after they got there, and were more comfortable that way. And there were some guys who just didn't hang around with anybody." Cary Hithon numbered among those who associated with other black midshipmen largely out of comfort.

Most of the black midshipmen who graduated in the 1960s were sponsored by Lillie Mae Chase. Many of the black midshipmen who graduated in the early 1970s were sponsored by Peggy Kimbo. Chuck Cole had no contact with African American families in town. Neither did Marv King. When his girlfriend came to visit, Marv arranged for her to stay in a white family's home. During this period, more and more local families, white as well as back, were making their homes available to black midshipmen.

Taken together, these changes in patterns of socialization amounted to a diffusion of the black midshipmen's subculture. Although there remained one or more groups of black midshipmen who counted other black midshipmen as their best friends at the Academy and partied among themselves outside the Yard, not every black midshipman identified with these groups. Diffusion of the black subculture was by no means tantamount to its disintegration, however, for black upperclassmen remained the most important source of support for black plebes.

The Academy itself increasingly became an important source of support for black midshipmen. The administration created and nurtured that impression by making genuine and visible attempts to tackle racial problems. The impulse toward reform came from the bottom up as well as from the top down. Because of President Johnson's personal interest in integration at the Academy, racial issues—and not just those connected with recruiting—appeared on Admiral Kauffman's agenda from the start of his superintendency.

Kauffman told Rear Admiral Lawrence Heyworth, commandant of midshipmen from August 1967 to November 1969, that he did not want any racial problems to arise. Kauffman didn't think there would be any problems, he said, if black plebes were treated the same as white plebes. Admiral Heyworth repeated that philosophy to company and battalion officers during weekly meetings. "I would make off-the-cuff remarks, repeating what the superintendent had said," Heyworth recalled. "But there weren't any specific guidelines."[6]

After appointing him to the Board of Visitors, President Johnson told Dr. James Nabrit that he wanted to see a black professor on the Academy's faculty. Nabrit recommended Samuel P. Massie. Dr. Massie interviewed for a position in the Academy's chemistry department in December 1965 and became its first African American professor on 1 February 1966. Having recently protested the lack of black faculty members at the Academy, the Annapolis branch of the NAACP greeted Massie's arrival with a great deal of fanfare. A native of Little Rock, Arkansas, Massie had graduated from high school at age thirteen and earned a B.S. degree in chemistry from what is now the University of Arkansas at Pine Bluff, an M.A. in chemistry from Fisk University, and a Ph.D. in organic chemistry from Iowa State University. Before coming to Annapolis, he had served as chairman of the chemistry departments at Langston University in Oklahoma, Fisk University, and Howard University; associate program director of the National Science Foundation; and president of North Carolina College. He later became chairman of the Naval Academy's chemistry department (1977–81); received five honorary degrees for his contributions in science, technology, education, and community service; became an honorary member of the class of 1993; and received numerous accolades from the African American and scientific communities.[7]

Sam Massie was both harbinger and agent of change. In November 1967, Admiral Kauffman established the Academy's first equal employment opportunity committee and appointed Dr. Massie chairman. The committee served as the principal instrument for reviewing cases of racial discrimination brought by civilian employees or job applicants. During the 1970s, the committee formulated the Academy's first affirmative action plan, in accordance with directives from the superintendent, Navy Department, and Civil Service Commission. The plan dealt mainly with the Academy's black employees. It acknowledged the need to increase the number of minorities and women on the faculty as well as opportunities for advancement for black janitors. Massie remained chairman of this committee until 1976, when a naval officer replaced him, but he continued to serve on the committee until 1980.[8]

Hard on the heels of hiring Professor Massie, Admiral Kauffman tackled the problem of discrimination against black naval personnel in the city of Annapolis. When black enlisted men assigned to the Academy's associated naval station had difficulty finding off-base housing, Kauffman set up a meeting with Annapolis city officials and local apartment and trailer court owners. Kauffman and the landlords gathered at the Academy on 16 June 1967 with Assistant Secretary of Defense (Manpower) Thomas H. Morris, Under Secretary of the Navy Robert Baldwin, Assistant General Counsel for the Defense Department Frank A. Bartimo, Annapolis mayor Roger W. Moyer, and other local and federal officials. Kauffman made it clear that landlords who did not promise to rent to African American servicemen and their families would have their properties placed off limits to *all* service families. The Defense Department officials confirmed that such a policy was fully in keeping with Secretary McNamara's directives. Faced with the prospect of losing a significant source of rental income, many of the owners and landlords caved in and signed nondiscrimination pledges.[9]

Nevertheless, the same kind of problem arose a year later. Each spring many firsties would rent houses for their families near the Academy for June Week. During the spring of 1968, Kauffman learned that Sherwood Forest, an attractive development of summer homes about fifteen minutes' drive from the Academy, "had a hard and fast rule against renting to blacks," as he recalled. To confirm the story, he asked Gil Lucas to try to rent a house there. Lucas was turned away. Kauffman then fired the opening shots of what he later dubbed the "Battle of Sherwood Forest." He spent hours on the phone and in meetings with lawyers, Defense Department officials, and members of the Sherwood Forest board. Once again he wielded the economic weapon. "Any establishment that would not serve *all* midshipmen," he told the board, "would serve *no* midshipmen." Kauffman also resorted to what he described as "a little indirect blackmail," implying that he would go to the press if the board did not change its policy. Kauffman won the battle. That June, Gil Lucas became the first African American midshipman to rent a house in Sherwood Forest.[10]

Despite Admiral Kauffman's victories, segments of the Annapolis real estate business remained unreconstructed. During his first semester on the Academy faculty, Sam Massie commuted on weekends to Durham, North Carolina, until he and his family moved to a rental property on Southgate Avenue. The Massies were one of two black families on the street, and they never ran into difficulties there. After renting for two years, Massie and his wife Gloria began looking for a house to buy. "The realtors would only show us houses in poor condition with structural problems and steered us away from neighborhoods where we knew decent and higher-priced homes existed," Massie recalled. "They showed me houses that I could buy three of. In earlier years there had been a sign posted on Southgate that read 'After Sundown, Colored Not Welcomed.' While the sign had disappeared long before my coming to Annapolis, it appeared that the attitude had not. Although my appointment and high position was accepted at the Academy, the community of Annapolis was not ready to accept the Massie family. Dismayed but not surprised, I shared my unhappiness about the discriminatory service provided by realtors with the local newspaper and so all of Annapolis was aware of the discrimination I faced. When a realty agent publicly challenged my discrimination claim, we decided to leave Annapolis, and we purchased a new house 25 miles away in the all-white Montpelier section of Laurel, Maryland. I was not happy about having to drive 50 miles a day to and from the Academy."[11]

The first African American naval officers to serve on the faculty and in the executive department came on board during Admiral Kauffman's and Admiral Calvert's superintendencies. In 1966, Lieutenant Maurice E. Clark, '59, began a tour in the engineering department. Two years later, Lieutenant William H. Norman, a naval flight officer, the same officer who later became Admiral Zumwalt's special assistant for minority affairs, joined the history faculty; Lieutenant Edward L. Green, USMC, began a tour in the naval science department; and Commander George I. Thomson became Sixth Battalion officer. After graduating from the Academy in 1969, Ensign Frederick E. Jones remained there in the physical education department as sailing instructor and football coach. In 1970, Lieutenant Commander William E. Kelley became 21st Company Officer. Lieutenant (later Commander) Ken Johnson joined the candidate guidance office that same year.[12]

Admiral Kauffman met with black midshipmen not only as a group but individually. He developed a particularly close relationship with Tony Watson. "Admiral Kauffman was probably my greatest mentor," Watson recalled. "I met him when I was president of my class as a plebe. He and his wife kind of took me in. They had me over to their house a lot and really made me feel at home. Admiral Kauffman and I sat one-on-one periodically in his library, just he and I. He frequently sought my opinion, which made me feel great. He'd ask how things are going for black midshipmen and he'd sit and listen."

In the spring of 1968, Watson was selected brigade commander of his class. A few days before Admiral Kauffman's change of command that summer, Watson's company officer, a marine, called him into his office. "He wanted me to learn how to use a sword," Watson said. "I figured it was because I was brigade commander of the class and he wanted to make sure I could do it right. He drilled me for a whole weekend. The night before the change of command, Admiral Kauffman called me over to his quarters. We went to the library in his quarters. He sat me down and he lit a cigarette as he so often did. 'Tomorrow at the change of command,' he said, 'I'm going to pass on to you my family sword.' The sword dated back to 1908. It had been worn by his grandfather, who was an admiral, by his father, who was an admiral, and by him. His son was not going to join the military. So he was doing me the honor of passing on his family sword and its tradition to me. I wore that sword for some twenty odd years."

Admiral Heyworth, then commandant, recalled the event. "It was a nice, balmy spring day outside of Bancroft Hall in the area where we all assembled for noon meal formation. Admiral Kauffman said some nice words about Tony Watson, his leadership, and how he exemplified what the Naval Academy was trying to achieve with all midshipmen, then presented him with the sword. It was quite an impressive thing." "Admiral Kauffman was the greatest admiral I've ever known," declared Tony Watson.

Admiral Calvert also met periodically with the black midshipmen individually and as a group. "We're here to do anything we can to help you," he would say. The midshipmen expressed discontent about the situation at hops and dances, "but nothing that really was a major problem," as Calvert recalled. Tony Watson in particular had the admiral's ear. On several occasions Calvert sought advice from Watson on how to handle racial issues. Before his epiphany at his mother's funeral, Don Montgomery teetered on the brink of separation for academic deficiency. "I dug a hole for myself plebe year," he recalled. "I wound up going to three academic boards. During that arrogant time, I would want to quit every other week. The superintendent—Admiral Calvert—had lunch with me twice. I thought it was because I was this hotshot athlete, but he felt sorry for my mom and dad. He knew that it would break their hearts if I left. He encouraged me. He was an unbelievable guy, a great guy. I stayed and finished the course. During my junior year we played Boston College at home and we just stomped them. They had an All-American defensive tackle. I blocked him all over the field that day. We won the game like 42–13. It was covered by Associated Press. I had a good game and they gave me some ink. Admiral Calvert had gotten out of the Navy by then. He was over in San Francisco working for Texaco and he saw an article in a local San Francisco paper about what a good game I had. He cut the article out of the paper. I got an envelope in the mail. I opened it. Inside was the article. He had written on it, 'Aren't you glad you stayed?' This man's one of the biggest big shots with Texaco. He was the man who landed the first submarine at the North Pole. He's got time to write me a letter? I thought that was pretty neat."

During the late 1960s and early '70s, the administration became more responsive to black midshipmen's needs. Young black and white Americans had different tastes in music. In general, white kids listened to rock and roll or country and western while black kids preferred soul and funk. Musical tastes among black and white midshipmen reflected these cultural differences. Student bands that performed at hops and other events had been in existence at the Academy since 1907.[13] Before and during Paul Reason's time, these bands catered to the tastes of the overwhelming white majority. In 1968, a dozen midshipmen formed the Academy's first student rhythm and blues group, dubbed the Jay Gees. Four African American midshipmen, Cliff Files, '72, Bert Freeman, Tony Watson, and Leo Williams, along with Bobby Woo, '70, whom the others called "our Chinese-Spanish-American soul brother," sang, and the rest played. "All of the guys in the seven-piece band were Caucasian," Williams recalled. "It was a real blending of cultures and it worked like a charm. We did some Blood, Sweat and Tears, some Chicago, and some pop, but 80 percent of the repertoire was rhythm and blues." "We did a lot of Temptations, a lot of Four Tops," recalled Bert Freeman. "Tunes of the day. Primarily black groups." "The band was the love of my life for the last two years," Williams said. "It's where I put 80 percent of my disposable energy outside of academics." The group achieved club status, enabling it to receive funding as an official extracurricular activity, play at hops, and travel and perform outside the Academy, including at women's colleges. The band lasted until 1971.

In 1972, James Jackson, Ken Dunn, several other African Americans, and one Hispanic midshipman started a band they called the Variations. Whereas the Jay Gees were integrated, the Variations were virtually all black. "The Academy did a bold thing," Jackson recalled. "They funded my band so that all of us could get outfits, they paid for equipment, and they let us perform at several midshipman dances. Everybody loved it. We played Temptations and James Brown. People who liked that came, and the black midshipmen participated in dances to a higher degree." Word of the band's existence reached Annapolis's black community, spread by the black workers at the Academy who heard the Variations practicing twice a week. As a result, more young black women from town attended hops. "It was an important group because it brought young ladies up to the Academy to various functions. That meant that we were able to get girlfriends and have dates and stuff," recalled Kerwin Miller. "I wasn't in the Variations. I was not musically inclined. But it was a great group. We enjoyed it. Those guys would play and girls would come. We'd get to talk to girls while they were playing. I think we were better off not being in the band. But they did get a chance to play outside the Academy, though. That was the good part. They got to go to places that we didn't get to go to." The Variations remained in existence through 1978.

In the fall of 1969, Lieutenant Norman suggested that the Academy establish a black studies program like those then springing up at civilian institutions across America. "A study of existing courses," Norman wrote in a letter to the head of the English, history and government department, "reveals that little, if any, emphasis is devoted to describing the black American accurately and naturally as a participant in and contributor to the life and development of the U.S." Academic dean A. Bernard Drought set up an ad hoc committee to develop a plan for such a program and asked Sam Massie to chair it. Massie accepted this responsibility on top of his research, teaching load, and chairmanship of the equal employment opportunity committee. The black studies planning committee consisted of six faculty members and six midshipmen, black and white, including Commander Clark, Major Green, Ensign Jones, Midshipman 1/C Leo Williams, Midshipman 2/C Hank Shaw, '71, and Midshipman 3/C Nelson Jones, '72. "Knowledge of black people and their contributions to American life is more important to a midshipman than to a student at a civilian institution," Massie declared. "The midshipman is going to be a leader." With the Navy becoming more racially diverse, he argued, officers should know something about different races under their command. The committee did not propose a full black studies curriculum like those being adopted in civilian schools. Instead it recommended development of courses in black history, culture, and contributions to America; the inclusion of these themes in existing courses, such as including black writers in plebe English courses; increasing the number of black faculty members; employing visiting black lecturers and professors; and increasing the number of presentations and activities with multicultural themes. The Academy approved these proposals in the spring of 1970 and elevated the black studies committee from an ad hoc to a standing committee. Massie continued as chairman. As a result of the committee's effort, the library acquired many new holdings on black history and culture; the English department created two elective courses, American Black Literature and Afro-American Culture; black ministers led chapel services; and prominent African Americans delivered Forrestal lectures, including Rear Admiral Sam Gravely, author Alex Haley, politician Julian Bond, and General Daniel James Jr., the U.S. Air Force's first African American four-star general. "They were very proactive in presenting very credible and viable role models," recalled James Jackson, who saw General James speak. "It was a key strategic element in trying to infuse diversity into the Academy and show the Academy's support."[14]

In conversations with the academic dean, Dr. Massie emphasized the need to hire more African American faculty members. In light of his own experience, he stressed the importance of official involvement in helping future black faculty members find housing and fight housing discrimination, if necessary. Massie pushed for minority faculty recruitment at national professional meetings attended by black scholars. These efforts paid off in 1978 when Dr. Marlene Brown joined the English department.[15]

Admiral Zumwalt put his stamp on the Academy by billeting officers there who supported his controversial "people programs" and "more relaxed 'mod Navy'":[16] R. Adm. Max K. Morris, who became commandant of midshipmen in June 1971, and V. Adm. William Mack.

In January 1972, Admiral Morris formed a midshipman-manned human relations committee (later called the Human Relations Council) to inform him of problems or situations that could negatively affect "intra-brigade morale and kinship," as he put it in a letter to Admiral Zumwalt, and to recommend solutions. The committee also assisted Morris in developing programs to make the brigade aware of problems in the fleet. About a dozen midshipmen, black and white, served on the committee.[17]

The human relations committee made the commandant aware of several issues and situations black midshipmen found galling. In one such situation, committee members pointed out that no Academy sports team had ever had a black coach. Shortly thereafter the Academy hired Terry Lewis as assistant football coach, making him the Academy's first black coach.[18]

Two grievances aired by the human relations committee involved social director Mary Marshall. Mrs. Marshall was an older southern belle brimming with warmth and social grace, but she harbored Jim Crow views on propriety in race relations. She had long maintained notebooks to help midshipmen find homes in and around Annapolis where their girlfriends and families could stay when visiting. "Any time I would go to the social director's office to obtain a drag house for a young lady," recalled Chuck Reddix, "I noticed that invariably it would be in the home of some black family in Annapolis." This didn't bother Reddix at the time, but it did bother his black shipmates on the human relations committee. They told the commandant that Mrs. Marshall had quietly been keeping two sets of notebooks—one for blacks and one for whites, even after the battle of Sherwood Forest—and that this practice had caused "considerable ill feeling" among black midshipmen. Morris quickly put a stop to segregated "drag houses" and adopted an "open-housing" policy. He obtained new commitments from homeowners to make their homes available without regard to race, dropped the names of the few who refused, and had the books reworked accordingly.

The other situation involved tea fights. Black midshipmen in the class of 1970 found that the old pattern still prevailed during their plebe year (1966/67). Ev Greene never stood in line to meet his first dance partner. "If any young black ladies were invited to the tea fight," he recalled, "the social director would always bring them over to where the black midshipmen would be. The unwritten rule was that you would not go through the line." As Leo Williams put it, "There was not going to be a possible incident because a young white debutante was brought together at the end of the curtain with a black midshipman." Williams recalled the social director as a "cordial woman and almost motherly to me, but when it came to those things that were socially acceptable, there was a clear line because of her heritage. I have both fond and not-so-fond memories of Mrs. Marshall." Bruce Henry recalled one not-so-fond memory. "If a black midshipman was seen dancing with a young white lady," he recalled, "the social director would come over and split you up. 'That is not allowed here,' she would say. 'You're in a southern state. We cannot condone that type of behavior.'"

On one occasion, Tony Watson found a unique solution to the awkward situation. "We weren't really allowed to stand in line with the rest, so I decided I'd get a date," he recalled. He took Peggy Kimbo's seven-year-old daughter Crystal. "She was a great dancer," he said. "We had a great time. She was the life of the party. She could out-dance anybody there."

All too often, Mrs. Marshall's lack of contacts in the black community resulted in too few black women attending the dances, or worse, none at all. To rectify the situation, in the summer of 1972 Admiral Morris hired Carol Henriquez, a graduate of Howard University and widow of an African American naval aviator, as assistant social director.[19] "I took the job because of the black midshipmen," Henriquez said, "not because of the Academy's salary incentive. None of the men has been deprived, as such. But the military establishment has not been sensitive to their needs. The Navy is aware that the social situation leaves much to be desired, but the command hasn't identified the changes that need to be made."[20]

Mrs. Henriquez identified those changes herself. She couldn't help but notice the dearth of black women at tea fights and began inviting women from Howard University, Bowie State, and other historically black colleges. Mrs. Henriquez treated black midshipmen with warmth and friendliness. She seemed to be "looking out for our best interests," recalled Cary Hithon. At social events, Mrs. Henriquez made sure that black midshipmen were enjoying themselves.

The hiring of Carol Henriquez heralded the doom of Jim Crow social etiquette at tea fights. That custom had vanished by James Jackson's plebe year. "The only criterion for the escort you would be linked up with was height," Jackson recalled. "On several occasions, I was introduced to a white escort." Chuck Cole recalled going through the line like everyone else. He, too, got paired with a white woman on one occasion. "Her eyebrows might have raised a little bit," Cole recalled, "but nobody else's eyebrows were raised. It wasn't a big deal."

Admiral Mack knew full well that Admiral Zumwalt accorded integration a high priority, so he took racial issues seriously. Born in 1915 into a Navy family, Mack was raised mostly in Illinois. Although few African Americans lived in the places where he grew up, his parents taught him to be tolerant of all races. After graduating from the Academy in 1937, Mack served in battleships, destroyers, and amphibious forces. As a senior officer, he served as aide to the secretary of the navy, chief of information, chief of legislative affairs, and deputy assistant secretary of defense for manpower and reserve affairs. Before returning to Annapolis, he commanded the Seventh Fleet during the mining of Haiphong Harbor.[21]

Mack's racial policy rested on the principle of nontolerance of discrimination. As he told reporters a week after becoming superintendent, the Academy had to "walk a fine path between no discrimination and no patronization" of black midshipmen. He took pains to ensure that the commandant, battalion and company officers, and everyone else in authority at the Academy understood the Navy's racial policies as well as his own.[22]

Mack took pains to inform the midshipmen, too. At the beginning of each academic year, he held an assembly of the entire brigade to "tell them my policies," as he recalled. In a very simple and straightforward manner, he declared that he would tolerate no racial discrimination. "Any person violating this dictate," he would say, "will immediately be discharged."[23]

In August 1972, Admiral Mack instituted a faculty and staff human relations advisory council to ensure that all civilians and military people working at the Academy and its associated naval station enjoyed equal opportunity to develop to their full potential. The council worked with similar organizations in the surrounding civilian communities.

The first group of appointees to the council included Stan Carter, who had become a lieutenant and returned to the Academy in 1972 as 10th Company officer, followed by Gil Lucas returning as 35th Company officer in 1973. That same year, Lieutenant Commander Otis Tolbert became 26th Company officer. Thereafter a steady stream of African American Navy and Marine Corps officers rotated into faculty and executive department billets at the Academy. Proportions of African Americans on the faculty and staff varied, but they would never again be lily-white.[24]

The first black company officers could not help but notice how the Academy had changed since they were midshipmen. The kind of treatment they had received as plebes had been outlawed. "If you touched a midshipman with one finger at any one time," Gil Lucas recalled, "you could be thrown out." But the most significant change from the racial perspective was the increasing numbers of black midshipmen entering the Academy each year.

Admiral Mack's responsibilities included administering the implementation of Phase I of the Navy's Race Relations Program throughout his command. During Phase I, BuPers required the superintendent and all of the officers and enlisted men and women assigned to the Academy to attend seminars to enhance racial awareness. By June 1974, all officers and many civilian employees had completed either the three-day, 24-hour Executive seminar or the two-and-a-half-day, 20-hour UPWARD seminar. "Everyone needed a certain amount of indoctrination," Mack recalled. "I thought they were doing a great deal of good."[25]

During phase I, BuPers also required the Academy to provide race relations education to each midshipman. The program began during the 1972/73 academic year. The commandant administered it through the battalion and company officers. Before training midshipmen, company officers attended at least two human relations seminars led by professionals from the National Training Laboratory covering group interaction, self-awareness, interpersonal relations, race relations, and similar topics.[26]

Company officers then presented eight hours of training to first classmen during the second semester, working with them in small groups in seminar-type settings and using case histories from the fleet as the basis for group discussion. The Division of Naval Command and Management devoted twenty-two additional hours to human relations in its junior officer course. The training aimed at preparing midshipmen for their responsibilities as junior officers out in the fleet. "By identifying the various elements of institutional racism, subtle expressions of discrimination, and developing an in-depth understanding of overt discriminatory practices," Admiral Mack told the Board of Visitors in April 1973, "our newly commissioned officers will be prepared better to deal effectively with the many leadership problems in the area of human relations, both as leaders of the Brigade of Midshipmen and as commissioned officers."[27]

Ric Samuels attended these human relations seminars. One of them left a vivid impression. "They gave what they called a chitlin test," he recalled. "I think there were twenty questions on the test. It was just to show how testing can be culturally biased, like the SAT. If you were an inner city black kid, you knew all the stuff on that test. It involved common things. They'd ask, 'What's a hog?' That was a slang term back then for a Cadillac. And 'How long does it take to cook chitlins?' and 'What's a do?' Things that kids in the city would know. A friend of mine, a black kid who grew up in a white suburban environment, bombed on the test, because he wasn't exposed to that. But most of us knew the answers. I guess the average black probably scored eighteen on the test out of twenty. The average white kid scored like a four or lower. Some missed every question. These guys were outraged to the point of wanting to go to blows over this stuff. The prof had to cool everybody down. That was a real eye-opener for me, to see how upset these guys could get over something that put them in a reverse situation."

Bobby Watts found the seminars "pretty brutal." Watts learned that some of his classmates from New Jersey, New York, and elsewhere in the Northeast harbored prejudice as deep as some of the southerners. "At one point one of my classmates jumped up. 'If you don't like it here,' he shouted, 'why don't you guys go back to Africa?' 'You're an Italian American,' I said. 'You're very proud of that. And you talk about when your family came over here in the '30s or '40s. My family's been here a whole lot longer than yours has. Maybe *you* should go back to where *you* came from.'" Some white midshipmen resented the fact that many of the ethnic slurs they had grown up hearing at home were no longer acceptable. "We spent a number of seminars just discussing why words are derogatory and why you have to be concerned about what you say," Watts recalled. "Some people—such as southerners who would use the word 'nigger' and not think anything of it—just couldn't understand that." By means of these sessions the administration put out the word that racial and ethnic slurs such "nigger" and "flip," an epithet applied to Filipino messmen, were now taboo.

On 21 August 1973, Admiral Mack issued an instruction establishing the Naval Academy Human Goals Program under the auspices of the broader Navy Department Human Goals Program, then being managed throughout the Navy by BuPers. The instruction brought all of the Academy's previously instituted equal opportunity and race relations education programs under one administrative umbrella. The objectives of the Human Goals Program both at the Academy and throughout the fleet included eliminating racism, ensuring equal opportunity, eradicating drug and alcohol abuse, preventing discrimination against women, and motivating people for naval careers. At bottom lay the goal of training managers to deal with an increasingly diversified fleet. Admiral Mack became the Academy's human goals officer, responsible for approving, monitoring, and providing resources for all plans developed in support of the program. The commandant administered the program for all executive department officers and midshipmen, and the academic dean did so for military and civilian faculty. In May 1974, Mack established four human goals committees chaired by the commandant, academic dean, commanding officer of Naval Station Annapolis, and deputy for operations, as well as a staff and faculty human goals advisory council to oversee the four human goals committees. The following July, Mack appointed a special assistant for human goals to direct and coordinate the various projects sponsored by the human goals programs and to serve as liaison with BuPers and the chief of naval education and training.[28]

All told, the various types of training mandated by BuPers could have absorbed up to a quarter of midshipmen's class time. Admiral Mack discerned the need for self-respect as a common thread in them all. With help from Rear Admiral John J. O'Connor, the Academy's senior chaplain, Mack put together a noncredit, 64-hour-long course dubbed "The Professional Officer and the Human Person" (POHP). Launched during the 1973/74 academic year, the course included instruction in ethics, morals, and world religions. The course consisted of short films or videotaped lectures presented to groups of some fifteen third classmen, followed by discussions of the lecture topic led by company officers.

That same year, all first classmen and plebes attended eight hour-long seminars in race relations and second classmen received six hours of race relations instruction in the leadership course taught by the Division of Naval Command and Management. Don Montgomery recalled that, although most people considered this "sensitivity training" a "waste of time . . . the reality was that it cleared up a lot of misconceived notions" and "gave us a chance to actually communicate, which we had never done. It brought us a lot closer together as a company."[29]

The POHP course aimed at familiarizing midshipmen with different cultures around the world, not just within the United States. "The point was to get you to understand that different people have different thoughts and concerns and religious backgrounds," recalled Chuck Cole. The course also included material specifically related to domestic concerns. "They made some films using midshipmen to give examples of things that constituted racism,"

Cole added. "I participated in the filming of two or three short vignettes. In one, a group of white guys were filmed walking and talking together. They passed a group of black guys who were doing the same thing. Then the camera panned to the white group, who stopped. They all kind of like looked at each other. 'You know,' one of them said, 'I wonder why they always congregate together.'" The idea that "diversity's a good thing," Ed Gilmore recalled, "was the punch line through the whole thing."

As 35th Company officer, Gil Lucas served as POHP course facilitator for the midshipmen in his company. "The idea was that after these canned presentations, you would shut off the TV and discuss them. I can remember my first session in the summer with the plebes. It was a session on race relations. There were about eighty plebes in the room. It was like somebody poured gasoline in the room and threw in a match. I was doing the best I could. The discussion involved race and what America was about. This one plebe stood up in the back, straight as an arrow, and said, 'All you people who don't like the Naval Academy, just get the hell out of here.' The plebes ranged in attitude from patriotic beyond belief to those who were just wondering, 'What have I gotten myself into?'" Lucas noticed that the course affected different individuals differently. "It heightened sensitivity," he said. "Some who weren't thinking about it much before thought about it more after that. Others got pissed off when they weren't pissed off earlier." "Some of the films were really very well done," he added. "Nothing that I've ever been associated with ever even approached that because you had a captive audience."

The Academy continued to offer the course during part of R. Adm. Kinnaird R. McKee's superintendency. McKee relieved Admiral Mack on 1 August 1975. After graduating from the Academy in 1951, McKee became a nuclear submariner. Before returning to Annapolis as superintendent, he served as commander of Submarine Group Eight, Fleet Ballistic Missile Submarine Force, and Submarine Force, Sixth Fleet.[30]

During the first year of Admiral McKee's superintendency, the Academy provided a broad spectrum of racial awareness training and education to all four classes. Plebes attended race relations training seminars with their company officers at the end of plebe summer 1975. They discussed the hows and whys of prejudice along with personal and institutional racism to prepare the plebes for life in Bancroft Hall after the brigade returned. During the second semester, firsties and segundos took a nonaccredited course dealing with contemporary leadership problems in the fleet, including topics on social problems affecting communication, ethics, values, racism, and naval officers' responsibilities to their people and to the oath of office. During both semesters, the Academy presented the POHP course to plebes and youngsters as it had the two previous years.[31]

In December 1975, Admiral McKee disbanded the human goals advisory council and in its place established a human relations advisory council. The new entity differed from the old in having a slightly larger membership, including nearly thirty black and white faculty members, officers and enlisted people, civilian employees, and one midshipman, but its function remained assisting the superintendent in running the human goals program and advising him on all matters concerning human relations and equal opportunity at the Naval Academy and naval station. Membership of the council in the spring of 1976 included Lieutenant Commander George L. Gaines, who had relieved Ken Johnson in the candidate guidance office, and Chuck Reddix, then a firsty. McKee directed that the council provide a forum for frank discussion of grievances, examine incidents concerning discrimination and propose solutions, and monitor the progress of the Academy's equal opportunity programs and affirmative action plans.[32]

Admiral McKee discontinued the POHP course during the 1976/77 academic year. He considered the course experimental and replaced it with a more permanent arrangement. In June 1976, in a minor reorganization, the Academy created the Division of Professional Development. The division consisted of two departments: seamanship and navigation, and leadership and law. The commandant assigned the director of professional development responsibility for providing "human relations training" to midshipmen by means of a new three-year leadership curriculum. Much of the content of the POHP course was recycled in the new curriculum. The commandant also ordered the director of professional development to designate one of his staff members as human goals officer, whose duties included an annual review of the Academy affirmative action plan.[33]

That same June the commandant established a human relations steering committee "to enhance inter-racial awareness and provide a sounding board for Brigade attitudes." The commandant placed the human goals officer in charge of the committee. The committee included more than three dozen black and white midshipmen—one representative from each company plus four officers—who met about once a month to discuss racial issues. "We would discuss racial slurs going around or if there was any tension between blacks and whites," recalled one of the black midshipmen appointed to the committee. "We would also discuss ways to break down barriers of communication. It was basically a way for midshipmen and the faculty to voice their concerns to each other."[34]

The commandant also directed company officers to conduct racial awareness seminars for the first and fourth classes. Cary Hithon, who participated in one of these seminars, vividly recalled the discussion. "We were talking about giving lesser-qualified people an opportunity," he said. At that time, the

Academy was accepting black candidates who barely had the minimum grade point averages and SAT scores while rejecting many white candidates whose numbers were well above the minimum.

"Hey, my father lost a job just like that to one of those people," declared one of Hithon's white classmates.

Hithon replied with a classic defense of affirmative action. "You have to do something like that to give other people opportunities," he said. "I'm not like you. If I'm going to be a productive part of society, you have to give me an opportunity. I didn't grow up speaking like you. I didn't grow up learning like you. I didn't grow up with what you have, so in order to make the playing field level, you have to give people like me this opportunity."

"You're different," argued the white classmate.

"What do you mean I'm different?" Hithon said. "I'm no different from any other black person." Hithon believed that given the opportunity, most black people could do well. His classmate seemed to believe that most black people could not and did not deserve the chance.

In 1977, student members of the black studies committee formed a new organization, the Black Studies Club. The club grew out of black midshipmen's involvement in Black History Week. The Academy first observed Black History Week in 1975 in accordance with a presidential proclamation declaring it a national event. Highlights included addresses by R. Adm. Samuel L. Gravely, who four years earlier had become the Navy's first black flag officer, and other prominent African Americans. That same year the Academy first celebrated the birthday of the Reverend Dr. Martin Luther King Jr. The black studies committee figured prominently in setting up and hosting these events that year and the next. Sam Massie realized that the Academy had only a limited amount of money for the black history program from special funds. Why not form a student club, he reasoned, and tap into appropriated funds? Admiral McKee agreed and launched the Black Studies Club, which took over sponsorship of Black History Week, turning it into Black History Month, featuring a major event each week during February. The black studies committee came to play primarily an advisory role for the academic dean and superintendent.[35]

For most of this period, black midshipmen sensed that the Academy was serious about integration, both in bringing African Americans on board and in countering discrimination after they arrived. "There was a very definite push to increase the number of minorities," recalled James Jackson. "It was not lost on me. Once students were accepted, the goal was to keep them at the Academy." "The Navy was trying to officially make efforts to improve the situation," recalled Ric Samuels. "The racial awareness part of leadership class. The proactive way they were recruiting minorities. Those were big statements." Samuels's classmate Bobby Watts felt the same way. "As the leadership gained awareness of black midshipmen's concerns," he said, "the Academy held discussion groups, conducted seminars, and made racial slurs unacceptable." Bruce Franklin believed the leadership was making an honest effort to diversify the brigade.

Fully Integrated

ACADEMICS PROVED the most difficult hurdle for black midshipmen to clear. The overall attrition rate for the classes of 1969–79 stood at 35 percent while the attrition rate for black midshipmen was 47 percent, a rise of 13 percent over the previous period. Of the 476 African Americans admitted to the Academy in this period, 240 graduated but 236 did not. Half of those who did not were discharged for academic deficiency, mostly during their plebe or youngster years. Of the black midshipmen who did not graduate, 30 percent resigned voluntarily, citing lack of motivation. The remaining 20 percent left for other reasons, including, marriage, medical discharges, inaptitude, and death. Only six were discharged for honor violations or bad conduct.

The class of 1971 suffered the highest black attrition rate, losing ten of thirteen African Americans admitted, or 77 percent. Two were discharged for academic reasons, four resigned for lack of motivation, and the rest left for other reasons. The classes of 1970, 1974, 1975, 1977, and 1978 each suffered 50 percent or higher attrition rates among black midshipmen. In contrast, the black retention rates for the classes of 1969, 1972, and 1973 equaled or excelled the overall retention rate.

The class of 1977 lost the highest number of black midshipmen, 60 of the 119 admitted. Of those who did not make it, 50 percent bilged for academic reasons, 35 percent resigned citing lack of motivation, and 15 percent left for other reasons.[1]

Part of the reason black midshipmen found the academic hurdle so high was the fact that, although they were academically qualified, they were not as well prepared on average as white candidates. The overall average SAT scores for incoming plebes in the class of 1977 were 564 verbal and 638 math. The African Americans of that class scored significantly lower, averaging 489 verbal and 561 math.[2]

Black midshipmen's poorer academic preparation resulted in large part from the separate and unequal education African Americans received under segregation and during the slow process of school integration. "Little did I realize that the public school education I had received was not quite at the level I needed to really excel in the Academy environment," Leo Williams recalled. "I was the valedictorian of my high school class of 550 graduates with a 3.96 GPA and about 1,200 on my SATs, so I thought I was king dog. I was just ready to go out there and continue a tradition of academic excellence. When I got to the Academy, it just hit me in the face that I was not as well prepared academically as I thought I was. It was absolutely a case of the facilities not being equal."

Although Chuck Cole graduated in the top 10 percent of his high school class, he found himself woefully underprepared in math. "I walked into calculus class," he recalled. "When the professor drew an integral sign on the board, I didn't know what it was. I thought I was in music class. It looked like a G clef to me. I didn't have a clue." Cole failed math three semesters in a row, but so many of his classmates, white as well as black, were having academic difficulties that he never had to appear before the academic board. Cole survived by studying with classmates, availing himself of the extra help the faculty offered, and developing better study habits.

Academic difficulties nearly led Jeff Sapp to resign. An average student in high school, Sapp struggled during his first two semesters at the Academy, finishing plebe year with a cumulative QPA of 1.61. During youngster year, Sapp found his course work overwhelming. "It would have been easier," he recalled, "to just quit and establish myself elsewhere as an athlete." He telephoned his parents to discuss the idea.

Art Sapp wouldn't hear of it. He boarded a plane for Annapolis to talk things over with his son in person. "If you're white and you drop out, people would think you're just taking a break to 'find yourself,'" Art said. "But since you're black, if you drop out of the Academy, people will think you're just another nigger who couldn't hack it."

His father's words forced Jeff Sapp to reevaluate his life. He determined not only to stick it out but to excel. "I decided that I didn't want to remember the Academy," he recalled. "I wanted the Academy to remember me." Sapp began devoting all his time to sports and studies, sacrificing any sort of social life. He never became an academic star as a midshipman, but he didn't quit either, graduating 871st in a class of 967 with a bachelor's degree in American political science.[3]

To African Americans who were upperclassmen when the class of 1977 entered, many of the black plebes seemed academically or otherwise unprepared. "A lot of these guys just didn't get it," recalled Kerwin Miller. "We were second class, so we were in charge of them. It was clear that what the Academy had done was to use the shotgun effect. The more we got there, the more would graduate. Some of those guys just didn't understand what they were getting into. They were having social problems with other midshipmen. Academic problems. A couple of them got put out for conduct. Honor offenses. They were just all over. A lot of them thought that they were just going to college. They didn't have the perception that the Academy was a military place and that they're going to be yelled at. A lot of them just went down."

Ed Gilmore had a similar impression. "There were black guys who should not have been there," he recalled. "I'm not an academician by any stretch of the imagination, but they had a guy from Watts with a 0.50. Didn't have a clue about grades. And he was overweight. It was obvious that some of those guys were academically unprepared. They weren't even close. The Navy did it to say, 'We're trying to fix this problem,' but clearly, they shouldn't have done it."

"They were really starting the push toward getting minorities there," Stan Carter recalled of his days as 10th Company officer. "The Academy was probably too lenient in terms of standards. The class of '77 started off with 119 and graduated 59 of them. Some of those guys should've gone to NAPS first instead of coming straight in. It wasn't that they didn't have the ability to eventually succeed, but rather the Academy was in such a hurry to rush them in to build up the numbers that they didn't do what they do now, and that is to send guys with potential to NAPS first and give them the training they need to be successful."

The administration tried a variety of tactics to combat the high attrition rates among black midshipmen. When Admiral Calvert first arrived, the Academy's core required curriculum included a five-hour plebe calculus course designed, in part, to weed out the academically unfit. After midterm exams, the head of the math department went to see Calvert. "Admiral," he said, "unless you do something now, you're going lose most of your black midshipmen." "They were *my* black midshipmen then," recalled Admiral Calvert. "They weren't qualified to do the calculus course at all, not because they weren't bright enough, but because their high schools were so poor. We realized we had to do something. I wasn't going to just give up and see them all fail." Calvert met with a member of the academic advisory board and the two of them devised a remedial math program "for anybody who comes in and is not really qualified to do the heavy math work," as the admiral put it. "It also helped some of the non-minority guys who were having trouble."

In 1972, Admiral Mack developed a program designed to enhance retention by sending midshipmen discharged for academic deficiency at the end
of their first semester to NAPS, where they received intensive instruction to
reduce their academic weaknesses, enabling them to reenter the Academy with
the next class. Although the program was theoretically open to all midshipmen, Mack touted it on the basis of its ability to help black midshipmen. In
February 1975, the vice chief of naval operations gave the program his formal
approval. No follow-up study on the success of the program seems to have
been done.[4]

During the 1970s, Sam Massie offered extra classroom instruction at night
in chemistry, math, and physics to anyone who needed it. Chuck Cole found
the sessions quite helpful. Massie "would try to bring in other professors,"
Cole recalled, "but more often than not, it was just him, and he might have
twenty or thirty midshipmen there. He helped a lot of blacks get through."

Such efforts doubtless helped, but they did not stanch the flow of black
midshipmen leaving the Academy during the mid-'70s. Little more was done
because the attrition rate for black midshipmen was not yet the barn-burning
issue for the administration that it would become by the next decade. "I finally
concluded that the goal we should seek was not how many minorities we could
admit," recalled Admiral McKee, "but how many we could *graduate*."[5]

Throughout the late 1960s and early '70s, black midshipmen who cleared the
academic hurdle encountered fewer and fewer racial barriers.

Early in this period, black midshipmen experienced a degree of racial social
separation on summer cruises. Bert Freeman took his youngster cruise on
board a destroyer. "I noticed that there was a goodly amount of segregation
aboard the ship," he recalled. "Not mandated segregation. It's just everybody
hung out with their own groups. Whenever I was on board ship, I associated professionally with white folks. Whenever I went on liberty, I went with
the black enlisted men rather than the white midshipmen. When we went
ashore at Galveston, Texas, we went straight to the black neighborhood. My
social life has always been that way." During Ev Greene's youngster cruise, a
country club in Lake Charles, Louisiana, invited the midshipmen on his ship
to a social function. The skipper told Greene, however, that the club did not
welcome black people, so Greene decided not to attend. Perhaps it should
have occurred to the skipper to turn down the invitation unless *all* of his
midshipmen were invited. Black petty officers and chiefs on the heavy cruiser
Columbus (CG-12) took Leo Williams and his black classmate Ed Shirley under their wing during youngster cruise. "They wanted to make sure that we
succeeded," Williams recalled, "so they took time to make sure that we knew
what we were doing. For the most part, the white midshipmen didn't get spe-

cial attention by the white sailors. The black staff noncommissioned officers [NCOs] took a different attitude. 'Let us tell you what we went through,' they would say, 'and the things you need to be looking out for and the things you need to be aware of and the things you need to do as you become an officer to help you succeed.' It was probably the best lesson I ever learned. Listen to the staff NCOs."

Social segregation did not seem to occur as much on cruises during the '70s. "I was the only black midshipman on my ship," recalled Kerwin Miller of his youngster cruise. "I didn't hang out too much with the black sailors at all. I hung out mainly with the white midshipmen. We had a pretty good time." What stands out in Eddie Graves's memory of summer cruises was the camaraderie he developed with classmates after he and his classmates bested Marine officers at Quantico in a race on the obstacle course for a keg of beer. During Marv King's youngster cruise, the enlisted men "sort of adopted the mids" and took them out to party.

Back at the Academy, prejudice still occasionally reared its ugly head. Although Ev Greene submitted his photo in time, it was excluded from the 1970 *Lucky Bag*. He attributed its exclusion to racism. Kerwin Miller and black classmates used to gather in the stairwell outside the wardroom on Sunday evenings to talk about how they had spent the weekend. On two or three occasions someone several floors up stuck his head in the stairwell and yelled racial epithets. The black midshipmen chased the culprit but never caught him.

At some point during the mid-1970s, probably during the 1974/75 academic year, someone put a hood over the statue of Tecumseh to make it look like a Ku Klux Klansman. Ed Gilmore recalled seeing the hooded statue on his way to class that morning. "The commandant made us have a stand-down to talk about it," he recalled. "One of my company classmates, a guy from California said, 'I don't see what the big deal is.' He thought it was funny. He didn't see anything wrong with it. I called him aside and said, 'What if you're out on a ship and it happens and you have a riot because of it. What are you going to do then?' He never got it, because it was something he just never had to deal with in his life before."

Jeff Sapp remembered seeing the hood over the statue upon returning to Bancroft Hall in the evening. Under the hood hung a sign that said something like "the Klan will ride again." Sapp recalled that a commissioned officer summoned him and a few other midshipmen to an office in Bancroft Hall and told them not to discuss the incident, that the authorities were on top of it, and that the Academy didn't need adverse publicity.

Fortunately, such incidents proved the rare exception rather than the rule. By and large, black midshipmen encountered less prejudice as upperclassmen than they had as plebes.

Sports continued to figure prominently in midshipmen's daily lives. Bert Freeman was on the varsity fencing team from his youngster through first-class years. During his second-class year, he was a first-team All-American and took third in the NCAA competition. As a firsty he became captain of the fencing team and NCAA foil fencer of the year. Ev Greene ran track and cross country. Bruce Henry rowed on the crew team all four years. Tony Watson boxed and played rugby. Leo Williams participated in basketball, football, and boxing. Ric Samuels wrestled and played football until sidelined by a knee injury and fear that such an injury would disqualify him from flying. Bobby Watts played 150-pound football and ran track. Don Montgomery played football all four years. Eddie Graves excelled in boxing. His penchant for knocking opponents to the floor earned him the nickname "Gravedigga." Chuck Cole played intramural football and softball and joined the YP (yard patrol craft) Squadron. James Jackson played junior varsity soccer during his first three years. Kerwin Miller was a boxer, coxswain on the crew team, and boxing manager. Chuck Reddix was plebe manager of the gymnastics team and then became varsity manager for his remaining three years. Marv King played 150-pound football and intramural football and did a little boxing. Byron Marchant ran track. Lloyd Prince sailed 44-foot Luder yawls.

Black midshipmen participated in the full range of Academy extracurricular activities. Besides fencing and singing in the Jay Gees, Bert Freeman was a member of the German Club, Catholic Choir, and Glee Club. He was also head cheerleader during his second- and first-class years. Leo Williams participated in the midshipman Big Brother organization. James Jackson marched with the Drum and Bugle Corps during his first-class year. Jeff Sapp played drums in the "NA Ten," a midshipman band. Marv King and Lloyd Prince worked on the midshipmen's radio station, WNRV. Prince also took photographs for the *Lucky Bag* and served on the hop committee. Chuck Cole was too busy studying to have time for extracurricular activities.

Black midshipmen varied in their participation in plebe indoctrination. Some did so to a moderate or normal degree. During the summer before second-class year, Bert Freeman served on the plebe training detail during the first set. On the last night he and his classmates assigned to the detail were in charge, they made the plebes sleep on their mattress springs. One of the plebes caught a cold and reported to sick bay. The doctor happened to ask how he caught the cold and found out about the order to sleep on the mattress springs. Because the order violated the new indoctrination standards then being enforced, Freeman and his classmates assigned to the first set of plebe detail nearly got dismissed. Instead, however, they each received 40 demerits.

Otherwise Freeman did the job as it was supposed to be done. "'Stick together!' I used to say until it was coming out of their ears," he recalled. "I always pushed fairness." In his opinion the worst thing a plebe could do was to mistreat another plebe. On one occasion he saw one plebe push another and knock the rifle out of his hands. Freeman had the errant plebe get down on "leaning rest" for twenty-five minutes. Leaning rest was essentially one push-up, held in the up position for as long as the upperclassman thought necessary or for as long as the plebe could take it.

Bruce Henry adopted a similar approach to plebe indoctrination. "I had a reputation of being fair and rather tolerant," he recalled. "I'd give you enough rope to hang yourself. If you hung yourself, then you really didn't want to come around to me more than once. But if you did what you needed to do, then you didn't have to come around to me."

Leo Williams took a middle-of-the-road approach. "I was not overzealous in wanting to give my plebes something that they would never forget," he recalled. "At the same time, by the time they finished plebe year, I wanted to make sure that they knew everything that they needed to know in order to survive the next three years. I did not go overboard, but I think I was pretty conscientious in ensuring that they knew what they needed to know."

Tony Watson loved serving on plebe detail. "Working to develop newly inducted plebes was one of the greatest leadership experiences I had," he said. "I was very confident that we could get these plebes trained up better than we were when we were plebes. I enjoyed it."

Ric Samuels was tough on plebes. The firsties ran the plebes during his first-class year. "I was on plebe detail," Samuels said. "When I took over, our company was at the very bottom of the totem pole. I was probably more of a disciplinarian than I needed to be, mainly because it was a turn-around situation. We went from last place to second place by the time we ended the set."

Bobby Watts also served on plebe detail as a firsty. One of Watts's classmates intended to treat plebes as badly as he had been treated. Watts thought that was wrong. "I didn't treat them the way I was treated," he recalled. "I treated them in a way I thought would allow them to be good midshipmen."

Kerwin Miller had plebe summer detail when he was a firsty. "There was a tendency that whatever you went through," he said, "you were going to put somebody else through that. I never adopted that philosophy. My philosophy was that the treatment had to be rationally related to things they would have to do later on when they became officers." Years later several of the men whom he had trained as plebes went out of their way to thank him for treating them fairly.

Some black midshipmen found indoctrination practices distasteful and shied away from participating in them. Eddie Graves hated the vicious hazing he had been subjected to plebe year. As an upperclassman he determined not to behave that way. As the 1975 *Lucky Bag* put it, he was known to "spoon plebes, spoon plebes, and spoon plebes."[6] Cary Hithon didn't spoon plebes on sight, but he wasn't hard on them either. "By no stretch of the imagination was I going to harass a plebe the way I was harassed," he recalled. He believed that minorities in general harassed plebes to a lesser extent than whites. Besides, football and academics left little time for running plebes. Marv King did not get involved in plebe indoctrination because he considered it "mickey mouse."

Black midshipmen achieved a number of firsts during this period. Charlie Bolden was elected president of the class of 1968 during his plebe and youngster years, the first African American class president. A speech he made in Mahan Hall during his plebe-year campaign cemented his reputation as a jokester. "The only other time I remember being out in front of this many white guys was back home in South Carolina," he said, "and I was running to get away from them."

Tony Watson broke several color barriers. A star man academically, he made regular appearances on the dean's list and superintendent's list. He was twice elected president of the class of 1970. At the end of his second-class year, he received the Carl Vinson Leadership Award for standing highest in his class in "Aptitude for the Naval Service." As a senior he became the first African American regimental commander, a five-striper, and received a commendatory letter from the superintendent for "having demonstrated outstanding officer-like qualities and contributing most by precept and example to the development of these qualities within the Brigade."[7]

"Tony Watson was kind of a groundbreaker for us," recalled Leo Williams, "because Tony was an incredibly popular, charismatic, and competent person. No doubt about it. Tony's powerful personality along with his competence broke down some of those barriers. Guys in the class loved him. For him to be the class president and the first five-striper certainly paved the way for others to get to that level and higher later on."

At the end of his first-class year, Bert Freeman became the first African American and the first fencer to receive the Naval Academy Athletic Association Sword for "personally excelling in athletics during his years of varsity competition." As part of the award his name was engraved on a tablet next to the names of past winners such as football star Roger Staubach. Freeman also received the Vice Admiral E. L. Cochrane Fencing Award for "contributing most to the promotion of fencing at the Naval Academy."[8]

Breaking color barriers picked up momentum in the '70s. In the 1972/73 academic year, Henderson Lawson, Cozy E. Bailey, Ronaldo A. Coulter, and Cleveland E. Cooper were elected, respectively, president, vice president, secretary, and treasurer of the class of 1975, the first time blacks occupied the four top elected spots in a class. Lloyd W. Keaser, '72, became a three-time EIWA wrestling champion. Each year since 1964, about 1 percent of the brigade were chosen to be Trident Scholars, who pursued individual research projects with faculty members. Charles M. Collier, '71, Owen D. Corpin, '74, and David A. Beam, '79, all became Trident Scholars.[9]

During his first-class year, Eddie Graves became the first black president of the Glee Club. At the time he was the club's only African American member. He considered winning the election to be one of his "crowning moments" at the Academy and one of the "highest honors" of his life. One moment in particular stood out in his memory. At a performance at an all-black school, a certain degree of racial tension permeated the atmosphere during the Glee Club's opening medley. After the last note faded into the chilly air, Graves walked out to the microphone in front of the group. "My name is Eddie Graves and I'm the president of this organization," he said. "As you can see, I brought my boys with me." The audience exploded in applause and shouts. "We had them the rest of the time," he recalled. "That was probably our best concert."

Late in the winter of 1977, the Annapolis chamber of commerce selected Midshipman 1/C Robert A. Goodrum as the first black midshipman of the year for his involvement in community activities, particularly the midshipman Big Brothers of America organization.[10]

Although Jeff Sapp never became a stellar student at the Academy, he excelled on the gridiron. Although standing only 5'11" tall and weighing around 200 pounds, he was named to three All-America teams as a defensive middle guard. During junior year, he was a key player in a defense that was ranked third in the country. In a particularly memorable game against Pitt that year (1975) he made fifteen tackles, helping Navy stop Heisman Trophy winner Tony Dorsett in a 17–0 shutout. As a firsty, he became not only the first African American co-captain of the football team but also the first athlete of any color to receive in the same year both the Thompson Trophy Cup, awarded to the midshipman who did the most to promote Academy athletics, and the Cooke Memorial Football Trophy, awarded to the top graduating football player.

The *Lucky Bags* from this period, the midshipmen's yearbooks, reflect the increasing integration of African Americans into all aspects of the Academy's culture. The 1966 *Lucky Bag* includes a photo of Charlie Bolden in the Popular Music Club and a sprinkling of photos of black underclassmen, but that's about it. The 1969 *Lucky Bag* features a picture of an African American studying, the first time a black midshipman appeared in the uncaptioned photo spread up front. It also has pictures of Lieutenant Norman serving on the faculty of the department of English, history and government, Commander

Thompson as Sixth Battalion officer, and the Jay Gees. The 1971 *Lucky Bag* was the first to include photos of black women among midshipmen's girl-friends. The 1975 *Lucky Bag* has photographs of the Variations, black female cheerleaders, black midshipmen and their dates, and the three black officers then in the executive department—Lieutenant Commander Carter, and Lieu-tenant Commander Tolbert, and Lieutenant Lucas. The 1979 *Lucky Bag* has photos of black men and women on approximately 150 of its 700-odd pages, or about 20 percent. The African American midshipmen are seen engaged in every Academy activity, from being sworn in as a plebe, getting a haircut, and scaling Herndon Monument to handling plebes, being a Trident scholar, and graduating.

During this period, black midshipmen achieved a more proportionate share of striper positions during their first-class year. Charlie Bolden served for one set as company commander, a three-striper position, then during the final set as regimental operations officer, a four-striper position. Bert Freeman had two stripes as company subcommander. Ev Greene was a squad leader. Leo Williams wore four stripes as a regimental operations officer. Eddie Graves wore three stripes and remained brigade parade officer throughout his first-class year. Ed Gilmore wore three stripes in the honor set. James Jackson became a company commander and a three-striper.

Black midshipmen also broke the barrier that kept their predecessors from reaching top striper positions. Tony Watson might have been the six-striper his first-class year if not for a sit-in outside the superintendent's house staged by about one hundred of his classmates during the fall of their second-class year (1968) over a policy instituted by the executive department that reduced the number of free weekends available to second classmen. Although Watson was not involved, the protest took place on his watch as second-class six-striper, so he did not make brigade commander as a firsty. As it was, he was a five-striper in the spring or honor set along with Leo Williams, a four-striper. James Jackson was interviewed to be brigade commander when he became a firsty but was not selected.

Ric Samuels was deputy brigade commander, a five-striper, during the honor set of his first-class year, in the spring of 1973. His white classmate Gary Roughead, who later became commandant (1997–99), was the six-striper during that set. "If you asked the blacks," Samuels recalled, "the reason I didn't become brigade commander was because I was black. If you asked whites, the reason I got five stripes was because I was black. Neither one is accurate. The truth of the matter was that Gary was better than I was at be-ing the brigade commander. I would never pick me over Gary, but I think I earned what I got." Samuels and Roughead roomed together that set and became good friends.[11]

In the spring of 1976, Chuck Reddix became the first African American brigade commander in the honor set. Reddix believed that his color influenced his selection as six-striper in a positive way. "I think I was chosen based on military performance, grades, personality, and, being realistic, race," he recalled. "Let's face it. However, having said that, you've got to remember that the black guys in my class were extremely capable. Derwood Curtis was the second regimental commander when I was the brigade commander. The color company commander at June Week that year, Jordan Smith, was black. In fact, Derwood's company officer, when I was brigade commander, took great delight in telling me that if it weren't for my grades being higher, then Derwood would have been the brigade commander. It actually says that my being in the seat was not a fluke; that I wasn't picked only because I was black. If they hadn't picked me, they could have easily picked Derwood, because he was good. Still is. I would say, though, they picked me because I majored in Navy. I happened to be at the right place at the right time with the right qualifications. They didn't have to lower any standards or reach down or play any stupid games to do it. And in the natural course of life, it would have happened sooner or later. That it happened sooner than later was a good deal."

Reddix's selection as six-striper created a modest amount of fanfare. Bernard Shaw, then a reporter for CBS news, interviewed him one afternoon after parade practice, and the interview aired on the CBS Evening News. Newspaper reporters covered the story as well. Articles on Reddix appeared in the *Afro-American*, the Annapolis *Evening Capital*, and other newspapers. An article in *Dawn Magazine*, a supplement to the *Afro-American*, pointed out that the Academy had come a long way since the 1930s when black midshipmen were "booted out of Annapolis simply because they were black."[12]

Reddix heard no grumbling from white midshipmen that he became the six-striper only because he was black. He did, however, receive two anonymous hate messages. He took them in stride. "The brigade commander has a telephone and can receive outside calls," he recalled. "I got one crank call. And somebody sent me an audio tape which had a little unpleasantness on it. 'It is the role of the black man to overpower the white man,' it said, and accused me of being the white man's lackey. Of course, you're batting national average, then. It was no big deal. You just kind of chuckle." Reddix also heard rumors that some of the older alumni referred to the third set of stripers in the class of 1976 as the "Black Set" or "Nigger Set."

Nothing negative attended the graduation ceremony that year, however. "The guys on the gymnastics team happily threw me into the wading pool," Reddix recalled. As commander of the 1976 Color Company, the 17th, Jordan Smith selected Stephanie B. McManus, whose family sponsored many black midshipmen, as color girl. She was the Academy's first African American color girl.

Distinguished African American educator Walter J. Leonard took stock of the Academy's racial policies after President Carter appointed him to the Board of Visitors in 1979. Leonard, president of Fisk University, a historically black institution in Nashville, Tennessee, and creator of a plan for equal opportunity in education and employment adopted by hundreds of American colleges, was particularly interested in the Academy's efforts to increase diversity. Throughout his two-year term, Leonard communicated regularly with other board members as well as with the Academy's leadership, enabling him to develop a view of the Academy firmly grounded in fact.

Leonard concluded that the Academy was doing as well or better than most American educational institutions in achieving equal opportunity, and he regarded the Academy as a "beacon to the rest of society" for diversity. To Leonard, Rear Admiral William P. Lawrence, superintendent and fellow Tennessean, symbolized the revolution in the Academy's racial policy. Leonard likened Lawrence to Justice John Marshall Harlan, who, despite being born into a slaveholding family, became a champion of civil rights, best known for writing the sole dissenting opinion in *Plessy v. Ferguson*. "Very often throughout our history," Leonard recalled, "it was the person that came from the area of the society most reluctant to accord equality who would lead the society in changing." The admiral and educator became close friends. Leonard himself became a symbol of change at the Academy when, on 1 April 1981, the other members of the Board of Visitors elected him chairman, thus making him the first African American accorded that honor.

Throughout the late 1960s and early '70s, greater proportions of black midshipmen selected the Marine Corps than their white classmates.[13] Bert Freeman became a marine because there seemed to be more camaraderie in the Corps than in the Navy. Bruce Henry entered the Corps because a dictatorial skipper during first-class cruise turned him off of the Navy. He believed the Marine Corps offered a better range of choices. Will Merrell selected the Marines because of a battalion officer who falsely accused him of hazing a plebe, called him a bigot, and recommended his dismissal for conduct unbecoming an officer when he was a segundo. Although the battalion officer apologized to Merrell when he found he had the wrong man, the experience left a bad taste in his mouth for the Navy. Leo Williams wanted to be a Marine Corps officer even before he entered the Academy. "Marines do what they say they're going to do," he recalled, "so integrity was a huge part of the reason to be a marine. But they also have a tremendous confidence and pride. When you see a marine, generally that marine is standing tall with his chest out. He looks like a million bucks, like he just came off of a poster. That's what the marines at the Academy looked like. It very strongly reinforced everything that I thought I wanted to be as a marine. There's also some of the macho tough, let's go out and kick some ass attitude that is also part of being a marine."

Some black alumni have led difficult lives after leaving Annapolis. Tony Jackson graduated from Princeton in 1971, bounced around from one job to another in state and federal government service, and suffered a long bout with depression in the late 1990s that cost him his job. At this writing he is struggling to reenter the job market. John Porter became a Marine aviator. He realized his potential as a fighter pilot and encountered no serious prejudice. In 1978 he left the Corps to pursue an airline career. In 1987 he joined the Air National Guard and four years later became a full-time F-16 instructor pilot. Unfortunately, he suffered a great deal of racially motivated harassment in the National Guard, particularly after a medical problem grounded him in 1996. Will Merrell left the Marines after twice being passed over for major and believed racism was largely responsible. He has since worked as a human resources executive, specializing in diversity, employee grievances, and affirmative action. Eddie Graves was honorably discharged from the Navy in 1977 for fraternization. For most of the 1990s, he fought a war against the HIV virus, both as an activist and a victim of AIDS.

Many black midshipmen who did not graduate went on to have rewarding careers. Lamar Chapman finished his education at the University of Illinois and the University of Chicago, earned a law degree, and forged a lucrative career for himself in law, marketing, management, and acquisition. Bruce Franklin, who resigned instead of turning back as the academic board had recommended at the end of his youngster year, served in the Air Force as an enlisted man, then embarked on a career as a computer systems field engineer and salesman.

Many black Academy graduates have done well in both the military and civilian worlds. Bruce Henry left the Marines after five years' active duty and started a career as an engineer with Mobil Oil Company. Bert Freeman stayed in the Marine Corps for eleven and a half years. Highlights of his career included commanding a bulk fuel company, building tank bridges in Okinawa, and starting a Marine Corps fencing team, winning the national championship in fencing in 1972, and representing his country in the Olympics that year. After leaving the Corps, Freeman worked for DuPont for a while and then set up his own management consultant business. He published his first book in 2006.[14] Ric Samuels fulfilled his dream of becoming a naval aviator. He earned his wings and flew A-6 Intruders. He then reached a point in his career where he would not be flying much. And he wanted to get married and start a family, which were difficult undertakings during the long deployments of the mid-

'70s. After getting out of the Navy he worked at IBM in sales and marketing for nine years, then started his own company. Charlie Boyd loved serving his country as an officer in the Marine Corps but disliked the "good old boy" attitude he found among many officers and hated the blatant racism he ran across on rare occasions. But he never encountered discrimination that hindered his career. He remained in the service until 1984, when he left the Corps to raise a family and earn more money in the civilian sector, working for a company in the nuclear industry in capacities ranging from engineering to management. Chuck Cole left the Navy after his five-year obligation. "I just didn't like the amount of sea time that I was putting in," he recalled. In the civilian world he found that having the Academy on his resume helped him land jobs. He worked for several defense contractors in program management, earned an M.B.A., and is currently employed by Lockheed Martin. Chuck Reddix survived Nuclear Power School and the surface warfare basic course, qualified as nuclear engineer officer on board the carrier *Enterprise* (CVN-65), earned a master's degree in mechanical engineering at the Naval Postgraduate School in Monterey, served as weapons officer on the cruiser *Josephus Daniels* (CG-27), and helped build the carrier *Abraham Lincoln* (CVN-72) as reactor training assistant. He left the Navy when the strain of being away from his family became too much and took a job running a nuclear power plant southwest of Houston. Byron Marchant served in submarines for five years, earned a law degree from the University of Virginia School of Law, and then forged a career in the telecommunications industry. At this writing he is executive vice president, chief administrative officer, and general counsel for Black Entertainment Television, Inc.

Many African American alumni left the regular service but kept their hand in as reservists. Kerwin Miller never thought of himself as a career naval officer. He made lieutenant, became a reservist, earned two law degrees and a master's in law, and has worked as a lawyer ever since. During the late 1980s and throughout the '90s, he involved himself heavily in alumni activities, serving on the board of trustees, in the Blue and Gold Program, and in the minority recruiting effort. Leo Williams became an artillery officer and held commands at every level of the Corps. He transferred to the reserve in 1978, rose to the rank of major general, and rarely encountered racial problems along the way. When he left the regular service, he took a job with the Ford Motor Company, eventually becoming brand manager for the Ford F-150 pickup and Ford Expedition sport utility vehicle. General Williams retired from the Marine Corps Reserve in 2004. Marv King's first tour involved minority recruiting in his hometown. After traveling extensively throughout the Far East and Mediterranean, he became a naval reservist in 1986 and rose to the rank of captain. When he left the regular navy he started a second career with Proctor and Gamble.

A few black alumni spent the bulk of their professional lives in uniform. After graduating from the Academy, Tony Watson entered the nuclear power program. In 1987, he became the second African American submarine skipper when he took command of the nuclear attack submarine *Jacksonville* (SSN-699). In 1992, he took command of Submarine Squadron Seven, becoming the first African American submarine squadron skipper. In 1994, he was promoted to rear admiral (lower half). He left the service in 1996 and became chief executive officer of U.S. Alliance Group, a recruiting firm that focuses on people leaving the military for jobs in the civilian sector. Ev Greene became the first African American commissioned officer to complete basic underwater demolition/SEAL training. He remained in the Navy for thirty years, largely in special warfare and equal opportunity billets, and retired as a captain. After earning his wings as a naval aviator and helicopter aircraft commander designation, Bobby Watts became commanding officer of Helicopter Combat Support Squadron Eight, commander of Training Air Wing Five, and a fellow in the CNO Strategic Studies Group. James Jackson remained in the Navy until 1995 and then became minority recruiter for Anne Arundel Community College near Annapolis. Ed Gilmore served as a surface line officer for twenty years after graduation. The highlight of his career was command of the frigate *Reuben James* (FFG-57). After leaving the Navy, he took a position as an executive assistant with Black Entertainment Television. Cary Hithon obtained his surface warfare officer qualification, commanded the minesweeper *Illusive* (MSO-448) and the frigate *Gary* (FFG-51), and rose to the rank of captain. Hithon's classmate and teammate Jeff Sapp commanded six ships and also became a captain. Despite his undistinguished academic record as a midshipman, Sapp earned three master's degrees while a commissioned officer. Lloyd Prince became a naval aviator and flew A-7 Corsairs and F/A-18 Hornets. He left the service in 1994 and became an airline pilot. Derwood Curtis, '76, Julius S. Caesar, '77, Victor G. Guillory, '78, Melvin G. Williams Jr., '78, Anthony L. Winns, '78, and Arthur J. Johnson Jr., '79, have risen to flag rank and remain in the service at this writing.

For some African American alumni, bitterness over their Academy experiences lingered for years after graduation. Tony Jackson believed the Academy accorded too much power to upperclassmen who were not mature enough to handle it responsibly. Bruce Franklin carried shame and resentment over not graduating for twenty years after leaving the Academy. He believed he would have stayed had he received better guidance on the implications of turning back. "I spent my life since then comparing where I am and what I'm doing to where my classmates who graduated are and what they're doing," he said. Despite his bitterness, he remained in touch with many of his classmates and active in the Naval Academy Alumni Association.

Other black alumni looked back on their four years by the Severn with mixed feelings. "It's hard to forget the bad experiences," recalled Ev Greene. "However, I did meet some outstanding individuals who epitomize the expression 'an officer and a gentleman.'" Bruce Henry had similar feelings. "If I had known what plebe year was going to be like," he recalled, "I probably would have never gone to the Academy. But I'm very proud to be a graduate. I got the diploma. I got the officer's commission. These are things that I hold my head high about even now. Obviously some of the social experiences were very unpleasant, but they were also growth experiences. It brings to mind something my parents said to me early on. Sometimes you have to try to be twice as good to get the same opportunities." Although John Porter enjoyed his Academy experience, it emphasized to him "how deeply ingrained racism was in America from top to bottom." "I graduated much more cynical and aggressive," he recalled. "My mother made particular note of my cynicism about racism after the Academy." Bobby Watts didn't wear his class ring or visit the Academy for ten years after graduating in 1973. "Professionally it provided me with the focus to succeed in the Navy," he recalled. "Personally it was a difficult, lonely, unhappy part of my life. If I could do it again, I wouldn't. But I would never stop my children from attending if they wanted to." Cary Hithon thought it was better to be *from* the Academy than be *at* the Academy. "I'm glad I did it," he said. "I wouldn't do it again." He believed that an NROTC program would have been a much less painful route to a commission as an ensign or second lieutenant. To Chuck Reddix, the Academy was "a pain in the butt most of the time." "As a rule," he recalled, "we thought of it then as 'a $55,000 education rammed up your ass a nickel at time.'" Reddix had two major complaints. "One, I felt I was trained more than educated. I got through there without ever taking an English course. You shouldn't be able to graduate from college without taking an English course. And two, it wasn't co-ed. We didn't get a good appreciation for women there. You never got to interact with them except on weekends when everybody was at their best trying to impress everybody. The real world doesn't work that way. If you were smart enough to figure that out, it didn't harm you. But if you weren't, you were in for some rude awakenings." On the whole, however, he considered his experience as a midshipman to be positive. "I never regret having gone," he added. "I don't have a whole lot of horrible memories. In fact, most of them are downright comical."

Many black graduates look back favorably on their time as midshipmen. "Graduation was probably one of the saddest days of my life," recalled Tony Watson, "because I was having so much fun at the Naval Academy, doing a lot of things." Bert Freeman said that "the Academy provided the best leadership experience I ever had in my life." Charlie Boyd summed up his Academy experience as "very tough and demanding, but also very worthwhile and ful-filling." The Academy taught Chuck Cole that even painful experiences can be beneficial. For Ed Gilmore, one of the most important benefits of going to the Academy was the lifelong friends he made.

Even African Americans who left before graduation derived benefit from their time at the Academy. Lamar Chapman, who attributed his departure to racism, considered his Academy experience to be "priceless." "I would not hesitate to recommend the Academy to any young man or woman looking for the finest education the world has to offer," he said, "particularly if they are in the minority. The Academy is a fine institution with a world-class reputation. Just having been there opened countless doors for me." The Academy imbued Bruce Franklin with discipline, leadership skills, and the ability to think on his feet. "It gave me the drive to be successful in whatever I do," he said.

Many black alumni from this period found that having the Academy on their resumes has benefited their careers. "When you say you graduated from the Naval Academy," recalled Bert Freeman, "it's like saying you graduated from Harvard University. It's helped me in terms of getting interviews, job offers, jobs, that sort of thing." Don Montgomery found that having the Academy on his resume opened doors. "The Naval Academy is an enabler," he said. "Before they know what color you are, you've already got the interview. Then they see that you have talent. They say, 'Either I'm going to hire this guy or my competition will.'" Ed Gilmore believed that the black alumni who graduated in the mid-'70s owed their success to the Academy. "Gene Ford, my classmate, is president of a construction company," he noted. "Maurice Tose, '78, has his own company. If you take the classes of '74, '75, '76, and '77 and look at where they came from and where they are now, there will be one common denominator. They all came from nothing and ascended to great things. It all started with the Academy. I feel good about being a Naval Academy graduate." Byron Marchant found that the education he received at the Academy served him well in business. "The Naval Academy has at the root of its curriculum discipline, analysis, judgment, and planning," he said. "Whether you're in command of a submarine or directing the legal and opera-tional areas of a multi-billion dollar multimedia conglomerate, these elements of management are mandatory."

While attending a Naval Academy minority alumni conference in 2000, Bert Freeman paused to reflect upon the accomplishments of black midship-men from his era. "You hardly think about yourself as a pioneer until you walk in a room one day and you're one of the oldest people there," he said. "Folks who are now captains and colonels see you and your classmates as legends. That's powerful. You've schooled some of these guys, taken them aside and given them advice, and they're captains and colonels today. And then to see my classmates and the guys who schooled us. Charlie Bolden was the commander of the space shuttle. Tony Watson was the first African American to command a nuclear-powered submarine squadron. Ev Greene, who was on the swimming sub squad for three years, was a Navy SEAL for thirty years. It's important for black midshipmen today to know that. Now you can look in a room and see ten African Americans, all Navy captains. For white folks, this might seem ordinary, but for African Americans here at the Naval Academy, and particularly for folks in our class, it is absolutely phenomenal to see this kind of growth, these kinds of accomplishments, and so many prominent people who look like you. We were lucky if we saw a black commander walk across the Naval Academy grounds back then. To feel like a pioneer is the most powerful thing. It makes you proud."

The revolution in the Navy's racial policy during the Vietnam era advanced the revolution that had begun during World War II but languished in the interim. Political pressures resulting from the civil rights movement and black unrest in the cities drove Defense Secretary McNamara and Admiral Zumwalt to lead the later effort. By the 1970s, the goal was to achieve proportionate representation of blacks throughout the Navy, including the officer corps. Official neglect gave way to affirmative action. By the nation's bicentennial in 1976, the Navy had institutionalized a policy of equal opportunity.

The Vietnam-era revolution in the Navy's racial policy forced the Naval Academy to develop and implement a sustained minority recruiting program for the first time in its history. No longer could the Academy remain unconcerned about the number of blacks who entered, nor could it afford to discourage publicity about African American midshipmen as it had done in November 1950 when reporters requested a photograph of Reeves Taylor and were turned down. Such a policy only exacerbated the Navy's World War II hangover. When the Navy finally did make a genuine effort to increase minority representation in the 1960s, the chickens came home to roost, to borrow a phrase from Malcolm X, in low interest and low turnout among African Americans. The Naval Academy in particular, as Admiral Kauffman discovered, suffered because of the bitterness in the black community over the lily-white legacy of the officer corps. As a result, the Navy had to hire advertising firms and assign Reeves Taylor, Ken Johnson, and other black and white officers the job of finding a cure.

Despite McNamara's course toward affirmative action, it took direct intervention by the president of the United States and the CNO to propel the Academy in that direction. The Gesell Committee goaded the chief of naval personnel into undertaking ad hoc, temporary, and ineffective recruiting measures during the early 1960s, but President Johnson's order to double the Academy's black enrollment in July 1965 shook the dickens out of Admiral Kauffman and spurred him into launching a formal, sustained minority recruiting effort. Before then, the Navy only had to make an effort; the president demanded results.

Although the Academy had doubled black enrollment by the time Admiral Zumwalt became CNO, it still was not moving fast enough toward proportional representation to suit him. If Zumwalt didn't shake the dickens out of Admiral Calvert, he certainly spurred him to intensify the Academy's minority recruiting effort and broaden the selection base of black candidates. As a result, the number of black plebes coming in each year skyrocketed from a handful to scores.

By the time of America's bicentennial celebration in July 1976, the Academy had a permanent, well-developed, and fully functioning minority recruiting program in place. The program consisted of four principal elements: informing the black community about the Academy, encouraging young black men to apply, educating them through BOOST and at NAPS to get them academically qualified, and assisting them in obtaining congressional appointments.

In 1965, BuPers spearheaded the Academy's recruiting effort, with help from the Academy's Blue and Gold Program. No office within BuPers dealt specifically with minority recruiting for Annapolis. In 1976, the director of candidate guidance spearheaded the Academy's overall recruiting effort. His organization included three minority affairs counselors whose specific mission was to increase minority enrollment.

When John F. Kennedy ran for office in 1960, the Academy ignored the black community. When Gerald R. Ford ran for office in 1976, the Academy marketed there. The most effective means for reaching the black community during this period proved to be the traveling done and personal contacts made by the minority affairs staff in the candidate guidance office.

Throughout this period, the greatest challenge in minority recruiting remained the dearth of fully qualified and motivated black candidates. As affirmative action became the law of the land, all the services, most civilian colleges, and large segments of private industry lined up to recruit the highly qualified "instant Negro," as *Ebony* magazine had put it. With school systems only slowly emerging from de jure and de facto segregation during this period, the pool of highly qualified African Americans remained small and competition for them remained fierce. The Navy not only had to overcome its World War II hangover but also had to compete with civilian schools offering full academic rides without the service obligation and prospect of long separation from loved ones. The solution the Academy hit upon was not to lower standards but to broaden the selection base by getting academically underqualified blacks up to speed scholastically. This strategy failed to meet the Academy's goal of proportional representation during this period. Nevertheless, it increased the number of black midshipmen from a token presence to a significant minority that more realistically reflected the population of the United States. It also represented a genuine effort to overcome the Navy's racist past.

African Americans were fully integrated into the brigade of midshipmen by the time the class of 1976 graduated. This does not mean that racial problems ended or that discrimination no longer occurred. It does mean, however, that African American midshipmen had virtually an equal chance at Academy opportunities.

Integration resulted from reform of the Navy and Naval Academy's racial policies. Before 1965, the Academy leadership considered race a non-issue. After President Johnson shook the dickens out of Admiral Kauffman and especially after Admiral Zumwalt mandated reform throughout the fleet, race appeared near the top of the leadership's agenda. While the classes of 1969–79 were passing through, the leadership diversified the Academy's faculty and staff, involved itself in off-base housing issues, created various equal opportunity and human relations committees and an affirmative action plan, provided racial awareness training for midshipmen, and supported extracurricular activities that celebrated black music and black culture. By 1976, monitoring the racial situation and ensuring equal opportunity for black midshipmen had become explicit parts of the superintendent and commandant's mission. Institutional racism had gone with the wind.

Reforms in the plebe indoctrination system and the Academy's racial policies changed the manner in which racist upperclassmen could act out their prejudices on black plebes. Early in this period, physical indoctrination methods were still the norm. Reforms in the plebe indoctrination system reduced the amount of physical hazing that occurred but did not eliminate it altogether. Eventually, the psychological supplanted the physical as the predominant form of indoctrination. Throughout the period, the intensity of either sort varied from one company to the next.

These changes positively affected black plebes' lives but did not eliminate negative racial attitudes and behavior. Although affirmative action brought people of different races and cultures together at the Academy, it did not teach them how to get along. It took the experience of living together to do that. And, despite these changes, prejudiced upperclassmen could still make life miserable for black plebes, and in some instances precipitate their departure.

The major element of the Navy's racial policy that affected the lives of black midshipmen of the classes of 1969–79 was the policy to increase their proportion. The most effective antidote to racially motivated hazing proved to be the presence of black upperclassmen. As their numbers increased during the 1970s, black midshipmen were no longer rare enough to be viewed as novelties; instead, they were present in each company and eventually in each class in each company. Racists could no longer easily escape the observation of those who would oppose them in venting their prejudices on black plebes. More than any of the racial awareness training the Academy offered, it was the growing presence of black midshipmen that reduced racially motivated hazing. Black upperclassmen provided moral support and occasionally ran interference for black plebes. Sometimes a black upperclassman had to have a talk with a classmate to get him to stop discriminating against black plebes. Sometimes the mere fact of his existence was all that was necessary to inhibit discriminatory practices in indoctrination.

Institutional reform and increasing black presence did not eliminate racially motivated mistreatment of black plebes, but they certainly reduced it. The upshot was that African Americans who became midshipmen toward the end of this period were less likely to encounter discrimination than their predecessors had been.

Early in the 1970s, the increasing numbers of black midshipmen solidified the black subculture that had gelled in the 1960s. In particular, the social and support network, the so-called Seventh Batt formed by black upperclassmen and Commander Ken Johnson, facilitated black plebes' passage across company and class lines to form and maintain friendships.

By the late 1970s, the black midshipmen's subculture, which had developed in part to meet black midshipmen's social needs not provided by the Academy, became more diffuse as the Academy became more responsive to their needs. African Americans who entered in the early '70s experienced a reformed plebe indoctrination system and more academic choices as well as increasing official recognition of their cultural diversity, evident in the administration's creation of black studies courses, support of music groups, and sponsorship of Black History Month events. The impetus for the administration to celebrate African American culture came from below, from Professor Massie and from the black midshipmen themselves. Though diffused, the black midshipmen's subculture never disappeared because as black people, African American midshipmen shared a common culture whose bonds survived the indoctrination process.

The boarding options available to black midshipmen's dates symbolized these changes. Before 1965, they stayed at Lil Chase's house. During the late '60s and early '70s, they could stay with any of several families on Mrs. Marshall's segregated drag house list or a hotel in town. By the end of the '70s, black midshipmen's dates could stay anywhere white midshipmen's dates could.

The greatest symbols of change in the Academy's racial policy were the elimination of the proscription against interracial dancing at tea fights and the ascendancy of black midshipmen to the top striper and elected leadership positions. By dropping the proscription against interracial dancing, the leadership removed the most prominent symbol of Jim Crow apartheid at the Academy. The elections of Charlie Bolden and Tony Watson as presidents of their respective classes proved that the majority of midshipmen judged their peers by their leadership abilities, not by the color of their skin. Chuck Reddix's holding the six-striper spot during the honor set symbolized the Academy's latent integration, for if an African American could hold the top position in the brigade, an African American could hold any other position if he had the right stuff.

Taken together, these changes mark a fundamental shift in the Naval Academy's culture. Responding to pressure for reform from above and below, successive superintendents and commandants between 1965 and 1976 instituted changes necessary to facilitate and complete the integration of African Americans into the brigade.

You can be Black, and Navy too.

Navy recruiting poster, 1972. United States Naval Historical Center.

Photograph, dubbed the "One Percent," including all thirty black midshipmen present at the Naval Academy, c. 1971. Special Collections and Archives Division, Nimitz Library, United States Naval Academy.

► Peggy Kimbo, 20 August 1990. Photograph by David W. Trozzo. Courtesy of the Maryland State Archives Special Collections (The Annapolis I Remember Collection) MSA SC 2140.

▼ The Jay Gees, 1970. Bert Freeman, future Olympic fencer, sits in the front row on the left; Leo Williams, future Marine Corps major general, stands in the second row, far left; and Tony Watson, future Navy rear admiral, appears in the second row, third from left. *Lucky Bag,* 1970, Nimitz Library, United States Naval Academy.

John F. Porter, Class of 1971, photographed at sea during youngster cruise, 1968. Naval Historical Center.

Robert D. Watts, Class of 1973. *Lucky Bag*, 1973, Nimitz Library, United States Naval Academy.

The Variations. *Lucky Bag*, 1975, Nimitz Library, United States Naval Academy.

▶ Donald Montgomery, Class of 1974. *Lucky Bag,* 1973, Nimitz Library, United States Naval Academy.

▼ Boyd E. Graves, Class of 1975, leading the Glee Club. *Lucky Bag,* 1975, Nimitz Library, United States Naval Academy.

◀ Kerwin E. Miller, Class of 1975. *Lucky Bag*, 1975, Nimitz Library, United States Naval Academy.

▲ Cary Hithon, Class of 1977. *Lucky Bag*, 1977, Nimitz Library, United States Naval Academy.

Left to right, Ensign Mason C. Reddix, the first black brigade commander; Midshipman 4/C Janie Mines, the first black female midshipman; and Professor Samuel P. Massie, the first black faculty member, September 1976. Special Collections and Archives Division, Nimitz Library, United States Naval Academy.

PART III
Unparalleled Opportunity: African American Men and Women, 1976–1999

Toward Proportional Representation

A FTER THE Navy adopted its first affirmative action plan in 1976, political attention to racial issues ebbed and flowed with the personal and political interests of individual policymakers, as it always had. But no matter who was sitting in Congress or the White House, racial issues remained near the top of the Navy's personnel policy agenda for the rest of the twentieth century. The Naval Academy's recruiting program strove to make the naval officer corps look more like America by striving to achieve proportional minority representation.

With the last vestiges of conscious institutional discrimination purged from the Naval Academy by 1976, by and large African Americans from the classes of 1980–99 enjoyed equal opportunity as midshipmen. This is not to say that racism had vanished. During the last quarter of the twentieth century, the Academy continued to attract midshipmen from all walks of life with all sorts of attitudes, including racial prejudice. Although official policy forbade discrimination, bigots still found ways to act out their prejudices. That said, there was perhaps less racial discrimination at the Academy than in most American institutions, whether federal, educational, corporate, or otherwise.

The Academy's chief social problem after the class of 1976 graduated was the integration of women into the brigade of midshipmen. The physical and social differences between the sexes were far more profound than any such differences among racial or ethnic groups. Within traditional U.S. military culture, service academies and combat duty billets had long been male bastions from which women were excluded. Even after the president authorized the appointment of women to the academies, a sizable proportion of male officers and midshipmen refused to let go of the notion that women didn't belong. As a result, women midshipmen faced sexual discrimination in varying degrees throughout this period, regardless of race. Black female midshipmen faced prejudice because of their race as well as their gender.

Throughout the period 1976–99, ultimate responsibility for equal opportunity in the Navy rested with the CNO, who sponsored the overall program, monitored the Navy's progress in implementing it, and reviewed various policies and procedures that supported it. The chief of naval personnel, division directors within OPNAV, and special assistants to the CNO and chief of naval personnel formulated and managed equal opportunity policy, and commanding officers and supervisors implemented the policy throughout the fleet.

The Navy's racial policy influenced the Naval Academy in two ways. First, throughout the period the Navy's leadership struggled to achieve proportional representation of African Americans in the officer corps, even as the criterion for "proportional" representation changed. As the source of about 20 percent of the officers commissioned into the Navy each year, the Academy strove to produce proportions of minority graduates in keeping with OPNAV policy. Second, as a naval command, the Academy implemented equal opportunity policy for its people, including the civilians, the uniformed officers, and, especially, the midshipmen.[1]

The Navy Affirmative Action Plan (NAAP) was the bedrock of the Navy's racial policy. The plan incorporated equal opportunity initiatives and provided guidance and direction for development of supporting plans throughout the Navy, including the Naval Academy. The plan covered professional growth, women in the Navy, equal opportunity and race relations training, and minority recruiting. It listed specific objectives along with procedures and a timetable for meeting them. It also called for an annual assessment of the implementation of affirmative action throughout the Navy. The NAAP did not, however, set goals for minority representation in terms of specific percentages.[2]

When the first NAAP appeared in June 1976, the Academy already had a well-developed recruiting program that pursued its objective along well-trodden avenues. Generally speaking, the Academy conducted recruitment through the Blue and Gold Program, which involved reserve officers, Academy alumni, and prominent citizens; Operation Information, which involved midshipmen; the Educator Visitation Program; local recruiters attached to the Navy Recruiting Command; the Naval Academy Athletic Association; and organizations affiliated with the Academy like the Naval Academy Foundation, the Naval Academy Alumni Association, and the Navy League of the United States. The Blue and Gold Program remained the most prominent and important means of recruiting, with more than 1,500 Blue and Gold officers and affiliates participating.

Although the Academy sought minority candidates through these organizations, it relied mainly upon the minority admissions counselors (MACs), as minority affairs counselors came to be called, for minority input. For the rest of the century, the Academy sought to recruit African Americans by traditional means as well as to refine the methods used by the MACs.

The candidate guidance staff continued efforts to increase minority involvement in the Blue and Gold Program, Operation Information, Educator Visitation Program, and other traditional recruiting avenues. Each issue of the *Blue and Gold Newsletter* carried a section on minority affairs, encouraging all Blue and Gold officers and affiliates to participate in minority recruitment and including tips for doing so. Travel by the Glee Club, Drum and Bugle Corps, and Gospel Choir, founded in the fall of 1985, served the overall recruiting effort because their sharp appearance and excellent performances generated interest in the Academy wherever they visited, and their itineraries increasingly included schools with large minority enrollments. Twenty African American members of the class of 1977 volunteered for six-month tours of recruiting duty after graduation before moving on to their permanent duty assignments, inaugurating a program that remained in operation for the rest of the 1970s. The three MACs on the candidate guidance staff specifically responsible for recruitment and guidance of minority candidates spent much of their time on the road visiting black communities.[3]

The Academy's minority recruiting effort bore fruit largely because of MAC efforts. The three MACs had an enormous territory to cover (the entire United States), their visitation-presentation approach to recruiting required a significant investment of time, and they faced stiff competition for the same pool of qualified blacks from other service academies and civilian institutions. Their efforts, however, paid big dividends. Between 1967 and 1977, the annual number of minority applicants soared from less than two hundred to more than a thousand. During the period 1976–80, an average of sixty-four African Americans entered the Academy each summer, accounting for an average of 4.8 percent of each incoming plebe class.[4]

Nevertheless, in June 1978, African Americans constituted only 2.1 percent of the Navy's officer corps. A 1979 study sponsored in part by the Office of Naval Research concluded that the Navy would have to recruit more effectively to achieve "proportionate representation" of minorities.[5]

In July 1979, the CNO, Admiral Thomas B. Hayward, chartered a minority officer accession study group to develop a plan to increase the proportion of African Americans in the Navy's officer corps to 6 percent by the end of 1985, with 3 percent Hispanic and 2 percent other minority representation. These percentages corresponded to the proportion of minority groups with college degrees, not to the higher proportions of minority groups in the country as a whole. This change marked the first time that minority representation goals were established as percentages of end strength. The 6-3-2 target represented a significant shift downward from previous goals based on the demographics of the overall population.

The minority officer accession study group met the following month. Its members examined existing recruiting policies and procedures in the Navy Recruiting Command and Naval Education and Training Command as well as for the Officer Candidate School, NROTC, and Naval Academy programs. To facilitate minority recruiting at the Academy, the group recommended increasing the number of MACs billeted there; expanding contacts with minority schools, counselors, and organizations; launching a direct mailing campaign to commanding officers who had enlisted people eligible for the Academy; authorizing enrollment to capacity in the NAPS and BOOST programs, with 50 percent minority students in the former and 70 percent in the latter; and recruiting minority applicants rejected by the Academy and NROTC program into NAPS or BOOST. The Academy increased the number of MACs to five and implemented the rest of the recommendations by August. "We're at the point now where people are realizing that minority recruiting hasn't just been a fad with the Naval Academy," declared Lt. Cdr. Monika Mitchell, the senior MAC, in a press release.[6]

Nevertheless, the Navy as a whole fell short of its minority officer recruiting goals. By the spring of 1981, it became evident that the Navy would not hit its targeted minority proportion for the officer corps by 1985. The issue arose at a CNO briefing held on 6 March 1981. Admiral Hayward believed the Navy was not doing enough to increase minority representation in the officer corps. At his behest, on 28 March, V. Adm. Lando W. Zech, deputy chief of naval operations for manpower, personnel, and training and chief of naval personnel, ordered R. Adm. James R. Hogg, director of the Military Personnel and Training Division (OP-13), to reconvene the minority officer accession study group to develop a plan for achieving the goal of 6 percent black, 3 percent Hispanic, and 2 percent other minority representation in the officer corps by the end of fiscal year 1988. Zech directed the group to examine "all parameters" of the NROTC, Aviation Officer Candidate School and AOCS Prep, Officer Candidate School and OCS Prep, Enlisted Commissioning, Minority Officer Recruitment Effort, NAPS, BOOST, and Academy programs, including recruiting methods and resources, admission standards, and curriculum, to maximize their effectiveness in achieving the goals.[7]

The group convened on 17 April under Admiral Hogg's deputy, Capt. John J. Gelke. It included representatives from the Naval Academy, Naval

Education and Training Command, Navy Recruiting Command, Naval Military Personnel Command, and divisions within the CNO's office. The group circulated a goals and recommendations statement to these various entities in July.

The superintendent of the Naval Academy, R. Adm. William P. Lawrence, considered the 6-3-2 goal unrealistic in the short term. For example, the study group had set a goal of sixty black officers commissioned in the Navy from the class of 1985, but only fifty-one African Americans had entered the class. Admiral Lawrence pointed out a problem that had plagued the Academy's minority recruiting effort for years—the relatively small pool of qualified African Americans. Less than 7 percent of all bachelor's degrees in the nation conferred in the 1978/79 school year went to African Americans. Worse, African Americans received less than 0.4 percent of the technical degrees conferred that year. To meet the goal of 6 percent black officer accessions, Lawrence estimated that the class of 1988 would have to admit ninety-nine African Americans. Attrition and Marine Corps accessions would whittle this number down to forty-nine blacks commissioned into the Navy, a figure representing an estimated 6 percent of the projected graduating class. Since only thirty-eight African Americans graduated in the class of 1981, the Academy would have to increase its minority recruiting effort significantly to meet the 6 percent black goal. Lawrence suggested several no-cost measures for doing so, such as inviting members of the National Naval Officers Association to become Blue and Gold officers, increasing the number of black Blue and Gold officers to fifty by the end of fiscal year 1982, and increasing minority enrollment at NAPS.[8]

With similar input from the other organizations represented, the minority officer accession study group developed a seven-year plan to achieve its 6-3-2 goal by the end of fiscal year 1988. Distributed in February 1982, the plan, dubbed the "minority officer accession study," included thirty-two recommendations to assist the Navy in reaching this goal. Twelve of these pertained to the Naval Academy. The study group acknowledged that the Academy had been "meeting its input goals," but minority attrition and a disproportionate number of minority graduates entering the Marine Corps denied the Navy the full benefit of this commissioning source. One recommendation suggested that the Academy develop and implement its own plan to meet the 6-3-2 goal, taking these factors into account. Another recommendation embodied Admiral Lawrence's idea to increase the number of minority Blue and Gold officers and to invite National Naval Officers Association members to participate. The study noted that only ten of the 1,500 members in the Blue and Gold Program were minorities. Three of the recommendations dealt with NAPS: the school should increase its minority enrollment effort, increase the minority proportion of its staff, and increase visual acuity waivers to increase the pool of eligible students. The study suggested that the Navy assert full control over BOOST program curriculum and instructors, contact minority enlisted men and women eligible for the program by personal letter, and consider a student's total performance in the BOOST program instead of just the SAT score in determining eligibility for the Academy. Other suggestions included filling the remaining four of the twenty billets for minority officers at recruiting districts recommended by the 1979 study and establishing a permanent two-person minority officer recruitment effort (MORE) team to recruit at high schools, junior colleges, and universities with significant minority enrollment. The study included a provision for the formation of a steering group to monitor progress in attaining its goals.[9]

Meanwhile, the Academy tackled the recruiting problem posed by the study group. To have 6 percent of each graduating class consist of blacks commissioned in the Navy, the candidate guidance office calculated that the number of African Americans entering the classes of 1986–88 would have to average 133 per class, factoring in losses through attrition and service selection for the Marine Corps. This meant more than doubling the present average number of African Americans coming in each year. Toward that end, the MACs developed a "minority marketing plan" that featured several "absolutely essential" actions necessary to increase minority input, including sending letters of assurance to all "early-offer" minority candidates as early in the cycle as possible, to preempt other institutions from getting them; soliciting more help in recruiting from black Academy alumni and their families; establishing "liaison with centers of influence in minority communities"; making contact with minority candidates even before their junior year in high school to help them shape the proper academic course; utilizing more black midshipmen in Operation Information; and increasing the number of black Blue and Gold officers.[10]

One of the principal authors of the minority marketing plan was James Jackson, now a lieutenant commander. After graduation, Jackson earned his wings as a naval flight officer and served a tour with Patrol Squadron Five before returning to the Academy in October 1980 for a tour as a MAC. In a press release on the Academy's minority recruiting effort, Jackson discussed some of the difficulties black applicants faced in gaining admission to the Academy. High admissions standards constituted a big stumbling block. They made it "as difficult for a black student to get into the Academy as to get into Harvard," Jackson said. "Only 14 percent of the black students who apply here are accepted . . . primarily because so few are academically prepared. . . . What we have to do is reach minority high school students early to get them on track to qualify for our program."[11]

Jackson later recalled that the minority marketing plan emphasized quality over quantity. "Our goal was to find what we called the 'golden 200' applicants and just work those students very carefully," he said. To identify those students, Jackson focused on academic criteria. "I looked for students who had scored well on the SAT exam and who had had high school chemistry and physics," he said. "I often would find those sorts of black students at parochial or private schools." Rather than scouring the entire county, Jackson focused on areas that had produced black midshipmen in the past. "I didn't recruit in public schools [or] the inner cities to a great degree," he said. "I recruited oftentimes from schools where current midshipmen had come from. I also asked chief petty officers if their sons or daughters were interested in coming. I didn't go to county fairs or to Boy Scout jamborees. I didn't do a lot of traditional things. I went right to where I thought the successful students were. Alaska probably wasn't going to be producing, but cities like Chicago and Washington, D.C., were probably going to yield four or five because they had a track record." Because most of the students Jackson tried to recruit were inundated by scholarships from top universities, "selling the Navy lifestyle," as he put it, became the greatest challenge. Jackson received criticism for not focusing more on inner city schools, but pressure to produce forced him to employ a strategy that placed results above casting the net wider.[12]

As a lieutenant, Cary Hithon served a tour as a MAC with James Jackson. Although Hithon reported to the deputy director and director of the candidate guidance office, any overarching minority recruiting issues came down to his level through Commander Jackson. Hithon was the MAC for the mid-Atlantic and Northeast region, from Maryland to Maine. Only rarely did he visit individual high schools other than standouts like Poly in Baltimore. "By and large," he recalled, "it was career days and college fairs." He did most of his traveling in the late spring and early fall, to attend these events. "Being out there talking to the kids and being an example, not just talking to them over the phone or sending them some cold piece of mail, was more effective," he said. "In person you could see their body language, see their reactions, and talk their language. And you're not just talking to the individual, but to their friends and family. You try and create a network." Hithon believed the biggest flaw in the system was that the director of candidate guidance viewed minority recruiting as a MAC responsibility, not a candidate guidance office responsibility.[13]

The Academy employed a slightly different process for admitting candidates recruited by Commander Jackson and the other MACs. Whereas the admissions board generally reviewed majority candidates only on paper, the dean of admissions, Capt. Robert W. McNitt, permitted the MACs to appear in person before the board to present each individual minority candidate.

As Commander Jackson recalled, Captain McNitt took this extra step because of a "moral commitment" to "increase numbers of black midshipmen of high quality."[14]

In the fall of 1981, the MACs launched a program to inform members of the Congressional Black Caucus and Congressional Hispanic Caucus about the minority marketing plan. Between them, these members of Congress had eighty-seven vacancies in the class of 1986. The program included making visits to members' Washington offices, sending letters and information packets to their home offices, and putting on a seminar with congressional staffers hosted by Dr. Domingo Reyes, special assistant secretary of the navy for minority affairs.[15]

The 1981 minority officer accession study recognized that the Navy still suffered from the "twin problems" of "image and awareness" throughout minority communities. On 20 August 1982, Admiral Zech hosted a luncheon in Washington for black community leaders. Zech hoped to overcome these problems and thereby enhance minority recruitment. Besides Zech and R. Adm. James D. Williams, commander of the Navy Recruiting Command, the Navy was represented by three other flag officers from personnel and human resource billets along with the National Naval Officers Association president, Capt. Buddie Joe Penn, whose previous tour was as First Battalion officer at the Academy and who was now the special assistant to CNO/Special Projects (OP-00E), and Stan Carter, '65, now a commander in the billet of special assistant to the chief of naval personnel for minority affairs. Black leaders in attendance included Dr. Althea Simmons, director of the Washington bureau of the NAACP; Dr. Calvin Rolark of the United Black Fund; Judge John D. Fauntleroy of the D.C. superior court; Maudine Cooper, vice president of the Washington chapter of the National Urban League; and Dr. Daniel Thomas, assistant to the executive director of the National Association for Equal Opportunity in Higher Education. Numerous suggestions arose during the luncheon. Those pertaining to the Naval Academy included sending more black midshipmen back to their high schools and communities to assist in recruiting and setting up programs in conjunction with local NAACP and Urban League chapters involving black midshipmen in community activities.[16]

Three weeks later one of the attendees at the luncheon, R. Adm. P. J. Mulloy, director of the Human Resource Management Division in the CNO's office, recommended that the Navy send representatives to major national minority conventions and conferences to help counter its "poor image" in minority communities. Among the organizations Mulloy mentioned were the NAACP, the National Council of Black Churchmen, the National Baptist Student Union, the National Association for Equal Opportunity in Higher Education, and the Congressional Black Caucus. He recommended that a

Naval Academy representative attend the conventions of the National Alliance of Black School Educators, National Naval Officers Association, and National Urban League.[17]

In the months that followed, representatives from the candidate guidance office participated in some twenty college fairs, career workshops, and conventions, twelve of which were sponsored by the National Scholarship Service and Fund for Negro Students (NSSFNS). The office continued direct mailings to students appearing on lists purchased from the NSSFNS as well as from the Educational Testing Service and nearly doubled the MAC travel budget. The Academy and the Navy Recruiting Command exchanged computer tapes of names of minority applicants to their respective programs. In the dean of admission's section of the Academy's command objectives statement for the 1983–84 academic year, achieving the admissions goals set by the CNO minority officer accession study group "while maintaining first year attrition of minorities no higher than the class average" ranked second only after the goal of finding the specified number qualified applicants for the incoming class. In preparing fitness reports on the other MACs, Captain McNitt graded them on the plebe-year performance of the minority recruits they signed up. This reinforced the emphasis on quality above quantity.[18]

Despite these efforts, the Academy fell short of 6 percent black enrollment. The African American proportions of incoming midshipmen in the classes of 1984, 1985, 1986, 1987, and 1988 were, respectively, 4.6 percent, 3.8 percent, 5.3 percent, 5.0 percent, and 3.6 percent. The steering group monitoring implementation of the minority officer accession study took note of these shortfalls and attributed them, in part, to minimal minority representation (5 percent) in the Blue and Gold Program, failure of Blue and Gold officers to recruit minorities actively in their regions, and failure of the Academy to utilize seats for minorities at NAPS.[19]

Capt. B. J. Penn agreed that low minority input into NAPS was one of the reasons for the shortfall. Other reasons, as he noted in an April 1984 memo to CNO Adm. James D. Watkins, included the fact that some of the people recommended for NAPS were admitted directly into the Military and Air Force academies and that the Naval Academy had not filled its MAC billets until recently. Admiral Watkins told R. Adm. Charles R. Larson, the superintendent, that he found the shortfalls "distressing" and encouraged him to develop "more effective initiatives" to increase minority accessions.[20]

In response to the CNO, Admiral Larson sponsored a minority recruiting and accessions meeting on June 28. Representatives from the Academy, Naval Education and Training Command, Navy Recruiting Command, BuPers, and secretary of the navy's office discussed minority recruiting issues in the same room at the same time—"a first to my knowledge," as Captain Penn put it.

They talked about various avenues into the Academy and ways to coordinate their efforts. Penn believed the Academy remained too dependent on the MACs for minority accessions. In a memo to Admiral Watkins, he suggested that the Academy ought to involve the entire Blue and Gold network in minority recruiting. "Doesn't take a minority to recruit a minority," he concluded. Watkins agreed.[21]

Commitment to the goal of achieving 6 percent African American representation at the Academy remained a top recruiting priority during the 1984–85 admission cycle. The Academy began the cycle with a full complement of six MACs, four coded for blacks, one for a Hispanic, and one for "any minority." In the spring of 1984, the candidate guidance staff mailed information packets to more than fifteen thousand minority students identified on lists purchased from the Educational Testing Service and the American College Testing Service. In the fall of 1984, the Glee Club made several trips to schools with large minority enrollments. Sixteen percent of midshipmen participating in Operation Information during the 1984/85 admissions cycle were minorities. In 1985, NAPS increased its black enrollment by 45 percent over the year before. That same year, MACs attended the NAACP and Urban League conventions and National Naval Officers Association and Association of Naval Services Officers conferences to market the Academy in the black community and increase minority participation in the Blue and Gold program. The candidate guidance staff included minority briefings at Blue and Gold training sessions and area coordinators' conferences. The staff also published a brochure titled *Opportunities for Ethnic Americans,* which it mailed to all black and Hispanic applicants. As the director of candidate guidance put it, this brochure soon became "*the most valuable* minority information piece available to the candidate guidance team." Throughout the 1984–85 cycle, the MACs increased visitation to homes and high schools, conducted a mail campaign to minority Academy alumni and their families to solicit their help in recruiting, and invited larger numbers of minority youth and more representatives from national minority organizations to visit the Academy. They followed the usual recruiting procedures as well, such as attending college fairs and career workshops.[22]

As a result of these efforts, the Academy met the minority officer accession study goal for black enrollment in the class of 1989. The study had set its sights on enrolling seventy-two African Americans during the summer of 1985; the Academy admitted seventy-seven of the 1,016 young black men and women who applied.[23]

Capt. Harry A. Seymour, who became director of candidate guidance that summer, soon realized that he had a tough job ahead of him. The difficulty stemmed from declining minority college enrollments relative to their proportion of the U.S. population. Articles in newsletters such as *Black Issues in Higher Education* and in news magazines like *U.S. News & World Report* declared this trend a crisis. One article pointed out that, although more African Americans were graduating from high school than ever before, fewer were entering college. Some 613,000 African Americans were enrolled in college in 1984, down 3.3 percent from 1980. A backlash from white students and professors against affirmative action, tougher academic standards, and a shift in financial aid from grants to loans contributed to the problem.[24]

In a memo to the superintendent, Captain Seymour attributed the success of the minority recruiting effort for the class of 1989 to "the performance of the minority admissions counselors and their one-on-one counseling efforts." But Seymour also warned that minority recruiting would "become more difficult each year" owing to falling percentages of African Americans enrolled in college. "Between 1975 and 1981, for example, the percentage of blacks going to college fell 11 percent," he noted, "even though there was an increase in the number of black high school graduates." He recommended increasing the number of authorized MAC billets from six to eight so that each Academy recruiting region would have a MAC working alongside the regional director. This would "allow for a more effective, flexible and efficient minority recruiting effort," he concluded. The superintendent subsequently authorized the two billets.[25]

Meanwhile, shortfalls in minority officer accessions prompted the CNO to convene in 1984 a minority officer accessions task force (MOATF) to review and validate minority accession goals, consider lessons learned from previous study groups, evaluate accession programs, and formulate new programs and initiatives.[26] The task force increased the African American admissions goals to 87 for the class of 1990, 105 for the class of 1991, and 113 for the class of 1992. Captain Seymour knew that these targets would be difficult to hit in the face of declining black college enrollment. The result would be more "fierce competition for the high quality minority student."

In the spring of 1986, Seymour sat down to analyze the status, strengths, and weaknesses of the Academy's minority recruiting effort. The number of applications from African Americans for the class of 1990 totaled 1,049 at that point, up from 1,016 for the previous class. Seymour attributed the increase to effective counseling and extensive follow-up efforts by the MACs, including greater emphasis on home visits. Problem areas included the fact that minority high school students still were not taking the courses necessary to qualify for direct appointment, nor were they completing the admissions packet in a timely manner.[27]

As a result of Captain Seymour's analysis, the candidate guidance staff refined their recruiting approaches. The MACs increased efforts to get minority candidates to complete application packages. They sent recruiting information and referral sheets with which to recommend prospective candidates to every member of the National Naval Officers Association. And they invited minority Marine Corps Reserve officers to join the Blue and Gold team. Captain Seymour mailed letters to minority Academy graduates inviting them to become Blue and Gold officers. He also asked Blue and Gold area recruiters to coordinate efforts with the MACs and minority alumni.

Travel remained a prominent aspect of MACs' duties. In one month alone (October 1985), MACs attended college fairs, visited schools, or hosted events in eight states and three Caribbean islands. During one four-day trip to Detroit, Michigan (14–17 April 1986), Lt. Cdr. L. B. Lastinger, regional director of the Academy's recruiting Region Four, and Ensign Napoleon McCallum, who remained at the Academy after graduating in 1985 to serve as a MAC, visited eight high schools; attended two meetings, a dinner, a reception, and a press conference; and did interviews with local television, radio, and newspaper reporters. The highlight of the trip was a reception held by a local judge to introduce Lastinger and McCallum to influential leaders of Detroit's black community, including the head of the Detroit chapter of the NAACP, two former professional football players, and a host of others. Ensign McCallum himself generated a lot of interest, for he had been a football star and a Heisman Trophy candidate at Navy. As a result of these efforts, ninety-two African Americans entered the Academy in the summer of 1986, exceeding the MOATF goal by five midshipmen and accounting for 6.6 percent of the incoming class of 1990.[28]

In 1987, with strong support from the CNO, the superintendent expanded the candidate guidance office, filling the two additional MAC billets as Captain Seymour had recommended. This increase resulted in the largest minority recruiting organization to date, with a total of eight MACs on board. Seymour designated one of the counselors senior MAC to coordinate the activities of the entire MAC organization. The duties of the senior MAC, whom the other counselors dubbed the "big MAC," included revising the minority marketing plan at the end of each candidate cycle; coordinating and monitoring execution of the marketing plan; serving as liaison with the director and deputy director of candidate guidance and the dean of admissions; and training MACs as they rotated in. Two other MACs served as black and Hispanic marketing coordinators. Their jobs entailed coordinating the national recruiting effort, monitoring the progress in marketing the Academy to their respective ethnic groups, and assisting the big MAC in revising the marketing plan at the end of each cycle. Each MAC was assigned to cover one of the Academy's eight recruiting regions, working in conjunction with the regional director.

The MACs almost completely revised the Academy's minority marketing plan for the 1987/88 admissions cycle. Captain Seymour believed that since 1982, when the plan was last revised, "any clear sense of direction has eroded and the efforts have been more individual and less collective."

Based on the goals set forth in the 31 October 1984 MOATF report, Dean McNitt established the target for black enrollment in the class of 1992 at seventy-seven African Americans and seventy-nine Hispanic Americans. The big MAC and his staff were responsible for meeting these goals and maintaining minority input into NAPS.

In the process of drawing up the 1987–88 minority marketing plan, the MACs studied census data, Enrollment Planning Service analyses, minority SAT scores, and a host of other sources to figure out which markets they were covering adequately and which they were not. They concluded that they were adequately reaching black communities in Detroit, Houston, Baltimore, Washington, D.C., and other cities that had traditionally produced black midshipmen but needed to do more in New York, Chicago, Philadelphia, Los Angeles, and the majority of the other major U.S. cities with large black populations. The MACs decided to focus their efforts on the latter cities during the class of 1992 candidate cycle.

The 1987–88 minority marketing plan identified high school visits as the most valuable means for identifying and meeting potential candidates. It suggested that MACs consult NROTC coordinators to identify which high schools were producing the best students. It also suggested that MACs coordinate with the Academy public affairs office to set up interviews with local newspapers and radio and television stations. If high schools made it difficult for MACs to meet students during the day, the plan suggested holding an "information seminar" at a conference room or auditorium after hours. The plan attributed past success in adequately covered cities to saturation with information about the Academy, a strong Blue and Gold organization, and visibility resulting from high school visits and attendance at college fairs. The plan listed tactics for making and maintaining contacts, such as obtaining names from Educational Testing Service and American College Testing Service lists and establishing ties to "centers of influence in the minority communities."

Candidates deemed high attrition risks would be channeled into NAPS instead of being admitted directly into the Academy. The staff used primarily academic criteria—SAT scores, high school class standing, and so forth—for determining whether an individual was at high risk for attrition. A policy statement produced in February 1988 by the candidate guidance office noted how the present "philosophy on the admission of high risk minority students varied" from that of the past. "The Class of 1978's Black population admitted was 94 midshipmen," it noted; "however, the Class suffered a 52.1 percent four-year Black attrition rate. The Class of 1985's Black population numbered 51; however, the Class four-year Black attrition was only 25.5 percent."

The minority recruiting effort during the 1987–88 admissions cycle again featured a blend of tried-and-true and refined procedures. Between June 1987 and June 1988, the MACs made 105 recruiting trips, a 53 percent increase in travel over the previous year. Refinements made during this cycle included increased involvement by minority midshipmen in counseling prospective candidates, particularly in mailing out letters and working the phones on Saturdays. The candidate guidance office sent letters under the superintendent's signature to the members of the Congressional Black Caucus, soliciting their help in cultivating interest in the Academy among their minority constituents and offering to make presentations to them on the Academy's program. After the class of 1992 entered, the minority members would be polled to determine which media influenced their decision to become midshipmen.[29]

These efforts yielded disappointing results. Sixty-four African Americans entered with the class of 1991, accounting for only 4.9 percent of the incoming class.[30]

In October 1987, the minority action group upped the ante. Consisting of representatives from OPNAV, the Naval Military Personnel Command, policy branches in BuPers, and the Academy and chaired by the head of BuPers's Equal Opportunity Division (Pers-61), the group met quarterly to review the Navy's equal opportunity policy and monitor implementation of the NAAP. The group recommended raising the yearly commissioning goal for each source, including the Academy, to 7 percent, to achieve the 6-3-2 goal sooner.

This recommendation caused Captain Seymour a great deal of consternation. Citing a study that projected continuing decline in the number of African Americans graduating from high school through 1999, Seymour suggested that the group establish a more realistic goal: if they assumed that each class produced one thousand graduates and used a 35 percent black attrition rate, he argued, to achieve a 7 percent black Navy commissioning figure they would need approximately 120 blacks in each incoming class. The Academy "has expended maximum effort to inform and attract Black students in the junior high school through community college level," he declared. With the Academy's minority recruiting effort operating at maximum level and given the declining numbers of black high school graduates, he concluded, an input of 120 blacks was not currently attainable.

Instead, Captain Seymour suggested that the black input goals for the classes of 1992–96 gradually increase from seventy-seven to ninety-two African Americans. Accounting for losses because of attrition and Marine Corps accessions, these inputs would yield proportions of blacks from each graduating class commissioned into the Navy increasing from 4 percent in 1992 to 6 percent in 1996.[31]

The candidate guidance office's recruiting efforts during the 1987–88 admissions cycle yielded a black enrollment in the class of 1992 of seventy-one midshipmen, falling short of its target of seventy-seven midshipmen by six. These seventy-one African Americans accounted for 5.2 percent of this 1,365-midshipmen class. Captain Seymour put the best face on it in a June 1988 memo to the chairman of the minority action group by reporting the number of African Americans accepted by NAPS as part of the results of that year's minority recruiting effort. The fifty incoming black NAPSters, when added to the seventy-one African Americans entering in 1992, brought the "total USNA/NAPS acceptances" to 121, a figure consistent with group goals.[32]

In July 1988, after the class of 1992 was sworn in, Capt. Seymour submitted the Academy's minority accessions plan update to R. Adm. Raymond G. Jones Jr., director of OP-13 (now called the Military Personnel Policy Division) and head of MOATF. The plan emphasized increasing African American enrollment at NAPS as the key to increasing the black population at the Academy. It also stated the candidate guidance office's intentions to increase involvement by the Blue and Gold organization and the National Naval Officers Association in minority recruiting.[33]

Throughout most of the 1980s, the BOOST program channeled a steady but small stream of African Americans into the Naval Academy. Between 1985 and 1988, an average of 254 people per year graduated from the program. Of these, 83 percent entered the NROTC. Only sixty-seven BOOST graduates entered the Academy during this period, and only fourteen of them were African Americans, for an average input into the Academy of four black BOOSTers per year. Despite these small numbers, the BOOST program remained a valuable tool for increasing the number of minority naval officers primarily through the NROTC program.[34]

Meanwhile, the equal opportunity assessment brief given to the CNO in the spring of 1988 revealed that, despite its best efforts, the Navy was still falling short of its equal opportunity goals in several areas, including minority officer promotion, minority enlisted advancement, "high minority involvement with Uniform Code of Military Justice violations," and minority officer accessions. In 1987, African Americans accounted for only 3.4 percent of the Navy's officer corps. In May 1988, the chief of naval personnel directed each commissioning source, including the Naval Academy, to recruit sufficient numbers of minority candidates so that African Americans constituted 7 percent and Hispanics 4 percent of officers commissioned each year. In the long run, this rate would enable the Navy to meet its 6-3-2 goal.

On 20 June 1988, Adm. Carlisle A. H. Trost, the CNO, chartered a group to examine the entire spectrum of racial policies in the Navy. Dubbed the "CNO Study Group on Equal Opportunity in the Navy" and chaired by R. Adm. Ralph W. West Jr., director of the Office of Pride, Professionalism and Personnel Excellence (OP-15), the group was to "review personnel policies concerning officer and enlisted accessions, attrition, and professional development" and to make recommendations "necessary to improve minority representation and enhance opportunities for minority personnel." Part of the group's mission entailed determining whether the 7 percent black/4 percent Hispanic commissioning goals were feasible.

For eight weeks beginning on 12 July, the group heard briefings from equal opportunity representatives, interviewed thousands of officers and enlisted people at dozens of commands, and sent questionnaires to thousands more. The group focused on five different areas of equal opportunity policy as well as on officer and enlisted accessions, distribution, and attrition in initial training. The group submitted its report to the CNO late that year.

The report concluded that the Navy had made "important gains and steady progress since the establishment of the Equal Opportunity Program in 1970." It noted that the Navy had achieved its goal for African American representation in the enlisted service in 1983 and exceeded it ever since. By the end of 1988, African Americans accounted for 15 percent of the enlisted service, a larger proportion than the black population of the United States, which stood at 12 percent. Despite extensive efforts in minority recruiting, education, and affirmative action, however, black representation in the officer corps remained below target, and black officers and enlisted people were not receiving promotions, advancement, and access to certain billets at rates commensurate with white sailors and officers.

For example, the group found problems in each area of equal opportunity policy it examined. In regard to command climate, most of the minority officers and enlisted men and women still heard racial jokes or slurs, almost half believed that incidents at their commands had racial overtones, and many lacked confidence in the Navy's grievance procedures and feared reprisal if they filed a grievance. Flag officers, commanding officers, executive officers, most department heads and division officers, and few chief petty officers received equal opportunity training commensurate with their respective positions. Large portions of the NAAP had become obsolete. The Navy's equal opportunity organization suffered from inadequate infrastructure and improper utilization. And the new command-managed equal opportunity (CMEO) program was not being adequately implemented.[35]

The CMEO program had emerged from problems with the Navy's equal opportunity program that became evident during the late 1970s. Although by 1977, Phase II was considered fully implemented in the fleet and most commands had affirmative action plans, human resource councils, and command training teams in place, many individuals remained unaware of their own personal equal opportunity obligations, even after undergoing training. At the same time, many commanding officers had come to resent Phase II as an external intrusion into their commands. By the end of the 1970s, the equal opportunity program had become stagnant.

In 1980, CNO Adm. Thomas Hayward sought to "reinvigorate" the Navy's approach. "We have not yet achieved genuine equal opportunity," he declared. Equal opportunity considerations "must be ingrained into all aspects of Navy life." New initiatives were required to make equal opportunity an integral part of leadership and management. The 1981 NAAP mandated a command-managed program designed to bring equal opportunity management within the commanders' own chains of command. The CNO introduced the CMEO program to the fleet on 5 February 1985. The program continued to emphasize the self-sustaining affirmative action aspects of Phase II but made each skipper, rather than an external agency, responsible for equal opportunity in his or her own command. By the end of 1986, the Navy had phased out any separate commands whose charter included human relations, race relations, or organizational effectiveness.[36]

The CNO study group found that some of the problems affecting minority recruiting at the Academy afflicted other officer programs as well. The group took note of declining African American college enrollment throughout the 1980s, and interviews with black and Hispanic midshipmen and officer candidates revealed that in many minority communities the Navy still had a negative image or no image at all. "A significant majority of those interviewed stated that the families, friends and peers often tried to dissuade them from entering officer programs," noted the group's report. "Many of the comments made to the minority officer candidates prior to their enlistment were negative. School counselors were also singled out as being uninformed on subjects required to prepare students for selection into officer programs, benefits offered by the Navy and availability of scholarships. Little or no officer recruiting literature was available in schools."

The CNO study group attributed the Navy's image problem to its low advertising budget. Analyses such as the Navy Advertising Effectiveness Study and the Youth Attitude Tracking Study ranked the Navy third among the services in advertising awareness and third in target population propensity to join the Navy. In 1987, the Navy spent less on advertising than the Army, Air Force, or Marine Corps. That year, the Navy spent $282,000 for Naval Academy, NROTC, and college-related advertising while the Army spent $9,775,000 for corresponding programs. Recruiters and midshipmen alike remarked on the severe shortage of available promotional materials.

As a result of its analysis of each officer program, the CNO study group concluded that the Navy would fall short of its goals for minority representation in the officer corps in fiscal years 1992 and 1996. Specifically, the group found that, although the Officer Candidate School and Aviation Officer Candidate School were commissioning enough officers to meet the 7 percent black/4 percent Hispanic representation goals, the NROTC program was not. And although BOOST and the Baccalaureate Degree Composition Program were effective in achieving affirmative action goals, the Officer Candidate Prep School was not.

As for Annapolis, which supplied the Navy with 20 percent of the officers commissioned annually, the study group concluded that the Academy was recruiting enough Hispanics but not enough blacks. Too few minorities were entering from BOOST and NAPS programs, and too many were commissioned in the Marine Corps. More than one-quarter of the African Americans who graduated in the classes of 1980–88 selected the Marines, compared to the overall rate of 16.7 percent. The group recommended that the Academy increase its input goals from NAPS and BOOST and encourage black firsties to select the Navy rather than the Marine Corps.

The study group found that the Academy's emphasis on high SAT scores exacerbated its recruiting problem. Educational Testing Service data indicated that, whereas 47 percent of whites who took the SAT in 1987 scored 500 or better in the math section, only 13 percent of blacks did so. According to the Academy's selection formula, 60 percent of a candidate's score depended on his or her high school class rank and SAT scores. The average SAT score for midshipmen selected for the class of 1992 was 1255, but blacks entering that class averaged only 1149. Most African American applicants scored below the Academy's minimum SAT standard. Beginning with the class of 1993, the Academy planned to change the relative weight of SAT math and verbal scores from 1:1 to 3:1, which the study group believed would only enhance the difficulty of finding African Americans who could meet this standard.

Nevertheless, the CNO study group declared that 7 percent black/4 percent Hispanic yearly commissions were "challenging but realistically achievable goals." Based on model projections, attainment of 6 percent black officer end strength would be attained by the year 2000 and Hispanic end strength by 1999.[37]

To meet these goals, the study group recommended funding and expanding upward mobility programs, investing more in advertising, and increasing enrollment in BOOST. As for the Naval Academy, the study group suggested enrolling seventy-five African Americans per year into NAPS, admitting fifteen black BOOST graduates per year into the Academy, and increasing efforts to encourage black firsties to select careers in the Navy instead of the Marines. To hit the 7 percent black target, the study group set the Academy's commissioning goals at fifty black ensigns for the class of 1993 and sixty-three black ensigns for each of the classes of 1994–2000. Thus the class of 1994 was slated to hit the target of 7 percent black Navy commissions. On 13 April 1989, the CNO issued an update of the Navy equal opportunity manual designed to correct the deficiencies identified by the study group.[38]

One of the officers responsible for implementing the CNO study group's recommendations was the special assistant for equal opportunity (OP-01J) to the deputy CNO for manpower, personnel and training (OP-01)/chief of naval personnel. Capt. Pete Tzomes, '67, held that billet from June 1988 to June 1990. Tzomes also reported to Rear Admiral West, chairman of the CNO study group.

In September 1988, Captain Tzomes visited Captain Seymour to review the Academy's minority recruiting program. Tzomes believed that, unless the Academy made "drastic changes" to its "procedures and philosophy," it would fail to hit the 7 percent black commissioning target. He favored an approach that involved looking beyond minority candidates' numbers on paper—particularly their SAT scores—and more deeply into their character. In the current system, a student who scored above the 1100 minimum on his SAT, came from a "perfect" family, and had good grades stood a chance of being admitted, whereas a student from a single-parent family, whose mother had to work nights and relied on him to care for his baby sister, who also made good grades, but who scored only 850 on his SAT had no chance of being admitted, despite having demonstrated responsibility and leadership. Tzomes believed the system needed to be altered to accommodate the latter type of candidate. Seymour thought this idea would lead to "reduced academic rigor for minorities or some variation on the old 'turnback' system for minorities requiring additional time to graduate" and pointed out the need to graduate technically competent naval officers. Tzomes agreed but thought that something had to be done to increase the number of blacks graduating from the Academy. Seymour declared that the Academy would not lower its qualification criteria "simply to 'make numbers.'" He believed lowering standards would only increase attrition, "causing nothing to be gained by graduation day," as he put it in a memo to the superintendent. A better solution, he argued, would be to establish a formal "academic intervention" program to reduce attrition.[39]

The superintendent agreed with Captain Seymour. The Academy remained committed to the goal of commissioning 7 percent black and 4 percent Hispanic officers into the Navy beginning with the class of 1994. The Academy intended to achieve that goal by increasing minority recruitment and decreasing minority attrition. To facilitate the latter, the Academy planned to establish an academic center to tutor those in need of academic help.[40]

The superintendent had already taken steps to reduce minority attrition and thereby increase minority officer accessions. During the summer of 1988, after being notified of the convening of the CNO study group, he formed a "minority midshipmen study group" to examine factors that impacted minority midshipmen recruiting and attrition. The group included the senior MAC and five faculty members and executive department officers, with Captain Seymour serving as chairman. The group met several times during the summer and fall of 1988.

That October, the group noted that the attrition rate of black plebes had climbed from 5.1 percent for the class of 1989 to 13.2 percent for the class of 1991. Although these rates compared favorably to the overall rates—10.5 percent for the class of 1989 and 13.7 percent for the class of 1991—they were still cause for concern. The group found life in Bancroft Hall "to be free from ethnic discrimination." Academic problems constituted the primary cause of attrition among African American midshipmen.

"If we are to meet minority commissioning goals," concluded Captain Seymour in a memo to the superintendent, "we will need to increase the input into each incoming class without increasing academic risk" and "find a way to decrease the attrition rates of minorities without creating a double standard within the Brigade." He recommended "an increased use of the stretch-out program for *all*" midshipmen as one possible antidote for attrition. The stretchout program, which evolved from the old turnback practice, enabled midshipmen with academic problems to remain at the Academy for up to a full extra year to accumulate sufficient credits for graduation. Seymour doubted that the Academy would attain the goal of admitting 105 black midshipmen "in the near future" given the competitive minority recruiting climate "while maintaining our current academic standards." Seymour later recommended improving the system of academic counseling and support, returning to the study skills program conducted in the early 1980s, reducing the first plebe semester academic load from nineteen to sixteen credit hours, and modifying the validation program.[41]

The minority midshipmen study group met several more times over the winter. On 10 March 1989, Captain Seymour forwarded to the superintendent an interim report containing the group's most important findings and recommendations. The group found that approximately one hundred midshipmen in each entering class were "at significant risk of attriting from USNA for academic reasons." These one hundred included both minority and majority midshipmen as well as several NAPS graduates and "blue chip" athletes. "At-risk midshipmen can be identified prior to entering USNA and at the end of first semester fourth-class year," Seymour noted. In the past, 60 percent of black midshipmen and 42 percent of white midshipmen in the bottom 10 percent of their class at the end of the first plebe semester eventually bilged for academic reasons. To counter this trend, the group recommended establishing by the start of the 1989–90 academic year a "proactive academic intervention system with counseling and academic remediation beginning during Plebe Summer for at-risk midshipmen." To staff such a program, the group suggested assigning two faculty members, a clinical psychologist, and the Naval Academy Alumni Association academic liaison officer. For midshipmen with "strong officer-like qualities" but low grades after the first plebe semester, the group recommended that they be given the option of attending NAPS during the second semester and following summer. "Such attendance would allow these midshipmen to improve their academic foundation," the group concluded, "re-enter the Naval Academy with the next class in August and improve their chances to graduate from USNA."

The group also recommended revising the book of professional knowledge that plebes were responsible for knowing, cutting back on activities that disrupted class work during the week before the Army-Navy game, and exempting academically deficient midshipmen from standing watches. This study should have been titled the "Academically At-Risk Midshipmen Study," noted Captain Seymour, since many majority midshipmen were also at risk.

As for the recruiting side, the minority midshipmen study group found that normal duty assignment rotation created a lack of continuity and ongoing expertise in recruiting and advertising in the candidate guidance office, and that computer support to enable electronic tracking of prospective candidates from the ninth through the eleventh grades did not exist. To remedy these problems, the group recommended hiring a civilian recruitment and marketing analyst like the one in place at the Air Force Academy and increasing computer staff support for recruiting.[42]

The minority midshipmen study group submitted its final report to the superintendent in August. Over the next two years the Academy implemented several of the group's recommendations, including establishing the academic center, expanding the stretchout program, reducing the scope of the plebe professional book, and reducing "non-spirit related Army Week activities." The Academy did not, however, increase computer staff support for admissions or add a civilian recruitment and marketing analyst to the candidate guidance office because of "monetary concerns and redirection of effort within the Admissions office," as Captain D. W. Davis, Seymour's successor as director of candidate guidance, put it.[43]

That same summer, eighty-six African Americans entered with the class of 1993. They accounted for 6 percent of the 1,433 midshipmen who entered the Academy in 1989. Although this marked only the second time since the establishment of the 6-3-2 goal in 1979 that the percentage of blacks among the incoming plebes reached 6 percent, the bar had already been raised to 7 percent.[44]

Further refinements to minority recruiting procedures gave the Academy a good chance of achieving that goal. In the spring of 1989, the candidate guidance office sent invitations to 543 black and Hispanic Academy graduates to get involved in the Blue and Gold Program. Sixteen of them became Blue and Gold officers or affiliates and dozens of others expressed interest. The following September, at the area coordinator's conference hosted by the candidate guidance office, all of the coordinators agreed to designate one of their Blue and Gold officers as the local minority marketing coordinator. The next month, minority representation in the program reached an all-time high, with fifty-nine black and twenty-four Hispanic Blue and Gold officers.[45]

The Academy also made its first effort to recruit candidates directly from the BOOST program. In January 1989, some fifty BOOSTers visited the Academy for three days and two nights over a weekend. The BOOSTers stayed in Bancroft Hall, interacting with midshipmen during their daily routine. Nearly a dozen of the African American BOOSTers enjoyed the stay so much that they decided to apply to the Academy.[46]

Operation Information for the spring of 1990 emphasized minority recruiting. Forty volunteers—sixteen black, thirteen Hispanic, one Asian, and ten white midshipmen—made 97 appearances before live audiences consisting of candidates and their parents to promote the Academy. Seventeen of the appearances were one-on-one sessions with undecided minority candidates who had received letters of assurance or appointments. All this was done without cost to the Academy.[47]

On 17 April 1990, the minority action group met to review the progress being made in several policy areas. Captain Tzomes chaired the meeting. The members of the group reaffirmed the 7 percent black commissioning goal for the class of 1994. They also reaffirmed the CNO study group's goal of enrolling at least seventy-five blacks per year in NAPS and accepting into the Academy at least fifteen black BOOST graduates per year. All of these goals were incorporated into the 1990 NAAP. Representatives from the Naval Academy, Navy Recruiting Command, and Naval Education and Training discussed a proposal to establish recruiting priorities for black midshipmen among their commands. The representatives agreed that steering candidates toward specific programs would be counterproductive, for it would eliminate the motivating factor of personal choice. They agreed that their commands already cooperated sufficiently and that no formal policy was needed.[48]

During the summer of 1990, 106 African Americans entered the Academy in the class of 1994, accounting for 8.6 percent of the total. If the black attrition rate approximated the overall attrition rate, the Academy stood a good chance of achieving the 7 percent commissioning goal.[49]

On 13 March 1991, a working group met to review and update the NAAP. The Academy representative succeeded in convincing the group to revise the part of the 1990 NAAP that dealt with NAPS and BOOST. Instead of enrolling seventy-five blacks per year into NAPS, African Americans were to account for 25 percent of the annual enrollment. And instead of accepting fifteen black BOOST graduates per year into the Academy, the goal became to "develop action to encourage Black and Hispanic BOOSTERS to apply for admission to USNA." The 7 percent black commissioning goal for the class of 1994 remained in force.[50]

The 1991 NAAP, issued in August, constituted a "complete revision" of the previous version. It sought to achieve a demographically balanced Navy, fair and equal treatment, upward and lateral mobility, and freedom from discrimination and sexual harassment for all officers and enlisted men and women. The plan addressed specific "functional areas" of personnel policy: composition, recruiting/accessions, augmentation/retention, professional military education, assignments, training and education, discipline, separations, utilization of skills, equal opportunity climate, promotions, and discrimination/sexual harassment complaints. The plan assigned oversight responsibilities to the CNO and chief of naval personnel and implementation responsibilities to the assistant chief of naval personnel for personal readiness and community support (Pers-6), fleet commanders-in-chief, second echelon commanders, commander of the Navy Recruiting Command, commanders, commanding officers, and officers in charge. It included provisions for monitoring the progress of implementation at all levels of command and chartered a working group sponsored by the chief of naval personnel, chaired by OP-15, and including a representative from the Academy to review and revise the NAAP annually. The 1991 NAAP remained in force until OPNAV cancelled it on 4 November 2003, declaring that the plan had "served its purpose."[51]

The NAAP defined equal opportunity as an "essential element of Navy leadership," an "integral part of the Navy's commitment to core values," and "fundamental to mission accomplishment, unit and personal readiness, and quality of life." The plan defined "affirmative actions" as "specific, positive steps to correct or eliminate institutional and personal discrimination on the basis of race, ethnic group, national origin, religion, or gender."

The plan assigned the Naval Academy, chief of naval education and training, OP-15, OP-13, commander of the Navy Recruiting Command, and commanders-in-chief "primary responsibility" in the functional area of officer accessions. The overall goal for composition of the officer corps was to "attain a minority officer population which, at a minimum, reflects the percentage of minorities with college degrees in the general population." Specifically, the plan called for a minimum officer inventory of 6 percent black by end of fiscal year 2000 and 3 percent Hispanic by end of fiscal year 1999. The plan projected these goals on the basis of "past recruiting performance and new initiatives."

To ensure that the Navy met these goals, the plan called for each accession source to commission a minimum of 7 percent black and 4 percent Hispanic officers annually. The NAAP directed the Naval Academy to commission at least 7 percent black officers annually starting with the class of 1994 and to ensure continued commissioning of at least 4 percent Hispanic officers annually. OP-13 was to monitor the Academy's progress in meeting these goals. The plan also directed commanders at various levels to encourage qualified minority enlisted people to apply to BOOST, NAPS, and the Academy.[52]

The class of 1994 graduated on 25 May. Among them were seventy-two African Americans, who accounted for 7.7 percent of the class, thus achieving the goal set forth in the NAAP. If the Academy could continue to keep the black attrition rate at about the same level as the overall rate, it stood a reasonable chance of achieving the 7 percent goal for the rest of the decade, for the proportions of African American men and women admitted into the classes of 1995, 1996, 1997, 1998, and 1999 stood, respectively, at 7.4 percent, 7.9 percent, 6.2 percent, 7.3 percent, and 7.4 percent. These figures left little room for error, however.[53]

The hats that the class of 1994 had tossed into the air had barely returned to earth when, in July, Secretary of the Navy John H. Dalton dropped a bombshell on the Academy's minority officer recruiting effort. Although the Academy was barely achieving the 7 percent black commissioning goals set forth in the 1991 NAAP, Dalton asked the Academy to commission minority officers at rates comparable to the demographic composition of the U.S. population. His "Enhanced Opportunities for Minorities Initiative" sought to achieve a naval officer corps composed of 12 percent black officers, 12 percent Hispanic officers, and 5 percent Asian-Pacific Islander/Native American officers by the year 2025. Dalton reasoned that by seeking proportional representation based college graduates, the earlier 6–3–2 goal placed artificial limits on the officer corps' demographic composition and excluded potential candidates who might be motivated by scholarships, enlisted commissioning programs, early acceptance, and other recruiting incentives. For the year 2000, Dalton set officer accession goals at 10 percent black, 10 percent Hispanic, and 4 percent Asian-Pacific Islander/Native American. Admiral Boorda shared Dalton's intention "to increase the goal in the minority officer area ASAP to reflect percentages in the civilian population," as he put it to an Army colleague.[54]

During the first year under Secretary Dalton's 12-12-5 goals, the Navy streamlined its minority scholarship process and, through aggressive recruiting, tripled the number of African Americans applying to the NROTC program. These changes helped the Navy increase the proportion of scholarships awarded to minorities from 11 to 19 percent without changing selection standards.[55]

Although no one at the Academy disagreed with the importance or desirability of the 12-12-5 goals, concerns arose over the availability of resources needed to attain them. The Academy estimated expenses rising from $570,000 in fiscal year 1997 to $1,050,000 in fiscal year 2001 for more instructors, recruiters, travel, and related expenses. Even with increases in funding, some naval leaders were skeptical that Secretary Dalton's goals could be attained because of the demographics of the feeder system.[56]

According to data assembled in the candidate guidance office, of the 110,462 African American high school seniors who took the SAT in 1995, only 892, or 0.8 percent, scored above 1100 in verbal and math combined, roughly the Academy's minimum requirement. Other service academies and colleges still competed for the same people, many of whom found other scholarship offers more attractive or were turned off by the service commitment or military lifestyle required of midshipmen. The small pool of qualified potential candidates constituted the first big hurdle in attaining Secretary Dalton's commissioning goal.[57]

The next big hurdle resulted from the perpetual problem of lack of awareness in minority communities of the opportunities available at the Academy. The BuPers Office of the Special Assistant for Minority Affairs (Pers-00J) found that, despite a quarter-century of effort by Ken Johnson and his MAC successors, far too many talented minority students still did not conceive of the Navy as a good career opportunity, on par with being a doctor or lawyer or business owner.

The admissions process itself was a major hurdle. Whereas most applicants normally initiated the process during their junior year of high school, most minorities did not do so until their senior year. Since many interested minority students did not find out about the admission requirements until late in high school, their records were not as strong or balanced as the majority of applicants. The application process consisted of three parts: scholastic/physical aptitude examination, medical examination, and nomination. The scholastic part included seven different forms for candidates to fill out or have filled out: "Personal Data," "Personal Statement," "Strong Interest Inventory," "Candidate Extra-Curricular Activity Form," math and English teacher recommendation forms, and a transcript request. Some students lost interest because the application seemed too complex. Others did not fully understand the process and never completed the application.[58]

Nevertheless, the Middle States Association Commission on Higher Education, which convened in Annapolis on 19–22 November 1995 to evaluate the Academy's educational objectives and the means used to attain them, declared that Dalton's commissioning goals were "attainable if there is a willingness to 'think outside the box' and to pursue aggressively the necessary financial resources for support services and recruitment."[59]

Meanwhile, in January 1995, Admiral Jeremy M. Boorda, the CNO, tasked V. Adm. Frank L. Bowman, the chief of naval personnel, to oversee a comprehensive review the Navy's equal opportunity program and to recommend ways to streamline and upgrade it. Boorda was committed to helping minorities, women, and, indeed, everyone in the Navy receive fair and equitable treatment. In fact, many top naval leaders compared Boorda's role in opening doors to women, including placing them on combatant ships, to the role played by Admiral Zumwalt in opening doors to minorities. Boorda was every bit as concerned about minority issues as he was about women's issues.[60]

Admiral Bowman convened an equal opportunity review task force to tackle the job. The task force consisted of twenty-five officers and enlisted people from fleet and shore commands. The group divided the review into two parts. The first assessed the current program and proposed actions to upgrade it. The second formulated a new definition and vision for Navy equal opportunity. Senior naval commanders, BuPers, and the Navy inspector general also provided input. Ideas were drawn from Secretary Dalton's Enhanced Opportunities for Minorities Initiative, the 1988 CNO study group report, and other previous work as well.

Robert D. Watts, '73, then a Navy captain, served on the task force. In 1993, Watts had become director of BuPers's Equal Opportunity Division (Pers-61). "Admiral Boorda challenged us to come up with a new vision for equal opportunity in the Navy, and we were able to do that," he recalled. "We got together folks throughout the fleet, throughout the world, and called them into Washington, D.C., for four to six weeks, for a working group. We looked at taking equal opportunity beyond gender and race and opening the programs to everybody. We wanted people to understand that the minute you come into the Navy, you're going to be provided the opportunity to succeed."[61]

The task force found the "main obstacle" to be that people in the Navy viewed equal opportunity "as a compartmented issue—one for the specialists—one for someone else to deal with." Admiral Boorda agreed. "The path to true equal opportunity," he wrote in a message disseminated throughout the fleet, "lies within all of us—in our personal commitment to an environment in which all hands have the opportunity to be their best." Boorda included the new definition in his message. Navy equal opportunity, he declared, "is 'fair and equitable treatment of all hands by all hands at all times.' This forward-looking definition emphasizes equal treatment for all hands, not just minorities and women. . . . Simply stated, it is the golden rule, which we all should always strive to follow."

The task force centered the review around five themes: leadership commitment, mainstreaming equal opportunity, improving the understanding of CMEO, incorporating equal opportunity in all levels of the leadership continuum, and "developing a career life mentoring cycle." Admiral Boorda succinctly expressed what the task force meant by leadership commitment. "We can't upgrade [equal opportunity] from headquarters," he said. "Change has to come from the fleet. All hands must take responsibility, first for their own actions, then for their peers and those under them." "Mainstreaming" meant transferring control of equal opportunity from specialists back to the chain of command. The "career life mentoring cycle" entailed measures to eliminate bias from fitness reports and to ensure that "all hands" had "an equal opportunity for success throughout their career." The other two themes involved more specific educational initiatives derived from the basic idea of making everyone responsible for equal opportunity. The CMEO theme also embodied the idea of providing commanders a "preventive maintenance tool" to identify concerns before they became problems. In all, the review resulted in twenty-four major recommendations based on these five themes.

In the short term, the task force intended to revise the equal opportunity manual to incorporate its recommendations. The long-term plan included incorporating the manual's contents into various instructions and regulations so that the manual itself could be done away with. The plan embodied an idealistic dream. By educating all hands and making each sailor and officer responsible for his or her own actions, prejudice among Navy people, whether it stemmed from racism, sexism, or any other -ism, could be controlled if not eliminated.[62] Tragically, probably as a result of Admiral Boorda's suicide on 16 May 1996, the plan was never fully implemented.[63]

Nevertheless, the updated Navy equal opportunity manual issued on 21 June 1996 reaffirmed Secretary Dalton's concept of proportional representation. One of its stated goals was to attain "an officer and enlisted population that reflects the general population." The manual embodied many of the recommendations made in the equal opportunity review.[64]

Meanwhile, during the summer of 1995, the Navy announced an aggressive campaign to increase black representation in the officer corps from 7 percent to 12 percent and raise the total minority enrollment from 18 percent to 30 percent by the year 2004.[65]

The proportion of African Americans graduating in the classes of 1995,

1996, 1997, 1998, and 1999, was, respectively, 7.2 percent, 6.3 percent, 5.5 percent, 6.4 percent, and 6.8 percent. These proportions failed to meet even the 7 percent black commissioning goal. Perhaps as Pete Tzomes had suggested, the Academy will have to make major changes to its minority recruiting program before it can meet the more ambitious 12 percent goal. Only time will tell. Nevertheless, these figures, along with the policies that brought them about, illustrate the tremendous distance integration at the Academy has traveled since 1976.[66]

In 1997, the Academy created a new position in the candidate guidance office—admissions outreach coordinator—and hired Don Montgomery, '74, for the job. Montgomery had left the Navy after serving out his five-year obligation and went into sales, working for Proctor and Gamble and Whitehall Laboratories. He did so well that he could afford to leave the latter position and do some fishing off his boat in the Chesapeake for a while before reentering the job market. He had just taken a lucrative job with a start-up company when the opportunity arose to become admissions outreach coordinator.

News that the Academy had never topped the 120 African Americans who entered with the class of 1977 during his first-class year shocked him. "Man," he thought, "I figured we'd be up to 200 by now." Then he was told the actual numbers of African Americans entering and graduating from the Academy each year. "That's pathetic," he thought. Even though it meant a substantial pay cut, he decided to take the job. He started on 8 January 1998.

Montgomery works closely with the dean of admissions, augmenting the MAC organization in the candidate guidance office. His principal responsibility as admissions outreach coordinator is to get the word out. "We want to do everything we can to make sure that every minority kid in America understands that there's an opportunity for qualified and motivated kids at the United States Naval Academy, regardless of what color they are," he said.

Montgomery approaches his responsibility along three main avenues: purchased name lists, visits to centers of influence, and minority alumni conferences. The first entails buying lists of names from marketing companies and sending out mass mailings. It also includes maintaining computerized lists of potential candidates. The second involves trips each April and November to meet with African American leaders in an effort to increase awareness about the Academy in the black community. The third involves inviting minority alumni back to the Academy each year to solicit their help in increasing minority enrollment. To date the Academy has sponsored nine admissions outreach conferences, the first in 1998. The creation of Montgomery's billet represents the implementation of the minority midshipmen study group's recommendations to hire a civilian recruitment and marketing analyst and to set up a computerized candidate tracking system, albeit nearly a decade after they were made.

If you ask Don Montgomery about what kind of opportunity exists at the Naval Academy for a black kid, be prepared for a long answer. "The United States Naval Academy graduates more kids of color, more African Americans in particular, with bachelor of science in engineering degrees than any other school in the state of Maryland. The environment here is conducive to excellence. If you've got ability and you're willing to demonstrate it, there won't be people holding you back. We have an opportunity for everybody. For motivated and qualified kids, we offer the opportunity of a lifetime, particularly for kids of color, because an Academy education opens doors."[67]

CHAPTER

Overall Improvement and Ongoing Inequality

IF MEASURED by distance traveled, black people took meaningful strides in all areas of American life during the twentieth century. Yet, at the century's end, the racial divide in the United States remained significant. This reality shaped how the 1,511 black midshipmen (including 167 women) admitted into in the classes of 1980–99 adapted to the Academy's culture and then left their mark upon it. As has always been the case, their individual backgrounds reflected their diversity.[1]

In 1999, the black population of the United States numbered 35.1 million people, or 13 percent of the total population. Most black people still lived in the South—55 percent—with 19 percent in the Northeast, 18 percent in the Midwest, and 8 percent in the West. Most African Americans no longer lived in rural areas but in metropolitan regions—about 86 percent—with 55 percent residing in inner cities.

Black ghettos and white suburbs still existed in big cities across the Rust Belt and in the Northeast. De facto segregation of churches, social centers, and private schools remained common. In some areas, white flight, the war on busing, and other factors resulted in resegregation of schools. In the South, the proportion of African American students going to school with whites reached 60 percent in 1971. By 1990, however, three-quarters of African American students in the urban South attended schools that were at least 90 percent black.

Nevertheless, according to the 2000 U.S. census, black and white Americans were more likely to live in integrated neighborhoods at the end of the 1990s than at the beginning of that decade. The trend toward increasing black-white integration held true in suburbs as well as cities. Nationwide, two-thirds of black people and nearly two-thirds of white people lived in integrated neighborhoods. People in the fast-growing West and South, as well as in smaller metropolitan areas—Atlanta, Austin, Baltimore, Charlotte, Denver, Nashville, New Orleans, San Jose, Seattle, Washington, D.C.—were more likely than people in other parts of the country to live in integrated neighborhoods. Segregation levels remained higher in midwestern cities and the largest and oldest urban areas—Boston, Chicago, Detroit, Philadelphia, New York, St. Louis—where blacks and whites had a long history of living separately.

The gap between blacks and whites in education closed in some areas but widened in others. In terms of illiteracy rates, school enrollment rates, and median years of schooling completed, blacks achieved near parity with whites by the mid-1990s. On the other hand, between 1972 and 1992 the proportion of black high school graduates who enrolled in college climbed from 27 to 32 percent, whereas the proportion for white high school graduates climbed from 32 to 42 percent. In 1999, 88 percent of non-Hispanic whites and 77 percent of blacks of age twenty-five years and older had finished high school, and 28 percent of non-Hispanic whites and 15 percent of blacks had bachelor's degrees.

Economic disparity between black people and white people remained pronounced. Although three-fourths of all black men were employed in 1960, barely half held jobs twenty years later. During the 1980s, two-thirds of all black workers in the South held low-income jobs, compared to one-third of whites. Half of all black workers did menial labor. Managers commonly assigned blacks to dead-end jobs, minimized their executive role, scrutinized them more harshly than comparably trained whites, and excluded them from the after-hours socializing that advances careers. In 1982 only one in thirty black men, compared with one in ten whites, filled management or administrative positions. By the mid-1980s, blacks earned, on average, 56 percent of white earnings, a drop of seven percentage points on the corresponding figure for 1975. In 1990, in every occupation and region of the country and at every educational level, the median African American income was lower than for whites. In 1999, the black unemployment rate remained double that for non-Hispanic whites (9 percent and 4 percent, respectively). The proportion of black men working in managerial and professional specialty occupations was roughly only half that of white men (17 percent and 32 percent, respectively), and black men were twice as likely as white men to work in service occupations.

The recession of the 1970s, the Reagan administration's cutting of aid programs, and the growth in single-parent families headed by women increased black poverty. By 1990, one-third of blacks and half of all black children lived below the poverty line. The proportion of single-parent, female-headed households rose from one-fifth of all black families in 1960 to nearly one-half in 1986, accounting for about 75 percent of all black children raised in poverty. In 1998, the black poverty rate was 26 percent, compared to the overall rate of 13 percent and the non-Hispanic white rate of 8 percent. Among all children under age eighteen, the poverty rate for African Americans (37 percent) more than tripled the rate for whites (11 percent).

The high incidence of poverty often resulted in a brutal existence for inner city black people. In 1984, the number of young blacks in prison exceeded by more than 25 percent the number of young blacks in college dormitories. In 1990, blacks constituted 54.7 percent of those accused of murder and 69.3 percent of those arrested for robbery. Poor African Americans were six times as likely as whites to suffer from violent crime. Homicide was the leading cause of death for blacks between the ages of eighteen and thirty-four. In April 1992, black rage against poverty exploded in a riot in Los Angeles following the acquittal of white police officers accused of beating a black motorist. The riot resulted in the deaths of fifty-two people and injuries to 2,300 others. It was the first major incident of urban unrest since 1968 and the deadliest since the draft riots in New York City in 1863. The mugging of eighty-one-year-old Rosa Parks in her own home in Detroit in August 1994 by a young black male in search of money for drugs symbolized the plight of inner-city blacks. "It was a fitting metaphor for the times," noted historian Robert Cook: "the woman whose name was legendary in civil rights folklore beaten and robbed by a man who had failed to benefit from the reforms of the 1960s." In October 1995, black males poured into Washington, D.C., for Black Muslim leader Louis Farrakhan's Million Man March to signal, peacefully, their concern about black-on-black violence and to reaffirm black pride.

Yet African Americans did advance on the economic front. By 1990, 47 percent of blacks and 74 percent of whites lived in households with incomes at least double the poverty line. The percentage of blacks in professional and semiprofessional occupations rose from 3.6 percent in 1940 to 5.9 percent in 1980. In 1990 dollars, 30 percent of black families earned more than $35,000 annually, up from 23.8 percent in 1970. Affirmative action played a large role in creating a black middle class which, by the mid-1990s, constituted roughly a third of the country's black population.

The black political record also reflects a blend of overall improvement and ongoing inequality. Since the Voting Rights Act of 1965, local government reorganization and gerrymandering schemes hampered the growth of black political strength. In 1992, African Americans held fewer than 2 percent of the nation's elective offices. Nevertheless, black people made significant advances in national as well as local politics. Jesse Jackson won 3.5 million primary votes in his 1984 bid for the Democratic presidential nomination and finished third in a field of eight candidates. He did even better in 1988, doubling his vote total and placing second. The Congressional Black Caucus numbered thirty-eight members after the 1992 elections. Enforcement of the Voting Rights Act of 1965 enabled the black proportion of registered voters to climb by 1990 to 11.2 percent, nearly their proportion of the population. The number of African Americans holding elective office across America rose from three thousand in 1975 to more than seven thousand in 1992. The number of cities and towns with black mayors rose from 120 in 1980 to 300 in 1992, even in municipalities with black minorities such as Seattle and New York.

Attitudes toward race both progressed and stagnated as well. In some areas, patterns of race relations continued to change at a glacial pace. In Durham, North Carolina, in 1982, a racist killed a black man for walking with a white woman. In Ludowici, Georgia, students picked separate black and white homecoming queens until 1984. The U.S. Department of Justice recorded a rise in racist attacks from 99 in 1980 to 276 in 1986. Kevin Nesmith, a black student at the Citadel, a military academy in Charleston, South Carolina, resigned after whites wearing Klan robes burst into his room at 2:00 in the morning shouting racial slurs and hazing him. In Georgia, a case in 1987 illustrated that killers of white persons were four times likelier to be executed than killers of black persons. In 1990, former Nazi and Klansman David Duke won 59 percent of the white vote in Louisiana in his unsuccessful bid for the U.S. Senate. In 1994, the trial of former football star and actor O. J. Simpson for the first-degree murder of his estranged white wife gripped the nation like a soap opera throughout its eight-month duration. When the court handed down a not-guilty verdict, many African Americans reacted with joy and many whites with disbelief, symbolizing the rift between black and white America.

Nevertheless, southern memories of black protests mellowed to the point where both races treat them as a part of their history of which they can be proud. Montgomery motorists now drive down the Martin Luther King Jr. Expressway, and the Dexter Avenue Baptist Church, where King was pastor, has become a national landmark.

Although there is no doubt that racism and prejudice exist in America, it is also true that racism and prejudice, on the whole, have declined since 1976. As the twentieth century ended, most major American institutions, including the armed forces, government, academia, and the professions, were more racially integrated than they had ever been. Opinion polls suggested that most white people eschewed beliefs in racial hierarchies. Martin Luther King's birthday had become a national holiday. Once the norm, overt expressions of white racial hostility had become the exception. A minority of individuals and groups still promoted hate in public forums such as the Internet, but society had become intolerant of overt expressions of racism and sexism in schools, government offices, the military, and other American institutions, as well as in the workplace and in most of society. Once upon a time southern whites used the word "nigger" without a second thought. At the end of the twentieth century, virtually the only whites who used the word freely were bigots, for most white people found the "n-word" too distasteful to say, even when quoting others. Even interracial dating and marriage, once the ultimate taboo, had become widely accepted.[2]

Karyn Reddick, a black student attending an integrated public high school in Selma, Alabama, in the late 1980s, had heard about Bloody Sunday but viewed it as part of a bygone age. "Try as you can, you can't believe that white people once treated black people that way," she said. "It seems like something that happened long, long ago."[3]

Beginning in the summer of 1976, a new minority appeared at the Naval Academy—women. There was nothing new about women in the Navy. American women first donned naval uniforms in 1908 with the establishment of the U.S. Navy Nurse Corps. During World War I women enlisted in the Navy as yeomen (F) to perform clerical duties and free deskbound men to fight, but only for the duration. During World War II women enlisted and were commissioned as officers in the WAVES (Women Accepted for Volunteer Emergency Service), again to free men to fight. WAVES served primarily in health care, clerical, and storekeeper billets. Navy nurses received relative rank and then temporary commissioned rank during the war, and in 1947 they gained a separate staff corps and permanent commissioned rank. In 1948, the Armed Services Integration Act gave women a permanent place in all the services, including the Navy. But the same legislation prohibited women from serving in combatant ships and aircraft. Thereafter the Navy maintained a trained cadre of female officers and enlisted women to serve as a nucleus in the event of mobilization, but for more than two decades neither Navy nurses nor Navy women not serving in the Nurse Corps transcended their traditional roles.[4]

The women's rights movement helped change all that. American women have taken political action on their own behalf since they began teaching in grammar schools and working in textile factories early in the nineteenth century. The women's rights movement went through cycles of reform and reaction ever since, but always with at least some women engaged in some form of activism. Before the 1960s, various women's groups fought for temperance and women's suffrage and against slavery, inhumane labor practices, and sexual harassment and abuse. The movement's most significant achievement before World War II was winning the right to vote for women in 1920. Since

World War II, increasing numbers of women sought employment outside the home. During the 1960s, a resurgent women's movement arose as women's organizations and activists called for legislation on numerous issues, including tax-supported child care and cessation of sex discrimination in employment and education. The women's rights movement was never a monolithic entity unified under one leader, but a diversity of organizations and activists with a wide variety of goals, ideas, and leadership styles.

As a result of efforts by national women's rights organizations, Congress changed the tax code to permit credits for child care and passed laws to prohibit discrimination against women in access to credit, in pension rights, and in employment. In other legislation, Congress prohibited workplace discrimination against pregnant women and barred sexual harassment of female employees.

Meanwhile, more and more women entered the workforce. By 1970, 41 percent of women worked outside the home. The number of women elected to state legislatures doubled in the decade after 1975. The number of women in Congress climbed from nineteen representatives in 1975 to thirty in 1991. By 1980, women constituted half of the student population at colleges, and more than 50 percent of adult women worked outside the home, where they made strong inroads into traditionally male professions such as law and medicine. In 1981, President Reagan appointed the first woman Supreme Court justice. Between 1973 and 1987, the proportion of women in the armed forces quintupled. Indeed, the role of women in American society had undergone a fundamental shift.

Admiral Zumwalt perceived the sea change in American society's approach toward women's rights as well as civil rights. Almost from the start, his Programs for People aimed at eliminating sexual discrimination for the roughly nine thousand women serving among the Navy's nearly half million men. In 1971, he convened a pair of study groups as the first step toward devising a comprehensive program for improving opportunities and conditions for Navy women. By the end of his watch, the Navy had increased women's eligibility for many more jobs and billets than before, promoted a woman to flag rank, commissioned the first female chaplain in any service, and permitted a half dozen women to become naval aviators.[5]

On 7 October 1975, President Gerald Ford signed a bill authorizing appointment of women to the service academies. The law specified that each service would determine the numbers admitted. In light of the prohibition against women serving in combatant ships or aircraft, the secretary of the navy established a goal for the number of women inducted into the class of 1980, the first to include women, at eighty, a number he considered "consistent with the needs of the naval service." The chief of naval personnel was authorized to determine admission goals for women in each succeeding year based on the needs of the service and attrition.

Over the next decade, admission goals for women climbed steadily. In 1985, the superintendent sought to increase the number of authorized women to 135, or roughly 10 percent of the incoming class. He argued that admitting more women would provide a better distribution of female midshipmen in the brigade; better reflect the upward trend in the proportion of female officers in the Navy, projected to be 9.9 percent in fiscal year 1987; increase the opportunity for successful participation and competition in women's sports; and foster greater acceptance of women by their male shipmates, leading, in turn, to greater retention rates for women. The chief of naval personnel gave the superintendent permission to increase the number of women to about 10 percent of each incoming class, beginning with the class of 1989.

African American women have been present in each class since the first women were admitted in July 1976. From one black woman in the class of 1980, the number admitted to successive classes climbed to an average of twelve per year in the classes of 1995–99, or roughly 7 percent of women admitted into each class.

The Academy's minority recruiting organization dealt with recruitment of minority women. MACs handled their cases and presented information on individual minority applicants to the admissions board in the same manner as for minority males. All women had to meet the same admissions standards as men, with adjustments made to the physical requirements to account for the physiological differences between the sexes.[6]

The 1,511 African Americans admitted into the classes of 1980–99 represented a quantum leap over the 476 black midshipmen who entered into the classes of 1969–79 and the fifty-one African Americans who entered in the classes of 1949–68. The demographics of the Academy's black population in the last quarter of the twentieth century more nearly reflected the demographics of America's black population than ever before. The Academy's Institutional Research Office has reliable home state and admission source data back to the class of 1988. The classes of 1988–99 included 956 African Americans. Of these, 503 received direct appointments, 405 entered from NAPS, forty-five came via the BOOST program, and three entered through the Naval Academy Foundation Program. These African Americans came from every state in the Union except Alaska, Montana, New Hampshire, North Dakota, South Dakota, Utah, Vermont, and Wyoming, all states with very small black populations. Maryland provided the most black midshipmen (105), followed by California (86), Virginia (67), Georgia (67), New York (63), Texas (56), Florida (55), New Jersey (39), Pennsylvania (34), South Carolina (33), and

Michigan (32). The remaining states each supplied fewer than thirty. About 55 percent of these black midshipmen came from the South, where about 55 percent of all African Americans lived.[7]

Wherever they came from, most black midshipmen from the classes of 1980–99 became aware at some point in their youth that a racial divide still existed in America.[8] Michael Greenwood, '85, was born in Montgomery, Alabama. Shortly after his birth, his father walked out on the family and his mother went north in search of work. His father's mother raised him until he was two years old, by which time his mother had settled in Meriden, Connecticut, and found employment as a worker in a chemical factory. Michael considered Meriden his hometown, for it was there that his mother raised him and his three brothers and one sister. Although Michael's paternal grandmother took great pride in her Cherokee heritage, his mother raised Michael and his brothers and sisters as black. Michael's father had grown up under segregation in the South and had served amid prejudice as an enlisted man in the Navy. Michael had little contact with him while growing up. During the few moments they did have together, it became apparent to Michael that his father "harbored a keen distrust of whites," as he recalled. Although his mother had encountered prejudice as well, she "appeared to harbor little of his hatred." She had worked for white families as a nanny and with white people in various jobs. "She felt very comfortable working in the 'white world,' and encouraged us to do the same," Michael said. "That's not to say she was unscarred by her experiences. She passed down many stories of the family's racial experiences: assaults, marches, etc. But she also taught her children to judge people as individuals."

The strongest influences on Michael's racial outlook came from growing up in an integrated neighborhood and attending integrated schools. "An overwhelming majority of people I interacted with were white," he recalled. "Throughout my youth, except for my mother and pastor, whites filled the positions of authority—teachers, athletic coaches, doctors, dentists. I had no choice but to be accepting because there were no alternatives. If I had continuously been subjected to debilitating racism through these experiences, my attitude toward whites would have been different. But, fortunately, that was not the case. Although I experienced a number of actual and some perceived racial slights, it was infrequent and definitely not debilitating. In fact, a number of whites frequently made themselves available during difficult periods of my life and served as important role models. Significant among many were my kindergarten teacher, my eighth grade English and history teachers, and my tenth grade biology teacher. Each one provided guidance, attention, and expressed an expectation of my eventual success. Similarly, the majority of my friends, and all of my 'best friends,' were white. Being human, my white friends could be insensitive and even cruel in regard to race. However, rarely did they direct such beliefs directly at me. Instead, racial insults and stereotypes were directed at other blacks, often without concern that I could hear what was said. As a result, I felt very isolated. Admittedly, this isolation was often self-imposed. But it resulted from my ability to be a part of both the black and white communities, yet not feeling fully accepted by either one."

Greenwood found athletics and academics effective antidotes to racism. "It appeared that most whites judged me by my athletic ability," he said, "and even racists (I knew a few) wanted to win. Despite the stereotypes, my junior high and high schools had few blacks participating in athletics. Secondly, I was academically sound. Not brilliant by any measure, but smart enough that many teachers were willing to invest time and effort to help me develop my abilities. As a consequence, my racial experiences were very different from what I observed of other minorities in my hometown."

Mario Maddox, '85, grew up in black neighborhoods in inner-city Atlanta. His father, born during the Depression, had left school after finishing the sixth grade to go to work. After serving in the Army in Germany during the Korean War, Mario's father got some technical training in Boston that enabled him to forge a career in the federal government, working for the Center for Disease Control in Atlanta in a mechanical shop, making contraptions to facilitate animal experiments. When Mario's mother was young, she was named Miss Sepia Atlanta (later Miss Black Atlanta). She attended Spellman College for a couple of years but did not graduate. She embarked on a business career, becoming manager of the bookkeeping department at the First National Bank of Atlanta and later at Coastal States Insurance.

In Mario's community, most people believed that African Americans "didn't get a fair chance in life," as he recalled. "There was this great white oppressor, 'the man.' Our parents didn't necessarily teach it, but that view was very prevalent where I grew up. Everybody thought that blacks were under class and that life wasn't fair." His parents tried to teach him and his two older brothers to be neutral on race. Mario never had a personal encounter with prejudice while growing up and never heard a white person utter a racial epithet, but his family lived and shopped in black areas. The schools that Mario attended were all black. Even when vacationing by the ocean, the family went to Fernadina Beach, a black beach north of Jacksonville, Florida.

Tracey James, '92, grew up mostly in Crownsville, Maryland. Her father was an Army chief warrant officer in intelligence. Tracey never knew him. He died of leukemia while her mother was pregnant with her. Her mother received a bachelor's degree from Morgan State University, majoring in foreign languages. After Tracey's father died, her mother supported her older brother and her by working variously in a library, as a substitute teacher, and in part-time administrative positions. Eventually she landed a full-time job at the Naval Academy on the early morning shift in the galley. Later she was promoted to the Midshipmen Food Services office, then to the Academy clinic as consult coordinator and supervisor of the medical records department.

Tracey's grandfather, a talented, hardworking man with a good job at Bethlehem Steel, had endured lots of prejudice in his day and formed definite views on race. When a story about a murder or other violent crime appeared on the news, the first thing he wanted to know was the perpetrator's race. He felt shame and disappointment if the person was black and relief if he or she wasn't.

Tracey's mother did not want her children exposed to prejudice or to stereotype others. "My mother did not permit us to discuss people in terms of race," she recalled. "We were forbidden from putting our arms against other people's arms to see who was the darkest, forbidden from comparing hair texture and eye color, forbidden from distinguishing anyone by their race. We had to get creative when we were trying to describe someone, because identifying people in terms of color was not permitted." Tracey's grandfather reinforced this teaching. "He would never permit anyone to say that another person had 'good hair,'" Tracey said. "His hair was thick and coarse, while his wife's hair was long and wavy. No eye color or hair texture was better than the other. He made it known to anyone and everyone that unless your hair was falling out from disease or your eyes were blinded, you had 'good hair' and 'pretty eyes.'"

Tracey lived in a black neighborhood and attended mostly white schools. At school she had lots of friends of many different ethnicities, but her closest friends were the other African American kids in the neighborhood. "My mother taught me that no one was better than me and that I was no better than anyone else, and certainly, race had little to do with character," Tracey recalled. "Since I was a teenager, my mother instilled in me that she did not care what color spouse my brother and I chose, but they had to be true Christians."

Arnoux Abraham, '93, a first-generation American of Haitian decent, grew up in inner-city Miami in predominantly minority neighborhoods. His mother worked as an interpreter in a hospital and his stepfather as a supervisor in a cement factory. His mother taught him to judge people by their principles and to "forgive and forget." Miami was a mosaic of different races and ethnicities and Arnoux saw everything from race riots to multicultural parades. He had many non-black friends and encountered no prejudice.

Reuben Brigety, '95, was born and raised in Jacksonville, Florida. His mother earned a bachelor's degree from Florida A&M University and worked as teacher of speech therapy. His father was the first African American graduate of the University of Florida medical school and had established a successful practice as an obstetrician/gynecologist in Jacksonville. Reuben grew up with a strong sense of family progress, with each generation providing a strong foundation for the growth of the next. "It was always my responsibility to understand where I was coming from and to help take our family one step further," he recalled. His great grandparents on his mother's side were children of slaves. His great grandfather, Jesse Aaron, whom the family called "Poppa Daddy," was a farmer. He left school after about the third or fourth grade to work. He rose early each morning at his little house in Gainesville and walked ten miles to the fields, worked all day, and walked home in the evening. He also carved wooden figures of animals and people, some of which can now be found at the University of Florida. When his maternal grandmother was young, she worked in wealthy white people's kitchens in Tallahassee. She later worked nights scrubbing floors and otherwise cleaning in the state capitol building. Many an evening Reuben's mother would work right alongside his grandmother.

This aspect of the family's heritage assumed a special poignancy during Reuben's junior year of high school. "When I was sixteen I went to a program called the American Legion Boy's State, a program run by the American Legion in every state, every summer. It's when boys who are juniors in high school go off and actually recreate the process of state government, starting in small cities and ultimately electing governors. Florida's Boys State is actually held in the capital in Florida. That year I happened to be elected the governor of Boy's State, which meant that I was able to make speeches in the state legislature building. We held meetings in the state cabinet room. Forty years before, my grandmother had swept the floor and cleaned spittoons in the same building. To have her grandson, figuratively, anyway, as the governor, was something that was very powerful for us as a family, and that sense of progression was not lost on me. As a matter of fact, it is something that weighs quite heavily in my view of the world."

Reuben's father often told him stories about the discrimination he had to overcome while attending medical school in Gainesville. He was not permitted to eat with the other students. His instructors suggested he apply to a black medical school and arbitrarily failed him his first year. When he took his shirts to a dry cleaner in town, the woman behind the counter said, "I'm sorry, sir, we don't do colored shirts here." "Well that's okay," said Brigety, "I don't have any colored shirts, anyway. They're all white." But it soon became clear that it was not the color of the shirt to which the woman was referring. Dr. Brigety persevered and succeeded by sheer hard work. Reuben didn't see much of him while growing up. "While some little kids go and play baseball with their dads," he recalled, "my early years were spent on rounds with my father."

Reuben grew up in a largely white neighborhood, went to largely white public schools, but attended a black church. "I grew up pretty much color-blind in the sense of having friends from all different backgrounds," he recalled. "My parents purposely put me in that sort of environment because they really wanted me to see that people are people." Church was not just a place of worship but a place to "experience my ethnicity," as he put it, "in the sense of experiencing my people." Nevertheless, his parents, aunts, and uncles instilled in him the belief that "ultimately, in America, if you are African American, you had to work twice as hard in order to be accepted as equal."

Quintin Jones, '98, was born and raised in a black neighborhood in Memphis, Tennessee. He spoke to his father only once, and that was during plebe year at the Academy. His mother raised Quintin by herself until he was twelve, when she married his stepfather. His mother worked as a sales representative for the *Commercial Appeal,* a local newspaper. His stepfather was a custodial manager at the University of Memphis. Quintin attended all-black schools until he was about halfway through high school, when the family moved to the eastern part of the city. He transferred to a high school that was about 50 percent black, took honors classes, and made many non-black friends. Although Quintin's mother and stepfather never espoused negative racial views, they remained wary of him getting into situations where his race could get him into trouble. On one occasion, one of Quintin's white friends wanted to meet him at the roller rink. His stepfather drove Quintin over, but when he realized that Quintin would be the only black kid at the rink he talked him out of going. "I don't think it's a good idea for you to put yourself in that situation," he said. "There may be people there who don't particularly welcome your presence. If something gets out of hand, and there's no one there to back you up except your friend, they may very well beat him up too, because he's with you." Quintin was quite upset, for such thoughts had never crossed his mind. He had only wanted to go roller skating with a friend.

Jerry Gray, '00, grew up in Lusby, Maryland. His father was an auto mechanic and his mother a supply and procurement clerk at the recreation center at Naval Air Station Patuxent River. His grandma, grandpa, aunt, and uncle loomed large in his upbringing. Jerry was raised in the church. Although born a Methodist, when he got older he attended a Baptist church. His family never espoused negative racial views. Instead they emphasized being careful about choosing his friends, whatever their color. Jerry grew up in a mixed neighborhood free of racial tension where everybody got along. One of his best friends was a white girl whose family treated him as one of their own. "They would joke all the time about how they adopted me and I was their darker kid," Gray recalled. "I came over any time I wanted to. I raided the fridge, watched TV. I was no different to them." Jerry was enrolled in the gifted and talented program in middle school and in honors classes in high school. He was usually one of three or four blacks in a class with twenty-five or thirty white students. He spent lots of time with white students outside of class because he knew them so well from class and they were his friends. It was a perfectly natural thing to do. A few black students not in his classes in middle school didn't see it that way, however. Occasionally they called him "AIW" for "African American in with white." They thought he shouldn't be spending so much time with white people. Older white people in town or at school who didn't know his family sometimes looked askance at him when he wore his Naval JROTC uniform or used technical language when speaking, because such behavior didn't fit their stereotype of a black kid his age.

As in earlier periods, black children raised in military families often encountered less prejudice than those from nonmilitary families. Ingrid M. Turner, '86, was born in Fort Riley, Kansas, and raised on various Army bases until fourth grade, when her father, an Army colonel, moved the family to Bowie, Maryland, for a tour at Walter Reed U.S. Army Medical Center, after which he retired and set up a private practice in optometry. Ingrid's mother was a teacher. While her father was on active duty, her mother taught classes to enlisted people who wanted to earn a GED. After her father retired, her mother taught the third grade. Ingrid grew up in integrated neighborhoods and attended integrated schools, both on Army bases and in Bowie, where she attended Elizabeth Seton High School, a Catholic girls' school. She had more white friends than black friends in high school. Her parents tried to shelter her from prejudice and never really taught her anything about race. She had no negative racial experiences growing up.

Nikki Peoples, '97, was born in New Jersey and raised in Milpitas, California, about five minutes from San Jose. Her father was a career military man, first an enlisted marine, then a Green Beret officer and jump master with the Army's Special Forces. He retired a major, earned a master's degree, and became a human resources and personnel management consultant. Nikki's mother earned a master's degree from Golden Gate University, worked as a federal probation officer, and later became a pretrial officer in San Jose. Nikki's parents taught her Martin Luther King's principle that people should be judged not by the color of their skin but by the content of their character. Although her parents stressed equality between the sexes as well as among races, she all too frequently encountered instances of racism or sexism while growing up. Her father taught her to put forth 100 percent effort in everything she did as an antidote to racism and sexism. He believed that a female could learn to play basketball just as well as a male and would take her to the YMCA or military bases to shoot hoops. Nikki often encountered sexism on the basketball court, but once she proved herself the males respected her.

For Jacqueline Jackson, '99, moving from a military to a civilian environment in the middle of her childhood brought America's racial divide into sharp relief. Jacqueline was born in the Philippines and raised in Germany and the United States in a military family. Her father, an African American, was an enlisted man in the Army. He walked out on the family when Jacqueline was in the ninth grade. Her mother, a native of the Philippines, served in the National Guard. Jacqueline spent her early years on military bases in Germany and inside U.S. military culture, growing up in racially mixed neighborhoods and attending mixed schools.

Jacqueline received mixed signals about race while growing up. Her mother did not want Jacqueline to engage in what she considered stereotypical black behavior—being loud, arrogant, and rude. Sometimes when Jacqueline misbehaved, her mother would say, "Don't act black." Jacqueline's father conveyed the impression that prejudice had held him back, preventing him from advancing as far in life as he should have. "White people are conniving," he would say. "Never trust them." Jacqueline herself never experienced prejudice while living in the military environment and never had a problem associating with white children. "I don't think color was that big a deal on a military base," she recalled.

When Jacqueline was about nine or ten, the family moved back to her father's old neighborhood, a predominantly black suburb of Columbus, Ohio, where she attended predominantly black schools. She remained there through high school and for two years at Ohio State University. Leaving the military environment marked another turn in her racial outlook. "When I came back to the United States," she recalled, "I had a big problem, because I didn't talk like them, I didn't act like them, I didn't look like them. I had a lot of negative experiences with black people. The first day I went into school in Germany, everyone was trying to sit with me. In the United States, I came back to a black school and everyone was ridiculing me."

For other black midshipmen in the classes of 1980–99, high school opened their eyes to America's racial divide. Troy Lee McSwain II, '84, grew up in south-central Los Angeles, about a mile from where the 1992 race riot started. His father, who had been a sonarman in the Navy, had an associate's degree from a junior college and worked as a computer engineer for Control Data Systems. His mother worked as a teacher's assistant and took care of the household. Troy lived in an all-black neighborhood and attended mostly white schools. His parents taught him to treat everyone as equal and not to judge people based on the color of their skin, "because you were the one being judged most of the time on the color of your skin," as Troy recalled. "Basically they taught me to just try to be fair with somebody until they mistreated you, and then deal with things accordingly." They also stressed the importance of education. Troy was enrolled in a gifted program in elementary school and junior high, then the regular program at Westchester High School. He spent the summer between his sophomore and junior years (1978) in a summer program at Phillips Academy in Andover, Massachusetts.

The culture of Los Angeles street gangs shaped Troy's daily routine during the school year. Troy lived in a "Crip" neighborhood and had to travel through a "Blood" (a rival gang) neighborhood to get to school. Bloods routinely harassed kids from outside their neighborhood who were passing through on their way home from school. Troy avoided violent confrontations and getting mixed up in gangs by playing football. He excelled on the gridiron, becoming first-team All League center, first-team All League linebacker, and captain of his team. "In the afternoon when kids who didn't have anything to do were joining gangs and being influenced by drug dealers and things like that, I was playing football," recalled McSwain. "By the time I got home, it was dark. It was nothing but eat dinner, do your homework, and go to bed."

McSwain, an excellent student, made As and Bs through junior high and high school, was a member of the California Scholastic Federation, Senior Steering Committee, and National Honor Society, and was selected as a delegate to the American Legion Boys' State in Sacramento. He graduated fifty-fifth in a class of five hundred. At church, he was a junior deacon and president of the youth department. But he didn't want his friends to think him a "square" or a "geek." So through high school he kept two sets of books, one at school and one at home, so neither his classmates nor the "gangbangers" would see him carrying books home to do homework.

McSwain and other black students who were bused to Westchester High had difficulty making friends with white students. "We went to a white school and lived in the 'hood, so we got stereotyped," he recalled. "The white kids didn't gravitate toward us. We were separate. We had to stick together because at the end of the day, we had to catch a bus home through gang neighborhoods." McSwain found that athletic excellence won over the white students. "The white kids didn't really accept me until I played sports," he said. "As a person, they didn't accept me, but as an athlete, they did, so that's where most of my white friends came from. In playing sports, I started to meet more white kids on the team. They started getting to know me as a person and they respected me as a person." He found, however, that the friendships he made with whites did not extend beyond school or school activities. "After football practice, I had to catch a bus home to my neighborhood with other black guys. The white guys weren't there with me. They'd go do their thing and I went and did my thing. It was nothing socially afterwards."

For Roger G. Isom, '88, the racial gap narrowed in high school. Roger was raised in a family of nine children in Monticello, Florida, a farming community about twenty miles east of Tallahassee. Both of his parents finished high school. His dad was a carpenter. His mother was a maid but worked only when each child was old enough for care by a sibling. Their house lacked indoor plumbing. "I bought our first bathtub and toilet when I joined the Navy and saved enough money to send them," Roger recalled. The family drew water from a well or borrowed water from neighbors. Even though Roger's father made minimum wage with eleven mouths to feed, the family never went without food. "We grew vegetables and raised hogs, chickens, and ducks," Isom recalled. "Dad and Mom taught us to be humble and thankful for the 'small things in life.' I would not trade my upbringing, because those humble beginnings shaped my core values."

Growing up in rural Florida only five miles from the Georgia line, Isom learned early about the social differences between races. "There were so many reminders," he recalled. "Our schools may have been integrated legally, but there were still very distinct places in my hometown that were considered 'white people places' and 'coloreds places.' The churches were not integrated. Even though whites were welcomed, I only saw white people at our churches during election periods. My parents taught me that some white people did not like me simply because of my color. We had marches by the KKK; we also had marches by the Black Panthers. We lived beside a large farming development called Norias Plantation. My grandfather worked on the plantation as a sharecropper. When he died and none of the kids volunteered to work for the plantation supervisor, my grandmother was forced to move. If nothing else, the Norias Plantation sign at the crossroad to our house was a constant reminder of the past and a symbol of a history that some whites and blacks would not escape."

Like fellow southerner Mario Maddox, Roger Isom never encountered prejudiced whites directly. "People in our community had defined norms and customs," he recalled. "You stay in your place and you will be alright," they would say. When Roger was thirteen, his church was firebombed and shots were fired through its windows. "To this day, I don't know who did it," he said, "but I do know that I was very afraid and saddened."

Like Troy McSwain, Roger Isom had white friends, but he saw them only at school or during school-related activities. Isom's high school class was 60 percent black and 40 percent white. In the ninth grade, Roger entered the gifted program. Throughout high school he attended at least one class per semester in the program. Being one of two African Americans in these classes, he was "truly a 'minority,'" as he put it. The rest of his classes were mostly black.

The gifted program made Roger apprehensive at first. "My initial fear had nothing to do with the academic courses," he recalled. "I was primarily afraid that I would not 'fit in' with this group of elite and middle- to upper-class students. I was coming into the program late and feared that they would make fun of my home, my parents' occupations, or my unfamiliarity with the fads and trends for 'wealthy youths.' I remember meeting two classmates at our crossroad for a carpool to the school's Brain Brawl. My biggest worry was for them to ask to use our bathroom." Nevertheless, Roger had no difficulty making friends with white students.

Roger worried that his acceptance among white students would alienate him from other black students. "I was somewhat of a class clown, who did crazy things so that I could fit in with the other classmates not in the gifted program," he recalled. "I did not want to be considered a sellout. In fact, I joined the high school band as a senior to play drums and show that I was a 'cool black dude.'"

Racial lines sometimes made friendships with white students difficult for Roger to maintain. The lines faded noticeably toward the end of his high school years. "One of my class's greatest accomplishments was hosting the first integrated senior prom," he recalled. "Before 1982, the white seniors refused to attend the official school prom with the blacks. Instead they would have their prom at the country club. Of course, no black membership there. My class decided to stop that division and we hosted the prom successfully."

Roger had to work to help support his family. He and his mother and younger brothers and sisters picked peas and beans for white farmers. "We only received fifty cents for a bushel of peas," he recalled. "The owners received on average eight dollars for the same bushel. Obviously there was an inequity in the payments, but the owners had the power. We were replaceable, because many black people in my community needed the work to pay the bills. One year, my father, a very proud man, refused to allow us to work for the white farmers unless they gave us a raise. You could call it a boycott or strike. To my surprise, it worked. We eventually got seventy-five cents a bushel. I will always respect my dad for taking a stand." During his last two years of high school, Isom took a job working in a supermarket. The job was "awesome," he said. "I was finally working in an air-conditioned space, with toilets."

William L. Carr, '97, grew up in a black neighborhood in Milwaukee's inner city. His father died two days before he was born. His mother worked at various jobs until William began high school, when she settled into a dual career as a private nurse and hairdresser. A devout Baptist, his mother always told him and his younger sister that "the Lord knows no color, He only knows attitudes and personalities," as he recalled. "You don't judge somebody by their color." William's close-knit churchgoing family shared that outlook, and his own experiences in high school reinforced it. William attended West Division High School, Milwaukee's school of the arts. He majored in music and played bass, clarinet, trumpet, saxophone, and other instruments as well as sang. Kids from all over the city were bused there. The student body included people of all manner of ethnicities and tastes, from "preppies" to "thrashers," as William put it. He got along well with them all. Back in the neighborhood, however, other African Americans often characterized white people as racist oppressors and talked about how "the man's been doing it for four hundred years." When Carr would argue that not all white people are bad and it's what's inside that counts, he would be called "preacher" or "grandma."

For black midshipmen in the classes of 1980–99, the desire for a military career weighed heavily in their decision to apply for the Academy. Reuben Brigety had been interested in the military for as long as he could remember. The summer before ninth grade, on the last day of his family's vacation in Orlando, Florida, Reuben was sitting in the hotel lobby while his parents were checking out. A pamphlet that a young man was reading on career opportunities for naval officers caught Reuben's eye. He asked the young man if he could read it. The fellow gave it to him. The pamphlet described some of the roles that naval officers played in the Department of Defense and the State Department. It included an illustration of an African American ensign. Reuben was intrigued. He wrote to the Navy Department, asking how to become a naval officer. The Navy sent him information on the Sea Cadets, a Navy League–sponsored program resembling Naval JROTC, except that the Sea Cadets trained with active duty naval units. Reuben joined the Sea Cadets when he turned fourteen. The program included water survival training, weapons training, drilling, marching, and naval customs. At the same time a retired flag officer who had just moved next door, V. Adm. Thomas R. Kinnebrew, filled Reuben with tales of his adventures in the Navy. Coincidently, a black naval officer who had recently joined the Brigetys' church, Lieutenant Wymon Winbush, '82, also told Reuben tales of his midshipman days. Reuben was hooked. These influences fueled his ambition to become a midshipman and to have a naval career. When the time came to send out applications for college, Reuben applied to only one school, the Naval Academy.

Jacqueline Jackson had developed the desire to go to the Naval Academy while she was in high school. "But I thought it was almost impossible," she recalled. "I was just intimidated by all the forms." When Ohio State offered her a full scholarship, she decided to go there. By sophomore year, Jackson was getting bored. She wanted more out of life than an engineering degree and a job. "I wanted to live a life that I could tell my kids and grandkids about," she said. A military career seemed to offer what she was looking for. Movies like *Top Gun* portrayed the Navy as the most glamorous service and rekindled her ambition to apply to the Academy.

Jerry Gray had begun thinking about a military career in ninth grade, when he joined the Naval JROTC program. Gray quickly developed a deep respect for his assistant instructor, a Marine master gunnery sergeant, and his unit's commanding officer, a Naval Academy graduate. These role models, together with a love of the water fostered by crabbing and fishing with his grandfather, sparked an ambition to make the Navy a career.

For some of these midshipmen, a military career was a family tradition. Nikki Peoples had long wanted to follow in her father's footsteps into the armed services. "However," she recalled, "I didn't want to enter the military without having gone to college first. Then I heard about the different academies from movies like *Space Camp* and *Top Gun,* and I knew a girl who was accepted to the Naval Academy. My original intention was to go to the Air Force Academy or West Point, but I was heavily recruited by the local Blue and Gold officer. He convinced me that there were more opportunities for women entering the Navy."

Roger Isom's family viewed military service as a "noble and effective means of escaping the farming life and becoming somebody," as he recalled. Three of his older brothers had enlisted in the Army. The supervisor of the county's gifted program told Roger's mother that Roger should consider going to a service academy. Roger had not heard much about service academies before then. On one occasion, he saw two West Point cadets visiting his school. "These guys are perfect," he thought. On another occasion, Roger had seen the Army-Navy game on TV. The announcers referred to the players with such phrases as "cream of the crop," "future national leaders," and "America's finest." "No way those institutions would accept me," he thought. Hearing that an appointment entailed a congressional nomination confirmed this perception. "I can't go to the academies," he thought. "Mom and Dad don't know any congressmen." Roger figured he would enlist in the Army, as had his three older brothers. "Despite being salutatorian of my class," he recalled, "I did not plan on going to college, because my parents couldn't afford it. Simply graduating from high school was a major accomplishment in our community. Then a Navy recruiter came to his school. Roger spoke with him. The recruiter described the BOOST program as the ticket to an NROTC scholarship or, possibly, an appointment to the Academy. The BOOST program would enable Roger to leave the farm, attend college without burdening his parents, and "accept the challenge of meeting the standard my brothers had set in the military." Roger decided to enlist in the Navy.

William Carr grew up wanting to join the Marine Corps because so many of the men in his family had been marines. His stepfather and uncle talked him out of enlisting in the Marines, however, arguing that from a career standpoint enlisting in the Navy or Air Force made better sense. College had not entered the picture. His mother simply could not afford to pay for it. So he enlisted in the Navy and went through the Basic Underwater Demolition/SEAL School. He then went out to the fleet. After about a year and a half on the carrier *Carl Vinson*, his division officer ordered him to apply to NAPS. Carr did so and was accepted.

Quintin Jones developed an ambition to go to West Point while he was in high school. After graduating, he entered West Point Preparatory School, the Army's equivalent of NAPS. "I found out that I should've been studying more instead of working," he recalled. He struggled academically throughout the year and was not accepted into West Point. The Army suggested that he spend a year at Valley Forge Military Academy, then reapply to West Point. Jones entered Valley Forge and pulled his grades up enough during first semester to get an early acceptance offer from West Point. He also played football and basketball. During a basketball game at Navy, he fell in love with the Naval Academy campus and redirected his ambition toward becoming a midshipman. The superintendent of Valley Forge, a retired Navy flag officer, made a few phone calls and got him into the Naval Academy.

Other African Americans from the classes of 1980–99 simply wanted to be midshipmen and had not pondered the future beyond graduation. Michael Greenwood's ambition to become a midshipman arose from being a Dallas Cowboys fan. "I idolized the team and its players," he recalled. "Roger Staubach, an Academy grad, led 'America's team.'" As Greenwood did research on Staubach's alma mater, he became infatuated with the Academy's history, traditions, and reputation and developed a strong interest in becoming a midshipman. At this point, however, he had not given much thought to whether he wanted a naval career. For William Triplett, '89, a boat ride past the Academy with his family doctor sparked the ambition to become a midshipman.

A few sought to become midshipmen for the chance at a career in aviation. "I knew that I wanted to fly," recalled Arnoux Abraham. "I narrowed my choices to the Air Force Academy and Naval Academy. I decided on the Naval Academy because I knew that being able to land on board a ship was far more prestigious and difficult than on land." Roger Grayson, '88, wanted to become a naval aviator, had an interest in engineering, and needed a good scholarship to minimize the financial burden on his parents. He considered civilian schools, the NROTC program, and the Naval Academy. The Academy seemed the best choice.

Economic considerations motivated many to apply to the Academy. Mary Alice Miles, '87, grew up in Lexington Park, Maryland, near Naval Air Station Patuxent River. Mary's mother had always emphasized the importance of a good education. Her parents wanted her to become the first in the family to graduate from college but could not afford to pay her way. Because her home was so near "the base," as her family called the naval air station, Mary had early developed a fascination for things military, so it seemed natural for her to consider opportunities offered by the Navy. During her senior year in high school, she read an article in the paper about students accepted to service academies. "My accomplishments are comparable to theirs," she thought. "Maybe I should look into this option. I could get a good education on full scholarship, have a job upon graduation, and lay a strong foundation for my life." She spoke with a Navy recruiter on the base about the Naval Academy. It turned out that four of her high school classmates had already accepted the appointments available that year, so the recruiter steered her toward NAPS. Ironically, Mary's class rank and GPA were higher than three of the four appointees, all of whom happened to be her friends. "They were and are good guys," recalled Mary, "so I harbored absolutely no resentment." She gladly accepted the opportunity offered to her and entered NAPS in 1982.

Tracey James was given a Naval Academy recruiting brochure during her junior year in high school. The idea of a free education at a top-tier school and a guaranteed job intrigued her. Plus the Academy was close to home. Her mother, who worked there, encouraged her to apply. Ingrid Turner also found the prospect of a free education and guaranteed job attractive. "Near the time I graduated high school," she recalled, "a lot of people were coming out of college and not getting jobs." Turner applied and was accepted to the Air Force Academy, the Military Academy, and the Naval Academy as well as to ROTC programs at Duke University and the University of North Carolina. She found the Navy more attractive than the other services because she liked the water and had swum on the Naval Academy's Junior Dependent Youth Activities swim team. She figured that a service academy would make her a better officer than an NROTC program, so she picked the Naval Academy.

Mario Maddox signed up for the JROTC program in tenth grade because he heard it was an easy A. He found that he liked the discipline and structure, so he remained in the program throughout high school. During his senior year, an Air Force Academy recruiter visited the school and tried to recruit Maddox's best friend. It was the first time Maddox ever heard of a service academy, so he began looking into them all. The school's guidance counselors seemed to know little about West Point and nothing about the Naval Academy, leaving Maddox to find information on his own. He liked the idea of a scholarship and a military career, particularly the scholarship. He applied to several civilian schools as well as to the service academies. Maddox was considering the Merchant Marine Academy and a dual-degree program through Georgia Tech and Morehouse when the Navy offered to send him to NAPS. He accepted.

In some cases, parental pressure provided the motive to apply. In high school Troy McSwain developed an ambition to become a fashion designer. "But because of homosexuality in the fashion business," he recalled, "my parents discouraged me from it. My father, because he was ex-Navy, talked me into going to the Naval Academy." As a fallback position, the Naval Academy did have a certain appeal for McSwain. When he was about eight or nine, one of his cousins became a midshipman in the class of 1974, an event that created considerable favorable comment in the family, not least because of the cousin's passing for white at the Academy. After graduating, the cousin came home to Los Angeles for a visit. He pulled up to the house in a Porsche 911 and filled McSwain's ears with stories about the Academy. "Wow," thought McSwain. "I want to do that if I can." By McSwain's junior year of high school, his grades, extracurricular activities, sports, and SAT scores made him a shoo-in for the Academy. After he initiated the application process, a MAC paid him several visits at home to ensure that he completed it correctly.

Some black midshipmen drew mixed responses for their decision to attend the Academy. Quintin Jones's family members, neighbors, and friends supported his decision to embark on a military career, but when the academic dean and assistant dean at Valley Forge Military Academy heard he wanted to go to Annapolis they tried to talk him out of it. Both of the deans had graduated from West Point. "We really don't think you should go to the Naval Academy," they said, arguing that the Navy tended to be more elitist than the Army. "There's a lot more racism in the Navy than there is in the Army." Jones had already given the matter a lot of thought. Although the Army had more minority officers than the Navy, he reasoned, the Navy offered more opportunities. Arnoux Abraham's family considered being a naval officer an honorable profession, but his friends thought the military "seemed to be a waste."

Those in Tracey James's family who understood what the Academy was about were proud that she had been accepted. Friends who didn't know what the Academy was about thought she was enlisting in the Navy. "Why are you enlisting in the military when you can go to college?" they would ask. Her boyfriend tried to discourage her from going, partly because he had had a negative experience in the Air Force and partly because he didn't want to lose her.

William Carr's mother and stepfather supported his decision to become a midshipman and thought it a wonderful opportunity. Most of his friends, however, didn't know anything about the Academy. Many considered him a sellout for going to what they perceived as a white school instead of to a historically black school.

When Michael Greenwood told his father that he was going to the Naval Academy, it proved to be the last conversation they ever had. "Although we never had a close relationship," Greenwood recalled, "what we did have ended when I decided to join an organization that had demeaned blacks and perpetuated the racism he had marched and fought against." And though his junior and senior high school teachers and guidance counselors nurtured Greenwood's interest in the Academy enthusiastically, his family, friends, and neighbors "showed little to no interest. Most of them didn't know that the Academy was a university and assumed that I was enlisting in the Navy."

By and large, most black midshipmen drew positive responses for their decision to attend the Academy. Roger Grayson was the first in his immediate family to attend college, making everyone proud. Troy McSwain's family, friends, and acquaintances were quite pleased for him, since they viewed the Academy as an institution comparable in prestige to an Ivy League school. Folks in Nikki Peoples's community were very supportive. "One of my friends even enlisted in the Air Force because of my decision to go into the military," she recalled. Ingrid Turner's decision met a similar reception. "Everybody was proud and excited," she said.

Roger Isom's friends laughed when they heard he had joined the Navy. He had never been in a swimming pool and couldn't swim a stroke. Nevertheless, he did well in the BOOST program, earning a nomination as sailor of the year. A distant cousin happened to be in the BOOST program at the same time. When the cousin applied to the Naval Academy, Isom did so as well. "The family has to stick together," he said. Isom thought his chances of being accepted were slim. In April 1984, Carey Hithon, then a lieutenant doing a tour as a MAC for the Academy, visited BOOST to interview candidates for the Academy. During an interview with Isom, Hithon couldn't help but comment on his demeanor. "Seaman Apprentice Isom," he said, "you're cocky."

"No sir," replied Isom, "just confident."

"Congratulations Roger," Hithon said at the end of the interview. "I'll see you at Annapolis this summer."

"I was in shock," recalled Isom, "but still skeptical." When the secretary of the navy's official appointment notification arrived in the mail a few weeks later, Isom was ecstatic. "It's true," he thought. "I'm going to the Naval Academy. I am going to get a college degree." He called home from a pay phone in the base library. He was so elated that he could barely talk. The news filled his mother with joy. Roger was the first of her children to attend college. She and her husband perceived Roger's appointment to the Academy "as a blessed opportunity from God."

Mario Maddox and his family greeted his appointment with the same level of enthusiasm. The day the letter arrived notifying him of his acceptance into NAPS was one of the happiest days of Mario's youth. "My father and I were standing in the front yard just jumping and cheering," he recalled. "I knew that this was my opportunity in life." Despite lingering traces of the Navy's World War II hangover, his neighbors, friends, and acquaintances overwhelmed him with support. "I became an instant hero in my neighborhood and in my family as someone who was really going to do something with their life. I enjoyed every moment of it. It made me feel really proud." "How in the world did your son ever get into the Naval Academy?" people would ask his parents.

Racism Was a Fringe Attitude,
Sexism Was Mainstream

AFRICAN AMERICANS entering the Naval Academy in the classes of 1980–99 generally encountered less prejudice than had their predecessors. Nevertheless, black midshipmen still saw a broad range of racial attitudes during plebe year. The Academy itself took stock of these attitudes along with other issues concerning African Americans through a minority midshipmen study group established on 1 August 1988 by R. Adm. Ronald F. Marryott, the superintendent, to examine minority recruiting and attrition. Chaired by Capt. Harry Seymour, director of candidate guidance, the group consisted of members of the admissions board, faculty, and candidate guidance staff and included three African Americans. The group met periodically for the next eight months, interviewed scores of midshipmen, faculty, and uniformed staff, and kept Admiral Marryott apprised of its progress. Its investigation focused on academic performance, brigade life, and marketing. Its full report, issued in May 1989, became the sine qua non for understanding minority recruitment and retention issues at the Academy in the 1980s and 1990s.[1]

Many black midshipmen of this period felt no negative racial attitudes from classmates or upperclassmen. "Race didn't seem to be an issue at the Academy," recalled Arnoux Abraham. Jerry Gray thought the full plebe schedule left no room for racism. To be sure, he noticed cultural differences among classmates. "I like Gospel and R&B," he said, "but I can't stand heavy metal." He couldn't stand gangsta rap either, which seemed to surprise some of his white classmates. Reuben Brigety never personally experienced discrimination at the Academy. The minority midshipmen study group found life in Bancroft Hall to be "free from ethnic discrimination."[2]

Most black midshipmen, however, encountered a little prejudice among a few classmates and upperclassmen. As the minority midshipmen study group report put it, "No overwhelming negative environmental issues exist for minority midshipmen since evidence of racial tension, prejudice, or overt hostilities occur rarely, if at all. Isolated situations and individual persons are sometimes annoying and unpleasant and minorities do find they must cope with occasional instances of insensitivity and lack of understanding by others."[3]

Michael Greenwood never observed any racially motivated threats or attacks at the Academy. Instead, as he recalled, prejudice manifested itself in "subtle hints, innuendos, and references" that surfaced "in anger or during controversial class lectures or speakers." Quintin Jones said that prejudice came across subtly in jokes or insensitive remarks.[4]

Mario Maddox found that some white midshipmen resented the existence of the Black Studies Club. "What if we had a white studies club?" they would say. According to the minority midshipmen study group report, "Most majority midshipmen feel that a homogenous brigade excludes the need for organizations based upon racial or ethnic identity. Minorities see this as a negative perception, but a necessary price to develop self-esteem and enjoy friendships with others who share common cultural backgrounds and interests."[5]

Interracial dating could still evoke prejudice. Tracey James began dating a white midshipman candidate while she was at NAPS. "He was very close with the black male midshipman candidates in his platoon," she recalled. "He was the company commander and well respected by all. When the black midshipman candidates found out that we were dating, though we were very discreet and professional about our relationship, they shunned me and asked me why I was 'crossing over.' I thought that was ironic, considering none of them gave me the time of day. When we broke up, the guys talked to me a little more. Even though they followed this white midshipman like he was all-seeing, all-knowing, they had a problem with my having the same admiration toward him."

While James was at the Academy, the thought of interracial dating aroused deep-seated, perhaps subconscious prejudice in her roommate, a white female midshipman. "We were very close and looked out for each other," James recalled of their relationship. "I felt I could trust her completely." As a varsity athlete, James's roommate enjoyed the privilege of choosing classes online before nonathletes. She signed up for a creative writing class. James wanted to take that class too, but by the time she was permitted to register the course was full. An English major, James was very disappointed. Her roommate offered to share her coursework with James. "She would show me the journal entries they had to write, telling me the subject, and I would write freestyle on the subject or go over in my head what my feelings were about the assigned topic," James said.

"One day, I had a free period and I decided to read what the creative writing class had been assigned the day before. I opened the green spiral notebook my roommate kept and turned to the last journal entry. I don't remember the subject, but it was her 'creative' thoughts on interracial dating. Brutally honest. She kept referring to black people as 'one of *them*' and I kept trying to figure out who she thought 'them' was. She referred to a very handsome black midshipman and how she thought he was gorgeous and athletic and funny. He was truly all of those things, and he was just simply a good person. But, she went on to say, she could never introduce him to her parents. They wouldn't understand the attraction. She could never bring one of 'them' home. What would her father think if she dated one of 'them'? After all, she had a black roommate and we were friends, but to actually date, marry and sleep with one of 'them'??? She couldn't do it. She questioned her feelings, whether they were right or wrong, and I felt like a bucket of cold water had been dumped over my head. I was stunned at what I was reading. How could this be? How could I have misjudged my own roommate? The man I was currently dating was Muslim and had introduced me to racial prejudice. We had countless arguments about racism, and I didn't believe racism still existed in America. I had been given so many opportunities and was successful and had a bright future. Who, exactly, was being held back, and by whom? He insisted that white people couldn't be trusted, and I insisted that he was paranoid and living in the sixties. For the first time, I questioned my position. I put the folder back in its place, and just sat there in a daze. Thinking. Pondering. Questioning. Wondering. I don't know how long I sat there, but my roommate came back from class, happy and smiling, threw her arms around me and gave me a big kiss on the forehead, and called me by the pet name she had given me. I couldn't fake a smile, or return the same greeting or pet name back. She asked me what I was thinking about. I was cold. I asked her, matter of factly, 'What do you think about Brenton [not his real name]?' This was the guy she said was so gorgeous but she couldn't take him home or date him."

'Brenton?' she responded. 'Oh, I think he's great!'

'So, you like him?' I asked.

'Of course, who doesn't?'

'I mean, you think he's good looking and all that?'

'Yeah, he's better than good looking!'

I was trying to analyze her answers. I couldn't believe I was this poor a judge of character. 'Would you date him? I mean, could you see yourself dating him?' I asked, hoping that this would spark a deeper discussion when she said no.

'Sure, I would date him in a heartbeat,' was her reply.

'You would date Brenton,' I questioned flatly, 'in a heartbeat?'

'In a heartbeat,' was her reply.

I was so sick with the response I just got up and left. There was tension in the room for a few days after that. I'm sure she realized later that afternoon that those weren't random questions. But while she was responding, she hadn't realized that I had read the journal. We have never spoken about it since."

Such incidents stood out in stark relief for James because prejudice rarely surfaced at the Academy. "I was completely blind to any prejudice and I got along well with everyone. The guys looked out for me like a little sister for the most part. I lived nearby and went home on the weekends, so I never felt as though the white midshipmen were excluding me. On a few occasions, I had all of the girls in the company over to my house for dinner. We were a close company, and we went to lectures together, waited for each other, and stayed up late with each other, studying or just talking. We shared our dreams and hopes with one another, and I was very trusting. I had another roommate who was an electrical engineer. I think she was even more naïve than I was. Racial issues never came up in our conversation. She was from Minnesota, and her parents treated me very kindly. We got along well, and she dated a Filipino midshipman. It never came up that he was a different race. If she didn't like someone, it was because of their character."

Only rarely did racial prejudice surface openly for other midshipmen as well. On the day the brigade returned after plebe summer, William Carr overheard upperclassmen talking in the hall outside his room. "Oh shit," said one of the upperclassmen. "I see you got some spooks in your company." Carr forgot himself and ran out into the hall to confront the upperclassman. "I was a plebe," he recalled. "I wasn't really thinking. I got shat on pretty bad."

Roger Isom found that some white midshipmen were "naïve or simply unaware of some of the negative things that blacks had experienced," as he recalled. "I remember one classmate from Michigan telling me that he had never seen a black person till he was fourteen. I was amazed."

William Carr had to deal with white classmates who feared him. One day a classmate asked, "Do you know why everybody's afraid of you?"

"No, why?" Carr replied. "Seriously. I want to know. I haven't done anything to anybody."

"You're a pretty good-sized black guy."

"What the hell does that mean? There's some pretty big white guys, bigger than me."

"You always have this serious look on your face."

Carr found this kind of attitude frustrating.

Tracey James dealt with unwelcome curiosity among white women at NAPS who hadn't spent much time around black females before. There were stares in the shower and she was bombarded with questions. "What's that stuff you put in your hair? Why do you put baby oil on your body? What happens if I put grease in my hair? How do you wash your hair? How come you don't wash your hair every day? Why is your body shaped like that? How come black women have big behinds? How come black women have big chests? Have you ever thought about getting the space between your front teeth closed?"

Troy McSwain found himself answering the same sorts of questions. During plebe year he roomed with two white classmates who hadn't known any black people before. One of the white plebes was visibly shocked when he found out that the only black plebe in the company was to be his roommate. "He liked to have died when I walked in that room," McSwain recalled. The two later discussed their first day as roommates. "I was watching you put your pants on," the roommate told McSwain, "because I didn't know if you were going to put your pants on the same way that I did." At first, McSwain had fun explaining things like hair grease to his roommates, but it quickly lost its charm as the relationship degenerated into almost constant bickering. Being from Los Angeles, McSwain wasn't used to Maryland's cold winter weather and preferred sleeping with the window closed. His roommates both came from the upper Midwest and weren't used to Maryland's warm winter weather and liked sleeping with the window open. McSwain didn't like much of the food served in the mess hall, so he snuck fruit or boxes of cereal into the room. His roommates liked the food in the mess hall and worried about being caught with food in the room, which violated regulations. McSwain and his roommates had different tastes in music, related to their girlfriends differently, and on and on. At one point one of the midwesterners hung up a rebel flag in the room. McSwain objected vigorously. After about two weeks, a black segundo in the company made the roommate take it down. McSwain attributed the constant bickering not to prejudice but to cultural differences. Still, whenever there was a disagreement, it always came down to two white guys against one black guy.

Reuben Brigety also encountered white classmates who had little exposure to black people before coming to Annapolis. Most such people, he recalled, were "completely color-blind to race, such that if you're black or Filipino or Hispanic, they didn't care." To such midshipmen it was performance that counted, not color or ethnicity.

Likewise, a few of the black midshipmen had not previously interacted much with white people. NAPS provided Mario Maddox with his first exposure to white people. "I found that white people think very differently than black people," he recalled. "They thought in ideal terms and we thought in real terms. It was a real culture shock for me." Despite such differences, he got along well with white people and found that he could trust and rely on them.

"If it wasn't for my white roommate to tutor me," he said, "there's no way I could have made it through the prep school."

A significant number of white midshipmen still believed that blacks were at the Academy only to meet the Navy's minority officer accession goals, echoing the idea prevalent in the 1970s that blacks did not deserve to be there. According to the minority midshipmen study group report, "Some majority midshipmen assume that minorities gain admission to meet a quota, do not meet the minimum standards needed for academic success, and receive more lenient treatment by the academic board."[6] This view persisted until the end of the century. A committee appointed in 1997 to review Academy problems found "a perception among some of the white male majority that standards are compromised in order to admit more minorities, and that those who are admitted are less qualified."[7] "Regardless of how smart you may be," Reuben Brigety said of such midshipmen, "they just really didn't want to accept you, or couldn't accept the fact that you were there because of your own merit." Such attitudes sometimes surfaced in stereotypical remarks. On one occasion a second classman asked two of Brigety's black classmates, "Why are you here? Are you athletes or are you from NAPS?" "Neither of them happened to be either," Brigety recalled. "They were just good students."

Jacqueline Jackson encountered this attitude during plebe summer when she played sports. Although she had never been athletic, some people assumed she was an athlete simply because of her race. "I can remember three distinct cases where they thought I was recruited for a particular sport," she said. "They didn't make that assumption about the white females in those sessions."

On one occasion, Jackson came in dead last on the obstacle course. She reported her time to one of the coaches, an older white man. "Where are you from?" he asked.

"I'm from Columbus, Ohio," she replied.

"You're not from Columbus. You're from one of the suburbs, right?"

"Yes, Worthington."

"I knew you weren't from the city. With this time I could tell you didn't have cops chasing you and neighbors shooting at you."

Jackson believed that this kind of attitude extracted a price from black midshipmen. "As a black person, you do have to work twice as hard to get equal respect, because you have to prove that you're supposed to be there first. Once you do that, you're home free. But no white males have to do that."

The minority midshipmen study group identified this attitude as the most important environmental issue facing minorities at the Academy. "An environment which stresses the model midshipman, successful in academics, physical education and military performance," the group's report noted, "makes the minority midshipmen who have difficulty reaching this ideal due to weak academic achievement feel frustrated and somewhat isolated. This may result in a perception of not being totally accepted."[8]

Prejudice was not limited to white people. "There were black midshipmen who came from predominantly black backgrounds, and because of that had an exceptionally difficult time adjusting to the lifestyle of the Naval Academy," Reuben Brigety recalled. "The social life is completely different. The type of music people listen to is different. The norms of behavior between people are different. Some became really quite bitter. They consistently only hung with black people and didn't really make much of an effort to try to socialize with whites." Troy McSwain dealt with white people only when he had to. "I tried not to interact," he recalled. "I didn't hang out with white guys. I hung out with brothers." McSwain avoided white people because he believed he could never know what they really thought about him.

Mario Maddox noticed that some black midshipmen felt oppressed by white midshipmen. He recalled one particular black classmate as the most racist person he ever met. "He absolutely despised white people," Maddox said. "He braced up a white plebe and told him to stay braced up while he went to church one Sunday morning. He had him braced up so long that the kid passed out. The kid eventually quit and wrote his congressman." The black firsty was severely disciplined.

Reuben Brigety found that some of the bitterness among black classmates toward whites was fueled by the inability or unwillingness among some of the whites to try to understand the lifestyle or backgrounds of African Americans. "The Los Angeles riots in 1992 happened while I was at the Academy. The riots began when police officers who had viciously beaten motorist Rodney King were acquitted. Like many Americans, many midshipmen believed it was simply a law-and-order matter. They refused to see the hopelessness and despair that went into the spine of that sort of thing." They failed to grasp that some of their black classmates had come from the same sort of urban environments.

During the 1980s and '90s, black people often sat together at the dining tables, just as they had during the '70s. The practice continued to attract attention from white midshipmen. Some of Reuben Brigety's white friends told him they thought they would be unwelcome at a black table and wondered why black midshipmen wanted to sit together. Tracey James noticed the same uneasiness. On one occasion she discussed the topic with a white male midshipman. "When they all sit together, it just makes me feel uncomfortable," he said. "Well, when you all sit together, it doesn't make us feel uncomfortable," she replied, "so why should it make you feel uncomfortable?" To Mario Maddox, such white midshipmen seemed to wonder, "What the hell are they plotting?" "Nobody was plotting anything," Maddox recalled. "We just liked to sit together and talk about the party we had or 'This course is kicking my butt' or 'Can somebody help me?' I guess we could kind of relate to each other's experiences in life."

By and large, most midshipmen—white or black—did not harbor racial prejudice. Reuben Brigety found that many of the midshipmen who were prejudiced before coming to the Academy "genuinely had their attitudes change" by working with minority midshipmen. Roger Grayson believed that the presence of renowned black athletes such as football star and Heisman Trophy candidate Napoleon McCallum, '85, and All-American basketball star David M. Robinson, '87, helped foster a favorable image of black midshipmen. ·

Although racial slights or open displays of prejudice among faculty members became increasingly rare in the 1980s and '90s, such incidents still occurred. Quintin Jones observed that some faculty members assumed that all black midshipmen were athletes. On William Carr's first day of swim class, the instructor asked, "Who wants to try to validate?" To validate, a midshipman had to pass certain skill tests. Those who passed didn't have to report to swim class for the rest of the semester. Carr, who had swum in high school, been a lifeguard, and gone through Basic Underwater Demolition/SEAL training, volunteered. "Oh come on," the instructor said. "You know black guys can't swim." Anger flashed through Carr's mind. He stood up, but his roommate, who happened to be white, pulled him back down. "Don't even say anything," Carr's roommate said. "Just jump in the water and show him." Carr did so. He did so well, in fact, that not only did he validate, but the instructor asked him to join the swim team.

The instructor's unfortunate remark stemmed from a stereotype with some basis in fact. A report based on a study of the classes of 1988–91 revealed that minority midshipmen wound up on the swimming sub squad at a much higher rate than whites. Black midshipmen accounted for 6.6 percent of the brigade during the academic year 1990/91, but they constituted 40 percent of the swimming sub squad in the spring of 1991.[9]

For the most part, however, black midshipmen encountered no racial hostility from faculty members. "The faculty was overwhelmingly supportive of racial integration," recalled Craig Symonds, who taught history at the Academy from 1976 to 2005. "We believed integration would make the institution stronger in the long run because it would be more closely representative of America."[10] Mario Maddox believed the faculty treated midshipmen like midshipmen, regardless of color.

Whereas many black midshipmen never encountered racism, most women did encounter sexism.[11] Prejudice against female midshipmen permeated the brigade. Racism was a fringe attitude; sexism was mainstream. "I don't think women were seen as equal to men," recalled Arnoux Abraham. Michael Greenwood said that women were "treated as second-class midshipmen." William Carr often saw derogatory remarks about women scrawled on bathroom walls and heard derogatory remarks about women uttered in Bancroft Hall. When Carr suggested in class one day that the Academy needed more female midshipmen, male classmates threw wads of paper at him. When women received senior striper positions, many male midshipmen believed that they did not deserve the positions or that they had received them to meet a quota rather than because of merit. During plebe summer a few midshipmen tried to make Mary Miles feel like a token. "You're only here because you're a black female," they would say. Jacqueline Jackson found that many male midshipmen did not take female midshipman officers seriously.

Sexist male midshipmen often vented their prejudice against women midshipmen through a broad range of unprofessional and discriminatory behavior, including voicing off-color marching songs and cadence calls, telling offensive jokes in the presence of women, and making derogatory comments about women. Several members of the class of 1979, the last class to graduate with no women, inscribed LCWB on their class rings, which stood for "Last Class with Balls."[12]

The sexism resulted from a wide variety of attitudes and beliefs. Many male midshipmen in the class of 1979 and earlier believed that the Academy would have to lower its standards to accommodate women.[13] Some male midshipmen resented the fact that some of the female midshipmen could not run as fast or do as many push-ups as they could. Others thought that the Academy took women only to meet a quota, as Jacqueline Jackson recalled, "so there's automatically no need to respect them." Quintin Jones observed that many male midshipmen openly expressed the opinion that women did not belong at the Academy. Mary Miles encountered the age-old attitude common in civilian institutions that women matriculated only to get a "Mrs. degree." Before 1993, women were excluded from combatant assignments in the fleet, leading many male midshipmen to conclude that women didn't belong at the Academy because female officers couldn't contribute as much to the fleet as males. Some male midshipmen resented women because they believed their presence debased the masculine warrior mystique long associated with the Naval Academy. Others resented women for taking appointments that otherwise would have been filled by male applicants.[14]

Ronald R. Evans, 24th Company officer from 1984 to 1986, recalled that when male midshipmen discussed female midshipmen, they cast them in a negative light. "I would routinely hear male midshipmen say things like, 'Women don't belong at the Naval Academy.' 'Women are holding us back in the company.' 'Women are causing morale problems in the company.' 'Women have too many excuses' to get out of various activities in the company, marching, for example. Either it's being on-their-period-related, or it's diet-related, or minor injury-related." Evans found that black males and white males alike espoused such views. Professor Symonds observed that sexism was not limited to one race—both white and black males could be sexist.[15]

For many midshipmen, the prophet of the belief that women did not belong at the Naval Academy was James Webb, '68. Highly decorated for his service as a Marine platoon commander in Vietnam, appointed secretary of the navy (1987–88) by President Ronald Reagan, and author of *A Sense of Honor,* Webb was brilliant, cocky, white, and what many would consider a dinosaur for his views on women in the military.

Webb outlined his objections to women at the Naval Academy in the 1979 *Washingtonian* magazine article "Women Can't Fight." Combat remained the principal mission of the armed forces, he argued. Although there is a place for women in military service, they do not belong in combat. Since the principal mission of the service academies is to groom combat leaders, women do not belong in the service academies. The presence of women at the academies was "poisoning" that mission, he declared. "By attempting to sexually sterilize the Naval Academy environment in the name of equality, this country has sterilized the whole process of combat leadership training, and our military forces are doomed to suffer the consequences." Presaging the lament of the demise of physical hazing in *A Sense of Honor,* Webb bemoaned the changes in the plebe indoctrination system from the time when he and his classmates were "pushed deep inside ourselves for that entire year, punished physically and mentally, stressed to the point that virtually every one of us completely broke down at least once. And when we finished our first year, we carried out the same form of abuse on other entering classes. That was the plebe system. It was harsh and cruel. It was designed to produce a man who would be able to be an effective leader in combat, to endure prisoner-of-war camps, to fight this country's wars with skill and tenacity. And it's all but gone. . . . Now, you cannot physically punish a plebe. You cannot unduly harass a plebe. God forbid that you should use abusive language to a plebe."

Webb concluded that the inclusion of women had changed the Academy for the worse. The indoctrination system had been "neutered to the point it can no longer develop or measure leadership," he declared. "Internally, sexual attractions and simple differences in treatment based on sex have created resentments and taken away much of the institution's sense of mission. . . . Plebe year has been eviscerated." In researching the article, Webb spoke to hundreds of midshipmen, female as well as male. Not one of them, according to Webb, actually believed "that women will ever be accepted as comrades, in the traditional sense, by the men." Male midshipman adherents to Webb's views proudly dubbed themselves "Webb-ites" and devised the acronym WEBB, for the expression "women except Bancroft, baby." Some even wore "Jim Webb Fan Club" T-shirts.[16]

Webb's article caused both female midshipmen and the administration no end of difficulty. It "was my single greatest problem as superintendent," recalled V. Adm. William P. Lawrence, who served in that role from August 1978 to August 1981. The Academy's library kept copies of "Women Can't Fight" on hand because so many midshipmen asked for it. The article continued to fuel sentiment among some male midshipmen that women did not belong because they degraded the school's program of instruction by reducing the stressful indoctrination process needed for proper development of combat leaders. "There was no way [to get] away from the intense, almost palpable resentment," recalled Jennifer Brooks, '82. "It was unbelievably demoralizing to be painted as a pampered slut who was just taking up classroom space and predestined to endanger the lives of the brave young men around me."[17]

The most common manifestation of sexist attitudes at the Academy during the 1980s and '90s was the "WUBA" joke. WUBA was the acronym for "Working Uniform Blue Alpha," one of the uniforms first issued to women in 1976. Among sexist midshipmen, it came to mean "Women Used by All" or "Women with Unusually Big Asses." It also became a generic derogatory nickname for female midshipmen. WUBA jokes that denigrated women became commonplace. "What do you call seven WUBAs in the Chesapeake?" went one such joke. "A bay of pigs." "What's the difference between a WUBA and an elephant?" went another. "Ten pounds. How do you make up the difference? You force-feed the elephant." "What do you call a mid who fucks a WUBA?" went a third. "Too lazy to beat off." The expression WUBA also appeared in graffiti, in productions of the Masqueraders, in the Academy drama group, and in catcalls.[18]

The "big ass" variant of WUBA reflected the perception among many males that female midshipmen were overweight. This perception stemmed from the difficulty many women had in maintaining their weight within Academy height-weight standards. "My body build did not fit neatly into the USNA package," recalled Tracey James. "I lost weight over plebe summer but was still considered outside the standards. I joined the powerlifting team, won every competition, two national titles, and was a three-time All-American, but I had to take a body fat measurement every quarter because I was over the height-weight standards. I was solid muscle, so tight that the medics couldn't pinch fat from the back of my arms with the caliper to perform the body fat test. 'Stop flexing,' they would say. 'I'm not flexing,' I would reply. 'I just have a lot of muscle weight.' It became almost a joke that I would have to routinely go to medical for body fat testing when it was apparent that I had such low body fat."

"I don't believe that the Navy is intentionally biased against black women, but I can say that the body fat tape-measuring test certainly puts many black women at a disadvantage. One of the three areas measured is around the buttocks and hips. I was pretty 'blessed' in that area and squats came real easy for me in the gym. I had developed quite a lot of inches, and it didn't do me any favors with the tape measurement. Even though I was physically fit, was one of only three women in the class who could do more than ten pull-ups, was captain of the men's and women's powerlifting team, and looked good in my uniform, I was considered out of standards."

"This did terrible things for my self-esteem, image, and eating habits. During my second and third trimesters at NAPS, I became consumed with counting calories, obsessed with potential weight gain, and fearful to be seen eating anything but salads or taking food back to my room. I was cautious about what I was eating, making myself throw the food back up, exercising like crazy, and doing a lot of other unhealthy things to lose the weight and lose it quickly, so as not to be kicked out of NAPS. It got to the point that I looked unhealthy. I talked to a female Navy captain, a doctor, who told me that I was the same height as a classmate. My classmate was tiny, very petite, built, really, like a little boy. The captain said, 'You're the same height. You should weigh the same.' 'Look at my shoe size,' I thought. 'Look at my chest size, look at the way I'm built. I'm not going to lose sixty pounds and look like this individual, ever.'"

"The weight standards serve a purpose, and I don't believe them to be deliberately racist or sexist, but they do a serious disservice to many black women who do not fit neatly into the standards set simply because of body composition and have severely affected the confidence and self-esteem of many women in the military." James said that one of her classmates found trying to lose weight to meet height-weight standards so stressful on top of everything else that she "opted to just leave."

Much of the difficulty women had in maintaining height-weight standards stemmed from the high-fat diet served in the mess hall. Although they exercised more than most women their age, many female midshipmen gained weight eating the Academy diet. "Harassment of females often revolved around physical standards," recalled Michael Greenwood, "primarily weight and uniform appearance." Eventually the Academy adopted less fattening menu items, but the harassment based on appearance had by then become embedded in Academy culture and continued unabated. Even though the Academy's rigorous physical requirements made overweight midshipmen—male or female—relatively rare, Quintin Jones observed that male midshipmen often referred to female midshipmen as "those fat girls." "There were many females at the Academy who I wouldn't even dare think of as overweight," recalled Nikki Peoples, "but were considered fat by the male midshipmen."

Kathleen Slevin, a white alumna of the class of 1980, noted that one of her biggest regrets about her Academy experience "was that I learned how to be ashamed of being a woman in the Navy." She found that many other women midshipmen thought that way as well. "Articles like 'Women Can't Fight' . . . and attitudes like 'Once a WUBA always a WUBA' help form this feeling of shame." When she graduated, however, Slevin felt nothing but pride in her accomplishment. This pride resulted, in large measure, from the support she had from family, friends, and Academy officers, particularly Admiral Lawrence.[19]

Black female midshipmen faced a more intricate set of prejudicial attitudes than did either white females or black males. Like Tracey James, they confronted the same sort of racial issues with white women that black midshipmen did with white men. Unlike black male midshipmen, black female midshipmen had to deal with the attitude that gave rise to WUBA jokes as well. Janie Mines was the first black woman to graduate from the Academy and the only black female in the class of 1980. She recalled plebe year—with breathtaking understatement—as a "difficult time." "On a good day I was referred to as a 'double insult,'" she said. "The other women did not know quite what to make of me and they had their own problems. The feeling of isolation was unbearable at times."[20]

For Nikki Peoples, racial prejudice combined with gender politics to create particularly galling situations. "It seemed like many of my white classmates felt that the Academy did not have racial issues," she recalled. "The white midshipmen thought everything at the Academy was okay as long as there weren't people walking around in KKK costumes or using the "n" word every five minutes. Many were naïve to the subtleties of racism. Many of the white females who had dealt with sexism were naïve to the existence of racism. I sat in a physics class where our instructor (a Navy commander) repeatedly called on a blonde girl sitting in the back row who rarely raised her hand when he asked a question. I was in the very front row and raised my hand often but was repeatedly ignored. The only person in the class who noticed was a black guy."

"The same instructor said I would never graduate from the Academy in four years, which I did. This instructor failed three people in my class: a black guy, a Hispanic female who eventually quit the Academy, and me. Even though I had a strong "C" in the class, I approached this instructor for help and was treated rather un-warmly. He admitted to having people in my company spy on me. However, he was the only racist faculty member I encountered."

"Unfortunately, some of us are more exposed to racism than others. Being a confident, outspoken, and assertive black female may often be misperceived as being a black female stereotype (loud, opinionated, aggressive). Most of my brushes with racial adversity occurred within Bancroft Hall. For example, during my sophomore year I raised my grades from a 1.39 my first semester to a 3.29 my second semester. I also volunteered to be the third-class training officer, as well as took part in other extracurricular activities. I was told repeatedly that I'd never get an A in military performance unless I raised my grades. I finally did, and I was still ranked last in my squad against a white guy who couldn't even do one push-up, although I always scored high on the physical fitness test. I was also ranked below a white female who was always injured and who fraternized with an upperclassman within the company. These were but a few of the experiences that led me to believe that racism is still quite prevalent in the Academy as well as in society."

"No White Midshipman in Their Right Mind"

THE EXTENT to which racist or sexist midshipmen could act upon their prejudices depended largely on how rigorously the Academy enforced its policies concerning race, gender, and plebe indoctrination. The racial policies that affected black midshipmen's lives (apart from the accession goals that affected their numbers) continued to evolve during the last quarter of the twentieth century, but at a much slower pace than during 1965–76. In June 1979, in accordance with CNO policy, the superintendent merged the military equal opportunity and civilian equal employment opportunity programs into a consolidated command human goals program. "Confrontation and elimination of racism and sexism" at the Academy numbered among the objectives of the new program. The superintendent created a temporary human goals steering committee to "study and implement" the combined program.

On 2 April 1980, the superintendent replaced the temporary steering committee with a permanent human relations advisory council. Its members included two representatives from the faculty, two from the uniformed staff, and two from the brigade, one of whom was chairman of the brigade human relations council, as well as eight others from elsewhere in the Academy and naval station. The superintendent appointed a new chairman each fiscal year. The human relations advisory council monitored the Academy's affirmative action plan and equal opportunity programs, examined all instances of discrimination and took "corrective action," and advised the superintendent on all matters relating to human relations at the Academy. In January 1983, the superintendent reduced brigade representation on the council to one midshipman.[1]

By 1990, the Academy's equal opportunity program employed three full-time civilians, including a deputy equal employment opportunity officer, an equal opportunity specialist/federal women's program manager, and an equal opportunity assistant. Collateral-duty counselors assisted the full-time staff by working to resolve problems in the informal stage of the complaint process. The superintendent retained responsibility for the overall program. The staff managed several special emphasis programs within the overall program that targeted specific needs, including the Federal Equal Opportunity Recruitment Program, Handicapped/Disabled Veterans Program, Federal Women's Program, Hispanic Employment Program, Upward Mobility Program, and the Federal Equal Employment Opportunity Advisory Committee. These programs aimed at reducing underrepresentation and resolving inequities in the Academy's civilian workforce. The overall objective was to create and maintain a civilian workforce "reflective of our nation's race, sex, and ethnic diversity."[2]

By 1981, the midshipman human relations council formed in January 1972 by the commandant had elaborated into brigade, battalion, and company human relations councils. Each company council included one representative from each class. The brigade council included a chairman, a vice chairman, one first-class representative from each battalion, and one representative each from the second, third, and fourth classes; it provided a forum for frank discussion of "real or imagined" issues related to racism, sexism, and hazing and a channel of communication for disseminating the Academy's equal opportunity policies down to midshipmen and for reporting any problems to the commandant. Any midshipman could bring matters to the council's attention.[3]

Some midshipmen perceived the human relations council "as ineffectual, a vehicle for punishment instead of a helping tool," as the minority midshipmen study group put it. "Majorities feel that a woman or other minority uses the HRC [human relations council] to strike back at unpleasant upperclassmen. Minorities feel that the HRC pays little attention to genuine concerns."[4] Other midshipmen thought that the council did, in fact, help improve midshipmen's interpersonal communications skills and resolve problems.

During this period the Academy made a firmer commitment to the diversification of its faculty and uniformed staff. In 1980, the superintendent had established a minority faculty review group to develop a plan for increasing minority representation on the faculty. By 1990, minority faculty members accounted for 5 percent of the civilian faculty. Although this proportion did not compare favorably with the overall population, it did constitute a respectable showing, considering that only 3.5 percent of engineering faculties nationwide were Hispanic, Native American, or African American. The difficulties the Academy experienced recruiting faculty members from the small pool of minority Ph.D.s amid stiff competition from other universities and industry mirrored the difficulties the candidate guidance office faced in recruiting minority midshipmen.[5]

In May 1983, Capt. Buddie Joe Penn, special assistant to the CNO for special projects (OP-00E), sent a memorandum to the CNO that the Academy was "doing better in terms of total numbers of minority officers assigned" there but needed to put them "in positions which are more visible and involve contact with the brigade." He noted that MACs had limited contact with midshipmen. He recommended raising the issue with the superintendent and expressing the desire for better minority representation among battalion and company officers to the chief of naval personnel. "We should also look for some sharp minority senior officers for high visibility positions such as Deputy Commandant," he added.[6]

Nothing immediate came of these suggestions, however, for a year later the CNO commented to the superintendent on the "paucity" of minority officers. At that time (April 1984), seventeen black officers were assigned to the Academy but only one was in the brigade organization. The rest were staff corps, instructors, or MACs.[7]

The next month R. Adm. David L. Harlow, commander of the Naval Military Personnel Command, took action to remedy the situation. "Black unrestricted line officers are underrepresented in both senior and junior USNA role model billets," he wrote in a memo to the chief of naval personnel. "There are no senior black officers in battalion or professional development billets, and there are no black U.S. Navy company officers (one black Marine)." In the short term, Harlow relieved two MACs and used them to fill company officer billets. In the long term, he intended to keep at least three of the thirty-six company officer billets filled with black officers. Although the Academy did not always thereafter have at least three black company officers, the administration made a conscious effort to place African American officers in role model billets.[8]

Ron Evans was one of the MACs whose billet was switched, to 24th Company officer. His presence pleased the minority midshipmen in the company. Two black midshipmen told him so. "Sir, I'm so happy to see you," they said. "I'm proud of you." "At that time," Evans recalled, "I realized that it was important for midshipmen of all colors to see staff and officers of all colors. It promoted a sense of belonging. It promoted in the minds and hearts of our minority midshipmen, although I hate to say it, a ray of hope, knowing that if this lieutenant made it, and was commissioned and was doing fairly well in the Navy, so could they. Having young minority mids see minority company officers and minority instructors in uniform I'm sure was a confidence builder and motivator."[9]

Yet only a few years later, black midshipmen still perceived a lack of minority role models among the commissioned staff. "This is a 'Catch-22' situation," noted the minority midshipmen study group. "The numbers in the Navy, Marine Corps, and throughout the brigade are small. Minority officers assigned to USNA are concentrated in the candidate guidance office for recruiting reasons. While not interacting with midshipmen in a classroom setting, these officers become very involved with minority midshipmen through various extra curricular activities and during counseling sessions conducted frequently in Leahy Hall."[10]

Some six months after the study group's report appeared, the Academy got its first black deputy commandant, Tony Watson, who served in that billet from November 1989 to March 1992 and was promoted to captain during the tour.[11] The next African American deputy commandant was Charlie Bolden, who held that job from June 1994 to June 1995. In 2005, sixty years after Wes Brown became a plebe, Capt. Bruce Grooms, '80, became commandant of midshipmen, the highest-ranking black leader in the Academy's history.[12]

In May 1990, the Academy established a CMEO program as required by all commands under the Navy's equal opportunity program. Its objectives included ensuring a positive equal opportunity environment within the brigade, monitoring various administrative practices, enhancing midshipmen's knowledge about the affirmative action plan, and indoctrinating midshipmen in the importance of equal opportunity and the evils of discrimination. The CMEO program included a command training team, which conducted equal opportunity training by means of annual "Rights and Responsibilities" workshops, and a command assessment team, which monitored the equal opportunity climate by reviewing data on conduct, military performance rankings, academic deficiencies, and physical education deficiencies; interviewing midshipmen; and conducting surveys. In instances where command assessments uncovered misperceptions that women or minorities received preferential treatment, midshipmen received training to correct these misperceptions.[13]

All of these initiatives conveyed the message that the Academy condemned discrimination, but nowhere was it put so bluntly as in the regulations. An explicit proscription against discrimination appeared in the regulations for the first time in 1981. "Midshipmen will not individually or collectively discriminate against another individual or group because of race, sex, religion, or cultural differences," said Regulation 0411. "To do so will be considered a violation of these regulations and established policy of both the U.S. Navy and Naval Academy. As used in this regulation, discrimination is defined as an intentional overt action which fails to promote equal opportunity or degrades another's character and/or self-esteem based on prejudices derived from race, sexual, religious, or cultural differences, as viewed by society as a whole." Similar statements appeared in the regulations thenceforward.[14]

While proscriptions against discrimination became firmly embedded in Naval Academy policy, training designed to enhance midshipmen's racial awareness became diluted within a broader scope of human relations training aimed at preventing sexual harassment as well as racial discrimination. Racial awareness training continued to be done under the Academy's human goals program, administered for midshipmen by the commandant through the naval leadership curriculum. In September 1980, the commandant issued an instruction outlining the plan to achieve the Navy's goals and training requirements in human relations and equal opportunity. Midshipmen received human goals training in their second-, third-, and fourth-class years. During plebe year they received four hours of "Human Relations and Equal Opportunity/Race Relations" training in the summer and three hours of "Human Relations and EO" instruction in the course Naval Leadership 102. During youngster year they received three hours of "training in EO/RR processes" in the course Naval Leadership 200. During second-class year they received five hours of "Human Relations and EO Instruction" in the course Naval Leadership 303. The human goals program included training in intercultural relations education, drug and alcohol abuse training, social programs, and organizational development and management training. Company officers also discussed racial discrimination among other topics periodically during formal "Company Officer Time" periods.[15]

In the spring of 1984, the amount of human relations and equal opportunity training was reduced to three hours during plebe summer and one hour in Naval Leadership 102, three hours in Naval Leadership 200, and three hours in Naval Leadership 303. Midshipman human relations council representatives also received additional orientation on the human goals program.[16]

Race appeared as but one among myriad topics covered in these courses. In the academic year 1990–91, for example, the eighth of nine objectives for Naval Leadership 102 was, as the secretary of the navy told a senator, "to present contemporary issues in drug and alcohol abuse, prejudice, equal opportunity, and the integration of women in the services as they relate to unit integrity and coordinated mission accomplishment." On completing the course, the student was expected to "understand the relationship between proper attitudes concerning equal opportunity/race and the effective use of all human resources present in the Navy" and "be acquainted with the different cultures present in the operating environment in the Navy." These were the eleventh and twelfth of thirteen "skills" supposed to be learned from the course. Three of the forty-five hours of Naval Leadership 303, "Ethics and Leadership Applications for the Naval Officer," were spent discussing and analyzing equal opportunity and examining "the sources, effects, and means for countering racism, sexism, discrimination, sexual harassment, and fraternization." The tenth of the twelve "skills" supposed to be learned in the course was "understand the effects of prejudice and bias on a military organization and the elements of the Navy's Equal Opportunity program" and "be able to discuss methods for eliminating racism, sexism, discrimination, sexual harassment, and fraternization within the organization."[17]

In 1988, the department of leadership and law introduced Naval Leadership 301, "Communication and Planning for Leaders," designed to hone public speaking skills while discussing topics like alcohol abuse, race and gender discrimination, honor, and peer pressure. The course aimed at training second classmen for indoctrinating plebes. Black midshipmen hailed the segment of the course that addressed racism "as an overwhelmingly positive experience," according to the minority midshipmen study group. "The topic forced a dialog between the majority midshipmen who believe there are no ethnic issues at the Academy and the minority midshipmen who disagree. Very often these issues are just perceptions by both parties easily rectified by discussions."

The study group gave an example to illustrate the need for such communication. "Consider a black midshipman who is out of the company area 'a lot.' Classmates see the black as a loner, not involved in company matters. But this sole black in his class within his company actually is away struggling with swimming and seeking academic help, reluctant to let company mates know of the extra time needed to meet standards. His music and leisure interests are completely different than those of his company mates. With little free time, he seeks those who share the same interests and background. Misperceptions result." Despite its success, however, NL 301 was discontinued in the 1992–93 academic year.[18]

In 1994, human relations training was shifted to the character development division, established that year. In the 1999/2000 academic year, racial themes appeared in the *Naval Academy Catalog* in six plebe summer human relations classes that addressed "issues such as stress management, conflict resolution, assertiveness, fraternization and prejudice and diversity"; in the human education resource officer program, which placed midshipmen trained in human relations and "peer issue resolution" in each company for each class; and in "several lessons" in "human-relations related General Military Training," such as "discrimination/cultural diversity, responsible relationships, sexual assault prevention, prevention of sexual harassment, suicide awareness, and conflict resolution," taught by professional development division officers and first-class human education resource officers.[19]

The upshot was that some black midshipmen perceived that the Academy offered little in the way of training to promote racial awareness. "Equal opportunity training was awful," recalled Jacqueline Jackson. "They're content with the status quo. No one's getting beat up or no one's blatantly getting harassed, so everything's okay." Nikki Peoples believed the Academy followed the wrong approach to promote awareness of diversity. "Diversity training seemed to be facilitated by people who had very little experience with racism or sexism," she said. Troy McSwain believed that the Academy did nothing to enhance midshipmen's racial awareness.

Although the amount of training dedicated to promote racial awareness shrank after 1980, extracurricular activities that promoted cultural diversity blossomed and flourished. By 1999, the Academy sponsored the Filipino-American Club, Japanese-American Club, Korean-American Club, Latin-American Club, and organizations for Catholic, Jewish, Protestant, Baptist, and Mormon midshipmen. "These clubs are organized not only to help those ethnic groups to associate with each other," William Carr observed, "but the doors are open within each club for other races and ethnic groups to come in to actually learn about the group." Jerry Gray thought the groups promoted awareness of diversity within the brigade.[20]

The Black Studies Club remained the Academy's premier organization for the celebration of African American heritage and achievements. Throughout the 1980s and '90s, the club remained active in sponsoring activities commemorating Martin Luther King's birthday and Black History Month, inviting guest lecturers like actor James Earl Jones, General Frank E. Peterson, the Marine Corps' first black aviator, Emmy award–winning local television news journalist Renee Poussaint, and civil rights leader Andrew Young. Roger Isom noted that the commandant attended many of these events, thereby signaling official support of activities to promote diversity. The club also sponsored numerous other events, including periodic meetings with the National Naval Officers Association to assist black midshipmen in making service selections and the Naval Academy/Benjamin Banneker Honors Math and Science Society Partnership, founded in 1989, in which black midshipmen tutored local high school students.[21]

The Black Studies Club remained central to the black midshipmen's subculture. Penny Vahsen, a writer who did a story on black midshipmen in 1987, equated the Black Studies Club with the Seventh Battalion. "The club sponsored many dances and socials in the town of Annapolis," she noted. "When it was first established, the Seventh Battalion's purpose was to provide the black midshipmen with a sense of ethnic cohesiveness. It became almost a 'clique,' and there was considerable pressure by blacks to join and stay together as a group. This pressure lessened as the 1980s arrived. [The club became] a serious cultural group which sponsored many guest speakers. It is less of a security blanket for the black students than it was in the past."[22]

Edward A. Meyers, '82, recalled that the "original intent was to get plebes to know upperclassmen and see who can help you—just a social thing. There was pressure to join. It was meant for just blacks alone, but that kind of died out. At the Academy they don't throw parties so it was someplace to go. By my junior year it was not just for blacks alone. It became a mix of everybody."[23]

In the fall of 1985, twenty black midshipmen founded another extracurricular activity that enhanced the brigade's awareness of African American culture, the Gospel Choir. The choir debuted at the 1986 Martin Luther King Jr. memorial service at the Naval Academy chapel. The group was so well received that they were invited to sing at Vassar College, the first of many appearances outside the Academy. Membership soon grew to some fifty singers and the organization evolved into a brigade support activity. It became a particularly important means of minority recruiting. During the academic year, the choir put on monthly performances at the chapel and appeared frequently at local churches, schools, and colleges. Each year during spring break the Gospel Choir went on tour, performing at high schools in cities across America.[24]

All in all, the Academy's racial policy in its various manifestations—regulations prohibiting discrimination, human resources organizations, extracurricular activities, racial awareness training, even the minority midshipmen study group—gave black midshipmen the sense that the Academy took racial issues seriously. Black midshipmen considered the interviews conducted by the minority midshipmen study group "a positive experience," the group noted, "because the administration was willing to listen to their concerns."[25] Reuben Brigety believed that the Naval Academy was very much a meritocracy. "If you are good and work hard," he said, "the sky is the limit and you can do whatever you would like to do." Quintin Jones perceived the Academy's racial policy as zero tolerance of discrimination. "We will not accept racism here at the Academy under any circumstance," as he put it. "No white midshipman in their right mind would openly use a racial slur, because they'd get kicked out."

The Academy's policy toward women resembled its racial policy in several respects. Equal opportunity and prohibition of discrimination and sexual harassment formed the bedrock of the policy. To facilitate the integration of women and their acceptance by the men, Academy officials, as they had done with African Americans, distributed female midshipmen evenly throughout the brigade, assigning about nine to twelve women to each company. Unlike black midshipmen, however, women roomed together from the start, normally with three women assigned to each room. The Academy's leadership sought to ensure that the faculty and uniformed staff included role models for women midshipmen. By the fall of 1991, six of the thirty-six company officers were women, as were about 19 percent of the faculty members.[26]

Despite these efforts, discrimination against women midshipmen remained endemic within the brigade throughout the 1970s and '80s. Sexism manifested itself not only in negative attitudes toward female midshipmen but also in negative action. Some male midshipmen went out of their way to find ways to fry other male midshipmen who talked to female midshipmen. On one occasion a male midshipman expressed displeasure at the presence of women by urinating on a female midshipman's door.[27] On another occasion one or more male midshipmen vandalized an overweight female midshipman's room, breaking some of her things and ruining some of her uniforms. The victim eventually left the Academy with an eating disorder.[28]

Elizabeth Anne Belzer had a particularly rough plebe year. On one occasion she found a dead rat in her Bancroft Hall mailbox. On several occasions a bra was stolen from her room and then returned in an envelope covered with signatures. She felt rejected by most of the male classmates in her company. One of the few who supported her was Stanley Lathorne Cooper, who happened to be black. The environment seemed so hostile that she even feared for her physical safety. Many a night she went to bed asking God that she not wake up in the morning.

The hostility lasted all four years. During youngster year, male classmates threw a pie in Belzer's face, snapped a picture, and printed it in *The Log*, a politically incorrect humor magazine published by midshipmen until it was outlawed in 2001. During the summer of 1979, Belzer became regimental commander, the Academy's first female five-striper. When the regimental subcommander learned that he was to be a woman's subordinate, he tried to resign from the position. "He gave me a hard time throughout the summer," Belzer recalled years later. "These are the kinds of things you just never get over." Nevertheless, driven by the need to prove she could take it, in 1980 she became the first woman to receive an Academy diploma.[29]

Melody Ann Wheeler, who entered the year after Liz Belzer graduated, also had a terrible plebe year. The presence of women in all four classes failed to inhibit a small group of upperclassmen from attacking her with a brutal and cowardly combination of sexual harassment and physical threat. They threw her in the shower with other male midshipmen and made her say she was "wet," an unsubtle sexual innuendo. They tossed condoms in her room at night. They hung her by the ankles out of a top story window in Bancroft Hall and made her describe the sound her head would make when it hit the pavement if they let go. They put a gun in her mouth and asked if she was ready to die for her country. The bullying lasted all year long. "They were literally determined to drive women out," Wheeler recalled. They almost succeeded in her case, for she left the Academy at the end of plebe year. Astonishingly, she decided to return the following fall, motivated by the desire to serve her country. She graduated in 1986.[30]

Although many women never experienced such vicious treatment, they were still made to feel outside the mainstream, like black males who had matriculated in the 1950s and '60s. Mary Miles did not encounter sexist attitudes among her male classmates until "Herndon," as the Plebe Recognition Ceremony was called. Herndon the monument is a 21-foot-tall gray granite obelisk honoring the officer associated with the custom of the captain being the last to leave a sinking ship. Herndon the ceremony is a revered tradition dating to the early twentieth century, heralding the end of plebe rates and the transition of plebes to youngsters. By the time Miles experienced it in 1984, the ceremony took place as the first in a week-long series of events culminating in the graduation of the first class. The ceremony symbolized the teamwork necessary to get through plebe year, for it involved the fourth classmen forming a human pyramid so that one of them could climb to the top of the monument and replace a plebe's "dixie cup" hat fastened there with an upperclassman's visored cap. The ceremony also embodied a little of the lighthearted sadism inherent in the plebe indoctrination process, for upperclassmen would smear the monument with some 200 pounds of lard beforehand to make the climb harder. Nevertheless, Herndon has been great fun for generations of midshipmen and their families.[31]

For Mary Miles, Herndon was "disillusioning." Since the first day of plebe summer she had been forging close bonds with her company classmates, male and female alike, in order to survive the crucible of plebe indoctrination. When the gun fired to signal the start of the ceremony, Mary raced toward the monument, eager as any of her classmates to get to the top. She twice tried to surmount the human pyramid, but each time male classmates reached up and pulled her down. "After the second time," she recalled, "I stood back and watched in disgust." She saw male classmates do the same thing to other women. "These guys had been my brothers all year," she recalled. Since the goal was to finish the climb as fast as possible, and since women on average weighed less than men, it would have been logical for men to boost women to the top. Instead it seemed that the males would rather take longer to finish than see a female get the dixie cup. Miles spoke with a few of her male classmates afterward. "Where did that come from?" she asked. "It's a tradition," replied one of them. "The upperclassmen told us, 'No WUBAs on Herndon.'"

In the late 1980s, a group of male midshipmen who believed that women did not belong at the Academy formed an underground group dubbed the "WUBA Ku Klux Klan." "The mission of these guys," recalled Reuben Brigety, "was to make women's lives really quite difficult. They did it by commenting on how much women ate at the tables, how fat they looked in the uniform, that sort of thing."

The WUBA KKK didn't last long. "Poetic justice reigned, as it does in most cases," Brigety said. "Ultimately this ring was found out. They had to go before the deputy commandant, who, at the time, was Anthony Watson. They had to go before this very large, esteemed black professional naval officer and explain how they possibly came up with the club called the WUBA KKK. They were put on restriction for a year."

Sexist attitudes and actions had a deleterious effect on female midshipmen's performance. Although women entered the Academy with higher average SAT and Academy success predictor scores than men, on average they attained lower grade point averages as plebes and youngsters and lower class standings as firsties. They also received lower military performance grades and rankings. Female plebes had higher conviction rates for conduct offenses, particularly for more serious offenses. For the classes of 1980–91, the average attrition rate for women was 33 percent, compared with 23 percent for men.[32]

Scandals involving female midshipmen made headlines. One of the most infamous scandals involved a white midshipman, Gwen Marie Dreyer, who resigned in the spring of 1990 near the end of her youngster year after an episode in which male midshipmen handcuffed her to a urinal in the men's room and snapped photos. The Academy investigated the incident and punished two male upperclassmen with demerits. Dreyer left because she believed Academy officials had neither taken appropriate action nor perceived it as a symptom of a much larger problem rather than an isolated incident. "This was not just a case of hazing," she said after she left Annapolis. "It has to do with being a woman. Women are integrated into the Academy, but they are not accepted. . . . After the whole thing was over, one of the guys told my roommate that this kind of thing was going to keep happening until we, the female midshipmen, got a sense of humor."[33]

In March 1996, James F. Barry, an Academy faculty member, published an opinion piece in the *Washington Post* declaring that the Academy "is plagued by a serious morale problem caused by a culture of hypocrisy, one that tolerates sexual harassment, favoritism and the covering up of problems." Barry cited the fall 1995 arrest of twenty-four midshipmen for alleged drug possession and the 1991 Tailhook scandal as outcomes of the Academy environment. He said one female officer told him that during her tour she saw some fifty or sixty female midshipmen, at the rate of about ten per semester, who had been sexually assaulted. Only four had gone forward with their claims. The article included excerpts from a letter written by a female midshipman that outlined her frustration at the treatment she had received:

> I have sat through lecture after lecture on sexual harassment, and I have been sexually harassed just about every day. . . . I cannot think of

a day that has gone by when I have not had to listen to rude, disgusting comments being made about women from my male counterparts. I have been slapped on the butt, pinched and bumped into. I have woken up in the middle of the night on numerous occasions to find some male standing in my doorway, standing in my room, sitting on my desk, or actually in bed with me. I have even mentioned this to officers and instead of concern I got labeled a problem child. I came to this institution with the high expectations of becoming a naval officer. Most of these ambitions have been crushed due to the "boys' club" that runs this institution.

Barry recounted another case in which a woman "was essentially driven out of the Academy when she complained that her roommate was having sex with an upperclassman in their dorm room."[34]

Such allegations precipitated a cascade of investigations of the Academy's policies. In August 1986, Cdr. Marsha J. Evans became the Academy's first female battalion officer. It was not long before she realized that "women were treated badly," as she put it. "After ten years of being there, there were still major problems." After three and a half months in the billet, Evans brought her concerns to the attention of the superintendent, Rear Admiral Marryott. In December, Marryott convened a study group to examine the progress of integration of women at the Academy, with Evans as chair. After almost a year of work, the group submitted its report to Admiral Marryott in November 1987: Although percentages of involuntary separations for male and female midshipmen had been comparable, the percentage of voluntary separation for women (24 percent) doubled that for men (12 percent). Academically, women made lower grades than men during their first two years, yet by the first-class year the women's overall academic performance exceeded the men's. Similarly, women's grades in military performance lagged considerably behind men's during plebe year and then caught up or surpassed the men as marginal performers improved or left the Academy. Varsity athletics provided female midshipmen with their most effective source of support. The attrition rate for women who participated on a varsity team plebe year was less than 20 percent, compared to almost 50 percent for women who never participated in a varsity sport.

The women midshipmen's study group noted the negative attitudes female midshipmen encountered and how these attitudes resulted in negative treatment. "Instances of sexual harassment, discrimination, and manifest prejudicial attitudes have occurred that escaped the attention of the chain of command," the report concluded. "The negative attitudes are rooted in the fact that because women are not allowed to hold combatant assignments, their contribution to the Naval Service is limited. This fuels a persistent belief that women do not belong at the Academy. This belief is sometimes manifested in such inappropriate behavior as the use of derogatory language in reference to women, the use of off-color or demeaning marching songs and cadence calls, and the telling of offensive jokes in the presence of women."

The report made forty-seven specific recommendations to improve the assimilation of women into the brigade. Basically, these recommendations called for adjusting the selection process to weed out applicants with low technical proficiency or aptitude, emphasizing the need for women to maintain their physical fitness, providing better sources of support for nonathletes, emphasizing the policy prohibiting sexual harassment, and improving the dissemination of information to all midshipmen about the roles women play in the Navy and the performance of female midshipmen. The Academy implemented them all.[35]

But it wasn't enough. By the end of May 1990, no fewer than five military and congressional investigations were under way into allegations of sexual harassment, unfair or unusually rough treatment, and academic improprieties at the Academy. A study of women midshipmen completed that July concluded that women were not as well assimilated into the brigade as women were in the fleet. According to the study, a persistent, vocal minority of male midshipmen, officers, faculty, staff, and alumni continued to express openly the opinion that women should not be midshipmen. The attitude and actions of this minority so pervaded the Academy's climate that most midshipmen readily acknowledged that women midshipmen were not accepted as equals. The study made recommendations to redress this problem, prompting the Academy to issue a plan of actions and milestones that included establishing a policy of zero tolerance of all forms of discrimination, increasing female representation among faculty and brigade officers, requiring that male and female plebes be indoctrinated in an identical fashion, and providing information to midshipmen regarding the role of women in the Navy and the performance of female midshipmen. The Academy also took steps to emphasize and reinforce for midshipmen its policies on equal opportunity, discrimination, and sexual harassment.[36]

The infamous September 1991 Tailhook Association convention focused intense scrutiny on the Navy's entire equal opportunity program. Trouble began when several dozen Navy and Marine Corps aviators formed a gauntlet on a third floor corridor of the Las Vegas Hilton. Some women ran the gauntlet willingly, but others were forced to do so against their will while men molested them. Twenty-six women, fourteen of them naval officers, were assaulted. Full details of the debauchery broke in the press some nine months later, when Lt. Paula Coughlin went public with an account of her sexual assault at the hands of fellow aviators. These revelations intensified the controversy swirling around the Navy's leadership. Stories involving strippers, shaving of women's legs, liquor dispensed from phalluses, and other lurid details surfaced in the wake of Lieutenant Coughlin's going to the press. Tailhook led to the resignation of the secretary of the navy and other top naval leaders and the delaying or withholding of promotion or transfers for some four thousand naval officers. The Navy severed all official ties with the Tailhook Association. Tailhook has since resounded with the same scandalous ring as Watergate.[37]

Tailhook spurred naval leaders to wage war on gender discrimination. Early in July 1992, a few weeks after Lieutenant Coughlin's story broke in the press, Undersecretary of the Navy Dan Howard, Adm. Frank B. Kelso II, the CNO, and Gen. Carl E. Mundy Jr., the commandant of the Marine Corps, summoned hundreds of senior naval leaders to the Pentagon for a detailed briefing on the Navy Department's new course of action to wipe out sexual harassment. "Anyone still wasting time disparaging women, fighting their integration or subjecting them to sexual harassment is a dragging anchor for the entire Navy and Marine Corps," declared Howard. "Anyone who still believes in the image of a drunken, skirt-chasing warrior back from the sea is about a half century out of date. If that's you, we don't need you." The new course of action entailed clarifying legal issues behind sexual harassment, measures to enhance equal opportunity for women in the Navy and Marine Corps, and steps to eliminate from naval culture demeaning behavior and attitudes toward women. "Unfortunate as it was," noted R. Adm. Paul E. Tobin, assistant chief of naval personnel for personal readiness and community support (PERS-6), "the Tailhook incident has prompted us to carefully review our policies and record of compliance" in prevention of sexual harassment and equal opportunity.

Ev Greene, '70, then a captain, was director of the Equal Opportunity Division (Pers-61) in BuPers at that time. "Most of my tour was dominated by looking at the Navy's policies and training regarding sexual harassment as a result of Tailhook," he recalled. "My staffing expanded. We set up a separate sexual harassment branch."[38]

In the wake of Tailhook, Congress required the leaders of the services to submit written certification "that appropriate measures have been taken to publish and enforce regulations which expressly prohibit discrimination on the basis of race, color, religion, sex, or national origin" before it would expend funds for military education in fiscal year 1993. "We are working to make our equal opportunity and sexual harassment prevention policies among the best in the world," declared Admiral Kelso in his certification statement. "Primarily, we have strengthened and streamlined the procedures for separation that commanding officers can take in cases of serious incidents of sexual

harassment." Kelso also declared that implementation of the recommendations made by the 1988 CNO study group on equal opportunity "resulted in
fundamental changes in our equal opportunity program and a steady improvement in our Navy-wide equal opportunity climate monitored by a comprehensive affirmative action plan." He added that, as the Navy "downsized" in
the wake of the end of the cold war, naval leaders were "taking special care to
ensure that minorities and women are not disproportionately affected. [The]
Navy still intends to increase minority representation in accordance with our
affirmative action plan goals."[39]

In the course of dealing with Congress's certification requirement, the
assistant secretary of the navy for manpower and reserve affairs requested a
policy statement from the Naval Academy. The Academy forwarded copies of
its sexual harassment policy and strategic plan. The latter provided "a strategy
to achieve our vision of the future," as R. Adm. Thomas C. Lynch, the superintendent, put it. Goal 3 of the plan was to "excel in equal opportunity."
The plan outlined several objectives, including to "achieve a composition of
midshipmen that equals or exceeds the diversity goals of the officer corps in
the Navy and Marine Corps"; "achieve a composition of military staff which
is representative of the diversity of the Naval Service"; and "encourage civilian
minority and women instructors to seek faculty positions at USNA."[40]

Sparked by accounts of Lt. Paula Coughlin's Tailhook horrors in the press,
the Academy had a "sexual harassment stand-down" on 22 August 1992, with
the day devoted to sexual harassment training and emphasis on the policies
prohibiting sexual harassment and discrimination. Thereafter the Academy
provided an hour of training on prevention of sexual harassment to all midshipmen annually.[41]

In the wake of Tailhook and the Gwen Dreyer incident, Sen. Sam Nunn
(D-Ga.), chairman of the Senate Committee on Armed Services, asked the
General Accounting Office to examine the treatment of women at the Academy. Shortly thereafter, following allegations of unfair treatment of Hispanic
midshipmen, Rep. Albert G. Bustamante (D-Tex.) asked the GAO to examine the treatment of minorities at the Academy. In April 1993, the GAO
released a report responding to both requests and concluded that neither
women nor minority midshipmen fared as well as white male midshipmen
in class standings, grades, outcomes of the disciplinary system, and attrition
rates. The report recommended that the Academy develop a database to enable routine analysis of midshipmen's performance, establish criteria for as-
sessing when disparities warranted corrective action, and prepare a plan of
action with milestones to track command assessment recommendations and
corrective actions as well as assess the effectiveness of the actions. In response
to these recommendations, the Academy established the Office of Institu-

tional Research to develop a consolidated database and to become the fount of statistical data on the Academy.[42]

The situation for women midshipmen improved significantly during the late 1990s. In part, some of the hard-line attitudes against women had softened. During his youngster year, Reuben Brigety attended airborne school with several former WUBA Klansmen, who were then firsties, who told Brigety that they regretted having been associated with the group. But, as Brigety recalled, "not everyone had this sort of Paul-esque epiphany about their attitudes toward gender." In large part, the situation for women had improved because of policy changes that the leadership enforced. William Carr observed that the Academy's sexual harassment policy frightened many midshipmen and served as a deterrent. Jerry Gray agreed. "We're lectured almost every other week on sexual harassment," he said. "It makes you aware that the relationship between plebes and upperclass shouldn't reach beyond professional. The sexual harassment thing is hammered day in and day out. You just don't do it."

But mostly it was the 1993 military bill permitting women on combatant ships that changed male midshipmen's attitudes toward their female shipmates. "I saw an immediate change almost overnight," noted Karen Flack, a mechanical engineering professor at the Academy at the time. "The men's attitudes towards the women completely changed for the better when it was clear women were able to perform the roles they were trained for."[43]

Nevertheless, sexism remained a problem. Fifty-nine percent of female midshipmen surveyed during the 2004/5 academic year said they had experienced some form of sexual harassment at the Academy. About two-thirds of midshipmen, both female and male, believed that sexual harassment training had little or no effect in reducing or preventing sexual harassment.[44]

"Women midshipmen today continue to be not fully accepted and integrated into the brigade," General Bolden said in a 2000 interview. "Women experience covert and sometimes overt opposition to their presence in *any* military organization. I am not impressed by the overall acceptance of women in the military, *period*. And the Naval Academy is a part of that establishment."[45]

In 2005, a Department of Defense task force deemed the culture at the service academies "hostile" to women. V. Adm. Rodney P. Rempt, who had become superintendent in August 2003, vowed to reverse that culture and adopted a zero-tolerance policy against behavior hostile to women. In response to a task force recommendation to increase the number of women in leadership positions, on 20 October 2006 Vice Admiral Rempt announced the appointment of the Academy's first female commandant, Capt. Margaret D. Klein, '81. The director of the advocacy group Ending Violence

Against Women said that a woman's presence in a leadership position could significantly improve the climate for female midshipmen.[46]

Throughout the last quarter of the twentieth century, the plebe indoctrination system evolved to keep pace with the Academy's gender policy. The 1981 mid-shipman regulations forbade hazing, required midshipmen to report instances of hazing to the commandant, and defined hazing as "any unauthorized as-sumption of authority by a midshipman whereby another midshipman suffers or is exposed to any cruelty, indignity, humiliation, hardship, or oppression, or the deprivation or abridgement of any right." The 1987–88 *Squad Leader's Manual* clarified the parameters of acceptable treatment: "The treatment of plebes by acts that degrade or humiliate is in violation of the principles of re-gard for human dignity and mutual respect." Physical maltreatment, defined as "any action taken for the sole purpose of inflicting physical discomfort on a person, the result of which serves no beneficial purpose," was a serious of-fense that would "result in grave punishment, up to and including discharge." The next year an instruction on "Fourth Class Indoctrination" issued by the commandant spelled out indoctrination procedures in detail. For example, it specified the exact information plebes had to know each day during plebe summer. The instruction also listed and defined prohibited activities, includ-ing sexual harassment, hazing, and discrimination.[47]

In the spring of 1990, after the departure of Gwen Dreyer, R. Adm. Virgil L. Hill, the superintendent, announced a series of steps that further tightened the noose on hazing, including creating an independent ombudsman to field complaints about treatment of plebes, issuing an order making physical con-tact with plebes grounds for dismissal, and reaffirming a ban on horseplay with involuntary participants. "No midshipman will touch, grab, punch or push another midshipman who has verbally or through other means expressed his or her objection to the activity," declared General Order 1-90.[48]

That July, R. Adm. Joseph Prueher, the commandant, told a reporter about how such changes in the indoctrination system had affected plebe sum-mer. "I'm not talking about a kinder, gentler plebe summer," Admiral Prue-her said. "What it is, is an indoctrination process for the Naval Academy. It is not a boot camp. We don't take the tack of 'Let's make plebe summer as tough as we can to see if we can winnow out the people we know are not go-ing to make it.' That's not our objective. Our objective is to make it strenu-ous, physically tiring, where they learn a lot of military behavior. Degradation, humiliation, things like that are not part of it. Being tired, a lot of physical stress and a lot of mental stress are part of it just because there's a lot to do." In this atmosphere, not only had rigging the rifle become taboo, but also the atomic sit-up.[49]

Tracey James lived through the change. She grasped the old concept quickly during plebe year. "Second class were supposed to intimidate, harass, humiliate, and make people look like fools in front of their peers and their seniors," she recalled. "I didn't look at it as something personal. I just looked at it as, 'You didn't know your rate and this is the consequence for not knowing that particular rate on that day.'" James and her classmates assumed that, when they became second classmen, their job would be to yell and scream and gang up on plebes and break them down. "That's all we knew," she said. "That's what we learned. When you're second class, you yell at the plebes, you train them, and you make life tough for them, and it builds character and makes them stronger. Going into second-class year [1990–91], the administration said, 'We're not going to do that anymore. We're going to do things more constructively. You're going to have to find other ways to get your points across.'" Yet resourceful midshipmen who objected to the presence of certain others still found ways to make their lives difficult. As James put it, "I saw men and women who people thought weren't going to cut it get run out."

Attitudes toward race and gender, along with the Academy's policies governing race, gender, and plebe indoctrination, shaped upperclassmen's behavior toward African American plebes. A few black plebes could point to nothing overtly racist in their treatment but suspected that prejudice might be behind at least some of it. "There were times I felt psychologically harassed," Michael Greenwood said, "but I was never able to confirm it was due to race. The manifestation of racism in much of present-day America is subtle and ambiguous. Even the perpetrator may not be aware of his motivations and actions."

Troy McSwain had no doubt that race figured prominently in his treatment. Apart from one black upperclassman, a junior, he was the only African American midshipman in his company. "When I walked down the hallway," he recalled, "I stood out like a sore thumb. I got picked on. I had daily comearounds. I had come-arounds until I went to bed at night. I walked around in a brace so much, shit, I thought it was damn near normal for me to try to put my chin on my chest."

McSwain never bought into the system the way Chuck Reddix, Roger Isom, and Reuben Brigety did. McSwain resented having what he considered a lot of unnecessary and trivial rules imposed on his personal freedom. He certainly didn't identify with most other midshipmen. "I just didn't fit in, dude," he said. "I mean, I didn't fit in at all."

To avoid trouble with upperclassmen, McSwain employed the same strategy he had used to avoid gang trouble back in Los Angeles—he went out for football. During the first semester of plebe year, he played on the 150-pound team and ate meals at the training table with his teammates instead of with his company mates. Most of the upperclassmen in his company weren't athletes, and they resented the extra privileges they thought he was getting as a football player. When the season ended, everyone on the 150-pound team had to resume eating with his company. "When I went back to the regular tables," he said, "I got shitted on."

Because of such treatment, he developed an aversion to upperclassmen. "I had a bunch of jerk-offs telling me what to do and how to live," he said, "which I didn't really appreciate." McSwain had little respect for the upperclassmen giving him a hard time, so he struck back at the system. He would get a note from the team doctor permitting him to wear sneakers instead of shoes, which meant that he could wear whiteworks and avoid formations and uniform inspections. To dodge come-arounds, he would strike up conversations with company officers or anyone else who outranked the upperclassmen who wanted him to come around. Such tactics only increased the ire of the upperclassmen in his company.

It was academics, not conduct, that nearly did in McSwain during plebe year. McSwain made an A in conduct each semester. "I was more worried about the Navy shit than I was the academic stuff," he recalled. "What could a teacher do to me? Nothing but fail me. So what? I didn't care. The guys I had to eat with and get yelled at by, those are the guys I worried about, the upper classmen." His grades suffered as a result. He finished first semester with a QPA of 1.67 and second semester with a 1.56. At the end of the second semester he appeared before the academic board, which voted to retain him, but "with great reservation." Nevertheless, he had survived plebe year.

Whatever role race played in McSwain's woes, prejudice did not generally translate from attitude into action. The presence of significant numbers of black upperclassmen, coupled with the explicitly stated policy prohibiting racial discrimination, must have inhibited most of the racist minority of upperclassmen from acting out their racial prejudices. It never occurred to Roger Isom, William Triplett, Arnoux Abraham, Reuben Brigety, or Quintin Jones that racism played any part in their indoctrination experiences. Roger Grayson underwent physical hazing, "but it was controlled and purposeful," as he recalled. "I had white male classmates who were treated worse than I was, so I can only surmise that the hazing was not racially motivated."

Mario Maddox got yelled at a lot during plebe year, as did his white classmates. Although he suffered no physical hazing, he did have to endure psychological hazing at the hands of two firsties who practiced archery while he did chow calls near their room. "They would shoot arrows right by your face," he recalled. "The target was behind your head over to the side and it would scare the living shit out of you because you'd think they'd miss and hit you right in the face." But Maddox didn't perceive any racial underpinnings to the treatment. "They did it to everybody," he said. "It was just a dangerous way of playing."

Early in plebe year, William Carr phoned his mother every couple of days asking for a plane ticket home. "You're having trouble now," she would say, "maybe shedding a couple of tears. But look at it this way, sweetheart. When you look back on it a couple of years from now, you're going to laugh." Carr gutted it out. Indeed, when he became a firsty, he did look back on plebe year and laugh. His difficulties were mostly academic. Racial problems never entered the picture in a debilitating sort of way.

Jerry Gray was the only African American plebe in his company. Like the rest of his classmates, he chopped down the hallways and sounded off when he squared corners, but he didn't shout "Go Navy, sir!" as loudly or with as much enthusiasm as the others. Some of the upperclassmen mistook his more laid-back attitude for a lack of motivation and began giving him extra attention. The thought crossed Gray's mind that the extra attention was racially motivated. "But then I realized it was because of the way I was acting," he recalled. "I don't think it was because I'm black."

Black female midshipmen were likelier than black males to experience negative attitudes translated into mistreatment. At the end of plebe summer, Ingrid Turner had the misfortune of landing in the 21st Company, nicknamed "Playboy 21." "Playboy 21 did not want women at all," she recalled. This attitude manifested itself in an effort to run her out of the Academy. The upperclassmen went out of their way to humiliate her, to make her feel stupid, to make her life so unpleasant that she would resign. "I had to walk down the hall and say 'Ping, ping, ping, ping, ping, ping, ping, ping, ping,' so they would know it was me coming," she recalled. On many occasions she found herself the only plebe in the hallway. "I'd be up against the bulkhead by myself," she recalled. "Not only would my squad leader be there, but the whole second class would be there, and any of the firsties that wanted to play in this little game. They would all be screaming at me, asking me stuff I didn't know, yelling at me. Sometimes they were so close they spit in my face."

The upperclassmen constantly tried to trip her up on her rates. They asked only legitimate questions, but they drew from such a broad range of knowledge that she could not possibly know all the answers. At tables she faced withering barrages of questions, so many that she often could not eat. Even when she did answer questions correctly, they would keep asking until they found questions she couldn't answer. They would make her do extra reports on professional topics, then criticize the reports in front of her to humiliate her. It was psychological warfare.

The upperclassmen made her feel as though she deserved what she was getting. They made her believe that she was stupid, which she wasn't, and that she had a bad memory, which she didn't. The hazing robbed her of self-esteem, tore at her self-confidence, and hampered her performance in the classroom. In fact, she nodded off in leadership class so often that the professor thought she was anemic. Turner never knew for certain what motive lurked behind her treatment, but she was the only black woman in the company, the upperclassmen running her were all white males, and none of the half-dozen or so white female plebes in the company were being treated as badly. Racism must have been her tormentors' motivation.

Even when Turner did know her rates, she still couldn't win. Each week plebes were assigned a new "professional" topic. Second classmen would quiz them and sign a "chit" if they passed. When "Army" was the subject of the week, Turner's father helped her learn it. "I knew everything," she recalled. She went around as usual to her second-class squad leader and answered every question he could throw at her. "You know what, Miss Turner," he said. "You know it, but I'm not signing it off." Nobody else would sign the chit, either. The episode brought Turner to the edge of resigning.

Trouble from NAPS followed Tracey James to the Naval Academy. She turned eighteen during her first semester at NAPS. That evening, James and a large group of friends went out to a nightclub to celebrate. They returned to the dormitory before midnight. Since James's roommate had gone home to New York for the weekend, as she did every weekend, her best friend, Mary Roaf, who was from another company, decided to spend the night and sleep in her roommate's rack. At about 2:00 in the morning, an acquaintance from the same company as Roaf, a black football player whose broken leg was in a cast and who was getting around on crutches, hobbled into James's room. He knew that her roommate had gone home, but he did not know that Roaf was asleep in the other rack. He thought James was alone. "He said he was coming to wish me a happy birthday," recalled James. "He shut the door, which was completely against the rules. I asked him to leave and turned back over." James had almost drifted back to sleep, but sensed something was wrong. "I woke up," she said. "He was leaning over me on my rack masturbating. I couldn't believe it. There was not a lot of light coming in the room, but I could tell what was going on. I told him to get out. He didn't leave immediately. Mary had awakened, but she didn't say anything. She was just listening. I wasn't yelling. I was more embarrassed than anything else and horrified that this was happening. I just couldn't understand how someone could do something like this. I saw myself as a midshipman, not a female midshipman, but just a midshipman candidate like everyone else was."

The next morning James felt humiliated. She did not know what to do. She sought advice from a midshipman candidate who held a leadership position and whom everyone respected. He had been an enlisted man before coming to NAPS. She figured he would know how to handle it. "Don't say anything about it," he told her. "Just leave it alone. Forget it happened."

Mary Roaf disagreed. "No," she said. "That's not the way things work." Before James had decided what to do, Roaf reported the incident to a female ensign. The ensign summoned James into her office. "I know who it is," the ensign said, "But I need you to tell me in order for me to pursue this." James vacillated. "If you don't say something," the ensign told her, "then this person is going to graduate with you, be commissioned with you, and serve beside you." James mulled over the implications and thanked the ensign but remained undecided about turning in her assailant.

Many of the assailant's black male friends acknowledged that what he did to her was wrong, but they encouraged her not to report him. "He will be a varsity football player," they said. "He's going to help us beat Army." They also played the racial card. "He's black," they said. "He's a 'brother.' We don't turn each other in. If his race had been different, then it would be a totally different story, but you just don't bilge one another."

Tracey James now wrestled with a classic dilemma. As Darlene Clark Hine and Kathleen Thompson put it in their excellent history of black women in America, "the terrible reality of [black women's] oppression by men of their own color . . . was personal and political dynamite. No one wanted to light the fuse. Black women anticipated, correctly, that exposing their private pain and the sexism in their community would be seen as a betrayal of black men. . . . On a broader level, they believed that disclosure would erode the moral authority their men held in relations with dominant white power. The tendency to close ranks, to keep silence in order to protect the community, was strong, too strong for most black women to oppose."[50]

All Tracey James really wanted was an apology. Instead her assailant made up a rap song declaring that he was untouchable and could do what he pleased. "That sealed it for me," recalled James. "I went ahead and reported it." The authorities handled the case swiftly and discreetly. James's assailant was separated from NAPS. His naval career was over.

Reaction among the midshipman candidates was mixed. Some adhered to the credo "never bilge a shipmate." Others believed that the punishment fit the crime. "I wouldn't want that to happen to my sister," they thought. "I wouldn't want that to happen to me."

But for James the episode was far from over. Both she and Mary Roaf began receiving hate e-mail on their computers, including vulgar messages. Mostly the messages castigated James for ruining the career of a black man. "We don't want you commissioned with us," the messages said. "We don't want you serving with us. He was a football player. You're not an athlete. Your grades are average. You have nothing to offer the Naval Academy." "Mary and

I were strongly encouraged to leave the prep school," James recalled. In public, the company officer in her assailant's company, a Navy lieutenant, refused to salute her or to return her salutes.

The harassment devastated James. "I was completely disillusioned," she recalled. "My well being, my safety, my life was violated, and it was being placed in a category below winning a sports event."

The harassment followed James to the Academy. She continued to receive hate e-mail, sent through accounts of people who had been separated. Football players whom she had not met before seemed to know that she was the reason a NAPster they had been counting on had been kicked out. She remained fearful of walking past the football team tables in the mess hall.

"They made my life a living hell," James recalled, "and influenced my decisions to keep silent about other wrong things that I had witnessed. I encouraged other people who came to me for guidance about whether or not to report violations of our military norms to keep silent because I knew what retribution they would face." For example, during plebe summer, one of James's roommates was dating a second-class midshipman in their squad. It was a clear case of fraternization, a violation of the regulations. "He would come into the room all hours of the night, drinking or not drinking," James recalled, "and they'd be intimate in the room while we were there. My other roommate said, 'What should we do?' I said, 'We should talk to her, but as far as reporting it, you don't want to do that. Remember the situation that happened at NAPS? Well, that was me, and I reported it, and these are the things that came out of it.'" James's roommate broke up with the segundo before the end of the summer, but James continued to wrestle with the dilemma of not bilging shipmates and not tolerating those who violated the honor code.

The harassment also affected James's participation in extracurricular activities. By first-class year, her main harasser had become a prominent figure in the Black Studies Club. "I withdrew my support and participation completely," recalled James. Because he had also been a member of the Gospel Choir, James had steered clear of that organization as well. Throughout her years as a midshipman, the NAPS-hangover harassment never brought her to the point of resigning, but it definitely tainted her experience. "The prejudice I encountered was toward the females," she concluded, "not necessarily the minorities."

During the 1980s and '90s, black midshipmen had a much more elaborate support network than their predecessors, enjoying access to a broader array of social groups. By and large, black midshipmen from the classes of 1980–99 joined or formed social groups on the basis of common interest rather than race. "On the weekends a lot of white male midshipmen would go off to a frat party at Towson State or the University of Maryland and drink beer and listen to country music," Reuben Brigety recalled. "A lot of the black midshipmen would go off to Howard University and watch Howard play football or go listen to jazz for the evening. Sometimes all the guys and girls from a company would get together for a barbecue at the home of someone who lived nearby. They just wanted to hang together. A lot of companies were like that. Or all the guys or girls from a sports team wanted to hang together because they spent so much time together while training."

Many black midshipmen formed deep and lasting friendships with white classmates. "White midshipmen were some of my best friends," Mario Maddox said. "One of my plebe year roommates was a groomsman in my wedding." Jacqueline Jackson's closest friends were her white roommates. "There were eight black females in my class," she said. "We got together when we first came to the Academy because we were black. Then I found out I really didn't have that much in common with them. I had more in common with white females. Friends don't become friends just because they're the same color." Ingrid Turner also formed friendships on the basis of common interest rather than race.

Yet some social groups did form along racial lines. "On both sides of the color bar there were people who were exceptionally open-minded and were able to make friends with everybody," Reuben Brigety said. "On both sides of the color bar there were people who chose simply to socialize with their own and continued to retain stereotypes of people on the other side of the fence." Jacqueline Jackson noticed that, although not all black midshipmen hung out together, there were several black cliques. At the extreme end of the spectrum, Tracey James heard rumors that both an underground white supremacy group and an underground black power group existed among midshipmen, although she never knew anyone connected to either rumored group.

Inside the Yard, midshipmen tended to group according to common interests, whether they took the same courses, belonged to the same company, came from the same hometown, or played the same sport. "But once we got off the Yard," recalled one black midshipman from the class of 1991, "it seemed like there were a lot of different minority groups that would go do things together. African Americans would go to Howard to visit and to date and do those kinds of things. Filipinos went to the University of Maryland Baltimore campus and hung out with the Filipino crowd there." William Carr recalled that black midshipmen often sat together at home football games under the sign commemorating the battle of New Georgia. They called it the New Georgia section. "We sat together because we were all friends," Carr recalled. "We were all in the Gospel Choir. We always hung out."

Social groups that seemed to be segregated by race or gender sometimes sent subtle or ambiguous messages to midshipmen outside the group. "White or black or women classmates often held informal gatherings—parties, study sessions, etc.—to which no blacks or whites or men were invited," recalled Michael Greenwood. "Now such events were not racist or sexist, but the psychological impact on the rejected shipmate could be quite debilitating. Thus many minority or female midshipmen were wounded by their Academy experience without the benefit of an identifiable assailant."

In most instances, however, the crucible of plebe year forged ties among classmates from all backgrounds. "We all had to get along," recalled one black midshipman. "You really learn to bond during plebe year. If a shipmate needed something, you'd help them out, because you knew that the next day, you could be in the exact same situation." Jerry Gray agreed. "The plebes in the company tend to become really close because you're getting through plebe year with these people." Gray added that the entire plebe class constituted a minority, outnumbered, as they were, nearly three to one by upperclassmen.

Like Jerry Gray, Roger Isom was the only black plebe in his company. Isom got along well with everyone. "I had superb support from my classmates, both white and black," he recalled. "I enjoyed being part of '88. As a matter of fact, our class president all four years, Kennon Artis, was black. The upperclassmen were also supportive. They considered me to be a leader in the company. I was selected as the third-class brigade commander by the upper class."

Tracey James found that her trouble from NAPS did not follow her into her company. "I had a very strong rapport with my classmates in my company, black and white, male and female," she recalled. "We had strong camaraderie." She also benefited from support of upperclassmen. "I remember one senior black midshipman in my company," she said. "He was from Baltimore and knew my brother. He looked out for me as much as he could. He didn't ask me difficult questions until he was sure I knew them, and then he would ask me in front of a large group of people to allow me to show off my knowledge. In the same respect, I remember a white midshipman doing the same thing. He would quiz me on a subject area, and when he was certain that I knew it completely, would ask me about it at tables in front of everyone. So I did have support from both black and white upperclassmen."

Mario Maddox also found many white upperclassmen to be supportive. During plebe summer his squad leader cut him slack because he couldn't memorize easily. His first-semester squad leader, Ernest Petzrick, was tough but fair. "Ernie had to have his jaw broken and reset because of a condition, so he couldn't yell at me," Maddox recalled. "He had his mouth wired shut. He tried to yell and it didn't work well. I always pretended I didn't understand what he said even though I did. But by the end of that semester, around Christmas time, I had really become a much better student and a much better plebe because of him. Ernie said, 'I've really seen a transformation in you and I'm proud of that.' He was pretty happy with me and he left me feeling pretty good."

Many black midshipmen found the Academy's sponsor program a great source of support. The program linked every new plebe who so desired with a volunteer family within twenty-two miles of the Academy.[51] These "sponsor families" served as an institutional analog for all midshipmen to what Lillie Mae Chase and Peggy Kimbo had provided for past generations of black midshipmen. "My sponsor family was white and treated me like family," recalled Roger Grayson. Roger Isom also enjoyed a warm relationship with his sponsor family. "They were a Catholic family," he recalled, "the Mazzeos. We had a great relationship. I will never forget my first visit to their home in 1984. After dinner, they told their little daughter Beth to say goodnight. To my surprise, she kissed me on the cheek as though I were her big brother. As a black midshipman who grew up in the South and never 'stayed in a white person's home' I learned a valuable lesson—stereotypes can limit one's horizons. Color truly did not matter to them."

Mario Maddox's sponsor was Mario O. "Duke" Green, an African American millionaire who had grown up with his father and happened to be Mario's godfather. Duke Green lived in D.C. "He was one of the top black businessmen," Maddox said. "I would go up and see him all the time. I got to meet some very influential people, and infamous people like Marion Barry, who was mayor then."

Many black midshipmen continued to find support in extracurricular activities that celebrated African American culture. Arnoux Abraham was a member of the Black Studies Club and Gospel Choir. Membership in these activities enabled him "to address any problems on a more familiar and personal level," as he recalled.

Not every black midshipman found certain sources of support to their liking. "The extracurricular activities didn't appeal to me," recalled Troy McSwain. "The Gospel Choir? I'm not a singer. The Black Studies Club? You think I want to meet with somebody to talk about Martin Luther King and Malcolm X? That's like asking a guy that's into cars and bikes, 'Let's go to the basket weaving class.'" McSwain did, however, enjoy the tradition of visiting families in Annapolis's black community, which remained an important source of support for black midshipmen through the end of the twentieth century. On several occasions McSwain visited Peggy Kimbo's home. He found the same sort of atmosphere at the homes of the Wilson and Bowman families. "You would go out on a Saturday," McSwain recalled, "and there would be twenty-five midshipmen between their two houses—Ma Bowman and Ma Wilson lived right across the street from each other—and we would go and hang out and they would cook us food that we were accustomed to. Whoever wanted to come that was black was welcome. We were happy to have some place to go." Many a time when Tracey James was out in town, people would stop her for a chat. "I did appreciate people talking to me on the streets," she recalled, "telling me how proud they were of me and asking me if I knew Wesley Brown. Putting me in that category made me proud."

Roger Isom developed particularly close relationships with people in Annapolis's black community. "My involvement in the Annapolis community was probably atypical," he recalled. "Consistent with my home roots, I was active in the local churches. I spoke to youth on Sundays about the Naval Academy and life in general. I attended Asbury Methodist Church on West Street. Mrs. Edna Booth, a member then eighty-two years old, 'adopted' me. She became my second sponsor. We are close today. She is age ninety-seven and we still talk and joke about the 'good old days.' My parents have stayed with her. I even stayed with her after graduation for three months. She is a mother, grandmother, and friend combined. Thank you, Mrs. Booth!" Isom also developed a close relationship with the Lewis family, who had a daughter his age named Lisa. After Roger graduated, he married Lisa.

Black workers employed by the Academy remained another important source of support. "I am still friends with Smitty and Leroy, the barbers," noted Roger Isom. Sheldon Harris, who worked as a janitor in Bancroft Hall from 1948 to 1983, befriended generations of black midshipmen. The Harris family's longevity in Maryland matched his own longevity in "Mother B." Harris lived near the Chesapeake Bay Bridge on property his great uncle had purchased in 1872, but his roots in Maryland date back to 1643. Shortly after Harris began working at the Academy, he met Wes Brown. Brown stuck out like a sore thumb, Harris recalled, but seemed to receive fair treatment. Harris became acquainted with many of the black midshipmen who followed. "I used to bring in goodies for them," he recalled. "Mostly on Fridays, so they'd have it on the weekend." He developed a particularly close relationship with Montel Williams, '80. "I knew him personally," Harris recalled. "Knew his family. Knew his father."[52]

But the black community no longer served as a universal source of support for all black midshipmen. Michael Greenwood considered Annapolis's black community "invisible" and therefore "inaccessible." Mario Maddox recalled that local black men his own age resented black midshipmen for having parties that local black young women would attend. "It was like in the movie *An Officer and a Gentleman*," he recalled. "Some of those guys would come in and try to bust up our parties. One guy even came in with a gun one time and we had to shut the party down."

Support from outside as well as inside the Academy saved Ingrid Turner's naval career. Month after month of racially motivated psychological hazing and sleep deprivation began taking its toll on her grades. She was barely passing. Friends warned her that, although she could not get kicked out for not knowing her rates, she could get kicked out for failing her classes. She put in the time she needed to pass, but doing so took time away from learning her rates and doing the professional reports. This gave the upperclassmen the excuse they needed to keep up the pressure.

Turner wasn't the sort of person who complained, nor would she ask others for help. Still, other midshipmen could not help but notice how she was being treated. Sometimes an upperclassman would intervene, momentarily stopping classmates from yelling at her or stopping them from making her say "ping, ping, ping, ping" as she walked down the halls. Much of her support came from fellow athletes. During plebe year she lettered in swimming and played varsity volleyball. Other swimmers and volleyball players would volunteer advice in the locker room.

The female firsties in the 21st Company area could not offer much help. To begin with, there were only three of them. One had transferred in from another company and had her own problems. Rumor had it that alcohol was involved. Another was an out-of-company striper living in the 21st Company area. "They wouldn't listen to her," Turner recalled. "She wasn't one of them." The last was a manager on the woman's basketball team who traveled a lot. But even when she was there, "You've got to know what they ask you" was the best advice she could offer. Turner later surmised that the three female firsties were too intimidated to do much of anything.

Turner's company officer, a female Marine major, did not intervene. "She was tough," Turner recalled. "She was hard. She had gone through hell. Her attitude seemed to be, 'If it had to be tough for me, by golly, it's going to be tough for you.'" Because Turner was always so busy with academics, rates, and sports, she did not have time for a social life. She was pretty much isolated.

Turner reached the edge in March just after her squad leader refused to sign her chit for Army professional knowledge. It happened at the table. The upperclassmen were bombarding her with questions as usual, preventing her from eating. She decided she'd had it. "This is ridiculous," she thought. "I can't take it anymore." She likened herself to a prisoner of war. But instead of answering every question with only her name, rank, and serial number, she said "I'll find out, sir." "My squad leader asked me a question," she recalled. "I said, 'I'll find out, sir.' Then the next person asked me a question. I said, 'I'll find out, sir.' They went around. 'I'll find out, sir.' 'I'll find out, sir.' 'I'll find out, sir.' They said, 'Oh, Miss Turner doesn't know anything today.' So they got everybody involved. 'Come over here, Johnny, ask Miss Turner something.' 'Miss Turner, . . . ?' 'I'll find out, sir.' 'I'll find out, sir.' 'I'll find out, sir.' So they all wrote me up for not knowing daily rates. Almost twenty people wrote me up." Shortly after that meal, she telephoned her parents and told them she wanted to quit.

Turner's older brother, a 1980 West Point graduate, divined what was going on. "They're probably trying to run her out," he told his father. Dr. Turner drove down to the Academy to talk to one of the chaplains, Lieutenant Shamburger.

After the chat with Turner's father, Shamburger summoned Ingrid to his office. "Do you still want to quit?" he asked.

"Yes," she said. "I'm ready to go home."

"Why don't we try you in another company? If you don't succeed, then you'll know you're not cut out for the Academy. But if you go to another company and you do okay, you'll know it wasn't you."

"Okay," said Ingrid. "I'll try another company." After all, she had nothing to lose by giving it one last shot.

Chaplain Shamburger could not make the transfer happen by himself. Ingrid had to put in a chit requesting the transfer, and the chain of command had to approve it. Her squad leader and midshipman company commander both denied the request. Her company officer, the white female Marine major, told her she couldn't handle the Academy and would be better off leaving; she also denied the request. Turner's battalion commander, a salty white male Marine colonel, was downright hostile. "You say if I don't let you change companies, you're quitting," he hissed. "I consider that a threat." Nevertheless, he approved Turner's request, perhaps because one of his superiors had ordered him to do so. Turner packed up her room and, on a Saturday night when nobody was around, moved her stuff over to the 16th Company, nicknamed "Sweet 16."

The difference between the old and new companies was like night and day. Sweet 16 was a more ethnically diverse company than Playboy 21. Turner had no difficulty making friends. One of the female plebes in the 16th, who happened to be a fellow swimmer, heard that Turner had been having difficulty in her old company and went out of her way to help her adjust. The upperclassmen in Sweet 16 held plebes responsible for knowing the rates printed on the daily sheets, a single page. When they would ask Turner her rates, she would rattle off the contents of the page with no difficulty. "Good," they would say, and sign her off. There were no questions drawn from deep in *Jane's Fighting Ships,* no yelling, and no spitting in her face.

Turner had no trouble in Sweet 16. She knew her rates. Her uniform was impeccable. Her room looked better than anybody else's. Her conduct was by the book. The upperclassmen as well as the plebes considered her squared away. They wondered why she had had such a hard time in Playboy 21.

"Blessed to Have Had the Opportunity"

ALTHOUGH RACISM proved to be far less of an obstacle to the goal of finishing plebe year for black midshipmen from the classes of 1980–99 than it was for their predecessors, the academic hurdle remained just as daunting. Whereas the overall attrition rate for these classes was 24 percent, the rate for black midshipmen stood at 30 percent. From year to year the black attrition rate varied across a broader range, with higher peaks and lower valleys than the overall attrition rate: 19–28 percent overall, 13–47 percent for the black subgroup. This variation caused the administration a great deal of heartburn.[1]

The primary cause of black attrition also differed from that for overall attrition. The majority of midshipmen who left the Academy before graduation did so voluntarily, but most black midshipmen who left before graduation bilged academically. In fact, for the classes of 1983–87, the black academic attrition rate was four times greater than the overall rate.[2]

The problem of minority academic attrition figured prominently in Rear Admiral Marryott's decision to launch the minority midshipmen study group in August 1988. His primary concern was that high minority attrition rates would prevent the Academy from achieving the CNO's 7 percent black officer commissioning goal.[3]

In early 1989, the minority midshipmen study group surveyed midshipmen about the Academy's academic climate. Most midshipmen, particularly African Americans, found academics tough. Black midshipmen tended to opt for less technical majors than whites. Midshipmen of all races admitted that they did not have enough time to study and did not know how to study. Although black midshipmen devoted more time to studying than white midshipmen, they still made lower grades. Black midshipmen's poorer performance seemed to stem from poorer academic preparation prior to matriculation. As a group, blacks entered the Academy with lower high school class standings and lower SAT scores than whites.[4] A report based on a study of the classes of 1988–91 indicated that whites consistently made significantly higher semester grade point averages than minorities.[5]

One of Captain Seymour's approaches to minority retention involved seeking ways to optimize existing aspects of the academic program. His recommendations to the superintendent included revising the study skills program, reducing the plebe first-semester course load from nineteen credit hours to sixteen, and modifying the validation program as ways to lower minority attrition rates.[6]

Seymour also examined other schools' approaches. Friends from Stanford, Notre Dame, Georgetown, the University of Virginia, and Lafayette College told him about different methods to support academically at-risk students. The methods he thought the Naval Academy should consider included early identification of academically at-risk students; spending more time honing study skills during plebe summer; assigning more experienced academic deans as academic advisors to at-risk students; and creating a learning assistance center where students could go throughout the year to get counseling or tutoring and take advantage of other support services. "What impressed me about these programs," Seymour concluded in a 19 December 1988 memo to the superintendent, "was the degree of personal involvement in supporting student academic performance at the institution. When reviewing the freshman success rates and graduation rates of these colleges and universities, this proactive approach obviously pays off." "The more I review minority (and majority) attrition data and the reasons contributing to the same," he noted to the superintendent ten days later, "the more I am convinced that a formal academic 'intervention program' is needed—particularly for those whom we admit of higher academic risk."[7]

Captain Seymour began reporting the findings and recommendations of the minority midshipmen study group to the superintendent in March 1989. The group found that about one hundred midshipmen in each entering class were at significant risk for academic attrition. Historical attrition data indicated that many of these midshipmen could be identified before entering the Academy and virtually all of them at the end of the first plebe semester. Unless the Academy modified its academic support system, Seymour warned, most such midshipmen would leave before graduation. He recommended establishing a "proactive academic intervention system," with academic counseling, remedial study, and computer tracking beginning as early as plebe summer for at-risk students.[8]

Two months later, the minority midshipmen study group's report laid out the minority attrition problem in detail. The group determined that, for the classes of 1983–92, academic difficulties accounted for 68 percent of black attrition, compared to 32 percent of overall attrition. "The small voluntary attrition that does occur among black midshipmen," the group noted, "is often linked with fear of academic failure in the future." Virtually all African American midshipmen (94 percent) who bilged for academic reasons had a first semester QPA in the bottom 30 percent of their class. "Because 10 percent of entering plebes" and "about 50 percent of entering blacks are at high risk of separation," the report noted, "a program to improve academic performance must occur immediately."

The report emphasized the need not to lower current minority admissions criteria to admit more minority midshipmen, for doing so would only raise the minority academic attrition rate with little likelihood of gains in the number of minority officer commissions. The report reiterated the need for a "midshipman academic intervention program" along the lines Captain Seymour had laid out the previous March. It also emphasized the need to identify at-risk midshipmen as early as possible and to enhance communication between a midshipman's military chain of command and faculty members.

Other recommendations included expanding the stretchout program, limiting Army-Navy week activities that interfered with study time, reducing the scope of professional knowledge plebes had to memorize, exempting at-risk students from watch-standing responsibilities during the week before final exams, prohibiting midshipmen in academic trouble from participating in club sports and brigade support activities, and sending selected students appearing before the academic board at the end of first semester to NAPS.[9]

In accordance with these recommendations, in August 1989, R. Adm. Virgil Hill, the superintendent, established an academic center with three full-time staff members for counseling at-risk students. Over the next several years, the administration implemented most of the study group's recommendations.[10] The black attrition rate still averaged about 30 percent for the classes of 1994–99, but there was less variation in the rates from one class to the next than there had been in times past.[11]

Despite the administration's close attention to minority issues in the 1980s and '90s, disparities in treatment of black midshipmen remained. In response to congressional inquiries made in the wake of Tailhook, the General Accounting Office (GAO) launched investigations of the treatment of women and minorities at the service academies. Its Naval Academy investigation focused on the classes of 1988–91. A report issued on 30 April 1993 enumerated the racial disparities in detail and indicated that academic disparities between white and black midshipmen persisted beyond plebe year. In each of the four classes reviewed, whites consistently made significantly higher semester grade point averages than minorities did. The report also revealed that minorities consistently received lower average military performance scores than whites did. Both midshipman officers and company officers tended to give African American midshipmen lower rankings than they did whites.

These lower military performance ratings were reflected in the proportion of brigade leadership positions held by black midshipmen. The report found that minority midshipmen were selected for leadership positions at a rate below their proportional representation in the brigade. For the academic years 1983–91, minority representation at the three-stripe level was consistently below their proportional representation in the classes. In 1983, when minorities constituted 12 percent of the class, they held only about 2 percent of the three-striper positions. Similarly, in 1991, minorities accounted for 15 percent of the class but only 7 percent of the three-striper positions.

These disparities demonstrated that the Academy's racial policy had not eliminated discrimination. The Academy developed the leadership potential of midshipmen, in part, by allowing them to police themselves. The Academy's culture emphasized toughness, obedience to regulations and to upperclassmen, loyalty to classmates and to company mates, non-interference with classmates, and, especially, "never bilge a shipmate." These folkways continued to enable prejudiced upperclassmen to discriminate under the cover of leadership development without revealing their true motive. And they induced observers not to get involved and victims not to complain.

Although the situation improved for the classes of 1990–93, racial disparities remained. Although minorities achieved proportional representation in striper positions, they were still underrepresented in striper staff positions. Midshipmen who held striper positions had less time for academics, and as a result their scores tended to drop during their striper tours. Since Academy officials did not want stripers to get in academic trouble, they tended not to select midshipmen deemed at academic risk for striper positions. This, Academy officials told GAO investigators, might explain the disparity in three-striper rates, as might heavy minority participation in varsity sports.

GAO investigators found that minority midshipmen were convicted at higher rates than whites for conduct and honor offenses. Minority plebes had higher conviction rates than white plebes for conduct offenses, but the rates were about the same for minority and white upperclassmen. For honor violations, minorities were charged with offenses at a higher rate, had their cases dropped at a lower rate, and were found guilty at a higher rate than whites.

There was even a gap in attitudes. GAO investigators found that, whereas most black and white midshipmen believed faculty members, company officers, conduct boards, honor boards, and academic boards treated all midshipmen the same, a higher percentage of whites than minorities believed that minorities were treated better, and a higher percentage of minorities believed that they were treated worse.[12]

Occasional racial incidents reflected the disparities and made for awkward moments. Roger Isom recalled one such incident that took place during his senior year. "An intruder entered a white female's room and stole some personal items," he said. "The room was dark and she was asleep. She startled him when she awoke and he ran. When the Naval Investigative Service [NIS] interviewed her, she said that the intruder was 'about 5 feet 10 inches tall, black, thin, and could run fast.' Based on her description and without authorization from the commandant, the NIS agents began pulling black male midshipmen from classes or rooms and photographing them as potential suspects. Fortunately, a black classmate told me what was going on. At the time, I was the Black Studies Club president and the brigade commander. I immediately went to the commandant's office to inquire about the NIS agents' actions. He denied having authorized the photographs and immediately directed the NIS to cease that part of their investigation. Furthermore, the commandant apologized to me for the NIS actions. I relayed his apology to the black midshipmen. This event was handled at our level. It reminded me that racism and stereotyping still existed among some members of the military. This event also reminded me to keep my guard up after I left the Academy for the Navy."

As the Academy became increasingly diversified, ethnic jokes and humor involving racial stereotypes became an increasingly sensitive issue. Many midshipmen had difficulty accepting the fact that some of their classmates took offense at forms of humor that they considered socially acceptable. During Quintin Jones's youngster year, a white midshipman circulated an e-mail titled "Christmas in the Hood," a racist parody of "The Night before Christmas."

Sometimes the line between acceptable and offensive remained fuzzy, with different people drawing it in different places. During Jacqueline Jackson's youngster year, the 1974 "blaxploitation" movie *Dolemite* became a fad among her company mates. The film starred Rudy Ray Moore, a black standup comedian whose act featured profanity and rhyming lines. The movie essentially showcased Moore's signature routine, based on the character "Dolemite." According to Moore's website, the movie's plot involved prostitution and drug dealing and featured an "all-girl kung fu army, pimpin' clothing and decor, and incredibly outlandish characters" whose dialog included phrases like "You no business, insecure, rat soup eatin,' junkyard motherfucker!" The movie became somewhat of a cult classic, revered by many 1990s rappers but reviled by people such as members of the group Young African Americans Against Media Stereotypes.[13]

A group of Jackson's white male company mates watched *Dolemite* time and again and had taken to repeating phrases from the movie among themselves, often in mocking tones amid derisive laughter. Sometimes Jackson believed her white shipmates were making fun not just of "this stupid black person" in the movie but of all black people, including her. When Jackson voiced her objections, her white company mates became angry and defensive, arguing that black people laughed at the film too, and chided her for being too "politically correct."

Stereotyping of any ethnic group bothered Jackson. To liven up the routine in navigation class, midshipmen would set aside time every now and then for telling jokes. On one occasion a classmate told a Mexican joke. "Something about how do you make a Mexican chilly," Jackson recalled. "Everyone was laughing. I stood up. 'No more ethnic jokes,' I said. Everyone booed. Afterward, a black guy in the class said, 'Why did you say that? Now we're not going to have joke day anymore.' I guess because it wasn't about blacks, he had no problem with it."

Tracey James had a similar experience. During first-class year her white roommate told a black joke at the dinner table that stunned their company mates into silence. All eyes turned toward James, who excused herself and left. The roommate later apologized, almost in tears, but James wasn't placated. "You couldn't see past yourself getting patted on the back for a clever joke," she thought. "You didn't see how it would embarrass me or embarrass your classmates." For James, the solution to the problem of determining what's funny and what's offensive was simply to not tell ethnic jokes at all.

Cultural differences sometimes resulted in far more dire consequences than mere occasional unpleasantness among midshipmen. Troy McSwain crossed company and class lines to gain support from other black midshipmen, but with a nontraditional twist. During McSwain's plebe year, three black upperclassmen secretly joined an international black college fraternity, Omega Psi Phi, through a local graduate chapter. During visits to Ma Bowman and Ma Wilson's houses, McSwain became acquainted with the three upperclassmen. He admired their bond. They seemed closer to each other than other black midshipmen did. Early in youngster year, McSwain and nine other black midshipmen pledged Omega Psi Phi through the upperclassmen. They were trying to form an underground Naval Academy chapter. All thirteen pledges and members of the fraternity would get up early in the morning to go running together and have fraternity meeting during the runs.

The close association with other black midshipmen had a positive impact on McSwain's overall performance. He finished first-semester youngster year with an A in military performance, an A in conduct, and a QPA of 2.61. "My grades improved because I wanted to make the fraternity," he recalled. "The fraternity really cared about my grades."

That Christmas break, McSwain went home to Los Angeles and returned with his car. Regulations permitted youngsters to have a car, but it had to be kept at least five miles from the Academy and could be driven inside the five-mile limit only when departing or returning from authorized leaves.[14] But, as McSwain recalled, "one night it was snowing and I didn't want to miss curfew, so I just took a chance and drove it right on campus and parked it." He left it in the midshipman parking lot for several days. Meanwhile, authorities took note of the unregistered vehicle. A bulletin over the loudspeaker asked its owner to report to the duty officer. McSwain turned himself in and admitted that the car was his. His punishment included eight weeks of restriction, which meant that he had to remain at the Academy over spring break.

The punishment proved to be his undoing. Despite being in such deep trouble over the car, McSwain continued breaking rules. He found himself endlessly marching off demerits. The more trouble he got into, the more rules he would break, desperate for relief from the Academy environment. "It got to the point where I didn't care," he said. "Going over the wall was nothing. The fact that I was black and didn't give a shit made it even worse. I didn't care if I got in trouble. 'I've got to do two more weeks on top of the eight I already got? So what.'" His grades in conduct and military performance for the second semester each dropped to a C, and his QPA plummeted to a 1.47.

To add insult to injury, the commandant summoned McSwain and the other members of his fraternity to his office just days after the ten pledges had crossed over into full brotherhood. Although no regulation forbade joining a fraternity, the commandant was concerned that the bond among the members would be stronger than their commitment to the honor concept. He asked whether they would report each other for infractions of the rules. "We looked at the commandant and said no," McSwain recalled. "Deep down inside we knew we'd never reprimand each other. The commandant basically said that if we were all the same class, it wouldn't have been a problem, but the fact that we were in different classes meant that we were kind of stepping over their chain of command." The commandant ordered them to disband the organization.

Terribly upset, McSwain returned to his room and told his roommates what had happened. One roommate admitted that he had been the one who reported McSwain and the others to the commandant. McSwain was shocked.

"I didn't know what you were doing," the roommate said.

"Well why didn't you ask me?" McSwain said.

"Because you were being so secretive," the roommate replied. "I wanted to make sure you weren't joining some cult or becoming a Black Panther. Everybody you were around was black."

"We were going through an initiation process," McSwain recalled. "My roommates were really puzzled. They didn't understand what I was doing. They didn't know it was just a fraternity." Many a time when McSwain and his roommates were in the room studying or just talking, one of the other fraternity members would come by. "Yo, man," he would say to McSwain, "can I talk to you?" "So we'd go out in the hallway and talk," McSwain said. "We wouldn't talk in front of them. Everything became a secret. That's why he turned us in. He thought it was some kind of a black alliance thing and we were going to do an uprising."

McSwain was astonished that his roommate had never bothered to ask what he was doing. The roommate was no doubt astonished that McSwain had never bothered to tell him what he was doing. The problem was that their relationship had degenerated to the point that they simply stopped talking to each other. The miscommunication had proven fertile ground for misunderstanding.

Several days later, McSwain made a second appearance before the academic board. This time the board voted to dismiss him. McSwain completed the separation process and left Annapolis quickly. He felt both frustration and relief. He was no quitter, but he was glad to be free of the Academy's constraints. He hopped into his car, the same one that had precipitated his downfall, and drove back to Los Angeles with no regrets.

McSwain became a professional model, appearing in magazines such as *GQ* and *Ebony Man*. In 1994, he did what he had always wanted to do—he entered the fashion business as a consultant and designer of men's clothing, specializing in custom suits for professional athletes, entertainment figures, and businessmen. Four years later he founded McSwain Enterprises, a men's fashion company based in Beverly Hills, California. His more than five hundred clients include basketball player Kobe Bryant, football player Michael Westbrook, sports announcer and former football player Terry Bradshaw, boxer Mike Tyson, and jazz musician Herbie Hancock. His work has been featured in the *New York Times*, magazines *In Style, Esquire, Black Enterprise,* and *Sports Illustrated,* and on ESPN and Fox television. In 1999, *Los Angeles Magazine* named him that city's "Best Wardrobe Designer."[15]

McSwain never believed racism was the sole cause of his Academy woes. But he certainly thought it was a contributing factor. The cultural differences between him and the upperclassmen in his company, all but one of whom were white, raised his profile as a target. "You had to deal with prejudices that weren't really bad prejudices," McSwain concluded. "But shit happens, you know what I mean?" The cultural differences between him and his room-mates, and white people in general, led him to socialize only with other black people. But the principal reasons for his difficulties were his defiant attitude and propensity for breaking regulations. At bottom, like most Americans, he was simply temperamentally unsuited to being a midshipman.

On the whole, race relations at the Academy continued to improve after the 1990s. A survey of upperclassmen conducted in October 2004 indicated declining perceptions of racism among midshipmen. Only 17 percent of black midshipmen believed racism impeded their development, down from 31 per-cent in 1996. Ninety-eight percent of all midshipmen described teamwork and cooperation among different racial and ethnic groups as positive.[16]

Black midshipmen in the classes of 1980–99 remained fully integrated into brigade life. African Americans continued to participate in the full range of Academy extracurricular activities. Michael Greenwood was vice president of his class for three years and president of the History Club for one year. Jerry Gray participated in the Black Studies Club and became president of the Gos-pel Choir. Mario Maddox marched on the drill team and served on the bri-gade social affairs committee.

Black midshipmen also helped create new extracurricular activities. During his second-class year, Reuben Brigety helped establish the Joint Service Multi-Ethnic Mentorship Program, which brought schoolchildren from Annapolis and the surrounding communities for a day-long series of workshops designed to demolish stereotypes and to develop team-building skills across racial and ethnic lines. That same year Brigety helped establish the Midshipman Leader-ship Library, a space in the basement of Bancroft Hall stocked with books, pamphlets, and videos about leadership.

Black midshipmen participated heavily in varsity sports.[17] Reuben Brigety was a varsity fencer. Michael Greenwood played junior varsity lacrosse and boxed. Ingrid Turner lettered in swimming during plebe and youngster years. Mary Miles played on the varsity women's basketball and softball teams. In 1987, David Robinson, '87, became the first midshipman, African-American or otherwise, to receive the Naismith Trophy and Wooden Award as player of the year in college basketball.[18]

African American midshipmen participated in intramural and club sports as well. Arnoux Abraham did gymnastics and karate. Mario Maddox played intramural football and tennis and joined the judo club. Nikki Peoples played intramural volleyball and basketball, joined the rock climbing club and the karate club, and became president of the women's rugby club.

Like midshipmen as a whole, black midshipmen varied in the degree to which they participated in indoctrinating plebes. Arnoux Abraham believed in passing what he had learned on to plebes. Ingrid Turner treated plebes the way she was treated in Sweet 16, not Playboy 21. As a squad leader during her first-class year, Turner required her plebes to know what was "on the page" but didn't grill them on professional knowledge beyond that. She didn't yell at plebes, preferring to lead by example. She let younger black females know that she was available, but none of them ever came to her for help.

Although there was nothing special about the way Mario Maddox ran plebes, his company mates considered him a "flamer"—one who was tough on plebes.[19] "For my company, I was considered a jerk," he recalled. "My company was 'Slack 6.' We were the easiest company and God knows I needed an easy company when I was a plebe. My NAPSter roommate went to 18th Company, which was the hardest company. I probably would have been considered a moderate or very easy-going guy in 18th Company, but in 6th Company I stood out as a jerk, as a junior. I would drill the plebes if they didn't know what they needed to know. I would scream at them at the table and that type of thing. But I didn't do anything above and beyond. I never messed up somebody's room."

Michael Greenwood considered "pushing plebes" as perhaps his best experience at the Academy. "Each of my upper-class years afforded me a new role and relationship with my plebes," he recalled. "As a youngster, I assumed the role of confidant, buddy, and even cheerleader. As a second class, I was an enforcer of the traditions of the past, the 'bad cop' to the first class 'good cop.' Finally, as a first class I saw myself as a mentor. By far first-class year was the most rewarding experience. As a regimental subcommander I honed the skills required to lead my peers, and later as a squad leader I developed many of the tools required to lead sailors. Helping the plebes transition from civilian life and mentoring the third and second class provided me with hands-on experience that continues to serve me well. The overall Academy experience taught me two valuable lessons: (1) Each person reflects the sum total of their personal experiences; and (2) Trust and respect will afford a leader the opportunity to fundamentally change an individual. An additional lesson learned was that leadership is a process: everyone and every situation require a response tailored for that specific person and situation."

Although not in proportion to their representation in the brigade, many African Americans did achieve striper positions during their first-class year. Arnoux Abraham and William Carr became squad leaders. Five African Americans from the classes of 1980–99 attained the rank of brigade commander or six-striper: Walter Nobles, '82; Roger Isom, '88; Geoffrey S. Royal, '93; Reuben Brigety, '95; and Lawrence Nance, '99.[20]

Roger Isom became regimental commander during the summer before his senior year and six-striper during the fall set of first-class year. He believed he had the full support of his classmates, the faculty, and the administration in each position. The Academy's African American workers were particularly proud of him. "Many of the black employees would grab me and say a kind word of encouragement," he recalled. "I remember the black tailors looking at my uniform and saying 'Midshipman Isom, we have to make sure that you look good now. You're going be in front and you represent us, you understand.' I could not let these employees down. They were so happy that another black midshipman was the brigade commander. I was as obligated to serve them as I was the brigade of midshipmen. Despite my rank, the civilian employees would give me advice as well as encouragement. You can imagine my joy when I returned to the Academy twelve years later to have Smitty cut my son's (Little Rog) hair at the local shop. My how time flies."

Like Isom, Reuben Brigety majored in Navy. Brigety became the first midshipman of any color to hold three of the Academy's top midshipman leadership positions: brigade sergeant major during second-class year, regimental commander during the following summer, and brigade commander during the fall set of first-class year. Brigety received a modest amount of media attention for being the six-striper. Most of the attention focused on his role as brigade commander, not the fact the he was black. He was featured in a television show broadcast from Baltimore called *On Time*. Articles about him appeared in the *Washington Post* and the *Navy Times*. Newspapers in his hometown of Jacksonville, Florida, covered the story in detail.

Being brigade commander gave Brigety another chance to meet Wesley Brown. The two had first met during Brigety's plebe year at a Black Studies Club function, where Brown talked about his own plebe year. "The thing that really amazed me about Mr. Brown was that he is so affable," Brigety recalled. "I mean he is a very warmhearted man, very endearing. He mentioned that it was sort of difficult being in the Naval Academy at that time, but he really didn't give us an indication of how difficult it was." The two occasionally crossed paths in succeeding years.

The most memorable meeting took place in 1995 after Brigety led a parade during homecoming, while the class of 1949 celebrated its forty-fifth reunion. For Brigety, the parade itself was nothing out of the ordinary. For Brown, however, the sight of a black midshipman out in front of the brigade was nothing short of extraordinary. "After the parade he came up to me," Brigety recalled. "This man, who was so affable, always had a smile, and had never talked about how hard it had been at the Academy, was crying like a baby. Tears were just streaming down his face. I had certainly never seen him so emotional. I had rarely seen anyone so emotional." For Brown, the moment symbolized how far the Academy had come since he was a midshipman. In 1945, he was the only African American midshipman. Fifty years later, an African American was leading the entire brigade of midshipmen.

When last I spoke with them, the younger African American alumni from the classes of 1980–99 had just begun their military service. William Carr entered the Marine Corps after graduating in 1997 and intended to make it a career. Nikki Peoples graduated that same year and went on to serve as weapons officer, R-Division officer, public affairs officer, and midshipman training officer on the *Pearl Harbor* (LSD-52), homeported in San Diego, and as operations officer and exercise planning officer at Command Maritime Prepositioning Squadron One, out of Rota, Spain. Quintin Jones graduated in 1998, entered the Marine Corps, and had risen to the rank of captain. Jerry Gray selected surface warfare (nuclear), graduated in 2000, and went to sea on board the Aegis destroyer *Mitscher* (DDG-57). Jacqueline Jackson also went surface warfare (nuclear).

Many African American alumni from the classes of 1980–99 are thriving in their military careers. William Triplett served on board three Aegis cruisers. He was the operations/combat information center division officer and anti-submarine warfare officer on the *Vincennes* (CG-49); electrical officer, damage control assistant, and main propulsion assistant on the *Lake Erie* (CG-70); and the combat systems officer on the *Cowpens* (CG-63). During one of his tours ashore, he received a master's degree in information technology management from the Naval Postgraduate School in Monterey, California. "I have had an equal opportunity for promotion in all of my jobs and currently hold a coveted billet in the surface warfare community," he said.

Tracey James embarked on a career in the general unrestricted line. She spent her first tour on Guam, where she met her husband, earned a master's degree, became a qualified scuba diver, and volunteered at the island's first rape/crisis center. She also won every case as legal officer and started the command's first newsletter. In 1994, she returned to the Washington area to work at the National Security Agency as a threat analyst. While there she worked part time for Charter Behavioral Health Systems as a counselor, started her doctorate at Loyola College, and bought her first home. In 1997, she returned to the Naval Academy, where she sponsored several young black female midshipmen and thereby fulfilled her dream to be a role model, taught leadership courses in the division of professional development, developed a women's mentoring program, and served as the sexual assault advocate and coordinator. After her tour in Annapolis, she became the director of fleet and family support in Fort Meade, Maryland. At this writing she holds the rank of lieutenant commander.

After graduating from Navy, Ingrid Turner embarked on a career as a general unrestricted line officer. "My first duty station was the Naval Postgraduate School," she recalled. "I spent three years there and earned my M.B.A. there. Then I came back to the Naval Academy and worked in the admissions office from 1989 to 1992. I started out as a minority admissions counselor for a region and then I became the big MAC. I was also a regional director and volunteered to coach softball and soccer." At night while stationed in Annapolis, she began law school. In 1992, she was one of five people throughout the Navy selected for the Law Education Program. She was also the first black female selected for the program. The Navy sent her to law school and, when she finished, changed her designator to judge advocate general corps. Since then she has served tours in San Francisco, Japan, and Virginia as a Navy lawyer, has earned an LL.M. degree in health care law, and has risen to the rank of commander. Neither her race nor her gender has kept her from getting a job for which she was qualified. "The Navy has given me everything I wanted," she said. "Every position I've asked for, I've gotten."

Early in her naval career, Michele Howard, '82, served on board *Hunley* (AS-31), *Lexington* (AVT-16), *Mount Hood* (AE-29), and *Flint* (AE-32). In 1987, she received the Secretary of the Navy/Navy League Captain Winifred Collins Award, given to one female officer each year for outstanding leadership. Her tours ashore included being instructor and course coordinator at the Steam Engineering Officer of the Watch course in Coronado, California, and serving in BuPers as the Navy liaison to the Defense Advisory Committee on Women in the Military Services.

In January 1996, Howard became executive officer of the dock landing ship *Tortuga* (LSD-46), making her the Navy's first female executive officer of a combatant. In 1998, she completed a master's degree in military arts and sciences from the Army's Command and General Staff College. In 1999, she assumed command of the dock landing ship *Rushmore* (LSD-47), becoming the Navy's first black female officer to command a ship. *Rushmore* at that time was the Navy's only amphibious "smart ship," designated to integrate and evaluate commercial off-the-shelf technologies for possible fleet application. In 2006, she became the first black female Academy graduate selected for flag rank.[21]

Some black alumni have had great careers but have had to battle prejudice to advance. "I served my first nine years in submarines," recalled Michael Greenwood. "I've also had tours with Amphibious Squadron Seven and Combined Forces Command/US Forces Korea. For the last eight years I have served as an intelligence officer. In general, I'm unaware of any prejudice impacting a promotion or denying me the necessary tours to be competitive. I have experienced racism within the Navy, but I was able to overcome it and minimize its impact. One experience is especially noteworthy. During my first tour, one of my commanding officers nearly ended my career. 'If it was up to me,' he said, 'there'd be no *niggers* in my navy.' His evaluations echoed this sentiment. However, I was fortunate in that he was blatant and publicly stated such opinions. Had he been subtle, I would have had no reasonable recourse to overcome his bias. I also had the support of my shipmates (officer and enlisted) and they went to bat for me. As a consequence, during my subsequent tour, I successfully applied to the Board of Correction of Naval Records and had his fitness reports expunged from my official record. As a result there appears to be no permanent damage and I've been able to continue my career."

Roger Isom went from the Academy into nuclear power training and served on board five different nuclear attack and fleet ballistic missile submarines, including duty as executive officer of the nuclear attack submarine *Cheyenne* (SSN-773). In between tours at sea, he taught naval science courses at Hampton University, earned a master's degree in engineering management from Old Dominion University, and, in 1999, returned to the Naval Academy to earn a master's degree in leadership and education development and serve as a company officer. "Unfortunately," Isom recalled, "I encountered prejudice on one tour. Although I did not want to acknowledge it as prejudice at the time, it did hinder my promotion. But the most discouraging aspect of the tour was having a white senior enlisted sailor tell me that a senior officer on the submarine 'did not like blacks.' True or not, the fact that the senior enlisted sailor would make such a statement in the mid-'90s confirmed my perception of prejudicial treatment. Nevertheless, I did not lose faith in the Navy. In fact I am glad that I experienced the event. It served as a reminder that there are still pockets of officers and sailors in the Navy who do not accept races or genders different from the traditional 'white man's navy.' The event was a timely reminder, because I survived the promotion halt and made it on my last 'look.' . . . Most of all, I obtained an important dose of reality which made me realize that more racial progress is needed as soon as possible. Fortunately, the number of bad apples is decreasing, based on the other seven senior officers that I have worked for. I had an equal opportunity to get jobs that I was qualified for. I am proud to be a submariner. In 1989 only thirty-six of 4,971 submarine officers were black. In 2000, eighty-six of 3,800 were black. We have a long way to go in terms of diversity, but one thing I appreciate about being black in the submarine force is that, once you get the dolphins, the respect from other communities is virtually automatic. Moreover, people in the submarine community know that you have 'earned' those dolphins. Regardless of what happens in the future, I take pride in being somewhat of 'a pioneer of hope' for future minority submarine officers." When last I spoke with him, Isom held the rank of commander.

Mario Maddox began his naval career on the fast track, but racial problems with the executive officer of his second ship and a personality clash with the skipper, coupled with his first wife's substance abuse, derailed it. He left the Navy in 1996 after twice being passed over for promotion to lieutenant commander. He moved back to Atlanta and eventually landed a great job with Manhattan Associates, a software engineering firm.

Many black Academy graduates have forged diverse and distinguished careers in both the military and the civilian sectors. Kevin Baugh, '82, compiled an impressive record as a naval officer. "I served as a SEAL until my retirement in 1998. My service included duty on six of seven continents; armed combat during operation Just Cause; work with the United Nations; work with the U.S. Southern Command; work with the Joint Special Operations Command; and work on the staff of the assistant secretary of defense for special operations and low intensity conflict. During my service I obtained a master's of science in foreign service degree from Georgetown University with honors. After my retirement from the Navy I formed a small start-up company with four friends and am currently finishing my Ph.D. in international relations."[22]

After graduating from the Academy in 1987, Mary Miles married Terry McElroy, '86, and served in the Marine Corps, attaining the rank of captain in three years. After resigning her commission in 1992, Mary Miles McElroy embarked on a career in collegiate athletics administration. In the first job of her second career, she worked as senior woman administrator of the Naval Academy Athletic Association as well as assistant athletic director for NCAA compliance. Four years later she moved to Atlanta, where, in 2000, she earned an M.S. in management from Georgia Tech. In July 2005, she became director of intercollegiate athletics at Georgia State University and thereby also became the first black woman at a major Division I institution that was not also a historically black college. A year later she was selected to receive the National Association of Collegiate Women Athletic Administrators' 2006 Administrator of the Year Award for her division.[23]

Reuben Brigety graduated in 1995 and then spent two years as a Pownall Scholar at Cambridge University in England, where he earned a master's degree in international relations. He had a change of heart about a career in the Navy and left the service honorably in the summer of 2000. He went on to complete his Ph.D. in international relations at Cambridge and took a job with the arms division of Human Rights Watch, the largest U.S.-based international human rights organization. "I have conducted humanitarian battle damage assessment missions in Afghanistan," he said, "as well as participated in major international diplomatic conferences in Geneva aimed at improving civilian protections under the law of armed conflict." In 2003, he left Human Rights Watch to become an assistant professor of international relations at

American University's School of International Service and later an assistant professor of government and politics at George Mason University.[24]

Roger Grayson qualified as a surface warfare officer while a young lieutenant j.g., was selected for department head on the first look, and qualified as a master training specialist while an instructor. "I did not experience any real prejudice while I was on sea duty," he recalled. "I served with other peer and senior black officers, which I believe helped. I was always promoted on time and did get the orders I asked for, with the exception of a lateral transfer to the intelligence community. After my first sea tour I made up my mind that surface warfare as a full-time job was not for me. I started working on my master's degree in business management while on shore duty and started researching careers in the civilian sector. The Navy was offering voluntary buyouts for my year group, so I felt the time was right for me to make the move. I left active duty in February 1995, finished my master's degree, and started working for a health care company in corporate marketing. I currently hold a position as a management consultant."

Dr. Leo S. Mackay Jr., '83, a Secretary of the Navy Distinguished Midshipman Graduate, finished pilot training at the top of his class in 1985, went on deployments to the North Atlantic, Mediterranean, and Indian Ocean, completed Naval Fighter Weapons School (Topgun), and logged 235 carrier landings and 1,000 hours in the F-14 fighter. From 1989 to 1993, Mackay was a Kennedy Fellow at Harvard University, where he earned a master's degree in public policy from the Kennedy School of Government and a doctorate in political and economic analysis from the Graduate School of Arts and Sciences. During that time he was a Harvard MacArthur scholar, a graduate prize fellow, and a research fellow at the Center for Science and International Affairs. In 1992, he returned to the Naval Academy to teach military history and western civilization and was a special guest fellow at the Brookings Institution.

After leaving Annapolis the second time, Mackay served in the Office of the Secretary of Defense as military assistant to the assistant secretary of defense for international security policy. In this role he coordinated two hundred people responsible for U.S. defense policy in nuclear weapons, export licensing, counterproliferation, and arms control.

Mackay left active duty in 1995 for a job at Lockheed Martin, where he became director of market development. Two years later, he took a job at Bell Helicopter, where he became vice president of the aircraft services business unit at Bell Helicopter Textron. In this role he had general management responsibility for Bell's global distribution and logistics, commercial spares and accessories sales, and aircraft production.

In July 2001, Mackay accepted a senior position in the Department of

Veterans Affairs, where, as second-in-command, he was the chief operating officer of the federal government's second-largest department. With an annual budget of $48 billion, the Department of Veterans Affairs employed some 219,000 people at hundreds of medical centers, clinics, benefits offices, and national cemeteries across America.[25]

Montel Williams, '80, enlisted in the Marine Corps in 1974 after graduating from high school in his hometown of Baltimore, Maryland. After receiving two meritorious promotions, he entered NAPS in 1975 and graduated from the Naval Academy in 1980. Williams was commissioned in the Navy, earned a degree in Russian from the Defense Language Institute in Monterey, California, and served nine years as a naval intelligence officer, specializing in cryptology. During his last year of service, he began conducting informal counseling for the spouses and families of people in his command to help them cope with the strain of six-month deployments. These sessions led to an invitation to speak to a group of children in Kansas City, Missouri. In the charismatic, nononsense style that has come to define him, he addressed the kids about the importance of staying off drugs and staying in school. The talk marked the beginning of a three-year career as a motivational speaker. After the Kansas City appearance, he received numerous requests from schools across the country and eventually gave up his naval commission to pursue motivational speaking full time. He has since reached out to thousands of parents, educators, and business leaders, encouraging them to work together to address youth issues and to motivate youngsters to reach their full potential.

Williams's success as a motivational speaker propelled him into a career in entertainment. During the 1990s, he appeared in several movies and television programs. In 1994, he launched *The Montel Williams Show*. Two years later he received the Daytime Emmy Award for outstanding talk show host, which ranked among television's highest honors. That same year he published a bestselling autobiography and motivational book, *Mountain, Get Out of My Way*.

Throughout the 1990s, Williams remained active in community service work. In 1996, he produced and directed two antidrug public service announcements, distributed by the Office of National Drug Control Policy. In 2002, he established a foundation to help support three organizations that specialize in finding a cure for multiple sclerosis. And he continued to make public speaking engagements, bringing his antidrug and stay-in-school messages to audiences across the country.

Williams has received numerous awards for his community service work, including the 1999 Tipper Gore Remember the Children Volunteer Award from the National Mental Health Association, the 1999 Dr. Martin Luther King Jr. Governor's Humanitarian Award from New York State, and the 1999

Larry Steward Leadership and Inspiration Award from the Entertainment Industries Council.[26]

Many black graduates linked their success in life to their Academy experience. Roger Grayson thought the Academy was tough academically but considered the overall experience to be positive and rewarding. William Carr would not do plebe year over again for a million dollars. Although he did not much like the Academy as a plebe, he came to love it as an upperclassman. "I learned a lot about other people," he said. "I learned a lot about myself." Mario Maddox had similar sentiments. "It was absolutely the best thing that ever happened to me, bar none," he said, "but there's no way in hell I would ever do it again." Mary Miles, on the other hand, would definitely do it again. Her Academy experience, she said in a recent interview, instilled confidence to tackle any challenge.

For Michael Greenwood, the benefits of being an Academy alumnus have far outweighed the drawbacks. "The Academy challenged me mentally, physically, and emotionally," he said. "It provided me with wonderful friends and experiences. It provided a foundation of discipline and honor. Finally, it allowed me the opportunity to observe and model the behavior I believe all should aspire to. But the experience also retarded my development in some areas of my life. With a fixed schedule, explicit rules, and continuous monitoring, it was easy to be successful. Consequently, I found my first years of commissioned service a little more challenging than most of my non-USNA peers. They appeared to have a better handle on personal finance and relationships. Generally speaking, however, the benefits have been life long while the shortcomings were temporary."

Tracey James said that, if she had to do it over, she would do it differently. "I came to the Academy very naïve, as far as just not knowing anything about the military," she recalled. "I would have come in more physically prepared. I would have learned more about military structure. It was completely new to me plebe year. I think it was new to a lot of people. I didn't really realize how the aircraft and the ships and the weapon systems fit together and how they fit into a career until I went on my youngster cruise. Before then it was just memorization of facts that you needed to know to pass the pro quiz. So I think I would've prepared myself more. I would've asked more questions from people who had been in the military about what to expect."

Jacqueline Jackson admitted that she had entered the Academy with unrealistic expectations. "I was naïve enough to expect utopia," she recalled. "I thought that a military institution could enforce things that other institutions couldn't. I thought the Academy could *make* people good, even against their will. But it was fun. I enjoyed it. I've seen presidents, been on TV, and jumped out of helicopters. At the airport, people think I'm a celebrity. It's worth it."

Some black graduates look back on their years by the Severn with un-abashed pride. "My Academy experience was absolutely great," recalled Ar-noux Abraham. "The Academy gave me tools that I have used throughout my career." For Reuben Brigety, the Academy experience was "defining." "It brought out things in me that I didn't know were there," he said. "For an awful lot of reasons, it made me stronger and capable of dealing with adver-sity, able to deal with sacrifice, and it really gave me an initial sense of what I would like to be doing for a life's profession. I am convinced that the Naval Academy is one of the best public resources our country has to offer. The service academies are the only places that systematically churn out leaders for this country."

Nikki Peoples expressed similar sentiments. "Despite the fact that I felt I was treated unfairly at times," she said, "I would do it all over again in a heartbeat. I love the Naval Academy, and I'm proud to say that it's my alma mater. I wouldn't trade it for the world. It was very exciting. I learned a lot about myself, and I was fortunate to be able to do things that some people will never do in a lifetime."

"I think I made the right decision to go to the Academy," said Quintin Jones. "I had a great time there. I've had so many opportunities to meet people that I know I wouldn't have had a chance to meet if I hadn't have gone there. I've been to so many places that I couldn't have gone to if I'd been in a civilian institution. The leadership experience is phenomenal. At no other place in the world are you given ten people straight out of high school, and whatever you say or do is going to affect their life. You just don't get that anywhere else. It's a good feeling. One of those ten might turn out to be the president, and you can say, 'Man, I trained that guy. Look where he's at now.' He may go to Fortune 500 Company one day and be the CEO. Who knows? I may need a job down the road, and I trained that guy, and he knows I'm a good guy, so, hey, he'll give me a job. It's great to know that the friends you made at the Academy will be your friends ten or fifteen years down the road. That's just the type of bond and family atmosphere that you have at the Acad-emy. I don't think you can get it anywhere else."

Many black alumni from the classes of 1980–99 found that having an Academy education on their resume has benefited them in the business world. "It opened doors that I think would've never been opened," said Mario Mad-dox. "Where I work now, when they hear I'm from the Naval Academy, there's oohing and ahhing, even to this day. In my previous job, one of the first things the president of the company told his people about me was, 'We got a Naval Academy graduate in our company.'"

Even African Americans who left before graduation derived benefit from having gone to Annapolis. "I learned a lot about business," said Troy Mc-

Swain. "The Naval Academy experience made me a more a disciplined person, more focused. My work ethic definitely comes from the Academy. My memory; I used to have to memorize the menu of the day, the officer of the day, this and that. I did that shit for a year. I can look at something and pretty much know it. I get a much larger respect factor from the business community as well as just people in general when I tell them I went to school at the Naval Academy. Anybody's that heard of the Naval Academy treats me totally different, just because I went there. I've been offered jobs because the Naval Academy appears on my resume. The fact that I went there has definitely opened up several doors. I don't have to use that anymore, but in the beginning, it did help. It helped with jobs. It helped with job interviews, all kinds of things."

Roger Isom looked back on the Academy as a source of unparalleled opportunity: "Opportunities to learn swimming, sailing, and karate, to lead clubs, to speak to youth, to lead your classmates and the brigade, to see the world (i.e., Japan, Hong Kong, Philippines, Cuba, Puerto Rico, and the Virgin Islands). Opportunities to get a college degree in aerospace engineering, to make Mom and Dad smile during your graduation as they place the ensign shoulder boards on your dress whites, to have your oldest brother (the pacesetter) be the first enlisted person to salute you. Opportunities to see and become a part of another family with skin colored different from you but a family who loves you no less, to get a third grandmother and friend four times your age. Opportunities to represent your race as the brigade commander of 'America's finest' despite the fact that the first black alumnus graduated so recently, in 1949. Opportunities to speak to congressmen (on the Board of Visitors) about the state of the Naval Academy when you said as a child 'Mom and Dad don't know any congressmen.' The opportunity to meet my future wife, Lisa, and wonderful in-laws. And finally, the opportunity to serve my classmates, the Academy, and the community with a cheerful heart."

"I spoke to the faculty during my last summer at the Academy," Isom added. "One new member asked me what I liked most about the Naval Academy. 'Sir,' I said, 'I feel blessed to have had the opportunity to go to this institution and experience what I once perceived as an impossible option for me.' My Academy experience is an opportunity that I did not waste and would not trade. What a journey!"

After dissemination of the first Navy affirmative action plan in 1976, each successive CNO remained committed to proportional representation of minorities in the officer corps and paid close attention to the number of African Americans entering the Academy each year. OPNAV's dedication to proportional representation, begun during Admiral Zumwalt's tour as CNO, put the Navy near the cutting edge of affirmative action for the rest of the twentieth century.

The definition of proportional representation articulated by OPNAV and the Navy secretariat changed several times during the last quarter of the twentieth century. In 1976, Navy leaders had only vaguely defined proportional representation, expressed variously as reflecting the demographics of the country or the enlisted service but never as a specific number. In 1979, Admiral Hayward defined proportional representation more concretely—corresponding to the proportion of African Americans with college degrees—and set a specific numerical goal, 6 percent, for each incoming class. Although the Academy achieved that goal only twice during the 1980s (with the classes of 1990 and 1993), in May 1988 the chief of naval personnel directed each commissioning source, including the Naval Academy, to recruit enough African Americans so that blacks constituted 7 percent of officers commissioned each year, with a view toward achieving the original 6 percent black officer composition goal sooner. The Academy had only twice achieved the 7 percent goal (with the classes of 1994 and 1995) when Secretary Dalton's 1994 Enhanced Opportunities for Minorities Initiative raised the bar to 12 percent, corresponding to the proportion of black people in America. This will doubtless prove a much harder target to hit.

The Academy generally resisted increases in minority accession goals throughout the period, arguing that its recruiting program was already bringing in as many black candidates as possible, given the size of the pool and the resources available. However, Academy officials always strove to meet the higher goals, often offering short-term compromises until they could develop new procedures or commit new resources.

OPNAV involved itself not only in setting the Academy's minority accession goals but also in devising procedures for meeting them. The minority officer accessions study groups in 1979 and 1981, minority officer accessions task force in 1984, and CNO study group on equal opportunity in 1988 each offered suggestions to facilitate minority recruiting and increase minority enrollment at the Academy. By and large the Academy accepted and implemented these recommendations, particularly when they involved refinements to existing procedures, such as increasing the number of MACs in the candidate guidance office or expanding the network of contacts in the black community. No doubt the representatives from the Academy serving on these groups helped shape palatable recommendations.

The Academy's overall recruiting effort has always depended heavily on volunteerism. Its principal recruiting tool has long been the Blue and Gold Program, whose officers and affiliates have done their work at no cost to the Academy beyond that necessary for administering and training them. Likewise, the Academy's minority recruiting effort has always depended heavily on volunteerism. Since 1976, the candidate guidance office has tried to encourage active-duty minority officers, minority alumni, members of the National Naval Officers Association, and even minority midshipmen to donate time to the minority recruiting effort. The position of outreach coordinator was initially funded by charitable contributions and sought to encourage volunteerism through minority alumni conferences.

The Academy's basic approach to minority recruiting evolved between 1976 and 1999 but was not revolutionized during that period. Changes embodied refinements to existing techniques rather than brand-new approaches. In the late 1990s, the Academy's minority recruiting effort still operated along the lines of the basic model Ken Johnson developed in the early 1970s, featuring extensive travel to black communities across the country and establishing personal contacts with black students, guidance counselors, and community leaders. Although the number of MACs grew from three in 1976 to eight in 1987 and remained at eight through 1999, their philosophical and procedural foundation remained the visitation-presentation approach. Most of the refinements made to the minority recruiting program arose from finding ways to use existing resources and methods more efficiently rather than developing radically different techniques. Time and again suggestions surfaced for increasing minority involvement in the Blue and Gold Program or tapping the National Naval Officers Association for help—in short, increasing volunteerism—or increasing the flow from NAPS and BOOST. Other refinements consisted of tweaks to marketing data research and analysis techniques, basic marketing tactics, and advertising, such as creating brochures and purchasing lists from new sources. Because their performance evaluations depended on finding candidates who could survive plebe year, MACs tended to do their fishing in areas that had produced successful minority midshipmen in the past rather than in uncharted waters, particularly inner-city schools. Pete Tzomes identified the crux of the problem in the fall of 1988 when he concluded that the Academy could not drastically increase minority officer accessions without making drastic changes to the minority recruiting program. No one has yet devised a viable alternative to the existing system, however.

Besides the lack of fundamental innovation to recruiting strategy and tactics, the other salient feature of the minority recruiting program since 1976 has been the Academy's refusal to alter admissions standards simply to boost numbers. The Academy has varied in the degree to which it accepted students deemed high attrition risks, but it has never wavered from its basic requirement for academic excellence as a criterion for admission. Although SAT and ACT scores and secondary school grades have their flaws and the "whole man" concept has evolved in an ongoing effort to broaden the base of motivated candidates, numerical measures of academic performance have enabled Academy officials to produce reliable methods for predicting whether students can survive the Academy's rigorous academics. The Academy has been quite right to rely on academic prowess in the process of producing technically competent naval officers. There is simply no substitute for academic prowess to succeed at the Academy. Although attrition predictors based on academic performance have proved reliable, no one has been able to come up with a reliable method for measuring academic *potential.*

As a result, whereas the numbers of African Americans entering the Academy each year produced a steep upward graph between 1965 and 1976, those numbers were relatively level between 1976 and 1999. The proportion of African Americans admitted into the classes of 1980–99 averages roughly 6 percent. Increases in resources and changes in techniques resulted in peaks as high 8.6 percent (with the class of 1994), but these have been offset by valleys as low as 3.8 percent (with the class of 1985). Refinements to recruiting methods have made the process more efficient but have not produced significantly higher minority accessions sustained consistently over a multiyear span.

The difficulty in securing enough black midshipmen to meet OPNAV accessions goals forced the Academy to adopt different procedures for admitting black midshipmen. The admissions board has generally reviewed majority candidates only on paper, but since the early 1980s MACs have personally presented each individual minority candidate to the board. And since Ken Johnson first reported on board in 1970, the Academy has relied on minorities to recruit minorities. Far from being a hangover from the Navy's racist past, the Academy employed this approach because a black man in gold braid—"someone who looks like us"—has far more credibility with black kids in presenting opportunities available for African Americans in the Navy. The same kind of attitude existed among black midshipmen who looked up to black officers in the executive department as role models.

Throughout the last quarter of the twentieth century, regardless of how OPNAV defined proportional representation, the principal and perennial challenges facing the Academy's minority recruiting effort have been finding enough qualified and motivated candidates and combating the Navy's negative or non-image in minority communities. Declining black college enrollments during the 1980s, resegregation of school districts in many areas, and poor education in inner cities limited the pool of potential candidates available to a system whose ticket for admission required at least the potential for academic excellence. As Vietnam-era antimilitary sentiment faded and the economy boomed during the 1980s and '90s, selling the Navy lifestyle, with its relatively low pay, limits on personal freedom, and time away from family, remained difficult. Many qualified minority students never heard of the Naval Academy, or continued to perceive the Navy as a racist institution, or received competing offers of partial or full scholarships to civilian colleges.

Personal contact with prospective candidates has always been the Academy's best minority recruiting tactic. Academy agents, whether MACs, Blue and Gold officers, black midshipmen, or National Naval Officers Association members, have achieved their best results at high schools, college fairs, and homes, meeting and talking to young candidates on an individual basis. Perpetual efforts to increase volunteerism by active duty and retired officers and reservists, Academy alumni, and midshipmen have explicitly recognized this fact. Presence in communities has been the best way not only to inspire prospective candidates but also to address the Navy's image problem. The presence of black midshipmen home on leave or black alumni home from the fleet remains the strongest antidote to lack of awareness of the Academy and the Navy in African American communities. Areas that have had a strong Blue and Gold organization and regular visits from Academy recruiting agents have tended to produce black midshipmen. Perpetual efforts to increase the Academy's outreach by sending representatives to meetings of national organizations such as the NAACP, National Urban League, and National Alliance of Black School Educators have explicitly recognized this fact. Outreach has always been and will always remain a necessity, for each new generation of potential midshipmen is born without knowledge of what the Naval Academy has to offer. The biggest challenge will be to reach and develop a largely untapped source—inner-city black youth.

African Americans remained fully integrated into the brigade of midshipmen through the end of the twentieth century. Although racial disparities and other problems reflecting America's racial divide still surfaced, black midshipmen continued to enjoy an equal chance at Academy opportunities.

While the classes of 1980–99 were passing through, monitoring the racial situation and ensuring equal opportunity for black midshipmen remained near the top of the superintendent's and commandant's agendas. Whether from the perspective of minority officer accession goals, revising the human relations program, or ensuring that the faculty and staff reflected the diversity of the fleet, consciousness of race and diversity was ingrained in the Academy's culture from top to bottom.

Open expressions of racism at the Academy were few and far between during the 1980s and '90s. Black midshipmen still ran up against negative racial attitudes and prejudice among some classmates and upperclassmen, but more often than not the kind of negative racial situations they encountered involved individuals who had no prior experience with people of other races making inappropriate or insensitive remarks without intending harm. Ignorance, immaturity, or inexperience were the culprits in such cases, not bigotry.

That said, true bigots—those who believed themselves racially superior to black people—still found ways to act out their prejudices under cover of plebe indoctrination, leadership development, and various other exercises of power. As long as some midshipmen had authority over others, the potential for clandestine discrimination remained. The Academy's racial policies had curbed but had not eliminated discrimination.

As a result, although racially motivated mistreatment of black midshipmen remained rare during this period, it did happen. From a policy standpoint, what inhibited racists from acting on their prejudices or drove bigots underground was not so much racial awareness training, which had become diluted and subsumed under the general mantle of human relations, but statements in regulations explicitly prohibiting discrimination. The most effective antidote to racially motivated mistreatment of black midshipmen, however, remained the presence of upperclassmen willing to confront bigots and speak out against discrimination.

Throughout the 1980s and '90s, black midshipmen generally moved within several social circles. They forged friendships among company mates, other players on their sports teams, fellow members of extracurricular activities, classmates in the same course section, and people with similar outside interests. Some of these social circles happened to form largely along racial lines, such as the memberships of the Black Studies Club and Gospel Choir and groups going off to party at historically black colleges. Generally speaking, however, most circles in which black midshipmen moved, particularly involving activities inside the Academy, included members of all races and ethnicities.

Black midshipmen could find support within any of these circles if they needed it. They could also turn to families they met through the Academy's sponsor program. Although black midshipmen could still find support from other black midshipmen and from Annapolis's black community, they were far less likely to rely exclusively on members of their own race. Common interest, not race, formed the basis of most social relationships among midshipmen by the end of the twentieth century. The Academy's racial policy, the ubiquitous presence of black upperclassmen throughout the brigade, the elaborate support system available to them, and the general decline of racism across the United States combined to minimize the amount of racial discrimination black midshipmen suffered.

Women, however, continued to face difficulties being accepted by the majority. Like its racial policy, the Academy's policy toward women rested on the principles of equal opportunity and prohibition of discrimination. But the Academy's culture proved far more resistant to the acceptance of women after the gender barrier had been broken in 1980 than it had been to the acceptance of African Americans after the color barrier had been broken in 1949. Despite support for female midshipmen from the administration and the equal opportunity policy, many male midshipmen clung to the belief that women did not belong at the Academy, even twenty years after the first female midshipmen had graduated in 1980. This belief translated into mistreatment of women more often than racial prejudice translated into mistreatment of African Americans during this period. To a large extent this attitude accounted for the significantly higher attrition rate among women than men. Black female midshipmen faced discrimination and disparities because of race as well as gender. Thus one could expect a black woman to have experienced more difficulties at the Academy than either a black man or a white woman. In part, the problems experienced by African American and women midshipmen resulted from lingering racism and sexism in the armed forces and throughout the country.

Sexual harassment and discrimination existed at the Academy through the 1980s because sexist midshipmen believed they could get away with such behavior. Only after the Academy's leadership cracked down on sexual harassment and discrimination in the wake of Tailhook and President Clinton signed the bill ending combat exclusion for women on combatant ships did these problems diminish in the mid-1990s.

By and large, black midshipmen, male and female, from the classes of 1980–99 looked back with pride at the Naval Academy as an unparalleled opportunity to obtain a first-class education, a gateway to the naval profession, and a ticket to a lucrative civilian career.

Conclusion

Wesley Brown stood at a podium on the seaward side of Bancroft Hall's seventh wing before a crowd of naval officers, sailors, Academy alumni, midshipmen, state and local officials, community leaders, area residents, family, and friends. This day, Brown declared, was the third most momentous day of his life, after the day he married his wife Crystal and the day he graduated from the Naval Academy. During a ceremony that Saturday, 25 March 2006, the Naval Academy broke ground for the Wesley Brown Field House, a 140,000-square-foot athletic facility named in his honor. It was the first building on the Yard named for an African American. Admiral Michael G. Mullen, the CNO, likened the historical significance of Brown's achievement in breaking the Academy's color barrier to Admiral William Halsey's leadership during World War II. The groundbreaking symbolized how far the Navy and the Naval Academy have come during Brown's lifetime in making equal opportunity a reality.[1]

Race relations at the Academy have always reflected race relations in American society. Whether or not black midshipmen could succeed in any given period depended on national politics, the Navy's racial policy, the attitudes of the Academy's leadership, midshipmen's racial attitudes, and black midshipmen's own abilities. During the latter half of the twentieth century, impulses from above and below transformed the Academy from a racist institution to one that ranked diversity and equal opportunity among its fundamental tenets. This transformation was not without its social cost, however, and black midshipmen bore the brunt of it.

Only a handful of African Americans graduated from the Academy in the two decades following Wes Brown's success in 1949. The classes of 1949–68 included fewer than three dozen black graduates. Racism and the Navy's neglect of racial issues explain the dearth of African American midshipmen during this period. Racism tarnished the Navy's image in the black community, discouraged black youth interested in the Academy from seeking admission, and denied blacks equal opportunity to enter the Academy. Neglect of racial issues by the Navy's leadership prevented the establishment of a permanent minority affairs organization or program charged with recruiting blacks for the Academy. By the mid-1960s, pressure from the civil rights movement on the federal government resulted in ad hoc minority recruiting efforts, but no policy of proportional minority representation in the officer corps yet emerged.

By and large, those African Americans who did gain admission to the classes of 1949–68 grew up under segregation and entered the Academy to become naval officers. Although they had no racial problems with the vast majority of midshipmen, they did encounter racial hostility from some upperclassmen. In a few instances, this hostility precipitated the departure of black midshipmen. To whatever degree of racially motivated hazing black midshipmen underwent, their plebe experiences were that much worse than those of their white classmates. Until they were forced to pay attention to racial issues by pressure from higher in the chain of command outside Annapolis, the Academy's leaders ignored racial issues. By ignoring racial issues, the leadership enabled discrimination to exist.

As they had done while growing up, black midshipmen turned primarily to other African Americans both inside and outside the Academy for support. By the early 1960s, a subculture had emerged to provide black midshipmen with an alternative mutual support structure and means for socialization denied them by the main Academy culture and segregation in Annapolis.

If black midshipmen from the classes of 1949–1968 survived plebe year, their experiences differed in key respects from those of their white classmates, for they suffered racial indignities in town and on cruise, often received lower "grease" marks than they deserved, and did not have equal opportunity for the top leadership positions in the brigade. Black midshipmen were not yet fully integrated, professionally or socially, and the leadership's policy toward them remained one of official neglect. True equal opportunity remained elusive until the Academy developed racial policies and black midshipmen achieved social equality and equal professional opportunity.

The Vietnam War era witnessed the most profound changes in the Navy's racial policy since World War II. Political pressures resulting from the civil rights movement, black unrest in the cities, and an enlightened sense of fairness among some of the Navy's top leaders drove the service to revive the racial policy revolution that had begun during World War II but languished in the interim. During this period, official neglect gave way to affirmative action, and the gap between written racial policy and actual racial practice began to close.

The second revolution unfolded in two phases. Sparked by the civil rights agendas of presidents Kennedy and Johnson and driven by Defense Secretary McNamara's Directive 5120.36, the first phase culminated in an equal opportunity program that sought to eliminate racial bias in recruiting, assigning, and promoting African Americans. President Nixon's redefinition of affirmative action sparked the second phase, which—driven by the policies of successive chiefs of naval operations, beginning with Admiral Elmo R. Zumwalt Jr.—culminated in an affirmative action program designed to achieve proportional representation of African Americans in all pay grades and occupational categories throughout the fleet. By the nation's bicentennial in 1976, the Navy had institutionalized a policy of affirmative action, equal opportunity, and proportional minority representation.

Despite the Navy's general course toward affirmative action, however, it was direct intervention by higher powers outside Annapolis—the president of the United States and the CNO—that propelled the Naval Academy in that direction. The Gesell Committee goaded the chief of naval personnel into undertaking ad hoc, temporary, and ineffective recruiting measures during the early 1960s, but President Johnson's order to double the Academy's black enrollment in July 1965 spurred the superintendent into developing and implementing the Academy's first sustained minority recruiting program. Although the Academy had met Johnson's goal of doubling black enrollment by the time Admiral Zumwalt became CNO, it still was not moving fast enough toward proportional representation to suit Zumwalt, so he prevailed upon the Academy to intensify its minority recruiting effort. During the 1970s, the minority recruiting program evolved into its modern form, featuring minority admissions counselors and minority accessions goals established as a percentage of incoming and later graduating midshipmen. As a result, the number of black plebes entering each year skyrocketed from a handful to scores, increasing the number of black midshipmen from a token presence to a significant minority that more realistically reflected the population of the United States. Minority recruiting at the Academy has remained an OPNAV concern since 1970.

The pattern of experiences of African Americans who graduated in the early 1970s differed little from that of those who graduated during the '60s. But for those who graduated in the mid-'70s and later, a new pattern emerged. This new pattern was the product of changes in the Academy's racial policy that resulted from both the Vietnam-era revolution in the Navy's racial policy and the impetus for reform from black midshipmen themselves.

Since World War II, the plebe system, when it functioned as intended, facilitated integration of black midshipmen into the brigade. At its best, the crucible of plebe indoctrination forged bonds among classmates that transcended racial boundaries. At the same time, however, it provided opportunities for bigots to act on their prejudices under the cover of indoctrinating plebes. Beginning in the 1960s, reform of the plebe indoctrination system reduced but did not eliminate racists' and, later, sexists' ability to do so.

Most African Americans from the classes of 1969–79 experienced some aspect of integration while growing up and decided to attend the Academy as the result of outreach efforts by the minority recruiting program. Most of the racial problems they had with classmates and upperclassmen resulted from ignorance or insensitive remarks instead of genuine prejudice, although many black midshipmen did encounter whites who believed that black midshipmen were underqualified and admitted only to meet a racial quota. And, occasionally, black midshipmen still ran up against genuine bigots who believed that white people were superior to people of color.

Equal opportunity occurred after the Academy's leadership created and enforced racial policies and black midshipmen achieved social equality. During the 1970s, the Academy openly espoused a policy of equal opportunity, non-discrimination, and affirmative action by instituting racial awareness training, establishing human relations committees, diversifying the faculty and staff, and sponsoring extracurricular activities that celebrated diversity. Together with reforms in the plebe indoctrination system, the Academy's policy made a profound impact on the experiences of black midshipmen. It was the growing presence of black upperclassmen, however, that proved the greatest barrier to any discrimination that manifested itself during plebe indoctrination. Institutional reform and increasing black presence did not eliminate racially motivated mistreatment of black plebes, but they certainly inhibited it. In sum, true equal opportunity occurred only after practice caught up with policy.

The academic hurdle proved the greatest barrier to a black midshipman's ultimate success during the period 1976–99. If African Americans maintained passing grades, their experiences largely resembled those of their white classmates. They were fully integrated into Academy life, sports, and social activities and had the opportunity to achieve top leadership positions in the brigade. The black midshipmen's subculture became more diffuse as white classmates and the institution itself became more responsive to their needs. In the early 1970s, a black midshipman's closest friends at the Academy were most likely other black midshipmen. A decade later, a black midshipman's closest friends were just as likely to be white as black.

After the Navy adopted the first navy affirmative action plan in 1976, racial issues remained near the top of the Navy's personnel policy agenda for the rest of the twentieth century. As a result of OPNAV's dedication to affirmative action, begun during Admiral Zumwalt's tour as CNO, the Academy strove to achieve proportional representation of African American midshipmen, even as the criterion for proportional representation changed from the ratio of blacks in the general population, to the ratio of college students, and back to the ratio in the general population again. During this period the Academy's basic approach to minority recruiting depended heavily on volunteer participation by active duty and retired officers and embodied refinements to existing techniques rather than truly innovative approaches. Accession goals for African Americans increased from 6 percent to 7 percent to 12 percent, but the proportion of black midshipmen admitted into the classes of 1980–99 averaged roughly 6 percent.

With the last vestiges of conscious institutional discrimination purged from the Naval Academy by 1976, African Americans in the classes of 1980–99 remained fully integrated into brigade life and enjoyed equal access to Academy opportunities. Although racial disparities and problems reflecting America's racial divide still surfaced, black midshipmen encountered less discrimination than in any time in the past. Equal opportunity and nontolerance of discrimination remained the bedrock of the Academy's racial policy, and racial issues continued to appear near the top of the administration's agenda.

Most black midshipmen in the classes of 1980–99 grew up in integrated circumstances in at least one area of their lives and attended the Academy for either military or economic motives. About half entered the Academy right out of high school; the other half went to NAPS first. Insensitive remarks or stereotyping constituted the bulk of racial problems these midshipmen faced. Open expressions of bigotry had become quite rare and were just as likely to be detrimental to the perpetrator as to the target. For support, black midshipmen had at their disposal all the resources available to the majority as well as the traditional black network. Although the black academic attrition rate exceeded the majority rate, Academy officials never lowered minority admission standards to boost numbers. The ratio of black stripers more nearly reflected their proportion of the brigade than in times past.

The Academy's chief social problem after the class of 1976 graduated was the integration of women. Female midshipmen faced sexual discrimination, regardless of race. Although the Academy's gender policy rested on the principles of equal opportunity and prohibition of discrimination, its culture proved far more resistant to the acceptance of women after the gender barrier had been broken in 1980 than it had been to the acceptance of African Americans after the color barrier had been broken in 1949. Only after the Academy's leadership more rigorously enforced policies prohibiting sexual harassment and discrimination in the wake of Tailhook did the atmosphere for women improve significantly. As in the case of black midshipmen, it took direct pressure from higher-ups outside Annapolis for the Academy's leadership to do so. Even twenty years after the first female midshipmen graduated in 1980, however, many male midshipmen clung to the belief that women did not belong at the Academy. As a result, black female midshipmen faced discrimination and disparities because of gender as well as race.

Nevertheless, by the end of the twentieth century, the Naval Academy had become an unparalleled opportunity for African American men and women.

Black midshipmen who cleared the academic hurdle obtained a first-class education and entrée into the naval profession or a lucrative civilian career. An Academy ring did not guarantee that a black person would rise to the Navy's senior ranks, attain top positions in government, or make a million dollars in civilian careers, but African American alumni have climbed to such heights, and they have the Naval Academy to thank for their start.

▲ Midshipmen standing in formation at a change of command ceremony, 29 June 1990. Department of Defense photo by Jeff Elliott.

◄ Napoleon McCallum, Class of 1986, running with football, c. 1985. Department of Defense photo by Phil Hoffman.

Black fourth classman reaching the top of Herndon Monument. *Lucky Bag,* 1986, Nimitz Library, United States Naval Academy.

David M. Robinson, Class of 1987, scoring. *Lucky Bag,* 1987, Nimitz Library, United States Naval Academy.

During the 1980s and '90s, drawings featuring the company nickname appeared before group photographs of the midshipmen in each company in Academy yearbooks. This drawing precedes the 15th Company photographs and symbolizes the attitude of many male midshipmen toward women in that period. *Lucky Bag,* 1986, Nimitz Library, United States Naval Academy.

Ingrid Turner, Class of 1986. *Lucky Bag*, 1986, Nimitz Library, United States Naval Academy.

Tracey James, Class of 1992. *Lucky Bag*, 1992, Nimitz Library, United States Naval Academy.

Nikki Peoples, Class of 1997. *Lucky Bag*, 1997, Nimitz Library, United States Naval Academy.

Jacqueline Jackson, Class of 1999. *Lucky Bag*, 1999, Nimitz Library, United States Naval Academy.

Reuben Brigety, Class of 1995, shaking hands with Adm. Charles R. Larson, superintendent of the Naval Academy, at the Dedication Parade held during Commissioning Week, May 1995. *Lucky Bag,* 1995, Nimitz Library, United States Naval Academy.

Capt. Bruce Grooms (left) standing beside Wesley A. Brown during the ground-breaking ceremony for the Wesley Brown Field House at the Naval Academy, 25 March 2006. Department of Defense photo by Matt Jarvis.

Notes

Abbreviations

BD	MacGregor, Morris J., and Bernard C. Nalty, eds. *Blacks in the United States Armed Forces: Basic Documents*, 13 vols. Wilmington, Del.: Scholarly Resources, 1977
CG	Candidate Guidance Papers, 1984–92, United States Naval Academy Records, United States Naval Academy Archives, Nimitz Library, United States Naval Academy, Annapolis, Md.
CNOSGR	U.S. Navy Department, Chief of Naval Operations, *CNO Study Group's Report on Equal Opportunity in the Navy* (Washington, D.C.: Office of the Chief of Naval Operations, 1988)
MPJ	Midshipman Personnel Jackets, Special Collections and Archives Division, Nimitz Library, United States Naval Academy, Annapolis, Md.
NAACPLC	National Association for the Advancement of Colored People Papers, Library of Congress, Washington, D.C.
OA	Operational Archives, Naval Historical Center, Washington, D.C.
RG 319	Records of the Army Staff, National Archives and Records Administration, Washington, D.C.
RG 405	Records of the United States Naval Academy, Annapolis, Md.
SR	Superintendent's Records, United States Naval Academy Records, Special Collections and Archives Division, Nimitz Library, United States Naval Academy, Annapolis, Md.
USNA	United States Naval Academy, Annapolis, Md.
USNACH	United States Naval Academy Command Histories, Special Collections and Archives Division, United States Naval Academy, Annapolis, Md.

Preface

1. Reminiscences of R. Adm. Draper L. Kauffman, Oral History Department, United States Naval Institute, vol. 2, 808–21.

Chapter 1

1. Adm. Joseph Paul Reason, Oral History, U.S. Naval Institute.

2. For a brief overview of the history of African Americans in the U.S. Navy through the Korean War, see Bernard C. Nalty, *Long Passage To Korea, Black Sailors*

and the Integration of the U.S. Navy (Washington, D.C.: Government Printing Office, 2003).

3. Morris MacGregor, *Integration of the Armed Forces, 1940–1965* (Washington, D.C.: Government Printing Office, 1981), 67–68.

4. MacGregor, *Integration of the Armed Forces,* 72.

5. Circular Letter No. 48–46, 27 February 1946, *BD* 7:407; "Freedom to Serve," 1950, *BD* 11:1381; Bernard Nalty, *Strength for the Fight: A History of Black Americans in the Military* (New York: Free Press, 1986), 210.

6. U.S. Navy Department, *Annual Report, Fiscal Year 1945,* A-19; Paul to Granger, 27 July 1945, file "U.S. Navy, General, 1940–47," box II B145, NAAC-PLC; Dennis D. Nelson, *The Integration of the Negro into the U.S. Navy* (New York: Farrar, Straus, and Young, 1951), 166–67; Regina Akers, "The Integration of Afro-Americans into the WAVES, 1942–1945" (M.A. thesis, Howard University, 1993).

7. MacGregor, *Integration of the Armed Forces,* 167–69, 236, 245–46, 416; Nalty, *Strength for the Fight,* 210–11, 219–21.

8. For a detailed discussion, see Robert J. Schneller Jr., *Breaking the Color Barrier: The U.S. Naval Academy's First Black Midshipmen and the Struggle for Racial Equality* (New York: New York University Press, 2005).

9. Edward S. Hope, "The Navy Salutes: Dr. Edward S. Hope—First Black CEC Officer," *Navy Civil Engineer* 26 (Winter 1986/87): 32.

10. Developed by a board headed by R. Adm. James L. Holloway Jr., it was dubbed the "Holloway Plan."

11. "The Holloway Plan: A Summary View and Commentary," 21 July 1947, box 49, James V. Forrestal Papers, Seeley G. Mudd Library, Princeton University; MacGregor, *Integration of the Armed Forces,* 247.

12. Hope to Chief of Bureau of Personnel, 17 January 1947, *BD* 8:252–59; MacGregor, *Integration of the Armed Forces,* 246.

13. Hope to Chief of Bureau of Personnel, 17 January 1947, *BD* 8:252–59; MacGregor, *Integration of the Armed Forces,* 248–50.

14. Alan Gropman, *The Air Force Integrates, 1945–1964* (Washington, D.C.: Office of Air Force History, 1985), 77; Nalty, *Strength for the Fight,* 208, 213, 215, 221–22, 236.

15. Harry S. Truman, Executive Order 9981, 26 July 1948, *BD* 8:687–89; William C. Berman, *The Politics of Civil Rights in the Truman Administration* (Columbus: Ohio State University Press, 1970), 97–100; Alan Fried, "And We'll All Be Free: The Role of the Press in the Integration of the United States Army, 1947–1950" (Ph.D. dissertation, University of Florida, 1994), 176; MacGregor, *Integration of the Armed Services,* 303; Nalty, *Strength for the Fight,* 240–42.

16. Berman, *Politics of Civil Rights,* 133.

17. Charles Fahy et al., *Freedom to Serve: Equality of Treatment and Opportunity in the Armed Services: A Report by the President's Committee* (Washington, D.C.: Government Printing Office, 1950), xii, 3, copy in *BD* 11:1355–1438; MacGregor, *Integration of the Armed Forces,* 314–15, 349–50, 375.

18. Fahy, *Freedom to Serve*, 23; MacGregor, *Integration of the Armed Services*, 331; Nalty, *Strength for the Fight*, 243.

19. Minutes, Meeting of the President's Committee on Equality of Treatment and Opportunity in the Armed Services, 26 April 1949, *BD* 10:1147, 1161–65.

20. Fahy et al., *Freedom to Serve*, 24–28.

21. Memorandum for the Chairman Personnel Policy Board, 22 December 1949, *BD* 12:95–98; Fahy et al., *Freedom to Serve*, 16, 27; MacGregor, *Integration of the Armed Forces*, 414; Nelson, *Integration of the Negro into the U.S. Navy*, 116.

22. Fahy et al., *Freedom to Serve*, 28; Paul B. Fay Jr., Memorandum for the Secretary of the Navy, 7 February 1963, file "Chap XXI," box 9, Entry "Integration of Armed Forces 1940–1965," RG 319.

23. Memorandum on Recruitment Trends, 16 July 1963, *BD* 12:527–59.

24. U.S. Bureau of Naval Personnel, "Memo on Discrimination of the Negro," 24 January 1959, *BD* 12:132–40.

25. C. Vann Woodward, *The Strange Career of Jim Crow* (New York: Oxford University Press, 1955), 139–42.

26. Obie Clayton Jr., ed., *An American Dilemma Revisited: Race Relations in a Changing World* (New York: Russell Sage Foundation, 1996), 187; Harvard Sitkoff, *The Struggle for Black Equality, 1954–1981* (New York: Hill and Wang, 1981), 20–23. For Marshall's campaign against *Plessy v. Ferguson*, see Juan Williams, *Thurgood Marshall: American Revolutionary* (New York: Times Books, 1998).

27. William H. Chafe, "America since 1945," in Eric Foner, ed., *The New American History* (Philadelphia: Temple University Press, 1990), 149; Al Hinman, "Confederate Flag Must Come Down, Says S.C. Governor," U.S. News Story Page, CNN Interactive, posted 27 November 1996, http://www.cnn.com/US/9611/27/rebel.flag/index.html; James T. Patterson, *Grand Expectations: The United States, 1945–1974* (New York: Oxford University Press, 1996), 395–98; Sitkoff, *Struggle for Black Equality*, 26–27.

28. Sitkoff, *Struggle for Black Equality*, 30–32.

29. John Hope Franklin and Alfred A. Moss Jr., *From Slavery to Freedom*, 6th ed. (New York: McGraw-Hill), 1988, 443–46; Patterson, *Grand Expectations*, 478–80; Sitkoff, *Struggle for Racial Equality*, 69–96, 129–49; Robert Weisbrot, *Freedom Bound: A History of America's Civil Rights Movement* (New York: Norton, 1990), 38–41, 66–67, 75.

30. Robert Cook, *Sweet Land of Liberty? The African American Struggle for Civil Rights in the Twentieth Century* (New York: Longman, 1998), 122–23; Arthur M. Schlesinger Jr., *A Thousand Days: John F. Kennedy in the White House* (Boston: Houghton Mifflin, 1965), 29, 40, 73; Patterson, *Grand Expectations*, 436–37, 440, 468–85; Sitkoff, *Struggle for Black Equality*, 105–108, 156–58, quoted on 106; Weisbrot, *Freedom Bound*, 45–54, 75–76, Kennedy quoted on 75.

31. Sitkoff, *Struggle for Racial Equality*, 160–61; Weisbrot, *Freedom Bound*, 76–83, King quoted on 82–83.

32. Cook, *Sweet Land of Liberty*, 142–43; Patterson, *Grand Expectations*, 524–

30, 542; Weisbrot, *Freedom Bound*, 87–91; Woodward, *Strange Career of Jim Crow*, 181–85, Johnson quoted on 185–86.

33. Franklin and Moss, *From Slavery to Freedom*, 449; Patterson, *Grand Expectations*, 544–46.

34. Cook, *Sweet Land of Liberty*, 150, 170–71; Patterson, *Grand Expectations*, 552–53; Sitkoff, *Struggle for Black Equality*, 116; Weisbrot, *Freedom Bound*, 95–114; Manning Marable, *Race, Reform and Rebellion: The Second Reconstruction in Black America, 1945–1982* (Jackson: University Press of Mississippi, 1984), 27.

35. Patterson, *Grand Expectations*, 579–80; Sitkoff, *Struggle for Racial Equality*, 187–97; Weisbrot, *Freedom Bound*, 136–49.

36. Patterson, *Grand Expectations*, 582–85, Johnson quoted on 582; Sitkoff, *Struggle for Racial Equality*, 197; Weisbrot, *Freedom Bound*, 152.

37. McNamara, Memorandum for the Secretaries of the Military Departments et al., 24 March 1961, *BD* 12:422; Department of Defense News Release, 27 March 1961, unfiled documents, box 8, Entry "Integration of Armed Forces 1940–1965," RG 319; MacGregor, *Integration of the Armed Forces*, 504, 530.

38. John B. Connally, "Personal Letter. . . . ," 12 May 1961, and Evans, Memorandum for Directorate for Military Personnel, OASD(M), 12 September 1962, file "Chap XX," box 8, Entry "Integration of the Armed Forces 1940–1965," RG 319.

39. Dutton, Memo for Yarmolinsky, 26 October 1961, *BD* 12:452–54; Mac-Gregor, *Integration of the Armed Forces*, 508.

40. Wofford to Runge, 18 September 1961, file "Chap XX," box 8, Entry "Integration of Armed Forces 1940–1965," RG 319; Evans, Memorandum for Mr. Runge, 22 September 1961, and Memorandum for Record, 25 September 1961, *BD* 12:447–51; MacGregor, *Integration of the Armed Forces*, 508; Nalty, *Strength for the Fight*, 276.

41. Dutton, Memo for Yarmolinsky, 26 October 1961, *BD* 12:452–54; Runge, Memorandum for the Under Secretary of the Army et al., 7 November 1961, file "Chap XX," box 8, Entry "Integration of Armed Forces, 1940–1965," RG 319.

42. "The Negro in the Armed Forces: 1963 Report of the U.S. Commission on Civil Rights," *BD* 12:481–559; MacGregor, *Integration of the Armed Services*, 500.

43. Carolyn P. DuBose, *The Untold Story of Charles Diggs: The Public Figure, the Private Man* (Arlington, Va: Barton, 1998), 29–30; MacGregor, *Integration of the Armed Forces*, 503, 520–22, 535; Bruce Ragsdale and Joel D. Treese, *Black Americans in Congress, 1870–1989* (Washington, D.C.: Government Printing Office, 1990), s.v. "Charles Cole Diggs, Jr."; Michael S. Williams, ed. *The African American Encyclopedia*, 6 vols. (New York: Marshall Cavendish, 1993), s.v. "Charles Cole Diggs, Jr."

44. Diggs to McNamara, 12 February 1962, file "Chap XX," box 8, Entry "Integration of Armed Forces 1940–1965," RG 319; Diggs to Kennedy, 27 June 1962, *BD* 12:466–70; Gropman, *Air Force Integrates*, 161, 173; MacGregor, *Integration of the Armed Forces*, 520–22, 530, 534–35.

45. Both McNamara and Adam Yarmolinsky, McNamara's deputy assistant

secretary of defense for international affairs, claim credit for the idea of creating the Gesell Committee. Carl Runge credited Diggs with the idea, as did historian Alan Gropman. See Runge to Diggs, 16 July 1962, file "Chap XX," box 8, Entry "Integration of Armed Forces 1940–1965," RG 319; Gropman, *Air Force Integrates,* 173; MacGregor, *Integration of the Armed Forces,* 530–37; Nalty, *Strength for the Fight,* 280–81.

46. Korth, Memorandum for the Under Secretary of the Navy, 24 January 1963, file "Chap XXI," box 9, Entry "Integration of the Armed Forces 1940–65," RG 319.

47. Gesell to Fay, 6 February 1963, file "Chap XXI," box 9, Entry "Integration of Armed Forces 1940–1965," RG 319; MacGregor, *Integration of the Armed Forces,* 537.

48. Fay, Memorandum for the Secretary of the Navy, 7 February 1963, file "Chap XXI," box 9, Entry "Integration of Armed Forces 1940–1965," RG 319.

49. Chief of Naval Personnel to Presidents, January–February 1963; Smedberg, Memorandum for the Under Secretary of the Navy, 20 May 1963; and Fay, Memorandum for the Secretary of the Navy, 15 July 1963, all in file "Chap XXII," box 10, Entry "Integration of Armed Forces 1940–1965," RG 319.

50. Nathaniel S. Colley et al., "The President's Committee on Equal Opportunity in the Armed Forces: Initial Report: Equality of Treatment and Opportunity for Negro Military Personnel Stationed within the United States," 13 June 1963, *BD* 13:21–93, quotations on 10, 11, 41; Abe Fortas et al., "The President's Committee on Equal Opportunity in the Armed Forces: Final Report: Military Personnel Stationed Overseas and Membership and Participation in the National Guard," November 1964, *BD* 13:125–52; MacGregor, *Integration of the Armed Forces,* 544–45.

51. Secretary of the Navy, Memorandum for the Assistant Secretary of Defense (Manpower), 10 July 1963, file "Chap XXI," box 9, Entry "Integration of Armed Forces 1940–1965," RG 319.

52. Robert S. McNamara, Department of Defense Directive 5120.36, 26 July 1963, *BD* 13:174–76; Editorial comment, *BD* 13:249; MacGregor, *Integration of the Armed Forces,* 548, 556.

53. Robert S. McNamara, Department of Defense Directive 5120.36, 26 July 1963, *BD* 13:174–76; Paul B. Fay, "Outline Plan for Implementing . . . Directive 5120.36," n.d., *BD* 13:244–46; Norman S. Paul, Memorandum for the Under Secretary of the Navy, 13 September 1963, *BD* 13:247; MacGregor, *Integration of the Armed Forces,* 561–64; Nalty, *Strength for the Fight,* 290.

54. Secretary of the Navy Instruction 5350.6, "Equal Opportunity and Treatment of Military Personnel," January 1965, and Memorandum for Mr. Paul, Policy Formulation, Planning and Action in the Office of the Deputy Assistant Secretary of Defense (Civil Rights), 21 September 1965, file "Chap XXII," box 10, Entry "Integration of Armed Forces 1940–1965," RG 319; U.S. Department of the Navy, *CNO Study Group's Report on Equal Opportunity in the Navy* (Washington, D.C.: Office of the Chief of Naval Operations, 1988), 1-A-2; MacGregor, *Integration of the Armed Forces,* 564–66.

55. Public Law 88–276, 3 March 1964, *United States Statutes at Large*, vol. 78 (Washington. D.C.: Government Printing Office, 1965), 148–53; Statement by R. Adm. Charles S. Minter, 5 March 1964, in "Report of the Board of Visitors to the United States Naval Academy, 1964," box 2, Entry 209A, Reports of Boards and Committees, Reports of the Board of Visitors, 1936–1977, RG 405; U.S., Department of the Navy, Bureau of Naval Personnel, *United States Naval Academy Admissions Regulations, 1965* (Washington, D.C.: Bureau of Naval Personnel, 1964), 5–10; R. L. Field, "The Black Midshipman at the U.S. Naval Academy," *Proceedings* 99 (April 1973): 31–33.

56. "Recapitulation of Admissions (4th Class) Class of 1963," 2 November 1959, folder 4, box 5, Entry 39B Records of the Superintendent, General Correspondence, Midshipmen, Policy and Administration, 1927–1964, RG 405; "Negroes Admitted to the U.S. Naval Academy as Midshipmen," n.d., U.S. Naval Academy Institutional Research office; The United States Naval Academy Alumni Association, Inc. *Register of Alumni: Graduates and Former Midshipmen and Naval Cadets* (Annapolis, Md.: U.S. Naval Academy Alumni Association, 1997). The total number of African Americans appointed—*including* those not admitted—cannot be determined for this or any other period. The Naval Academy has never kept permanent records on appointees not admitted, nor has every member of Congress.

57. "Negroes Admitted to the U.S. Naval Academy as Midshipmen," n.d., U.S. Naval Academy Institutional Research office; U.S. Naval Academy, *Annual Register of the United States Naval Academy*, 1959 (Washington. D.C.: Government Printing Office, 1959), 107–132.

58. "Negroes Admitted to the U.S. Naval Academy as Midshipmen," n.d., U.S. Naval Academy Institutional Research office; Bruce Ragsdale, ed., *Biographical Directory of the United States Congress, 1774–1989* (Washington, D.C.: Government Printing Office, 1989).

59. Schneller, *Breaking the Color Barrier*, 163–64, 175–77.

60. "Negroes Admitted to the U.S. Naval Academy as Midshipmen," n.d., U.S. Naval Academy Institutional Research Office; Lt. Cdr. Wesley Anthony Brown, Oral History, U.S. Naval Institute; Stanley Jerome Carter, interview by author, 5 January 2000; Ragsdale and Treese, *Black Americans in Congress*, s.v. "William Levi Dawson," "Charles Cole Diggs, Jr.," "Augustus Freeman Hawkins," "Robert Nelson Cornelius Nix, Sr.," and "Adam Clayton Powell, Jr." For detailed discussions of black congressmen's efforts to integrate the Academy through World War II, see Schneller, *Breaking the Color Barrier.*

61. Adm. Joseph Paul Reason, Oral History, U.S. Naval Institute.

62. *Pittsburgh Courier*, 4 June 1960; Carter interview; "Negroes Admitted to the U.S. Naval Academy as Midshipmen," n.d., U.S. Naval Academy Institutional Research Office; U.S. Naval Academy, *Annual Register*, 1962, 179.

63. U.S. Congress, House, Office of the Historian, *Women in Congress, 1917–1990* (Washington, D.C.: Government Printing Office, 1991), s.v. "Edna Flannery Kelly."

64. Malvin D. Bruce, interview by author, 9 April 1998.

65. Patrick M. Prout, interview by author, 6 August 1999.

66. Cohelan to Berquist, 19 May 1959, Chief of Naval Personnel to Superintendent, 26 May 1959, and Superintendent to Chief of Naval Personnel, 19 June 1959,
folder 4, box 5, Entry 39B, Records of the Superintendent, General Correspondence, Midshipmen, Policy and Administration, RG 405; and Chief of Naval
Personnel to Superintendent, 10 August 1959, folder 9, box 5, Entry 39B, Records
of the Superintendent, General Records, Midshipmen, Brigade of Midshipmen, RG
405; "Negroes Admitted to the U.S. Naval Academy as Midshipmen," n.d., U.S.
Naval Academy Institutional Research Office.

67. Ruth D. Wilson, "Statement of American Civil Liberties Union concerning
Segregation and Discrimination in the U.S. Navy, Submitted to the Department of
the Navy, June, 1955," *BD* 12:303–308.

68. Carter interview; Prout interview; Abraham R. Stowe, interview by author, 8
June 1999; Taylor interview; Chancellor A. Tzomes, interview by author, 24 August
1999. The 1950–65 editions of the *Pittsburgh Courier* contain few articles on the
Navy and even fewer on the Academy. Similarly, very few articles published in *Ebony*
and *Jet* during this period mention the Academy, and those that do are very short.

69. Fay, Memorandum for the Secretary of the Navy, 7 February 1963, file
"Chap XXI," box 9, Entry "Integration of Armed Forces 1940–1965," RG 319;
Superintendent, U.S. Naval Academy to Secretary of the Navy, 10 November 1950,
folder 8, box 5, "Brigade of Midshipmen," Entry 39B, RG 405.

70. Parry to White, 31 July 1951, policy statement, 31 August [sic] 1951;
Lochard to Superintendent, 2 October 1951; and Parry to Lochard, 10 October
1951, all in folder 9, box 5, "Brigade of Midshipmen," Entry 39B, RG 405.

71. *Afro-American,* 13 June 1953.

72. Heise to Marchbanks, 30 November 1954; Heise to Hagan, 1 December
1954; statement by "ESD," 14 January 1958; and Heise to Thompson, 2 April
1958, all in folder 9, box 5, "Brigade of Midshipmen," Entry 39B, RG 405.

73. Stowe interview; Tzomes interview; Norman quoted in Gerald Astor, *The
Right to Fight: A History of African Americans in the Military* (Novato, Calif.:
Presidio, 1998), 425.

74. Fay, Memorandum for the Secretary of the Navy, 7 February 1963, file
"Chap XXI," box 9, Entry "Integration of Armed Forces 1940–1965," RG 319;
Memorandum for the Secretary of the Navy, 4 August 1965, "Naval Academy" file,
1966 box 34, 00 Files, OA; Memorandum for Mr. Paul, 21 September 1965, file
"Chap XXII," box 10, Entry "Integration of Armed Forces 1940–1965," RG 319;
MacGregor, *Integration of the Armed Forces,* 569–70.

Chapter 2

1. Unless otherwise cited, chapters 2–5 are based on the following: Lou Adams,
interview by author, 19 July 1999; Harold S. Bauduit, interview by author, 13 July
1999; Charles F. Bolden Jr., interview by Cathleen Lewis and Ian Cooke, National

Air and Space Museum, 13 February 1995, and interview by author, 4 and 11 December 2000; Wesley A. Brown, interviews by author, 19 December 1995 (first interview), 23 January 1997 (second interview), 17 October 1997 (third interview), 17 December 1998 (fourth interview), 16 September 1999 (fifth interview); Malvin D. Bruce, interview by author, 9 April 1998; Willie Z. Byrd, MPJ; Stanley J. Carter Jr., interview by author, 5 January 2000; Lawrence C. Chambers, interview by author, 7 November 1996, and MPJ; Kevin F. Delaney, interview by author, 18 November 1999; Richard A. Drew, MPJ; George M. Fennel Jr., MPJ; James Frezzell, interview by author, 2 August 1999, and MPJ; Floyd Grayson, interview by author, 5 May 2000; Lucius P. Gregg Jr. to author, 20 March 2001; John T. Jackson III, interview by author, 10 August 1999; William C. Jones, interview by author, 30 November 1999; Robert G. Lucas, interview by author, 2 December 1999; Donald McCray, MPJ; Charles S. Minter Jr., interview by author, 18 May 2000; James K. Orzech, interview by author, 24 August 1999; Patrick M. Prout, interview by author, 6 August 1999; John D. Raiford to author, 13 December 2000 and 30 January 2001; Adm. Joseph Paul Reason, Oral History, U.S. Naval Institute; Edward A. Sechrest, MPJ; David F. Simmons to author, 4 August 1999; Reeves R. Taylor, interview by author, 2 December 1996, letter to author, 15 January 1997, and MPJ; Chancellor A. Tzomes, interview by author, 24 August 1999.

2. U.S. Census Bureau, "Race for the United States, Regions, Divisions, and States: 1950," http://www.census.gov/population/documentation/twps0056/tabA-09.pdf, downloaded 16 August 2006; U.S. Census Bureau, "Race for the United States, Regions, Divisions, and States: 1960," http://www.census.gov/population/documentation/twps0056/tabA-08.pdf, downloaded 16 August 2006.

3. U.S. Census Bureau, "Educational Attainment, by Race and Hispanic Origin: 1960 to 1998," http://www.census.gov/prod/99pubs/99statab/sec04.pdf, downloaded 16 August 2006; William H. Chafe, "The Gods Bring Threads to Webs Begun," *Journal of American History* 86 (March 2000): 1531–51; Pete Daniel, *The Shadow of Slavery: Peonage in the South, 1901–1969* (Urbana: University of Illinois Press, 1990); Franklin and Moss, *From Slavery to Freedom;* Gunnar Myrdal, *An American Dilemma: The Negro Problem and Modern Democracy,* 2 vols. (New York: Harper, 1944); Joel Williamson, "Wounds Not Scars: Lynching, the National Conscience, and the American Historian," *Journal of American History* 83 (March 1997): 1221–53; Woodward, *Strange Career of Jim Crow.*

4. Schneller, *Breaking the Color Barrier,* 166–76.

5. Schneller, *Breaking the Color Barrier,* 175–78.

6. Although Reason earned enough merit badges, he did not become an eagle scout, for political reasons. He did, however, become a life scout.

7. Jack Sweetman, *The U.S. Naval Academy: An Illustrated History* (Annapolis, Md.: Naval Institute Press, 1979), 213.

8. *Afro-American,* 25 June 1955.

9. Paul Reason to Joseph Reason, 18 May 1961, Adm. J. Paul Reason, Personal Papers, Special Collections and Archives Division, Nimitz Library, USNA.

Chapter 3

1. U.S. Naval Academy, *Regulations of the U.S. Naval Academy, 1945* (Annapolis, Md.: U.S. Naval Academy, 1945); David F. Sellers, "The United States Naval Academy: It Belongs to the Fleet," *Proceedings* 62 (October 1936): 1433.

2. U.S. Naval Academy, *Regulations of the U.S. Naval Academy, 1945;* Kendall Banning, *Annapolis Today,* 5th ed. (Annapolis, Md.: U.S. Naval Institute, 1957), 21.

3. Ross Mackenzie, *Brief Points: An Almanac for Parents and Friends of U.S. Naval Academy Midshipmen* (Annapolis, Md.: Naval Institute Press, 1993), 39–55.

4. "Parents of USNA Midshipman" website, http://www.usna-parents.org/resources/plebesummer.htm, downloaded 27 March 2006.

5. Schneller, *Breaking the Color Barrier,* 193.

6. Paul Reason to Joseph Reason, 4 June 1961, Adm. J. Paul Reason, Personal Papers, Special Collections and Archives Division, Nimitz Library, USNA.

7. Ingrid Bowers, *A Greater Challenge: U.S. Naval Academy Black History* (Bethesda, Md.: Phase II Productions, 1979), video documentary.

8. U.S. Congress, Senate, *The United States Naval Academy: A Sketch Containing the History, Entrance Requirements, Curriculum, Athletics, After Graduation Service, and Other Factual Information,* S. doc. 181, 75th Cong., 3d sess., 1938, pp. 32–34.

9. W. D. Puleston, *Annapolis: Gangway to the Quarterdeck* (New York: D. Appleton-Century, 1942), 206.

10. Banning, *Annapolis Today,* 37–46; Norlin J. Jankovsky, ed., *Reef Points, 1945–1946* (Annapolis, Md.: United States Naval Academy, 1945), 88.

11. Jankovsky, *Reef Points,* 39. For specific anecdotes, see Jimmy Carter, "Excerpts from President Carter's Speech in the Naval Academy Chapel," *Shipmate* (September 1996): 12; Jimmy Carter, *Why Not the Best?* (Nashville, Tenn.: Broadman, 1975), 43; Joseph P. Flanagan, interview by author, 19 March 1997; Howard A. Weiss, interview by author, 11 May 1996 (first interview); Richard E. Whiteside, interview by author, 9 October 1996.

12. Schneller, *Breaking the Color Barrier,* 185.

13. Taylor interview; Reeves R. Taylor, to author, 15 January 1997; "Fourth Class Organization—Officers," 24 June 1949, folder 3, box 1, Entry 39B, Records of the Superintendent, General Correspondence, Office of the Commandant, 1926–1956, Commandant of Midshipmen, RG 405.

14. Sheldon Harris, interview by author, 15 May 2001; U.S. Naval Academy, *Reef Points 1936–1937* (Annapolis, Md.: Naval Academy, 1936), 157; Trident Society, ed., *The Book of Navy Songs* (New York: Doubleday, 1937), 32, 126; U.S. Congress, Senate, *Centennial of the United States Naval Academy, 1845–1945,* S. Doc. 91, 79th Cong., 1st sess., 1945, 11; Puleston, *Annapolis,* 237; Paul E. Tobin Jr., to author, 27 March 2006, containing material from a Naval Academy "concerned alumni" blog. Although the Navy song book cited above is the 1937 edition, midshipmen present during Wesley Brown's time knew the songs. Although the word "moke" is absent from 1945–75 editions of *Reef Points,* the 1970/71 edition contains the following

term: "MOC (Rhymes with Coke)—Marine Officer Candidate, the local sanitation man on each deck of Mother 'B.'" (165). Sheldon Harris, who worked as a janitor in Bancroft Hall for thirty-five years (1948–83), recalls that midshipmen's use of the term "moke" faded toward the end of his employment there.

15. Bernice Lott and Diane Maluso, eds., *The Social Psychology of Interpersonal Discrimination* (New York: Guilford, 1995), xi–xii, 4.

16. Wilks received an honorable discharge for academic deficiency after the first semester.

17. Philip L. Brown, *The Other Annapolis, 1900–1950* (Annapolis, Md.: Annapolis Publishing, 1994).

18. Paul Reason to Dr. and Mrs. Reason, 28 August 1961, Personal Papers of Adm. J. Paul Reason, Special Collections and Archives Division, Nimitz Library, USNA.

19. Paul Reason to Dr. and Mrs. Reason, 21 November 1961, Personal Papers of Adm. J. Paul Reason, Special Collections and Archives Division, Nimitz Library, USNA.

20. Schneller, *Breaking the Color Barrier,* 211–34.

21. Leighton W. Smith, interview by John D. Sherwood, 22 January 2001.

22. Schneller, *Breaking the Color Barrier,* 205–207.

23. Ernest B. Brown, to author, 26 July 1999.

24. Milton Gussow, interview by author, 27 October 1997; Milton Gussow, to author, 18 September 1997.

Chapter 4

1. Lt. Cdr. Wesley Anthony Brown, Oral History, U.S. Naval Institute; Chambers interview; Taylor interview; U.S. Naval Academy, *Lucky Bag,* 1949.

2. Schneller, *Breaking the Color Barrier,* 222.

3. *Washington Post,* 4 March 2004.

4. Program, "Home Going Service for Our Beloved Lillie Mae Chase," author's files; *The Capital,* 9 March 2001.

5. *Washington Post,* 13 May 1960; *Washington Star,* 4 June 1961 and 24 March 1963.

6. John Greenya, "Black Man on a White Field," *Washington Post Magazine,* 1 February 2004, 16–18, 26–28.

7. "Negroes Admitted to the U.S. Naval Academy as Midshipmen," n.d., U.S. Naval Academy Institutional Research Office.

Chapter 5

1. *New York Times,* 6 May 1969; Jack Engeman, *Annapolis: The Life of a Midshipman* (New York: Lothrop, Lee, and Shepard, 1965), 53; Sweetman, *U.S. Naval Academy,* 211–12.

2. *New York Times,* 6 May 1969.

3. *New York Times,* 6 May 1969.

4. John A. Fitzgerald, "Changing Patterns of Officer Recruitment at the U.S. Naval Academy," *Armed Forces and Society* 8 (Fall 1981): 111–28.

5. *Jet*, 26 May 1960, 7.

6. "Negroes Admitted to the U.S. Naval Academy as Midshipmen," n.d., U.S. Naval Academy Institutional Research Office.

7. Class standing data and average percentile calculated from "Negroes Admitted to the U.S. Naval Academy as Midshipmen," n.d., U.S. Naval Academy Institutional Research Office, and U.S. Naval Academy, *Annual Register*, 1952–69 editions.

8. U.S. Naval Academy, *Regulations of the United States Naval Academy, 1945*, 46–48; Reeves R. Taylor, interview by author, 2 December 1996. "Negroes Admitted to the U.S. Naval Academy as Midshipmen," n.d., U.S. Naval Academy Institutional Research Office, and U.S. Naval Academy, *Annual Register*, 1952–69 editions.

9. Bruce interview; Prout interview.

10. Chambers interview; Grayson interview.

11. *Afro-American*, 9 June 1956, 13 June 1964.

12. *Afro-American*, 6 January 1955.

13. June Week was renamed "Commissioning Week" in 1979, when the Academy moved graduation to May.

14. Statistics compiled from U.S. Naval Academy, *Annual Register*, 1952–69 editions. Statistics from the class of 1959 served as the basis for comparison with black midshipmen. See also Mackenzie, *Brief Points*, 45–46.

15. Gerald L. Hoewing and Delilah D. Rumburg et al., *Report of the Defense Task Force on Sexual Harassment & Violence at the Military Service Academies* (Washington, D.C.: Government Printing Office, June 2005), ES1.

16. Lt. Cdr. Wesley Anthony Brown, Oral History, U.S. Naval Institute; Brown, first interview; Official Service and Medical Record, s.v. Wesley Anthony Brown, service number 521291, National Personnel Records Center, St. Louis, Mo.; *Baltimore Sun*, 17 March 1998; resume and letter, Ryan to Brown, 5 June 2002, courtesy of Wesley A. Brown.

17. Robert A. Rosenberg, "The Annapolis Connection: The Salty Saga of Naval Academy Graduates Who Rose to Star Rank in the Air Force," *Air Force Magazine* 67 (February 1984): 74–78.

18. Official Biography for Charles F. Bolden Jr., http://www.usmc.mil, 11 May 2000.

19. "Negroes Admitted to the U.S. Naval Academy as Midshipmen," n.d., U.S. Naval Academy Institutional Research Office.

20. U.S. Bureau of Naval Personnel, "Memo on Discrimination of the Negro," 24 January 1959, *BD* 12:132–40.

21. Other than in Wesley Brown's case; see Schneller, *Breaking the Color Barrier*, 197–234.

Chapter 6

1. Johnson, Memorandum for the Secretary of the Navy, 3 July 1965, file 1531, 1967 box 13, 00 Files, OA.

2. Patterson, *Grand Expectations*, 524–71, Johnson quoted on 524 and 562.

3. Cook, *Sweet Land of Liberty*, 260–61; Marable, *Race, Reform, and Rebellion*, 210; Patterson, *Grand Expectations*, 642, 723–24; Weisbrot, *Freedom Bound*, 293; Williams, *African American Encyclopedia*, s.v. "affirmative action."

4. Johnson, Memorandum for the Secretary of the Navy, 3 July 1965, file 1531, 1967 box 13, 00 Files, OA; *Washington Star*, 20 July 1965; UPI wires 154 and 159, 3 August 1965, "Naval Academy" file, 1966 box 34, 00 Files, OA; *Washington Post*, 4 August 1965; Reminiscences of R. Adm. Draper L. Kauffman, Oral History Department, United States Naval Institute, vol. 2, 808–21.

5. Officer Biographical Files, s.v. "Draper L. Kauffman," OA.

6. Reminiscences of R. Adm. Draper L. Kauffman, Oral History Department, United States Naval Institute, 2: 808–21; Lucas interview.

7. Nitze, Memorandum for the President, 5 August 1965, file 1531, 1967 box 13, 00 Files, OA.

8. Reminiscences of R. Adm. Draper L. Kauffman, Oral History Department, United States Naval Institute, 2: 808–21.

9. "Report of the Board of Visitors to the United States Naval Academy," 5 November 1965, pp. 5–6, 15, box 2, Entry 209A, RG 405; Reminiscences of R. Adm. Draper L. Kauffman, Oral History Department, United States Naval Institute, 2: 808–21; Lucas interview.

10. "Report of the Board of Visitors to the United States Naval Academy," 5 November 1965, box 2, Entry 209A, RG 405.

11. McNamara, "Memorandum for Educators," 6 October 1965, file "Chap XXII," box 10, Entry "Integration of the Armed Forces 1940–1965," RG 319.

12. "Bugle Call for Negro Cadets," *Ebony*, June 1966, 73–78.

13. Taylor interview; *Afro-American*, 2 May 1970.

14. Abraham R. Stowe, interview by author, 29 January 2000; *New York Times*, 25 October 1965; *Christian Science Monitor*, 4 September 1967; *Navy Times*, 8 November 1967; *Washington Post*, 28 October 1967; Photos NH 76534-KN and NH 76528-KN, Curator Branch, Naval Historical Center, Washington, D.C.; *CNOSGR*, 1–7, 1-A-2; Byron A. Wiley, "Equal Opportunity: Challenge to Navy's Management," *Proceedings* 96 (September 1970): 36; John W. Bodnar, "How Long Does It Take to Change a Culture? Integration at the U.S. Naval Academy," *Armed Forces and Society* 25 (Winter 1999): 301; Nalty, *Strength for the Fight*, 314.

15. Herbert R. Northrup et al., *Black and Other Minority Participation in the All-Volunteer Navy and Marine Corps* (Philadelphia: Industrial Research Unit, Wharton School, University of Pennsylvania, 1979), 3; Nalty, *Strength for the Fight*, 313; Wiley, "Equal Opportunity," 36.

16. "Report of the Board of Visitors to the United States Naval Academy," 5 November 1965, pp. 5–6, 15, box 2, Entry 209A, RG 405; Long, Memorandum for the Executive Assistant and Senior Aide to the Chief of Naval Personnel, 6 December 1967, file 1531, box 13, 00 Files, OA; Fitt, Memorandum for the Under Secretaries of the Army and Air Force, 27 December 1967, file 1531, 1967 box 13, 00 Files, OA; Reminiscences of R. Adm. Draper L. Kauffman, Oral History Department, United States Naval Institute, 2: 817.

17. Long, Memorandum for the Executive Assistant and Senior Aide to the Chief of Naval Personnel, 6 December 1967, file 1531, 001967 box 13, 00 Files, OA; Baird, Memorandum for the President, 26 December 1967, file 1531, 1967 box 13, 00 Files, OA. One of the African American graduates of the class of 1971, a turnback from the class of 1970, was not listed among those who entered in 1967.

18. Rhinelander, Memorandum for Mr. Baird, 6 December 1967, file 1531, 1967 box 13, 00 Files, OA; "Report of the Board of Visitors to the United States Naval Academy," 5 May 1965, pp. 31–32, box 2, Entry 209A, RG 405.

19. "Report of the Board of Visitors to the United States Naval Academy," 5 May 1965, pp. 31–32, box 2, Entry 209A, RG 405; "The Superintendent's Report to the Naval Academy Alumni Association, June 1965–June 1968," 1968 folder, entry 5213/36, SR.

20. James F. Calvert, *Silent Running: My Years on a World War II Attack Submarine* (New York: Wiley, 1995), 274–75.

21. James F. Calvert, interview by author, 10 August 2000; USNACH, 1970/71, vol. 1, 6.

22. "Report of the Board of Visitors to the United States Naval Academy," 5 May 1965, pp. 31–32, box 2, Entry 209A, RG 405; Calvert interview.

23. Superintendent, USNA Instruction 5420.16, 14 March 1969, folder 4, box 1, and DRCG (Director Recruitment and Candidate Guidance Instruction) 5450.1, 6 January 1970, Record Group 1, Sub Group Office of the Superintendent, series Superintendent's Office Files, Box Vice Admiral James Calvert, USN/Reference Files, Naval Academy Records (unprocessed), USNA; "Report of the Board of Visitors to the United States Naval Academy," 1 December 1969, folder 4, box 2, entry 209A, RG 405; Calvert to Anderson, 22 December 1970, Record Group 1, Sub Group Office of the Superintendent, series Personal/Private Affairs, Box 8, Naval Academy Records (unprocessed), USNA; McMullen to Bafalis, 24 March 1975, file 1531 1 January–28 February, 1975 box 13, 00 Files, OA; Calvert interview.

24. Edwin D. Etherington, "Recruiting and Admissions, United States Naval Academy," August 1968, folder 4, box 3, RG-11, Standing Committees Series, Admissions Committee, SR; *Blue and Gold Newsletter,* May 1969, box 4, CG.

25. "Negroes Admitted to the U.S. Naval Academy as Midshipmen," n.d., U.S. Naval Academy Institutional Research Office.

26. Chief of Naval Personnel to Commanding Officer, Naval Academy Preparatory School, 19 December 1968, BuPers Notice 5400, 11 January 1969, Commanding Officer, Naval Academy Preparatory School to Chief of Naval Personnel, 18 February 1969, and Frosch to Teague, 28 February 1969, folder 4, box 3, Record Group 1 Superintendent, Sub Group Office of the Superintendent, series Superintendent's Office Files, Box Contents Vice Admiral James Calvert, USN/Reference Files, RG 405; BOOST, September 1988, file "BOOST-Class of 1989," box 1, CG; Field, "Black Midshipman," 34–35; James Talmadge Jackson Jr. and Mario Renara Maddox, "The Role of the Broadened Opportunity for Officer Selection and Training (BOOST) Program in Supporting the Navy's Minority Accession Policies"

(unpublished M.S. thesis, Naval Postgraduate School, Monterey, Calif., 1990), 8, 28, 32, 54. In 1973, the Navy expanded the scope of BOOST to include "all educationally disadvantaged individuals"; Norman, Memo for Executive Assistant to CNO (OP-002), 7 February 1973, folder 7, drawer 4, safe 3, Adm. Elmo R. Zumwalt Personal Papers, OA.

27. Officer Biographical Files, s.v. "Elmo R. Zumwalt, Jr.," OA; Astor, *Right to Fight,* 445–46; Thomas C. Hone, *Power and Change: The Administrative History of the Office of the Chief of Naval Operations, 1946–1986* (Washington, D.C.: Government Printing Office, 1989), 85.

28. Elmo R. Zumwalt Jr., *On Watch: A Memoir* (New York: Quadrangle, 1976), 168.

29. Norman Friedman, "Elmo Russell Zumwalt, Jr.," in Robert W. Love Jr., ed., *The Chiefs of Naval Operations* (Annapolis, Md.: Naval Institute Press, 1980), 365–79; James D. Hessman, "Z Is for Z-Gram," *Armed Forces Journal* 108 (7 December 1970): 30–33, 42. Zumwalt used the term "Z-gram" to personalize the standard Naval Operations messages (NAVOPS) that were originated in the office of the CNO and disseminated to the entire service.

30. Zumwalt, *On Watch,* 198–202; Hessman, "Z Is for Z-Gram," 30.

31. Zumwalt, *On Watch,* 202–204; Chester A. Wright, "The U.S. Navy's Human Resource Management Programs: In the Aftermath of the U.S.S. *Kitty Hawk/Constellation* Racial Incidents" (unpublished paper presented at the 35th Military Operations Research Society Symposium, U.S. Naval Academy, 2 July 1975), 27–28.

32. CNO/VCNO Action Sheet 339–70, 21 August 1970, file 1531, 1970 box 37, 00 Files, OA; CNO/VCNO Action Sheet 677–70, 23 November 1970, file "Equal Opportunity in the Armed Forces 5350/1, 1970–1971," SR.

33. Kinney, Memorandum of the CNO, 15 December 1970, file 1531, 1970 box 37, 00 Files, OA; *Blue and Gold Newsletter,* September 1971, box 4, CG.

34. Norman, Memorandum for the Special Assistant to CNO/VCNO for Decision Coordination, 5 January 1971, and Tidd, Memorandum for the CNO, 13 January 1971, file 1531, 1970 box 37, 00 Files, OA.

35. USNACH, 1970/71, vol. 1, 59; Calvert interview; Calvert, telephone conversation with author, 2 November 2000.

36. *Evening Sun* (Baltimore), 28 September 1970; *Evening Capital* (Annapolis), 21 October 1970; "Report of the Board of Visitors to the United States Naval Academy," 5 December 1970, file 1531, 1971 box 84, 00 Files, OA; Norman, Memorandum for the Special Assistant to CNO/VCNO for Decision Coordination, 5 January 1971, file 1531, 1970 box 37, 00 Files, OA; "Report of the Board of Visitors to the United States Naval Academy," 30 April 1971, file 1531, 1972 box 78, 00 Files, OA; *Evening Sun,* 6 June 1973; Del Malkie, "Blacks at the Naval Academy," *All Hands,* September 1976, 28–31; *Blue and Gold Newsletter,* October 1970 and November 1972, box 4, CG; *Christian Science Monitor,* 6 June 1974; Penny Vahsen, "Blacks in White Hats," *Proceedings* 113 (April 1987): 67.

37. "Negroes Admitted to the U.S. Naval Academy as Midshipmen," n.d., U.S.

Naval Academy Institutional Research Office; *Blue and Gold Newsletter,* July 1971 and July 1972, box 4, CG; U.S. Naval Academy Alumni Association, *Register of Alumni.*

38. *Blue and Gold Newsletter,* September 1971 and November 1972, box 4, CG.

39. http://www.nnoa.org/origin.php and http://www.nnoa.org/mission.php, 28 June 2002.

40. Cook, *Sweet Land of Liberty,* 255–62; Patterson, *Grand Expectations,* 701, 723–25; Weisbrot, *Freedom Bound,* 288, 294–98.

41. Department of Defense Directive 1322.11, 24 June 1971, *BD* 13:441–44; Northrup, *Black and Other Minority Participation,* 14.

42. Secretary of the Navy Instruction 5350.10A, 9 July 1971, *BD* 13:445–46, and BuPers Notice 1611, n.d. [9 July 1971], *BD* 13:440.

43. Whittet, Memo for the CNO, 9 November 1972, folder 7, drawer 4, safe 3, Adm. Elmo R. Zumwalt Personal Papers, OA; Zumwalt, *On Watch,* 220–21; Northrup, *Black and other Minority Participation,* 16–17.

44. Zumwalt, *On Watch,* 210–19, 234–39, 222–33; Nalty, *Strength for the Fight,* 299–326; John Darrell Sherwood, *Black in Blue: Racial Unrest in the Navy during the Vietnam War Era* (New York: New York University Press, 2007). For details on other minor incidents, see folders 6 and 7, drawer 4, and folder 1, drawer 3, safe 3, Adm. Elmo R. Zumwalt Personal Papers, OA.

45. U.S. Department of the Navy, Bureau of Naval Personnel, *Phase II Equal Opportunity/Race Relations Program: Equal Opportunity Program Specialist Consultant Guide, Volume II,* NAVPERS 15260 (Washington, D.C.: Bureau of Naval Personnel, [1974]), III-1; Navy Inspector General, Memorandum for the CNO, "NAVINSGEN Study of the Command Managed Equal Opportunity (CMEO) Program," 9 August 1993, and "EO Overview," n.d., enclosed under Director, Equal Opportunity Division (Pers-61) to Equal Opportunity Review Task Force Member, 23 January 1995, Working Papers, Office of Special Assistant to Minority Affairs, Chief of Naval Personnel; Northrup et al., *Black and Other Minority Participation,* 22–25, 32; Wright, "U.S. Navy's Human Resource Management Programs," 30–39.

46. U.S. Department of the Navy, Bureau of Naval Personnel, *Phase II,* III-1– III-2; *CNOSGR,* 1–10; Navy Inspector General, Memorandum for the CNO, "NAVINSGEN Study of the Command Managed Equal Opportunity (CMEO) Program," 9 August 1993, and "EO Overview," n.d., enclosed under Director, Equal Opportunity Division (Pers-61) to Equal Opportunity Review Task Force Member, 23 January 1995, Working Papers, Office of Special Assistant to Minority Affairs, Chief of Naval Personnel; Northrup et al., *Black and Other Minority Participation,* 15, 23–30; Nalty, *Strength for the Fight,* 326.

47. Nalty, *Strength for the Fight,* 327, 338–39.

48. Northrup et al., *Black and Other Minority Participation,* 33–34, 185.

49. W. Montague Cobb, "New Spirit in the Navy," *Journal of the National Medical Association* 68 (November 1976): 540.

50. William P. Mack, interview with author, 13 November 2000; Reminiscences of V. Adm. William P. Mack, Oral History, U.S. Naval Institute.

51. USNACH, 1971/72, vol. 1, 61–65; "Report of the Board of Visitors to the United States Naval Academy," 5 December 1974, file 1531 1 January–28 February, 1975 box 13, 00 Files, OA; "U.S. Naval Academy Minority Recruiting," 17 February 1988, file "Candidate Guidance Office Goals and Objectives 1983–86 & 1988," box 1, CG.

52. "Negroes Admitted to the U.S. Naval Academy as Midshipmen," n.d., U.S. Naval Academy Institutional Research office; USNACH, 1973/74, vol. 1, 87; Walsh, Memorandum for the CNO, 31 May 1974, file 15311 April–15 June, 1974 box 42, 00 Files, OA; Haynes, Memo for the CNO, 29 May 1975, file 1531 1 June–30 June, 1975 box 14, 00 Files, OA; "Report of the Board of Visitors to the United States Naval Academy," 15–16 July 1975, file 1531 1 July–31 August, 1975 box 14, 00 Files, OA. The first document states that 120 blacks entered in 1973; the second document sets the figure at 112.

53. Haynes, Memo for the CNO, 29 May 1975, file 1531 1 June–30 June, 1975 box 14, 00 Files, OA.

54. Holloway, Memorandum for the Chief of Naval Personnel, 5 June 1975, file 1531 1 June–30 June, 1975 box 14, 00 Files, OA.

55. Bagley to Mack, 27 March 1975, "U.S. Navy Minority Recruiting Communications Pilot Plan for NROTC and U.S. Naval Academy Candidates," 16 April 1975, and Commander, Navy Recruiting Command, to Superintendent, 18 April 1975, file 1531 1 June–30 June, 1975 box 14, 00 Files, OA.

56. *Blue and Gold Newsletter,* June–July–August 1976, box 4, CG; "Report of the Board of Visitors to the United States Naval Academy," 19–20 November 1975, p. 4, file 1531 1 January–10 February, 1976 box 7, 00 Files, OA; "Report of the Board of Visitors to the United States Naval Academy," 29–30 November 1976, file 1531 1 July–31 December, 1976 box 8, 00 Files, OA; "U.S. Naval Academy Minority Recruiting," 17 February 1988, file "Candidate Guidance Office Goals and Objectives 1983–86 & 1988," box 1, CG.

57. "Negroes Admitted to the U.S. Naval Academy as Midshipmen," n.d., U.S. Naval Academy Institutional Research Office.

Chapter 7

1. Franklin and Moss, *From Slavery to Freedom,* 459; Patterson, *Grand Expectations,* 656–62; Sitkoff, *Struggle for Black Equality,* 185–217; Weisbrot, *Freedom Bound,* 154–211, 258.

2. John Whiteclay Chambers II et al., eds., *The Oxford Companion to American Military History* (New York: Oxford University Press, 1999), s.v., "Vietnam Antiwar Movement," "Vietnam War (1960–1975)"; Muhammad Ali quoted in Randall Kennedy, *Nigger: The Strange Career of a Troublesome Word* (New York: Pantheon, 2002), 35–36.

3. Cook, *Sweet Land of Liberty,* 257–62; Patterson, *Grand Expectations,* 701, 723–25, 771–78; Sitkoff, *Struggle for Black Equality,* 211–13; Weisbrot, *Freedom Bound,* 288, 294–98.

4. Cook, *Sweet Land of Liberty,* 264–65; Franklin and Moss, *From Slavery to Freedom,* 463; Patterson, *Grand Expectations,* 731.

5. "Negroes Admitted to the U.S. Naval Academy as Midshipmen," n.d., U.S. Naval Academy Institutional Research Office; U.S. Naval Academy, *Annual Register,* 1969/70.

6. Bodnar, "How Long Does it Take?" 300.

7. Chief of Naval Training to CNO, 15 February 1973; Superintendent, United States Naval Academy, to CNO, 17 April 1973; and OPNAV Notice 5450, 10 August 1973, file 1531, 1973 box 36, 00 Files, OA.

8. "Negroes Admitted to the U.S. Naval Academy as Midshipmen," n.d., U.S. Naval Academy Institutional Research Office.

9. Unless otherwise cited, chapters 7–10 are based on the following: Charles F. Bolden, interview by author, 4 and 11 December 2000; Charlie C. Boyd Jr. to author, 11 February 2000; Lamar C. Chapman III to author, 24 July 1999; Charles D. Cole, interview by author, 27 January 2001; Kenneth D. Dunn to author, 27 August 1999; Scott Fontaine to author, 5 July 1999; Bruce R. Franklin to author, 6 November 2000, and interview by author, 14 November 2000; Joseph B. Freeman, interview by author, 15 November 2000; Edward J. Gilmore, interview by author, 1 December 1999; Boyd E. Graves, interviews by author, 17 November 2000 and 22 March 2001; Everett L. Greene to author, 8 September 1999, and interview by author, 20 September 1999; Ronald O. Grover to author, 10 September 1999; Bruce A. Henry, interview by author, 13 July 1999; Cary Hithon, interview by author, 28 November 2000; Anthony L. Jackson, MPJ and interview by author, 13 July 1999; James T. Jackson Jr., interview by author, 9 September and 5 October 1999; Marvin E. King to author, 4 December 2000; Byron F. Marchant, interview by author, 4 January 2000; William Merrell to author, 17 September 1999; Kerwin E. Miller, interview by author, 12 December 2000; Donald Montgomery, interview by author, 8 September 1999; John Porter to author, 27 December 1999; Lloyd Prince to author, 30 October 2000; Mason C. Reddix, interview by author, 6 January 1997; Richard G. Samuels to author, 16 July 1999, and interview by author, 3 August 1999; Jeffrey K. Sapp, interview by author, 21 September 2006; Anthony J. Watson, interview by author, 10, 18, and 22 October 2001; "Rear Admiral Anthony Watson: From the Projects to the Pentagon," *Ebony,* June 1994, 85–86, and "Watson Takes NAACP Award," in file "Blacks in the Navy, U.S. Naval Academy," Ready Reference Files, OA; Robert D. Watts to author, 3 August 1999, and interview by author, 25 August 1999; Leo V. Williams, interview by author, 16 November 2000.

Chapter 8

1. See for example *Lucky Bag,* 1978, 293, and *Lucky Bag,* 1979, 283.

2. *Evening Sun* (Baltimore), 6 June 1973.

3. *Evening Sun* (Baltimore), 6 June 1973.

4. Kauffman to McDonald, 12 April 1966, file 1351, 1967 box 13, 00 Files, OA; "Report of the Board of Visitors to the United States Naval Academy, 1960," box 2,

Entry 209A, RG 405; draft, "Report of the Middle States Association of Colleges and Secondary Schools Evaluation Team for the United States Naval Academy," March 1966, file 1531, 1967 box 13, 00 files, OA; U.S. Naval Academy, *Annual Register,* 1960, 114; Sweetman, *U.S. Naval Academy,* 215–24.

5. Middendorf, Memo for the Assistant Secretary of Defense (Manpower and Reserve Affairs), 19 February 1975, file 1531 1 January–28 February, 1975 box 13, 00 Files, OA; Sweetman, *U.S. Naval Academy,* 226, 230–33.

6. Calvert interview.

7. Adm. David L. McDonald, Memorandum for the Under Secretary of the Navy, "Plebe Indoctrination Policy at the U.S. Naval Academy," 19 August 1966, and Superintendent, U.S. Naval Academy, to the Chief of Naval Personnel, 1 August 1966, file 1531, 1967 box 12, 00 Files, OA; Hoof to Chief of Naval Personnel, 2 November 1966, file 1531, 1967 box 12, 00 Files, OA.

8. COMDTMIDN (Commandant of Midshipmen) Instruction 1531.2A, 6 August 1964, folder 3, box 5, Entry 3, RG 405; "Fact Sheet" enclosed in Adm. David L. McDonald, Memorandum for the Secretary of the Navy, 26 November 1966, file 1531, 1967 box 12, 00 Files, OA.

9. Kauffman to Semmes, 1 August 1966, file 1531, 1967 box 12, 00 Files, OA; COMDTMIDN Instruction 1531.2A, 17 August 1965, folder 3, box 5, Entry 3, RG 405; Adm. David L. McDonald, Memorandum for the Under Secretary of the Navy, 19 August 1966, file 1531, 1967 box 12, 00 Files, OA.

10. Kauffman to McDonald, 12 April 1966, file 1531, 1967 box 13, 00 Files, OA.

11. *Washington Post,* 2, 3, 5, and 6 April 1966; *Congressional Record,* Senate, 7 April 1966, pp. 7603–7606; Kauffman to McDonald, 12 April 1966, file 1531, 1967 box 13, 00 Files, OA.

12. *Congressional Record,* Senate, 7 April 1966, pp. 7603–7606.

13. Baldwin, Memorandum for the CNO, 27 July 1966, and Semmes, Memorandum for CNO, 1 August 1966, file 1531, 1967 box 12, 00 Files, OA.

14. COMDTMIDN Instruction 1531.2C, 1 August 1966, file 1531, 1967 box 12, 00 Files, OA; Kauffman to Semmes, 1 August 1966, file 1531, box 1967 12, 00 Files, OA; Adm. David L. McDonald, Memorandum for the Under Secretary of the Navy, 19 August 1966, file 1531, 1967 box 12, 00 Files, OA; "Fact Sheet" enclosed in Adm. David L. McDonald, Memorandum for the Secretary of the Navy, 26 November 1966, file 1531, 1967 box 12, 00 Files, OA; Kauffman to Semmes, 29 November 1966, file 1531, 1967 box 12, 00 Files, OA.

15. Hoof to Chief of Naval Personnel, 2 November 1966, file 1531, 1967 box 12, 00 Files, OA; "Fact Sheet" enclosed in Adm. David L. McDonald, Memorandum for the Secretary of the Navy, 26 November 1966, file 1531, 1967 box 12, 00 Files, OA; "The Superintendent's Report to the Naval Academy Alumni Association, June 1965–June 1968," 1968 folder, entry 5213/36, SR.

16. Alex Roland to author, 9 March 2003; http://www.aaup.org/index.htm, 3 October 2003.

17. Seager to Kauffman, 19 October 1966, file 1531, 1967 box 12, 00 Files, OA.

18. Anthony L. Jackson, MPJ and interview with author, 13 July 1999.

19. Hoof to Chief of Naval Personnel, 2 November 1966, file 1531, 1967 box 12, 00 Files, OA; Chief of Naval Personnel to the Secretary of the Navy, 16 December 1966 and 17 January 1967, file 1531, 1967 box 12, 00 Files, OA; R. Adm. Draper Kauffman, Statement to the Board of Visitors, 28 April 1967, file 1531, 1967 box 13, 00 Files, OA; "The Superintendent's Report to the Naval Academy Alumni Association, June 1965–June 1968," 1968 folder, entry 5213/36, SR; *Washington Post*, 7 September 1969; Todd A. Forney, "Four Years Together by the Bay: A Study of the Midshipman Culture at the United States Naval Academy, 1946–1976" (Ph. D. dissertation, Ohio State University, 2000), 400–425.

Chapter 9

1. Program, "Home Going Service for Our Beloved Lillie Mae Chase"; *The Capital*, 9 March 2001 and 4 March 2004.

2. Ethelda Peggy Kimbo, interview by Mame Warren, 28 April 1990, box MSA SC 2140 00/11/10/11, "The Annapolis I Remember Collection," Special Collections, Maryland State Archives, Annapolis, Md.

3. James T. Jackson to author, 24 September 2001.

4. *Lucky Bag*, 1979, 245.

5. Kenneth D. Dunn, conversation with author, 4 March 2004.

6. R. Adm. Lawrence Heyworth Jr., interview with author, 9 August 2000.

7. Samuel P. Massie, "Catalyst: The Autobiography of an American Chemist: Dr. Samuel P. Massie," with Robert C. Hayden (unpublished draft book manuscript, c. May 2001).

8. USNA Notice 12713, 31 July 1975, annex 117, vol. 6, USNACH, 1975/76; USNA Notice 12713, 23 June 1976, annex 14, vol. 2, USNACH, 1976/77; Massie, "Catalyst."

9. *Evening Capital*, 20 June 1967; *Baltimore Sun*, 3 and 4 August 1967.

10. Reminiscences of R. Adm. Draper L. Kauffman, Oral History Department, United States Naval Institute; Lucas interview; Wiley, "Equal Opportunity," 36.

11. Massie, "Catalyst," 37.

12. *Lucky Bag*, 1969–72 editions; *Afro-American*, 14 June 1969.

13. Sweetman, *U.S. Naval Academy*, 163.

14. Academic Dean Notice 5420, 9 December 1969, file "Black Studies Committee 5420/49," SR; *Evening Capital*, 17 April 1970; Massie, "Catalyst."

15. Massie, "Catalyst."

16. *Washington Post*, 22 June 1972.

17. Officer Biographical Files, s.v. "Max K. Morris," OA; Morris, Memorandum for Admiral Zumwalt, 7 September 1972, file 1531, 1972 box 78, 00 Files, OA; USNACH, 1972/73, vol. 1, 56; COMDTMIDN Notice 5420, 31 October 1975, annex 52, vol. 4, USNACH, 1972/73.

18. Morris, Memorandum for Admiral Zumwalt, 7 September 1972, file 1531, 1972 box 78, 00 Files, OA.

19. Morris, Memorandum for Admiral Zumwalt, 7 September 1972, file 1531, 1972 box 78, 00 Files, OA; USNACH,1972/73, vol. 1, 56.

20. "Four at the Helm," *Ebony,* January 1973, 105–107.

21. Officer Biographical Files, s.v. "William P. Mack," OA; William P. Mack, interview with author, 13 November 2000.

22. *Washington Post,* 22 June 1972; Mack interview.

23. Mack interview.

24. Superintendent, USNA Notice 5420, 9 August 1972, annex 36, and Superintendent, USNA Instruction 5420.21, annex 58, USNACH, 1972/73, vol. 4; *Lucky Bag,* 1973–75 editions.

25. "Racial and Minority Affairs Program," 26 March 1974, and Ruland to Leist, 31 May 1974, 1974 folder, entry 5390/1 Human Goals 1973–77, SR; Mack interview.

26. USNACH, 1972/73, vol. 1, 55–56; Statement by the Superintendent, "Report of the Board of Visitors to the United States Naval Academy," 12 April 1973, file 1531, 1973 box 36, 00 Files, OA; Reminiscences of V. Adm. William P. Mack, Oral History, U.S. Naval Institute, 677–78.

27. USNACH, 1972/73, vol. 1, 55–56; Statement by the Superintendent, "Report of the Board of Visitors to the United States Naval Academy," 12 April 1973, file 1531, 1973 box 36, 00 Files, OA.

28. USNA Instruction 5390.1, 21 August 1973, 1973 folder, entry 5390/1 Human Goals 1973–77, SR; USNACH, 1973/74, vol. 1, 74–84; USNACH, 1974/75, vol. 1, 94–99.

29. Vice Chief of Naval Operations, memorandum for the CNO, 30 January 1974, file 1531 1 January–31 March, 1974 box 42, 00 Files, OA; USNACH, 1973/74, vol. 1, 74–84; Reminiscences of V. Adm. William P. Mack, Oral History, U.S. Naval Institute, 674–77; Montgomery interview.

30. Officer Biographical Files, s.v. "Kinnaird R. McKee," OA.

31. USNACH, 1975/76, vol. 1, 96–97.

32. USNA Instruction 5420.21B, 4 December 1975, 1976 folder, entry 5390/1 Human Goals 1973–1977, SR; USNA Notice 5420, 5 March 1976, annex 116, vol. 6, USNACH, 1975/76; USNACH, 1975/76, vol. 1, 95.

33. USNACH, 1975/76, vol. 1, 42, 97; COMDTMIDN Instruction 5390.1C, 11 June 1976, annex 75, vol. 4, USNACH, 1976/77; annex A, vol. 2, USNACH, 1977/78; Reminiscences of V. Adm. William P. Mack, Oral History, U.S. Naval Institute, 677–78.

34. COMDTMIDN Instruction 5390.1C, 11 June 1976, annex 75, vol. 4, USNACH, 1976/77.

35. Superintendent to W .C. Haskell, 8 January 1975, file 5060/27, SR; USNACH, 1974/75, vol. 1, 137; Massie, "Catalyst."

Chapter 10

1. "Negroes Admitted to the U.S. Naval Academy as Midshipmen," n.d., U.S. Naval Academy Institutional Research Office; U.S. Naval Academy Alumni Association, *Register of Alumni.*

2. J. H. Morris, Memorandum for the CNO, 13 July 1973, file 1531, 1973 box 36, 00 Files, OA.

3. U.S. Naval Academy, *Annual Register United States Naval Academy,* 5 June 1974 (Annapolis, Md.: U.S. Naval Academy, 1974), 110; U.S. Naval Academy Alumni Association, *Register,* 482; Jimmy Lawrence, "Colorado Springs' Jeffrey Sapp—He's an Officer and a Gentleman," *Odyssey West* 2 (December 1983): 24–27; Sapp interview.

4. Superintendent to CNO, 17 December 1974, and Vice Chief of Naval Operations, Memo for the Superintendent, 19 February 1975, file 1531 1 January–28 February, 1975 box 13, 00 Files, OA.

5. R. Adm. Kinnaird R. McKee, interview by David Winkler, 21 March 2000, Naval Historical Foundation, Washington, D.C.

6. *Lucky Bag,* 1975, 362–63.

7. U.S. Naval Academy, *Annual Register,* 1969/70 (Washington, D.C.: Government Printing Office, 1969), 163; U.S. Naval Academy, *Annual Register,* 1970/71, 169; Heyworth interview.

8. U.S. Naval Academy, *Annual Register,* 1970/71, 174.

9. "Four at the Helm," 100–106; Bodnar, "How Long Does it Take?" 294, 305.

10. *Afro-American,* 8–12 March 1977.

11. Gary Roughead, interview by author, 27 March 2001.

12. *Afro-American,* 13–17 April and 8–12 June 1976; *Dawn Magazine,* June 1976; *Evening Capital,* 12 April 1976.

13. See Chapter 11.

14. J. Bert Freeman, *Taking Charge of Your Positive Direction* (New Bern, N.C.: Trafford, 2006).

Chapter 11

1. *CNOSGR,* 2-31–2-38, 3-14. The implementation of equal opportunity policy is examined in chapter 14.

2. *CNOSGR,* 3-3; Northrup et al., *Black and Other Minority Participation,* 33–34.

3. Owen D. Corpin, "Development of a Model for Minority Recruitment at the United States Naval Academy" (unpublished Trident Scholar Project Report, 21 May 1974, National Technical Information Service document AD-784 111); *Blue and Gold Newsletter,* June 1977 and May–June 1979, box 4, and Recruiting Objectives Statement, 30 August 1984, file "Candidate Guidance Office Goals and Objectives 1983–86 and 1988," box 1, CG.

4. "Negroes Admitted to the U.S. Naval Academy as Midshipmen," n.d., U.S. Naval Academy Institutional Research Office; Superintendent to CNO, 2 March 1977, file 1531 8 February–30 June, 1977 box 13, 00 Files, OA; Memo, Dean of Admissions to Superintendent, 15 September 1982, file "Letters Signed by Dean of Admissions May '81–Dec. '79," box 4, CG.

5. *Blue and Gold Newsletter,* November 1978, box 4, CG; Northrup et al., *Black and Other Minority Participation,* v, 203.

6. Deputy Chief of Naval Operations (Manpower, Personnel and Training), Memorandum for Director, Military Personnel and Training Division, 28 March 1981, file "Minority Recruiting 1135," 1981, Central Files, Office of the Superintendent, USNA Records, USNA; "POA&M to Implement [1979] Minority Officer Accession Study Recommendations," enclosed under Gelke, Memorandum on Reconvening of the Minority Officer Accession Study Group, 2 April 1981, file "Minority Recruiting 1135," 1981, Central Files, Office of the Superintendent, USNA Records, USNA; Press Release, 18 May 1981, annex 82, vol. 4, USNACH, 1980/81; Hogg, Memorandum, 5 February 1982, "Minority Recruiting 1135," 1982, Central Files, Office of the Superintendent, USNA Records, USNA; *CNOSGR*, 3-3.

7. Memo for the Record, 11 March 1981, file "Minority Recruiting 1135," 1981, Central Files, Office of the Superintendent, USNA Records, USNA.

8. Lawrence, Memorandum for the Director, Military Personnel and Training Division, 13 August 1981, file "Minority Recruiting 1135," 1981, Central Files, Office of the Superintendent, USNA Records, USNA.

9. 1981 Minority Officer Accession Study, enclosed under Hogg, Memorandum, 5 February 1982, "Minority Recruiting 1135," 1982, Central Files, Office of the Superintendent, USNA Records, USNA.

10. *Blue and Gold Newsletter,* Fall 1981, box 4, CG.

11. Press Release, 30 March 1982, annex 71, vol. 5, USNACH, 1981/82.

12. James T. Jackson, interviews with author, 9 September and 5 October 1999.

13. Cary Hithon, interview with author, 28 November 2000.

14. Jackson interview.

15. *Blue and Gold Newsletter,* Spring 1982, box 4, CG.

16. 1981 Minority Officer Accession Study; CNO to Superintendent, 3 September 1982, "Minority Recruiting 1135," 1982, Central Files, Office of the Superintendent, USNA Records, USNA.

17. CNO to Superintendent, 8 September 1982, and Mulloy, Memorandum, 27 September 1982, "Minority Recruiting 1135," 1982, Central Files, Office of the Superintendent, USNA Records, USNA.

18. Memo, Dean of Admissions to Deputy for Management, 25 August 1983, Superintendent, USNA Notice 1531, 13 October 1983, and Recruiting Objectives Statement, 30 August 1984, file "Candidate Guidance Office Goals and Objectives 1983–86 and 1988," box 1, CG; Jackson interview.

19. "ORB Pitch," 5 September 1984, file "Candidate Guidance Office Goals and Objectives 1983–86 and 1988," box 1, CG; Memo, Seymour for the Superintendent, 7 October 1985, file "Captain Chip Seymour, USN, Dir., CGO, File I," box 4, CG; "Negroes Admitted to the U.S. Naval Academy as Midshipmen," n.d., U.S. Naval Academy Institutional Research Office; U.S. Naval Academy Alumni Association, *Register of Alumni*.

20. Penn, Memo for the CNO, 16 April 1984, and Watkins to Larson, 30 April 1984, file 1531 April–June, box 1984, 1531–1600 (September), 00 Files, OA.

21. Penn, Memo for the CNO, 29 June 1984, file 1531 April–June, box 1984 1531–1600 (September), 00 Files, OA.

22. Commander, Naval Military Personnel Command, Memo to the Chief of Naval Personnel, 14 May 1984, file 1531 April–June, 1984 box 1531–1600 (September), 00 Files, OA; "ORB Pitch," 5 September 1984, file "Candidate Guidance Office Goals and Objectives 1983–86 and 1988," box 1, CG; Memo for the Blue and Gold, 21 February 1985, *Blue and Gold Newsletter* file, box 4, CG; Memo, Seymour for the Superintendent, 7 October 1985, file "Captain Chip Seymour, USN, Dir., CGO, File I," box 4, CG; Memo, Superintendent for OP-130, 5 December 1985, file "Captain Chip Seymour, USN, Dir., CGO, File I," box 4, CG; Memo, Director of Candidate Guidance for the Public Affairs Officer, 25 November 1986, file "Capt. H. A. Seymour, Jr., Director Cand. Guidance file II," box 4, CG. Emphasis in original.

23. These seventy-seven accounted for 5.6 percent of the 1,376 midshipmen who entered that summer, still below the 6 percent goal.

24. Seymour, Memo to the Dean of Admissions, 22 July 1985, file "Capt. Chip Seymour, USN, Dir., CGO, File 1," box 4, CG. Newsletters from files "Superintendent's Meeting on Minority Efforts 1987–88" and "Minority Game Plan 1987–88," box 2, CG.

25. Memo, Seymour for the Superintendent, 7 October, and Memo, Seymour to the Superintendent, 15 October 1985, file "Captain Chip Seymour, USN, Dir., CGO, File I"; Memo, Dean of Admissions to Superintendent, 8 August 1986, file "Letters Signed by Dean of Admissions, May 1981–Dec. 1989," box 4, CG.

26. *CNOSGR*, 1-11.

27. Point paper, "Minority Recruiting," n.d. (c. April 1986), file "Superintendent's Meeting on Minority Efforts '87-'88," box 2, CG.

28. Memo, Director of Candidate Guidance to Superintendent, 6 November 1985, file "Capt. Chip Seymour, USN, Dir., CGO, File I"; Lastinger to Director, Candidate Guidance, 21 April 1986, file "LCDR L. Scott DepDirCGO"; Memo, Director of Candidate Guidance for the Public Affairs Officer, 25 November 1986, file "Capt. H. A. Seymour, Jr., Director Cand. Guidance file II"; Memo, Superintendent to OP-130, 2 December 1986, file "Capt. H. A. Seymour, Jr., Director Cand. Guidance file II"; Letter, Seymour to Area Coordinators, 17 February 1987, file "Capt. H. A. Seymour, Jr., Director Cand. Guidance file II," all in box 4, CG; Briefing Materials, "Admissions," August 1986, file "Candidate Guidance Office Goals and Objectives 1983–86 and 1988," box 1, CG.

29. Minority Marketing Plan, n.d. (c. 1987) and Letter, Superintendent to Members of the Congressional Black Caucus, n.d. (c. 1987–88), file "Minority Game Plan 1987–88," box 2, CG; "U.S. Naval Academy Minority Recruiting," 17 February 1988, file "Candidate Guidance Office Goals and Objectives 1983–86 and 1988," box 1, CG; and Memo, Superintendent to CNO (OP-130), 26 July 1988, file "Capt. H. A. Seymour, Jr., file IV," box 4, CG.

30. "Negroes Admitted to the U.S. Naval Academy as Midshipmen," n.d., U.S.

Naval Academy Institutional Research Office; U.S. Naval Academy Alumni Association, *Register of Alumni*.

31. Memo, Director of Candidate Guidance to Chairman, Minority Action Group, file "Superintendent's Meeting on Minority Affairs, '87-'88," box 2, CG.

32. Memo, Director of Candidate Guidance to Chairman, Minority Action Group, 13 June 1988, file "Capt. H. A. Seymour, Jr., File IV," box 4, CG.

33. Memo, Superintendent to CNO OP-130, 26 July 1988, file "Capt. H. A. Seymour, Jr., File IV," box 4, CG.

34. "BOOST Input to USNA," April 1988; Ada Hunt, BOOST Briefing Slides, September 1988, file "BOOST—Class of 1989"; and "BOOST Visit," 13 January 1989, box 1, CG; James Talmadge Jackson Jr. and Mario Renara Maddox, "The Role of the Broadened Opportunity for Officer Selection and Training (BOOST) Program in Supporting the Navy's Minority Accession Policies" (unpublished M.S. thesis, Naval Postgraduate School, Monterey, Calif., 1990), iii.

35. *CNOSGR*, ES-1–ES-15, 1-2, 1-13, A-1–A-3, 3-4.

36. *CNOSGR*, 1-11–1-12, 2-5; "Navy EO Overview," enclosed under Director, Equal Opportunity Division (Pers-61) to EO Review Task Force Member, 23 January 1995, Office of the Special Assistant for Minority Affairs to the Chief of Naval Personnel.

37. *CNOSGR*, ES-1–ES-16, 3-7–3-8, 3-15–3-17, 3-26–3-29.

38. *CNOSGR*, 3-28–3-31, 3-E-1; "Navy EO Overview," enclosed under Director, Equal Opportunity Division (Pers-61) to EO Review Task Force Member, 23 January 1995, Office of the Special Assistant for Minority Affairs to the Chief of Naval Personnel.

39. Seymour, Memo for the Record, 22 September 1988; and Memo, Director of Candidate Guidance to Superintendent, 29 December 1988, file "Capt. H. A. Seymour, Jr., File IV," box 4, CG; Tzomes, telephone conversation with author, 24 April 2001.

40. Memo, CNO to Superintendent, 18 December 1989, in binder labeled "Supporting Data," under cover of NAAP, OPNAVINST 5354B, 17 February 1989, Office of the Special Assistant for Minority Affairs, Chief of Naval Personnel.

41. Memos, Seymour to Superintendent, 20 October and 22 November 1988, file "Capt. H. A. Seymour, Jr., File IV," box 4, CG.

42. Memo, Seymour to Superintendent, 10 March 1989, file "Capt. H. A. Seymour, Jr., File IV," box 4, CG.

43. Memo, Davis to the Superintendent, 12 July 1991, file "Memos for the Superintendent July 1986–December 1991," box 4, CG.

44. "Negroes Admitted to the U.S. Naval Academy as Midshipmen," n.d., U.S. Naval Academy Institutional Research Office; U.S. Naval Academy Alumni Association, *Register of Alumni*.

45. Memo, Superintendent to OP-01J, 24 October 1989, file "1531/Naval Academy 10/89–12/89," box 4, CG.

46. Memo, Laurel to Director, Candidate Guidance, 26 January 1989, file "BOOST-Class of 1989," box 1, CG.

47. Memo, Director, Candidate Guidance to the Superintendent, 23 May 1990, file "Memos for the Superintendent, July 1986–December 1991," box 4, CG.

48. Memo, Director of Candidate Guidance to Superintendent, 19 April 1990, file "Memos for Superintendent July 1986–December 1991," box 4, CG.

49. USNA Institutional Research Office.

50. Memo, Director, Candidate Guidance to Superintendent, 13 March 1991, file "Memos for Superintendent July 1986–December 1991," box 4, CG.

51. Memo, Deputy Chief of Naval Operations for Manpower and Personnel, 4 November 2003, author files, Naval Historical Center, Washington, D.C.

52. OPNAV Instruction 5354.3D, Navy Affirmative Action Plan, 19 August 1991, Office of the Special Assistant for Minority Affairs, Chief of Naval Personnel.

53. USNA Institutional Research Office.

54. Office of the Under Secretary of Defense for Personnel and Readiness, *Career Progression of Minority and Women Officers* (Washington, D.C.: Department of Defense, August 1999), 20; "Minority Officer Accession Data," 30 June 1994, enclosed under Dalton to CNO, 17 June 1994, file 1000 DCN April–June 94, box 1 of 17, acc. 957205, 00 Files, OA; Handout, "Year 2000 Diversity," Second USNA Outreach Conference, 11 November 1999; Boorda to McCaffrey, 2 June 1994, enclosed under "Minority Officers Assigned to SOUTHCOM, 6 June 1994, file 853 on, April–June 1994, box 1 of 17, acc. 957205, 00 Files, OA.

55. Office of the Under Secretary of Defense for Personnel and Readiness, *Career Progression of Minority and Women Officers,* 20.

56. Middle States Review Report, 19–22 November 1995, www.usna.edu, 30 January 2001.

57. Handout, "Year 2000 Diversity," Second USNA Outreach Conference, 11 November 1999.

58. Draft Briefing Slides, c. 1997, Office of the Special Assistant for Minority Affairs, Bureau of Naval Personnel.

59. Middle States Review Report, 19–22 November 1995, www.usna.edu, 30 January 2001.

60. Tzomes, telephone conversation with author, 24 April 2001; Nick Kotz, "Breaking Point," *Washingtonian,* December 1996, 112–13.

61. Robert D. Watts, interview, 25 August 1999.

62. Chief of Naval Personnel, memo for the CNO, "Equal Opportunity Review Initiatives—Action Memorandum," 25 May 1995, and enclosures, file 1522–1873 April–June 1995, box 2 of 24, acc. 977572, 00 Files, OA.

63. Watts interview.

64. OPNAV Instruction 5354.1D, Navy Equal Opportunity Manual, 21 June 1996, Office of the Special Assistant for Minority Affairs, Chief of Naval Personnel.

65. Office of the Under Secretary of Defense for Personnel and Readiness, *Career Progression of Minority and Women Officers,* 20.

66. USNA Institutional Research Office.

67. Donald Montgomery, interview with author, 8 September 1999.

Chapter 12

1. USNA Institutional Research Office.

2. Obie Clayton Jr., ed., *An American Dilemma Revisited: Race Relations in a Changing World* (New York: Russell Sage Foundation, 1996), 54, 141, 176–77, 189; Cook, *Sweet Land of Liberty,* 279–86, quotation on 286; Philip A. Klinkner, *The Unsteady March: The Rise and Decline of Racial Equality in America,* with Rogers M. Smith (Chicago: University of Chicago Press, 1999), 306–307; Marable, *Race, Reform and Rebellion,* 203; Jesse McKinnon and Karen Humes, *The Black Population in the United States: March 1999,* U.S. Census Bureau, Current Population Reports, Series P20–530 (Washington, D.C.: Government Printing Office, 2000); Sitkoff, *Struggle for Black Equality,* 220–25; Weisbrot, *Freedom Bound,* 305–17. For an excellent discussion of the history of the "n-word," see Kennedy, *Nigger.*

3. Karyn Reddick quoted in Weisbrot, *Freedom Bound,* 317.

4. Susan H. Godson, *Serving Proudly: History of Women in the U.S. Navy* (Annapolis, Md.: Naval Institute Press, 2001).

5. Zumwalt, *On Watch,* 261–65.

6. Marsha J. Evans et al., *The Integration of Women in the Brigade of Midshipmen, Report to the Superintendent* (Annapolis, Md.: Naval Academy, November 1987), 11–12, 19; USNA Institutional Research Office.

7. USNA Institutional Research Office.

8. Unless otherwise cited, chapters 12–15 are based on the following: Arnoux Abraham to author, 20 December 2000; Reuben E. Brigety II, interview by author, 16 December 1996; William L. Carr, interview by author, 10 December 1996; Jerry R. Gray, interview by author, 16 December 1996; Roger S. Grayson to author, 27 December 1999; Michael D. Greenwood to author, 10 June 2001; Tracey Nicole James Hayes to author, 29 February 2000, and interview by author, 5 April 2000; Roger Isom to author, 14 March 2000; Jacqueline R. Jackson, interview by author, 10 December 1996; Quintin Jones, interview by author, 10 December 1996; Jason Jorgensen to author, 11 December 2000; Mario R. Maddox, interview by author, 7 December 2000; Troy L. McSwain II, interview by author, 4 January 2001, and MPJ; Nikki-Nicole Peoples to author, 12 February 2001; William M. Triplett to author, 30 November 2000; and Ingrid M. Turner, interview by author, 3 January 2001. One of the Academy alumni who sat for an interview wishes to remain anonymous.

Chapter 13

1. Marryott, Memorandum, 1 August 1988; Seymour, Memorandum for the Superintendent, 29 August 1988; and "Report to the Superintendent on Study of Minority Midshipmen," [May 1989], file Minority Midshipmen Study Group 1989, Admissions Division, USNA Records, USNA.

2. Seymour, Memorandum for the Superintendent, 20 October 1988, file Minority Midshipmen Study Group 1989, Admissions Division, USNA Records, USNA.

3. "Report to the Superintendent on Study of Minority Midshipmen," p. 34, file Minority Midshipmen Study Group 1989, Admissions Division, USNA Records, USNA.

4. *Baltimore Sun,* 17 March 1998.

5. "Report to the Superintendent on Study of Minority Midshipmen," p. 34, file Minority Midshipmen Study Group 1989, Admissions Division, USNA Records, USNA.

6. "Report to the Superintendent on Study of Minority Midshipmen," p. 35, file Minority Midshipmen Study Group 1989, Admissions Division, USNA Records, USNA.

7. *Baltimore Sun,* 17 March 1998.

8. "Report to the Superintendent on Study of Minority Midshipmen," p. 35, file Minority Midshipmen Study Group 1989, Admissions Division, USNA Records, USNA.

9. United States General Accounting Office, *Naval Academy: Gender and Racial Disparities* (Washington, D.C.: General Accounting Office, 1993), 43. See chapter 9 for an explanation of the sub squad.

10. Craig Symonds, interview by author, 30 August 2006.

11. Social scientists have defined sexism as "the oppression or inhibition of women through a vast network of everyday practices, attitudes, assumptions, behaviors, and institutional rules. It is structural and systemic, and results in the privileging of men." See Lott and Maluso, *Social Psychology of Interpersonal Discrimination,* 13.

12. Evans et al., *Integration of Women.*

13. *Evening Capital,* 7 June 1978.

14. Evans et al., *Integration of Women,* 88.

15. Capt. Ronald Richard Evans, interview by author, 4 May 2000; Symonds interview.

16. James Webb, "Women Can't Fight," *Washingtonian,* November 1979, 144–48, 273–82; Navy *Times,* 7 May 1990; Carol Burke, "Dames at Sea: Life in the Naval Academy," *New Republic,* 17 and 24 August 1992, 20; Jean Zimmerman, *Tailspin: Women at War in the Wake of Tailhook* (New York: Doubleday, 1995), 234–35; Bob Lewis, "Female Naval Academy Grads Say Webb Column Caused Harassment," Associated Press, 13 September 2006, http://content.hamptonroads.com/story.cfm?story=110936&ran=145117.

17. *Navy Times,* 7 May 1990; William P. Lawrence and Rosario Rausa, *Tennessee Patriot: The Naval Career of Vice Admiral William P. Lawrence, U.S. Navy* (Annapolis, Md.: Naval Institute Press, 2006), 184; Lewis, "Female Naval Academy Grads."

18. Maddox interview; Burke, "Dames at Sea," 20.

19. Slevin to Lawrence, 24 January 1981, folder 1 January 31–March 1981, ON/1531 Supt. 1956–1981, SR.

20. Janie L. Mines, "The Jewish Chapel," *Shipmate,* January–February 1995, 28.

Chapter 14

1. Superintendent, USNA Notice 5420, 8 June 1979, annex 17, vol. 2, USNACH, 1978/79; Superintendent, USNA Instruction 5420.21C, 2 April 1980, annex

6, vol. 4, USNACH, 1979/80; Superintendent, USNA Instruction 5420.21D, 12 January 1983, annex 62, vol. 5, USNACH, 1982/3.

2. USNACH, 1989/90, vol. 1, 108–20.

3. Commandant, COMDTMIDN Notice 5420, 2 December 1980, annex 66, and COMDTMIDN Notice 5420.3C, 12 January 1981, annex 65, vol. 4, USN-ACH, 1980/81; Evans et al., *Integration of Women*, 85.

4. "Report to the Superintendent on Study of Minority Midshipmen," p. 35, file Minority Midshipmen Study Group 1989, Admissions Division, USNA Records, USNA.

5. Superintendent's Statement to the Board, Report of the Board of Visitors to the United States Naval Academy, 7–8 October 1980, file 1531 1 January–31 March, 1981 box 1500–1531 (31 March), 00 Files, OA; USNACH, 1989/90, vol. 1, 111–12.

6. Penn, Memorandum for the CNO, 25 May 1983, file January–March 1983, box 1983 1500 (30 December)-1533 (30 September), 00 Files, OA.

7. Penn, Memorandum for the CNO, 16 April 1984, and Watkins to Larson, 30 April 1984, file 1531 April–June, 1984 box 1531–1600 (September), 00 Files, OA.

8. Harlow, Memorandum for the Chief of Naval Personnel, 14 May 1984, file 1531 April–June, 1984 box 1531–1600 (September), 00 Files, OA.

9. Capt. Ronald Richard Evans, interview by author, 4 May 2000.

10. "Report to the Superintendent on Study of Minority Midshipmen," p. 35, file Minority Midshipmen Study Group 1989, Admissions Division, USNA Records, USNA.

11. Officer Biographical Files, s.v. "Anthony J. Watson," OA.

12. Officer Biographical Files, s.v. "Charles F. Bolden," OA; *Baltimore Sun*, 21 May 2005.

13. COMDTMIDN Instruction 5420.3F, 29 May 1990, annex 20, vol. 2, USNACH, 1989/90; U.S. General Accounting Office, *Gender and Racial Disparities*, 55–57.

14. Regulation 0411, Midshipman Regulations, 1981, Nimitz Library, USNA.

15. COMDTMIDN Instruction 5390.1E, 10 September 1980, annex 65, vol. 4, and vol. 1, 36, USNACH, 1980/81.

16. COMDTMIDN Instruction 5390.1F, 9 May 1984, annex 50, vol. 4, USNACH, 1983/84.

17. Howard (Acting Secretary of the Navy) to Senator Robert C. Byrd, 30 May 1991, file 1000 DCN (1 of 2), box "00 SUBJ FILES APR-JUN 1000 DCN 1991 (box 2 of 2)," 00 Files, OA.

18. Annex 43, vol. 4, USNACH, 1988/89; annex 46, vol. 4, USNACH, 1989/90; annex 54, vol. 4, USNACH, 1990/91; annex 48, vol. 5, USNACH, 1991/92; annex 33, vol. 3, USNACH, 1992/93; "Report to the Superintendent on Study of Minority Midshipmen," p. 36, file Minority Midshipmen Study Group 1989, Admissions Division, USNA Records, USNA.

19. File://A:\USNA Doc 2.htm, 14 February 2001; U.S. Naval Academy,

United States Naval Academy 1999–2000 Catalog (Annapolis, Md.: Naval Academy, 1999), 64–65.

20. U.S. Naval Academy, *United States Naval Academy 1999–2000 Catalog,* 44.

21. 1979 folder, 5420/49 Black Studies Committee, SR; annex 165, vol. 4, USNACH, 1976/77; *Blue and Gold Newsletter,* winter 1980/81, box 4, CG; USNACH, 1982/83, vol. 1, 115; Penn, Memorandum for Executive assistant to CNO, 31 January 1983, file January–March 1983, box 1983 1500 (30 December)–1533 (30 September), 00 Files, OA; Speller to Kelso, 13 April 1993, file 1000 DCN April–June 1993, box 1000 DCN April–June 1993, 00 Files, OA.

22. Vahsen, "Blacks in White Hats," 69.

23. Vahsen, "Blacks in White Hats," 69.

24. *Lucky Bag,* 1991, vol. 2, 281; United States Naval Academy Gospel Choir, "Down by the River" (compact disc, 1997).

25. "Report to the Superintendent on Study of Minority Midshipmen," p. 36, file Minority Midshipmen Study Group 1989, Admissions Division, USNA Records, USNA.

26. U.S. General Accounting Office, *Gender and Racial Disparities,* 10–11, 54.

27. Michele Howard, presentation at the Naval Historian's Seminar, 19 February 2002, Naval Historical Center, Washington, D.C.

28. Hayes interview.

29. *The Log,* 26 April 1978, 15; Elizabeth Anne Belzer Rowe, interview by author, 7 September 2006, and e-mail to author, 25 October 2006.

30. Melody Wheeler Spradlin, interview by Curtis Utz, 7 September 2006.

31. "The Charge of 1000: The History and Traditions of the Herndon Monument Climb," http://www.usna.org/HerndonPAO.html, downloaded 17 October 2006.

32. U.S. General Accounting Office, *Gender and Racial Disparities,* 2–3.

33. U.S. General Accounting Office, *Gender and Racial Disparities,* 12; Zimmerman, *Tailspin,* 233.

34. James F. Barry, "Adrift in Annapolis," *Washington Post,* 31 March 1996, C1, C4.

35. Evans et al., *Integration of Women;* Zimmerman, *Tailspin,* 181–82.

36. *Washington Post,* 30 May 1990; U.S. General Accounting Office, *Gender and Racial Disparities,* 53–54.

37. "Deepening Shame," *Newsweek,* 10 August 1992; Kotz, "Breaking Point," 98–99; Richard B. Linneken, "Tailhook 1991 and Other Perplexities," *Proceedings,* September 1992, 36–40.

38. Everett L. Greene, interview by author, 20 September 1999. Howard quoted in *All Hands,* August 1992, 4.

39. CNO, Memo for the Assistant Secretary of Defense (Force Management and Personnel), 12 January 1993, and enclosures, file 1000 DCN January–March 1993, box 1000 DCN January–March 1993, 3 of 3, 00 Files, OA.

40. "USNA Strategic Plan," n.d., enclosed under CNO, Memo for the Assistant

Secretary of Defense (Force Management and Personnel), 12 January 1993, file 1000 DCN January–March 1993, box 1000 DCN January–March 1993, 3 of 3, 00 Files, OA.

41. Division of Professional Development Command History, annex 33, vol. 3, USNACH, 1992/93; "Sexual Harassment (S.H.) Training," enclosure in CNO, Memo for the Assistant Secretary of Defense (Force Management and Personnel), 12 January 1993, file 1000 DCN January–March 1993, box 1000 DCN January–March 1993, 3 of 3, 00 Files, OA.

42. U.S. General Accounting Office, *Gender and Racial Disparities*, 3, 12–13, 59.

43. Sharon Hanley Disher, "30 Years of Women at USNA—A Success Story," *Shipmate*, September 2006, 15.

44. Paul J. Cook et al., *Service Academy 2005 Sexual Harassment and Assault Survey* (Arlington, Va: Defense Manpower Data Center, 2005), v–vi. See also General Accounting Office, *DoD Service Academies: Update on Extent of Sexual Harassment* (Washington, D.C.: General Accounting Office, March 1995); Hoewing and Rumburg et al., *Report of the Defense Task Force*.

45. Charles F. Bolden Jr., interview by author, 11 December 2000.

46. Cook, *Service Academy 2005 Sexual Harassment*, 25; *Baltimore Sun*, 21 October 2006.

47. Regulation 0417, Midshipman Regulations, 1981, Nimitz Library, USNA; Squad Leader's Manual, pp. 1–18, annex 13, vol. 2, USNACH, 1987/88; COM-DTMIDN Instruction 1520.1M, "Fourth Class Indoctrination," annex 34, vol. 4, USNACH, 1988/89.

48. General Order 1–90, 26 May 1990, annex 19, vol. 2, USNACH, 1989/90; *Washington Post*, 30 May 1990.

49. *Navy Times*, 9 July 1990.

50. Darlene Clark Hine and Kathleen Thompson, *A Shining Thread of Hope: The History of Black Women in America* (New York: Broadway Books, 1998), 302.

51. Mackenzie, *Brief Points*, 111.

52. Sheldon Harris, interview by author, 15 May 2001.

Chapter 15

1. Seymour, Memorandum for the Superintendent, 10 February 1988, file "Superintendent's Meeting on Minority Efforts 87–88," box 2, CG; "Negroes Admitted to the U.S. Naval Academy as Midshipmen," n.d., U.S. Naval Academy Institutional Research Office; Memo, Pat Stroop, USNA Institutional Research Office, to author, 7 March 2001; U.S. Naval Academy Alumni Association, *Register of Alumni*; U.S. Department of Defense, *Black Americans in Defense*, 255–64.

2. Seymour, Memorandum for the Superintendent, 20 October 1988, file "Capt. H. A. Seymour, Jr., File IV," box 4, CG; Seymour, Memorandum for the Superintendent, 3 February 1989, file Minority Midshipmen Study Group 1989, Admissions Division, USNA Records, USNA.

3. Marryott, Memorandum, 1 August 1988, and Hill, Memorandum for the

DCNO (Manpower, Personnel and Training), 18 August 1989, file Minority Midshipmen Study Group 1989, Admissions Division, USNA Records, USNA.

4. "Report to the Superintendent on Study of Minority Midshipmen," file Minority Midshipmen Study Group 1989, Admissions Division, USNA Records, USNA.

5. U.S. General Accounting Office, *Gender and Racial Disparities,* 39.

6. Seymour, Memoranda for the Superintendent, 20 October and 22 November 1988, file "Capt. H. A. Seymour, Jr., File IV," box 4, CG.

7. Seymour, Memorandum for the Superintendent, 19 December 1988, file Minority Midshipmen Study Group 1989, Admissions Division, USNA Records, USNA; Seymour, Memorandum for the Superintendent, 29 December 1988, file "Capt. H. A. Seymour, Jr., File IV," box 4, CG.

8. Seymour, Memorandum for the Superintendent, 10 March 1989, file "Capt. H. A. Seymour, Jr., File IV," box 4, CG.

9. "Report to the Superintendent on Study of Minority Midshipmen," file Minority Midshipmen Study Group 1989, Admissions Division, USNA Records, USNA.

10. Hill, Memorandum for the Deputy Chief of Naval Operations for Manpower, Personnel and Training, 18 August 1989, file Minority Midshipmen Study Group 1989, Admissions Division, USNA Records, USNA; U.S. General Accounting Office, *Gender and Racial Disparities,* 54–55; U.S. Naval Academy Alumni Association, *Register of Alumni,* lxxxiv.

11. Seymour, Memorandum for the Superintendent, 10 February 1988, file "Superintendent's Meeting on Minority Efforts 87–88," box 2, CG; "Negroes Admitted to the U.S. Naval Academy as Midshipmen," n.d., U.S. Naval Academy Institutional Research Office; Memo, Pat Stroop, USNA Institutional Research Office, to author, 7 March 2001; U.S. Naval Academy Alumni Association, *Register of Alumni;* U.S. Department of Defense, *Black Americans in Defense,* 255–64.

12. U.S. General Accounting Office, *Gender and Racial Disparities,* 1–7, 39–48.

13. http://www.delafont.com/comedians/rudy-ray-moore.htm, 26 February 2002; http://www.yaaams.org/hollywooderas.shtml, 26 February 2002.

14. MacKenzie, *Brief Points,* 92.

15. http://www.troymcswain.com, 3 January 2003; http://www.washingtonpost.com/wp-srv/sports/nba/longterm/1999/draft/articles/rites1.htm, 7 November 2002; http://www.nfl.com/ce/feature/0,3783,5526446,00.html, 7 November 2002.

16. *Navy Times,* 28 February 2005.

17. U.S. General Accounting Office, *Gender and Racial Disparities,* 46.

18. U.S. Naval Academy Alumni Association, *Register of Alumni,* lxxxiv.

19. *Lucky Bag,* 1985, 386.

20. U.S. Naval Academy Alumni Association, *Register of Alumni,* lxxxii.

21. "Biography Michelle Janine Howard," author files.

22. Kevin Baugh to author, 20 October 2000.

23. "Georgia State University Names Mary McElroy as New Director of

Intercollegiate Athletics," http://www2.gsu.edu/~wwwath/050630-new_ath_ad2 .htm, posted 30 June 2005; "Alumni Profile: Mary McElroy Blazing Trail in Athletics Administration," http://mgt.gatech.edu/news_room/news/2005/marymcelroy/ index.html, posted 20 September 2005.

24. Reuben E. Brigety II to author, 20 August 2002 and 14 July 2003.

25. "Annapolis Grads Sworn in to VA Posts," *Shipmate* 64 (September 2001): 18.

26. http://www.usna.com/News_Pubs/Publications/Shipmate/2001/ 2001_04/Williams.htm, 15 June 2001; http://www.montelshow.com/montel/bio .htm, 14 March 2002.

Conclusion

1. Digital Video Disk, "Wesley Brown Fieldhouse Groundbreaking Ceremony," raw footage, U.S. Naval Academy Public Affairs Office, 25 March 2006. The $45 million construction project is slated for completion around 2008.

Bibliography

Primary Sources
Archives, Manuscripts, and Special Collections

Library of Congress, Washington, D.C.

National Association for the Advancement of Colored People Papers

Maryland State Archives, Annapolis, Md.

"The Annapolis I Remember Collection," Peggy Kimbo, interview by Mame
Warren, 28 April 1990

Moorland-Spingarn Research Center, Howard University, Washington, D.C.

Wesley Anthony Brown Papers

William Levi Dawson Papers

National Air and Space Museum, Washington, D.C.

Oral Histories

Maj. Gen. Charles Frank Bolden Jr., United States Marine Corps, Class of
1969, interview by Cathleen Lewis and Ian Cooke, 13 February 1995

National Archives and Records Administration, Washington, D.C.

RG 319: Records of the Army Staff

Entry "Integration of Armed Forces 1940–1965"

National Personnel Records Center, St. Louis, Mo.

Official Service and Medical Record, s.v. Wesley Anthony Brown, service number
521291.

Naval Historical Center, Washington, D.C.

Operational Archives

Official Files

Records of the Immediate Office of the Chief of Naval Operations
(Double Zero or 00 Files)

Adm. Elmo R. Zumwalt Personal Papers

Contemporary History Branch

Author Correspondence Files (all correspondence is addressed to the author
and includes letters, faxes, e-mails, and audio tapes)

Arnoux Abraham, Class of 1993, 20 December 2000

Kevin A. Baugh, Class of 1982, 20 October 2000

Charlie C. Boyd Jr., Class of 1976, 11 February 2000

Ernest B. Brown, Class of 1949, 26 July 1999

Jimmy Carter, Class of 1947, 10 April 1996 and 24 September 1997

Lamar C. Chapman III, Class of 1975, 24 July 1999

Kenneth D. Dunn, Class of 1974, 27 August 1999

Joseph P. Flanagan, Class of 1947, 19 March 1997

Scott Fontaine, Class of 1971, 5 July 1999

Bruce R. Franklin, Class of 1976, 6 November 2000

Roger S. Grayson, Class of 1988, 27 December 1999

Everett L. Greene, Class of 1970, 8 September 1999

Michael D. Greenwood, Class of 1985, 10 June 2001

Lucius P. Gregg Jr., Class of 1955, 20 March 2001

Ronald O. Grover, Class of 1975, 10 September 1999

Milton Gussow, Class of 1949, 18 September 1997

Tracey Nicole James Hayes, Class of 1992, 29 February 2000

Thomas J. Hudner Jr., Class of 1947, 29 August 1996

Roger Isom, Class of 1988, 14 March 2000

Jason Jorgensen, Class of 1991, 11 December 2000

Marvin E. King, Class of 1978, 4 December 2000

Harry M. Krantzman, Class of 1949, 27 September 1996

Thomas F. Lechner, Class of 1949, 25 September 1996

Earle K. McLaren, Class of 1934, 20 May 1997

Walter M. Meginniss, Class of 1947, 4 June 1997

William Merrell, Class of 1975, 17 September 1999

Donald R. Morris, Class of 1948B, 19 October 1996

Nikki-Nicole Peoples, Class of 1997, 12 February 2001

John Porter, Class of 1971, 27 December 1999

Lloyd Prince, Class of 1978, 30 October 2000

John D. Raiford, Class of 1954, 13 December 2000 and 30 January
    2001

Elizabeth Anne Belzer Rowe, Class of 1980, 25 October 2006

Richard G. Samuels, Class of 1973, 16 July 1999

David F. Simmons, Class of 1968, 4 August 1999

Reeves R. Taylor, Class of 1953, 15 January 1997

William M. Triplett, Class of 1989, 30 November 2000

Stansfield Turner, Class of 1947, 26 August 1996

Robert D. Watts, Class of 1973, 3 August 1999

J. C. G. Wilson, Class of 1935, 12 May and 10 June 1997

Oral Histories (all interviews by author unless otherwise stated)

Lou Adams, Class of 1958, 19 July 1999

Anonymous, 28 October 1996

Eugene A. Barham, Class of 1935, 29 April 1997

Harold S. Bauduit, Class of 1956, 13 July 1999

Charles F. Bolden, Class of 1968, 4 and 11 December 2000

Reuben E. Brigety II, Class of 1995, 16 December 1996

Wesley Anthony Brown, Class of 1949, 19 December 1995 (first inter-
    view), 23 January 1997 (second interview), 17 October 1997 (third
    interview), 17 December 1998 (fourth interview), 16 September 1999

(fifth interview); interview by Jean-Paul Reveyoso and Martha Dey, 8 May 1991, General Accounting Office, Washington, D.C.

Malvin D. Bruce, Class of 1959, 9 April 1998

James F. Calvert, Class of 1943, 10 August 2000

William L. Carr, Class of 1997, 10 December 1996

Stanley J. Carter Jr., Class of 1965, 5 January 2000

Lawrence C. Chambers, Class of 1952, 7 November 1996

Charles D. Cole, Class of 1976, 27 January 2001

Kevin F. Delaney, Class of 1968, 18 November 1999

Joseph P. Flanagan Jr., Class of 1947, 23 September 1996

Ronald R. Evans, 4 May 2000

Bruce R. Franklin, Class of 1976, 14 November 2000

Joseph B. Freeman, Class of 1970, 15 November 2000

James Frezzell, Class of 1968, 2 August 1999

Edward J. Gilmore, Class of 1976, 1 December 1999

Boyd E. Graves, Class of 1975, 17 November 2000 and 22 March 2001

Jerry R. Gray, Class of 2000, 16 December 1996

Floyd Grayson, Class of 1965, 5 May 2000

Everett L. Greene, Class of 1970, 20 September 1999

Milton Gussow, Class of 1949, 27 October 1997.

Sheldon Harris, 15 May 2001

Tracey Nicole James Hayes, Class of 1992, 5 April 2000

Lawrence Heyworth Jr., Class of 1943, 9 August 2000

Cary Hithon, Class of 1977, 28 November 2000

Thomas J. Hudner Jr., Class of 1947, 21 October 1996

Anthony L. Jackson, Class of 1970, 13 July 1999

Jacqueline R. Jackson, Class of 1999, 10 December 1996

James T. Jackson, Class of 1975, 9 September and 5 October 1999

John T. Jackson III, Class of 1962, 10 August 1999

Quintin Jones, Class of 1998, 10 December 1996

William C. Jones, Class of 1964, 30 November 1999

Graham W. Leonard, Class of 1949, 16 April 1997

Walter Leonard, member and chairman, Board of Visitors (1979–81), 1 September 2006

Robert G. Lucas, Class of 1968, 2 December 1999

William P. Mack, Class of 1937, 13 November 2000

Mario R. Maddox, Class of 1985, 7 December 2000

Byron F. Marchant, Class of 1978, 4 January 2000

Edward J. McCormack Jr., Class of 1947, 23 October 1996

Mary A. Miles McElroy, Class of 1987, interview by Gary Weir, 7 September 2006

Kinnaird R. McKee, Class of 1951, interview by David Winkler, 21 March 2000

Troy L. McSwain II, Class of 1984, 4 January 2001

Kerwin E. Miller, Class of 1975, 12 December 2000

Charles S. Minter Jr., Class of 1937, 18 May 2000

Donald Montgomery, Class of 1974, 8 September 1999

Walter G. Moyle Jr., Class of 1947, 12 August 1997

James K. Orzech, Class of 1968, 24 August 1999

Patrick M. Prout, Class of 1964, 6 August 1999

Mason C. Reddix, Class of 1976, 6 January 1997

Elizabeth A. Belzer Rowe, Class of 1980, 7 September 2006

Richard G. Samuels, Class of 1973, 3 August 1999

Jeffrey K. Sapp, Class of 1977, 21 September 2006

Leighton W. Smith, Class of 1962, interview by John D. Sherwood,
22 January 2001

Melody A. Wheeler Spradlin, Class of 1986, interview by Curtis Utz,
7 September 2006

Abraham R. Stowe, 8 June 1999 and 29 January 2000

William H. Sword, Class of 1949, 24 October 1996

Craig Symonds, United States Naval Academy history faculty member
(1996–2005), 30 August 2006

Reeves R. Taylor, Class of 1953, 2 December 1996

Ingrid M. Turner, Class of 1986, 3 January 2001

Chancellor A. Tzomes, Class of 1967, 24 August 1999

Anthony J. Watson, Class of 1970, 10, 18, and 22 October 2001

Robert D. Watts, Class of 1973, 25 August 1999

Howard A. Weiss, Class of 1947, 11 May 1996 (first interview),
22 October 1997 (second interview)

Richard E. Whiteside, Class of 1949, 9 October 1996

Leo V. Williams, Class of 1970, 16 November 2000

Nimitz Library, United States Naval Academy, Annapolis, Md.

RG 405: Records of the United States Naval Academy

Entry 3. "Commandant of Midshipmen, Office of the Commandant,
Published Documents, Commandant Instructions and Notices 1959–
1971"

Entry 39B. "Records of the Superintendent."

Entry 204. "Journals of the Academic Board, 1845–1979"

Entry 209A. "Records of Boards and Committees, Board of Visitors, Reports
of the Board of Visitors, 1936–77"

Special Collections and Archives Division

"Black Midshipmen" Reference File

Midshipmen Personnel Jackets

Naval Academy Records.

Admissions Division

Superintendent's Files, 1960–81

Candidate Guidance Office Papers, 1984–92

United States Naval Academy Command Histories, 1970–99
United States Naval Institute, Annapolis, Md.
   Lt. Comm. Wesley Anthony Brown, Civil Engineer Corps, United States Navy
      (Ret.), Class of 1949, Oral History
   Adm. Joseph Paul Reason, United States Navy (Ret.), Class of 1965, Oral
      History
   Reminiscences of R. Adm. Draper L. Kauffman, United States Navy (Ret.), Class
      of 1933, 2 vols., Oral History
   Reminiscences of V. Adm. William P. Mack, United States Navy (Ret.), Class of
      1937, Oral History

Published Documents and Reports
Cook, Paul J., et al. *Service Academy 2005 Sexual Harassment and Assault Survey.*
   Arlington, Va.: Defense Manpower Data Center, 2005.
Evans, Marsha J., et al., *The Integration of Women in the Brigade of Midshipmen,*
   Report to the Superintendent, Submitted by the Women Midshipmen Study Group,
   November 1987. Annapolis, Md.: Naval Academy, 1987.
Fahy, Charles, et al. *Freedom to Serve: Equality of Treatment and Opportunity in the*
   Armed Services: A Report by the President's Committee. Washington, D.C.:
   Government Printing Office, 1950.
Hoewing, Gerald L., and Delilah D. Rumburg et al. *Report of the Defense Task Force*
   on Sexual Harassment & Violence at the Military Service Academies. Washington,
   D.C.: Government Printing Office, June 2005.
Jankovsky, Norlin J., ed. *Reef Points, 1945–1946.* Annapolis, Md.: United States
   Naval Academy, 1945.
Johnson, Warren, transcriber. "Excerpts from President Carter's Speech in the Naval
   Academy Chapel, Tuesday, 4 June 1996." *Shipmate,* September 1996, 12–13, 45.
MacGregor, Morris J., and Bernard C. Nalty, eds. *Blacks in the United States Armed*
   Forces: Basic Documents. 13 vols. Wilmington, Del.: Scholarly Resources, 1977.
McKinnon, Jesse, and Karen Humes, *The Black Population in the United States:*
   March 1999. U.S. Census Bureau, Current Population Reports, Series P20–530.
   Washington, D.C.: Government Printing Office, 2000.
Northrup, Herbert R., et al. *Black and Other Minority Participation in the All-*
   Volunteer Navy and Marine Corps. Philadelphia: Industrial Research Unit,
   Wharton School, University of Pennsylvania, 1979.
Office of the Under Secretary of Defense for Personnel and Readiness. *Career*
   Progression of Minority and Women Officers. Washington, D.C.: Department of
   Defense, August 1999.
U.S. Congress. House. *Memorial Services Held in the House of Representatives and*
   Senate of the United States, Together with Tributes Presented in Eulogy of William
   L. Dawson, Late a Representative from Illinois. Washington, D.C.: Government
   Printing Office, 1971.
———. House. Office of the Historian. *Women in Congress, 1917–1990.* Washing-
   ton, D.C.: Government Printing Office, 1991.

U.S. Department of Defense. *Black Americans in Defense of Our Nation: A Pictorial Documentary of the Black American Male and Female Participation and Involvement in the Military Affairs of the United States of America.* Washington, D.C.: Government Printing Office, 1991.

————. *The Negro Officer in the Armed Forces of the United States of America.* Washington, D.C.: Department of Defense, 1960.

U.S. General Accounting Office. *DoD Service Academies: Update on Extent of Sexual Harassment.* Washington, D.C.: General Accounting Office, 1995

————. *Report to the Chairman, Committee on Armed Services, U.S. Senate: Naval Academy: Gender and Racial Disparities.* Washington, D.C.: General Accounting Office, 1993.

U.S. Naval Academy. *Annual Register of the United States Naval Academy,* 1936–1979. Washington, D.C.: Government Printing Office, 1945–1979.

————. *Lucky Bag* (yearbook). Various years.

————. *Regulations of the United States Naval Academy, 1945.* Annapolis, Md.: U.S. Naval Academy, 1945.

United States Naval Academy Alumni Association, Inc. *Register of Alumni: Graduates and Former Midshipmen and Naval Cadets.* Annapolis, Md.: U.S. Naval Academy Alumni Association, 1997.

U.S. Navy Department. Bureau of Naval Personnel. *Phase II Equal Opportunity/Race Relations Program: Equal Opportunity Program Specialist Consultant Guide,* Volume 2: NAVPERS 15260. Washington, D.C.: Bureau of Naval Personnel, n.d. [1974].

————. Bureau of Naval Personnel. *United States Naval Academy Admissions Regulations, 1965.* Washington, D.C.: Bureau of Naval Personnel, 1964.

————. Office of the Chief of Naval Operations. *CNO Study Group's Report on Equal Opportunity in the Navy.* Washington, D.C.: Office of the Chief of Naval Operations, 1988.

United States Statutes at Large. Washington, D.C., Government Printing Office, 1874–.

Memoirs and Contemporary Publications

"Annapolis' First." *Time,* 13 June 1949, 19–20.

"Annapolis Grads Sworn in to VA Posts." *Shipmate* 64, September 2001, 18.

Banning, Kendall. *Annapolis Today,* 5th ed. Annapolis, Md.: U.S. Naval Institute, 1957.

Barry, James F. "Adrift in Annapolis." *Washington Post,* 31 March 1996, C1, C4.

Bowers, Ingrid. *A Greater Challenge: U.S. Naval Academy Black History.* Bethesda, Md.: Phase II Productions, 1979 (video documentary).

Brown, Wesley A. "The First Negro Graduate of Annapolis Tells His Story." *Saturday Evening Post,* 25 June 1949, 26–27, 110–12.

"Bugle Call for Negro Cadets." *Ebony,* June 1966, 73–78.

Burke, Carol. "Dames at Sea: Life in the Naval Academy." *New Republic,* 17 and 24 August 1992, 16–20.

Calvert, James F. *Silent Running: My Years on a World War II Attack Submarine.* New York: Wiley, 1995.

Carter, Jimmy. *Why Not the Best?* Nashville, Tenn.: Broadman, 1975.

Cobb, W. Montague. "New Spirit in the Navy." *Journal of the National Medical Association* 68 (November 1976): 540–42.

Davis, Benjamin O., Jr. *American: An Autobiography.* Washington, D.C.: Smithsonian Institution Press, 1991.

"Deepening Shame." *Newsweek,* 10 August 1992.

Engeman, Jack. *Annapolis: The Life of a Midshipman.* New York: Lothrop, Lee, and Shepard, 1965.

"Four at the Helm." *Ebony,* January 1973, 105–107.

Hessman, James D. "Z Is for Z-Gram." *Armed Forces Journal* 108 (7 December 1970): 30–33, 42.

Hinman, Al. "Confederate Flag Must Come Down, Says S.C. Governor." U.S. News Story Page, CNN Interactive, posted 27 November 1996, http://www.cnn.com/US/9611/27/rebel.flag/index.html.

"Historical News." *Journal of Negro History* 49 (July 1964): 219–23.

"Historical Notes." *Journal of Negro History* 53 (July 1968): 281–82.

Hope, Edward S. "The Navy Salutes: Dr. Edward S. Hope—First Black CEC Officer." *Navy Civil Engineer* 26 (Winter 1986/87): 16, 28–32.

Kotz, Nick. "Breaking Point." *Washingtonian* 32 (December 1996): 94–121.

"Largest Negro Group at U.S. Academies." *Jet* 16 (1 October 1959): 3.

Lawrence, William P., and Rosario Rausa. *Tennessee Patriot: The Naval Career of Vice Admiral William P. Lawrence, U.S. Navy.* Annapolis, Md.: Naval Institute Press, 2006.

Linneken, Richard B. "Tailhook 1991 and Other Perplexities." *Proceedings,* September 1992, 36–40.

Malkie, Del. "Blacks at the Naval Academy." *All Hands,* September 1976, 28–31.

Mines, Janie L. "The Jewish Chapel." *Shipmate,* January–February 1995, 28.

Powell, Adam Clayton, Jr. *Adam by Adam: The Autobiography of Adam Clayton Powell, Jr.* New York: Dial Press, 1971.

Schlesinger, Arthur M., Jr. *A Thousand Days: John F. Kennedy in the White House.* Boston: Houghton Mifflin, 1965.

Trident Society, ed. *The Book of Navy Songs.* New York: Doubleday, 1937.

United States Naval Academy Gospel Choir. "Down by the River." (Compact Disc) Annapolis, Md.: United States Naval Academy, 1997.

Webb, James. "Women Can't Fight." *Washingtonian,* November 1979, 144–48, 273–82.

White, Walter. *A Man Called White: The Autobiography of Walter White.* New York: Viking, 1948.

———. *A Rising Wind.* Garden City, N.Y.: Doubleday, 1945, reprint ed., Westport, Conn.: Negro Universities Press, 1971.

Wiley, Byron A. "Equal Opportunity: Challenge to Navy's Management." *Proceedings* 96 (September 1970): 34–38.

Zumwalt, Elmo R., Jr. *On Watch: A Memoir.* New York: Quadrangle, 1976.

Newspapers and Periodicals

Afro-American
All Hands
Army and Navy Journal
Chicago Defender
Christian Science Monitor
Cleveland Call and Post
Evening Capital (Annapolis)
Evening Star (Washington, D.C.)
Evening Sun (Baltimore)
Navy Times
New York Daily Tribune
New York Times
Newsweek
Pittsburgh Courier
Post and Courier (Savannah)
Time
Washington Post
Washington Tribune

Secondary Sources
Books

Astor, Gerald. *The Right to Fight: A History of African Americans in the Military.*
    Novato, Calif.: Presidio, 1998.
Barlow, Jeffrey G. *Revolt of the Admirals: The Fight for Naval Aviation, 1945–1950.*
    Washington, D.C.: Government Printing Office: 1994.
Berman, William C. *The Politics of Civil Rights in the Truman Administration.*
    Columbus: Ohio State University Press, 1970.
Bourne, Peter G. *Jimmy Carter: A Comprehensive Biography from Plains to Postpresi-
    dency.* New York: Scribner's, 1997.
Brown, Philip L. *The Other Annapolis.* Annapolis, Md.: Annapolis Publishing, 1994.
Buchanan, A. Russell. *Black Americans in World War II.* Santa Barbara, Calif.: ABC-
    CLIO Books, 1983.
Cary, Francine Curro, ed. *Urban Odyssey: A Multicultural History of Washington,
    D.C.* Washington, D.C.: Smithsonian, 1995.
Chambers, John Whiteclay II, et al., ed. *The Oxford Companion to American
    Military History.* New York: Oxford University Press, 1999.
Clayton, Obie, Jr., ed. *An American Dilemma Revisited: Race Relations in a
    Changing World.* New York: Russell Sage Foundation, 1996.
Coletta, Paolo Enrico, ed. *American Secretaries of the Navy.* 2 vols. Annapolis, Md.:
    Naval Institute Press, 1980.

Cook, Robert. *Sweet Land of Liberty? The African American Struggle for Civil Rights in the Twentieth Century.* New York: Longman, 1998.

Dabney, Lillian G. *The History of Schools for Negroes in the District of Columbia, 1807–1947.* Washington: Catholic University of America Press, 1949. Published Ph.D. dissertation.

Daniel, Pete. *The Shadow of Slavery: Peonage in the South, 1901–1969.* Urbana: University of Illinois Press, 1990.

Dictionary of American Biography. 10 vols. plus supplements. New York: Scribners, c. 1964.

Disher, Sharon Hanley. *First Class: Women Join the Ranks at the Naval Academy.* Annapolis, Md.: Naval Institute Press, 1998.

Drago, Edmund L. *Initiative, Paternalism, and Race Relations: Charleston's Avery Normal Institute.* Athens: University of Georgia Press, 1990.

DuBose, Carolyn P. *The Untold Story of Charles Diggs: The Public Figure, the Private Man.* Arlington, Va.: Barton, 1998.

Fitzpatrick, Sandra, and Maria R. Goodwin. *The Guide to Black Washington: Places and Events of Historical and Cultural Significance in the Nation's Capital.* Revised ed. New York: Hippocrene Books, 1999.

Foner, Eric, ed. *The New American History.* Philadelphia: Temple University Press, 1990.

Franklin, John Hope, and Alfred A. Moss Jr. *From Slavery to Freedom.* 6th ed. New York: McGraw-Hill, 1988.

Freeman, J. Bert. *Taking Charge of Your Positive Direction.* New Bern, N.C.: Trafford, 2006.

Gatewood, Willard B., Jr. *Aristocrats of Color: The Black Elite, 1880–1920.* Bloomington: Indiana University Press, 1990.

Gelfand, H. Michael. *Sea Change at Annapolis: The United States Naval Academy, 1949–2000.* Chapel Hill: University of North Carolina Press, 2006.

Green, Constance McLaughlin. *The Secret City: A History of Race Relations in the Nation's Capital.* Princeton: Princeton University Press, 1967.

Greene, Robert Ewell. *Black Defenders of America, 1775–1973: A Reference and Pictorial History.* Chicago: Johnson, 1974.

Grimshaw, William J. *Bitter Fruit: Black Politics and the Chicago Machine, 1931–1991.* Chicago: University of Chicago Press, 1992.

Gropman, Alan L. *The Air Force Integrates, 1945–1964.* Washington, D.C.: Office of Air Force History, 1985.

Grossman, James R. *Land of Hope: Chicago, Black Southerners, and the Great Migration.* Chicago: University of Chicago Press, 1989.

Hamilton, Charles V. *Adam Clayton Powell, Jr.: The Political Biography of an American Dilemma.* New York: Atheneum, 1991.

Haygood, Wil. *King of the Cats: The Life and Times of Adam Clayton Powell, Jr.* Boston: Houghton Mifflin, 1993.

Hill, Robert A., et al., eds. *The FBI's RACON: Racial Conditions in the United States during World War II.* Boston: Northeastern University Press, 1995.

Hine, Darlene Clark, and Kathleen Thompson. *A Shining Thread of Hope: The History of Black Women in America.* New York: Broadway Books, 1998.

Holt, Thomas Cleveland. *Black over White: Negro Political Leadership in South Carolina during Reconstruction.* Urbana: University of Illinois Press, 1977.

Hone, Thomas C. *Power and Change: The Administrative History of the Office of the Chief of Naval Operations, 1946–1986.* Washington, D.C.: Government Printing Office, 1989.

Hoopes, Townsend, and Douglas Brinkley. *Driven Patriot: The Life and Times of James Forrestal.* New York: Knopf, 1992.

Hundley, Mary Gibson. *The Dunbar Story, 1870–1955,* with an introduction by Robert C. Weaver. New York: Vantage Press, 1965.

Janowitz, Morris. *The Professional Soldier: A Social and Political Portrait.* New York: Free Press, 1971.

Johnson, Jesse J., ed. *Black Armed Forces Officers, 1736–1971: A Documented Pictorial History.* Hampton, Va.: Hampton Institute, 1971.

Karsten, Peter. *The Naval Aristocracy: The Golden Age of Annapolis and the Emergence of Modern American Navalism.* New York: Free Press, 1972.

Katz, William Loren. *Eyewitness: A Living Documentary of the African American Contribution to American History.* New York: Simon and Schuster, 1995.

Kennedy, Randall. *Nigger: The Strange Career of a Troublesome Word.* New York: Pantheon Books, 2002.

Klinkner, Philip A., with Rogers M. Smith. *The Unsteady March: The Rise and Decline of Racial Equality in America.* Chicago: University of Chicago Press, 1999.

Lee, Ulysses. *The Employment of Negro Troops.* Washington, D.C.: Government Printing Office, 1994.

Lott, Bernice, and Diane Maluso, eds. *The Social Psychology of Interpersonal Discrimination.* New York: Guilford Press, 1995.

Love, Robert W., Jr., ed. *The Chiefs of Naval Operations.* Annapolis, Md.: Naval Institute Press, 1980.

MacGregor, Morris J. *Integration of the Armed Forces, 1940–1965.* Washington, D. C.: Government Printing Office, 1981.

Mackenzie, Ross. *Brief Points: An Almanac for Parents and Friends of U.S. Naval Academy Midshipmen.* Annapolis, Md.: Naval Institute Press, 1993.

Marable, Manning. *Race, Reform, and Rebellion: The Second Reconstruction in Black America, 1945–1982.* Jackson: University Press of Mississippi, 1984.

McCullough, David. *Truman.* New York: Simon and Schuster, 1992.

Moebs, Thomas Truxtun. *Black Soldiers, Black Sailors, Black Ink: Research Guide on African Americans in U.S. Military History, 1526–1900.* Chesapeake Bay: Moebs, 1994.

Mooney, James L., et al., eds. *Dictionary of American Naval Fighting Ships.* Washington, D.C.: Government Printing Office, 1959–.

Myrdal, Gunnar. *An American Dilemma: The Negro Problem and Modern Democracy.* 2 vols. New York: Harper and Brothers, 1944.

Nalty, Bernard C. *Long Passage to Korea: Black Sailors and the Integration of the U.S. Navy.* Washington, D.C.: Government Printing Office, 2003.

———. *Strength for the Fight: A History of Black Americans in the Military.* New York: Free Press, 1986.

Nelson, Dennis D. *The Integration of the Negro into the U.S. Navy.* New York: Farrar, Straus, and Young, 1951.

Nordin, Dennis S. *The New Deal's Black Congressman: A Life of Arthur Wergs Mitchell.* Columbia: University of Missouri Press, 1997.

Patterson, James T. *Grand Expectations: The United States, 1945–1974.* New York: Oxford University Press, 1996.

Ploski, Harry A., and Ernest Kaiser. *Afro USA: A Reference Work on the Black Experience.* New York: Bellwether, 1971.

Puleston, W. D. *Annapolis: Gangway to the Quarterdeck.* New York: D. Appleton-Century, 1942.

Ragsdale, Bruce, ed. *Biographical Directory of the United States Congress, 1774–1989.* Washington, D.C.: Government Printing Office, 1989.

Ragsdale, Bruce, and Joel D. Treese. *Black Americans in Congress, 1870–1989.* Washington, D.C.: Government Printing Office, 1990.

Schneller, Robert J., Jr. *Breaking the Color Barrier: The U.S. Naval Academy's First Black Midshipmen and the Struggle for Racial Equality.* New York: New York University Press, 2005.

Shellum, Brian G. *Black Cadet in a White Bastion: Charles Young at West Point.* Lincoln: University of Nebraska Press, 2006.

Sherwood, John Darrell. *Black in Blue: Racial Unrest in the Navy during the Vietnam War Era.* New York: New York University Press, 2007.

Sitkoff, Harvard. *The Struggle for Black Equality, 1954–1980.* New York: Hill and Wang, 1981.

Stillwell, Paul, ed. *The Golden Thirteen: Recollections of the First Black Naval Officers.* Annapolis, Md.: Naval Institute Press, 1993.

Sweetman, Jack. *The U.S. Naval Academy: An Illustrated History.* Annapolis, Md.: Naval Institute Press, 1979.

Timberg, Robert. *The Nightingale's Song.* New York: Simon and Schuster, 1995.

Weisbrot, Robert. *Freedom Bound: A History of America's Civil Rights Movement.* New York: W.W. Norton, 1990.

Williams, Juan. *Thurgood Marshall: American Revolutionary.* New York: Times Books, 1998.

Williams, Michael S., ed. *The African American Encyclopedia.* 6 vols. New York: Marshall Cavendish, 1993.

Woodward, C. Vann. *The Strange Career of Jim Crow.* New York: Oxford University Press, 1955.

Zimmerman, Jean. *Tailspin: Women at War in the Wake of Tailhook.* New York: Doubleday, 1995.

Articles

Anderson, Jervis. "A Very Special Monument." *New Yorker*, 20 March 1978, 97–121.

Bodnar, John W. "How Long Does It Take to Change a Culture? Integration at the U.S. Naval Academy." *Armed Forces and Society* 25 (Winter 1999): 289–306.

Brown, Wesley A. "Eleven Men of West Point." *Negro History Bulletin* 19 (April 1956): 147–57.

Chafe, William H. "America since 1945." In Eric Foner, ed., *The New American History*. Philadelphia: Temple University Press, 1990.

———. "The Gods Bring Threads to Webs Begun." *Journal of American History* 86 (March 2000): 1531–51.

Disher, Sharon Hanley. "30 Years of Women at USNA: A Success Story." *Shipmate*, September 2006, 14–19.

Field, R. L. "The Black Midshipman at the U.S. Naval Academy." *Proceedings* 99 (April 1973): 28–36.

Fitzgerald, John A. "Changing Patterns of Officer Recruitment at the U.S. Naval Academy." *Armed Forces and Society* 8 (Fall 1981): 111–28.

Friedman, Norman. "Elmo Russell Zumwalt, Jr." In Robert W. Love Jr., ed., *The Chiefs of Naval Operations*. Annapolis, Md.: Naval Institute Press, 1980.

Greenya, John. "Black Man on a White Field." *Washington Post Magazine*, 1 February 2004, 16–18, 26–28.

Haygood, Wil. "Keeping the Faith." *American Legacy* 3 (Winter 1998): 23–28.

Holt, Thomas C. "African-American History." In Eric Foner, ed., *The New American History*. Philadelphia: Temple University Press, 1990.

Lawrence, Jimmy. "Colorado Springs' Jeffrey Sapp: He's an Officer and a Gentleman." *Odyssey West* 2 (December 1983): 24–27.

Reddick, L. D. "The Negro in the United States Navy during World War II." *Journal of Negro History* 32 (1947): 201–19.

Rosenberg, Robert A. "The Annapolis Connection: The Salty Saga of Naval Academy Graduates Who Rose to Star Rank in the Air Force." *Air Force Magazine* 67 (February 1984): 74–78.

Schneller, Robert J., Jr. "Oscar Holmes: A Place in Naval Aviation." *Naval Aviation News* 80 (January–February 1998): 26–27.

Sowell, Thomas. "Black Excellence: A History of Dunbar High." *Washington Post*, 28 April 1974, C 3.

Vahsen, Penny. "Blacks in White Hats." *Proceedings* 113 (April 1987): 65–71.

Williamson, Joel. "Wounds Not Scars: Lynching, the National Conscience, and the American Historian." *Journal of American History* 83 (March 1997): 1221–53.

Unpublished Works

Akers, Regina. "The Integration of Afro-Americans into the WAVES, 1942–1945." M.A. thesis, Howard University, 1993.

Brown, Gerald R. "Military Training in the Public Schools of the District of Columbia." M.A. thesis, Howard University, 1963.

Corpin, Owen D. "Development of a Model for Minority Recruitment at the United States Naval Academy." Trident Scholar Project Report, 21 May 1974, National Technical Information Service document AD-784 111.

Forney, Todd Alan. "Four Years Together by the Bay: A Study of the Midshipman Culture at the United States Naval Academy, 1946–1976." Ph.D. dissertation, Ohio State University, 2000.

Fried, Alan. "And We'll All Be Free: The Role of the Press in the Integration of the United States Army (1947–1950)." Ph.D. dissertation, University of Florida, 1994.

Jackson, James Talmadge, Jr., and Mario Renara Maddox. "The Role of the Broadened Opportunity for Officer Selection and Training (BOOST) Program in Supporting the Navy's Minority Accession Policies." M.S. thesis, Naval Postgraduate School, Monterey, Calif., 1990.

Massie, Samuel P. "Catalyst: The Autobiography of an American Chemist: Dr. Samuel P. Massie," with Robert C. Hayden. Unpublished draft book manuscript, c. May 2001.

Neyland, Leedell W. "The Messman's/Steward's Branch: A Haunting Chapter in the History of the U.S. Navy, 1919–1942." Lecture given at the Naval Historical Center, 17 May 1994.

Salter, Krewasky Antonio. "'Sable Officers': African-American Military Officers, 1861–1948." Ph.D. dissertation, Florida State University, 1996.

U.S. Navy Department. "United States Naval Administration in World War II, Bureau of Naval Personnel, The Negro in the Navy in World War II." Washington, D.C.: Navy Department, 1947.

Wender, Harry S. "An Analysis of Recreation and Segregation in the District of Columbia." Manuscript, Historical Society of Washington, D.C., May 1949.

Wright, Chester A. "The U.S. Navy's Human Resource Management Programs: In the Aftermath of the U.S.S. *Kitty Hawk/Constellation* Racial Incidents." Paper presented at the 35th Military Operations Research Society Symposium, U.S. Naval Academy, 2 July 1975.

Index

ISBN-13: 978-1-60344-000-4
ISBN-10: 1-60344-000-3

54500

9 781603 440004